Lecture Notes in Computer Science 16237

Founding Editors

Gerhard Goos
Juris Hartmanis

Editorial Board Members

Elisa Bertino, *Purdue University, West Lafayette, IN, USA*
Wen Gao, *Peking University, Beijing, China*
Bernhard Steffen, *TU Dortmund University, Dortmund, Germany*
Moti Yung, *Columbia University, New York, NY, USA*

The series Lecture Notes in Computer Science (LNCS), including its subseries Lecture Notes in Artificial Intelligence (LNAI) and Lecture Notes in Bioinformatics (LNBI), has established itself as a medium for the publication of new developments in computer science and information technology research, teaching, and education.

LNCS enjoys close cooperation with the computer science R & D community, the series counts many renowned academics among its volume editors and paper authors, and collaborates with prestigious societies. Its mission is to serve this international community by providing an invaluable service, mainly focused on the publication of conference and workshop proceedings and postproceedings. LNCS commenced publication in 1973.

Zhiming Liu · Adnane Saoud · Heike Wehrheim
Editors

Theoretical Aspects of Computing – ICTAC 2025

22nd International Colloquium
Marrakech, Morocco, November 24–28, 2025
Proceedings

Editors
Zhiming Liu
Southwest University
Chongqing, China

Adnane Saoud
University Mohammed VI Polytechnic
Ben Guerir, Morocco

Heike Wehrheim
Carl von Ossietzky Universität Oldenburg
Oldenburg, Germany

ISSN 0302-9743   ISSN 1611-3349 (electronic)
Lecture Notes in Computer Science
ISBN 978-3-032-11175-3   ISBN 978-3-032-11176-0 (eBook)
https://doi.org/10.1007/978-3-032-11176-0

Preface

This volume contains the papers presented at ICTAC 2025, the 22nd International Colloquium on Theoretical Aspects of Computing, held during November 24–28, 2025, in Marrakech, Morocco.

The International Colloquium on Theoretical Aspects of Computing is a series of annual events founded in 2004 by the United Nations International Institute for Software Technology. ICTAC aims to bring together researchers and practitioners from academia, industry and government to present research and exchange ideas and experiences in theoretical aspects of computing and methods and tools for system development. ICTAC also aims to promote research cooperation between the Global South and the Global North.

In 2025, ICTAC received 64 submissions, including 5 tool and 5 short papers. Each submission was reviewed by at least three program committee members. Reviewing was single-blind. After an extensive discussion, the program committee decided to accept 21 full and two short papers as well as two tool papers. These proceedings furthermore contain four contributions from the invited speakers and one tutorial. The program contained keynote speeches by Antoine Girard on "Set Invariance for Assume-Guarantee Contracts in System Design", Klaus Havelund on "Fuzz Testing with Temporal Constraints", Joost-Pieter Katoen on "Facing Uncertainty in AI: From Verification To Synthesis" and Kim G. Larsen on "Timed Monitoring and Monitorability". Apart from the scientific program, ICTAC 2025 included two days of tutorials given by Dines Bjørner, Antoine Girard, Joost-Pieter Katoen and Kim G. Larsen.

We thank all authors for submitting their papers to the conference, and the Program Committee members and external reviewers for their excellent work in the review, discussion and selection process. We furthermore thank the Organization Committee, including Ahmed Bouajjani, Mohammed Erradi, Abderrahim Ait Wakrime, Sadek Belamfedel Alaoui, Khaoula Boukir, Karam Kharraz and Adnane Saoud, for their hard work in organizing the conference, as well as the College of Computing, University Mohammed VI Polytechnic, for logistical help. We also acknowledge our gratitude to the Steering Committee of ICTAC, in particular Martin Leucker, for their constant support.

Thanks go to EasyChair for significantly simplifying reviewing and the construction of the final proceedings and to the University of Oldenburg, Germany, for sponsoring EasyChair's conference licence. Finally, we thank Springer for their cooperation in publishing the proceedings and sponsoring a best paper award.

November 2025

Zhiming Liu
Adnane Saoud
Heike Wehrheim

Organization

General Chairs

Ahmed Bouajjani   Université Paris Cité, France
Mohammed Erradi   ENSIAS, UM5R, Morocco

Program Committee Chairs

Zhiming Liu   Southwest University, China
Adnane Saoud   UM6P, Morocco
Heike Wehrheim   Carl von Ossietzky Universität Oldenburg, Germany

Steering Committee

Martin Leucker (Chair)   University of Lübeck, Germany
Zhiming Liu   Southwest University, China
Tobias Nipkow   Technische Universität München, Germany
Augusto Sampaio   Universidade Federal de Pernambuco, Brazil
Natarajan Shankar   SRI, USA
Tarmo Uustalu   Reykjavik University, Iceland

Program Committee

Abderrahim Ait Wakrime   Mohammed V University, Morocco
Marcello Bonsangue   Leiden University, The Netherlands
Yuxin Deng   East China Normal University, China
Chelsea Edmonds   University of Sheffield, UK
Laurent Fribourg   LSV, France
Kim Guldstrand Larsen   Aalborg University, Denmark
Peter Habermehl   IRIF University Paris Cité, France
Ichiro Hasuo   National Institute of Informatics, Japan
Inigo Incer   University of Michigan, USA
Pushpak Jagtap   Indian Institute of Science, India
Jan Kretinsky   Masaryk University, Czech Republic

Zhiming Liu	Southwest University, China
Annabelle McIver	Macquarie University, Australia
Rosemary Monahan	Maynooth University, Ireland
Kirstin Peters	Universität Augsburg, Germany
Jorge A. Pérez	University of Groningen, The Netherlands
Augusto Sampaio	Federal University of Pernambuco, Brazil
Adnane Saoud	University Mohammed VI Polytechnic, Morocco
Maike Schwammberger	Karlsruhe Institute of Technology, Germany
Emil Sekerinski	McMaster University, Canada
Hussein Sibai	Washington University in St. Louis, USA
Julien Signoles	CEA LIST, France
Marjan Sirjani	Mälardalen University, Sweden
Ana Sokolova	University of Salzburg, Austria
Sadegh Soudjani	Newcastle University, UK
Silvia Lizeth Tapia Tarifa	University of Oslo, Norway
Maurice ter Beek	CNR, Italy
Cong Tian	Xidian University, China
Tarmo Uustalu	Reykjavik University, Iceland
Tomas Vojnar	Masaryk University and Brno University of Technology, Czech Republic
Heike Wehrheim	University of Oldenburg, Germany
Sarah Winkler	Free University of Bozen-Bolzano, Italy
Jim Woodcock	Southwest University, China
Zhilin Wu	Chinese Academy of Sciences, China
Lina Ye	LMF, Paris-Saclay University, France
Miaomiao Zhang	Tongji University, China

Additional Reviewers

Sharareh Alipour	Arthur Franz
Jakub Balabán	Hu Fu
Luís Soares Barbosa	Jens Chr. Godskesen
Avner Bensoussan	Marta Grobelna
Ivan Bliznets	Kush Grover
Roderick Bloem	Qais Hamarneh
François Bobot	Florian Horn
Syed Ali Asadullah Bukhari	Sacha Huriot
Zhenbang Chen	Juliano Iyoda
Adenilton J. da Silva	Juan Camilo Jaramillo
Masoud Ebrahimi	Stephane Le Roux
Luc Edixhoven	Yong Li
Jean-Christophe Filliatre	Davide Li Calsi

Lucas Lima
Jiaxiang Liu
Wanwei Liu
Hendrik Maarand
Marius Mikučionis
Zahra Moezkarimi
Stefanie Mohr
Jan Obdrzalek
Danny Bøgsted Poulsen
José Proença
Ivan Prokić
Maximilian Prokop
Qi Qiu
Sabine Rieder
Ahmed Shalaby

Meng Sun
Ihab Tabbara
Hellis Tamm
Renaud Vilmart
Cheng-Syuan Wan
Damien Woods
Hao Wu
Peng Wu
Yuxuan Yang
Mingyue Zhang
Hengjun Zhao
Shengggen Zheng
Paolo Zuliani
Nicolaj Østerby Jensen

Contents

Session Types

Logic and Theorem Provers

Probabilistic Systems

Automata

Cryptography and Choreography

Algorithms and Complexity

Tool and Short Papers

Invited Papers

Fuzz Testing with Temporal Constraints

Klaus Havelund[(✉)], Tracy Clark, and Vivek Reddy

Jet Propulsion Laboratory, California Institute of Technology, Pasadena, USA
`Klaus.Havelund@jpl.nasa.gov`

Abstract. Testing is in practice commonly performed by executing carefully planned scripts, which exercise particular planned scenarios. Fuzz testing can be applied as a complementary approach, to exercise a system outside the boundaries of the expected. However, fuzz testing can be too random. In this work, we explore an approach to fuzz testing using an expressive temporal logic named MaTL (Matching Temporal Logic) for expressing constraints on tests, restricting generated tests to only such that satisfy the provided constraints. MaTL is a linear temporal logic that supports future and past time operators and a match construct that selects argument values from events, similar to pattern matching in functional programming languages. Constraint solving is performed using the Z3 SMT solver.

1   Introduction

Our scenario is a software system, such as e.g. a spacecraft or rover, that is controlled by commands. A command is defined as a data record consisting of a name and a sequence of named arguments. Obviously, a wrong sequence of commands can have undesired consequences. Typically, such a software system, referred to as SUT (System Under Test), is tested by submitting carefully planned sequences of commands, referred to as tests, to it and verifying that observations of returned data satisfy expectations. This careful approach to test design is necessary. However, it may miss corner cases. It may be fruitful to produce more randomized tests, which humans have not designed the exact details of. Fuzz testing [30] can be used to exercise a system outside the boundaries of the expected in an attempt to break the system. In this paper, we explore, as a complementary approach to careful test design, how to fuzz test such systems by generating randomized tests (sequences of commands), constrained by temporal constraints, which can then be submitted to the SUT.

The given is a collection of predefined types of commands which can be submitted to the SUT, with their names and argument types. We refer to these as *command signatures*. A completely randomizing test generator will generate tests, each consisting of a completely randomized sequence commands, each with randomized arguments over the command signature. Although this may identify bugs in the SUT, it may be desirable to limit the randomness, and control it to avoid some scenarios, or dually, to explore some desired scenarios. To this end, we present both (i) a temporal logic, MaTL (Matching Temporal Logic), for constraining test generation, and (ii) an implementation in the form of the `fuzz` tool

Z. Liu et al. (Eds.): ICTAC 2025, LNCS 16237, pp. 3–26, 2026.
https://doi.org/10.1007/978-3-032-11176-0_1

[8] that automatically generates such tests from a collection of MaTL formulas. This allows a user to control the randomness by writing test specifications that restrict the generated tests to only those that satisfy a collection of formulas. Note that in this work, we do not explore how to evaluate the results of applying tests to the SUT. We assume that this is done in a separate activity, e.g. with runtime verification approaches [1,7,11,15].

Specifically, MaTL is a linear temporal logic that supports future and past time operators, and a *match* construct, matching commands in a test, similar to pattern matching in functional programming languages. Given a collection of such temporal formulas, the Z3 SMT solver [29] is applied to generate tests that satisfy the formulas. However, although an SMT solver supports the generation of tests satisfying a formula, it may not generate sufficiently random tests satisfying the formula. For example, if a formula states that a test with 10 commands must be generated that contains at least one drive command, an SMT solver may generate a test with 10 drive commands. For this reason, we have to refine the tests generated by the SMT solver by randomizing as much as possible while still satisfying the constraints.

The paper is organized as follows. Section 2 introduces the MaTL temporal logic by defining its syntax and semantics. Section 3 provides a collection of example properties for testing a planetary rover. Section 4 explains how a first-order predicate logic SMT formula is generated from the collection of MaTL formulas. Section 5 explains how an SMT generated test is refined by randomizing its contents while still satisfying the SMT formula generated from the collection of MaTL formulas. Section 6 evaluates `fuzz` on the MaTL formulas presented in Sect. 3. Section 7 discusses related work. Finally, Sect. 8 concludes the paper.

2   The MaTL Temporal Logic

The MaTL temporal logic allows specification of future and past time properties, as well as matching on events (commands) and their data arguments. We shall use the terms *event* and *command* interchangeably. MaTL is interpreted on finite traces.

Traces. In order to get an intuition behind the logic to be presented, we need to define the models of the logic, namely traces, that the formulas in the logic denote. A *trace* is a finite sequence of events: $\langle e_1, e_2, ..., e_n \rangle$, where each event is a named record $id(id_1 = v_1, ..., id_n = v_n)$ with a name id, and $n \geq 0$ arguments named $id_1, ..., id_n$ with respective values $v_1, ..., v_n$. Later we shall see that commands are just a form of events.

Syntax. The core formulas of MaTL are defined by the following grammar:

$$\varphi ::= \mathtt{tt} \mid \neg\varphi \mid \varphi \vee \varphi \mid \langle id(m)\rangle\varphi \mid e \diamond e \mid e \vdash r$$
$$\bigcirc\varphi \mid \varphi\,\mathcal{U}\,\varphi \mid \ominus\varphi \mid \varphi\,\mathcal{S}\,\varphi \mid \Sigma^{+}_{[a,b]}\varphi \mid \Sigma^{-}_{[a,b]}\varphi$$
$$m ::= \epsilon \mid m\,m \mid id = p$$
$$p ::= x? \mid x \mid c \mid id.id$$
$$e ::= x \mid c \mid id.id \mid e \otimes e$$
$$\diamond ::= \; < \mid \leq \mid = \mid \neq \mid \geq \mid >$$
$$\otimes ::= \; + \mid - \mid \times \mid \div$$

Here c can be an integer, a float, or a string, and a and b are non negative integers. In addition, parentheses are allowed with the obvious meaning. At a high level, this is effectively future and past-time LTL, extended with a few additional operators such as pattern matching over events (the most important one), and some more experimental ones such as matching strings against regular expressions, and counting how many times a formula is true.

The formulas $\mathtt{tt}$, $\neg\varphi$ and $\varphi \vee \varphi$ are the Boolean formulas for truth, negation and disjunction. We postpone the explanation of the match formula $\langle id(m)\rangle\varphi$ for a moment. The formula $e \diamond e$ compares the values of two arithmetic expressions using the classical relational operators. The formula $e \vdash r$ is true if the string value denoted by the expression e matches the regular expression r. Note that we have not specified the details of regular expressions. The formula $\bigcirc\varphi$ is true if φ is true in the next future state. The formula $\varphi_1\,\mathcal{U}\,\varphi_2$ is true if φ_2 is true at some point in the future, and until then, not including, φ_1 is true. The formula $\ominus\varphi$ is true if φ is true in the previous state (the past dual of $\bigcirc$). The formula $\varphi_1\,\mathcal{S}\,\varphi_2$ is true if φ_2 is true at some point in the past, and since then, not including, φ_1 is true (the past dual of $\mathcal{U}$). The formula $\Sigma^{+}_{[a,b]}\varphi$ is true if, over the entire future trace starting at the current position, the formula φ holds between a and b times ($0 \leq a \leq b$). The past-time dual $\Sigma^{-}_{[a,b]}\varphi$ is true if, over the entire past trace up to and ending at the current position, the formula φ holds between a and b times. Note that the interval $[a,b]$ refers to the number of trace positions where φ holds, not to a time window.

The match operator $\langle id(m)\rangle\varphi$ matches the current event being processed in the trace against $id(m)$, matching the event name against id and the event parameters against m as we shall see. In case $id = \mathbf{any}$, any command matches if the arguments match. The match must succeed and potentially yield new value bindings due to the parameters, after which the formula φ must be true at the same position in the trace, in the scope of these bindings. Recall that an event is a named record of the form: $id(id_1 = v_1, ..., id_n = v_n)$. The parameter match m is either the empty match ϵ (which means that there are no requirements on the parameters[1]), a match followed by a match $m\,m$, which means that both must match and their produced bindings are combined, or the matching $id_i = p_i$ of a specific parameter id_i against a pattern p_i. Patterns p can have one of four forms, matching against a parameter value v. The pattern $x?$ causes the variable x to be bound to the value v of the parameter and is now in scope of the following

---

[1] Note that it does not mean that the event must have no parameters.

formula φ. The pattern x is a variable already in scope, that must denote a value equal to the parameter v. The pattern c, a constant of integer, float, or string type, must be equal to v. The pattern $id_1.id_2$ denotes the enumerated value id_2 of the enumerated type $id_1 = \{..., id_2, ...\}$, and which must be equal to v. Enumerated types are used to define command argument types.

Derived Operators. We define the following derived operators.

$$
\begin{aligned}
\mathbf{ff} &= \neg\mathbf{tt} & \text{false} && (1) \\
\varphi_1 \wedge \varphi_2 &= \neg(\neg\varphi_1 \vee \neg\varphi_2) & \text{and} && (2) \\
\varphi_1 \rightarrow \varphi_2 &= \neg\varphi_1 \vee \varphi_2 & \text{implication} && (3) \\
e_1 \diamond_1 e_2 \diamond_2 e_3 &= e_1 \diamond_1 e_2 \wedge e_2 \diamond_2 e_3 & \text{ternary relation} && (4) \\[2mm]
[id(m)]\varphi &= \neg\langle id(m)\rangle\neg\varphi & \text{universal modality} && (5) \\
id(m) \Rightarrow \varphi &= [id(m)]\varphi & \text{universal modality} && (6) \\
id(m) \bullet \varphi &= \langle id(m)\rangle\varphi & \text{existential modality} && (7) \\
id(m) &= \langle id(m)\rangle\mathbf{tt} & \text{event occurrence} && (8) \\[2mm]
\Diamond\varphi &= \mathbf{tt}\,\mathcal{U}\,\varphi & \text{eventually in the future} && (9) \\
\Box\varphi &= \neg\Diamond\neg\varphi & \text{always in the future} && (10) \\
\Diamond\!\!\!\!\diagdown\; \varphi &= \mathbf{tt}\,\mathcal{S}\,\varphi & \text{sometime in the past} && (11) \\
\boxminus\varphi &= \neg\,\Diamond\!\!\!\!\diagdown\;\neg\varphi & \text{always in the past} && (12) \\
\varphi_1\,\mathcal{U}_{\mathrm{w}}\,\varphi_2 &= (\varphi_1\,\mathcal{U}\,\varphi_2) \vee \Box\varphi_1 & \text{weak until} && (13) \\
\varphi_1\,\mathcal{S}_{\mathrm{w}}\,\varphi_2 &= (\varphi_1\,\mathcal{S}\,\varphi_2) \vee \boxminus\varphi_1 & \text{weak since} && (14) \\
\bigcirc_{\mathrm{w}}\varphi &= \bigcirc\varphi \vee \neg\bigcirc\mathbf{tt} & \text{weak next} && (15) \\
\ominus_{\mathrm{w}}\varphi &= \ominus\varphi \vee \neg\ominus\mathbf{tt} & \text{weak previous} && (16) \\[2mm]
\Sigma_a^{+}\varphi &= \Sigma_{[a,a]}^{+}\varphi & \text{future exact count} && (17) \\
\Sigma_a^{-}\varphi &= \Sigma_{[a,a]}^{-}\varphi & \text{past exact count} && (18) \\
\bigcirc_a\varphi &= \bigcirc\bigcirc\ldots\bigcirc\varphi \quad a\text{ times} & \text{a steps in future} && (19) \\
\ominus_a\varphi &= \ominus\ominus\ldots\ominus\varphi \quad a\text{ times} & \text{a steps in past} && (20)
\end{aligned}
$$

Notes. Forms (1–4) are the standard Boolean logic forms. The universal modality (5) expresses that if the current event matches $id(m)$ then subsequently φ must hold. Note that this is different from the existential modality $\langle id(m)\rangle\varphi$ in the core syntax, which means that the current event must match $id(m)$ and thereafter φ must hold[2]. We have introduced alternative notations (6–7) for these modalities, reflecting more closely implication and sequential composition. (8) is yet a shorthand for just an event that occurs. The abbreviations (9–16) define the usual temporal logic operators for future and past time logic. The counting operators (17–20) should be obvious.

Example. Let us look at a few example properties. Consider the following trace consisting of three events:

$$\langle open(file = \texttt{"log"}, mode = \texttt{"r"}), read(file = \texttt{"log"}), close(file = \texttt{"log"})\rangle$$

---

[2] These opeartors are also known from modal logics, see e.g. [13,17].

This trace satisfies the following three properties:

(1) $\Box(open(file = f?) \Rightarrow \Diamond close(file = f))$

(2) $\Box(read(file = f?) \Rightarrow \neg close(file = f)\, \mathcal{S}\, open(file = f, mode = \texttt{"r"}))$

(3) $\Sigma_1^+ open(mode = \texttt{"r"})$

Their meanings are as follows. (1) Whenever a file f is opened, it is eventually closed. (2) Whenever a file f is read from, in the past it has been opened in read mode, and not closed since. (3) There should be one open event in read mode.

Semantics. A MaTL formula denotes a set of finite traces as explained in the following.

Assignments. The bookkeeping of which variables are assigned to which event argument values is recorded in *assignments*, which map variables to values. Let X be a set of variables, and let V be a set of values that represent event arguments. An assignment $\gamma \in \Gamma = X \xrightarrow{m} V$ is a finite mapping from variables to values. We write $[x_1 \mapsto v_1, ..., x_n \mapsto v_n]$ to denote the assignment that maps each variable x_i to the value v_i. We denote by ϵ the empty assignment, also written $[]$. We denote by $\gamma[x \mapsto v]$ the assignment that differs from γ only by associating the value x to v. We denote by $\gamma_1 \dagger \gamma_2$ the assignment γ_1 overridden by the assignment γ_2.

Semantic Functions. We shall introduce some semantic functions used in defining the semantics of MaTL. First, we give some functions for which we do not give definitions since these are either trivial or out of scope of the paper. The function $\mathsf{Op} : \otimes \to V \times V \to V$ represents the semantics of arithmetic operators, mapping an operator $\otimes$ to a function that when applied to two numbers returns a number. The function $\mathsf{Rel} : \diamond \to V \times V \to \mathbb{B}$ represents the semantics of relational operators, mapping an operator $\diamond$ to a function that, when applied to two numbers, returns a Boolean. Finally, the function $\mathsf{Reg} : r \to V \to \mathbb{B}$ represents the semantics of regular expressions, mapping a regular expression to a function that when applied to a string returns a Boolean (match or not, regular expressions here do not bind values).

The function $\mathsf{Eval} : e \to \Gamma \to V$ represents the semantics of expressions, evaluating an expression e in an environment Γ, returning a value V. It is also fairly obvious and requires no additional comments, but we provide its definition since it involves variables.

$$\mathsf{Eval}[\![x]\!]\,(\gamma) = \gamma(x)$$
$$\mathsf{Eval}[\![c]\!]\,(\gamma) = c$$
$$\mathsf{Eval}[\![id.id]\!]\,(\gamma) = id.id$$
$$\mathsf{Eval}[\![e_1 \otimes e_2]\!]\,(\gamma) = \mathsf{Op}[\![\otimes]\!]\,(\mathsf{Eval}[\![e_1]\!]\,(\gamma),\, \mathsf{Eval}[\![e_2]\!]\,(\gamma))$$

The function $\mathsf{Match} : m \to \Gamma \to C \to \Gamma_\bot$ is the core function. It gives semantics to the multi-argument pattern m occurring in a command pattern $id(m)$, given an environment Γ and a command C. The result is a new environment $\Gamma_\bot$, which is either a proper environment or $\bot$, which represents a failed match. The empty pattern ϵ matches all commands. Pattern composition $m_1\ m_2$ combines the results of each. Finally, the pattern $id = p$ matches if p matches the value of field id in the command χ.

$$\mathsf{Match}[\![\epsilon]\!]\,(\gamma)\,(\chi) = [\,]$$
$$\mathsf{Match}[\![m_1\ m_2]\!]\,(\gamma)\,(\chi) = \mathsf{Match}[\![m_1]\!]\,(\gamma)\,(\chi) \dagger \mathsf{Match}[\![m_2]\!]\,(\gamma)\,(\chi)$$
$$\mathsf{Match}[\![id = p]\!]\,(\gamma)\,(\chi) = \mathsf{Pat}[\![p]\!]\,(\gamma)\,(\chi.id)$$

The function $\mathsf{Pat} : p \to \Gamma \to V \to \Gamma_\bot$ is the other core function. It matches the argument pattern p against the argument value v. Note that a resulting empty environment $[\,]$ denotes a match but without any new bindings.

$$\mathsf{Pat}[\![x?]\!]\,(\gamma)\,(v) = [x \mapsto v]$$
$$\mathsf{Pat}[\![x]\!]\,(\gamma)\,(v) = \textbf{if } v = \gamma(x) \textbf{ then } [\,] \textbf{ else } \bot$$
$$\mathsf{Pat}[\![c]\!]\,(\gamma)\,(v) = \textbf{if } v = c \textbf{ then } [\,] \textbf{ else } \bot$$
$$\mathsf{Pat}[\![id_1.id_2]\!]\,(\gamma)\,(v) = \textbf{if } v = id_1.id_2 \textbf{ then } [\,] \textbf{ else } \bot$$

Trace Acceptance. Let σ be a finite trace of events of length $|\sigma|$ and i a natural number, where $0 \le i < |\sigma|$. Then $(\gamma, \sigma, i) \models \varphi$ denotes that φ holds at position i of σ with the assignment γ. The formal semantics of MaTL is defined below. The most important formula is $\langle id(m)\rangle\varphi$, which matches the current event at position i against the command pattern $id(m)$, and requires φ to be satisfied in the same position in the scope of possible new variable bindings[3]. The semantics of the counting operators require that the cardinality of the set of trace positions for which the formula φ holds (in the future or past) be in the interval $a..b$.

- $(\gamma, \sigma, i) \models \mathsf{tt}$.
- $(\gamma, \sigma, i) \models \neg\varphi$ **iff not** $(\gamma, \sigma, i) \models \varphi$.
- $(\gamma, \sigma, i) \models \varphi_1 \vee \varphi_2$ **iff** $(\gamma, \sigma, i) \models \varphi_1$ **or** $(\gamma, \sigma, i) \models \varphi_2$.
- $(\gamma, \sigma, i) \models \langle id(m)\rangle\varphi$ **iff** $(name(\sigma(i)) = id$ **or** $id = \textbf{any})$ **and**
                       let $\gamma' = \mathsf{Match}[\![m]\!]\,(\gamma)\,(\sigma(i))$ **in**
                       $\gamma' \neq \bot$ **and** $(\gamma', \sigma, i) \models \varphi$.
- $(\gamma, \sigma, i) \models e_1 \diamond e_2$ **iff** $\mathsf{Rel}[\![\diamond]\!]\,(\mathsf{Eval}[\![e_1]\!]\,(\gamma)\,, \mathsf{Eval}[\![e_2]\!]\,(\gamma))$.
- $(\gamma, \sigma, i) \models e \vdash r$ **iff** $\mathsf{Reg}[\![r]\!]\,(\mathsf{Eval}[\![e]\!]\,(\gamma))$.
- $(\gamma, \sigma, i) \models \bigcirc\varphi$ **iff** $i < |\sigma| - 1$ **and** $(\gamma, \sigma, i+1) \models \varphi$.
- $(\gamma, \sigma, i) \models \varphi_1 \mathcal{U} \varphi_2$ **iff** $(\gamma, \sigma, j) \models \varphi_2$ **for some** $i \le j < |\sigma|$
                       and for all $i \le k < j$ $(\gamma, \sigma, k) \models \varphi_1$.
- $(\gamma, \sigma, i) \models \ominus\varphi$ **iff** $i > 0$ **and** $(\gamma, \sigma, i-1) \models \varphi$.
- $(\gamma, \sigma, i) \models \varphi_1 \mathcal{S} \varphi_2$ **iff** $(\gamma, \sigma, j) \models \varphi_2$ **for some** $0 \le j \le i$
                       and for all $j < k \le i$ $(\gamma, \sigma, k) \models \varphi_1$.

---

[3] One could, as an alternative solution, argue that φ should hold in position $i + 1$, which could then lead to a request for a dual past operator requiring φ should hold in position $i - 1$.

– $(\gamma, \sigma, i) \models \Sigma^+_{[a,b]}\varphi$ **iff let** $s = \{j \in [i..|\sigma| - 1] \mid (\gamma, \sigma, j) \models \varphi\}$ **in**
     $a \leq |s| \leq b.$

– $(\gamma, \sigma, i) \models \Sigma^-_{[a,b]}\varphi$ **iff let** $s = \{j \in [0..i] \mid (\gamma, \sigma, j) \models \varphi\}$ **in**
     $a \leq |s| \leq b.$

We say that a trace σ satisfies a formula φ, written $\sigma \models \varphi$, if and only if $(\epsilon, \sigma, 0) \models \varphi$.

3   Example

In this section, we provide an example, illustrating the input to the **fuzz** tool, and the results it produces. The input constraint language for the **fuzz** tool uses ASCII characters. The mapping from the symbols used in Sect. 2 to ASCII format is as follows. $\neg$: not, $\vee$: or, $\bigcirc$: next, $\mathcal{U}$: until, $\ominus$: prev, $\mathcal{S}$: since, $\Sigma^+_{[a,b]}$: count (a,b), $\Sigma^-_{[a,b]}$: countpast (a,b), $\wedge$: and, $\Diamond$: eventually, $\square$: always, $\diamondsuit$: once, $\boxminus$: sofar, $\mathcal{U}_{\mathrm{w}}$: wuntil, $\mathcal{S}_{\mathrm{w}}$: wsince, $\bigcirc_{\mathrm{w}}$: wnext, $\ominus_{\mathrm{w}}$: wprev, Σ^+_a : count a, Σ^-_a : countpast a, $\bigcirc_n$: next n, $\ominus_n$: prev n. Note that all keywords also have ASCII symbol alternatives, although we do not use these here. For example eventually can be written as <>.

3.1   The Rover Command Example

We shall write constraints for generating tests for a planetary rover, which is controlled by commands. The rover can rotate, move (forward and backward), take pictures (of low, medium, or high quality), store them on a file system, send files to an orbiting satellite, collect samples (such as soil, rocks, etc.), and execute scripts. We operate with two enumerated types. The type **direction** represents the direction of driving, and the type **image_quality** represents the quality of pictures taken:

```
direction = { forward, backward }
image_quality = { low, medium, high }
```

The specific commands are as follows, written in an informal format, with arguments of types **uint** (unsigned integers), **float**, **string**, **direction** and **image_quality**. All commands have a number identifying the instance of that command, and a time stamp. Command numbers range from 0 to 1000 and time ranges from 0 to 10000. For some additional arguments, constraints are specified.

```
ROTATE(number:uint, time:uint, angle:float)
   where − 180 ≤ angle ≤ 180
GOTO(number:uint, time:uint, x:float, y:float)
   where − 10000 ≤ x,y ≤ 10000
MOVE(number:uint, time:uint, dir:direction, distance:float)
   where 1 ≤ distance ≤ 1000
PIC(number:uint, time:uint, quality:image_quality, images:uint)
   where 1 ≤ images ≤ 10
STORE(number:uint, time:uint, file:string, images:uint)
   where 1 ≤ images ≤ 10
SEND(number:uint, time:uint, file:string)
COLLECT(number:uint, time:uint, file:string, sample:string)
SCRIPT(number:uint, time:uint, script:string, file:string)
```

The command ROTATE rotates the rover an angle. The command GOTO moves to a given position (x, y) in the two-dimensional coordinate system that represents the planetary surface. The command MOVE moves the rover forward or backward a given distance provided in meters. The command PIC takes a given number of pictures of a given quality. The command STORE stores a given number of pictures on the camera in a file. The command SEND sends a file to an orbiting satellite (which can then send them to ground). The command COLLECT collects a given kind of sample and stores information about it in a file. The command SCRIPT executes a script given by name with a file as input.

3.2   Representation of Commands in XML

Command types (such as those above) are formally represented in XML files. The commands above are defined in an XML file, some of which is shown in Fig. 1. The XML format was chosen because of its use in the context in which the tool was developed. We are looking into supporting shorter formats, including JSON and Yaml. The file shows the definition of the `direction` enumerated type and the MOVE command, and should be self-explanatory.

3.3   Running `fuzz`

The main function of the **fuzz** library is the `generate_tests` function, which has the following type:

```
Command  =  Dict[str, Union[int, float, str]]
Test  =  list[Command]

def generate_tests(spec: Optional[str]  =  None,
                   test_suite_size: Optional[int]  =  None,
                   test_size: Optional[int]  =  None) -> list[Test]:
```

The function takes as argument a specification `spec` of constraints, represented as a text string, how many tests to generate `test_suite_size`, and how many commands there shall be in each test `test_size` (all tests contain the same number of commands). The function returns a list of tests, each of which is a list of commands, each represented as a dictionary mapping a command field and parameter names to values. Arguments to the function are optional, with default values extracted from a configuration file, an example of which is shown here:

```
{
    "cmd_files": ["xml/rover_commands.xml"],
    "spec_file": "spec.txt",
    "test_suite_size": 10,
    "test_size": 10
}
```

We can run the test generator without any constraints as follows.

```
from fuzz import generate_tests

tests  =  generate_tests(spec='', test_suite_size=100, test_size=10)
for test in tests:
    for cmd in test:
        print(cmd)
```

```
<command_dictionary>
  <enum_definitions>
    <enum_table name = "direction">
      <values>
        <enum numeric = "0" symbol = "forward"/>
        <enum numeric = "1" symbol = "backward"/>
      </values>
    </enum_table>
    ...
  </enum_definitions>

  <command_definitions>
    ...
    <fsw_command class = "FSW" opcode = "0x0003" stem = "MOVE">
      <arguments>
        <unsigned_arg bit_length = "32" name = "number">
          <range_of_values>
            <include min = "0" max = "1000"/>
          </range_of_values>
          <description>Command number.</description>
        </unsigned_arg>
        <unsigned_arg bit_length = "32" name = "time" units = "seconds">
          <range_of_values>
            <include min = "0" max = "10000"/>
          </range_of_values>
          <description>The dispatch time.</description>
        </unsigned_arg>
        <enum_arg bit_length = "8" enum_name = "direction" name = "dir">
          <description>Direction to move.</description>
        </enum_arg>
        <float_arg bit_length = "64" name = "distance" units = "meters">
          <range_of_values>
            <include min = "1" max = "1000"/>
          </range_of_values>
          <description>Distance to move.</description>
        </float_arg>
      </arguments>
    </fsw_command>
    ...
  </command_definitions>
</command_dictionary>
```

Fig. 1. XML representation of example command type.

This will in less than a second generate 100 completely random tests, one of which is the following (text strings are randomly generated and are here shortened to just '...').

```
{'name': 'ROTATE', 'number': 51, 'time': 944, 'angle': -150.42}
{'name': 'SCRIPT', 'number': 75, 'time': 287, 'script': '...', 'file': '...'}
{'name': 'PIC', 'number': 64, 'time': 491, 'quality': 'low', 'images': 8}
{'name': 'SCRIPT', 'number': 48, 'time': 598, 'script': '...', 'file': '...'}
{'name': 'COLLECT', 'number': 39, 'time': 583, 'file': '...','sample': '...'}
{'name': 'COLLECT', 'number': 89, 'time': 78, 'file': '...', 'sample': '...'}
{'name': 'ROTATE', 'number': 87, 'time': 28, 'angle': 76.22}
{'name': 'GOTO', 'number': 90, 'time': 2, 'x': -8132.07, 'y': 4708.92}
{'name': 'PIC', 'number': 58, 'time': 531, 'quality': 'high', 'images': 6}
{'name': 'STORE', 'number': 74, 'time': 981, 'file': '...', 'images': 3}
```

We may conclude that such sequences are just too random, and that we might want to constrain their form. This is what is achieved by filling out the `spec` parameter with constraints.

3.4 Writing Constraints

We shall now write 10 constraints illustrating the constructs of the temporal logic. The first two constraints apply to all commands (**any**). The first constraint, named p1, specifies that for every command with a time argument t_1, if there is a next command (weak next), and it has a time value t_2, then it must hold that $t_2 \geq t_1 + 10$. In other words, time must progress with steps no less than 10. The second constraint, named p2, requires that command numbers increase by 1. Note how the values of arguments are bound using the x? notation. Note also that if a parameter is not mentioned, there are no constraints on it.

```
rule p1: # time increases
  always [any(time = t1?)] wnext [any(time = t2?)] t2 ≥ t1 + 10

rule p2: # command numbers are consecutive
  any(number = 1)
  and
  always [any(number = n1?)] wnext [any(number = n2?)] n2 = n1 + 1
```

The next two constraints, p3 and p4, further constrain the arguments of the ROTATE and MOVE commands (compared to the constraints provided in the XML file in Fig. 1).

```
rule p3: # rotation within range
  always [ROTATE(angle = a?)] −90 ≤ a ≤ 90

rule p4: # distance within range
  always [MOVE(distance = d?)] (d = 1 or d = 2 or d = 3)
```

The next two constraints are more complicated and illustrate the power of the match construct. The constraint p5 specifies that if there is a MOVE command at a position in the test, going backward, and with a distance d, then eventually later in the test there must be a ROTATE command, rotating with an angle depending on the distance (simulating that the further backward the rover moves, the less it needs to rotate to get out of the situation it may be in). The next constraint, p6, states that every GOTO command must be followed only by GOTO commands that move "northeast" (increasing in both x and y).

```
rule p5: # move backward leads to rotation
  always [MOVE(dir = direction.backwards, distance = d?)]
    eventually <ROTATE(angle = a?)>
              ((d ≤ 1 and a = 45) or (d > 1 and a = 20))

rule p6: # go northeast
  always [GOTO(x = x1?, y = y1?)]
    always [GOTO(x = x2?, y = y2?)]
      (x2 > x1 and y2 > y1)
```

Now were are adding a bit more complexity to the constraints. The constraint p7 states that if i high quality images are taken, then eventually a subset j $(0 < j \leq i)$ of those images must be stored in a file with a name matching the regular expression \d\d\d\.img (e.g. 134.img), and after that, this file must be sent to the orbiting satellite.

```
rule p7: # image taking leads to storage and sending
  always [PIC(quality = image_quality.high, images = i?)]
    eventually <STORE(file = f?, images = j?)>
      (
```

```
            f ⊢ /\d\d\d\.img/
            and
            0 < j ≤ i
            and
            eventually SEND(file = f)
        )
```

The next constraint p8 is an example of a past time property and shows how
data values can also be related backward in time. The constraint states that if j
images are stored in a file, then (from the previous step) this file must not have
been stored before, and also there must have been taken a high quality picture
in the past of a number of images i where $i \geq j$, and no file is stored since then
except the current one.

```
  rule p8: # image storing requires past image taking
    always [STORE(file = f?,images = j?)]
        prev (
          not once STORE(file = f)
          and
          (
            not STORE()
            since
            <PIC(images = i?, quality = image_quality.high)> i ≥ j
          )
        )
```

The next constraint p9 illustrates how operations can be applied to data. It states
that if a sample collection named s is collected and the analysis result is stored
in a file f, then later, without any other collection in between, a script execution
is commanded on that file f, where the script is named by concatenating "run_"
with the sample name s and then ".py".

```
  rule p9: # sample collection leads to script execution
    always [COLLECT(file = f?, sample = s?)]
      next (
        not COLLECT()
        until <SCRIPT(script = k?, file = f)> k = "run_" + s + ".py"
      )
```

All of our constraints so far have been on the form: *"if ... then ..."*, which would
be satisfied by a test even if none of the antecedents were true. In order to enforce
some events to definitely happen, the last constraint p10 states that we want to
see a MOVE, a PIC with high image quality, and a COLLECT command.

```
  rule p10: # required commands
    eventually MOVE() and
    eventually PIC(quality = image_quality.high) and
    eventually COLLECT()
```

3.5   Running fuzz with Constraints

If we now call generate_tests with this specification as follows:

```
spec = """
  rule p1: # time increases
    always [any(time = t1?)] wnext [any(time = t2?)] t2 ≥ t1 + 10
...
"""
tests = generate_tests(spec = spec, test_suite_size = 100, test_size = 10)
...
```

we will see a test like the following.

```
{'name': 'SCRIPT', 'number': 1, 'time': 1, 'script': '...', 'file': '...'}
{'name': 'PIC', 'number': 2, 'time': 11, 'quality': 'high', 'images': 10}
{'name': 'STORE', 'number': 3, 'time': 21, 'file': '...', 'images': 8}
{'name': 'SEND', 'number': 4, 'time': 31, 'file': '...'}
{'name': 'MOVE', 'number': 5, 'time': 41, 'dir': 'forward', 'distance': 1.0}
{'name': 'PIC', 'number': 6, 'time': 51, 'quality': 'high', 'images': 10}
{'name': 'STORE', 'number': 7, 'time': 61, 'file': '482.img', 'images': 7}
{'name': 'COLLECT', 'number': 8, 'time': 71, 'file': 'm', 'sample': 'm'}
{'name': 'SCRIPT', 'number': 9, 'time': 81, 'script': 'run_m.py', 'file':'m'}
{'name': 'SEND', 'number': 10, 'time': 91, 'file': '482.img'}
```

The reader is encouraged to verify that the test satisfies the above constraints. For example, wrt. rules p1 and p2 we observe that command numbers increase in steps of 1, and time progresses with steps no less than 10 – in fact, steps of 10, there is a limit to the randomness which will be discussed below. Another example is rule p7 where we observe that commands number 2 and 6 request a high quality PIC to be taken, which is followed by a STORE command 7 in the file 482.img, followed by a SEND command 10 of that file. Note that our constraints do not exclude two PIC commands that match one SEND command, and there are also other random STORE and SEND commands.

We also have to talk execution time. The first test is generated in less than a second, but subsequent tests take longer. In total, for 100 tests this sums up to 38 min for generating 100 tests, averaging 23 s per test. The reason for this low speed is the regular expression predicate $f \vdash$ /\d\d\d\.img/ in rule p7. In general, string operations are very costly when using an SMT constraint solver such as Z3. If we remove this string predicate, **fuzz** generates the 100 tests in 68 s, averaging 0.7 s per test. Efficiency issues will be discussed in more detail in Sect. 6.

4   Generation of SMT Constraints

In this section, we shall try to give the reader an idea about the SMT formula generated from a user-provided specification in the MaTL temporal logic and how the SMT solver generates tests from it.

SMT Solving. An SMT solver finds an assignment to free variables in a first-order predicate logic formula constraining the free variables. As a very simple example, consider the quantifier free formula $x > 10$ referring to the free variable x. If we ask an SMT solver to find a satisfying assignment to x it may come up with, e.g. $[x \mapsto 11]$. Let us look at a slightly more interesting example. Let $f : \mathbb{Z} \to \mathbb{Z}$ be a function, and consider the following constraint, stating that the function is injective:

$$\forall x, y \in \mathbb{Z}, \ f(x) = f(y) \Rightarrow x = y$$

This problem can be encoded in SMT-LIB [24] (which has Lisp format) as follows.

```
(declare-fun f (Int) Int)
```

```
(assert
  (forall ((x Int) (y Int))
    (=> (= (f x) (f y)) (= x y))
  )
)

(check-sat)
(get-model)
```

The function f is referred to as an *uninterpreted function*. As a result, the SMT solver might return with the following assignment to f, which is basically the identity function $f(x) = x$ for all $x \in \mathbb{Z}$:

```
sat
(model
  (define-fun f ((x Int)) Int
    x)
)
```

Timelines and Commands. We shall apply this very idea by considering a test, our free variable, as a time line function from natural numbers to commands, $timeline : \mathbb{Z} \to Command$, here programmed in Z3's Python API:

```
timeline: Function  =  Function('timeline', IntSort(), Command)
```

A test of size N (containing N commands) will be considered an assignment to the `timeline` variable, where we are only interested in the value returned by this function for the arguments $0..N - 1$. So, e.g. $timeline(0)$ will denote the first command in the test, $timeline(1)$ the second command, and $timeline(N - 1)$ the last command. The SMT constraint generated from the MaTL formulas will determine which assignments (tests) are assigned to the variable.

We first need to define the type `Command` of commands. This is done by parsing the XML file defining the commands shown in Fig. 1. The definition of this datatype corresponding to our example is shown below in the SMT-LIB format, and consists of a list of constructors of the type, one for each command, and for each of these, a list of reverse selector functions, selecting the field values from a command of that type. As an example, let R be the command (ROTATE 2 9873 45) then (ROTATE_angle R) = 45. With each command C follows also a test predicate is_C, in this case is_ROTATE(R) = true.

```
(declare-datatypes ()
  (
    (Command
      (ROTATE (ROTATE_number Int)(ROTATE_time Int)(ROTATE_angle Real))
      (GOTO (GOTO_number Int)(GOTO_time Int)(GOTO_x Real)(GOTO_y Real))
      (MOVE (MOVE_number Int)(MOVE_time Int)
            (MOVE_dir direction)(MOVE_distance Real))
      (PIC (PIC_number Int)(PIC_time Int)
           (PIC_quality image_quality)(PIC_images Int))
      (STORE (STORE_number Int)(STORE_time Int)
```

```
            (STORE_file String)(STORE_images Int))
      (SEND (SEND_number Int)(SEND_time Int)(SEND_file String))
      (COLLECT (COLLECT_number Int)(COLLECT_time Int)
            (COLLECT_file String)(COLLECT_sample String))
      (SCRIPT (SCRIPT_number Int)(SCRIPT_time Int)
            (SCRIPT_script String)(SCRIPT_file String))
    )
  )
)
```

Generated SMT Formulas. We first schematically present the translation approach, ignoring in first instance the capturing of data values in events across the *timeline*. As we shall see, this boils down to simple indexing in the *timeline*. Assume two predicates p and q, and assume the temporal MaTL formula (always if p then eventually q):

$$\Box(p \to \Diamond q)$$

Note that this formula is equivalent to the MaTL formula $\Box([p]\Diamond q)$. If we consider the predicates to be predicates on commands, $p, q : Command \to \mathbb{B}$, we can interpret this temporal formula over our *timeline* function as follows, if we are interested in tests of length k.

$$\forall i \in \{0..k-1\},\ p(timeline(i)) \to \exists j \in \{i..k-1\}, q(timeline(j)))$$

We could use this formula as a guiding principle and translate our MaTL temporal logic formulas in this manner using universal and existential quantifiers. However, SMT solvers are known to be potentially inefficient on nested quantifiers as we have in this case. We therefore chose the alternative approach of unfolding the conditions as shown in the following formula for $k = 3$, which effectively states the same property ($\forall$ translates to $\wedge$ and $\exists$ translates to $\vee$ on a finite trace), recalling that $p \to q \equiv \neg p \vee q$.

$$
\begin{aligned}
&\neg p(timeline(0)) \vee q(timeline(0)) \vee q(timeline(1)) \vee q(timeline(2)) \\
\wedge\ &\neg p(timeline(1)) \vee q(timeline(1)) \vee q(timeline(2)) \\
\wedge\ &\neg p(timeline(2)) \vee q(timeline(2))
\end{aligned}
$$

The same principle is applied for past-time temporal logic. To illustrate a more complicated constraint, we will show the SMT constraint generated from MaTL rule p5 from Sect. 3.4, repeated here:

```
rule p5: # move backward leads to rotation
  always [MOVE(dir = direction.backwards ,distance = d?)]
    eventually <ROTATE(angle = a?)>
              ((d ≤ 1 and a =  45) or (d > 1 and a =  20))
```

To recall, it states that if we observe a MOVE command with direction backward and a distance d, then eventually we must observe a ROTATE command with an angle a that is a function of d.

We shall define the following shorthands. Let $\mathtt{isM}(i) = \mathsf{is}(\mathsf{MOVE}, \mathsf{timeline}(i))$, $\mathtt{isR}(i) = \mathsf{is}(\mathsf{ROTATE}, \mathsf{timeline}(i))$, $\mathtt{Mdir}(i) = \mathsf{MOVE\_dir}(\mathsf{timeline}(i))$, $\mathtt{Mdist}(i) = \mathsf{MOVE\_distance}(\mathsf{timeline}(i))$, and $\mathtt{Rangle}(i) = \mathsf{ROTATE\_angle}(\mathsf{timeline}(i))$. $\mathtt{fuzz}$ generates a formula with the shape shown in Fig. 2, for a test of size n. As in our small example above, we see n conjuncts. Each of these states that either the command at position i in *timeline* is not a MOVE command with direction backward, or (if it is), then one of the remaining disjuncts from position i to $n-1$ must be true, that is, that we observe a ROTATE command where the angle is correctly related to the MOVE distance observed at the time point i. Note how data capturing is represented by referring back to the position in the *timeline* (trace) where the data is collected.

$$\bigwedge_{i=0}^{n-1} \Big(\neg \big(\mathtt{isM}(i) \wedge \mathtt{Mdir}(i) = backward \big)$$

$$\vee \bigvee_{j=i}^{n-1} \Big(\mathtt{isR}(j) \wedge \big((\mathtt{Mdist}(i) \leq 1 \wedge \mathtt{Rangle}(j) = 45) \vee (\mathtt{Mdist}(i) > 1 \wedge \mathtt{Rangle}(j) = 20) \big) \Big) \Big)$$

Fig. 2. SMT constraint for rule p5.

Show me the Code. The reader is referred to [8] for a full exposition of the $\mathtt{fuzz}$ implementation. Here we shall just extract a few definitions, which illustrate the main principles. MaTL rules are parsed using the Lark parsing toolkit [14] for Python. The parser generates from a specification an abstract syntax tree of Python class instances, representing language constructs used in the specification. As a representative example for a temporal operator, the class $\mathtt{LTLUntil}$ in Fig. 3 represents the until formula $\varphi_1 \, \mathcal{U} \, \varphi_2$ (φ_1 until φ_2), requiring φ_2 to hold eventually and until then φ_1 must hold. This is represented as $\mathtt{LTLUntil} \, (\varphi_1, \varphi_2)$.

The class defines two methods (among others not shown here). The method $\mathtt{to\_smt}$ generates the SMT formula for this formula and exemplifies how these methods work. The method generates an SMT constraint according to the following pattern, here shown if we evaluate the formula at position 0:

$$\varphi_1 \, \mathcal{U} \, \varphi_2 = \varphi_2(0) \vee (\varphi_2(1) \wedge \varphi_1(0)) \vee (\varphi_2(2) \wedge \varphi_1(0) \wedge \varphi_1(1)) \vee \ldots$$

Since $\Diamond \varphi = \mathtt{tt} \, \mathcal{U} \, \varphi$ one can easily see that the temporal formula $\Diamond \varphi$ will generate an SMT formula of the form $\varphi(0) \vee \varphi(1) \vee \varphi(2) \vee \ldots \vee \varphi(k-1)$. Note, however, that the implementation for efficiency reasons does not rewrite all formulas to the core logic.

While $\mathtt{to\_smt}$ is used to generate traces that satisfy a formula, the other method, $\mathtt{evaluate}$, works in the other direction and verifies that a trace satisfies formula $\varphi_1 \, \mathcal{U} \, \varphi_2$. For this formula, it checks that the current $\mathtt{index}$ is within the trace and that φ_2 is true at $\mathtt{index}$, or φ_1 is true, and then it recurses, checking that the formula is true for $\mathtt{index} + 1$. This corresponds to the equation $\varphi_1 \, \mathcal{U} \, \varphi_2 = \varphi_2 \vee (\varphi_1 \wedge \bigcirc(\varphi_1 \, \mathcal{U} \, \varphi_2))$. The methods $\mathtt{evaluate}$ reflect the semantics in Sect. 2 without concern about efficiency. This turns out to be sufficient for our purposes since the scalability is determined by the `to_smt` methods, and the traces that can be generated using them can easily be verified with the simple `evaluate` methods in milliseconds. These methods are used by a function `verify_test( test: Test, spec: str) -> bool:` for testing all traces generated, providing an elegant automated testing technique. This function is also available to the user for testing user-generated tests.

```python
@dataclass
class LTLUntil(LTLFormula):
  left: LTLFormula
  right: LTLFormula

  def to_smt(self, env: Environment, t: int, end_time: int) -> BoolRef:
    return Or(
        [
          And(
            self.right.to_smt(env, t_prime, end_time),
            And([self.left.to_smt(env, t_i, end_time)
                  for t_i in range(t, t_prime)])
          )
          for t_prime in range(t, end_time)
        ])

  def evaluate(self, env: Environment, test: Test, index: int) -> bool:
    if within(index, test):
      return self.right.evaluate(env, test, index) or (
        self.left.evaluate(env, test, index)
          and
        self.evaluate(env, test, index + 1)
      )
    return False

  ...
```

Fig. 3. The LTLUntil class representing the formula $\varphi_1 \, \mathcal{U} \, \varphi_2$.

Another class is `LTLCommandMatch`, see Fig. 4, which represents the pattern matching formula $\langle id(m) \rangle \varphi$. The `to_smt` method consists of five parts. First, it generates a formula `right_command` checking that the command is right (in the case of **any**, any command matches). Second, it generates a list `right_arguments` of formulas, checking that the actual arguments match the formal parameter specifications. This list is then composed in conjunction `event_constraint` with the formula that checks that it is the right command. Third, the environment `env_plus`, being a copy of the incoming environment, is built, mapping any binding variable names to the values on the time line at that time. Fourth, the subformula `subformula_constraint` is then evaluated in that new environment. Finally, the conjunction of `event_constraint` and `subformula_constraint` is returned. The method `evaluate` (not shown) operates in a very similar manner, except that it works with real values in the trace rather than with constraints.

The last class `LTLVariableConstraint` that we show, see Fig. 5, represents argument matches of the form $command(..., field = x, ...)$ and is relatively self-explanatory.

```python
@dataclass
class LTLCommandMatch(LTLFormula):
  command_name: str
  constraints: list[LTLConstraint]
  subformula: LTLFormula

  def to_smt(self, env: Environment, t: int, end_time: int) -> BoolRef:
    if self.command_name == 'any':
      right_command: BoolRef = True
    else:
      is_method: str = f'is_{self.command_name}'
      right_command: BoolRef = getattr(Command, is_method)(timeline(t))
    right_arguments: list[BoolRef] =
      [constraint.to_smt(env,t,end_time) for constraint in self.constraints]
    event_constraint = And([right_command] + right_arguments)
    env_plus = env.copy()
    bindings =
      [c for c in self.constraints if isinstance(c, LTLVariableBinding)]
    for binding in bindings:
      env_plus[binding.variable] =
        extract_field(binding.command_name, binding.field, timeline(t))
    subformula_constraint = self.subformula.to_smt(env_plus, t, end_time)
    return And(event_constraint, subformula_constraint)

  ...
```

Fig. 4. The LTLCommandMatch class representing the formula $\langle id(m)\rangle\varphi$.

```python
@dataclass
class LTLVariableConstraint(LTLConstraint):
  variable: str

  def to_smt(self, env: Environment, t: int, end_time: int) -> BoolRef:
    actual_value =
      extract_field(self.command_name, self.field, timeline(t))
    return actual_value == env[self.variable]

  ...
```

Fig. 5. The LTLVariableConstraint class representing the argument match $command(..., field = x, ...)$.

5   Test Refinement

An SMT solver such as Z3 is not a great randomizer. It will find assignments that satisfy the constraints provided but will not necessarily attempt to randomize the assignments, either within an assignment or between assignments. Rather, it may try to minimize the job it has to do. As an example, suppose that we generate tests using only the two constraints p1 and p2 on Page 10, which require command numbers to increase by 1 and time to increase by at least 10. Our generate_tests function will first ask Z3 to generate a test for these formulas, which (if we ask for 5 commands per test) may be (actual output):

```
{'name': 'SCRIPT', 'number': 1, 'time': 363, 'script': '', 'file': ''}
{'name': 'SCRIPT', 'number': 2, 'time': 373, 'script': '', 'file': ''}
{'name': 'SCRIPT', 'number': 3, 'time': 383, 'script': '', 'file': ''}
{'name': 'SCRIPT', 'number': 4, 'time': 393, 'script': '', 'file': ''}
{'name': 'SCRIPT', 'number': 5, 'time': 403, 'script': '', 'file': ''}
```

As we can see, it has generated a test consisting of five SCRIPT commands, which satisfies the specification, but it is not very interesting. The `generate_tests` script therefore subsequently begins a refinement process, where it attempts to randomize each command, including its arguments, and if that fails, each argument of the original command. After each change, it calls `verify_test`, which calls the `evaluate` methods on the resulting test, and if it fails, that randomization is rejected. This procedure is described in Algorithm 1. After this process, it will generate a more randomized test, as e.g. the following (again, where random text strings have been replaced with ʼ...ʼ).

```
{'name': 'SEND', 'number': 1, 'time': 363, 'file': '...'}
{'name': 'SCRIPT', 'number': 2, 'time': 373, 'script': '...', 'file': '...'}
{'name': 'SEND', 'number': 3, 'time': 383, 'file': '...'}
{'name': 'COLLECT', 'number': 4, 'time': 393, 'file': '...', 'sample': '...'}
{'name': 'STORE', 'number': 5, 'time': 403, 'file': '...', 'images': 8}
```

The algorithm is a heuristic. One can approach this in different ways. A simpler version of Algorithm 1 was tried that consisted of not including lines 10–18 that randomize arguments. This solution was less effective. Another tried solution consisted, instead of lines 5–19, of invoking the SMT solver repeatedly with new random commands, and if it succeeded in generating a new test, the new command was kept. However, this turned out to be a very costly approach which does not scale well. Note that for each test, we call the SMT solver only once, with a new seed. We do not use a common approach of negating parts of the previous constraints used to obtain a new solution.

Algorithm 1. Refine (further randomize) Test

 1: **Input:** A MaTL specification and a test satisfying the specification
 2: **Output:** A more randomized test still satisfying the specification
 3: **for** each command c in the test **do**
 4:     Replace c with a random command c'
 5:     **if** the modified test satisfies the specification **then**
 6:         Keep the replacement c'
 7:     **else**
 8:         Restore original command c
 9:         # *Randomize arguments:*
10:         **for** each argument a of c **do**
11:             Replace a with a random argument a'
12:             # *Test whether new argument works:*
13:             **if** the modified test satisfies the specification **then**
14:                 Keep the replacement a'
15:             **else**
16:                 Restore original argument a
17:             **end if**
18:         **end for**
19:     **end if**
20: **end for**
21: **return** randomized test

---

6   Evaluation

We evaluated test generation on (modifications of) the ten properties p1-p10 introduced in Sect. 3.4. We performed two experiments. The first experiment used the scenario presented where some commands have string arguments, and where there are constraints on these (in particular properties p7, p8, p9). Strings turn out to be less efficient for SMT solving, and in particular regular expressions[4]. For this reason, we performed a second experiment, where we replaced string types with integer types and modified the formulas accordingly. This also includes enumerated types, which are represented as strings; these were mapped to numbers as well. This allows us to measure the price paid for operating with string constraints. The evaluation was carried out on an Apple MacBook Pro, with an M1 Max chip, and 64 GB of memory. The operating system was MacOS Sequoia, and applications were run in PyCharm 2023.1.2.

For each property, we generated tests of increasing length (10 commands, 20 commands, etc.). We also solved for all properties together for different test lengths in the two experiments. We measured the SMT formula generation time, the SMT solving time, and the total execution time (approximately the sum of the formula generation and solving time). Results are shown as logarithmic scaled plots, with solid green curves (scenario without strings) and red dashed curves (scenario with strings). For each setting, we generated three tests per length in order to keep runtime manageable.

Figure 6 shows the combined execution time for solving all the ten properties. Figure 7 shows the execution time per property. Figure 8 shows the relationship between the formula generation time and the formula solving time for selected test sizes. Note that the overhead of test refinement (randomization) as described in Sect. 5 is negligible relative to formula generation and solving. All times reported in the figures are totals for generating three tests at each length. Formula generation is performed once per length, while SMT solving is repeated per test. Consequently, the average per test *SMT time* is $(T_{\text{total}} - T_{\text{formula-generation}})/3$.

The results clearly show the impact of string constraints on scalability. In the setting without strings, execution times grow moderately with test length, remaining within practical limits even for the combined case at lengths up to 100. In contrast, the with-strings setting shows a much steeper growth, with certain properties (notably p7-p9) exhibiting exponential blow-ups and the combined case becoming infeasible beyond length 50. The stacked bar plot further indicates that the dominant cost in the with-strings setting lies in SMT solving, while formula generation remains a relatively minor contributor. The results suggest that improving the handling of strings is essential for referring to strings in specifications. It is also clear that the approach has scalability issues on tests beyond 100 events. Note that scalability also depends on the number of commands involved. For test generation in practice, we anticipate that tests of around 50 commands are reasonable to expect, although the exact number will depend on the application scenario.

---

[4] In property p7 we had to comment out the regular expression constraint `f ⊢ /ddd.img/` in order to get somewhat reasonable solving times.

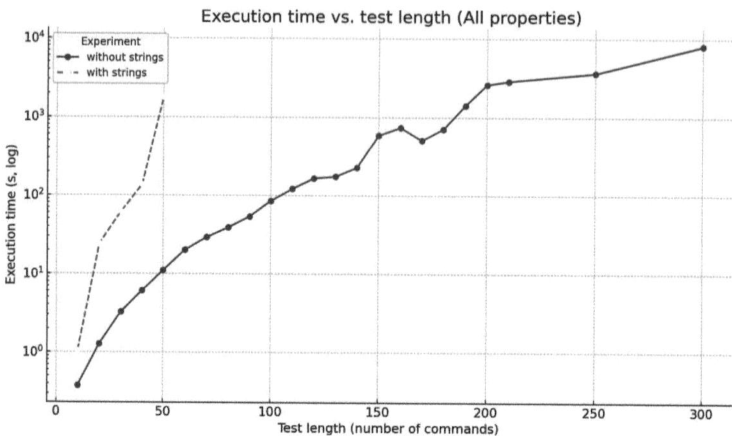

Fig. 6. Execution times (log scale) for all properties combined.

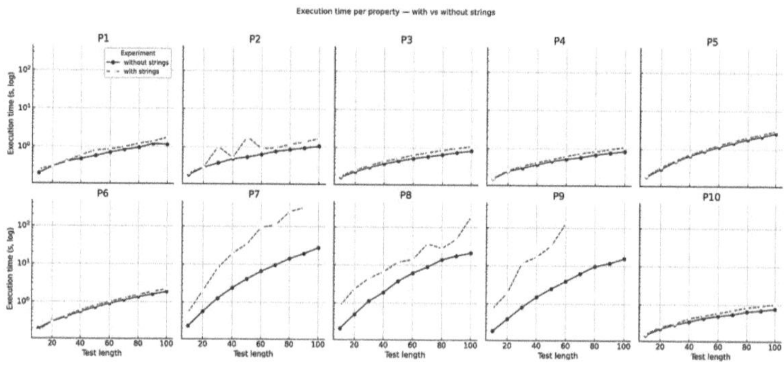

Fig. 7. Execution times (log scale) per property.

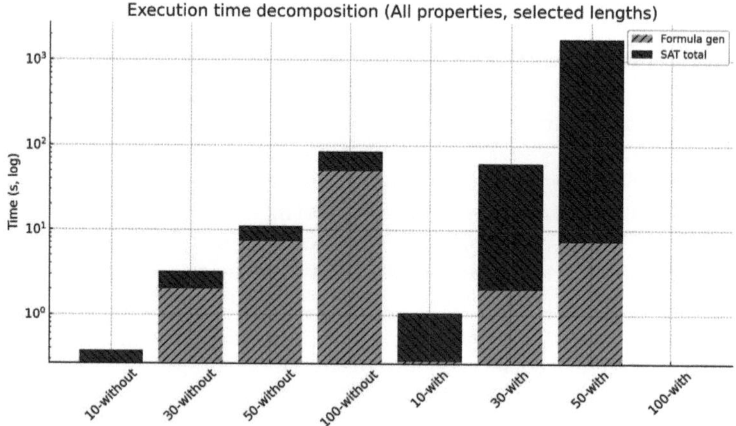

Fig. 8. Formula generation versus SMT solving time for selected test sizes (10, 30, 50, 100), without and with strings.

7   Related Work

The MaTL temporal logic is based on LTL [20], augmented with past-time operators, and a matching construct over events that carry data from potentially infinite domains, in the style of pattern matching in functional programming languages such as Scala [22]. The matching construct is related to the *freeze operator* in LTL logics and register automata over data words, see, e.g. [6], which supports storing data in registers in trace positions and comparing these with data in other trace positions with equality. MaTL goes beyond equality. Furthermore, register automata can store only as many data as the finite number of registered declared. The matching construct comes in two forms (*box modality* and *diamond modality*) corresponding to the modal operators of Hennessy-Milner logic [13,17]. Similar ideas appear in runtime verification logics [5,12,25], where the objective is to *monitor* traces rather than *generating* them. In particular, the Hawk logic [5] supports two modal operators similar to those provided by MaTL. The counting operators in MaTL correspond to similar operators in the temporal logic SALT [2].

The amount of work performed in the field of fuzz testing is overwhelming, and it will be impossible to provide a fair survey here. Generation of test cases from LTL is related to grammar-based fuzzing, which generates tests (strings) that satisfy a context-free grammar (rather than parsing such strings as grammars are normally used for). An excellent exposition on Python fuzz testing, including grammar-based fuzzing, is provided in [30]. Model-based testing uses higher-level models such as state machines. An example is [18], which translates SysML system models into bounded model checking problems, which are solved with SMT to produce tests. Our work can be seen as a form of model-based fuzzing, where the model is expressed in temporal logic. Constraint solving has long been employed for test generation. DART [10], CUTE [23], and KLEE [4] pioneered the concolic execution paradigm, where programs are run with concrete inputs while collecting symbolic path constraints, which are systematically negated and solved with an SMT solver to explore new paths beyond random fuzzing.

Generation of tests from an LTL formula is specifically closely related to checking satisfiability. Most work in this direction concerns future time temporal logics over atomic propositions (no data). Intuitively, if an LTL formula φ is satisfiable, then there must exist at least one trace that makes φ true, and such a trace can be used as a test. Satisfiability checking can be reduced to model checking by introducing a *universal model* M that denotes all possible traces over the set of propositions. In this model, φ is satisfiable precisely when $M \not\models \neg\varphi$, yielding an error trace, our test. A detailed study of translations from LTL to Büchi automata and their use in model checkers is provided in [21]. In [16] the authors investigate satisfiability checking for Mission-Time LTL (MLTL), a time-bounded variant of temporal logic. They develop reductions that map MLTL satisfiability into existing frameworks, including LTL satisfiability via automata-based techniques, and model checking with nuXmv. In addition, they propose an SMT-based encoding of MLTL satisfiability using Z3. The SMT encoding is similar to ours, although they use universal and existential quantification over trace positions, whereas we, for efficiency reasons, have chosen to unfold the quantifiers using conjunction and disjunction. A similar translation to SMT is pursued in [3] for MITL (Metric Interval Temporal Logic) satisfiability checking. In [26] the authors derive auxiliary sub properties from a future time propositional LTL requirement and use a model checker to generate execution scenarios (traces) for them. These scenarios are then used for monitoring the implementation, and coverage is achieved when every such scenario has been exercised by at least one observed execution.

A subject closely related to test generation from temporal formulas is planning [19, 28]. E.g. the PDDL3 [9] planning language standard extends the Planning Domain Definition Language (PDDL) with a fragment of LTL over finite traces. In [27] the authors introduce LTL-RE, which combines LTL operators with regular expressions, which are translated into alternating automaton, used to restrict classical planners. However, in classical planning languages such as PDDL, actions are parameterized over a finite set of typed objects. By contrast, MaTL operates on data values from potentially infinite domains.

8   Conclusion

We have presented the `fuzz` tool for generating tests, which are sequences of commands, from formulas in the MaTL temporal logic with future and past time operators, and a match construct matching events and their carried data. We defined the syntax and semantics of MaTL, and provided a collection of example properties. We explained how formulas are translated to SMT formulas, and also how monitors are generated, which verify that generated tests are valid. Since the Z3 solver cannot be relied upon to randomize its solutions, we described an extra randomization of the tests generated by Z3. The evaluation shows that the framework applied to our example properties is practical for tests of length 100 or less. We believe that tests normally would fall in this range. However, the approach faces a scalability challenge. Especially if there are many commands. In our case we operated with five commands. We demonstrated that string arguments to commands and constraints on these severely influence scalability in a negative direction. The format of commands, namely named data records with named fields, is very general, and many other formats can be generated from this format. This makes the approach more broadly applicable beyond applications being controlled by commands. Future work includes studying how strings can be handled more efficiently. Other SMT encodings can also be investigated, e.g. by using universal and existential quantification over trace positions instead of the use of conjunction and disjunction. It remains to be seen whether one performs drastically better than the other. Finally, the tool is currently based on the Z3 SMT solver. Future work can include also interfacing to other solvers.

Acknowledgments. The research was carried out at Jet Propulsion Laboratory, California Institute of Technology, under a contract with the National Aeronautics and Space Administration. We thank the reviewers for their helpful comments.

References

1. Bartocci, E., Falcone, Y., Francalanza, A., Leucker, M., Reger, G.: An introduction to runtime verification. In: Lectures on Runtime Verification - Introductory and Advanced Topics. LNCS, vol. 10457, pp. 1–23. Springer (2018)
2. Bauer, A., Leucker, M.: The theory and practice of SALT. In: Bobaru, M., Havelund, K., Holzmann, G.J., Joshi, R. (eds.) NFM 2011. LNCS, vol. 6617, pp. 13–40. Springer, Heidelberg (2011). https://doi.org/10.1007/978-3-642-20398-5_3
3. Bersani, M. M., Rossi, M., San Pietro, P.: An SMT-based approach to satisfiability checking of MITL. Inf. Comput. **245**, 72–97 (2015). https://doi.org/10.1016/J.IC.2015.06.007
4. Cadar, C., Dunbar, D., Engler, D.: KLEE: unassisted and automatic generation of high-coverage tests for complex systems programs. In: Proceedings of the 8th USENIX Symposium on Operating Systems Design and Implementation (OSDI), pp. 209–224. USENIX (2008)
5. d'Amorim, M., Havelund, K.: Event-based runtime verification of Java programs. ACM SIGSOFT Softw. Eng. Not. **30**(4), 1–7 (2005)
6. Demri, S., Lazić, R.: LTL with the Freeze Quantifier and Register Automata. Proceedings of the 21st Annual IEEE Symposium on Logic in Computer Science (LICS), pp. 17–26. IEEE (2006)
7. Falcone, Y., Havelund, K., Reger, G.: A tutorial on runtime verification. In: Broy, M., Peled, D., Kalus, G. (eds.) Engineering Dependable Software Systems. NATO Science for Peace and Security Series - D: Information and Communication Security, vol. 34, pp. 141–175. IOS Press (2013)
8. The Fuzz test case generator. https://github.com/havelund/fuzzing
9. Gerevini, A., Long, D.: Plan constraints and preferences in PDDL3, the language of the deterministic part of the fifth international planning competition. In: Fifth International Planning Competition, ICAPS (2006)
10. Godefroid, P., Klarlund, N., Sen, K.: DART: directed automated random testing. In: Proceedings of the 2005 ACM SIGPLAN Conference on Programming Language Design and Implementation (PLDI), pp. 213–223. ACM (2005)
11. Havelund, K., Goldberg, A.: Verify your runs. In: Meyer, B., Woodcock, J. (eds.) VSTTE 2005. LNCS, vol. 4171, pp. 374–383. Springer, Heidelberg (2008). https://doi.org/10.1007/978-3-540-69149-5_40
12. Havelund, K., Reger, G., Thoma, D., Zălinescu, E.: Monitoring events that carry data. In: Bartocci, E., Falcone, Y. (eds.) Lectures on Runtime Verification. LNCS, vol. 10457, pp. 61–102. Springer, Cham (2018). https://doi.org/10.1007/978-3-319-75632-5_3
13. Hennessy, M., Milner, R.: Algebraic laws for nondeterminism and concurrency. J. ACM **32**(1), 137–161 (1985). https://doi.org/10.1145/2455.2460
14. Lark - a parsing toolkit for Python. https://github.com/lark-parser/lark
15. Leucker, M., Schallhart, C.: A brief account of runtime verification. J. Logic Algebraic Program. **78**(5), 293–303 (2008). https://doi.org/10.1016/j.jlap.2008.08.004
16. Li, J., Vardi, M.Y., Rozier, K.Y.: Satisfiability checking for mission-time LTL. In: Computer Aided Verification, vol. 11562, pp. 3–22. Springer (2019). https://doi.org/10.1007/978-3-030-25543-5_1
17. Milner, R.: A modal characterisation of observable machine-behaviour. In: CAAP 1981: Colloquium on Trees in Algebra and Programming, vol. 112, pp. 25–34. Springer (1981)
18. Peleska, J., Vorobev, E., Lapschies, F.: Automated test case generation with SMT-solving and abstract interpretation. In: Bobaru, M., Havelund, K., Holzmann, G.J., Joshi, R. (eds.) NFM 2011. LNCS, vol. 6617, pp. 298–312. Springer, Heidelberg (2011). https://doi.org/10.1007/978-3-642-20398-5_22

19. Planning.Wiki. https://planning.wiki
20. Pnueli, A.: The temporal logic of programs. In: 18th Annual Symposium on Foundations of Computer Science, pp. 46–57. IEEE Computer Society (1977)
21. Rozier, K.Y., Vardi, M.Y.: LTL satisfiability checking. Int. J. Softw. Tools Technol. Transf. 12, 123–137 (2010). https://doi.org/10.1007/s10009-010-0140-3
22. Scala Programming Language. http://www.scala-lang.org
23. Sen, K., Marinov, D., Agha, G.: CUTE: a concolic unit testing engine for C. In: Proceedings of the 10th European Software Engineering Conference (ESEC/FSE), pp. 263–272. ACM (2005)
24. SMT-LIB. https://smt-lib.org
25. Stolz, V., Bodden, E.: Temporal assertions using AspectJ. In: Proceedings of the 5th International Workshop on Runtime Verification (RV 2005), vol. 144(4), pp. 109–124. Elsevier (2006)
26. Tan, L., Sokolsky, O., Lee, I.: Specification-based testing with linear temporal logic. In: Proceedings of the 2004 International Conference on Information Reuse and Integration, pp. 493–498. IEEE (2004). https://doi.org/10.1109/IRI.2004.1431509
27. Triantafillou, E., Baier, J., McIlraith, S.: A unifying framework for planning with LTL and regular expressions. In: Proceedings of the Workshop on Model-Checking and Automated Planning (MOCHAP) at ICAPS, pp. 23–31 (2015)
28. Unified planning library. https://unified-planning.readthedocs.io/en/latest
29. The Z3 SMT solver. https://github.com/z3prover/z3
30. Zeller, A., Gopinath, R., Böhme, M., Fraser, G., Holler, C.: The Fuzzing Book. https://www.fuzzingbook.org

Facing Uncertainty in AI: From Formal Verification To Synthesis

Joost-Pieter Katoen[1,2]($^{(\boxtimes)}$) (iD)

[1] Software Modelling and Verification, RWTH Aachen University, Aachen, Germany
[2] Formal Methods and Tools, University of Twente, Enschede, The Netherlands
`katoen@cs.rwth-aachen.de`

Abstract. Uncertainties occur in different forms: data may be noisy, mechanisms may be inherently randomised, the visibility (of e.g. a robot) may not be optimal, and the environment in which a system needs to operate may behave in an unknown manner. The central question that we will address is "Can we guarantee that AI systems are safe and resilient in the presence of such uncertainty?" We advocate using model-based, formal verification and synthesis with a particular focus on automation. We will present techniques to (a) verify uncertainty aspects modeled as randomness and to (b) use formal synthesis to complete partial designs. Several example AI models—Bayesian networks, partially observable Markov decision processes, and probabilistic programs – will illustrate the capabilities of these approaches.

The probabilistic model-checking problem is: given a probabilistic model M, a property φ and a threshold p in the interval $[0,1]$, is the probability that $M \models \varphi$ at least p? In this setting, all probabilities in M are fixed constants, φ is a reachability property (or more general, an ω-regular property) and p is a fixed constant. If M is a finite-state Markov chain, or Markov decision process (MDP)[1], this problem can be solved in polynomial time. Algorithmically, it basically amounts to solving a linear equation system or a linear program, respectively whose size is linear proportional to the number of states in M. Iterative methods do exist that compute $\Pr(M \models \varphi)$ with a guaranteed accuracy of $\epsilon > 0$. Models with several millions of states can be verified efficiently with tools such as Storm. Model checking of certain classes of infinite-state Markov models such as e.g., probabilistic pushdown automata and decisive Markov chains is decidable too.

Why is this of relevance to AI models under uncertainty? Popular models such as Bayesian networks can be rather straightforwardly be interpreted as Markov chains. The central NP-hard problem of conditional inference on Bayesian networks reduces to a (conditional) reachability objective. Ergo: Bayesian inference in probabilistic graphical models such as Bayesian networks can be tackled using probabilistic model-checking techniques. Another application in the

---

[1] In this case, the model-checking problem is the to ask whether the minimal or maximal reachability problem exceeds p.

Z. Liu et al. (Eds.): ICTAC 2025, LNCS 16237, pp. 27–30, 2026.
https://doi.org/10.1007/978-3-032-11176-0_2

field of AI are probabilistic programs with discrete probabilities. Such programs with finitely many control states can readily be seen as symbolic representations of finite (possibly huge) Markov chains, or MDPs in case non-determinism is included. This e.g., enables the automated verification of finite instance of discrete sampling algorithms [6], or the verification of pre-postcondition pairs on finite-state recursive probabilistic programs [8].

A major question is: where do the probabilities in the model M come from? For certain applications such as randomized algorithms, these values are provided, but e.g., exact values of the failure probability of equipment, the probability that a slippery robot does not move correctly, etc. are rarely at our disposal. This motivates to consider parametric Markov models. Here, the transitions are equipped with rational functions (such as $1-x$ and x) over a finite set of real-valued variables. The values of these variables can be constrained, expressing e.g., that x lies between $1/2$ and $3/4$, defining the set of admissible values. The feasibility problem is: given a parametric probabilistic model M over the variables x_1 through x_k, a property φ and a threshold p in the interval $[0, 1]$, is there a possible admissible valuation of the variables such that $\Pr(M \models \varphi) \geq p$? If M is finite state, this problem is ETR-complete [5], i.e., it is as hard as solving whether a sentence in the existential theory of the reals is satisfiable. (ETR lies between NP and PSPACE.). Other relevant parameter synthesis problems are to verify whether for all admissible parameter values $\Pr(M \models \varphi) \geq p$, or to find the parameter values that maximise (or minimise) $\Pr(M \models \varphi)$. Due to algorithmic developments in the last decade, the feasibility problem can be solved for parametric Markov models with hundreds of parameters [3].

These parameter synthesis techniques are readily applicable to parametric Bayesian networks with arbitrarily many, possibly dependent, parameters that may occur in multiple conditional probability tables (CPTs). This lifts restrictions, e.g., on the number of parametrized CPTs, or on parameter dependencies between several CPTs, that exist in the AI literature. Experiments on several benchmarks show that these parameter synthesis techniques can treat parameter synthesis for Bayesian networks (with hundreds of unknown parameters) that are out of reach for existing techniques [7].

There is more to this. Partially observable MDPs (POMDPs) are a central model in AI planning. They differ from MDPs in the sense that sets of observations are associated to each state. Policies that resolve the non-determinism can thus only see the state observations rather than the states themselves. States with the same observations cannot be distinguished. Whereas pure policies can attain maximal reachability probabilities in MDPs, for POMDPs policies need infinite memory. This renders the model-checking problem: given POMDP M, a reachability property φ, and a threshold p in the interval $[0, 1]$, is the maximal probability that $M \models \varphi$ is at least p? to be undecidable. Note that reachability means eventually reaching a state in some set regardless of the number of steps needed to reach this set. To remedy this, an often used technique is to restrict the set of possible policies to an a priori fixed finite memory size. (In AI, it is also common to consider bounded reachability, i.e., reachability within a given maximal number of steps.) Such policies can be seen as finite automata that based on their control state and the observation from the POMDP, provide the action to be taken.

The interesting fact is that finding an optimal finite-state controller for POMDP reachability is as hard as the feasibility problem in parametric Markov chains [4]. Ergo: finding optimal finite-state POMDP controllers for reachability is ETR-complete. This connection closed a gap in the known complete bounds for finding finite-state POMDP controllers. In addition, algorithmic techniques for the feasibility problem in parametric Markov chains can directly be applied to synthesise optimal finite-state controllers in POMDPs.

The parameter synthesis problem seeks for real-valued parameter values. A discrete version of this is the following problem: given an MDP M, a specification φ, and a—possibly huge but finite—design space of policies, find a policy in the design space (if any) such that the induced Markov chain satisfies φ. Constraints on the design space can be quite diverse. They can limit the size of the policy or encode domain-specific knowledge as in program sketching. Variations of this problem are e.g., the optimal feasibility problem that aims at finding a policy that satisfies φ under all given constraints in an optimal manner. Evidently, this is a more challenging problem. A relaxed version of this problem is to find a policy that is almost optimal, achieving a result that is close (but not exactly) the optimal value. An approach insipred by syntax-driven guided program synthesis yields promising results [1].

Main challenges are to consider these problems for probabilistic programs that induced infinitely many control states. Deductive frameworks for such programs using Hoare logics or weakest precondition frameworks do exist. They can be used to prove—using user-provided loop invariants—whether they terminate with probability one on all possible inputs, or establish an expectation over the program variables. Variations of the feasibility problem have not been deeply investigated yet so far in this setting though. Some initial work in that direction is [2].

References

1. Andriushchenko, R., Ceska, M., Macák, F., Junges, S., Katoen, J.P.: An oracle-guided approach to constrained policy synthesis under uncertainty. J. Artif. Intell. Res. **82**, 433–469 (2025)
2. Batz, K., Biskup, T.J., Katoen, J.P., Winkler, T.: Programmatic strategy synthesis: resolving nondeterminism in probabilistic programs. Proc. ACM Program. Lang. **8**(POPL), 2792–2820 (2024)
3. Junges, S., et al.: Parameter synthesis for Markov models: covering the parameter space. Formal Methods Syst. Des. **62**(1), 181–259 (2024)
4. Junges, S., et al.: Finite-state controllers of pomdps using parameter synthesis. In: UAI, pp. 519–529. AUAI Press (2018)
5. Junges, S., Katoen, J.P., Pérez, G.A., Winkler, T.: The complexity of reachability in parametric markov decision processes. J. Comput. Syst. Sci. **119**, 183–210 (2021)

6. Mertens, H., Katoen, J.P., Quatmann, T., Winkler, T.: Computing expected visiting times and stationary distributions in Markov chains: fast and accurate. J. Autom. Reason. **69**(3), 23 (2025)
7. Salmani, B., Katoen, J.P.: Automatically finding the right probabilities in bayesian networks. J. Artif. Intell. Res. **77**, 1637–1696 (2023)
8. Winkler, T., Gehnen, C., Katoen, J.P.: Model checking temporal properties of recursive probabilistic programs. Log. Methods Comput. Sci. **19**(4) (2023)

Timed Monitoring and Timed Monitorability

Kim Guldstrand Larsen[✉]

Aalborg University, 9220 Aalborg, Denmark
`kgl@cs.aau.dk`

Abstract. Runtime verification of temporal properties over timed observations is essential in cyber-physical systems such as autonomous vehicles, smart grids, and medical devices. This talk presents recent advances in predicting property satisfaction or violation in continuous real-time settings.

We focus on monitoring properties expressed in Metric Interval Temporal Logic (MITL) or Timed Büchi Automata [2,4]. Our symbolic online algorithms exploit zone-based techniques from Timed Automata model checking, enabling efficient handling of challenges like time divergence, timing uncertainty, and fluctuating parametric delays–without relying on costly parametric verification.

Assumptions about system behavior, expressed as Timed Automata, can further enhance monitoring [1]. We propose an assumption-based runtime verification framework and discuss its extension to probabilistic settings using Stochastic Timed Automata. Implemented in UPPAAL, our algorithms show promising initial results.

Finally [3], we also present new findings on monitorability, showing decidability and computable verdict bounds for deterministic Timed Muller Automata, while proving undecidability for nondeterministic Timed Büchi Automata. In addition we introduce and settle decidability of step- and time-bounded monitorability.

References

1. Cimatti, A., Grosen, T.M., Larsen, K.G., Tonetta, S., Zimmermann, M.: Exploiting assumptions for effective monitoring of real-time properties under partial observability. In: Madeira, A., Knapp, A. (eds.) Software Engineering and Formal Methods - 22nd International Conference, SEFM 2024, Aveiro, Portugal, November 6-8, 2024, Proceedings. Lecture Notes in Computer Science, vol. 15280, pp. 70–88. Springer (2024). https://doi.org/10.1007/978-3-031-77382-2_5
2. Fränzle, M., Grosen, T.M., Larsen, K.G., Zimmermann, M.: Monitoring real-time systems under parametric delay. In: Kosmatov, N., Kovács, L. (eds.) Integrated Formal Methods - 19th International Conference, IFM 2024, Manchester, UK, November 13-15, 2024, Proceedings. Lecture Notes in Computer Science, vol. 15234, pp. 194–213. Springer (2024).https://doi.org/10.1007/978-3-031-76554-4_11

3. Grosen, T.M., Kauffman, S., Larsen, K.G., Zimmermann, M.: Time for timed monitorability. In: Bouyer, P., van de Pol, J. (eds.) 36th International Conference on Concurrency Theory, CONCUR 2025, August 26-29, 2025, Aarhus, Denmark. LIPIcs, vol. 348, pp. 19:1–19:20. Schloss Dagstuhl - Leibniz-Zentrum für Informatik (2025). https://doi.org/10.4230/LIPICS.CONCUR.2025.19
4. Grosen, T.M., Kauffman, S., Larsen, K.G., Zimmermann, M.: Monitoring timed properties (revisited). In: Bogomolov, S., Parker, D. (eds.) Formal Modeling and Analysis of Timed Systems - 20th International Conference, FORMATS 2022, Warsaw, Poland, September 13-15, 2022, Proceedings. Lecture Notes in Computer Science, vol. 13465, pp. 43–62. Springer (2022). https://doi.org/10.1007/978-3-031-15839-1_3

Set Invariance for Assume-Guarantee Contracts in Cyber-Physical Systems Design
- Extended Abstract -

Antoine Girard[✉]

CNRS, CentraleSupélec Laboratoire des signaux et systèmes, Université Paris-Saclay,
91190 Gif-sur-Yvette, France
`Antoine.Girard@centralesupelec.fr`

Abstract. Contract theory is an appealing framework for rigorous component-based design of highly dynamic and distributed cyber-physical systems. Formally, a contract is a specification consisting of pairs of assumptions and guarantees. A guarantee describes the task that the component must fulfill when its environment (made of other components and of the external environment) satisfies the associated assumption. Assume-guarantee contracts make it possible to design components that can adapt under dynamic and uncertain working conditions. Moreover, compositional reasoning makes it possible to prove properties of a system based on the contracts satisfied by its components. In this presentation, we will explore the connections between assume-guarantee contracts and set invariance, a concept which forms one of the cornerstones of modern control theory. We will introduce a class of assume-guarantee contracts whose satisfaction can be characterized through invariant sets of an auxiliary dynamical system. We will discuss theoretical and computational aspects of the proposed framework and show illustrative applications in the design of hierarchical and distributed control systems.

Keywords: Assume-guarantee contracts · Invariant sets · Control systems

1 Contract-Based Design of CPS

Cyber-physical systems (CPS) consist of physical systems enhanced with computing and communication capabilities. CPS research is a driver of innovation in various technological fields: smart vehicles, smart grids, smart buildings, etc. While the term CPS refers to very different objects, these often share similar characteristics: they evolve in highly dynamic and uncertain environment (no stationary or nominal behavior), they are often integrated in large dynamic networks of CPSs (interactions via both cyber and physical channels), and they are subject to safety critical requirements. These characteristics make the design of CPS a challenging problem. An attractive approach to address these challenges

Z. Liu et al. (Eds.): ICTAC 2025, LNCS 16237, pp. 33–36, 2026.
https://doi.org/10.1007/978-3-032-11176-0_4

is through contract-based design [2,5,8]. In such approaches, a CPS is viewed as a component of a broader system. A contract for a component is a formal specification that provides an abstracted view of the interactions of the component with its environment, which typically includes other components of the system as well as the external environment, and that describes the expected behavior of the component. Assume-guarantee contracts are a common type of contracts and consist of an assumption together with a guarantee. The assumption can be viewed as formal behavioral abstraction of the environment, while the guarantee describes the expected behavior of the component when the assumption is effectively satisfied. Assume-guarantee contracts are suitable to address the challenges of CPS design. By assigning a collection of contracts to a CPS, one can design systems that can adapt to various environments. Moreover, contracts enable compositional reasoning, which makes it possible to reason on large networks of CPS. Finally, since contracts are formal specifications, they are suitable for designing safety critical systems by resorting to formal synthesis or verification.

2   Invariant Sets for Assume-Guarantee Contracts

In this presentation, we consider discrete-time *systems* of the form:

$$z_{t+1} \in F_S(z_t), \; z_0 \in \mathbb{Z}_0, \; t \in \mathbb{N} \tag{1}$$

where $z_t \in \mathbb{Z}$ is a variable that aggregates the states, inputs and outputs of the system S, $\mathbb{Z}_0 \subseteq \mathbb{Z}$, and $F_S : \mathbb{Z} \to 2^{\mathbb{Z}}$ is a set-valued map. This formalism is sufficiently general to include numerous systems of interest.

An *assume-guarantee contract* C is given by a pair of set-valued maps, that is, $C = (F_A, F_G)$ with $F_A, F_G : \mathbb{Z} \to 2^{\mathbb{Z}}$. We say that C is satisfied by S, denoted by $S \models C$, if the following property holds for all trajectories $(z_t)_{t \in \mathbb{N}}$ of (1) and for all $t \in \mathbb{N}$:

$$(\forall s \leq t, \; z_{s+1} \in F_A(z_s)) \implies z_{t+1} \in F_G(z_t). \tag{2}$$

Given a system S and a contract C, one is interested in checking whether S satisfies C. We showed in [4] that a necessary and sufficient condition for $S \models C$ is the existence of an invariant set $\mathbb{Z}_C \subseteq \mathbb{Z}$ for the set-valued map $F_{S \cap A} = F_S \cap F_A$ such that the following inclusions hold

$$\mathbb{Z}_0 \subseteq \mathbb{Z}_C \subseteq \mathbb{Z}_C^0 \tag{3}$$

$$F_{S \cap A}(\mathbb{Z}_C) \subseteq \mathbb{Z}_C \tag{4}$$

where $\mathbb{Z}_C^0 = \{z \in \mathbb{Z} |\; F_{S \cap A}(z) \subseteq F_G(z)\}$. This result can serve as theoretical basis for the development of computational approaches to the verification and synthesis of systems under assume-guarantee contracts, which will be discussed later. Moreover, similar results can be established for continuous-time systems [8].

Assume-guarantee contracts are particularly adapted to compositional reasoning, which makes it possible for instance to reason about networks of CPS from contracts satisfied by their components. However, contracts given by (2) are in general too weak to reason about arbitrary system interconnections, which generally include feedback loops. Therefore, it is useful to define the notion of strong satisfaction for assume-guarantee contracts [6]. We say that C is strongly satisfied by S, denoted by $S \models_s C$ if the following property holds for all trajectories $(z_t)_{t \in \mathbb{N}}$ of (1) and for all $t \in \mathbb{N}_{\geq 1}$:

$$(\forall s \leq t - 1,\ z_{s+1} \in F_A(z_s)) \implies z_{t+1} \in F_G(z_t). \tag{5}$$

Strong satisfaction makes it possible to break the circular dependencies in compositional reasoning. A characterization based on invariant sets similar to (3) and (4) can also be established.

3   Computational Aspects

The characterization of assume-guarantee contract satisfaction, given by (3) and (4), provides a theoretical basis for developing effective computational methods for CPS verification and synthesis.

For CPS described by linear dynamics, one draws on well-established techniques in control engineering. On the one hand, set-theoretic methods [3] make it possible to use polyhedral computations to compute invariant sets that are arbitrarily close to the maximal one. On the other hand, approaches based on linear matrix inequalities [9] allow us to compute ellipsoidal invariant sets using convex semidefinite optimization. In the presence of nonlinear dynamics, symbolic control approaches [1,7], which are based on the use of finite abstractions of the CPS dynamics, can be used to compute invariant sets with formal guarantees.

In the presentation, we will discuss these computational approaches and consider illustrative examples inspired by the design of hierarchical and distributed control systems.

Acknowledgements. This presentation is based on joint work with Adnane Saoud, Laurent Fribourg, Alessio Iovine, Grace Chiza Bulonza, and Sofiane Benberkane. The author gratefully acknowledges their valuable contributions. This work received funding from the Labex DigiCosme (project ANR-11-LABEX-0045-DIGICOSME) operated by ANR as part of the program "Investissement d'Avenir" Idex Paris Saclay (ANR-11-IDEX-0003-02), the European Research Council (ERC) under the European Union's Horizon 2020 research and innovation programme (grant agreement No 725144), and from the RTE-CentraleSupélec Chair.

References

1. Belta, C., Yordanov, B., Aydin Gol, E.: Formal methods for discrete-time dynamical systems. Springer (2017)
2. Benveniste, A., et al.: Contracts for system design. Found. Trends® Electron. Des. Autom. **12**(2-3), 124–400 (2018)

3. Blanchini, F., Miani, S.: Set-theoretic methods in control. Springer (2015)
4. Girard, A., Iovine, A., Benberkane, S.: Invariant sets for assume-guarantee contracts. In: IEEE Conference on Decision and Control, pp. 2190–2195 (2022)
5. Sangiovanni-Vincentelli, A., Damm, W., Passerone, R.: Taming Dr. Frankenstein: contract-based design for cyber-physical systems. Eur. J. Control **18**(3), 217–238 (2012)
6. Saoud, A., Girard, A., Fribourg, L.: On the composition of discrete and continuous-time assume-guarantee contracts for invariance. In: European Control Conference, pp. 435–440 (2018)
7. Saoud, A., Girard, A., Fribourg, L.: Contract-based design of symbolic controllers for safety in distributed multiperiodic sampled-data systems. IEEE Trans. Autom. Control **66**(3), 1055–1070 (2020)
8. Saoud, A., Girard, A., Fribourg, L.: Assume-guarantee contracts for continuous-time systems. Automatica **134**, 109910 (2021)
9. Tarbouriech, S., Garcia, G., da Silva Jr, J.M.G., Queinnec, I.: Stability and stabilization of linear systems with saturating actuators. Springer Science and Business Media (2011)

Tutorial

Domain Analysis and Description:
A Tutorial

Dines Bjørner$^{(\boxtimes)}$

Technical University of Denmark Fredsvej 11, 2840 Holte, Denmark
bjorner@gmail.com

Abstract. We present a summary of a domain analysis & description method. Domains are the realm in which [large scale] software is embedded – in order to serve human actions in predominantly man-made "surroundings". The method, with its *principles, procedures, techniques* and *tools*, are outlined. A main principle is that of delineating observable **phenomena** into describable **entities**; these into **endurants** and **perdurants**, i.e., roughly speaking "statically" and "dynamically" observable **entities**; entities into **endurants** and **perdurants**; endurants into **solids** and **fluids**; solids into **parts** and **living species**; parts into **atomic** and **compound parts**; and compound parts into **Cartesians** and **part sets**. Endurants are then "endowed" with **unique identities, mereologies, attributes** and **intentional "pull"**. Endurants are then, by transcendental deduction, "morphed" into **perdurants: behaviours** that *communicate*, and where unique identities, mereologies and attributes serve as possible updateable behaviour arguments.

The Triptych Dogma

In order to *specify* $\mathbb{S}$*oftware*, we must understand its $\mathbb{R}$*equirements.*
In order to *prescribe* $\mathbb{R}$*equirements* we must understand the $\mathbb{D}$*omain.*
So we must **study, analyze** and **describe** $\mathbb{D}$*omains.*
$\mathbb{D},\mathbb{S} \models \mathbb{R}$: In **proofs** of $\mathbb{S}$*oftware* correctness,
with respect to $\mathbb{R}$*equirements*,
assumptions are made with respect to the $\mathbb{D}$*omain*

1 Introduction

We encourage the reader to carefully study the above triptych[1] – and the abstract with its *slanted text* and **bold face** highlighted terms. We are **not** concerned with computing; **neither** are we concerned with software **nor** with requirements to software. Computability and correctness of software is **not** our concerns. **We**

This paper is the basis for an invited tutorial for ICTAC 2025, Marrackesh, Morocco, 24–29 November 2025.

[1] The domain modeling approach of this paper has been extensively covered in books and lectures notes [2,21]. The present paper is derived from [24].

Z. Liu et al. (Eds.): ICTAC 2025, LNCS 16237, pp. 39–66, 2026.
https://doi.org/10.1007/978-3-032-11176-0_5

are concerned with understanding domains such as *railways, insurance, banking, retail and wholesale trading, health care, container terminal ports*, etcetera. How can we analyze and describe domains? That is our concern. So we propose a rigorous method for analyzing and describing domains. The mandate that this paper suggests is that software development begins with *domain analysis & description*, continues with *requirements prescription* [2, *Chapter 9*], and and "ends" with *software design* [1] and coding. This is the new approach: the strict separation of concerns. It was first carried out in the commercial development of the DDC Ada Compiler [26]. Nobody has suggested the separate development of domain models before. Michael A. Jackson [29] discusses a role for domains, in the context of requirements, software and the *machine* – but does not suggest a separate, let alone, formal description of domains.

One of the novel aspects of the domain modeling approach that is advocated here is the somewhat "strict" methodological approach. Here the method is seen as a set of *principles, procedures, techniques* and *tools*. The main principle is *abstraction* and the combined *narration & formalization* of the domain description. The main principle is that of following a specific *domain analysis & description ontology*. The main techniques are predominantly "mental": to be carried out by the domain analyzer cum describer and are those of calculating type names and types of *endurants, unique identifiers, mereologies* and *attributes*, as well as the definitions of *behaviours*[2] And the main *tools* are those of the dozen or so *prompts* and nine *schemas*.

● ● ●

We structure this paper in a perhaps unusual form. Instead of compact paragraphs interspersed with definitions cum characterizations, examples, etc., You shall mostly find itemized and enumerated statements. For a more conventional presentation form we refer to the longer 37 page [24].

2   Domains

Characterization 1 *Domain*:

By a *domain* we shall understand a *rationally describable* segment of a *discrete dynamics* fragment of a *human directed & assisted* reality:

- the world that we daily observe
- in which we work and act –
- a reality made significant by human-created entities ∎

Characterization versus Definition

○ It is important to observe that we use the term 'characterization' and not the term 'definition'.
○ The reason is the following:

---

[2] The *slanted* font terms will soon be revealed!.

    ∗ The describable concepts of the domains that we wish to delineate / encircle are not formal[3].

    ∗ Were they formal, then we could use the term 'definition'.

    ∗ The aim of a 'domain description' is to formalize an instance of a domain.

    ∗ But the formal instances do not mean that the underlying concepts are formal.

An Aside: From Algorithmics to Domains

- "In the beginning" there were **algorithms**
- About 1948 came the von Neumann **computers**
- 1960s: Focus was on **software** implementing algorithms on data
- Late 1970s" **requirements**
- 2010s: **domain engineering**

Domain Engineers face the 𝔻omain.
– end of an aside

Informal Example 1 *Some Domain Examples*: [4]

- **Rivers:** sources, deltas, tributaries, waterfalls, etc., and their man-made dams, harbours, locks, etc. – and their conveyage of materials (ships, barges, etc.) [22, *Chapter B*].
- **Road nets:** street segments and intersections, traffic lights and automobiles – and the flow of these, etc. [22, *Chapter E*].
- **Pipelines:** liquids (oil, gas, or water), wells, pipes, valves, pumps, forks, joins and wells and the flow of fluids, etc. [22, *Chapter I*].
- **Container terminals:** – container vessels, containers, cranes, trucks, etc. – and the movement of these [22, *Chapter K*]
- **Retailing:** customers, shops, distributors, manufacturers, … ∎

Characterization 1 relies on the understanding of the terms

- *'rationally'*
- *'discrete'*
- *'human'*

By **rationally describable** we mean that what is described can be understood, including reasoned about, in a rational, that is, logical manner – in other words **logically tractable**. By **discrete dynamics** we imply that we shall basically rule out such domain phenomena which have properties which are continuous with respect to their time-wise, i.e., dynamic, behaviour. By **human-directed & assisted** we mean that the domains – that we are interested in modeling – have, as an important property, that they possess man-made and utilized entities.

---

[3] The describable/underlying concepts are those of *entities, endurants, perdurants, solids, fluids, parts, living species, atomic parts, compound parts, Cartesians, part sets*, etc. These concepts will all be 'characterized'.

[4] Some examples are informal, as is this, some are "formal". We shall alert You to the formal ones!.

3   A Domain Modeling Analysis & Description Ontology

So how do we approach analyzing and describing the kind of domains that we attempted to outline above ? We propose an altogether new approach. It is partly motivated by the philosophy of Kai Sørlander, a Danish philosopher [31]. The approach, as already revealed in the **abstract**, consists of inquiring, when You, as a domain analyzer cum describer, physically observe a domain and mentally reflect on what You observe in that domain: which are the phenomena; which of these are rationally describable, i.e., are entities, and, of the entities, which are endurants, i.e., somehow "statically" observable, and which are perdurants, i.e., somehow "dynamically" observable, etc.

The terms: phenomena, entities, endurants, perdurants, etc., will be explained now in detail. Their ontological relationship is captured in Fig. 1.

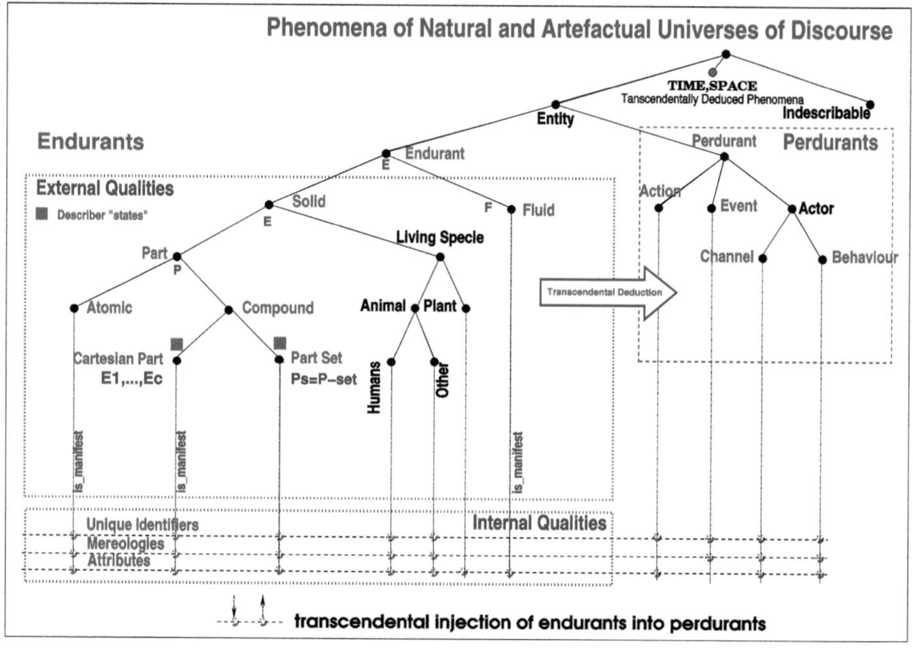

Fig. 1. A Domain Modeling Analysis & Description Ontology

4   Phenomena and Entities. Endurants and Perdurants

The are "things" in domains we can rationally describe, and there are "things" we cannot, at present, rationally describe.

4.1 Phenomena

Characterization 2 *Phenomena*:

- By a *phenomenon*
  we shall understand a fact
  that is observed to exist or happen ∎

Some phenomena are rationally describable – to some degree – others are not.

Informal Example 2 *Phenomena*: For a transport domain we identify the following phenomena: *trains, unpleasant smell of automobile exhaust, the flight of an aircraft* ∎

4.2 Entities

Characterization 3 *Entities*:

- By an entity an *entity*
- we shall understand a [more-or-less]
- rationally describable phenomenon ∎

Informal Example 3 *Entities*: For a transport domain we identify the following entities: *the way bill* and *bill of lading* for a transport, the *inquiry* as to a transport of specific goods, the *departure* of a train ∎

- **Prompt 1** is_entity(ϕ)

  * is_entity(ϕ) holds
  * for phenomenon ϕ
  * if ϕ is describable ∎

By a prompt (*cue*[5], *schlüsselwörter, mots-clés, spunto, ...*) we shall here understand: a mental note – something for the domain analyze & describer to do – according to the domain analysis & description ontology.

4.3 Endurants

Characterization 4 *Endurants*:
Endurants are those quantities of domains that we can observe (see and touch), in *space*, as "complete" entities at no matter which point in *time* – "material" entities that persists, endures – capable of enduring adversity, severity, or hardship [Merriam Webster] ∎

---

[5] cue: thing said or done that serves as a signal to an actor or other performer to enter or to begin their speech or performance.

Endurants are either *natural* ["God-given"] or *artefactual* ["man-made"]; and either **solid** or **fluid**; and either *manifest*, or *conceptual*; and either *mobile*, or *immobile* – or are *immobile* but can be moved!

Informal Example 4 *Endurants*: In a transport domain we can identify the following endurants:*streets, street intersections, automobiles, trucks, buses, rails, trains, sea, container vessels, air and aircraft* ∎

Endurants are:

- **"God-given" vs. Man-made:**
    * Lakes, rivers, mountains, fish, and roses – are "God-given".
    * Roads, automobiles and aircraft – are man-made.
- **Solid vs. Fluid:**
    * An automobile and a mountain is solid.
    * The milk in a carton, and the water in a lake is fluid.
- **Manifest vs. Conceptual:**
    * An automobile is manifest.
    * The "assembly" of automobiles and roads is seen as conceptual.
- **Mobile vs. Immobile:**
    * A ship is mobile.
    * A road is immobile.
    * Most cargo on a ship, or on-shore, is immobile – but can be moved!

- **Prompt 2** $is\_endurant(e)$:
    * $is\_endurant$ holds
    * for entity e
    * if e is an endurant ∎
    * **pre:** $is\_entity(e)$

4.4   Perdurants

Characterization 5 *Perdurants*: Perdurants are those quantities of domains for which only a fragment exists, in *space*, if we look at or touch them at any given snapshot in *time* [Merriam Webster]∎

Perdurants are here considered to be *actions*, *events* and *behaviours*.

Informal Example 5 *Perdurants*: In a transport domain we can identify the following perdurants: *moving automobiles, moving trucks, moving trains, moving ships, moving aircraft.* ∎

- **Prompt 3** $is\_perdurant(e)$:
    * $is\_perdurant(e)$ holds
    * for entity e
    * if e is a perdurant ∎
    * **pre:** $is\_entity(e)$

5   External and Internal Endurant Qualities

Characterization 6 *External Qualities*: External qualities of endurants of a manifest domain are, in a simplifying sense, those we can see, touch and have spatial extent. They, so to speak, "take form".

Informal Example 6 *External Qualities*: the Cartesian of sets of solid atomic street intersections, and of sets of solid atomic street segments, and of sets of solid automobiles of a road transport system reflect external qualities ∎

Characterization 7 *Internal Qualities*: Internal qualities are those properties [of endurants] that do not occupy *space* but can be measured or spoken about or have occurred ∎

Informal Example 7 *Internal Qualities*: the distinct identity of each automobile; the [mereological] relations between street segments [links] and intersections [hubs]; the position of an automobile on a street segment; the state of a hub: green–red ∎

6   External Qualities

External qualities of endurants are, simplifying, those that we can see and touch and which have spatial extent.

6.1   The Universe of Discourse

The "outermost" quality of a domain is the "entire" domain – "itself" ! Any domain analysis starts by identifying that "entire" domain ! We it a name, say UoD, for *universe of discourse*, We describe it, in *narrative* form,
that is, in natural language
containing terms of professional/technical nature, the domain. Finally, *formalizing* just the name:
giving the name "status" of being a type name,
that is, of the type of a class of domains
whose further properties will be described subsequently.

Schema 1 *The Universe of Discourse*

> **Narration:**
> > The name, and hence the type, of the domain is UoD
> > The UoD domain can be briefly characterized by ∎∎∎
> **Formalization:**
> > type UoD ∎

Formal Example 1 *Multi-modal Transport*: [6]

> **Narration:**
>> The domain is that of multi-modal transport T: land, sea and air,
>> of goods, G: passengers and merchandise,
>> by conveyors, C: bus, truck, train, ship and aircraft.
>> "K"ustomers, K, inquire, order, deliver and receive goods.
>> Firms, F, offer, confirm order and convey goods.
>> Conveyors load and unload merchandise at nodes, N,
>> travel along links, L of a transport net, N, and
>> keep firms and customers informed by messages, M.
>> Etcetera, etcetera.
>
> **Formalization:**
>> **type**
>>> T, M, C, K, G, F, ..., N, L, N, M, ...
>>
>> **value**
>>> inq, ordr, deliv, recv, offr, conf_ordr, convey, load, unload, travel, inf, ...
>>
>> **axiom**
>>> ... ■

6.2   Solid Endurants

Given then that there are endurants we now postulate that they are either [mutually exclusive] *solid* (i.e., discrete) or *fluid*.

Characterization 8 *Solid Endurants*:

- By a *solid* endurant
    * we shall understand an endurant
    * which is separate, individual or distinct in form or concept,
  or, rephrasing,
    * have body (or magnitude) of three-dimensions:
        * length/height,
        * breadth/width and
        * depth ■

Informal Example 8 *Solid Endurants of a Pipeline System*: Some are: wells, pipes, pigs, valves, pumps, forks, joins and sinks ■

Prompt 4 `is_solid`:

- `is_solid(e)` holds
- for endurant e
- if e is solid ■
- **pre:** `is_endurant(e)`

---

[6] This example is listed as 'formal' – although it is mostly "sketchy informal" !.

6.3   Fluids

Characterization 9 *Fluid Endurants*: By a *fluid endurant* we shall understand an endurant which is prolonged, without interruption, in an unbroken series or pattern; [] or, rephrasing: a substance (liquid, gas or plasma) having the property of flowing, consisting of particles that move among themselves ∎

Informal Example 9 *Fluid Endurants*: Examples of fluid endurants are: *water, oil, gas, compressed air, smoke*∎

Fluids are otherwise liquid, gaseous, plasmatic, granular, or plant products, et cetera.

Prompt 5 *is_fluid*: is_fluid(e) holds for endurant e if e is fluid ∎
pre: is_endurant(e)

6.4   Parts and Living Species Endurants

Given then that there are solid endurants we now postulate that [mutually exclusive] they are either *parts* or *living species*.

6.4.1   Parts

Characterization 10 *Parts*: The non-living-species solids are what we shall call parts∎

Parts are the "work-horses" of man-made domains.

Informal Example 10 *Parts*: *Pipeline Units*: wells, pumps, pipes, pigs, valves, forks, sinks ∎

Prompt 6 *is_part*:

- is_part(e) holds
- for solid endurants e
- if e is a part∎
- **pre:** is_solid(e)

6.4.2   Atomic and Compound Parts We distinguish between atomic and compound parts.

- It is an empirical fact that
- parts can be composed from parts.
- That possibility exists.
- Hence we can [philosophy-wise] reason likewise.

6.4.2.1 Atomic Parts

Characterization 11 *Atomic Part*:

- By an *atomic part*
- we shall understand a part
- which the domain analyzer considers to be indivisible
- in the sense of not meaningfully consist of sub-parts ∎

Informal Example 11 *Atomic Parts*: hubs, H, i.e., street intersections links, L, i.e., the roads between two neighbouring hubs automobiles, A ∎

Prompt 7 *is_atomic*:

- is_atomic(p) to hold
- for parts p if
- p is atomic ∎
- **pre:** is_part(e)

6.4.2.2 Compound Parts

Characterization 12 *Compound Part*: Compound parts are those which are observed to consist of several parts ∎

Informal Example 12 *Compound Parts*:

- A **road net** consists of a **Cartesian** of [∘] a **set of hubs**, i.e., street intersections or "end-of-streets", and [∘] a **set of links**, i.e., street segments (with no contained hubs) ∎

Prompt 8 *is_compound*:

- is_compound(p) holds
- for parts p
- if p is a compound ∎
- **pre:** is_part(e)

—Cartesians

Characterization 13 *Cartesians*: Cartesian parts are those compound parts which are observed to consist of two or more distinctly sort-named endurants (solids or fluids) ∎

Formal Example 2 *Road Transport*: [7]

Narrative:

---

[7] This example is 'formal' in the sense that it adheres to the *narrative/RSL formalization* dogma.

1. A road transport, rt:RT, is abstracted as a Cartesian of
2. a road net, RN and
3. an aggregate of automobiles, SA –
4. where the road net is a Cartesian of a set of hubs, AH,
5. and a set of links, AL.
6. An aggregate of automobiles is a set of automolbiles.
7. Automobiles are here considered atomic.

Formalization:

type
1. RT
2. RN
3. SA
4. AH = H-set
5. AL = L-set
6. AS = A-set
7. A

value
2. **obs_RN**: RT $\rightarrow$ RN
3. **obs_SA**: RT $\rightarrow$ SA
4. **obs_AH**: RN $\rightarrow$ AH
5. **obs_AL**: RN $\rightarrow$ AL
6. **obs_AS**: SA $\rightarrow$ AS ∎

Prompt 9 *is_Cartesian*: is_Cartesian(p) holds for compound parts p if p is Cartesian ∎
pre: is_compound(e)

A Cartesian part, say p:P, consists of two or more endurants. Which are the type names of the endurants of which it consists? The inquiry: record_Cartesian_part_type_names(p:P), yields the *type names* of the constituent endurants.

Prompt 10 *record-Cartesian-part-type-names*:

value
    record_Cartesian_part_type_names: P $\rightarrow$ $\mathbb{T}$-set
    record_Cartesian_part_type_names(p) as $\{\eta E1, \eta E2, ..., \eta En\}$ ∎

Here $\mathbb{T}$ is the **name** of the type of all type names, and ηEi is the **name** of type Ei.

Informal Example 13 *Cartesian Parts*:

- The Cartesian parts of a road transport, rt:RT, consists of
    * an aggregate of a road net, rn:RN, and
    * an aggregate set of automobiles, sa:SA:

50   D. Bjørner

- That is:
  - `record_Cartesian_part_type_names(rt:RT)` $= \{\eta RN, \eta SA\}$
  - `record_Cartesian_part_type_names(rn:RN)` $= \{\eta AH, \eta AL\}$ ∎

—Part Sets
Characterization 14 *Part Sets*:

- Part sets are those compound parts
- which are observed to consist of
- an indefinite number of zero, one or more parts ∎

Prompt 11 *is_part_set*:

- `is_part_set(p)` to holds
- for compound parts e
- if e is a part set ∎
- **pre:** `is_compound(e)`

The inquiry: `record_part_set_part_type_names`, yields the (single) type of the constituent parts.

Prompt 11 *record-part-set-part-type-names*:

value
    `record_part_set_part_type_names`: $E \rightarrow \mathbb{T}Ps \times \mathbb{T}P$
    `record_part_set_part_type_names(e:E)` **as** $(\eta\, Ps, \eta\, P)$ ∎

Example 1. *Part Sets: Road Transport*: The road transport contains a set of automobiles. The part set type name has been chosen to be SA.
    It is then determined (i.e., analyzed) that SA is a set of Automobile of type A

- `record_part_set_part_type_names(sa:SA)` $= (\eta\, As, \eta\, A)$ ∎

6.4.2.3 Compound Observers

Prompt 13 *describe_compound(p): P $\rightarrow$* RSL-**Text**:

value
    let $\{\eta\, P1, \eta\, P2, ..., \eta\, Pn\}$=`record_Cartesian_part_type_names(e:E)` **in**
    " **type**
           P1, P2, ..., Pn;
        value
           obs_P1: E$\rightarrow$P1, **obs**_P2: E$\rightarrow$P2,...n **obs**_Pn: E$\rightarrow$Pn "

let $(\eta\,\mathsf{Ps},\eta\,\mathsf{P})$ = record_part_set_part_type_names(e:E) **in**
" **type**
$\qquad$ P, Ps = P-**set**,
$\quad$ **value**
$\qquad$ **obs**_Ps: E→Ps "
end end ∎

6.5 States

Characterization 15 *States*:

- By a *state*
- we shall mean any subset of the parts of a domain ∎

Formal Example 3 *Road Transport State*:

8. There is the set of all hubs,
9. and the set of all links,
10. and the set of all automobiles.
11. The union of these form a state.

variable
8. $\quad hs$:AH := **obs**_AH(**obs**_RN(rt))
9. $\quad ls$:AL := **obs**_AL(**obs**_RN(rt))
10. $\quad as$:SA := **obs**_AS(**obs**_SA(rt))
11. $\quad \sigma$:(H|L|A)-**set** := $hs \cup ls \cup as$ ∎

6.6 Summary of Endurant Prompts

6.6.1 Analysis Prompts

- is_entity
- is_endurant
- is_perdurant
- is_solid
- is_fluid

- is_part
- is_atomic
- is_compound
- is_Cartesian
- is_part_set

6.6.2 Description Prompts

- record_Cartesian_part_type_names
- record_part_set_part_type_names
- describe_compound: Cartesians, Part Sets

7   Internal Qualities Intangibles

Characterization 16 *Internal Qualities* Internal qualities are those properties [of endurants] that do not occupy *space* but can be measured or spoken about ∎

Example 2. *Internal qualities* Examples of internal qualities are **uid_**: the *unique identity* of a part, **mereo_**: the *mereological relation* of parts to other parts, and **attr_**: the attribute query of endurants ∎

7.1   Unique Identity

Characterization 17 *Unique Identity*: An immaterial property that distinguishes any two *spatially* distinct solids. The unique identity of a part p of type P is obtained by the postulated observer **uid_P**:

Schema 2 *Describe-Unique-Identity-Part-Observer*:

> " **type**
>> P, PI
>> **value**
>>> **uid_P**: $P \rightarrow PI$ " ∎

Here PI is the type of the unique identifiers of parts of type P.

Formal Example 4 *Unique Road Transport Identifiers*: The unique identifierss of a road transport, rt:RT, is here limited:

12. each hub has a unique identifier,
13. each link has a unique identifier, and
14. each automobile has a unique identifier.

```
type
12. HI
13. LI
14. AI
value
15. uid_H: H → HI
16. uid_H: L → LI
17. uid_H: A → AI  ∎
```

Schema 3 *Describe-Unique-Identifiers*:

> let $\{\eta\,\mathsf{P1}, \eta\,\mathsf{P2}, ..., \eta\,\mathsf{Pn}\}$ = **record_domain_part_type_names**(p:P) in
> " **type**
>   P1I, P2I, ..., PnI;
>   **value**
>   **uid_P1**: P1→P1I, **uid_P2**: P2→P2I,..., **uid_Pn**: Pn→PnI "
> **end** ∎

We have thus introduced a core domain modeling tool the **uid_**... observer function, one to be "applied" mentally by the domain describer. The **uid_**... observer function is "applied" by the domain describer. It is not a computable function.

No two parts have the same unique identifier.

Formal Example 5 *Road Transport Uniqueness*:

The unique identifiers of a road transport, rt:RT, consists of the unique identifiers of

15. the set of all hub identifiers,
16. the set of all link identifiers,
17. the set of all automobile identifiers.
18. Together they form a unique identifier state.
19. There are as many hubs, links and automobiles as there are hub, link and automobile identifiers.

variable

15. hs_{uids}:HI-**set** := { **uid_H**(h) | h:H • h $\in \sigma$}
16. ls_{uids}:LI-**set** := { **uid_L**(l) | l:L • l $\in \sigma$}
17. as_{uids}:AI-**set** := { **uid_A**(a) | a:A • a $\in \sigma$}
18. σ_{uids}:(HI|LI|AI)-**set** := $hs_{uids} \cup hs_{uids} \cup hs_{uids}$
19. **card**σ = **card**σ_{uids}

7.2 Mereology

The concept of mereology is due to the Polish mathematician Stanisław Leśniewski (1886–1939)

Characterization 18 *Mereology*: Mereology is a theory of the relations of an [endurant] parts to a whole and the relations of [endurant] parts to [endurant] parts within that whole∎

From Mereology to Communication Channels
We shall analyze and describe: narrate and formalize the mereology of manifest parts. This form of description serves to explain how parts relate to one another. These relationships "reappear" in the part-perdurant behaviours in the form of CSP-like communications over channels between mereologically prescribed sub-channels.
Mereologies can be expressed in terms of unique identifiers.

Formal Example 6 *Road Traffic Mereology*: We shall be concerned onlt with the mereology of some manifest parts.

20. The mereology of links is a 2 element set of hub identifiers of the road net[8].
21. The mereology of a hub is a possibly empty set of hub identifiers of the road
    net.
22. The mereology of an automobile is [some subset of] a set of hub and link
    identifiers[9]

type
20. ML = LI-set **axiom** $\forall$ ml:MK • **card** ml = 2 $\wedge$ ml $\subseteq$ ls_{uis}
21. MH = HI-set **axiom** $\forall$ mh:MH • mh $\subseteq$ hs_{uis}
22. MA = (HI|LI)-set **axiom** $\forall$ ma:MA • ma $\subseteq$ as_{uis}
value
20. **mereo_L**: L $\rightarrow$ ML
21. **mereo_H**: H $\rightarrow$ MH
22. **mereo_A**: A $\rightarrow$ MA ∎

In general:

Schema 4 *Describe-Mereology*:

> " **type**
>   PMer = $\mathcal{M}$(PI1,PI2,...,PIm)
>   **value**
>   **mereo_P**: P $\rightarrow$ PMer
>   **axiom**
> $\mathcal{A}$(pm:PMer) " ∎

where $\mathcal{M}$(PI1,PI2,...,PIm) is a type expression over unique identifier types of
the domain; **mereo_P** is the mereology observer function for parts p:P; and
$\mathcal{A}$(pm:PMer) is an axiom that secures that the unique identifiers of any part
are indeed of parts of the domain ∎

7.3   Attributes

Attributes are what finally gives "life" to endurants: The external qualities
"only" named [i.e., typed] and gave structure to their atomic or compound types.
The internal qualities of uniqueness and mereology are intangible quantities.
The internal quality of attributes gives "flesh & blood" to endurants: they let us
express endurant properties that we can more easily, i.e., concretely, relate to.

---

[8] This is a simplified version: it allows for automoblie traffic in both directions of the
   link. We leave it to the reader to "cook" up othe such traffic possibilities.

[9] – a full set means that the specific automobile is allowed to travel all over the net.

Characterization 19 *Attributes*: are properties of endurants that can be measured either physically or can be objectively spoken about ∎

Attributes are of types and, accordingly have values.

An informal domain analysis function, `record_attribute_type_names`: analyzes parts, $p{:}P$, into the set of attribute names of parts $p{:}P$

Schema 5 *record-attribute-type-names*:

value

    record_attribute_type_names: P $\to$ $\eta\mathbb{T}$**-set**
    record_attribute_type_names(p:P) **as** ηT**-set** ∎

Formal Example 7 *Road Net Attributes, I*:
Example attributes are:

23. Hubs have states, hσ:HΣ: the set of pairs of link identifiers, ($f$li,$t$li), of the links $f$rom and to which automobiles may enter, respectively leave the hub.
24. Hubs have state spaces, hω:HΩ: the set of hub states "signaling" which states are open/closed, i.e., green/red.
25. Links that have lengths, LEN; and
26. Automobiles have road net positions, APos,
27. either *at a hub*, atH,
28. or *on a link*, onL, some fraction, f:**Real**, down a link, identified by li, from a hub, identified by fhi, towards a hub, identified by thi.
29. Links have states, lσ:LΣ: the set of pairs of link identifiers, ($f$li,$t$li), of the links $f$rom and to which automobiles may enter, respectively leave the hub.
30. Links have state spaces, lω:LΩ: the set of link states "signaling" which states are open/closed, i.e., green/red.
31. Hubs, links and automobiles have *histories:* time-stamped, chronologically ordered sequences of automobiles entering and leaving links and hubs, with automobile histories similarly recording hubs and links entered and left.
32. Link positions have well-defined identifiers and fractions.

ss

type
23. HΣ = (LI×LI)**-set**
24. HΩ = HΣ**-set**
25. LEN = **Nat**
26. APos = atH | onL
27.   atH :: HI
28.   onL :: LI × (fhi:HI × f:**Real** × thi:HI)
29. LΣ = (HI×HI)**-set**
30. LΩ = LΣ**-set**
31. HHis,LHis = (TIME×AI)*
31. AHis = (TIME×(HI|LI))*

value
23. attr_HΣ: H $\to$ HΣ
24. attr_HΩ: H $\to$ HΩ
25. attr_LEN: L $\to$ LEN
26. attr_APos: A $\to$ APos
29. attr_LΣ: L $\to$ LΣ
30. attr_LΩ: L $\to$ LΩ
31. attr_HHis: H $\to$ HHis
31. attr_LHis: L $\to$ LHis
31. attr_AHis: A $\to$ AHis

axiom
32. $\forall$ mk_onL(li,(fhi,f,thi)):onL • 0<f<1 $\wedge$ li$\in ls_{uids}$ $\wedge$ {fhi,thi}$\subseteq hs_{uids}$ $\wedge$ ... ∎

Schema 6 *Describe-endurant-attributes(e:E)*:

> **let** $\{\eta\,\text{A1},\eta\text{A2},...,\eta\text{An}\}$ = record_attribute_type_names(e:E) **in**
> " **type**
>   A1, A2, ..., An
>   **value**
>   **attr__A1**: E $\rightarrow$ A1, **attr__A2**: E $\rightarrow$ A2, ..., **attr__An**: E $\rightarrow$ An
>   **axiom**
> $\forall$ a1:A1, a2:A2, ..., an:An: $\mathcal{A}$(a1,a2,...,an) "
> **end** ∎

7.4   Michael A. Jackson's Attribute Categories

Michael A. Jackson [28] has suggested a hierarchy of attribute categories:

- `static` values, `is_static(v)`, are constants, cannot change;
- `dynamic` values, `is_dynamic(v)`, are variable, can change – and within the dynamic value category:
  - `* inert` values, `is_inert(v)`, can only change as the result of external stimuli where these stimuli prescribe new values;
  - `* reactive` values, `is_reactive(v)` if they vary, change in response to external stimuli, where these stimuli either come from outside the domain of interest or from other endurants;
  - `* active` values, `is_active(v)`, can change (also) on their own volition – and within the dynamic active value category:
    - `* autonomous` values, `is_autonomous`, change only "on their own volition" – the values of an autonomous attributes are a "law onto themselves and their surroundings";
    - `* biddable` values, `is_biddable(v)` are prescribed, but may fail to be observed as such; and
    - `* programmable` values, `is_programmable`, can be prescribed.

We refer to [28] and [2] [*Chapter 5, Sect. 5.4.2.3*] for details. We suggest a minor revision of Michael A. Jackson's attribute categorization, see left side of Fig. 2. We single out the inert from the ontology of Fig. 2, left side. Inert attributes seem to be "set externally" to the endurant. So we now distinguish between `is_external` and `is_internal` dynamic attributes. We summarize Jackson's attribute [L] and our revised categorization [R] in Fig. 2.

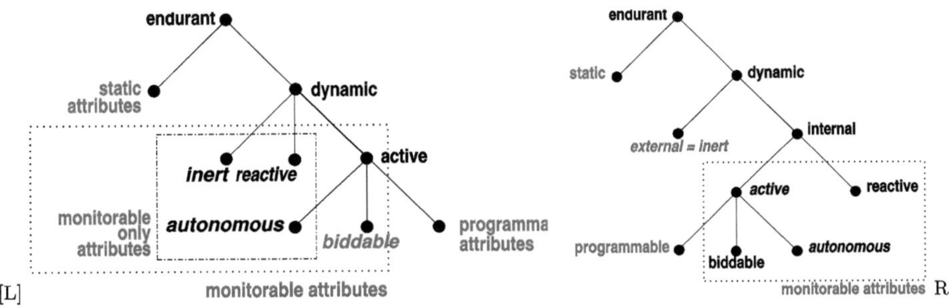

. Michael Jackson's [Revised] Attribute Categories

Fig. 2. Michael Jackson's [Revised] Attribute Categories

7.5 Intentional Pull

Two or more parts of different sorts, but with overlapping sets of intents[10] may excert an intentional "pull" on one another. This *intentional "pull"* may take many forms. Let $p_x : X$ and $p_y : Y$ be two parts of *different sorts* (X, Y), and with *common intent*, ι. *Manifestations* of these, their common intent must somehow be *subject to constraints*, and these must be *expressed predicatively*.

Example 3. *Road Transport Intentionality Automobiles* include the *intent*: transport, as do *hubs* and *links*. *Manifestations* of transport are reflected in *hubs, links* and *automobiles* having the *history* attribute. The *intentional "pull"* of these manifestations is this: For every automobile, if it records being in some hub or on some link at time τ, then the designated hub, respectively link, records exactly that automobile; and vice versa: for all hubs [links], if it records the visit of some automobile at time τ, then the designated automobile records exactly that hub [link] ∎

Example 4. *Double-entry Bookkeeping* Another example of intentional "pull" is that of double-entry bookkeeping. The *incomes/expenses ledger* must *balance* the *actives/passives ledger* ∎

Example 5. *The Henry George Theorem* states that under certain conditions, *spending* by government on *public goods* will increase *rent* based on *land value* more than that amount, with the benefit of the last marginal investment equaling its cost ∎

For example: *Increase in land value around a new bridge "equals" the cost of the bridge.*

---

[10] Intent: purpose; God-given or human-imposed!.

8   Transcendental Deduction

8.1   Some Characterizations

Characterization 20 *Transcendental*:

- By transcendental we shall understand
  * the philosophical notion:
  * the a priori or intuitive basis of knowledge,
  * independent of experience ∎

Characterization 21 *Transcendental Deduction*:

- By a transcendental deduction we shall understand
  * the philosophical notion:
  * a **transcendental** "conversion"
  * of one kind of knowledge
  * into a seemingly different kind of knowledge ∎

8.2   On Manifest Deductions

Definition 1 *Manifest Parts*: By a manifest part we shall understand a part which we have endowed with internal qualities: unique identification, mereology and attributes ∎

That is: You, the domain analyzer cum describer decides which are the manifest parts and which are not the manifest parts

Informal Example 14 *Manifest Road Traffic Parts*: We decide, for our "running" road traffic formal example that the manifest parts are those of hubs, links, and automobiles ∎

Comments:
We could have chosen otherwise. We could, for example, have chosen the aggregate of automobiles to be manifest and represent, for example, either the department of vehicles, or a nation-wide automobile club !

9   Perdurants

- We shall deploy the notion of transcendental deduction when
  * "moving" from **endurant** parts
  * to **perdurant** behaviours !
- And we shall apply transcendental deduction only to manifest parts.

9.1   Actions

- Actions [instantaneously] change state.
- Actions are prescribed.

9.2   Events

- Events [instantaneously] change state.
- Events are not planned.
- They "do so" surreptitiously.

9.3   Behaviours

Characterization 22 *Behaviours*:   Behaviours are sets of sequences of actions, events and behaviours – and take place "over time" ! ∎

Concurrency is modeled by the *sets* of behaviours. Synchronization and communication of behaviours are effected by CSP *output/inputs*:

- ch[{i,j}] ! value – and
- ch[{i,j}] ?.

Informal Example 15 *Road Net Traffic*:   Road net traffic actions: of **automobiles:** start, stop,turn right, turn left, etc.; of **links:** automobiles entering, leaving, and move on the link, etc.; of **hubs:** automobiles entering, leaving, and move, etc. within the hub; etc.

9.4   Channel

Characterization 23 *Channel*: A channel is anything that allows synchronization and communication of values between behaviours ∎

Schema 7 *Channel*:

We suggest the following schema for describing channels:

   " **channel** { ch[{ui,uj}] | ui,ij:UI • ... } M "

where ch is the describer-chosen name for an array of channels; ui,uj are channel array indices of the unique identifiers; UI, of the chosen message domain ∎

Formal Example 8 *Road Transport Interaction Channel*:

33. There is a set of channels between hubs, links and automobiles.
34. These channels communicate messages, M. M will "transpire" frm the behaviour definitions.

channel
33. { ch[{ui,uj}] | {ui,ij}:(HI|LI|AI)-**set** • ui$\neq$uj$\wedge${ui,uj}$\subseteq\sigma_{uids}$ } M
type
33. M ∎

9.5   Behaviour Signatures

Schema 8 *Behaviour Signature*:

Behaviour signatures[11] reflect the internal qualities of the part endurants from which they emerge by transcendental deduction:

value B_p: name of behaviour
$\rightarrow$ Uid_p its unique identifier
$\rightarrow$ $Mereo_p$ mereology
$\rightarrow$ Sta_Vals_p static attributes
$\rightarrow$ $Inert\_Vals_p$ inert attributes
$\rightarrow$ Mon_Refs_p monitorable attributes
$\rightarrow$ $Prgr\_Vals_p$ programmable attributes
$\rightarrow$ { ch[{i,j}] | ... } communication channels
$\rightarrow$ **Unit**   "ad infinitum"

Formal Example 9 *Road Transport Behaviour Signatures*:

35. The signature of hub behaviours follow the "Schönfinkel'ed pattern" of *unique identifier* $\rightarrow$ *mereo* $\rightarrow$ *static attributes* $\rightarrow$ *programmable attributes* $\rightarrow$ *channel arrays* and **Unit**.
36. The signature of link behaviours likewise.
37. The signature of automobile behaviours likewise.

We hint at these signatures.

---

[11] We 'Schónfinkel'/'Curry' function signatures.

value

35. hub: HI
  $\rightarrow$ MereoH
    $\rightarrow (H\Omega \times ...)$
      $\rightarrow (H\Sigma \times HHist \times ...)$
        $\rightarrow \{ch[\{\textbf{uid\_H}(p),ai\}]|ai:AI\bullet ai\in as_{uid}\}$ **Unit**

36. link: LI
  $\rightarrow$ MereoL$\rightarrow$
    $\rightarrow (L\Omega \times LEN \times ...)\rightarrow$
      $\rightarrow (L\Sigma \times LHist \times ...)$
        $\rightarrow \{ch[\{\textbf{uid\_L}(p),ai\}]|ai:AI\bullet ai\in as_{uid}\}$ **Unit**

37. automobile: AI
    $\rightarrow$ MereoA
      $\rightarrow (...)$
        $\rightarrow (AVel \times HAcc \times ... \times APos \times AHist)$
          $\rightarrow \{ch[\{\textbf{uid\_H}(p),ri\}]|ri:(HI|LI)\bullet ri\in hs_{uid}\cup ls_{uid}\}$ **Unit**

Here we have suggested additional and omitted some part attributes ∎

9.6 Behaviour Invocation

Schema 9 *Behaviour Invocation*:

Behaviours are invoked as follows:

" B($\textbf{uid\_B}$(p))
   ($\textbf{mereo\_P}$(p))
    ($\textbf{attr\_staA}_1$(p),...,$\textbf{attr\_staA}_s$(p))
     ($\textbf{attr\_inertA}_1$(p),...,$\textbf{attr\_inertA}_i$(p))
      ($\textbf{attr\_monA}_1$(p),...,$\textbf{attr\_monA}_m$(p))
       ($\textbf{attr\_prgA}_1$(p),...,$\textbf{attr\_prgA}_p$(p)) "

- All arguments are passed *by value*.
- The *uid* value is never changed.
- The *mereology* value is usually not changed.
- The *static attribute* values are fixed, never changed.
- The *inert attribute* values are fixed, but can be updated by receiving explicit input communications.
- The *monitorable attribute* values are functions, i.e., it is as if the "actual" monitorable values are passed *by name*!
- The *programmable attribute* values are usually changed, "updated", by actions described in the behaviour definition.

9.7   Behaviour Description An Example

Formal Example 10 *Automobile Behaviour at Hub*:

38. We abstract automobile behaviour at a Hub (hi).
    (a) Either the automobile remains at the hub,
    (b) or, internally non-deterministically,
    (c) leaves the hub entering a link,
    (d) or, internally non-deterministically,
    (e) stops.

```
38  automobile(ai)(ris)(...)(atH(hi),ahis,_) ≡
38a     automobile_remain_at_hub(ai)(ris)(...)(atH(hi),ahis,_)
38b     ⌐⌐
38c     automobile_leaving_hub(ai)(ris)(...)(atH(hi),ahis,_)
38d     ⌐⌐
38e     automobile_stop(ai)(ris)(...)(atH(hi),ahis,_)
```

39. [38a] The automobile remains at a hub:
    (a) time is recorded,
    (b) informing the hub behaviour, whereupon
    (c) the automobile remains at that hub, "idling",

```
39  automobile_remain_at_hub(ai)(ris)(...)(atH(hi),ahis,_) ≡
39a     let τ = record_TIME in
39b     ch[{ai,hi}] ! τ ;
39c     automobile(ai)(ris)(...)(atH(hi),⟨(τ,hi)⟩^ahis,_) end
```

40. [38c] The automobile leaves the hub entering link li:
    (a) time is recorded;
    (b) hub is informed of automobile leaving and link that it is entering;
    (c) "whereupon" the vehicle resumes (i.e., "while at the same time" resuming) the vehicle behaviour positioned at the very beginning (0) of that link.

```
40  automobile_leaving_b(ai)({li}∪ris)(...)(atH(hi),ahis,_) ≡
40a     let τ = record_TIME   in
40b     (ch[{ai,hi}] ! τ ‖ ch[{ai,li}] ! τ) ;
40c     automobile(ai)(ris)(...)(onL(li,(hi,0,_)),⟨(τ,li)⟩^ahis,_) end
40      pre: [hub is not isolated]
```

41. [38e] Or the automobile stops, "disappears—off the radar" !

41 automobile_stop(ai)(ris),(...)(atH(hi),ahis,_) $\equiv$ **stop** ▪

9.8 Behaviour Initialization

Formal Example 11 *Road Transport Initialization*:
We "wrap up" the main example of this tutorial:

42. Let us refer to the system initialization as an action;
43. all hubs are initialized,
44. and
45. all links are initialized,
46. and
47. all automobiles are initialized.

value
42. rts_initialisation: **Unit** → **Unit**
42. rts_initialisation() $\equiv$
43.   ‖ { hub(**uid_H(l)**)(**mereo_H(l)**)(**attr_HΩ(l)**,...)(**attr_HΣ(l)**,...)| h:H • h $\in hs$ }
44.   ‖
45.   ‖ { link(**uid_L(l)**)(**mereo_L(l)**)(**attr_LEN(l)**,...)(**attr_LΣ(l)**,...)| l:L • l $\in ls$ }
46.   ‖
47.   ‖ { automobile(**uid_A(a)**)(**mereo_A(a)**)(**attr_APos(a)attr_AHis(a)**,...) | a:A • a $\in as$ }

10   Conclusion

- This talk was **not** about computers, computing or Software.
- This talk was about Domain *descriptions*.   [2, Chapters 3–8]
- From these we develop Requirements *prescriptions*.   [2, Chapter 9]
- And from requirements we develop Software *designs*.   [1]

Acknowledgments. I owe debt to Michael A. Jackson for his [28]. The general idea, to me, of [28], has been Jackson's emphasizing dand clarifying a great number concepts. I am sure his "lexicon" was part of my subconsciousness when I, some 10+ years ago, thought out the ontology of this paper. Included in this was Jackson's categorization which, in my "rendition" evolved into attribute categories – and their enunciation as behaviour arguments.

Postscript

In [3] we "small scale", experimentally, analyze & describe a number of domains. In [23, 25] we apply the domain modeling approach to non-trivial, i.e., medium-to-large scale domains: banking and transport. The *Railway Book* [27], although not in the style of the current domain modeling method, presents a number of models from the railway domain.

References

1. Bjørner, D.: Software Engineering, Vol. 1: Abstraction and Modelling; Vol. 2: Specification of Systems and Languages; Vol. 3: Domains, Requirements and Software Design. Texts in Theoretical Computer Science, the EATCS Series. Springer, Heidelberg (2006)
2. Bjørner, D.: Domain Science & Engineering – A Foundation for Software Development. In: EATCS Monographs in Theoretical Computer Science. A revised version of this book is [4]. Springer, Heidelberg (2021)
3. Bjørner, D.: Domain Modeling Case Studies: Experimental research reports carried out to "discover", try-out and refine method principles, techniques and tools (2023)
4. Bjørner, D.: Domain Modeling Case Studies: Experimental research reports carried out to "discover", try-out and refine method principles, techniques and tools, 2023. 2023: Nuclear Power Plants, A Domain Sketch (2023). www.imm.dtu.dk/~dibj/2023/nupopl/nupopl.pdf
5. Bjørner, D.: Domain Modeling Case Studies: Experimental research reports carried out to "discover", try-out and refine method principles, techniques and tools, 2023. 2021: Shipping (2021). www.imm.dtu.dk/~dibj/2021/ral/ral.pdf
6. Bjørner, D.: Domain Modeling Case Studies: Experimental research reports carried out to "discover", try-out and refine method principles, techniques and tools, 2023. 2021: Rivers and Canals – Endurants – A Technical Note (2021). www.imm.dtu.dk/~dibj/2021/Graphs/Rivers-and-Canals.pdf
7. Bjørner, D.: Domain Modeling Case Studies: Experimental research reports carried out to "discover", try-out and refine method principles, techniques and tools, 2023. 2021: A Retailer Market (2021). www.imm.dtu.dk/~dibj/2021/Retailer/BjornerHeraklit27January2021.pdf
8. Bjørner, D.: Domain Modeling Case Studies: Experimental research reports carried out to "discover", try-out and refine method principles, techniques and tools, 2023. 2019: Container Terminals, ECNU, Shanghai, China (2023). www.imm.dtu.dk/~dibj/2018/yangshan/maersk-pa.pdf
9. Bjørner, D.: Domain Modeling Case Studies: Experimental research reports carried out to "discover", try-out and refine method principles, techniques and tools, 2023. 2018: Documents, TongJi Univ., Shanghai, China (2023). www.imm.dtu.dk/~dibj/2017/docs/docs.pdf
10. Bjørner, D.: Domain Modeling Case Studies: Experimental research reports carried out to "discover", try-out and refine method principles, techniques and tools, 2023. 2017: Urban Planning, TongJi Univ., Shanghai, China (2023). www.imm.dtu.dk/~dibj/2017/urban-planning.pdf

11. Bjørner, D.: Domain Modeling Case Studies: Experimental research reports carried out to "discover", try-out and refine method principles, techniques and tools, 2023. 2017: Swarms of Drones, Inst. of Softw., Chinese Acad. of Sci., Peking, China (2023). www.imm.dtu.dk/~dibj/2017/swarms/swarm-paper.pdf

12. Bjørner, D.: Domain Modeling Case Studies: Experimental research reports carried out to "discover", try-out and refine method principles, techniques and tools, 2023. 2013: Road Transport, Technical University of Denmark (2023). www.imm.dtu.dk/~dibj/road-p.pdf

13. Bjørner, D.: Domain Modeling Case Studies: Experimental research reports carried out to "discover", try-out and refine method principles, techniques and tools, 2023. 2012: Credit Cards, Uppsala, Sweden (2023). www.imm.dtu.dk/~dibj/2016/credit/accs.pdf

14. Bjørner, D.: Domain Modeling Case Studies: Experimental research reports carried out to "discover", try-out and refine method principles, techniques and tools, 2023. 2012: Weather Information, Bergen, Norway (2023). www.imm.dtu.dk/~dibj/2016/wis/wis-p.pdf

15. Bjørner, D.: Domain Modeling Case Studies: Experimental research reports carried out to "discover", try-out and refine method principles, techniques and tools, 2023. 2010: Web-based Transaction Processing, Techn. Univ. of Vienna, Austria, p. 186 (2023). www.imm.dtu.dk/~dibj/wfdftp.pdf

16. Bjørner, D.: Domain Modeling Case Studies: Experimental research reports carried out to "discover", try-out and refine method principles, techniques and tools, 2023. 2010: The Tokyo Stock Exchange, Tokyo Univ., Japan (2023). www.imm.dtu.dk/~db/todai/tse-1.pdf. www.imm.dtu.dk/~db/todai/tse-2.pdf

17. Bjørner, D.: Domain Modeling Case Studies: Experimental research reports carried out to "discover", try-out and refine method principles, techniques and tools, 2023. 2009: Pipelines, Technical University of Graz, Austria (2023). www.imm.dtu.dk/~dibj/pipe-p.pdf

18. Bjørner, D.: Domain Modeling Case Studies: Experimental research reports carried out to "discover", try-out and refine method principles, techniques and tools, 2023. 2007: A Container Line Industry Domain, Technical University of Denmark (2023). www.imm.dtu.dk/~dibj/container-paper.pdf

19. Bjørner, D.: Domain Modeling Case Studies: Experimental research reports carried out to "discover", try-out and refine method principles, techniques and tools, 2023. 2002: The Market, Technical University of Denmark (2023). www.imm.dtu.dk/~dibj/themarket.pdf

20. Bjørner, D.: Domain Modeling Case Studies: Experimental research reports carried out to "discover", try-out and refine method principles, techniques and tools, 2023. 1995–2004: Railways, Technical University of Denmark - a compendium (2023). www.imm.dtu.dk/~dibj/train-book.pdf

21. Bjørner, D.: Domain Modelling – A Primer. A short and significantly revised version of [2]. xii+202 (This book is currently being translated into Chinese by Dr. Yang ShaoFa, IoS/CAS (Institute of Software, Chinese Academy of Sciences), Beijing and into Russian by Dr. Mikhail Chupilko and his colleagues, ISP/RAS (Institute of Systems Programming, Russian Academy of Sciences), Moscow) (2023)

22. Bjørner, D.: Domain Models – A Compendium. Internet (2024). http://www.imm.dtu.dk/~dibj/2024/models/domain-models.pdf. This is a very early draft. 19 domain models are presented

23. Bjørner, D.: Banking – A Domain Description. Technical report, Technical University of Denmark, Fredsvej 11, DK-2840 Holte (2025). https://www.imm.dtu.dk/~dibj/2025/banking/main.pdf

24. Bjørner, D.: Domain Analysis & Description. Technical report, Technical University of Denmark, Fredsvej 11, DK-2840 Holte (2025)
25. Bjørner, D.: Transport – A Domain Description. Technical report, Technical University of Denmark, Fredsvej 11, DK-2840 Holte (2025). https://www.imm.dtu.dk/~dibj/2025/transport/main.pdf
26. Bjørner, D., Nest, O.N. (eds.): Towards a Formal Description of Ada. LNCS, vol. 98. Springer, Heidelberg (1980). https://doi.org/10.1007/3-540-10283-3
27. Bjørner, D., Pĕnička, M.: Towards a **TRAIN** Book for **The RAI**lway Domai**N**. Technical reports, Technical University of Denmark, Fredsvej 11, DK-2840 Holte, Denmark (2004). http://www.imm.dtu.dk/~dibj/train-book.pdf
28. Jackson, M.A.: Software Requirements & Specifications: a lexicon of practice, principles and prejudices. ACM Press. Addison-Wesley, Reading (1995)
29. Jackson, M.A.: Program verification and system dependability. In: Boca, P., Bowen, J., Siddiqi, J. (eds.) Formal Methods: State of the Art and New Directions, London, UK, pp. 43–78. Springer, Heidelberg (2009)
30. Sørlander, K.: Den rene fornufts struktur [The Structure of Pure Reason]. Ellekær, Slagelse, Denmark. See [14] (2022)
31. Sørlander, K.: The Structure of Pure Reason. Springer, Heidelberg (2025). This is an English translation of [13] – done by Dines Bjørner in collaboration with the author

Verification and Synthesis

Multi-perspective Correctness of Programs

Eduard Kamburjan[1,2(✉)] and Dilian Gurov[3]

[1] IT University of Copenhagen, Copenhagen, Denmark
`eduard.kamburjan@itu.dk`
[2] University of Oslo, Oslo, Norway
[3] KTH Royal Institute of Technology, Stockholm, Sweden
`dilian@kth.se`

Abstract. Traditionally, programs are formally specified and verified with respect to their *computational domain*, disregarding the domain in which they are to be applied. This, however, is inadequate for programs that simulate processes in a specific application domain, or programs that generate data that must conform to external, domain-specific specifications. Such programs need also to be correct with respect to their *application domain*. This work presents a Hoare Logic that manages two different perspectives on a program during a correctness proof: the computational view and the domain view. This enables us to specify the correctness of a program in terms of the domain *without* referring to the computational details, but at the same time to interpret failed proof attempts in the domain. For domain specification, we illustrate the use of description logics and base our approach on semantic lifting, an approach to interpret a program as a knowledge graph. We present a calculus that uses translations between both kinds of assertions, thus separating the concerns in specification, but enabling the use of description logic in verification.

1 Introduction

Programs are typically developed in the context of some domain and must truthfully represent the knowledge about this domain to be considered correct. When reasoning about a program, it is, therefore, interpreted as both a *computational structure* and as a *model* for the domain: At the very minimum, the implemented computational logic must correspond to the intended business logic, but in extreme cases, such as simulators, the domain is directly encoded in the program. Even if the program does not encode any business logic in its statements, it may generate output data that must be correct w.r.t. some external specification from the domain, for example for data exchange.

Deductive program verification [13] approaches employ logical reasoning to prove functional correctness, but currently rely on a singular specification language that focuses on the computational nature of programs: a program logic (PL), such as Hoare logic, that refers to statements and program elements (e.g., variables, expressions) within a first-order logic. Consequently, specification languages in deductive verification are disconnected from domain-focused logical approaches to knowledge representation, such as Description Logics (DL). DLs are an established tool to model domain knowledge with elaborate pragmatics in the form of, e.g., ontologies; yet, making use of them for program specification and verification remains unexplored.

© The Author(s), under exclusive license to Springer Nature Switzerland AG 2026
Z. Liu et al. (Eds.): ICTAC 2025, LNCS 16237, pp. 69–86, 2026.
https://doi.org/10.1007/978-3-032-11176-0_6

However, a direct translation of a DL specification into the contracts of the program logic would still not enable us to interpret intermediate steps of proofs in the domain: We require a way to manage both views (computational view and domain view) and their relation throughout a proof attempt for functional correctness, such that (a) we can investigate an intermediate step from both perspectives, e.g., to extract information from failed proofs, and (b) use both DL and PL for functional specification of programs.

We investigate reasoning about the correctness of programs with specifications for both the *implementation* (i.e., the program specifics) and its connection to the application *domain*. Domain-specific specification, in the form of description logic assertions, enables domain experts to be involved in modeling and programming, by giving them a tool to express their constraints without exposing them to implementation details. We aim to retain as much of the DL pragmatics during verification as possible, while making use of their logical foundation to recover assertions about the program: Failed proof attempts should be interpreted and explained [7,30] in the domain. Similarly, keeping DL separate from program assertions enables the use of specialized solvers. Nonetheless, these assertions are used by a Hoare logic that operates only on the program state, and not on its interpretation in the domain.

Specification. To connect program state and description logics, we use ideas from *semantically lifted programs* [18]. The state of a semantically lifted program is *lifted* into the domain in the form of a *knowledge graph*. This graph can then be enriched with DL axioms to interpret the program state in terms of the domain.

At the core of our approach are *two-tier* specifications. A two-tier assertion $\{\frac{\Delta}{\Phi}\}$, also written $\{\Delta;\ \Phi\}$, contains an assertion Φ about the program state, and an assertion Δ about the domain, which specifies the *lifted* state in terms of the domain. To connect the two assertions in the calculus, we lift not only the state, but also *the specifications*, in order to recover information for Φ from Δ.

Figure 1 illustrates the relations between state specification, the lifted state specification and the domain specification containing the lifted state specification. It is critical that the domain specification is using only the notions and vocabulary of the enriched state, and is not describing the lifted program state directly – it is describing the lifted state *enriched with additional axioms*. Thus, the program logic must be able to infer possible program states from the domain specification.

Verification. Consider a program that models the assembly of a car. Its final state must be data that describes the assembled car. This data is specified using a domain ontology, which expresses concepts such as `Has4Wheels`(c). This concept states that car c has four wheels. Let us consider the following statement, that sets the variable `wheels` to

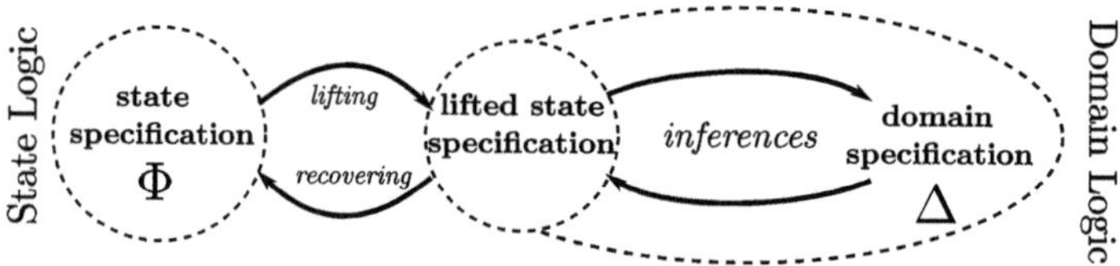

Fig. 1. Relation between domain and state specifications in their respective logics.

the parameter `nrWhls`. In the domain, the specification expresses that after execution, the modelled car has four wheels. For the implementation, it states that the parameter `nrWhls` must be 4.

$$\left\{ \begin{matrix} - \\ \texttt{nrWhls} \doteq 4 \end{matrix} \right\} \texttt{wheels := nrWhls} \left\{ \begin{matrix} \texttt{Has4Wheels}(c) \\ - \end{matrix} \right\} \tag{1}$$

From the perspective of the domain experts, the precondition cannot be stated, since they do not know how the car c is modelled, and are not aware of the encoding of wheels as integers, or even the very *existence* of the variable `wheels`. Thus, both parts of the contract are stated from different perspectives and uphold the separation of concerns between domain and computation. But given a suitable specification lifting, we can transform the above two-tier triple into the following, and derive that to ensure the domain post-condition, the state must have set the variable `wheels` to 4. This is easily shown using a standard assignment rule.

$$\left\{ \begin{matrix} - \\ \texttt{nrWhls} \doteq 4 \end{matrix} \right\} \texttt{wheels := nrWhls} \left\{ \begin{matrix} \texttt{Has4Wheels}(c) \\ \texttt{wheels} \doteq 4 \end{matrix} \right\} \tag{2}$$

The connection between the two tiers enables us to investigate a failed proof attempt. Consider the specification $\{-;\ \texttt{wheels} \doteq 3\}$. It does not allow one to infer that the car is member of the concept `Has4Wheels`, even though the user expects it. But using the lifting we can use standard abductive and deductive reasoning in DL [21] to explain why the expected entailment cannot be derived: From the implementation specification `wheels` $\doteq 3$ we cannot deduce that $\texttt{Has4Wheels}(c)$. But when we try to abduce an explanation for the specification target $\texttt{Has4Wheels}(c)$, we arrive at the implementation specification `wheels` $\doteq 4$, which very clearly indicates where the program fails to output data according to the specification.

This enables us to tackle another bottleneck of deductive program verification – the notoriously difficult task to understand intermediate proof states [11], where specification is intermingled with proof and implementation specifics.

To enable this overall explanation approach, abductive reasoning in the domain logic, deductive reasoning in the program logic, and lifting must be compatible with each other. In the remainer of this work, we give a precise characterization when the logics and lifting can be composed in a sound way.

Contribution. Our main contributions are (1) a Hoare logic that manages two connected views on a program correctness proof, (2) a characterization when a domain logic can be plugged in into the two-tier logic, and (3) an instantiation for description logic. The remainder of this paper gives a precise description of the connection between state and domain specification required to set up a two-tier Hoare logic to enable such inferences.

2   Preliminaries

We give the basic definitions for the logic that we use to describe the states of the implemented program directly, as well as definitions for description logics for domain specification. To simplify terminology, we refer to the former as *state logic* and to the later as *domain logic*. Both logics are based on semantics defined over values Val that include data values, which in our case will be the integers $\mathbb{Z}$ only, and names ∇, which correspond to nominals in description logic.

To ease the later connection between the two logics, we split function symbols into functions that result in a name, and data functions that result in a data value, and consider the set of program variables in the signature.

Definition 1 (Signatures). *A* state signature $\Sigma = \langle V, F, F_d, P \rangle$ *is a tuple of variable names* V, *function symbols* F, *data function symbols* F_d, *and predicate symbols* P. *A* domain signature $\Sigma_d = \langle N, R, T, A \rangle$ *is a tuple of nominals* N, *abstract roles* R, *concrete roles* T, *and atomic concepts* A. *We say that a (state or domain) signature Σ is a sub-signature of Σ' ($\Sigma \subseteq \Sigma'$) if all its components are subsets.*

In general, we refrain from treating arities formally and assume the usual syntactical checks to make formulas and interpretation respect the arity of symbols.

Definition 2 (Interpretations). *A* state interpretation $\mathcal{I}$ *over a state signature* $\Sigma = \langle V, F, F_d, P \rangle$ *is a map from: 1. function symbols $f \in F$ to functions from values to values, 2. data function symbols $f \in F_d$ to functions from values to integers, and 3. predicate symbols $p \in P$ to functions from values to booleans.*

A domain interpretation $\mathcal{I}_d$ *over a domain signature* $\Sigma_d = \langle N, R, T, A \rangle$ *is a map from: 1. nominal symbols $o \in N$ to names in ∇, 2. abstract role symbols $R \in R$ to relations over names, 3. concrete role symbols $T \in T$ to relations over names and $\mathbb{Z}$, and 4. atomic concepts symbols $A \in A$ to subsets of ∇. The set of all state interpretations is denoted $\mathbf{I}$, while the set of all domain interpretations is denoted $\mathbf{I}_d$.*

Program variables are not interpreted by I, but are part of the program state. Numerical constants are treated as special 0-ary function symbols.

Definition 3 (States and State Logic). *Let* V *be the set of program variables. A program state $\sigma : V \to Val$ is a mapping from variables to values. Let* S *denote the set of all program states. Let $\Sigma = \langle V, F, F_d, P \rangle$ be a state signature. State formulas Φ are defined by the following grammar, where v ranges over* V, *p over* P, *and f over* $F \cup F_d$. *The set of all state formulas over Σ is denoted $\Phi(\Sigma)$.*

$$\Phi ::= \Phi \wedge \Phi \mid \neg\Phi \mid t \doteq t \mid p(\bar{t}) \qquad\qquad t ::= v \mid f(\bar{t})$$

The semantics of the state logic $\sigma, \mathcal{I} \models \Phi$ is defined relative to a program state and a state interpretation, and is given in the technical report [17].

We use the usual abbreviations such as $\vee$ and $\to$ and omit $\mathcal{I}$ in the satisfiability relation if it is understood. We define a simple description logic, $\mathcal{ALCO}(D)$, following mostly the semantics of Horrocks and Sattler [16] for $\mathcal{SHON}(D)$. We stress that our approach is not relying on any particular property of this logic (or any description logic), except for the presence of data types, but we consider description logics as the most suited formalism for domain specification in our framework.

Definition 4 (Description Logic). *Let $\Sigma_d = \langle \mathrm{N}, \mathrm{R}, \mathrm{T}, \mathrm{A} \rangle$ be a domain signature. The syntax of domain formulas δ is defined by the following grammar, where A ranges over* A, *R over* R, *T over* T, *o over* N, *and n over literals from* $\mathbb{Z}$. *The set of all domain formulas over Σ_d is denoted $\Delta(\Sigma_d)$. We use Δ to range over sets of domain formulas.*

$$\delta ::= C \sqsubseteq C \mid C(o) \mid R(o,o) \mid R(o,n)$$
$$C ::= \top \mid \bot \mid A \mid \neg C \mid C \sqcup C \mid C \sqcap C \mid \exists R.\,C \mid \forall R.\,C \mid \exists T.\,n \mid \forall T.\,n$$

The semantics $\mathcal{I}_d \models \delta$ is defined relative to a domain interpretation, and is given in the technical report [17]. We use the usual logic abbreviations, such as $\equiv$.

Given a formula Φ (resp. a domain formula Δ), we denote the signature containing just the symbols it uses by sig Φ (resp. sig Δ). Semantic entailment is defined as usual: Given two formulas Δ, Δ', we say that Δ entails Δ' ($\Delta \models \Delta'$) if every interpretation that satisfies Δ, also satisfies Δ'. This naturally generalizes to sets of formulas. Given a set of domain formulas $\mathbf{K}$, we write $\Delta \models^{\mathbf{K}} \Delta'$ to denote that every interpretation that satisfies formula Δ and all elements of $\mathbf{K}$ also satisfies Δ'.

3   Motivating Example

Scenario. Consider a program that models the assembly of a small car, where a car is considered to be small if it has two doors and four wheels. This can be formalized in the domain logic using the following formula.

$$\texttt{SmallCar} \equiv \texttt{Has2Doors} \sqcap \texttt{Has4Wheels} \sqcap \texttt{Car}$$

Additionally, everything that has a body is a car, and everything that has a chassis has a body. For doors, wheels, and the body of the car, we can formulate the following, to express that everything that has 2 doors is part of the concept `Has2Doors`, and analogously for `HasFourDoors` and `HasBody`. We use the common pattern of *stubs* [22]: instead of modeling the number of doors using a `hasDoors` relation that maps to a number, we use a relation `doors` that maps to an individual that has some number associated with it using relation `hasValue`. As we see later, we can relate the stubs with variables in the programming language to connect the two formalisms.

$$\texttt{HasChassis} \sqsubseteq \texttt{HasBody} \sqsubseteq \texttt{Car} \qquad \exists \texttt{doors.}\exists\texttt{hasValue.2} \equiv \texttt{Has2Doors}$$
$$\exists\texttt{wheels.}\exists\texttt{hasValue.4} \equiv \texttt{Has4Wheels} \qquad \exists\texttt{body.NonZero} \equiv \texttt{HasBody}$$
$$\neg\exists\texttt{hasValue.0} \equiv \texttt{NonZero}$$

The program itself is given in Fig. 2. The assembly is old-fashioned: it starts with a chassis, and has three substeps, namely adding the body by assigning a non-zero id, then adding the wheels (`addWheels`), and adding the doors. It is operating on a single car, which is modelled by the variable `bodyId` for the id of the body, where `bodyId = 0` models that no body is attached, the variable `doors` which models the number of doors on the body, and `wheels`, which models the number of wheels. The assembled car has a chassis, which is not explicit in the program.

Specification. Our aim is to specify that procedure `assembly` indeed assembles a small car. However, the domain expert has no knowledge about the computational encoding of the process, e.g., that the wheels are modelled as a global variable. The contract of procedure `assembly` is as follows. In the beginning we get the number of doors (which must be 2) and the id of the body (which must be non-null), and in the end it is a small car. The individual c is implicit in the program – in our example, the program assembles exactly one car, but this information is not relevant for the domain expert. As specifications, we use pairs $\{\frac{\Delta}{\Phi}\}$ that express that domain formula Δ and state formula Φ must hold.

$$\left\{ \begin{array}{c} - \\ \mathtt{nrDrs} \doteq 2 \wedge \mathtt{bodyId} \neq 0 \end{array} \right\} \mathtt{assembly}() \left\{ \begin{array}{c} \mathtt{SmallCar}(c) \\ - \end{array} \right\}$$

Let us now turn to the specification of `addWheels`. The domain specification explains what is expected from the view of the car assembly (the car already has a chassis), while the implementation specification ($\mathtt{nrWhls} = 4$) specifies additional conditions *not visible in the domain* to ensure correctness. The former is specified by the domain expert, while the latter is added by the programmer.

$$\left\{ \begin{array}{c} - \\ \mathtt{nrWhls} \doteq 4 \end{array} \right\} \mathtt{addWheels}(\mathtt{nrWhls}) \left\{ \begin{array}{c} \mathtt{Has4Wheels}(c) \\ - \end{array} \right\}$$

The fact that the car has a chassis is not part of the specification—$\mathtt{HasChassis}(c)$ is not the domain precondition. The reason is that the modelled car by default has a chassis. Thus, the fact $\mathtt{HasChassis}(c)$ is part of the connection of the state with the background knowledge.

The post-condition is obvious - it states that afterwards the car being assembled is part of class `Has4Wheels`. Note that the implementation details are hidden from the domain experts – they do not know how c is modelled, whether it always has a chassis in the program, or whether this is explicit. They are, thus, not able to state the state precondition, as they are not aware of the encoding of wheels. Thus, the two parts of the contracts are stated from different perspectives and uphold the *separation of concerns* between domain and computation. Furthermore, we stress that the specification at the level of procedure contracts enables the participation of the domain expert in a more fine-grained specification, without being exposing too many technicalities, but requires that we must be able to switch between a domain and a state view in the middle of the analyzed statement.

```
1 var bodyId = 0; var wheels = 0; var doors = 0;
2 proc addWheels(nrWhls) begin wheels := nrWhls; end;
3 proc assembly(id, nrDrs) begin
4   bodyId := id; addWheels(4); doors := nrDrs;
5 end
```

Fig. 2. An assembly line program.

$$\text{hasValue}(\text{wheelsVar}, 4) \qquad \text{HasChassis}(c)$$

$$\text{wheels}(c, \text{wheelsVar}) \qquad \text{body}(c, \text{bodyVar}) \qquad \text{doors}(c, \text{doorsVar})$$

Fig. 3. The first formula is (part of) the lifted state, the other connect lifted state and domain.

Verification. To verify that `addWheels` adheres to its specification, we have to show that its procedure body indeed transforms a car into one with four wheels, which is exactly Eq. 1 (p. 3). In a classical weakest precondition calculus, we would now substitute `wheels` by `nrWhls` in the post-condition – the post-condition obviously needs to be `wheels` $\doteq 4$. But in out setting we only have the domain specification. Instead of introducing redundancy in the specification, which would also break our separation between tasks for the domain expert and tasks for the programmer, we can retrieve a state post-condition as follows.

At its basis, we rely on semantic lifting, which generates a domain state from a program state. Let us consider the program state σ_0 with $\sigma_0(\text{wheels}) = 4$. Its lifting consists of axioms for the program state, information about the domain *and* additional formulas that connect the domain concepts with those describing the lifted program state. Those are given in Fig. 3. Note that the resulting knowledge graph has two parts: lifted program state, and domain knowledge. However, the domain specification is only concerned with the domain knowledge. The first part is generic for the program, e.g., the existence of variables – instead of designing a new lifting for every application, this *direct lifting* can be used as a basis to simplify modeling [18].

Still, we can deduce knowledge about the state: For example, if the car has four wheels (i.e., `Has4Wheels`(c)), then the corresponding variable must be set to 4 (i.e., `hasValue(wheels, 4)`). This information, in turn, can be interpreted in the program logic as `wheels` $\doteq 4$, in order to strengthen our specification into Eq. 2 (p. 3).

Using the rule for assignment, we can prove the correctness of `addWheels` w.r.t. to its specification. We must consider the relation of `Has4Wheels`(c) and `wheels` $\doteq 4$ – as the program must establish both conditions, but only controls the state post-conditions, the state post-condition `wheels` $\doteq 4$ must imply the complete domain post-condition `Has4Wheels`(c). Having established our example and illustrated the challenges therein. we now give a formal treatment of the underlying Hoare logic. We return to the assembly line, and show it correct, after presenting the calculus in Sect. 5.

Explanation. Given the above framework, it is easy to see that we can not only investigate two perspectives on pre- and post-conditions of procedures, but also explain proof state. For example, consider a slight variant of the program, where `addWheelsBug` contains a bug: it always assigns 3 to the `wheels` variable, but uses the same contract.

```
1 var bodyId = 0; var wheels = 0; var doors = 0;
2 proc addWheelsBug(nrWhls) begin wheels := 3;   end;
3 proc assembly(id, nrDrs) begin
4   bodyId := id; addWheelsBug(4); doors := nrDrs;
5 end
```

Applying the weakest-precondition calculus results in the following triple, which cannot be proven: the post-condition is not consistent and the state specification does not entail the domain specification.

$$\left\{ \begin{array}{c} - \\ \texttt{nrWhls} \doteq 4 \end{array} \right\} \texttt{wheels} := 3 \left\{ \begin{array}{c} \texttt{Has4Wheels}(c) \\ \texttt{wheels} \doteq 3 \end{array} \right\}$$

One can use *abduction* to retrieve a possible explanation of how $\texttt{Has4Wheels}(c)$ could be inferred, and obtain the axiom $\texttt{hasValue}(\texttt{wheelsVar}, 4)$ to see where the program went wrong – critically, it uses the domain to explain what the state should be, an explanation mechanism normally not available in program verification.

4   A Two-Tier Hoare Logic

Our task now is to ensure that the program indeed models the assembly of a small car at the domain level, not just through the name of its variables and procedures. Our approach is based on two-tier assertions: A two-tier assertion has two parts, or tiers, in different logics, that are connected through a lifting mechanism for translation. Each tier corresponds to a different perspective. To do so, we must first define how to interpret a state in the domain and define the semantic lifting of a state.

Definition 5 (State and Specification Lifting). *A* state lifting *is defined as a function* $\mu : \mathbf{S} \times \mathbf{I} \to \mathbf{I}^d$ *from program models to domain models. A* specification lifting $\hat{\mu} : \Phi(\Sigma) \to \Delta(\Sigma^d)$ *is a mapping from program formulas to domain formulas. We denote the signature of the images of $\hat{\mu}$ as its* kernel, *written* $\ker \hat{\mu} = \bigcup_{\Psi \in \Phi(\Sigma)} \mathsf{sig}(\hat{\mu}(\Psi))$.

State and specification lifting must be compatible, such that if a state satisfies a state formula, then its lifting must satisfy the lifted formula. This is required for the soundness of lifting $\hat{\mu}$ – the state lifting μ is not used in the calculus we give later.

Definition 6 (Compatibility). *A pair* $(\mu, \hat{\mu})$ *is* compatible *w.r.t. a state interpretation* $\mathcal{I}$ *and a set of domain formulas* $\mathbf{K}$ *iff lifting state and formula preserves satisfaction:* $\forall \sigma \in \mathbf{S}. \, (\sigma, \mathcal{I} \models \Phi \Rightarrow \mu(\sigma) \models^{\mathbf{K}} \hat{\mu}(\Phi))$.

The domain logic is less expressive than the state logic, as its task is to specify in terms of the domain without exposing implementation details. Applying $\hat{\mu}$ allows one to interpret an intermediate state specification in the domain, for example to examine what this state is modelling. Similarly, the domain specification is not only part of the pre- and post-condition of the program, but also part of the pre- and post-condition of *procedures*. The lifting $\hat{\mu}$ is, thus, needed to add information to apply these contracts.

However, the program itself is analyzed in terms of the state logic. For example, the effect of an assignment can be clearly expressed for the state specification, but not for the domain. Here, we require to *recover* information from the domain specification by applying the inverse $\hat{\mu}^{-1}$. Consider the state specification $\phi = \texttt{wheels} \doteq 4$ and the domain specification $\delta = \texttt{HasFourWheels}(c)$. The lifting $\hat{\mu}$ enables us, together with further inferences and assuming a fitting pair of liftings, to derive δ from ϕ, and the recovering mapping $\hat{\mu}^{-1}$ enables us to derive ϕ from δ. Before we connect state and domain specification further, we give a direct lifting. The recovering mapping $\hat{\mu}^{-1}$ is only well-defined on the kernel of $\hat{\mu}$.

The characteristic formula χ_σ of a state σ is defined as $\bigwedge_{v \in \mathbf{dom}\,\sigma} v \doteq \sigma(v)$.

Definition 7 (Direct Lifting). *The specification lifting $\hat{\mu}_{\mathsf{direct}}$ is defined as follows, where* $\mathtt{var}_v$ *is a symbol identified by its index.*

$$\hat{\mu}_{\mathsf{direct}}(v \doteq n) = \{\mathsf{hasValue}(\mathtt{var}_v, n)\} \qquad \hat{\mu}_{\mathsf{direct}}(v \neq 0) = \{\mathsf{NonZero}(\mathtt{var}_v)\}$$
$$\hat{\mu}_{\mathsf{direct}}(\Phi_1 \wedge \Phi_2) = \hat{\mu}_{\mathsf{direct}}(\Phi_1) \cup \hat{\mu}_{\mathsf{direct}}(\Phi_2)$$

The state lifting is defined by: $\mu_{\mathsf{direct}} = \mathcal{I}$ *such that* $\mathcal{I} \models \hat{\mu}_{\mathsf{direct}}(\chi_\sigma)$.

The pair $(\mu_{\mathsf{direct}}, \hat{\mu}_{\mathsf{direct}})$ is compatible, and the example in Fig. 3 is an application of it with $\mathbf{K} = \{\mathsf{HasChassis}(c), \mathsf{wheels}(c, \mathsf{wheelsVar}), \dots\}$. The variables are also modelled as stubs – the formula $\mathsf{wheels}(c, \mathsf{wheelsVar})$ indeed expresses that the variable $\mathsf{wheelsVar}$ (i.e., $\mathtt{var}_{\mathsf{wheels}}$) is the stub that can be used in the domain to reason about the wheels of the car c. The kernel of $\hat{\mu}_{\mathsf{direct}}$ is as follows

$$\mathbf{ker}\,\hat{\mu}_{\mathsf{direct}} = \{\mathsf{hasValue}, \mathsf{NonZero}\} \cup \{\mathtt{var}_v \mid v \in \mathbf{dom}\,\sigma\} \cup \mathsf{sig}(\mathbf{K})$$

Note the explicit addition of $\mathsf{NonZero}$, which enables us to lift (and recover from) more abstract specifications than characteristic formulas.

4.1   Assertions

Equipped with a formal definition of lifting, we now define specifications that have both a domain and a state component. We refer to such specifications as *two-tier assertions*.

Definition 8 (Two-Tier Assertion). *Let $(\mu, \hat{\mu})$ be a compatible set of liftings (w.r.t. some $\mathcal{I}$ and $\mathbf{K}$). Let Δ range over sets of domain formulas over Σ_d and Φ over state formulas over Σ. A two-tier assertion has the form*

$$\left\{ \begin{array}{c} \Delta \\ \Phi \end{array} \right\}$$

written $\{\Delta; \Phi\}$ for brevity, and has the following semantics

$$\sigma \models^{\mathbf{K}} \{\Delta; \Phi\} \quad \textit{iff} \quad \sigma, \mathcal{I} \models \Phi \text{ and } \mu(\sigma), \hat{\mu}(\Phi) \models^{\mathbf{K}} \Delta$$

We say that a two-tier assertion is strongly consistent *if $\hat{\mu}(\Phi) \models^{\mathbf{K}} \Delta$.*

In a strongly consistent assertion, the domain is determined entirely by the state, which is exactly the condition we discussed above for post-conditions.

A contract is where domain specification can be used – we do not expect the domain expert to annotate intermediate specification in sequences of statements, but to interact with the developer on the level of procedures and other, abstracting language constructs.

$$\mathsf{cond}(P, R_1, R_2) = \{(\sigma, \sigma') \mid (\sigma \in P \wedge (\sigma, \sigma') \in R_1) \vee (\sigma \notin P \wedge (\sigma, \sigma') \in R_2)\}$$

$$[\![\mathsf{v} := \mathsf{expr}]\!]_{\mathbf{C,K}} = \{(\sigma, \sigma') \mid \sigma' = \sigma[\mathsf{v} \mapsto \mathcal{A}[\![\mathsf{expr}]\!]]\}$$

$$[\![s_1 ; s_2]\!]_{\mathbf{C,K}} = [\![s_1]\!]_{\mathbf{C,K}} \circ [\![s_2]\!]_{\mathbf{C,K}} \qquad [\![\mathsf{skip}]\!]_{\mathbf{C,K}} = \{(\sigma, \sigma) \mid \sigma \in \mathsf{S}\}$$

$$[\![\mathbf{if}\ (\mathsf{expr})\ \mathbf{then}\ s_1\ \mathbf{else}\ s_2\ \mathbf{fi}]\!]_{\mathbf{C,K}} = \mathsf{cond}(\mathcal{B}[\![\mathsf{expr}]\!], [\![s_1]\!]_{\mathbf{C,K}}, [\![s_2]\!]_{\mathbf{C,K}})$$

$$[\![\mathbf{while}\ (\mathsf{expr})\ \mathbf{do}\ s\ \mathbf{od}]\!]_{\mathbf{C,K}} = \mathsf{LFP}\ F_{\mathbf{C,K}}$$

$$\text{where } F_{\mathbf{C,K}}(R) = \mathsf{cond}(\mathcal{B}[\![\mathsf{expr}]\!], [\![s]\!]_{\mathbf{C,K}} \circ R, \mathsf{id}_{\mathsf{S}})$$

$$[\![\mathsf{p}(\mathsf{expr})]\!]_{\mathbf{C,K}} = \{(\sigma, \sigma') \mid \sigma \models_{\mathbf{K}} \mathsf{Prec}_{\mathbf{C}}(\mathsf{p}, \mathcal{A}[\![\mathsf{expr}]\!]_{\sigma}) \wedge \sigma' \models_{\mathbf{K}} \mathsf{Post}_{\mathbf{C}}(\mathsf{p}, \mathcal{A}[\![\mathsf{expr}]\!])\}$$

Fig. 4. Program semantics for statements s.

Definition 9 (Procedure Contract). *A* contract *for a procedure* $\mathsf{p}(\mathsf{v})$ *is a pair of two-tier assertions* $\left(\{{}^{\Delta_1^{\mathsf{p}}}_{\Phi_1^{\mathsf{p}}}\}, \{{}^{\Delta_2^{\mathsf{p}}}_{\Phi_2^{\mathsf{p}}}\}\right)$, *called the* precondition *and the* postcondition, *respectively. The set of all contracts in a program is denoted* $\mathbf{C}$. *Retrieving the precondition (resp. postcondition) of a procedure* p *with parameter* e *replacing its argument variable* v *is denoted:*

$$\mathsf{Prec}_{\mathbf{C}}(\mathsf{p}, \mathsf{e}) = \left\{ {}^{\Delta_1^{\mathsf{p}}}_{\Phi_1^{\mathsf{p}}[\mathsf{v} \setminus \mathsf{e}]} \right\} \qquad \mathsf{Post}_{\mathbf{C}}(\mathsf{p}, \mathsf{e}) = \left\{ {}^{\Delta_2^{\mathsf{p}}}_{\Phi_2^{\mathsf{p}}[\mathsf{v} \setminus \mathsf{e}]} \right\}$$

We can now introduce a simple, imperative programming language with procedure calls that operates on states. As we are not concerned with expressive power here, we limit expressions to a minimum, and procedures to only one parameter. The semantics of the language is relative to a set of contracts. This simplifies the later definition; a non-relative version is easily obtained by inlining. All variables are global, and we forbid recursive calls in preference of loops.

Definition 10. *The* syntax *of our programming language is defined by the following grammar. Let* v *range over variables,* n *over literals, and* p *over procedure names.*

$$\mathsf{prog} ::= \overline{\mathbf{var}\ \mathsf{v}\ =\ \mathsf{expr}\ ;}\ \overline{\mathsf{proc}} \qquad \mathsf{proc} ::= \mathsf{p}(\mathsf{v})\ \mathbf{begin}\ s\ \mathbf{end} \qquad procedures$$

$$\mathsf{expr} ::= n \mid \mathsf{v} \qquad\qquad\qquad\qquad\qquad\qquad\qquad\qquad expressions$$

$$s ::= \mathsf{v} := \mathsf{expr};\ \mid\ s\ ;\ s\ \mid\ \mathbf{if}\ (\mathsf{expr})\ \mathbf{then}\ s\ \mathbf{else}\ s\ \mathbf{fi}$$

$$\mid\ \mathbf{while}\ (\mathsf{expr})\ \mathbf{do}\ s\ \mathbf{od}\ \mid \mathsf{p}(\mathsf{expr}) \mid \mathbf{skip} \qquad\qquad statements$$

The semantics *of our language is defined relative to a contract set* $\mathbf{C}$ *and a set of formulas* $\mathbf{K}$, *as a binary relation on states, i.e., as a* denotational semantics $[\![s]\!] \subseteq \mathsf{S} \times \mathsf{S}$, *shown in Fig. 4, where we use* $\mathsf{LFP}\,F$ *to denote the least fixed-point of a function* F.

Our semantics is *procedure-modular*, i.e., we define the semantics of a procedure call as the semantics of the contract of the called procedure. This is why our semantics is based on binary relations on states rather than on partial functions. The evaluation functions $\mathcal{A}[\![\cdot]\!]$ and $\mathcal{B}[\![\cdot]\!]$ of arithmetic and boolean expressions are standard and omitted for brevity. For an extended treatment of the used kind of denotational semantics we refer to the standard texts [28, 31], and for details about the treatment of contracts to [12].

4.2 Hoare Triples

A two-tier assertion specifies a state, while two-tier Hoare triples relate the initial and final states of a program execution: If the precondition holds in the initial state, and the program terminates, then the postcondition holds in the final state. In our case, the pre- and post-conditions are lifted assertions.

Definition 11 (Two-Tier Hoare Triple). *A two-tier Hoare triple with respect to a compatible mapping $(\mu, \hat{\mu})$ has the following form*

$$\{\Delta_1;\ \Phi_1\}s\{\Delta_2;\ \Phi_2\}$$

with the expected semantics (given sets of formulas $\mathbf{K}$ and contracts $\mathbf{C}$)

$$\models_{\mathbf{C},\mathbf{K}} \left\{\begin{matrix}\Delta_1 \\ \Phi_1\end{matrix}\right\} s \left\{\begin{matrix}\Delta_2 \\ \Phi_2\end{matrix}\right\} \quad \textit{iff.} \quad \forall(\sigma,\sigma') \in [\![s]\!]_{\mathbf{C},\mathbf{K}} \cdot \left(\sigma \models_{\mathbf{K}} \left\{\begin{matrix}\Delta_1 \\ \Phi_1\end{matrix}\right\} \rightarrow \sigma' \models_{\mathbf{K}} \left\{\begin{matrix}\Delta_2 \\ \Phi_2\end{matrix}\right\}\right)$$

Let us now turn to the recovering mapping $\hat{\mu}^{-1}$. This faces the challenge of "delifting" arbitrarily formulas, while $\hat{\mu}$ must merely lift a limited set of expressions, on which we can easily enforce a normal form. Recovering could only operate on the limited signature $\mathbf{ker}\ \hat{\mu}$. For this reason, we must be able to infer formulas from a domain specification that are within this limited signature. While in some cases we may be able to deduce them, in the general case we may have to rely on *abduction*.

Fortunately, abduction is feasible in our setup – we have a clear notion of abductibles through the signature, and we only require formulas about individuals, not arbitrary formulas. This is exactly the well-explored setting of ABox abduction with abductibles [21]. We abstract from the exact mechanism to generate the inversible kernel and merely assume some function that realizes it.

Definition 12 (Kernel-Generator). *Let $\hat{\mu}$ be a specification lifting. A kernel-generator is a function $\alpha_{\mathbf{K}} : 2^{\Delta} \rightarrow 2^{\Delta}$ that, given a set of domain formulas Δ, generates another set of domain formulas $\alpha_{\mathbf{K}}(\Delta)$ such that $\mathsf{sig}(\alpha_{\mathbf{K}}(\Delta)) \subseteq \mathbf{ker}\ \hat{\mu}$ and $\alpha_{\mathbf{K}}(\Delta) \models_{\mathbf{K}} \Delta$.*

A kernel-generator can either perform abduction or deduction. In the case of abduction, most formulas are essentially implications that have $\mathbf{ker}\ \hat{\mu}$ as the consequent and the rest of the signature in the antecedent (e.g., *"if the program variable has this value, then the domain individual belongs to this concept"*). Abduction is not sound, but may still be useful to generate a condition for program correctness. One can precisely specify abduction with the usual conditions on $\alpha_{\mathbf{K}}$ [27]. In case of deduction, the kernel-generator infers the only possible values for the variables.

Given a state specification, we can lift it using $\hat{\mu}$ to a set of formulas with signature $\mathbf{ker}\ \hat{\mu}$. From there, we can deduce further formulas about the domain using description logic reasoning. To compare a given set of domain formulas, we use the kernel generator α to get formulas with signature $\mathbf{ker}\ \hat{\mu}$, from which we can inverse the lifting $\hat{\mu}^{-1}$. Implication on assertions is lifted as expected.

Definition 13. *One two-tier assertion implies another if the following holds.*

$$\{\Delta;\ \Phi\} \rightarrow_{\mathbf{K}} \{\Delta';\ \Phi'\} \quad \textit{iff.} \quad \forall\sigma.\,(\sigma \models_{\mathbf{K}} \{\Delta;\ \Phi\} \rightarrow \sigma \models_{\mathbf{K}} \{\Delta';\ \Phi'\})$$

Formally, we can now express the relations between $\hat{\mu}$, α and $\hat{\mu}^{-1}$ with the following lemma, on which our calculus will heavily rely.

Lemma 1. *The following three implications and equivalences hold.*

1. Generating the kernel of a domain specification implies the input:

$$\{\Delta, \alpha_{\mathbf{K}}(\Delta); \; \Phi\} \rightarrow_{\mathbf{K}} \{\Delta; \; \Phi\}$$

2. Adding lifted specification preserves satisfiability: $\{\Delta; \; \Phi\} \leftrightarrow_{\mathbf{K}} \{\Delta, \hat{\mu}(\Phi); \; \Phi\}$.
3. Adding recovered specification preserves satisfiability:

$$\left\{ \begin{matrix} \Delta, \Delta' \\ \Phi \end{matrix} \right\} \leftrightarrow_{\mathbf{K}} \left\{ \begin{matrix} \Delta, \Delta' \\ \Phi \wedge \hat{\mu}^{-1}(\Delta') \end{matrix} \right\} \; where \; \mathsf{sig}(\Delta') \subseteq \mathbf{ker} \; \hat{\mu}$$

5   A Calculus for the Two-Tier Hoare Logic

The calculus combines the concepts introduced previously by integrating two systems of rules: The first implements a weakest-precondition calculus on the implementation-specification for each statement, except for procedure calls. These rules erase domain information, as every change in the implementation can potentially affect any formula in the lifted specification. The second system of rules implements the kernel-generation, lifting and recovering that enables us to restore this information, or to add information to the implementation from the domain before it is erased. Verification is compositional, i.e., local to a single procedure and relative to the context: the contracts and background knowledge. Our judgement is, thus, verifying a lifted Hoare triple in a fixed context.

Definition 14 (Calculus). *Let $\mathbf{C}$ be the set of contracts for a given program, and $\mathbf{K}$ a set of formulas. A* judgement *of the calculus has the following form.*

$$\mathbf{C}, \mathbf{K} \vdash \{\Delta_1; \; \Phi_1\}s\{\Delta_2; \; \Phi_2\}$$

We say that the judgement is valid, *if for every state, in every terminating run where all procedures adhere to their respective contract, the Hoare triple holds.*

$$\mathbf{C}, \mathbf{K} \vdash \left\{ \begin{matrix} \Delta_1 \\ \Phi_1 \end{matrix} \right\} s \left\{ \begin{matrix} \Delta_2 \\ \Phi_2 \end{matrix} \right\} \quad iff \quad \models_{\mathbf{C}, \mathbf{K}} \left\{ \begin{matrix} \Delta_1 \\ \Phi_1 \end{matrix} \right\} s \left\{ \begin{matrix} \Delta_2 \\ \Phi_2 \end{matrix} \right\}$$

Let $P_1, \ldots, P_n$ and C be judgements. A rule *has the following form.*

$$\frac{P_1 \ldots P_n}{C}$$

The rule is sound, *if validity of premises $P_1, \ldots, P_n$ implies validity of the conclusion C.*

To connect the two specifications, we require a set of rules to modify the lifted assertions that serve as pre- and postconditions, as well as to strengthen the precondition or weaken the postcondition. These rules, given in Fig. 5, are all given relative to some $\mathbf{K}, \alpha_{\mathbf{K}}, \mathcal{I}$ and a compatible pair $(\mu, \hat{\mu})$, and implement the connection between domain and computation specification. In detail, rules **(pre-lift)** and **(post-lift)** enable to lift the state

$$\textbf{(pre-lift)}\ \ \frac{\mathbf{C},\mathbf{K} \vdash \left\{{}^{\Delta_1,\hat\mu(\Phi_1)}_{\quad\Phi_1}\right\}s\left\{{}^{\Delta_2}_{\Phi_2}\right\}}{\mathbf{C},\mathbf{K} \vdash \left\{{}^{\Delta_1}_{\Phi_1}\right\}s\left\{{}^{\Delta_2}_{\Phi_2}\right\}} \qquad\qquad \textbf{(post-lift)}\ \ \frac{\mathbf{C},\mathbf{K} \vdash \left\{{}^{\Delta_1}_{\Phi_1}\right\}s\left\{{}^{\Delta_2,\hat\mu(\Phi_2)}_{\quad\Phi_2}\right\}}{\mathbf{C},\mathbf{K} \vdash \left\{{}^{\Delta_1}_{\Phi_1}\right\}s\left\{{}^{\Delta_2}_{\Phi_2}\right\}}$$

$$\textbf{(pre-core)}\ \ \frac{\Delta_1 \models^{\mathbf{K}} \alpha_{\mathbf{K}}(\Delta_1) \qquad \mathbf{C},\mathbf{K} \vdash \left\{{}^{\Delta_1,\alpha_{\mathbf{K}}(\Delta_1)}_{\qquad\Phi_1}\right\}s\left\{{}^{\Delta_2}_{\Phi_2}\right\}}{\mathbf{C},\mathbf{K} \vdash \left\{{}^{\Delta_1}_{\Phi_1}\right\}s\left\{{}^{\Delta_2}_{\Phi_2}\right\}}$$

$$\textbf{(post-core)}\ \ \frac{\Delta_2 \models^{\mathbf{K}} \alpha_{\mathbf{K}}(\Delta_2) \qquad \mathbf{C},\mathbf{K} \vdash \left\{{}^{\Delta_1}_{\Phi_1}\right\}s\left\{{}^{\Delta_2,\alpha_{\mathbf{K}}(\Delta_2)}_{\qquad\Phi_2}\right\}}{\mathbf{C},\mathbf{K} \vdash \left\{{}^{\Delta_1}_{\Phi_1}\right\}s\left\{{}^{\Delta_2}_{\Phi_2}\right\}}$$

$$\textbf{(post-inv)}\ \ \frac{\mathsf{sig}(\Delta_2) \subseteq \ker \hat\mu \qquad \mathbf{C},\mathbf{K} \vdash \left\{{}^{\Delta_1}_{\Phi_1}\right\}s\left\{{}^{\Delta,\Delta_2}_{\Phi_2\wedge\hat\mu^{-1}(\Delta_2)}\right\}}{\mathbf{C},\mathbf{K} \vdash \left\{{}^{\Delta_1}_{\Phi_1}\right\}s\left\{{}^{\Delta,\Delta_2}_{\quad\Phi_2}\right\}}$$

$$\textbf{(pre-inv)}\ \ \frac{\mathsf{sig}(\Delta_1) \subseteq \ker \hat\mu \qquad \mathbf{C},\mathbf{K} \vdash \left\{{}^{\Delta,\Delta_1}_{\Phi_1\wedge\hat\mu^{-1}(\Delta_1)}\right\}s\left\{{}^{\Delta_2}_{\Phi_2}\right\}}{\mathbf{C},\mathbf{K} \vdash \left\{{}^{\Delta,\Delta_1}_{\quad\Phi_1}\right\}s\left\{{}^{\Delta_2}_{\Phi_2}\right\}}$$

$$\textbf{(cons)}\ \ \frac{\mathbf{C},\mathbf{K} \vdash \left\{{}^{\Delta_1'}_{\Phi_1'}\right\}s\left\{{}^{\Delta_2'}_{\Phi_2'}\right\} \qquad \left\{{}^{\Delta_1}_{\Phi_1}\right\} \to_{\mathbf{K}} \left\{{}^{\Delta_1'}_{\Phi_1'}\right\} \qquad \left\{{}^{\Delta_2'}_{\Phi_2'}\right\} \to_{\mathbf{K}} \left\{{}^{\Delta_2}_{\Phi_2}\right\}}{\mathbf{C},\mathbf{K} \vdash \left\{{}^{\Delta_1}_{\Phi_1}\right\}s\left\{{}^{\Delta_2}_{\Phi_2}\right\}}$$

Fig. 5. Rules for manipulating pre- and post-conditions.

specification. Rules **(pre-core)** and **(post-core)** abduct a core in the domain specification. We remind here that we define α so that the signature of its range indeed is the kernel. Rules **(pre-inv)** and **(post-inv)** apply the inverse lifting on the core. The consequence rule enables to strengthen, respectively weaken, the specification. We stress here that **(pre-core)** and **(post-core)** (and **(var)**, see below) invoke a DL reasoner – keeping Φ and Δ separate enables us to do so, an approach which merely translates DL into first-order logic would require to pass the verification condition to a solver for less tractable logics.

The rules for statements are given in Fig. 6. Using the previously introduced rules we can easily derive more complex ones that operate on both levels.

Rule **(var)** is the assignment rule for variables. On the state level, it is exactly the rule from the original Hoare calculus, expressing the precondition as the syntactically updated post-condition. On the domain level, it expresses that any domain knowledge in the domain post-condition must be justified by the state post-condition. As the domain pre-condition, however, it erases all information as the assignment may have arbitrary effects on the domain. Note that we can erase the domain knowledge in practice – strong consistency does not imply equivalence. In detail, **(skip)** expresses that the skip statement has no effect on the state. Branching, handled by rule **(branch)**, also erases the domain precondition, as it modifies the state precondition. Rule **(inv)** handles loops by unrolling. Lastly, rule **(contract)** just checks that the contract is adhered to, and **(seq)** is as expected completely analogous to the original rule. It is worth noting that rule **(contract)** uses domain specification only to syntactically match it with the Pre and Post predicates. Our main result is the soundness of the rules for lifted Hoare triples.

Theorem 1 (Soundness). *The rules in Fig. 5 and Fig. 6 are sound.*

Given the above rules, we can easily combine several operations to derive sound rules that operate in the domain as well. One simple way is to merely lift before and after the statement, such as in the following derived rule.

$$\text{(var)} \quad \frac{\hat{\mu}(\Phi) \models^{\mathbf{K}} \Delta}{\mathbf{C}, \mathbf{K} \vdash \{{}_{\Phi[v\backslash\text{expr}]}^{\emptyset}\}v := \text{expr}\{{}_{\Phi}^{\Delta}\}} \qquad\qquad \text{(skip)} \quad \frac{}{\mathbf{C}, \mathbf{K} \vdash \{{}_{\Phi}^{\Delta}\}\text{skip}\{{}_{\Phi}^{\Delta}\}}$$

$$\text{(branch)} \quad \frac{\mathbf{C}, \mathbf{K} \vdash \{{}_{\Phi\wedge\text{expr}}^{\emptyset}\}s_1\{{}_{\Phi}^{\Delta}\} \qquad \mathbf{C}, \mathbf{K} \vdash \{{}_{\Phi\wedge\neg\text{expr}}^{\emptyset}\}s_2\{{}_{\Phi}^{\Delta}\}}{\mathbf{C}, \mathbf{K} \vdash \{{}_{\Phi}^{\emptyset}\}\text{if (expr) then } s_1 \text{ else } s_2 \text{ fi } \{{}_{\Phi}^{\Delta}\}}$$

$$\text{(loop)} \quad \frac{\mathbf{C}, \mathbf{K} \vdash \{{}_{\Phi_1}^{\Delta_1}\}\text{if (expr) do } s; \text{ while (expr) do } s \text{ od else skip fi}\{{}_{\Phi_2}^{\Delta_2}\}}{\mathbf{C}, \mathbf{K} \vdash \{{}_{\Phi_1}^{\Delta_1}\}\text{while (expr) do } s \text{ od } \{{}_{\Phi_2}^{\Delta_2}\}}$$

$$\text{(contract)} \quad \frac{}{\mathbf{C}, \mathbf{K} \vdash \text{Pre}(\mathbf{C}, \mathbf{p}, \text{expr}) \; \mathbf{p}(\mathbf{e}) \; \text{Post}(\mathbf{C}, \mathbf{p}, \text{expr})}$$

$$\text{(seq)} \quad \frac{\mathbf{C}, \mathbf{K} \vdash \{{}_{\Phi_1}^{\Delta_1}\}s_1\{{}_{\Phi_3}^{\Delta_3}\} \qquad \mathbf{C}, \mathbf{K} \vdash \{{}_{\Phi_3}^{\Delta_3}\}s_2\{{}_{\Phi_2}^{\Delta_2}\}}{\mathbf{C}, \mathbf{K} \vdash \{{}_{\Phi_1}^{\Delta_1}\}s_1; \; s_2\{{}_{\Phi_2}^{\Delta_2}\}}$$

Fig. 6. Rules for weakest precondition reasoning with lifted assertions.

$$\text{(lift-var)} \quad \frac{}{\mathbf{C}, \mathbf{K} \vdash \{{}_{\Phi[v\backslash\text{expr}]}^{\hat{\mu}(\Phi[v\backslash\text{expr}])}\}v := \text{expr}\{{}_{\Phi}^{\hat{\mu}(\Phi)}\}}$$

While (lift-var) is sound, it does not transfer any information from the domain postcondition; the domain precondition is computed by a function of only the state precondition – it is, thus, not computing the weakest domain-precondition.

Using the mechanisms of the lifted core, we can give more precise versions of the rules for statements. Let $\text{DPre}(\Delta, \Phi)$ be the domain knowledge constructed by abducting a lifted core from the domain postcondition ($\alpha(\Delta)$), delifting it into the state logic (via $\hat{\mu}^{-1}$), performing the substitution on the delifted core and the computation specification ($[v \backslash e]$), and lifting the result back into the state logic ($\hat{\mu}$), thus realizing one full cycle of the information flow in Fig. 1: $\text{DPre}(\Delta, \Phi) = \hat{\mu}\big((\Phi \wedge \hat{\mu}^{-1}(\alpha_{\mathbf{K}}(\Delta)))[v\backslash\text{expr}]\big)$

However, for soundness it remains to show that the generated core is indeed implied by the domain specification. As discussed, this may not be the case if we use abduction for core generation. In this case, the open proof branches witness the abducted core and can be examined by the user. The following rule, for example, does so by integrating all steps to derive the domain precondition too.

$$\text{(total)} \quad \frac{\Delta \models^{\mathbf{K}} \alpha_{\mathbf{K}}(\Delta) \qquad \hat{\mu}(\Phi) \models^{\mathbf{K}} \Delta}{\mathbf{C}, \mathbf{K} \vdash \{{}_{\Phi\wedge\hat{\mu}^{-1}(\alpha_{\mathbf{K}}(\Delta))}^{\text{DPre}(\Delta,\Phi)}\}v := \text{expr}\{{}_{\Phi}^{\Delta}\}}$$

Proposition 1. *Rule (lift-var) is sound. Rule (total) is sound.*

Completeness. Our system contains standard Hoare logic (when not using domain specification), which is complete up to the theory of terms [6]. Thus, for every domain logic strictly weaker than first-order logic, our system has the same property.

$$\frac{\dfrac{\text{hasValue}(\texttt{wheelsVar},4)\models^{\mathbf{K}}\text{HasFourWheels}(c),\text{hasValue}(\texttt{wheelsVar},4)}{\mathbf{C},\mathbf{K}\vdash\left\{{}_{\texttt{nrWheels}\doteq4}^{\quad-}\right\}\texttt{wheels}:=\texttt{nrWheels}\left\{{}_{\texttt{wheels}\doteq4}^{\text{HasFourWheels}(c),\text{hasValue}(\texttt{wheelsVar},4)}\right\}}{\mathbf{C},\mathbf{K}\vdash\left\{{}_{\texttt{nrWheels}\doteq4}^{\quad-}\right\}\texttt{wheels}:=\texttt{nrWheels}\left\{{}_{-}^{\text{HasFourWheels}(c),\text{hasValue}(\texttt{wheelsVar},4)}\right\}}}{\mathbf{C},\mathbf{K}\vdash\left\{{}_{\texttt{nrWheels}\doteq4}^{\quad-}\right\}\texttt{wheels}:=\texttt{nrWheels}\left\{{}_{-}^{\text{HasFourWheels}(c)}\right\}}$$

$$\mathbf{K}=\big\{\texttt{SmallCar}\equiv\texttt{Has2Doors}\sqcap\texttt{Has4Wheels},\quad\texttt{HasBody}\sqsubseteq\texttt{HasChassis}\sqsubseteq\texttt{Car}$$
$$\exists\texttt{doors}.\exists\texttt{hasValue}.2\equiv\texttt{Has2Doors},\quad\exists\texttt{wheels}.\exists\texttt{hasValue}.4\equiv\texttt{Has4Wheels}$$
$$\exists\texttt{body}.\texttt{NonZero}\equiv\texttt{HasBody},\ \neg\exists\texttt{hasValue}.0\equiv\texttt{NonZero},\quad\texttt{doors}(c,\texttt{doorsField})$$
$$\texttt{HasChassis}(c),\texttt{wheels}(c,\texttt{wheelsVar}),\texttt{body}(c,\texttt{bodyVar})\big\}$$

$$\texttt{Prec}_{\mathbf{C}}(\texttt{addWheels},\texttt{nrWheels})=\{-;\ \texttt{nrWheel}\doteq4\}$$
$$\texttt{Post}_{\mathbf{C}}(\texttt{addWheels},\texttt{nrWheels})=\{\texttt{Has4Wheels}(c);\ -\}$$
$$\texttt{Prec}_{\mathbf{C}}(\texttt{assembly})=\{-;\ \texttt{nrDoors}\doteq4\wedge\texttt{id}\neq0\}\quad\texttt{Post}_{\mathbf{C}}(\texttt{assembly})=\{\texttt{SmallCar}(c);\ -\}$$

Fig. 7. Proof of the running example

Example. We return to the assembly line, where we can now finally give a formal proof of our running example in Fig. 7. The domain knowledge $\mathbf{K}$ are the axioms from Sect. 3, given in Fig. 7 together with the contracts for all procedures. The proof of addWheels's contract is below. The lifting is $\hat{\mu}(\texttt{wheel}\doteq n)=\{\texttt{HasValue}(\texttt{wheelsVar},n)\}$.

Rule (**post-core**) is applied first and adds hasValue(wheelsVar, 4) in the kernel generation through deduction – this follows from the *equivalence* axiom for HasFourWheels, as well as wheels(c, wheelsVar). The second applied rule is (**post-inv**), where this axiom is used to recover wheel $\doteq$ 4. The third applied rule is (**var**), where we must show that the post-condition is strongly consistent. The proof for the contract of assembly is given in the technical. That proof uses a stronger contract for addWheels including framing, i.e., expresses which variables do not change, but bears no insights into the interplay of program and domain.

6 Related Work

While specification is a long-standing challenge for deductive verification [2, 13, 29], integration of description logics, or related technologies, such as the semantic web stack, into deductive verification of mainstream programming languages has not been explored. However, there are investigations on the direct integration of description logics into programming languages and subsequent model checking.

(Con)Golog [10, 26] is an action programming language based on the situation calculus, designed to program agents that must access the current situation of their dynamic context. Golog has been connected with description logics to achieve decidable verification [32, 33] of temporal logic properties, based on abstraction into a system where model checking is decidable [1]. To do so, the external world is modeled as a description logic model. In contrast, we target mainstream imperative programming languages, where description logics are used only for specification. As we aim for better specification, questions of decidability are of lesser interest here. Knowledge and action bases [14] allow programs to access and manipulate a knowledge base using two abstraction operators, `ask` and `tell`. Again, verification of temporal properties based on model checking has been considered [14] with a focus on decidability [4,5], but no deductive system is given. Similarly, knowledge-based programs [9] use epistemic operators and have only been considered for analysis of simple temporal properties [20].

The original work on semantically lifted programs [18] uses integrated queries to access the lifted state. A similar mechanism is used by the probabilistic, ontologized programs [8], which also give a model checker for temporal properties based on SPIN. For semantically lifted programs, a type system is given in [19], which uses description logic entailments to verify graph query containments that ensure safety of the language-integrated queries. Leinberger et al. [25] also give a type system, but base their system not on liftings and graph queries, but on a tight integration of the class systems and graph shapes [23], which are again reduced to description logic entailments [24].

Refinement, e.g., using abstract state machines [3], is an alternative, formal approach to correct software based on refining an abstract specification into correct code. Many of our results, such as the interpretation of proof steps and domain specification, can conceptually carry over, but we stress that our tiers are *different* views on the same state – the domain view is not more abstract, but a genuinely alternative interpretation.

7   Conclusion

This work provides a new approach to tackle the long-standing specification and explanation bottlenecks in verification using techniques developed for knowledge representation. By using description logics as a second tier for software specifications, we can retain their pragmatics without sacrificing the expressive power needed to specify computational functionality.

The conditions on the lifting and its integration into the calculus are our main result, and the used programming language is consequently kept minimal. Thus, questions of expressive power and complexity are left for future work. For an implementation of our approach, we require to extend a program logic of a realistic programming language, and provide a lifting for its specification language. We consider Java as the most promising candidate: semantic lifing has been investigated for the JVM [15] and a rich ecosystem of verification tools, program logics and specificatin languages is available.

A full implementation for Java, however, is beyond the scope of this work and would merely obfuscate the generalicity of the core concept introduced here: Managing several perspectives on a correctness proofs by integrating a domain logic as a special view.

Future Work. Beyond such investigations of complexity and implementation, it remains an open question whether it is possible to retain information in the domain specification without explicitly generating the kernel.

Acknowledgments. This work was partially supported by the SM4RTENANCE EU project (grant nr. 101123490).

References

1. Baader, F., Zarrieß, B.: Verification of golog programs over description logic actions. In: Fontaine, P., Ringeissen, C., Schmidt, R.A. (eds.) FroCoS 2013. LNCS (LNAI), vol. 8152, pp. 181–196. Springer, Heidelberg (2013). https://doi.org/10.1007/978-3-642-40885-4_12
2. Baumann, C., Beckert, B., Blasum, H., Bormer, T.: Lessons learned from microkernel verification – specification is the new bottleneck. In: SSV. EPTCS, vol. 102, pp. 18–32 (2012)
3. Börger, E., Stärk, R.F.: Abstract State Machines. A Method for High-Level System Design and Analysis. Springer, Heidelberg (2003). http://www.springer.com/computer/swe/book/978-3-540-00702-9
4. Calvanese, D., Ceylan, İİ, Montali, M., Santoso, A.: Verification of context-sensitive knowledge and action bases. In: Fermé, E., Leite, J. (eds.) JELIA 2014. LNCS (LNAI), vol. 8761, pp. 514–528. Springer, Cham (2014). https://doi.org/10.1007/978-3-319-11558-0_36
5. Calvanese, D., Gianola, A., Mazzullo, A., Montali, M.: SMT safety verification of ontology-based processes. In: AAAI, pp. 6271–6279. AAAI Press (2023)
6. Cook, S.A.: Soundness and completeness of an axiom system for program verification. SIAM J. Comput. **7**(1), 70–90 (1978). https://doi.org/10.1137/0207005
7. Deng, X., Haarslev, V., Shiri, N.: A framework for explaining reasoning in description logics. In: ExaCt. AAAI Technical Report, vol. FS-05-04, pp. 55–61. AAAI Press (2005)
8. Dubslaff, C., Koopmann, P., Turhan, A.: Enhancing probabilistic model checking with ontologies. Formal Aspects Comput. **33**(6), 885–921 (2021)
9. Fagin, R., Halpern, J.Y., Moses, Y., Vardi, M.Y.: Reasoning About Knowledge. MIT Press, Cambridge (1995)
10. Giacomo, G.D., Lespérance, Y., Levesque, H.J.: ConGolog, a concurrent programming language based on the situation calculus. Artif. Intell. **121**(1–2), 109–169 (2000)
11. Grebing, S., Ulbrich, M.: Usability recommendations for user guidance in deductive program verification. In: Ahrendt, W., Beckert, B., Bubel, R., Hähnle, R., Ulbrich, M. (eds.) Deductive Software Verification: Future Perspectives. LNCS, vol. 12345, pp. 261–284. Springer, Cham (2020). https://doi.org/10.1007/978-3-030-64354-6_11
12. Gurov, D., Westman, J.: A hoare logic contract theory: an exercise in denotational semantics. In: Principled Software Development, pp. 119–127. Springer, Cham (2018). https://doi.org/10.1007/978-3-319-98047-8_8
13. Hähnle, R., Huisman, M.: Deductive software verification: from pen-and-paper proofs to industrial tools. In: Steffen, B., Woeginger, G. (eds.) Computing and Software Science. LNCS, vol. 10000, pp. 345–373. Springer, Cham (2019). https://doi.org/10.1007/978-3-319-91908-9_18
14. Hariri, B.B., Calvanese, D., Montali, M., Giacomo, G.D., Masellis, R.D., Felli, P.: Description logic knowledge and action bases. J. Artif. Intell. Res. **46**, 651–686 (2013)
15. Haubner, A.W.: Inspecting Java Program States with Semantic Web Technologies. Master's thesis, Technische Universität Darmstadt, Darmstadt (2022). https://doi.org/10.26083/tuprints-00022143, the software developed as part of this thesis is available on GitHub. The Semantic Java Debugger: https://github.com/ahbnr/SemanticJavaDebugger The jdi2owl library: https://github.com/ahbnr/jdi2owl
16. Horrocks, I., Sattler, U.: Ontology reasoning in the SHOQ(D) description logic. In: IJCAI, pp. 199–204. Morgan Kaufmann (2001)
17. Kamburjan, E., Gurov, D.: A Hoare logic for domain specification (full version) (2024). https://arxiv.org/abs/2402.00452

18. Kamburjan, E., Klungre, V.N., Schlatte, R., Johnsen, E.B., Giese, M.: Programming and debugging with semantically lifted states. In: Verborgh, R., et al. (eds.) ESWC 2021. LNCS, vol. 12731, pp. 126–142. Springer, Cham (2021). https://doi.org/10.1007/978-3-030-77385-4_8

19. Kamburjan, E., Kostylev, E.V.: Type checking semantically lifted programs via query containment under entailment regimes. In: Description Logics. CEUR Workshop Proceedings, vol. 2954. CEUR-WS.org (2021)

20. Knapp, A., Mühlberger, H., Reus, B.: Interpreting knowledge-based programs. In: ESOP. Lecture Notes in Computer Science, vol. 13990, pp. 253–280. Springer, Heidelberg (2023). https://doi.org/10.1007/978-3-031-30044-8_10

21. Koopmann, P., Del-Pinto, W., Tourret, S., Schmidt, R.A.: Signature-based abduction for expressive description logics. In: KR, pp. 592–602 (2020)

22. Krisnadhi, A., Hitzler, P.: The stub metapattern. In: WOP@ISWC. Studies on the Semantic Web, vol. 32, pp. 39–45. IOS Press (2016)

23. Leinberger, M., Lämmel, R., Staab, S.: The essence of functional programming on semantic data. In: Yang, H. (ed.) ESOP 2017. LNCS, vol. 10201, pp. 750–776. Springer, Heidelberg (2017). https://doi.org/10.1007/978-3-662-54434-1_28

24. Leinberger, M., Seifer, P., Rienstra, T., Lämmel, R., Staab, S.: Deciding SHACL shape containment through description logics reasoning. In: Pan, J.Z., et al. (eds.) ISWC 2020. LNCS, vol. 12506, pp. 366–383. Springer, Cham (2020). https://doi.org/10.1007/978-3-030-62419-4_21

25. Leinberger, M., Seifer, P., Schon, C., Lämmel, R., Staab, S.: Type checking program code using SHACL. In: Ghidini, C., et al. (eds.) ISWC 2019. LNCS, vol. 11778, pp. 399–417. Springer, Cham (2019). https://doi.org/10.1007/978-3-030-30793-6_23

26. Levesque, H.J., Reiter, R., Lespérance, Y., Lin, F., Scherl, R.B.: GOLOG: a logic programming language for dynamic domains. J. Log. Program. **31**(1–3), 59–83 (1997)

27. Mayer, M.C., Pirri, F.: First order abduction via tableau and sequent calculi. Log. J. IGPL **1**(1), 99–117 (1993)

28. Nielson, H.R., Nielson, F.: Semantics with Applications: An Appetizer. Springer, Heidelberg (2007)

29. Rozier, K.Y.: Specification: the biggest bottleneck in formal methods and autonomy. In: Blazy, S., Chechik, M. (eds.) VSTTE 2016. LNCS, vol. 9971, pp. 8–26. Springer, Cham (2016). https://doi.org/10.1007/978-3-319-48869-1_2

30. Schlobach, S.: Explaining subsumption by optimal interpolation. In: Alferes, J.J., Leite, J. (eds.) JELIA 2004. LNCS (LNAI), vol. 3229, pp. 413–425. Springer, Heidelberg (2004). https://doi.org/10.1007/978-3-540-30227-8_35

31. Winskel, G.: The Formal Semantics of Programming Languages: An Introduction. MIT Press, Cambridge (1993)

32. Zarrieß, B.: Verification of golog programs over description logic actions. Ph.D. thesis, Dresden University of Technology, Germany (2018)

33. Zarrieß, B., Claßen, J.: Verification of knowledge-based programs over description logic actions. In: IJCAI. AAAI Press (2015)

A Rely-Guarantee-Based Simulation
for Cooperative Semantics

Kevin Tran[1(✉)], Johannes Åman Pohjola[2,3] , Rob Sison[1] ,
and Gerwin Klein[1,4]

[1] UNSW Sydney, Sydney, Australia
{k.q.tran,r.sison}@unsw.edu.au
[2] Chalmers University of Technology, Gothenburg, Sweden
pohjola@chalmers.se, johannes.aman.pohjola@gu.se
[3] University of Gothenburg, Gothenburg, Sweden
[4] Proofcraft, Sydney, Australia
gerwin.klein@proofcraft.systems

Abstract. Compared to semantics with preemptively executing
threads, ones with cooperative threads permit easier specification of
atomicity in concurrent programs. We introduce a semantics of cooperative programs, and a simulation notion compatible with rely-guarantee
proofs. We prove our simulation composes in parallel and sequentially,
and that it can establish a standard trace-based notion of refinement.

Keywords: Concurrency · rely-guarantee reasoning · simulation

1 Introduction

Most semantics of concurrency suitable for reasoning about implementations use
a *preemptive* semantics, where execution may alternate between threads after
each step. This fine-grained concurrency is needed to model many efficiently
executing programs, but makes reasoning about them more difficult. To limit
concurrency, there might be constructs like atomic blocks which specify that the
code inside must execute atomically. However, consider the example below on
the left, a client of a lock-protected stack:

```
lock()                          while ¬isEmpty(stack) do
while ¬isEmpty(stack) do          x ← pop(stack)
  x ← pop(stack)                  yield
  unlock(); f(x); lock()          f(x)
```

How do we specify the desired critical section, where checking the stack
is empty and then popping it must be atomic, but the computation f(x) on
the popped value need not be? This is awkward, because atomic blocks are

constrained by syntactic structure. Instead, consider a *cooperative* semantics, where a thread, once executed, keeps executing until it decides to yield. The desired granularity of atomicity is shown to the right.

The purpose of our cooperative semantics is not to be implementable for all programs, but to describe programs with arbitrary granularity of atomicity, from fine-grained efficient implementations with many yields to coarse-grained specifications with few yields. We are not advocating for (or against) cooperative multitasking as an implementation technique. Using cooperative semantics is a choice that can be made independently of whether the implementation is cooperative; a program that executes preemptively can be modelled in a cooperative semantics by yielding after every step.

Programs with coarse-grained atomicity are usually easier to reason about. For example, when verifying a program using Owicki-Gries [13] or rely-guarantee [7], one needs to consider interference at the yield points, of which there are fewer with coarse-grained atomicity. We want the properties of the specification we have proven to carry over to the fine-grained implementation, which requires a notion of *atomicity refinement* to justify. We use a standard *event trace refinement* based on set inclusion of (partial) traces of events.

We aim to prove atomicity refinement as part of the future verification of multicore configurations of the seL4 kernel [8]. There are two such configurations: one where most in-kernel execution is protected by one lock around the entire kernel, and a *multi-kernel* configuration where separate kernel instances run on separate cores and share no or almost no data structures. In both cases, the goal is to use atomicity refinement to reduce a large part of the concurrency verification to the existing sequential proofs about seL4 and only deal with concurrency in those parts where it matters. A cooperative semantics is well suited to specify such parts. However, event trace refinement is not compositional with respect to parallel composition. To scale, we therefore need a proof method for refinement that supports compositional reasoning.

To the best of our knowledge, this paper develops the first compositional technique for proving refinement between cooperatively executing concurrent programs. We prove soundness with respect to refinement (Theorem 2), transitivity (Sect. 5.1), and derive decomposition principles for parallel composition (Sect. 5.2) and sequential composition (Sect. 5.3). All these results are formalized in the proof assistant Isabelle/HOL [12].

Our technique is based on the rely-guarantee-based simulation of Liang et al. (RGSim) [11], a compositional proof technique for refinement in a preemptive semantics. Adapting it to cooperative semantics is non-trivial: the treatment of sequential composition is subtle, and requires decoupling the tracking of interference points from the tracking of the current state.

2   Syntax

Our language is based on Complx [2], a preemptively concurrent extension of Simpl [14], used in the seL4 verification to model the behavior of C programs [16].

We choose Complx because our aim in the future is to reason about the multicore configurations of seL4. The syntax is as follows:

$$op : \quad \text{State} \to \text{State} \qquad b, g \subseteq \text{State}$$
$$f \in \quad \text{Fault} \qquad\qquad e : \quad \text{State} \to \text{Event}$$
$$c, c' \in \text{Com} ::= \textbf{skip} \mid \textbf{basic } op \mid c; c' \mid \textbf{if } b \textbf{ then } c \textbf{ else } c' \mid \textbf{while } b \textbf{ do } c$$
$$\mid \textbf{yield } g \mid \textbf{assert } f \, b \mid \textbf{print } e$$

The first line of the definition of Com (for *command*) consists of standard imperative programming constructs [18] (**basic** used to update state), while the second line has more unusual constructs. The syntax is parametrized on a set of states State, and does not fix any particular syntax for expressions. Instead, conditions and state updates are shallowly embedded as sets and functions on states, respectively. The command **assert** $f \, b$ checks if the current state satisfies b, faults with f if it does not, and resumes execution otherwise. It is used to model undefined behavior in C.

These two commands are our additions, and are not present in Complx:

- **yield** g yields control, permitting other threads to execute. A thread that has yielded becomes blocked until the state satisfies the guard g. This permits various synchronization mechanisms like blocking locks to be defined outside the core language.
- **print** e emits an event based on the current state. It has no effect on the state, but will be important for defining refinement and simulation later.

Unlike Complx, there is no syntax for parallel composition. Instead, a concurrent program is represented by a thread pool which includes one command (element of *Com*) per thread. Thread pools will be discussed further in Sect. 3.

3 Semantics

Our semantics is a small-step reduction semantics inspired by Abadi and Plotkin's [1] cooperative semantics. The steps are between *configurations*, which consist of a thread pool, the thread id of the active thread (if any), and a status (either a normal state or a fault). A thread pool is a partial map from thread ids to a command and a guard. The guard controls when the thread can be activated. For thread ids, $\mathbb{N}$ is merely a convenient choice of a countable set with equality.

Definition 1 (Configuration). *A configuration cfg* $= (i, T, st)$ *consists of:*

- *an optional thread id* $i \in \text{dom}(T) \sqcup \{\text{None}\}$
- *a partial map* $T : \mathbb{N} \rightharpoonup \text{Com} \times \mathcal{P}(\text{State})$
- *and a status* $st \in \text{Status}$.

$$s \in \text{State} \qquad f \in \text{Fault} \qquad st \in \text{Status} ::= \text{N } s \mid \text{F } f$$

Given $T(i) = (c, g)$, we say $\text{com}(T(i)) = c$ and $\text{guard}(T(i)) = g$. In this paper, we write thread pools as sets of pairs i.e. $T = \{(i, (c, g)), \ldots\}$.

For brevity in later definitions, we define some types of configurations. Those where the status is a fault, such as by failing an assertion, we call *faulting*. Configurations with an active thread, we call *active* configurations. Configurations without an active thread, and for convenience, not faulting, we call *inactive* configurations.

Definition 2. *We say that a configuration* (i, T, st) *is*

1. faulting *if there exists* f *such that* $st = \text{F } f$*;*
2. active *if* $i \in \text{dom}(T)$*, where* $\text{com}(T(i))$ *is called the* active command*;*
3. inactive *if* $i = \text{None}$ *and there exists* s *such that* $st = \text{N } s$*; and*
4. terminated *if it is inactive and, for all* $i \in \text{dom}(T)$*, it holds that* $\text{com}(T(i)) = $ ***skip***.

The semantics uses *evaluation contexts*, inductively defined by the grammar

$$\mathcal{C} \in \text{ECtxt} ::= [\,] \mid \mathcal{C}; c$$

As usual, $[\,]$ is a hole, and $\mathcal{C}[\cdot]\colon \text{Com} \to \text{Com}$ fills the hole in a context $\mathcal{C}$ with a command. In this case, $\mathcal{C}$ allows us to select the first command in a series of potentially nested (or empty) sequential compositions, which simplifies the formulation of our small-step rules.

We can now define the main step relation $\to$ of the semantics. See below for a selection of the rules. Here, we denote updating the function f at x to y by $f(x := y)(z)$, which is y if $z = x$ and $f(z)$ otherwise. The omitted rules for constructs such as if, while, etc. are standard. We focus here on the rules that are non-standard or important for cooperative semantics. If there is an active command, we perform a step by finding a redex and a corresponding evaluation context. Based on the redex, we can apply the appropriate rule. Exactly one redex exists, except in the case of **skip** where there are none. Otherwise, if there is no active command, the Activate rule lets us nondeterministically choose a thread whose guard holds, and whose command is not **skip**, to activate.

$$\text{Basic} \frac{i \in \mathbb{N} \qquad T(i) = (\mathcal{C}[\textbf{basic } op], g)}{(i, T, \text{N } s) \to (i, T(i := (\mathcal{C}[\textbf{skip}], g)), \text{N } op(s))}$$

$$\text{SeqSkip} \frac{i \in \mathbb{N} \qquad T(i) = (\mathcal{C}[\textbf{skip}; c], g)}{(i, T, \text{N } s) \to (i, T(i := (\mathcal{C}[c], g)), \text{N } s)}$$

$$\text{Yield} \ \frac{i \in \mathbb{N} \qquad T(i) = (\mathcal{C}[\textbf{yield } g], \_)}{(i, T, \text{N } s) \to (\text{None}, T(i := (\mathcal{C}[\textbf{skip}], g)), \text{N } s)}$$

$$\text{AssertTrue} \ \frac{i \in \mathbb{N} \qquad T(i) = (\mathcal{C}[\textbf{assert } f \ b], g) \qquad s \in b}{(i, T, \text{N } s) \to (i, T(i := (\mathcal{C}[\textbf{skip}], g)), \text{N } s)}$$

$$\text{AssertFalse} \ \frac{i \in \mathbb{N} \qquad T(i) = (\mathcal{C}[\textbf{assert } f \ b], g) \qquad s \notin b}{(i, T, \text{N } s) \to (i, T(i := (\mathcal{C}[\textbf{skip}], g)), \text{F } f)}$$

$$\text{Print} \ \frac{i \in \mathbb{N} \qquad T(i) = (\mathcal{C}[\textbf{print } e], g)}{(i, T, \text{N } s) \to (i, T(i := (\mathcal{C}[\textbf{skip}], g)), \text{N } s)}$$

$$\text{Activate} \ \frac{i \in \mathbb{N} \qquad T(i) = (c, g) \qquad c \neq \textbf{skip} \qquad s \in g}{(\text{None}, T, \text{N } s) \to (i, T, \text{N } s)}$$

Following Abadi and Plotkin, we call steps using the Activate rule *choice steps*, and write $\to_c$, and the other steps *active steps*, and write $\to_a$. As befits a semantics for cooperative execution, once a thread has been activated, it continues execution until it yields, faults, or reaches **skip**. Unlike Abadi and Plotkin, we do not automatically yield when the active command is **skip**. Instead, execution is suspended in what is called an *incomplete* configuration, a notion that will be important for sequential compositionality because in a cooperative semantics, not every sequential composition is a preemption point. For a thread to "properly" terminate, it must end with a **yield** rather than a **skip**.

Definition 3 (Incomplete configuration). *A configuration (i, T, st) is incomplete if $i \in \mathbb{N}$, $\text{com}(T(i)) = \textbf{skip}$ and there exists s such that $st = \text{N } s$. Incomplete configurations are active: they have a thread that is still selected for execution, but that cannot make any further progress.*

Example 1. We now give a sample execution from our semantics, where State $= \mathbb{N}$. We abbreviate **basic**$(x \mapsto x + 2)$ to $x \leftarrow x + 2$. We name the rules used at each step and underline the redex when taking an active step.

$$
\begin{array}{ll}
(\text{None}, \ \{(1, \ (x \leftarrow x + 2; \textbf{yield } \top, \{0, 42\}))\}, \ \text{N } 0) & \\
\to_c (1, \ \{(1, (\underline{x \leftarrow x + 2}; \textbf{yield } \top, \{0, 42\}))\}, \ \text{N } 0) & (\text{Activate}) \\
\to_a (1, \ \{(1, (\underline{\textbf{skip}; \textbf{yield } \top}, \{0, 42\}))\}, \ \text{N } 2) & (\text{Basic}) \\
\to_a (1, \ \{(1, (\underline{\textbf{yield } \top}, \{0, 42\}))\}, \ \text{N } 2) & (\text{SeqSkip}) \\
\to_a (\text{None}, \ \{(1, (\textbf{skip}, \top))\}, \ \text{N } 2) & (\text{Yield})
\end{array}
$$

We start in an inactive but not terminated configuration, and the last configuration is terminated. Since the status is N 0 in the initial configuration and the guard contains 0, the thread can be chosen for execution in the first Activate step. The next two steps, Basic and SeqSkip, are thread-internal, and the last step, Yield, returns execution to the thread pool, which contains no other active threads. Execution therefore terminates.

Example 2. Now suppose the thread did not end in a yield. We instead have:

$$(\text{None}, \ \{(1, \ (x \leftarrow x + 2, \{0, 42\}))\}, \ \text{N } 0)$$
$$\rightarrow_c \ (1, \ \{(1, (\underline{x \leftarrow x + 2}, \{0, 42\}))\}, \ \text{N } 0) \qquad \text{(Activate)}$$
$$\rightarrow_a \ (1, \ \{(1, (\textbf{skip}, \{0, 42\}))\}, \ \text{N } 2) \qquad \text{(Basic)}$$

The last configuration is not terminated, but incomplete.

4   Event Trace Refinement

This section defines our notion of event trace refinement. To define our traces of events, we will not use the small-step relation directly, but introduce an analog of a preemptive step, which we call a *fragment*.

4.1   Fragments

With cooperative execution, other threads cannot run while a thread is running, so intermediate states between yield points are inaccessible from the outside. Intermediate states can be made observable via **print**, but they cannot be affected by other threads. That means execution between yield points is sequential.

We can therefore coalesce the fine-grained small-step execution of the program into a more coarse-grained sequence of *fragments* that model the state transition and events output between yield points, or an initially active configuration and a yield point.

It is also here that **print** comes into play: when executing a fragment, we track the sequence of events $e(s)$ emitted by each **print** e command at state s.

Definition 4. *If we can execute a sequence of zero or more active steps from one configuration cfg to another cfg′, emitting the event sequence es, we write*

$$cfg \xrightarrow[a]{es}{}^{*} cfg'.$$

For compositionality later, it will be important to track not just the current state, but also the state at the most recent yield point. We therefore extend configurations as follows:

Definition 5 (Extended configuration). *An extended configuration is a pair* $xcfg = (cfg, s)$ *of a configuration* $cfg = (i, T, st)$ *and the state* $s \in$ State *at the last yield command. When cfg is inactive, we require the (normal) status and the last yield state to coincide:* $st = $ N s.

Now we can define fragments.

Definition 6 (Fragments). *Given extended configurations* (cfg, s) *and* (cfg', s')*, let* $(cfg, s) \overset{es}{\Longrightarrow} (cfg', s')$ *denote a fragment from* (cfg, s) *to* (cfg', s') *emitting the sequence of events es. We define it as the conjunction of:*

1. *cfg is not faulting or incomplete*
2. *cfg' is inactive, faulting, or incomplete*
3. *if cfg is inactive, then there exists* cfg'' *s.t.* $cfg \rightarrow_c cfg''$ *and* $cfg'' \overset{es}{\underset{a}{\rightarrow}}{}^* cfg'$
4. *if cfg is active, then* $cfg \overset{es}{\underset{a}{\rightarrow}}{}^* cfg'$
5. *if cfg' is active (including faulting or incomplete), then* $s' = s$*.*

Definition 7. *If we can execute a sequence of zero or more fragments from an extended configuration xcfg to another configuration* $xcfg'$*, emitting the sequence of events es, we write*

$$xcfg \overset{es}{\Longrightarrow}{}^* xcfg'$$

In the previous two definitions, if *es* is omitted, it is taken to mean the empty list, that is, no events being emitted.

We now give an example of a fragment, with State = Event = N. We use **print** x to emit the current state as an event. Steps with something above $\rightarrow$ emit an event, the rest emit no event. Consider the following small-step sequence:

$$(\text{None}, \{(2, (\mathbf{print}\ x; \mathbf{yield}\ \top, \top))\}, \text{N}\ 0)$$
$$\rightarrow_c (2, \{(2, (\mathbf{print}\ x; \mathbf{yield}\ \top, \top))\}, \text{N}\ 0) \qquad\qquad (\text{Activate})$$
$$\overset{0}{\rightarrow}_a (2, \{(2, (\mathbf{skip}; \mathbf{yield}\ \top, \top))\}, \text{N}\ 0) \qquad\qquad (\text{Print})$$
$$\rightarrow_a (2, \{(2, (\mathbf{yield}\ \top, \top))\}, \text{N}\ 0) \qquad\qquad (\text{SeqSkip})$$
$$\rightarrow_a (\text{None}, \{(2, (\mathbf{skip}, \top))\}, \text{N}\ 0) \qquad\qquad (\text{Yield})$$

Example 3. The sequence forms a single fragment that we can write as follows:

$$((\text{None}, \{(2, (\mathbf{print}\ x; \mathbf{yield}\ \top, \top))\}, \text{N}\ 0), 0)$$
$$\overset{[0]}{\Longrightarrow} ((\text{None}, \{(2, (\mathbf{skip}, \top))\}, \text{N}\ 0), 0)$$

94   K. Tran et al.

We can also conclude that

$$((2, \{(2, (\textbf{print } x; \textbf{yield } \top, \top))\}, \text{N } 0), 0)$$
$$\xrightarrow{[0]} ((\text{None}, \{(2, (\textbf{skip}, \top))\}, \text{N } 0), 0)$$

Example 4. Here is an example execution of several fragments:

$$((\text{None}, \{(1, (x \leftarrow x + 1; \textbf{yield } \top; x \leftarrow x + 1; \textbf{yield } \top, \top))$$
$$, (2, (\textbf{print } x; \textbf{yield } \top, \top))\}, \text{N } 0), 0)$$
$$\Rightarrow ((\text{None}, \{(1, (\textbf{skip}; x \leftarrow x + 1; \textbf{yield } \top, \top))$$
$$, (2, (\textbf{print } x; \textbf{yield } \top, \top))\}, \text{N } 1), 1)$$
$$\xrightarrow{[1]} ((\text{None}, \{(1, (\textbf{skip}; x \leftarrow x + 1; \textbf{yield } \top, \top))$$
$$, (2, (\textbf{skip}, \top))\}, \text{N } 1), 1)$$

4.2   Refinement

Given the notion of fragments from the previous section, we can now define
event trace refinement. When executing fragments, a trace of events is generated. This trace could be partial or end in a terminated, faulting or incomplete
configuration. We denote these results P, T, F, I, respectively.

We define the partial traces PT from an extended configuration $xcfg$ inductively by the following rules. Here we use @ for list concatenation and [] for the
empty list. Note that, as the name suggests, the trace only records events, not
states.

$$\frac{xcfg = ((i, T, \text{N } s), s')}{([], P) \in \text{PT}(xcfg)} \qquad \frac{xcfg = ((i, T, \text{F } f), s')}{([], F) \in \text{PT}(xcfg)}$$

$$\frac{xcfg = (cfg, s) \qquad cfg \text{ is terminated}}{([], T) \in \text{PT}(xcfg)} \qquad \frac{xcfg = (cfg, s) \qquad cfg \text{ is incomplete}}{([], I) \in \text{PT}(xcfg)}$$

$$\frac{xcfg \xrightarrow{es} xcfg' \qquad (tr, r) \in \text{PT}(xcfg')}{(es@tr, r) \in \text{PT}(xcfg)}$$

Using the first of the above rules and the execution from Example 1:

$$\{([], P), ([], T)\} \subseteq \text{PT}(((\text{None}, \{(1, (x \leftarrow x + 2; \textbf{yield } \top, \{0, 42\}))\}, \text{N } 0), 0)) \tag{1}$$

The program does not emit any events, so both traces record the empty list. For an example where PT is instead bound from above, we take a slightly different program that increments x twice, and yields in between. By induction on PT,

$$\mathrm{PT}(((\mathrm{None}, \{(1, (x \leftarrow x + 1; \mathbf{yield}\ \top; x \leftarrow x + 1; \mathbf{yield}\ \top, \top))\}, \mathrm{N}\ 0), 0))$$
$$\subseteq \{([], P), ([], T)\}\ (2)$$

We can now define event trace refinement as follows:

Definition 8 (Event trace refinement). *Let xcfg, xcfg$'$ be extended configurations. We say that xcfg $\sqsubseteq$ xcfg$'$ (xcfg refines xcfg$'$) if* $\mathrm{PT}(xcfg) \subseteq \mathrm{PT}(xcfg')$.

Refinement states that after executing some number of fragments from the concrete extended configuration, we can match the event trace and result by executing some number of fragments from the abstract extended configuration. The number of fragments may differ. This admits atomicity refinement where we decrease or increase the number of yield points between abstract and concrete levels, which our work aims to enable. Note that the statement of refinement here is for configurations $xcfg$ and $xcfg'$, not for programs. That is, the definition is for specific initial states of the thread pool, not over all of them.

Example 5 (Refinement). Since we showed in Eq. 1 and 2 that the traces of one program are above $\{([], P), ([], T)\}$ and the other below, we have

$$((\mathrm{None}, \{(1, (x \leftarrow x + 1; \mathbf{yield}\ \top; x \leftarrow x + 1; \mathbf{yield}\ \top, \{0, 42\}))\}, \mathrm{N}\ 0), 0)$$
$$\sqsubseteq ((\mathrm{None}, \{(1, (x \leftarrow x + 2; \mathbf{yield}\ \top, \top))\}, \mathrm{N}\ 0), 0)$$

If the programs emitted their state as events before the last yield, refinement would still hold, but only for configurations starting in the same state. Refinement would no longer hold if these threads were composed with another set of abstract and concrete threads that also modify x, even if refinement were to hold separately for these threads.

Example 6 (Non-refinement). Let

$$xcfg_c = ((\mathrm{None}, \{(1, (x \leftarrow x + 1; \mathbf{yield}\ \top; x \leftarrow x + 1; \mathbf{yield}\ \top, \{0, 42\}))$$
$$, (2, (\mathbf{print}\ x; \mathbf{yield}\ \top, \top))\}, \mathrm{N}\ 0), 0)$$
$$xcfg_a = ((\mathrm{None}, \{(1, (x \leftarrow x + 2; \mathbf{yield}\ \top, \top))$$
$$, (2, (\mathbf{print}\ x; \mathbf{yield}\ \top, \top))\}, \mathrm{N}\ 0), 0)$$

From Example 4, we have $([1], P) \in \mathrm{PT}(xcfg_c)$. By induction on PT, we have $\mathrm{PT}(xcfg_a) \subseteq \{([], P), ([0], P), ([0], T), ([2], P), ([2], T)\}$. Hence $xcfg_c \not\sqsubseteq xcfg_a$.

Together with Example 5 and Example 3 (noting that the fragment ends in a terminated configuration), this shows that event trace refinement is not compositional with respect to parallel composition (to be defined in Sect. 5.2).

5   Simulation

As just mentioned, although event trace refinement is an intuitive notion of behavioral preservation, it does not compose with respect to parallel composition. Since compositionality is indispensable for scalable reasoning, we follow the usual path of defining a compositional simulation instead that can be used for reasoning. To this end, we adapt the rely-guarantee-based simulation RGSim [11] to a cooperative semantics. We prove it implies our event trace refinement and is compositional with respect to parallel (Sect. 5.2) and sequential composition (Sect. 5.3).

The key difference between cooperative and preemptive semantics is that in preemptive semantics, every execution step is a yield point and therefore observable as a step. In cooperative semantics, we need to distinguish between execution states in the middle of a fragment and execution states that have reached a yield point where interference from other threads is possible. For the simulation to stay compositional, this needs additions to both the internal definition of the simulation itself, and the parameters the simulation operates on.

Our simulation is between two extended configurations, one concrete and one abstract, with additional parameters we introduce below. Let CState and AState be the concrete and abstract state set, respectively. The extra parameters are:

- $R_c, G_c \subseteq \text{CState} \times \text{CState}$, the *concrete rely and guarantee relations*
- $R_a, G_a \subseteq \text{AState} \times \text{AState}$, the *abstract rely and guarantee relations*
- $\alpha \subseteq \text{CState} \times \text{AState}$, the *state relation*
- $Q \subseteq \text{CState} \times (\mathbb{N} \rightharpoonup \mathcal{P}(\text{CState})) \times \text{AState} \times (\mathbb{N} \rightharpoonup \mathcal{P}(\text{AState}))$, the *normal postcondition*, which is a predicate on the states and the guards of all threads.
- $Q_i \subseteq \text{CState} \times \text{CState} \times \text{AState} \times \text{AState}$, the *incomplete postcondition*, which is a predicate on the current states and the states at the last yield point.

The first three items are the same as in the original RGSim, but the normal postcondition now keeps track of the guards. The incomplete postcondition is a new addition needed for sequential compositionality in Sect. 5.3. As is customary with rely-guarantee reasoning, we assume the rely relations R_c, R_a are reflexive.

As with the original RGSim, we will need the following definition:

Definition 9 (α-related transitions). *We call $\langle R_c, R_a \rangle_\alpha$ the α-related transitions in R_c and R_a. They are the set of all tuples $(s_c, s_c', s_a, s_a') \in \text{CState} \times \text{CState} \times \text{AState} \times \text{AState}$ such that $(s_c, s_a) \in \alpha$, $(s_c, s_c') \in R_c$, $(s_a, s_a') \in R_a$ and $(s_c', s_a') \in \alpha$.*

Let $xcfg_c = (cfg_c, s_c)$ be the concrete extended configuration, where $cfg_c = (i_c, T_c, st_c)$, and similarly for the abstract extended configuration $xcfg_a$. We now define the simulation between $xcfg_c$ and $xcfg_a$ coinductively.

Definition 10. *If $R_c, G_c, \alpha, R_a, G_a \vdash xcfg_c \preceq xcfg_a \; Q, Q_i$ then all of the following must hold:*

1. $(s_c, s_a) \in \alpha$

2. *if $i_c = $ None then $i_a = $ None*
3. *neither cfg_c nor cfg_a are faulting or incomplete*
4. *if cfg_c is terminated, then there exists an extended configuration $xcfg'_a$ such that $xcfg_a \Rightarrow^* xcfg'_a$, cfg'_a is terminated, $(s_c, s_c, s_a, s'_a) \in \langle G_c, G^*_a \rangle_\alpha$ and $(s_c, \mathrm{guard} \circ T_c, s'_a, \mathrm{guard} \circ T'_a) \in Q$, where $\circ$ is function composition.*
5. *if $xcfg_c \xRightarrow{es} xcfg'_c$ and cfg'_c is inactive, then there exists an extended configuration $xcfg'_a$ such that $xcfg_a \xRightarrow{es}{}^* xcfg'_a$, cfg'_a is inactive, $(s_c, s'_c, s_a, s'_a) \in \langle G_c, G^*_a \rangle_\alpha$ and $R_c, G_c, \alpha, R_a, G_a \vdash xcfg'_c \preceq xcfg'_a \ Q, Q_i$.*
6. *if $xcfg_c \xRightarrow{es} xcfg'_c$ and $st'_c = \mathrm{F} \ f$, then there exists an extended configuration $xcfg'_a$ such that $xcfg_a \xRightarrow{es}{}^* xcfg'_a$ and $st'_a = \mathrm{F} \ f$.*
7. *if $xcfg_c \xRightarrow{es} xcfg'_c$ and cfg'_c is incomplete, then there exists an extended configuration $xcfg'_a$ such that $xcfg_a \xRightarrow{es}{}^* xcfg'_a$, cfg'_a is incomplete, $(s_c, s_c, s_a, s'_a) \in \langle G_c, G^*_a \rangle_\alpha$ and there exists s''_c, s''_a such that $st'_c = \mathrm{N} \ s''_c$, $st'_a = \mathrm{N} \ s''_a$ and $((s_c, s''_c), (s'_a, s''_a)) \in Q_i$.*
8. *if $xcfg'_c$ and $xcfg'_a$ are extended configurations such that cfg'_c and cfg'_a are inactive and $(s_c, s'_c, s_a, s'_a) \in \langle R_c, R^*_a \rangle_\alpha$, then $R_c, G_c, \alpha, R_a, G_a \vdash xcfg'_c \preceq xcfg'_a \ Q, Q_i$.*

Case 1 states that the last yield states of the concrete and abstract configurations must be related by the state relation. Case 2 states that if the concrete configuration is inactive, then the abstract one must be too. It is used to prevent situations where we are free to pick a thread on the concrete level, but on the abstract level, we are forced to execute a thread. For case 3, the simulation only includes inactive configurations and active, but not faulting or incomplete configurations. Faulting and incomplete configurations are dealt with by executing fragments from a configuration in the simulation. Case 4 is the "base case" of the simulation, when the concrete configuration is terminated. The abstract configuration is allowed to do some work before terminating. The final states and guards of all threads must satisfy the normal postcondition. Cases 5, 6, 7 require that when we execute a fragment on the concrete level, we must match it with zero or more fragments on the abstract level. The fragments must preserve the state relation and also obey the guarantee relations (if we end in an inactive configuration). Case 7 also requires that when we end up in an incomplete configuration, that the last yield states and current states obey the incomplete postcondition. Case 8 requires that the simulation be robust against interference from the environment, bounded by the rely relations and the state relation.

We can strengthen rely relations and weaken the guarantee relations and postconditions:

Theorem 1. *If $R_c, G_c, \alpha, R_a, G_a \vdash xcfg_c \preceq xcfg_a \ Q, Q_i$ and*

- *$R'_c \subseteq R_c$ and $R'_a \subseteq R_a$ (strengthening relies)*
- *$G_c \subseteq G'_c$ and $G_a \subseteq G'_a$ (weakening guarantees)*
- *$Q \subseteq Q'$ and $Q_i \subseteq Q'_i$ (weakening postconditions)*

then $R'_c, G'_c, \alpha, R'_a, G'_a \vdash xcfg_c \preceq xcfg_a \ Q', Q'_i$.

We then prove the simulation sound with respect to the more intuitive trace refinement. First we prove a lemma, then obtain soundness as a corollary:

Lemma 1. *Let* Id *be the identity relation and* $\top$ *be the universal relation. If* Id$, \top, \alpha,$ Id$, \top \vdash xcfg_c \preceq xcfg_a \ Q, Q_i$, *then* $\mathrm{PT}(xcfg_c) \subseteq \mathrm{PT}(xcfg_a)$.

Proof. By induction over PT.

Theorem 2 (Soundness). *Let* R_c, R_a *be reflexive rely relations.*
     If $R_c, G_c, \alpha, R_a, G_a \vdash xcfg_c \preceq xcfg_a \ Q, Q_i$, *then* $xcfg_c \sqsubseteq xcfg_a$.

Proof. Using Theorem 1, we strengthen the relies to the Id relation and weaken the guarantees to the $\top$ relation. Unfold the definition of $\sqsubseteq$ and apply Lemma 1.

5.1   Transitivity

By focusing on the extended configurations, we can think of the simulation as a binary relation. Thus we might wonder whether or not our simulation is transitive, which would allow stepwise simulation proofs. Assuming that the rely relations and state relations are in some sense compatible, we can answer in the affirmative. The compatibility condition can informally be described as: given $\alpha \circ \beta$-related transitions, we can factor them into some α-related transitions and β-related transitions. More formally,

Definition 11. *Let* R_l, R_m, R_h *be rely relations on the low, middle and high levels. Let* α *be a state relation between the low and middle levels, and let* β *be a state relation between the middle and high levels. We say that* $\mathrm{compat}(R_l, \alpha, R_m, \beta, R_h)$, *if for all* $(s_l, s'_l, s_h, s'_h) \in \langle R_l, R_h \rangle_{\alpha \circ \beta}$ *and* s_m *s.t.* $(s_l, s_m) \in \alpha$ *and* $(s_m, s_h) \in \beta$, *there exists* s'_m *s.t.* $(s_l, s'_l, s_m, s'_m) \in \langle R_l, R_m \rangle_\alpha$ *and* $(s_m, s'_m, s_h, s'_h) \in \langle R_m, R_h \rangle_\beta$.

Theorem 3 (Transitivity). *Let* R_l, R_m, R_h *be rely relations on the low, middle and high levels. Let* α *be a state relation between the low and middle levels, and let* β *be a state relation between the middle and high levels. If*

- $R_l, G_l, \alpha, R_m, G_m \vdash xcfg_l \preceq xcfg_m \ Q, Q_i$
- $R_m, G_m, \beta, R_h, G_h \vdash xcfg_m \preceq xcfg_h \ Q', Q'_i$
- *and* $\mathrm{compat}(R_l, \alpha, R_m, \beta, R_h^*)$

then $R_l, G_l, \alpha \circ \beta, R_h, G_h \vdash xcfg_l \preceq xcfg_h \ Q \circ Q', Q_i \circ Q'_i$, *where* $\circ$ *means relational composition and* R_h^* *is the reflexive transitive closure.*

5.2   Parallel Composition

Although our language lacks a parallel composition operator, by taking the disjoint union of thread pools, we can obtain a somewhat restricted analog of it. This shallow embedding as a disjoint union allow us to inherit properties like associativity automatically. We can break down a simulation into simulations on each part of the disjoint union, abstracting away the behavior of the other part of the disjoint union using the rely and guarantee relations.

Given normal postconditions Q, Q' for the parts, what should the normal postcondition of the whole be? We need the states to agree, and the guards to be the disjoint union of the guards for the parts. Thus, we define $Q \sqcup Q'$, the set of tuples $(s_c, gs_c \cup gs'_c, s_a, gs_a \cup gs'_a)$ where $(s_c, gs_c, s_a, gs_a) \in Q$, $(s_c, gs'_c, s_a, gs'_a) \in Q'$, $\mathrm{dom}(gs_c) \cap \mathrm{dom}(gs'_c) = \emptyset$ and $\mathrm{dom}(gs_a) \cap \mathrm{dom}(gs'_a) = \emptyset$.

As with rely-guarantee reasoning, we need the normal postconditions to be stable under interference from the environment. Let $Q \subseteq \mathrm{CState} \times (\mathbb{N} \rightharpoonup \mathcal{P}(\mathrm{CState})) \times \mathrm{AState} \times (\mathbb{N} \rightharpoonup \mathcal{P}(\mathrm{AState}))$ be a normal postcondition and $\Lambda \subseteq \mathrm{CState} \times \mathrm{CState} \times \mathrm{AState} \times \mathrm{AState}$. We say $\mathrm{Sta}(Q, \Lambda)$, if for all $(s_c, gs_c, s_a, gs_a) \in Q$ and $(s_c, s'_c, s_a, s'_a) \in \Lambda$, we have $(s'_c, gs_c, s'_a, gs_a) \in Q$.

We now can state our parallel composition rule:

Theorem 4 (Parallel composition). *If*

1. $R_c, G_c, \alpha, R_a, G_a \vdash ((i_c, T_c, st_c), s_c) \preceq ((i_a, T_a, st_a), s_a)\ Q, Q_i$
2. $R'_c, G'_c, \alpha, R'_a, G'_a \vdash ((i'_c, T'_c, st'_c), s_c) \preceq ((i'_a, T'_a, st'_a), s_a)\ Q', Q_i$
3. $G_c \subseteq R'_c,\ G'_c \subseteq R_c,\ G_a \subseteq R'_a$ *and* $G'_a \subseteq R_a$
4. $\mathrm{dom}(T_c) \cap \mathrm{dom}(T_a) = \emptyset$ *and* $\mathrm{dom}(T'_c) \cap \mathrm{dom}(T'_a) = \emptyset$
5. $\mathrm{Sta}(Q, \langle R_c, R^*_a \rangle_\alpha)$ *and* $\mathrm{Sta}(Q', \langle R'_c, R'^*_a \rangle_\alpha)$
6. $(i''_c, st''_c, i''_a, st''_a, \mathrm{None}, \mathrm{None}) \in \{(i_c, st_c, i_a, st_a, i'_c, i'_a), (i'_c, st'_c, i'_a, st'_a, i_c, i_a)\}$

then

$$R_c \cap R'_c, G_c \cup G'_c, \alpha, R_a \cap R'_a, G_a \cup G'_a \vdash$$
$$((i''_c, T_c \cup T'_c, st''_c), s_c) \preceq ((i''_a, T_a \cup T'_a, st''_a), s_a)\ Q \sqcup Q', Q_i$$

Assumptions 1 and 2 are the simulations on the "parallel components". Assumption 3 states the rely and guarantee relations between the components are compatible. Assumption 4 states that the thread pools must have disjoint thread ids. Assumption 5 states that the normal postconditions are stable under interference. Assumption 6 is meant to formalize the idea of picking one half of the parallel composition to execute.

5.3   Sequential Composition

Even for concurrent programs, there is often a substantial amount of sequential reasoning to be done. In the preemptive case, every sequential composition is a preemption point, but with cooperative semantics this is not always the case. When executing a fragment with a sequential composition, we could either yield or not before executing the second part. This leads us to distinguish between normal and incomplete execution of a fragment. To propagate information from the first part to the second part of a sequential composition, we use the distinction between normal and incomplete postconditions. The normal postcondition, in addition to states, tracks thread guards at the end of executing the first part so that the second part can reason about them. The incomplete postcondition of the first part allows us to take the first part of the execution into account for checking the guarantee and state relations when the second part encounters a yield instruction. We now state our sequential composition rule:

Theorem 5 (Sequential composition). *If*

1.
$$R_c, G_c, \alpha, R_a, G_a \vdash$$
$$((i_c, \{(t_c, (c_c, g_c))\}, st_c), s_c) \preceq ((i_a, \{(t_a, (c_a, g_a))\}, st_a), s_a) \ Q, Q_i$$

2. *For all* $(s_c', gs_c', s_a', gs_a') \in Q$ *such that* $(s_c', s_a') \in \alpha$,

$$R_c, G_c, \alpha, R_a, G_a \vdash ((\text{None}, \{(t_c, (c_c', gs_c'(t_c)))\}, \text{N } s_c'), s_c')$$
$$\preceq ((\text{None}, \{(t_a, (c_a', gs_a'(t_a)))\}, \text{N } s_a'), s_a') \ Q', Q_i'$$

3. *For all* $(s_c', s_c'', s_a', s_a'') \in Q_i$ *and guards* g_c', g_a',

$$R_c, G_c, \alpha, R_a, G_a \vdash ((t_c, \{(t_c, (c_c', g_c'))\}, \text{N } s_c''), s_c')$$
$$\preceq ((t_a, \{(t_a, (c_a', g_a'))\}, \text{N } s_a''), s_a') \ Q', Q_i'$$

4. *For all* $(s_c', gs_c', s_a', gs_a') \in Q$, *we have* $t_c \in \text{dom}(gs_c')$ *and* $t_a \in \text{dom}(gs_a')$, *and* $s_c' \in \text{guard}(gs_c'(t_c))$ *and* $s_a' \in \text{guard}(gs_a'(t_a))$

5. $c_c' \neq \mathbf{skip}$ *and* $c_a' \neq \mathbf{skip}$

then

$$R_c, G_c, \alpha, R_a, G_a \vdash$$
$$((i_c, \{(t_c, (c_c; c_c', g_c))\}, st_c), s_c) \preceq ((i_a, \{(t_a, (c_a; c_a', g_a))\}, st_a), s_a) \ Q', Q_i'$$

Assumption 1 is the simulation on the first part of the sequential composition. Assumption 2 is the simulation on the second part, assuming the first part terminated normally. Assumption 3 is the simulation on the second part of the sequential composition, assuming the first part terminated in an incomplete configuration. The guards are actually irrelevant since we deal with active configurations. Assumption 4 specifies that when the first part terminates normally, we are not in a state blocked by the guard.

5.4   Example

We borrow the following example from Liang et al. [11, Section 4.3]. We wish to establish a simulation between incrementing an abstract atomic counter $x \in \mathbb{N}$ by 2 and incrementing a concrete lock-protected counter by 1 twice. The concrete state consists of a counter $x \in \mathbb{N}$, an optional thread id $i \in \mathbb{N} \sqcup \{\text{None}\}$ indicating the lock owner, and a ghost copy X of the abstract state. Then define for $i \in \mathbb{N}$:

$$\textbf{lock } i = (\textbf{if } \text{owner} = \text{None } \textbf{then skip else yield } \text{owner} = \text{None}); \ \text{owner} \leftarrow i$$
$$\textbf{unlock } i = \textbf{assert } (\text{owner} = i); \ \text{owner} \leftarrow \text{None}$$

The commands on each level are:

$$c_c = (\textbf{lock } w; \textbf{yield } \top); (x \leftarrow x + 1; \textbf{yield } \top); (x \leftarrow x + 1; \textbf{yield } \top);$$
$$\textbf{unlock } w; \textbf{yield } \top$$
$$c_a = x \leftarrow x + 2; \textbf{yield } \top$$

We have rely and guarantee relations, parametrized by a thread id $i \in \mathbb{N}$.

$$R_c(i) = \{(s_c, s_c') \mid \text{owner}(s_c) = i \implies s_c = s_c'\}$$
$$G_c(i) = \{(s_c, s_c') \mid s_c' = s_c \vee ((\text{owner}(s_c) = \text{None} \implies \text{owner}(s_c') = i)$$
$$\wedge (\exists i' \in \mathbb{N}. \ \text{owner}(s_c) = i' \implies i' = i \wedge \text{owner}(s_c') \in \{i, \text{None}\}))\}$$

The rely relation states that if a thread i holds the lock, then the environment is not allowed to change the state. The guarantee relation states that thread i can take, hold or release the lock, and cannot make any other state changes unless they have the lock.

The state relation says that X on the concrete level indeed copies the abstract x, and that when the lock is not held, the abstract and concrete x are equal:

$$\alpha = \{(s_c, s_a) \mid x(s_a) = X(s_c) \wedge (\text{owner}(s_c) = \text{None} \implies x(s_c) = X(s_c))\}$$

Our normal postcondition Q is just α on the states, and that the writer's guard is $\top$. The incomplete postcondition Q_i is not used for this example.

$$Q = \{(s_c, gs_c, s_a, gs_a) \mid (s_c, s_a) \in \alpha \wedge gs_c = \{(w, \top)\} \wedge gs_a = \{(w, \top)\}\}$$

Example 7. For any pair of states (s_c, s_a) in α, we have:

$$R_c(w), G_c(w), \alpha, \top, \top \vdash$$
$$(\text{None}, \{(w, (c_c, \top))\}, \mathbb{N} \ s_c) \preceq (\text{None}, \{(w, (c_a, \top))\}, \mathbb{N} \ s_a) \ Q, Q_i$$

Example 8. When we repeat the execution of c_c and c_a, we would also expect the simulation to hold. Indeed, using the sequential composition rule, we have:

$$R_c(w), G_c(w), \alpha, \top, \top \vdash$$
$$(\text{None}, \{(w, (c_c; c_c, \top))\}, \mathbb{N} \ s_c) \preceq (\text{None}, \{(w, (c_a; c_a, \top))\}, \mathbb{N} \ s_a) \ Q, Q_i$$

Liang et al.'s example also contains printer threads. Our Isabelle formalization similarly proves the simulation between these, and uses the parallel composition rule to prove simulation for the entire system.

6   Limitations and Future Work

The aim to use this work in the multicore seL4 verification informs some of its limitations. For instance, constructs for dynamically creating threads are not necessary for a static number of concurrent kernel instances. Parallel composition in a cooperative semantics is challenging to specify. A fork command would be a more natural extension but is unnecessary for our purposes.

The language we present is based on Complx [2]. Complx has exceptions, which are useful for modelling C constructs such as **break** and **continue**. We leave this for future work to focus on the main compositionality results first.

In our semantics there are "deadlocked" configurations: inactive configurations with threads that have not reached **skip**, but no guards are satisfied so no thread can run. Also, an active thread may run forever without yielding. Neither situation creates any fragments, thus satisfying our simulation and consequently, event trace refinement. Thus, deadlock freedom and termination are not preserved by our simulation, only safety properties on states.

We have not investigated how weak memory models would affect the semantics and have so far targeted sequential consistency only.

7   Related Work

Our mechanization of cooperative semantics is loosely based on the ideas of Abadi and Plotkin [1]. Their aim is not program verification, but instead exploring denotational semantics and connections to algebraic effects.

Liang et al. [11] introduce RGSim, a rely-guarantee-based simulation compositional with respect to constructs like parallel and sequential composition. Their work is formalized in Coq using a language with preemptive semantics. We adapt the simulation to a language with cooperative semantics while preserving parallel and sequential composition. As preemptive semantics can be expressed using cooperative semantics, our work in some ways generalizes RGSim.

For the treatment of atomicity refinement more broadly, linearizability [6] is a safety property widely used as a correctness condition for concurrent objects. It roughly states that each history of method invocations and responses is equivalent to a history where methods are executed sequentially. However, not all programs are naturally expressed as objects with methods; in particular, not those that we are interested in applying our method to.

Later work by the RGSim authors Liang and Feng [10] enables the use of liveness properties for blocking synchronization in addition to linearizability, so the same generalization may be possible in our setting. For our application, event trace refinement is sufficient, so we have not yet explored this direction further.

Elmas et al. [3,4] prove atomicity refinement and linearizability using reduction, which checks whether individual steps of a thread commute with steps of other threads, and which does not compose with respect to parallel composition. Elmas et al. use a preemptive semantics, but Civl [9] extends this line of work to use cooperative semantics. Their notion of refinement associates program steps with assertions, and checks for preservation of end-to-end behavior and absence of assertion failures. These methods are not proven sound in a proof assistant.

Compositional notions of refinement have been used to verify concurrent compiler optimizations. Simuliris [5] uses a separation logic-based simulation to prove a fair termination preserving contextual refinement of concurrent optimizations. Contextual refinement considers the termination behavior of a program (terminating with a value, infinite execution or getting stuck) when composed with arbitrary well-formed contexts. Their language has preemptive semantics, does not consider I/O and assumes non-blocking execution.

Timany and Birkedal [15] provide a compositional separation logic-based proof method for refinement of programs with continuations, which they use as a compilation target for a cooperative concurrent language. Although they prove refinement between the target and source programs, they do not define refinement between programs in the cooperative source language. The compiler eliminates some nondeterminism on the concrete level by assuming a particular scheduling implementation using a queue, whereas we continue to allow for arbitrary interleaving of threads at yield points. Arbitrary interleaving better models the possible range of behavior of programs at the implementation level, such as when running on multiple cores and using different schedulers.

Vistrup et al. [17] use interaction trees [19] to enable reusable program logic fragments for effects on top of a pure language, including cooperative concurrency. Their program logics deal with single programs and not refinement relations between programs.

8 Conclusion

This paper has presented a concurrent imperative language with cooperative execution semantics. The language is generic over state and can be instantiated to model the behavior of a variety of more concrete imperative languages.

A cooperative semantics, unlike the usual preemptive concurrency semantics, lets us easily model different degrees of atomicity of executions within the same language without being constrained by the block structure of the language.

We have adapted the standard notion of trace refinement for cooperative semantics as a basis for the soundness of a compositional simulation that can be used for reasoning about such programs.

Our simulation for cooperative concurrent semantics is based on RGSim [11], an existing simulation formalization for the preemptive setting. The cooperative setting requires a number of subtle changes to enable compositional proof rules for reasoning about parallel and sequential composition. We have proved in Isabelle/HOL that the simulation is sound with respect to refinement, that it is compositional, and that it satisfies basic desirable properties such as transitivity.

Acknowledgement. This research was funded by the Australian Government's RTP scholarship. We thank the reviewers and Thomas Sewell for their feedback.

Disclosure of Interests. The authors have no competing interests.

References

1. Abadi, M., Plotkin, G.: A model of cooperative threads. In: Proceedings of the 36th Annual ACM SIGPLAN-SIGACT Symposium on Principles of Programming Languages, POPL '09, pp. 29–40. Association for Computing Machinery, New York (2009). https://doi.org/10.1145/1480881.1480887
2. Amani, S., Andronick, J., Bortin, M., Lewis, C., Rizkallah, C., Tuong, J.: COMPLX: a verification framework for concurrent imperative programs. In: International Conference on Certified Programs and Proofs, pp. 138–150. SIGPLAN Notices, Paris (2017)
3. Elmas, T., Qadeer, S., Sezgin, A., Subasi, O., Tasiran, S.: Simplifying linearizability proofs with reduction and abstraction. In: Esparza, J., Majumdar, R. (eds.) TACAS 2010. LNCS, vol. 6015, pp. 296–311. Springer, Heidelberg (2010). https://doi.org/10.1007/978-3-642-12002-2_25
4. Elmas, T., Qadeer, S., Tasiran, S.: A calculus of atomic actions. In: Proceedings of the 36th Annual ACM SIGPLAN-SIGACT Symposium on Principles of Programming Languages, POPL '09, pp. 2–15. Association for Computing Machinery, New York (2009). https://doi.org/10.1145/1480881.1480885
5. Gäher, L., et al.: Simuliris: a separation logic framework for verifying concurrent program optimizations. Proc. ACM Program. Lang. 6(POPL) (2022). https://doi.org/10.1145/3498689
6. Herlihy, M.P., Wing, J.M.: Linearizability: a correctness condition for concurrent objects. ACM Trans. Program. Lang. Syst. 12(3), 463–492 (1990). https://doi.org/10.1145/78969.78972
7. Jones, C.B.: Tentative steps towards a development method for interfering programs. ACM Trans. Program. Lang. Syst. 5(4), 596–619 (1983)
8. Klein, G., et al.: Comprehensive formal verification of an OS microkernel. ACM Trans. Comput. Syst. 32(1), 2:1–2:70 (2014)
9. Kragl, B., Qadeer, S.: The civl verifier. In: 2021 Formal Methods in Computer Aided Design (FMCAD), pp. 143–152 (2021)
10. Liang, H., Feng, X.: A program logic for concurrent objects under fair scheduling. In: Proceedings of the 43rd Annual ACM SIGPLAN-SIGACT Symposium on Principles of Programming Languages, POPL '16, pp. 385–399. Association for Computing Machinery, New York (2016). https://doi.org/10.1145/2837614.2837635
11. Liang, H., Feng, X., Fu, M.: A rely-guarantee-based simulation for verifying concurrent program transformations. SIGPLAN Not. 47(1), 455–468 (2012). https://doi.org/10.1145/2103621.2103711
12. Nipkow, T., Paulson, L., Wenzel, M.: Isabelle/HOL—A Proof Assistant for Higher-Order Logic, Lecture Notes in Computer Science, vol. 2283. Springer, Heidelberg (2002)
13. Owicki, S., Gries, D.: An axiomatic proof technique for parallel programs I. Acta Informatica 6, 319–340 (1976)
14. Schirmer, N.: Verification of Sequential Imperative Programs in Isabelle/HOL. Ph.D. thesis, Technische Universität München (2006)
15. Timany, A., Birkedal, L.: Mechanized relational verification of concurrent programs with continuations. Proc. ACM Program. Lang. 3(ICFP) (2019). https://doi.org/10.1145/3341709
16. Tuch, H., Klein, G., Norrish, M.: Types, bytes, and separation logic. In: ACM SIGPLAN-SIGACT Symposium on Principles of Programming Languages, pp. 97–108. ACM, Nice (2007)

17. Vistrup, M., Sammler, M., Jung, R.: Program logics à la carte. Proc. ACM Program. Lang. **9**(POPL) (2025). https://doi.org/10.1145/3704847
18. Winskel, G.: The Formal Semantics of Programming Languages: An Introduction. MIT Press, Cambridge (1993)
19. Xia, L.Y., et al.: Interaction trees: representing recursive and impure programs in coq. Proc. ACM Program. Lang. **4**(POPL) (2019). https://doi.org/10.1145/3371119

Verification of the Release-Acquire Semantics

Parosh Aziz Abdulla[1] [ID], Elli Anastasiadi[2]([✉]) [ID], Mohamed Faouzi Atig[1] [ID], and Samuel Grahn[1] [ID]

[1] Uppsala University, Uppsala, Sweden
{parosh.abdulla,mohamed_faouzi.atig,samuel.grahn}@it.uu.se
[2] Aalborg University, Aalborg, Denmark
ellia@cs.aau.dk

Abstract. The Release-Acquire (`RA`) semantics and its variants are some of the most fundamental models of concurrent semantics for architectures, programming languages, and distributed systems. Several steps have been taken in the direction of *testing* such semantics, where one is interested in whether a single program execution is consistent with a memory model. The more general *verification* problem, i.e., checking whether all allowed program runs are consistent with a memory model, has still not been studied as much. The purpose of this work is to bridge this gap. We tackle the verification problem, where, given an implementation described as a register machine, we check if any of its runs violates the `.RA` semantics or its Strong (`.SRA`) and Weak (`.WRA`) variants. We show that verifying `WRA` in this setup is in $\mathcal{O}(n^5)$, while verifying `RA` and `SRA` is both NP- and coNP-hard, and provide a PSPACE upper bound. This answers some fundamental questions about the complexity of these problems, and provides insights on the expressive power of register machines as a model.

Keywords: Weak Memory · Release-Acquire · Verification · Register Machines

1 Introduction

Over the years, numerous consistency models have been proposed to capture the subtle concurrency semantics of hardware architectures, programming languages, and distributed systems. The Release-Acquire (`RA`) semantics and its variants are some of the most fundamental consistency models weaker than sequential consistency, which are especially common and well-studied in programming languages and distributed data stores. Such consistency models allow different processes (threads) to have different views of the order of certain memory updates and maintain a looser global consensus on all events. This allows for much faster

The authors were supported by Grant VR 2020-04430 of the Swedish Research Council. Elli Anastasiadi's work is funded by the Villum Investigator Grant S4OS of the Danish Independent Research Fund.

implementations while still providing the user an intuitive and deterministic understanding of the underlying concurrency model.

RA is a fragment of the C11 model [20], obtained by restricting the threads' read and write instructions to be release and acquire accesses, respectively. The RA model is appropriate as a rigorous foundational semantics on its own, independently of particular architectures and compilers, and it has verified compilation schemes to popular platforms such as the x86-TSO, POWER, and ARM architectures [8,9,24]. Several variants of the RA semantics have been proposed in the literature in recent years. Notably, the Strong-Release-Acquire (SRA) semantics [20] strengthens RA by forbidding behaviors that require the re-ordering of write instructions, but coincides with RA for programs that do not contain write-write races. In [20], it is shown that SRA captures precisely the guarantees provided by POWER compilers for programs compiled from RA. Another variant is the Weak-Release-Acquire (WRA) semantics that has been considered an alternative to RA in the semantics of shared-memory concurrent programs, permitting more efficient verification frameworks such as stateless model checking [17].

The relevance of RA and its siblings goes beyond compilers and hardware architectures. At the distributed systems level, they are equivalent to standard and well-studied variants of causal consistency [19]. SRA corresponds to the causal convergence consistency semantics implemented in data stores [10,11], while WRA corresponds to the classical definition of causal consistency [10].

One of the most fundamental computational problems for a given consistency model CM is *consistency checking*. Consistency checking comes in two flavors: *testing* and *verification* [2,6,16,21,27]. In testing, we are given the consistency model CM, often described using a set of axioms, and a program run ρ consisting of a sequence of events. The sequence is typically generated by an implementation, e.g., a hardware architecture, a compiler, or a distributed protocol, that is supposed to guarantee CM. The task is to check whether ρ satisfies CM. The verification problem is more general: we are given an *implementation* and asked to check whether *all* executions of the implementation satisfy CM.

The relevance and intricacy of the RA-like semantics have led to several recent works checking their consistency. All these works consider the *testing* problem. The first results showed that testing consistency under the RA semantics is of polynomial complexity [2,18]. Recently, it was shown that testing consistency for SRA and WRA also has polynomial complexity [27]. Despite the above results on testing consistency, little is known about the complexity of *verifying* consistency under the RA semantics. As far as we know, the problem is still poorly understood. The goal of this work is to bridge this gap.

Contribution: We consider the complexity of the consistency verification problem under the RA semantics. To state our results, we use the classical *register machine* model to describe the underlying implementation that handles memory access. The model is an extended finite-state machine with a finite set of registers that store data values from an unbounded domain. The machine interacts with a finite set of external threads through write (where the register machine inputs a value to a register) and read (outputting a stored value) operations performed on a finite set of variables. Furthermore, the machine can perform internal transitions to transfer (i.e., copy) data between registers. We do not allow data-dependent transitions, as is common in the literature for the type of architecture we are modeling. The model is conceptually simple, providing a concise framework to state our complexity results. At the same time, it is sufficiently robust to model relevant features needed to model cache protocols or distributed systems, such as rendezvous communication, broadcasting fences, vector clocks, broadcast communication and store buffers [10,12]. Moreover, recent works use automata-like formalisms for learning models of implementations and detecting bugs [13,15]. Such works enhance the relevance of register machines for verifying program behaviors, such as consistency with weak memory.

Given a register machine, we consider the verification problem, i.e. that regardless of the interacting program, it cannot produce a *bad behavior*, i.e., store and return values in a way that violates any one of the RA-family of models (namely, RA, WRA, and SRA). To do this, one must explore all possible runs of a given register machine. The state space of the register machine is infinite (since the data domain is infinite), and the set of paths is also infinite, so the problem's decidability is not obvious. Here, we show the decidability for all considered models, and in the case of large complexity also provide lower bounds. Our main contributions are the proofs that:

- The verification problem for WRA is in $\mathcal{O}(n^5)$ time (Sect. 3.1).
- The verification problem for the RA and SRA semantics is in PSPACE, and
- it is both NP, and coNP-hard (Sect. 4).

Our main technical contribution lies in determining a way to explore only finite (and thus finitely many) runs of the register machine. For our hardness results reduce from the boolean satisfiability and tautology problems. Due to space constraints all omitted proofs (marked with ∗) can be found in [1].

2   Preliminaries

In what follows, we will use the following notation:

- Given a relation R, $\mathbf{dom}\,(R)$ denotes its domain; $R^?$ and R^+ denote its reflexive and transitive closures; and R^{-1} denotes its inverse.
- Given a function f, we write $f\,[x \to y]$, to denote a new function f', where $f'(x) = y$, and $f'(x') = f(x')$, if $x' \neq x$.
- Given an expression S, we denote as $S(^a/_b)$, the expression S, where all occurrences of b have been replaced with a.
- For a set S and an element a, we let $S \oplus a$ denote the union $S \cup a$.

2.1   Register Machines

A *register machine*, or shortly a *machine*, is an extended finite-state automaton with a finite set of registers that store data values from an unbounded domain. The machine performs input (write) operations and output (read) operations

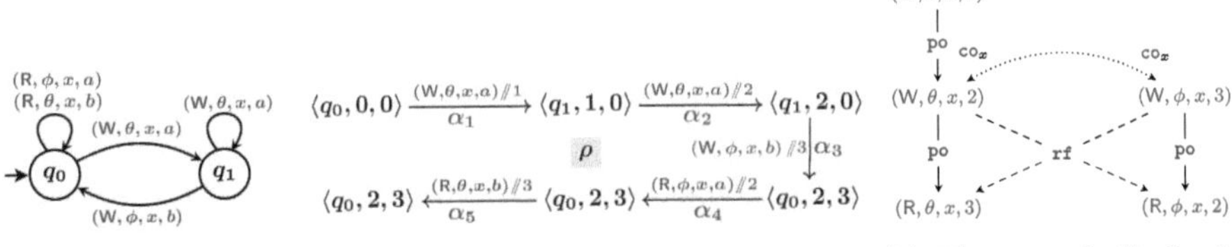

(a) A register machine $\mathcal{M}_1$ and a run ρ of $\mathcal{M}_1$

(b) The egraph G of ρ (see Section 2.3)

Fig. 1. Register machines and operational semantics

on a finite set of variables. Read and write operations correspond to external actions that synchronize the machine with its environment, i.e., with an external program consisting of a finite set of threads that run on the machine. Figure 1a (left) depicts a register machine $\mathcal{M}_1$ with two states q_0, q_1, and two registers a and b. The machine $\mathcal{M}_1$ manages two threads θ and ϕ accessing a (single) shared variable x. It starts executing from the initial state q_0 with the initial register values 0. Each transition of the machine is labeled by an *operation*. For instance, the transition label from q_0 to q_1 is the write operation $(\mathsf{W}, \theta, x, a)$. Here, the machine $\mathcal{M}_1$ accepts a request from the thread θ to write a new value to the variable x, upon which the machine stores the written value in the register a. The machine allows the program running on it to choose the written value. In q_1, the machine loops performing a sequence of write operations as the one above. The label of the transition from q_1 to q_0 is the write operation (W, ϕ, x, b), in which ϕ performs a write operation, and $\mathcal{M}_1$ stores the written value in b. In q_0, the machine accepts read requests from the threads. The operation $(\mathsf{R}, \theta, x, b)$ means that $\mathcal{M}_1$ accepts a request from the thread θ to read the value of the variable x, upon which the machine returns the value currently stored in the register b. We can explain the operation (R, ϕ, x, a) similarly. In the general case, a register machine is meant to allow *any* kind of request (i.e., a read or write from any thread to any variable) from the environment (program) at any time, no matter what state it is in. Such a register machine will be called *reactive*. We note that the machine we give as an easy example in Fig. 1 is not reactive, but we provide a reactive version of it (for completeness) in [1].

Definition 1. *Assume a set Θ of threads, a set $\mathcal{V}$ of variables, and a set **Regs** of registers. We assume that the variables and the registers range over a (potentially infinite) set $\mathcal{D}$ of data values with the particular value $0 \in \mathcal{D}$. A **register machine** $\mathcal{M}$ is a tuple $\langle Q, q_{\mathrm{init}}, \Delta \rangle$ where Q is the finite set of states, $q_{\mathrm{init}} \in Q$ is the initial state, and Δ is the finite set of transitions. A transition is a triple of the form $\langle q, \mathsf{o}, q' \rangle$ where $q, q' \in Q$ are states, and o is an operation. The operation o can be in one of the following three forms:*

- $(\mathsf{W}, \theta, x, a)$ *receives the value of the variable x from θ and writes (stores) the value in register a. The environment selects the written value (the program running on $\mathcal{M}$).*

- $(\mathsf{R}, \theta, x, a)$ *reads the value of the variable x from the register a and delivers the stored value to θ.*
- $a := a'$ *copies the value stored in the register a' to the register a.*

For any register machine, it is clear we can pre-process it to omit any unreachable states (from Q). We state and prove all remaining algorithms after this pre-processing has taken place, and thus with all remaining states being reachable by at least some path.

2.2   Operational Semantics

We define the operational semantics of a register machine by defining the transition system it induces, i.e., by defining the set of configurations of the machine together with a transition relation on them.[1] A *configuration* γ is of the form $\langle q, \mathcal{R} \rangle$ where $q \in Q$ defines the state of the machine, and $\mathcal{R} : \mathsf{Regs} \to \mathcal{D}$ defines the value $\mathcal{R}(a)$ of each register $a \in \mathsf{Regs}$. The *initial configuration* γ_{init} is the pair $\langle q_{\mathtt{init}}, \lambda\,\mathsf{Regs}.\,\emptyset \rangle$, i.e., the machine $\mathcal{M}$ starts running from a configuration where it is in its initial state and all its registers contain a dummy value $\emptyset$.

For example, a configuration of the machine $\mathcal{M}_1$ from Fig. 1a is a triple $\langle q, i_a, i_b \rangle$ describing the local state, and the contents of the registers a and b. In this example we see that a run ρ consists of a sequence of transitions. The run starts from the initial configuration where $\mathcal{M}_1$ is in its initial state q_0, and the registers contain their initial values 0. When executing a transition, we use the operation of the transition to generate an *action* describing an observable interaction between $\mathcal{M}_1$ and its environment. We use Γ to denote the set of configurations. A transition is of the form $\gamma_1 \xrightarrow{\alpha} \gamma_2$ where $\gamma_1, \gamma_2 \in \Gamma$ are configurations, and α is an operation augmented with a concrete value to be read or written. We define the transition relation between configurations according to the inference rules of Fig. 2. In the write rule, the machine executes a transition from q to q' while processing a write operation. The configuration changes state accordingly and updates the value of the relevant register as implied by the operation. In the read rule, the machine processes a read operation that returns the

$$
\begin{array}{ccc}
\text{Write} & \text{Read} & \text{Copy} \\[4pt]
\langle q, (\mathsf{W}, \theta, x, a), q' \rangle \in \Delta & \langle q, (\mathsf{R}, \theta, x, a), q' \rangle \in \Delta & \langle q, a := a', q' \rangle \in \Delta \\[4pt]
\mathsf{v} \in \mathcal{D} \quad \mathcal{R}' = \mathcal{R}[a \to \mathsf{v}] & \mathcal{R}(a) = \mathsf{v} & \mathcal{R}' = \mathcal{R}[a \to \mathcal{R}(a')] \\[4pt]
\hline
\langle q, \mathcal{R} \rangle \xrightarrow{(\mathsf{W},\theta,x,a)/\!/\mathsf{v}}_{\mathcal{M}} \langle q', \mathcal{R}' \rangle & \langle q, \mathcal{R} \rangle \xrightarrow{(\mathsf{R},\theta,x,a)/\!/\mathsf{v}}_{\mathcal{M}} \langle q', \mathcal{R} \rangle & \langle q, \mathcal{R} \rangle \xrightarrow{\tau}_{\mathcal{M}} \langle q', \mathcal{R}' \rangle
\end{array}
$$

Fig. 2. The semantics of a register machine's three operations. Write and copy operations update the state of the memory $\mathcal{R}$, while read operations only update the state of the register machine.

---

[1] We use the term *transition* to refer both to the set of transitions in the syntax of the machine (Definition 1) and to the transition relation on configurations. The meaning will always be clear from the context.

relevant register's value. The machine performs a register assignment operation in the copy rule. The operation is not visible to the external threads; hence, it is labeled by the silent event τ.

A run ρ of the program is a sequence $\gamma_0 \xrightarrow{\alpha_1} \gamma_1 \xrightarrow{\alpha_2} \cdots \xrightarrow{\alpha_n} \gamma_n$ of transitions, where each α_i is one of the operations described in Fig. 2. We say that ρ is **differentiated** if, all the write events in ρ all use different values.

2.3   Execution Graphs

We will be using execution graphs to both represent a run, but also to describe our models in the classic axiomatic style [25]. The nodes of an *execution graph* (*egraph* for short) are *events*. Figure 1b contains an example of an egraph. An event corresponds to an action performed by a register machine when interacting with its environment. The egraph edges specify different relations on the events. In this paper, to define our consistency models, we will work with three binary relations [19]: (a) the *program-order relation* (**po**), depicted by solid edges, totally orders the events in each thread; (b) the *reads-from* relation (**rf**), depicted by dashed edges, associates every read event with the write event it reads from; and (c) the *coherence-order* relation (**co**), depicted by dotted edges, partially orders the writes on each variable. Different consistency models are defined by forbidding different types of cycles in the egraph (as described in Sect. 2.4 below). We associate the runs of a register machine with egraphs.

Definitions. An *event* e is of the form $(\mathsf{ty}, \theta, x, \mathsf{v})$ where $\mathsf{ty} \in \{\mathsf{W}, \mathsf{R}\}$ is the type of the event (write or read), $\theta \in \Theta$ is the thread performing the event, $x \in \mathcal{V}$ is the variable on which θ conducts the event, and v is the value that is either written or read from memory. We define $e\text{·}\mathsf{type} := \mathsf{ty}$, $e\text{·}\mathsf{thread} := \theta$, $e\text{·}\mathsf{val} := \mathsf{v}$, and $e\text{·}\mathsf{var} := x$. We will use a set $\mathtt{InitEvents} = \{init^x \mid x \in \mathcal{V}\}$ of *initial* write events, where $init^x$ represents a dummy event writing the initial value 0 to x. We assume that the initial events do not belong to any threads. We use $\mathtt{Events}$ to denote the set of all events.

For a set of events $E \subseteq \mathtt{Events}$, we define the relation $[E] := \{\langle e, e \rangle \mid e \in E\}$, i.e., it is the restriction of the identity relation to the set of events in E. For $\mathsf{ty} \in \{\mathsf{W}, \mathsf{R}\}$, we define the relation $[\mathsf{ty}] := \{\langle e, e \rangle \mid e\text{·}\mathsf{type} = \mathsf{ty}\}$, i.e. it is the restriction of the identity relation to the set of events of type ty. Similarly, for a thread $\theta \in \Theta$, we define the relation $[\theta] := \{\langle e, e \rangle \mid e\text{·}\mathsf{thread} = \theta\}$. Sometimes, we view these relations as sets and write, e.g., $e \in [\mathsf{R}]$ to denote that e is of type R. We also consider boolean combinations of these relations, so we write $[E \wedge \mathsf{R}]$ to denote the set of events in E of type R. Fix a set $E : \mathtt{InitEvents} \subseteq E \subseteq \mathtt{Events}$ of events.

- A *program-order* on E is a relation po defined as a union $\cup_{\theta \in \Theta} \mathsf{po}_\theta$ such that po_θ is a total order on the set of events in $[E \wedge \theta]$. In other words, po totally orders all the events in E belonging to each thread.
- A *reads-from* relation $\mathsf{rf} \subseteq [E \wedge \mathsf{W}] \times [E \wedge \mathsf{R}]$ assigns to each read event r a single write event w in E with $\mathsf{r}\text{·}\mathsf{var} = \mathsf{w}\text{·}\mathsf{var}$ and $\mathsf{r}\text{·}\mathsf{val} = \mathsf{w}\text{·}\mathsf{val}$. We will write, $\mathsf{w}\,[\mathsf{rf}]\,\mathsf{r}$ to mean that r takes its value from w.

- A *partial-coherence-order* on E is a relation pco defined as a $\cup_{x \in \mathcal{V}} \text{pco}_x$ such that pco_x is a partial order on the set of write events on x. We require that $init^x$ is the smallest element in the sub-relation pco_x. A *total-coherence-order*, co on Events is a coherence-order in which the x-sub-relations are total. In other words, $\text{co} = \cup_{x \in \mathcal{V}} \text{co}_x$ and co_x is a total order on the set of write events on x. In this paper, we only use coherence-order relations that can be derived from the po- and rf-relations.

We also define the *happens-before* relation $\text{hb} := (\text{po} \cup \text{rf})^+$. A *partial execution graph* G is a tuple $\langle E, \text{po}, \text{rf}, \text{pco} \rangle$ where: (i) $E \subseteq \text{Events}$ is a set of events, (ii) po a program-order on the set E, (iii) rf is a reads-from relation on E, and (iv) pco is a partial coherence-order relation on E. A *total execution graph* is a partial execution graph in which the coherence-order relation is total.

For a relation R, an event $e \in E$, and a thread $\theta \in \Theta$, we write $e\,[R]\,\theta$ if $e\,[R]\,e'$ for some $e' \in [E \wedge \theta]$. The initial egraph is defined by $G_{\text{init}} := \langle \text{InitEvents}, \emptyset, \emptyset, \emptyset \rangle$, i.e., it only contains the initial events, and all its relations are empty.

Adding Events. We define an operation $\oplus$ that adds a new event to an egraph, according to the rules given in Fig. 3. If the new event w is a write event performed by a thread θ, we add w to the set of events. Adding a write event does not affect the rf and co relations.

$$\frac{e = (\text{W}, \theta, x, \text{v}) \quad E' = E \cup \{e\} \qquad \text{po}' = \text{po} \cup \{(e', e) \mid e' \in E \wedge e'\cdot\text{thread} = \theta\}}{\langle E, \text{po}, \text{rf}, \text{pco} \rangle \xrightarrow{e} \langle E', \text{po}', \text{rf}, \text{pco} \rangle}$$

$$\frac{e = (\text{R}, \theta, x, \text{v}) \quad \exists e' \in E : \; e'\cdot\text{type} := \text{W} \quad e'\cdot\text{var} = x \quad e'\cdot\text{val} = \text{v} \qquad E' = E \cup \{e\}, \quad \text{rf}' = \text{rf} \cup \{(e', e)\} \qquad \text{po}' = \text{po} \cup \{(e'', e) \mid e'' \in E \wedge e''\cdot\text{thread} = \theta\} \qquad \text{pco}' = \text{pco} \cup \{(e'', e') \mid e''\cdot\text{type} = \text{W} \wedge e''\cdot\text{var} = x \wedge e'' \in E \wedge e''\,[\text{po} \cup \text{rf}]^+ e\}}{\langle E, \text{po}, \text{rf}, \text{pco} \rangle \xrightarrow{e} \langle E', \text{po}', \text{rf}', \text{pco}' \rangle}$$

Fig. 3. The rules for adding events to an egraph. A write event only causes an update to the program order relation po, while a read event creates also rf and co edges. For the co update we consider only $e'' \neq e'$. Since co edges are added only when necessary, then the resulting co is a partial one.

For a new read event r, we also need to provide a write event w that already belongs to E from which r will read its value. The events r and w should have identical variables and values. We modify the po-relation in the same manner as for write events. We modify the rf-relation by adding the new pair $\langle \text{w}, \text{r} \rangle$ indicating that r is reading from w. Finally, we update the coherence-order, as defined in [2], so that we maintain the invariant that the latter is a modification-order as defined in [20]. To do so, we consider w and r to be sources and targets, and then search for write events w' that are hb-before r to connect to w.

From Runs to Egraphs. We associate to each run ρ of a register machine a corresponding egraph $G := \mathsf{mkEgraph}(\rho)$. To do so we will need to match the observable register machine operations (not copies) o with egraph events e. For an operation $\mathsf{o} = \mathsf{o} \mathbin{/\!\!/} \mathsf{v}$ (from Fig. 2), the corresponding egraph event inherits the type, thread, variable, and value of o, but not the register. Thus, $e((\mathsf{ty}, \theta, x, a) \mathbin{/\!\!/} \mathsf{v}) = (\mathsf{ty}, \theta, x, \mathsf{v})$. We define the function $\mathsf{mkEgraph}$ as follows:

Definition 2. *For a run ρ, we define*

$$- \quad \mathsf{mkEgraph}\left(\rho \xrightarrow{\mathsf{o}/\!\!/\mathsf{v}} \gamma_n\right) = \mathsf{mkEgraph}(\rho) \oplus e(\mathsf{o} \mathbin{/\!\!/} \mathsf{v}).$$

$$- \quad \mathsf{mkEgraph}\left(\rho \xrightarrow{\tau} \gamma_n\right) = \mathsf{mkEgraph}(\rho)$$

$$- \quad \mathsf{mkEgraph}(\epsilon) = G_{\mathsf{init}}.$$

Note here that the egraph corresponding to a run will not be a **total** one in the general case, as for example the run might not include any r, which means we will have no co edges. Moreover, this construction is **non-deterministic**, as for example, there might be several write events with the same value that could be read in a read event r. However as we have defined our register machines to be ***data independent*** we will soon see this is not a problem for the verification, and in fact we will have a single execution graph per run. Finally, it is possible that $\mathsf{mkEgraph}(\rho)$ fails in some step as for example there might be no source write event for a given read. Our definitions over consistency models assume this does not happen, and later on the algorithm will indeed check this separately.

2.4   Consistency Models

A declarative memory model is formulated as a collection of constraints on execution graphs, which determine the consistent execution graphs—the ones allowed by the model. In this section, we will formulate the three consistency models (CM) we work with. All our memory models are weaker than Sequential Consistency (SC), and allow for less restrictive memory accesses. SC requires that as soon as some value has been written in some variable, this is immediately visible to all threads.

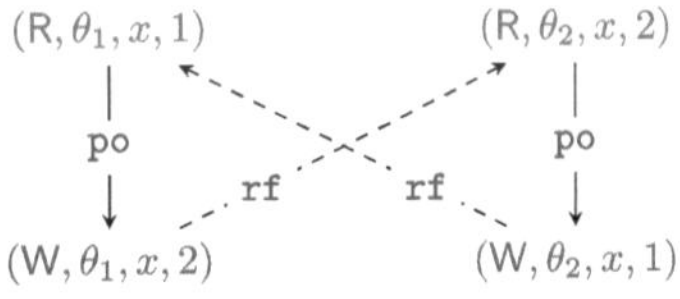

Fig. 4. An execution graph that contains a cycle on hb

The models we study instead allow for several threads to still view older values written in the variable, until they become "aware" of a new write on some path that "hides" the old value.

We define a consistency model CM by forbidding different forms of cycles in egraphs. All the consistency models we consider in this paper require the hb-relation to be acyclic, i.e., the transitive closure of po $\cup$ rf is a (strict) partial order. For instance, the egraph of Fig. 4 contains a cycle on hb and hence it does not satisfy any of our consistency models. Besides this condition on hb, our consistency models impose additional constraints on the egraph [19,20].

Definition 3. *Let* $G = \langle E, \mathrm{po}, \mathrm{rf}, \mathrm{pco} \rangle$ *be a (possibly partial) execution graph.*

- *We write* $G \models \mathrm{WRA}$ *to denote that for any* w *event in the graph, the relation* $[\mathrm{W} \wedge \mathrm{w \cdot var}] \cdot \mathrm{hb} \cdot \mathrm{w} \cdot \mathrm{hb} \cdot \mathrm{rf}^{-1}$ *is acyclic.*
- *We write* $G \models \mathrm{RA}$ *to denote that* $[\mathrm{po} \cup \mathrm{rf} \cup \mathrm{pco}_x]^+$ *is irreflexive for each variable* $x \in \mathcal{V}$.
- *We write* $G \models \mathrm{SRA}$ *to denote that the relation* $[\mathrm{po} \cup \mathrm{rf} \cup \mathrm{pco}]^+$ *is acyclic.*

For a set E of events, a program-order relation po on E, and a reads-from relation rf on E, we write $\langle E, \mathrm{po}, \mathrm{rf} \rangle \models \mathrm{RA}$ if there is a total coherence-order relation co on E such that $\langle E, \mathrm{po}, \mathrm{rf}, \mathrm{co} \rangle \models \mathrm{RA}$ (rsp. SRA, and WRA). We write $\langle E, \mathrm{po} \rangle \models \mathrm{RA}$ if there is a reads-from relation rf and a coherence-order relation co on E such that $\langle E, \mathrm{po}, \mathrm{rf}, \mathrm{co} \rangle \models \mathrm{RA}$ (rsp. SRA, and WRA).

Definition 4 (Memory models over runs). *For a run* ρ, *we write* $\rho \models \mathrm{RA}$ *to denote that* $\mathsf{mkEgraph}(\rho) \models \mathrm{RA}$ *(rsp. SRA, and WRA).*

Differentiated Runs: As we highlighted earlier, so far there might be several execution graphs associated with a single run. We write $\rho \models^{\mathtt{Diff}} \mathrm{RA}$ if ρ is differentiated and $\rho \models^{\mathrm{RA}}$. Note that for differentiated runs, the transition rules of Fig. 3 become deterministic. We prove:

Lemma 1. $*$ *For each (general) run* ρ *of a register machine* $\mathcal{M}$, *there exists a differentiated run* $\rho^{\mathtt{Diff}}$ *such that* $\rho \models \mathrm{RA}$ *iff* $\rho^{\mathtt{Diff}} \models \mathrm{RA}$ *(rsp. SRA, and WRA).*

For the remainder of this paper **we only consider differentiated runs** against any of our memory models. Below we also prove that for a (differentiated) run it suffices to check the partial execution graph that is formed by the rules of Fig. 3 against our memory models:

Lemma 2. $*$ *Let* $\mathcal{M}$ *be a register machine,* $\rho \in \mathsf{Runs}(\mathcal{M})$, *and* $\mathsf{mkEgraph}(\rho) = \langle E, \mathrm{po}, \mathrm{rf}, \mathrm{pco} \rangle$. *If* $\mathsf{mkEgraph}(\rho) \models \mathrm{RA}$, *then there exists a total coherence order* co, *with* $\mathrm{pco} \subseteq \mathrm{co}$, *such that* $\langle E, \mathrm{po}, \mathrm{rf}, \mathrm{co} \rangle \models \mathrm{RA}$. *(rsp. SRA, and WRA).*

Definition 5 (Memory models over register machines). *For a register machine* $\mathcal{M}$, *we write* $\mathcal{M} \models \mathrm{RA}$ *if* $\forall \rho \in \mathsf{Runs}(\mathcal{M}) \, . \, \rho \models \mathrm{RA}$. *(rsp. SRA, and WRA). We will refer to the problem of determining whether a register machine satisfies these semantics as* RA-Cons. *(rsp.* WRA-Cons *and* SRA-Cons).

Essentially, a register machine satisfies the RA-semantics if all its runs do so.

3   Algorithmic Results for WRA

We are now ready to state our results for the RA-Cons, WRA-Cons, and SRA-Cons problems. The results are stated in Theorem 1. We prove that all the above problems are decidable. In the case of WRA the complexity is polynomial to the size of the register machine, while for RA and SRA it is in PSPACE and it is both NP and coNP-hard. For WRA-Cons we prove it is sufficient to keep a constant amount of information regarding paths in memory, and thus manage polynomial time complexity. In the case of RA-Cons and SRA-Cons the size of the data structures increases, which implies an increment of the number of possible paths. In these cases it is not sufficient to keep in memory only a constant number of information for each paths we are exploring, but instead a polynomial one, which still yields a PSPACE algorithm, but the time complexity is no longer polynomial.

Theorem 1. *For a given a register machine $\mathcal{M}$ of size n:*

- RA-Cons *is in* PSACE *and it is both* NP *and* coNP-*hard.*
- SRA-Cons *is in* PSPACE *and it is both* NP *and* coNP-*hard.*
- WRA-Cons *is in* $\mathcal{O}(n^5)$.

The remainder of this section is dedicated to describing the idea of our algorithm, the hardness results, and proof sketches.

3.1   Algorithmic Method for WRA-Cons

Our P-TIME algorithm for WRA takes place in three modules. All modules are based on a type of backwards reachability approach. The different modules start from potential violations of the condition they correspond to and try to find paths leading to this violation by backtracking to the initial state. The register machine states are marked with some summary information about possible violating paths starting from them, and on each iteration we process edges leading a state and propagate relevant information of existing paths backwards. The reason for choosing to have a backward search is that it handles the copy operation better. We can apply the standard weakest pre-condition operator (see rule ⑨ in Fig. 5) to maintain optimal complexity. Having a forward search would lead to exponential branching over equivalence classes (where registers with identical values are kept in the same equivalence class). Our modules concern the following correctness aspects for all runs of a register machine $\mathcal{M}$:

- $\mathcal{M}$ does not allow for *ghost reads*. Those are read events that can read the value of a register that is empty.
- $\mathcal{M}$ does not allow for *mismatched variable reads*. I.e. all reads on variable x read from registers which were inputed with variable x.
- $\mathcal{M}$ does not allow for cyclic variable edit dependencies. This last condition is the one that truly defines the WRA semantics, as the other two are conditions that are required so that an execution graph can be formed.

The above conditions are implied by the execution graph semantics stated in Fig. 3. However, in order to simplify our algorithm we check them separately. In this way when we get to the most difficult condition of the above, which is the third, we do not need extra checks for the previous ones. For example, consider encountering a register a in some execution, and storing some information about this. It is not necessary to keep track of which variable x was stored in a, since we have already confirmed that there are no executions allowing operations on other variables to access registers that do not correspond to x. We formalize the above statements as:

Proposition 1. *Let* $\mathcal{M} = \langle Q, q_{\text{init}}, \Delta \rangle$, *we have that* $\mathcal{M} \models$ WRA *iff:*

1. *For all* $\rho \in$ Runs $(\mathcal{M})$, $\rho = \rho' \cdot$ r, *with* r $= (\mathsf{R}, \theta, x, a)$, *there exists an event* $e \in$ Events, *such that* $\rho = \rho_0 \cdot e \cdot \rho_1$, *and* e *is either a copy or write event that targets register* a.
2. *For all* $\rho \in$ Runs $(\mathcal{M})$, $\rho = \rho' \cdot$ r, *with* r $= (\mathsf{R}, \theta, x, a)$, *there exists an event* $\mathsf{w}_x \in$ Events, *such that* $\rho = \rho_0 \cdot \mathsf{w}_x \cdot \rho_1$, *and* w_x *writes some value* v *on register* b *(possibly* $b = a$*), and* v *is the last value assigned to* a *during* ρ_1.
3. *For each run* $\rho \in$ Runs $(\mathcal{M})$, *and for* $G_\rho =$ mkEgraph $(\rho) = \langle E, \text{po}, \text{rf}, \text{co} \rangle$, $[\mathsf{W} \wedge \mathsf{w}{\cdot}\mathsf{var}] \cdot \text{hb} \cdot \mathsf{w} \cdot \text{hb} \cdot \text{rf}^{-1}$ *is acyclic for each write event* w *of* E.

The proof along with the algorithms for checking the first and second condition are given in [1]. Note that the two first conditions can also be solved with a classical (low polynomial cost) reachability analysis. We add them there, along with the proofs of their correctness, as an easy demonstration of our method, which can prepare the reader for the final module and proof.

3.2   Exposed Read Violations

Let $\mathcal{M} = \langle Q, q_{\text{init}}, \Delta \rangle$ be a register machine operating on a set θ of threads, a set $\mathcal{V}$ of variables, a set Regs of registers, and a set $\mathcal{D}$ of data values. Algorithm 1 checks whether all runs of $\mathcal{M}$ respect Condition 3. of Proposition 1.

The key contributor to the complexity is the size of the largest data structure necessary. For WRA-Cons we need data structures of size $\mathcal{O}(|Q| * |\mathcal{V}| * |\text{Regs}| * |(\Theta \cup \text{Regs})|)$, which simplifies to $\mathcal{O}(|\mathcal{M}|^4)$. These data structures are used to store *summaries* of possible runs in $\mathcal{M}$. We only keep information for

---

Algorithm 1: WRA, Input: $\mathcal{M}$

```
1  tuple_added := true
2  paths := ∅
3  for read_edge ∈ M do
4  |   paths := paths ∪ Rule1.(read_edge)
5  while tuple_added do
6  |   tuple_added := false
7  |   for Rule ∈ Fig. 5 do
8  |   |   if Rule.condition ∈ paths then
9  |   |   |   if Rule.update ==Unsafe then
10 |   |   |   |   return Unsafe
11 |   |   else
12 |   |   |   paths' = paths ∪
           Rule.update
13 |   |   |   if paths' ≠ paths then
14 |   |   |   |   tuple_added := true
```

---

runs that might cause violations as the ones described in Proposition 1. The addition of information (in the form of state-summary tuples) to our data structures is monotonic, meaning once we have discovered a path from some state q exists, this information is never removed. Thus the data structure size bounds the number of iterations of our main loop (line 5, Algorithm 1). For each iteration, the algorithm checks if an existing possible violation path can be combined with more transitions of $\mathcal{M}$ (a search which is linear to the size of the machine), and creates more tuples to new states. The conditions for guranteeing existence

$$\dfrac{q_1\,[\mathrm{R}\wedge\theta\wedge x\wedge a]\,q_2}{q_1\,[\mathsf{fragile}\,(a)\,(\theta)\,(x)]}\;\text{\textcircled{1}}$$

$$\dfrac{\begin{array}{c}q_0\,[\mathrm{R}\wedge\theta\wedge y\wedge b]\,q_1\\ q_1\,[\mathsf{status}\,(a)\,(\theta)\,(x)]\;\text{\textcircled{2}}\end{array}}{q_0\,[\mathsf{status}\,(a)\,(b)\,(x)]}$$

$$\dfrac{\begin{array}{c}q_0\,[\mathrm{W}\wedge\theta\wedge y\wedge b]\,q_1\\ q_1\,[\mathsf{status}\,(a)\,(b)\,(x)]\;\text{\textcircled{3}}\end{array}}{q_0\,[\mathsf{status}\,(a)\,(\theta)\,(x)]}$$

$$\dfrac{\begin{array}{c}q_0\,[\mathrm{W}\wedge\theta\wedge x\wedge b]\,q_1\\ q_1\,[\mathsf{status}\,(a)\,(\theta\text{ or }b)\,(x)]\;\text{\textcircled{4}}\end{array}}{q_0\,[\mathsf{exposed}\,(a)\,(\theta)\,(x)]}$$

$$\dfrac{\begin{array}{c}q_0\,[\mathrm{R}\wedge\theta\wedge x\wedge b]\,q_1\\ q_1\,[\mathsf{status}\,(a)\,(\theta)\,(x)]\;\text{\textcircled{5}}\end{array}}{q_0\,[\mathsf{exposed}\,(a)\,(b)\,(x)]}$$

$$\dfrac{\begin{array}{c}q_0\,[\mathrm{R}\wedge\theta\wedge x\wedge (a\text{ or }b)]\,q_1\\ q_1\,[\mathsf{exposed}\,(a)\,(\theta)\,(x)]\;\text{\textcircled{6}}\end{array}}{q_0\,[\mathsf{exposed}\,(a)\,(a)\,(x)]}$$

Detecting failures.   Handling copy events

$$\dfrac{\begin{array}{c}q_0\,[\mathrm{W}\wedge\theta\wedge x\wedge a]\,q_1\\ q_1\,[\mathsf{exposed}\,(a)\,(\theta\text{ or }a)\,(x)]\;\text{\textcircled{7}}\end{array}}{\mathtt{Unsafe}}$$

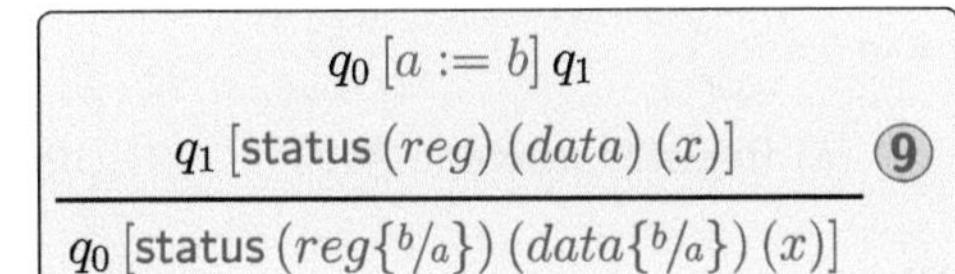

$$\dfrac{\begin{array}{c}q_0\,[a:=b]\,q_1\\ q_1\,[\mathsf{status}\,(reg)\,(data)\,(x)]\;\text{\textcircled{9}}\end{array}}{q_0\,[\mathsf{status}\,(reg\{{}^b\!/\!a\})\,(data\{{}^b\!/\!a\})\,(x)]}$$

Transparency rules propagate ANY tuples to states when the occurring event
does not affect the stored information.

$$\dfrac{\begin{array}{c}q_0\,[\mathrm{W}\wedge c]\,q_1\\ q_1\,[\mathsf{status}\,(a)\,(\theta\text{ or }b)\,(x)]\;\text{\textcircled{8}}\end{array}}{q_0\,[\mathsf{status}\,(a)\,(\theta\text{ or }b)\,(x)]}$$

$$\dfrac{\begin{array}{c}q_0\,[\mathrm{R}]\,q_1\\ q_1\,[\mathsf{status}\,(a)\,(\theta\text{ or }b)\,(x)]\;\text{\textcircled{8'}}\end{array}}{q_0\,[\mathsf{status}\,(a)\,(\theta\text{ or }b)\,(x)]}$$

Fig. 5. The rules for updating the exposed, and fragile data structures. status means either exposed or fragile. These rules are sufficient to detect violations of WRA, and for tracking $\mathsf{po}\cup\mathsf{rf}$. When a rule is stated with an "or" description it stands for two rules, one for each version of this clause.

of new (relevant) paths is characterized by the rules of Fig. 5, which produce new tuples (see lines 4 and 13). If no update takes place in one iteration, we are guaranteed we have arrived at a fixed-point and the procedure stops (lines 1, 6, and 14). Our data structures are:

- fragile : $Q\to 2^{\mathcal{V}\times(\Theta\cup\mathtt{Regs})\times\mathtt{Regs}}$. If $q\,[\mathsf{fragile}\,(a)\,(\theta)\,(x)]$ then there is a run ρ of $\mathcal{M}$ starting at q in which θ has a $[\mathsf{po}\cup\mathsf{rf}]^{+}$ path to a read event r on x, whose value is stored in register a when ρ is in q (for example rule ① in Fig. 5). A tuple $q\,[\mathsf{fragile}\,(a)\,(b)\,(x)]$ is created when, along an existing path to such an r, we encounter a new read event r', which reads from the value of register b on θ' (see rule ②). The tuple stands for an *expectation* of a tuple $q'\,[\mathsf{fragile}\,(a)\,(\theta')\,(x)]$, as, when an event that inputs the value for r', we should get a new $[\mathsf{po}\cup\mathsf{rf}]^{+}$ path, and thus we should get the tuple $q'\,[\mathsf{fragile}\,(a)\,(\theta')\,(x)]$ (see rule ③). We refer to Example 1 for a demonstration of this procedure.

- exposed : $Q \to 2^{\mathcal{V} \times (\Theta \cup \texttt{Regs}) \times \texttt{Regs}}$. These tuples are essentially an extension of the fragile tuples, with the addition that the paths that were described above can now refer to $[\texttt{po} \cup \texttt{rf}]^{+}\texttt{w}_x [\texttt{po} \cup \texttt{rf}]^{+}$ paths instead (for all $x \in \mathcal{V}$).

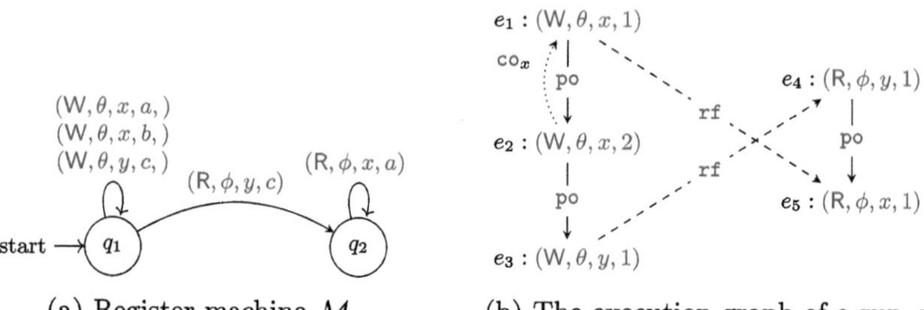

(a) Register machine $\mathcal{M}$.

(b) The execution graph of a run ρ of $\mathcal{M}$.

Fig. 6. A machine that produces an execution graph violating the WRA semantics.

Proposition 2. * *For a register machine $\mathcal{M}$, $\mathcal{M} \models$ WRA iff running Algorithm 1 on $\mathcal{M}$ flags no* Unsafe *configurations.*

Example 1. Consider the register machine $\mathcal{M}$ shown in Fig. 6a, and its run ρ shown in Fig. 6b. This execution graph does not respect WRA, as reversing the rf edge from e_1 to e_5, which means that the rules of Fig. 5 should flag Unsafe. We show the application of the rules for checking WRA, as stated by Proposition 2.

1. The edge $q_2 \xrightarrow{(\mathsf{R},\phi,x,a)} q_2$ matches rule ①, creating the tuple $q_2 [\mathsf{fragile}\,(a)\,(\phi)\,(x)]$. This tuple keeps track of the path that starts in q_2, and performs a read on x (the event e_5) which is $[\texttt{po} \cup \texttt{rf}]^{+}$ connected to earlier ϕ events.

2. $q_1 \xrightarrow{(\mathsf{R},\phi,y,c)} q_2$ together with $q_2 [\mathsf{fragile}\,(a)\,(\phi)\,(x)]$ matches rule ②, which in turn adds the tuple $q_1 [\mathsf{fragile}\,(a)\,(c)\,(x)]$. This event is relevant to the $[\texttt{po} \cup \texttt{rf}]^{+}$ path in the execution graph that we are keeping track of. Namely, any thread that will input the value that will be stored in c when reaching q_1 will gain a $[\texttt{po} \cup \texttt{rf}]^{+}$ path to e_5.

3. $q_1 \xrightarrow{(\mathsf{W},\theta,y,c,)} q_1$ together with $q_1 [\mathsf{fragile}\,(a)\,(c)\,(x)]$ match rule ③, adding the tuple $q_1 [\mathsf{fragile}\,(a)\,(\theta)\,(x)]$. Here, we see that indeed θ performs the input that was marked by the tuple in q_1. Thus, as can be confirmed at the execution graph in Fig. 6, an rf edge now relates θ to e_5.

4. $q_1 \xrightarrow{(\mathsf{W},\theta,x,b,)} q_1$ together with $q_1 [\mathsf{fragile}\,(a)\,(\theta)\,(x)]$ matches rule ④, which adds the tuple $q_1 [\mathsf{exposed}\,(a)\,(\theta)\,(x)]$. This update now initializes a exposed-type tuple. This is because now not only we have confirmed the $[\texttt{po} \cup \texttt{rf}]^{+}$ path to e_5, but also we have observed an input on the thread θ for x, which means that all other prior input events that will take place on it, should be "hidden" from e_5.

5. $q_0 \xrightarrow{(W,\theta,x,a,)} q_1$ together with $q_1 [\text{exposed}\,(a)\,(\theta)\,(x)]$ matches rule ⑦, and produces the **Unsafe** flag.

Example 1 only demonstrates the functionality of rules ①, ②, ③, ④, and ⑦. The rest of the rules capture different ways of how paths can be propagated to new states in a register machine.

4   Upper and Lower Bounds for RA-Cons and SRA-Cons

As we discussed above we were not able to provide an equally efficient algorithm for RA-Cons and SRA-Cons. In this section we focus on the complexity of these two problems. We first show that both RA-Cons and SRA-Cons are coNP and NP-hard. Then we provide a PSPACE upper bound.

Our first reduction is from the problem of tautology to RA-Cons. Namely, given a boolean formula φ over propositional variables $x, y, z, \ldots$, we will construct, in polynomial time, a register machine $\mathcal{M}$ such that $\mathcal{M} \models \text{RA}$ if and only if φ is a tautology. The key idea is to create a register machine that creates one run for each assignment of variables in the formula. The values of different writes are copied to neighboring (in some order) threads if this assignment is violating some clause of the formula. If the formula is a tautology then there is no run in which this procedure is so extensive that it creates a cycle.

The full details are given in [1]. There we also give the modifications necessary for proving NP hardness. We note that we chose to give the reduction over RA-Cons, as any algorithm detecting violations of more restrictive semantics (such as SRA, PSI, or SC), would also detect this violations, and thus this hardness result directly translates to them. In the case of SC, the hardness result already was implied by [16], but the final complexity could be much harder (or even undecidable) in this setup. Moreover, even though in the reduction we use ϵ transitions and several copy instructions, neither of these is truly the cause of the complexity. We can in fact create a similar construction, where we replace ϵ transitions with writes on some irrelevant thread, and copy commands with carefully ordered overwrites of registers, and retain the same effect. This implies that the cause of the coNP and NP hardness does not lie in this part of the expressiveness of the register machines. However, it is likely that the lack of a better than PSPACE algorithm is indeed caused by the copy commands.

4.1 Membership in **PSPACE**

The key idea of our PSPACE algorithm is that if the register machine $\mathcal{M}$ can produce an arbitrarily long violating run ρ, with arbitrarily many events in the corresponding execution graph mkEgraph (ρ), then it must also be able to produce a shorter run ρ_s, which has at most length $2 \times |\Theta|^2$, and whose egraph contains the same cycle. This is because if a cycle "enters" the same thread multiple times we are able to short-circuit the egraph cycle by jumping directly from the first entry event (say e_1) point to the event where the cycle exits that thread for the final time (say e_2) without performing the

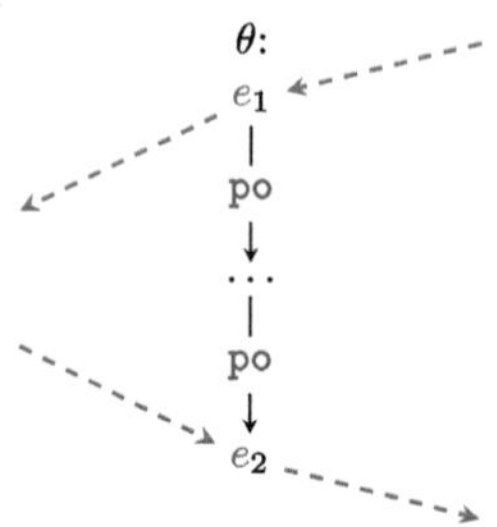

Fig. 7. Short circuiting a large cycle (in red) in the execution graph of a run, by following the **po** edges of θ. (Color figure online)

intermediate steps and instead following **po** edges, as seen in Fig. 7. Thus we know that a minimal cycle for each thread enters each thread at most once and exits each thread at most once. We therefore know that if a cycle can be created in some egraph, the relevant events in such cycle are linear to the size of the register machine. The full algorithm is available in [1].

5 Conclusion and Future Work

In this paper, we have taken the first steps towards a framework for verification under the RA semantics and its variants. To that end, we prove a polynomial space upper bound (and polynomial time in the case of WRA-Cons) when the implementation is described in the classical register machine model.

Our first future endeavor is to close the complexity gap left by Theorem 1. There, we were able to prove that the RA-Cons and SRA-Cons problems are both NP- and coNP-hard. We are aware of the gap in complexity, and we did try to provide either a faster algorithm, or a matching lower bound. However, at the current state our results are already establishing the decidability, and our algorithms utilize non-trivial ideas, and provide a platform for future improvements and approximations. Moreover we already have a prototype tool implementation [7] of our algorithms which would also heavily benefit from such progress. We also plan to leverage abstraction and stateless model-checking techniques to achieve more efficient verification.

Aside from the above, we plan to consider more expressive modeling languages that make our results applicable to a wider class of protocols at the cache, compiler, and application levels. One such extension would be to consider data-dependent register machines, which could model for example compare-and-swap events. This suggests that one would have to study a theory of equality/inequality to create an augmented register machine space and characterize all the possible executions. In this case, we would expect a (much) higher complexity as we would need to work in the framework of well-structured systems [3,14]. Another exciting extension to our register machine formalism would be to allow for transitions encoding more complex actions, such as `broadcast`, `rendezvous`, and `fences`. We already know that these operations can be encoded with a series of transitions in the simple model, but having them explicitly as part of the syntax would create more succinct models and potentially speed up the verification. Finally, another extension to the register machines would be in the direction of *parameterized verification*. We would be particularly interested in enhancing the model with the ability to handle arbitrarily many threads interacting with the memory without having to hard-code them as part of the register machine.

Another direction of future work is to study the decidability and complexity of consistency checking for other memory models such as PSI [26], SC, TSO, and RC11. A fundamental characteristic of our approach is using the declarative definition style for a consistency model. We highlight for example the declarative definition of PSI [23, Definition 4], which requires the acyclicity of $\mathsf{co} \cdot [\mathsf{po} \cup \mathsf{rf} \cup \mathsf{pco}]^+ \cdot \mathsf{rf}^{-1}$, i.e. only slightly more restrictive from the definition of `SRA` (Definition 3). Since the only relations necessary for this consistency model are already present in this work, this will be a natural and feasible next step. On the other hand, SC, even though it is also defined declaratively (as an acyclicity condition of $[\mathsf{po} \cup \mathsf{rf} \cup \mathsf{pco} \cup \mathsf{fr}]^+$), is much harder to capture with our existing rules, as it uses a whole new type of relation, namely the from-read (fr [5]) relation. Moreover, the *testing* problem of whether a run ρ is SC is known to be NP-complete, a bound that trivially also applies to the consistency checking problem since we can create a register machine that generates only ρ.

Related Work. In their seminal work [16], Korach and Gibbons showed consistency testing under the SC semantics is NP-hard. Alur et al. showed that the verification problem under the SC semantics [6] is undecidable, albeit for a data-dependent implementation model.

Several examples of protocols [4,22] are designed to enforce different consistency models. Such works guarantee the designed mechanisms' correctness and provide a good baseline for implementing practices. However, they do not produce uniform frameworks to answer the general consistency-checking question.

Bouajjani et al. [10] consider the verification problem for semantics, which is equivalent to `WRA`, but with a model that allows unbounded numbers of pending messages. They show the problem is EXPSPACE-complete.

Another primary direction is verifying *single runs*, expressed as sequences of memory access events, to determine whether that run satisfies a consistency model. This problem is quite complex in general, as, for at least all the memory models studied in this work, there is an unbounded number of possible reorderings of the observed events from one local view to the other. Several works consider the testing problem under the `RA` semantics [2,27]. These works show that the testing problem has polynomial complexity for `RA`. Bouajjani et al. [10] show that the testing problem for the `WRA` semantics has polynomial complexity.

Both works focus on providing a specific implementation or verifying a single run from an unknown implementation.

References

1. Abdulla, P., Anastasiadi, E., Atig, M.F., Grahn, S.: Verification of the release-acquire semantics. arXiv entry (2025)
2. Abdulla, P.A., Atig, M.F., Jonsson, B., Ngo, T.P.: Optimal stateless model checking under the release-acquire semantics. Proc. ACM Program. Lang. $\mathbf{2}$(OOPSLA), 135:1–135:29 (2018)
3. Abdulla, P.A., Cerans, K., Jonsson, B., Tsay, Y.-K.: General decidability theorems for infinite-state systems. In: Proceedings, 11th Annual IEEE Symposium on Logic in Computer Science, New Brunswick, New Jersey, USA, 27–30 July 1996, pp. 313–321. IEEE Computer Society (1996)
4. Ahamad, M., Neiger, G., Burns, J.E., Kohli, P., Hutto, P.W.: Causal memory: definitions, implementation, and programming. Distrib. Comput. $\mathbf{9}$(1), 37–49 (1995)
5. Alglave, J., Maranget, L., Tautschnig, M.: Herding cats: modelling, simulation, testing, and data mining for weak memory. ACM Trans. Program. Lang. Syst. $\mathbf{36}$(2), 7:1–7:74 (2014)
6. Alur, R., McMillan, K.L., Peled, D.A.: Model-checking of correctness conditions for concurrent objects. Inf. Comput. $\mathbf{160}$(1–2), 167–188 (2000)
7. Anonymous. Ccchecker. Anonymized implementation
8. Batty, M., Memarian, K., Owens, S., Sarkar, S., Sewell, P.: Clarifying and compiling C/C++ concurrency: from C++11 to POWER. In: Field, J., Hicks, M. (eds.) Proceedings of the 39th ACM SIGPLAN-SIGACT Symposium on Principles of Programming Languages, POPL 2012, Philadelphia, Pennsylvania, USA, 22–28 January 2012, pp. 509–520. ACM (2012)
9. Batty, M., Owens, S., Sarkar, S., Sewell, P., Weber, T.: Mathematizing C++ concurrency. In: Ball, T., Sagiv, M. (eds.) Proceedings of the 38th ACM SIGPLAN-SIGACT Symposium on Principles of Programming Languages, POPL 2011, Austin, TX, USA, 26–28 January 2011, pp. 55–66. ACM (2011)
10. Bouajjani, A., Enea, C., Guerraoui, R., Hamza, J.: On verifying causal consistency. In: Castagna, G., Gordon, A.D. (eds.) Proceedings of the 44th ACM SIGPLAN Symposium on Principles of Programming Languages, POPL 2017, Paris, France, 18–20 January 2017, pp. 626–638. ACM (2017)
11. Burckhardt, S.: Principles of eventual consistency. Found. Trends Program. Lang. $\mathbf{1}$(1–2), 1–150 (2014)
12. Delzanno, G.: Constraint-based verification of parameterized cache coherence protocols. Formal Methods Syst. Des. $\mathbf{23}$(3), 257–301 (2003)
13. Dierl, S., Fiterau-Brostean, P., Howar, F., Jonsson, B., Sagonas, K., Tåquist, F.: Scalable tree-based register automata learning. In: Finkbeiner, B., Kovács, L. (eds.) Tools and Algorithms for the Construction and Analysis of Systems, TACAS 2024. LNCS, vol. 14571, pp. 87–108. Springer, Cham (2024). https://doi.org/10.1007/978-3-031-57249-4_5
14. Finkel, A., Schnoebelen, P.: Well-structured transition systems everywhere! Theor. Comput. Sci. $\mathbf{256}$(1–2), 63–92 (2001)
15. Fiterau-Brostean, P., Jonsson, B., Sagonas, K., Tåquist, F.: Automata-based automated detection of state machine bugs in protocol implementations. In: 30th Annual Network and Distributed System Security Symposium, NDSS 2023, San Diego, California, USA, 27 February–3 March 2023. The Internet Society (2023)

16. Gibbons, P.B., Korach, E.: Testing shared memories. SIAM J. Comput. **26**(4), 1208–1244 (1997)
17. Kokologiannakis, M., Lahav, O., Sagonas, K., Vafeiadis, V.: Effective stateless model checking for C/C++ concurrency. Proc. ACM Program. Lang. **2**(POPL), 17:1–17:32 (2018)
18. Kokologiannakis, M., Lahav, O., Vafeiadis, V.: Kater: automating weak memory model metatheory and consistency checking. Proc. ACM Program. Lang. **7**(POPL), 544–572 (2023)
19. Lahav, O., Boker, U.: What's decidable about causally consistent shared memory? ACM Trans. Program. Lang. Syst. **44**(2), 8:1–8:55 (2022)
20. Lahav, O., Giannarakis, N., Vafeiadis, V.: Taming release-acquire consistency. In: Bodík, R., Majumdar, R. (eds.) Proceedings of the 43rd Annual ACM SIGPLAN-SIGACT Symposium on Principles of Programming Languages, POPL 2016, St. Petersburg, FL, USA, 20–22 January 2016, pp. 649–662. ACM (2016)
21. Luo, W., Demsky, B.: C11tester: a race detector for C/C++ atomics. In: Sherwood, T., Berger, E.D., Kozyrakis, C. (eds.) ASPLOS 2021: 26th ACM International Conference on Architectural Support for Programming Languages and Operating Systems, Virtual Event, USA, 19–23 April 2021, pp. 630–646. ACM (2021)
22. Perrin, M., Mostéfaoui, A., Jard, C.: Causal consistency: beyond memory. In: Asenjo, R., Harris, T. (eds.) Proceedings of the 21st ACM SIGPLAN Symposium on Principles and Practice of Parallel Programming, PPoPP 2016, Barcelona, Spain, 12–16 March 2016, pp. 26:1–26:12. ACM (2016)
23. Raad, A., Lahav, O., Vafeiadis, V.: On parallel snapshot isolation and release/acquire consistency. In: Ahmed, A. (ed.) ESOP 2018. LNCS, vol. 10801, pp. 940–967. Springer, Cham (2018). https://doi.org/10.1007/978-3-319-89884-1_33
24. Sarkar, S., et al.: Synchronising C/C++ and POWER. In: Vitek, J., Lin, H., Tip, F. (eds.) ACM SIGPLAN Conference on Programming Language Design and Implementation, PLDI 2012, Beijing, China, 11–16 June 2012, pp. 311–322. ACM (2012)
25. Shasha, D., Snir, M.: Efficient and correct execution of parallel programs that share memory. ACM Trans. Program. Lang. Syst. **10**(2), 282–312 (1988)
26. Sovran, Y., Power, R., Aguilera, M.K., Li, J.: Transactional storage for geo-replicated systems. In: Wobber, T., Druschel, P. (eds.) Proceedings of the 23rd ACM Symposium on Operating Systems Principles 2011, SOSP 2011, Cascais, Portugal, 23–26 October 2011, pp. 385–400. ACM (2011)
27. Tunç, H.C., Abdulla, P.A., Chakraborty, S., Krishna, S., Mathur, U., Pavlogiannis, A.: Optimal reads-from consistency checking for C11-style memory models. Proc. ACM Program. Lang. **7**(PLDI), 761–785 (2023)

Iteratively Synthesizing ϵ-Robust Barrier Certificates for Neural Network Controlled Systems

Yi Luo, Xin Chen(✉), Jin Dai, Enyi Tang, and Xuandong Li

State Key Laboratory For Novel Software Technology, Nanjing University, Nanjing, China
{602024320005,652025320002}@smail.nju.edu.cn,
{chenxin,eytang,lxd}@nju.edu.cn

Abstract. Ensuring the safe operation of neural network-controlled systems in the presence of uncertain measurements is a critical challenge. Inaccurate state estimation can lead to unsafe controller behavior, necessitating safety guarantees that can effectively handle measurement errors. Existing methods rely on pre-determining the measurement error bound ϵ and synthesizing ϵ-robust barrier certificates based on this bound. However, in practical applications, ϵ is often unavailable during the design phase, which limits the applicability of existing techniques. This paper addresses the problem from a novel perspective by proposing an iterative method for synthesizing robust barrier certificates. First, we synthesize a barrier certificate for a given system, and then the maximum tolerable error bound and the most vulnerable region is calculated through an optimization problem. Second, we design an iterative optimization framework that progressively strengthens the barrier certificate by repairing its most vulnerable regions, resulting in certificates with increasingly larger tolerable error bounds. Experiments on benchmark examples demonstrate that the proposed approach can generate barrier certificates that are more robust than those of state-of-the-art work.

Keywords: ϵ-robust barrier certificate · Neural network controlled system · formal verification · uncertain measurement

1 Introduction

Recent advances in deep learning have made neural networks a new class of adept and adaptable controllers for autonomous systems, considerably facilitating the design process. Deploying autonomous systems for safety-critical applications, such as medical devices, self-driving cars, and industrial robotics, ensures that safety is the priority among all system design and implementation requirements. Formal methods provide rigorous techniques for verifying autonomous systems subject to safety specifications. Thus, the ability to formally verify the safety specifications of neural network-controlled systems becomes imperative [23,25] before the systems are deployed.

Z. Liu et al. (Eds.): ICTAC 2025, LNCS 16237, pp. 124–141, 2026.
https://doi.org/10.1007/978-3-032-11176-0_9

In autonomous systems, controllers rely on state feedback from measurement components to determine safe control actions. However, state measurement may show great uncertainty in practice due to sensor errors, equipment inaccuracy, or even adversarial attacks [26,27]. Measurement uncertainty degrades the safety guarantees provided by the controllers if they are assumed to have perfect access to the measurement of system states. The controller's robustness to measurement uncertainty should be quantified in safety verification, ensuring that verified controllers do not put the system into unsafe states if the measurement errors are bounded by the obtained limits.

Barrier certificates have become increasingly popular as a tool for formally establishing the safety of systems within an infinite time horizon. A barrier certificate is a continuously differentiable function of states that assigns the over-approximation of the reachable set and the unsafe region with reals of opposite signs, respectively [12,14]. It acts as a barrier that prevents all trajectories originating from a given initial set from entering the unsafe region, thereby establishing a sound guarantee of safety.

To accommodate the measurement uncertainty in the safety verification of neural network-controlled systems, the ϵ-robust barrier certificates that are immune to constraint measurement errors are proposed. Here, ϵ is the bound of tolerable measurement errors within which a ϵ-robust barrier certificate can provide safety guarantee. Hence, in the presence of measurement uncertainty, how to synthesize the ϵ-robust barrier certificate with a bigger ϵ becomes the key problem in verifying a neural network-controlled system, Existing methods address the verification problem with imperfect measurement by following these steps. They first specify ϵ, the bound of measurement errors, and then synthesize the corresponding ϵ-robust barrier certificate (or control barrier function) using different construction conditions [5,20,29]. At design time, the bound ϵ is typically estimated from an offline dataset of states and measurements, or the physical characteristics of the sensor and perception. However, reliable estimation of maximal measurement errors is not always attainable due to the unaffordable cost of collecting data from the real world [13]. Furthermore, existing methods lack an effective way to evaluate the ϵ of the synthesized barrier function, resulting in an overly conservative estimation of ϵ (see example evaluation). These drawbacks limit their practical applicability.

Inspired by the observation that ϵ, the bound of tolerable measurement errors, is an inherent characteristic of the given barrier certificate, it can be derived from the barrier certificate and the system together. The paper addresses the problem of generating ϵ-robust barrier certificates from the reverse direction. Rather than specifying the bound ϵ before synthesizing barrier certificates, we propose an iterative approach to progressively synthesizing a sequence of increasingly robust barrier certificates, where a barrier certificate permitting larger measurement errors is created by repairing the vulnerable region of its predecessor.

Specifically, we synthesize a neural network as a ϵ-robust barrier certificate using an iterative framework. Initially, a neural network barrier certificate is trained and verified according to the construction conditions of barrier certificates for neural network-controlled systems. Then, the bounds of tolerable measurement errors associated with the neural network barrier certificate are derived by solving a quadratic optimization problem that encodes the measurement errors into constraints. The solution to the optimization problem reveals the most vulnerable region of the neural network. By augmenting the training data set with data from the region, a successor neural network barrier certificate that is potentially more robust is constructed, on which the next iteration proceeds to verify and identify the most vulnerable region, ultimately leading to the training of a refined neural network as a barrier certificate.

Compared with existing approaches, our method has two advantages. First, we can conclude that the actual bound within which a ϵ-robust barrier certificate provides a safety guarantee for neural network-controlled systems with measurement errors helps prevent the barrier certificate from being used conservatively. Second, the iterative approach leverages the flexibility of neural networks, gradually strengthening their robustness, which enables the production of a robust barrier certificate that surpasses the reach of existing methods.

The main contributions of the paper are summarized as follows:

- We propose a novel approach to determining the bound of tolerable measurement errors concerning a barrier certificate. We provide both rigorous proof and a computational method that constitutes quadratic programming.
- We propose an iterative approach to synthesizing more robust neural network barrier certificates for neural network-controlled systems, which gradually refines a neural network to make it more robust by repairing its most vulnerable region.
- We implement the safety verification tool *RobustNBC* and evaluate its performance on several benchmark examples. The experimental results show that *RobustNBC* can produce barrier certificates that are more robust than those of state-of-the-art work.

The remainder of this paper is organized as follows. Section 2 presents a formal definition of ϵ-robust barrier certificates and provides a proof of the theorems. Section 3 focuses on calculating the robust bound of a given barrier certificate. Section 4 discusses barrier certificate training, verification, and iterative improvement of the robust bound. Section 5 includes three examples of neural network-controlled systems and a benchmark comparison with the state-of-the-art method. Finally, Sect. 6 offers an overview of related work.

2 ϵ – Robust Barrier Certificates

In this section, we formalize the safety verification problem of neural network-controlled systems in the presence of uncertain measurements. We define ϵ-robust barrier certificates and prove their guarantee of safety when the measurement errors passed to the controllers are less than the bound ϵ.

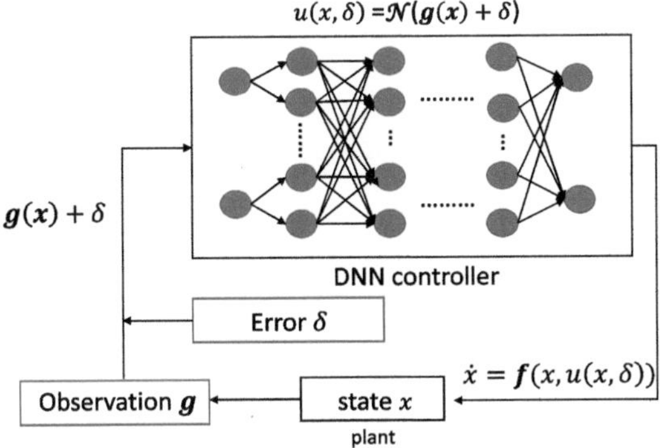

Fig. 1. A neural network controlled system with uncertain measurements.

Figure 1 depicts the structure of a neural network-controlled system. The observation function g measures the states x as $g(x)$. Stochastic errors δ are placed on the measurements of states, inputting $g(x) + \delta$ to the neural network controller, based on which the controller sends control signals $u(x,\delta)$ to the dynamics that model the evolution of the actual system states. Note that, in the presence of measurement errors, the controller is forced to calculate control signals using an inaccurate estimate of the states.

The paper assumes that the observation function $g(x)$ always returns the actual values of states. Thus, the following definition omits g for simplicity.

Definition 1 (Neural Network controlled system with uncertain measurements). *A neural network controlled system with uncertain measurement consists of a tuple $\mathcal{S}\langle V, I, \Psi, \mathcal{N}, \delta, f \rangle$, where*

- *$V = \{x_1, \cdots, x_n\}$, a set of real-valued system variables;*
- *$I \subset \mathbb{R}^n$, the initial condition;*
- *$\Psi \subset \mathbb{R}^n$, the state invariant;*
- *$\mathcal{N} : \mathbb{R}^n \to \mathbb{R}^m$, the neural network producing control signals $\mathcal{N}(x + \delta)$;*
- *$\delta : \mathbb{R}^n$, the uncertain measurement errors;*
- *$f : \mathbb{R}^n \times \mathbb{R}^m \to \mathbb{R}^n$, the local Lipschitz continuous vector field i.e., $\dot{x} = f(x, \mathcal{N}(x + \delta))$.*

Starting from one state in the initial region I, under the control of a neural network controller $\mathcal{N}$, the system $\mathcal{S}$ evolves according to the vector field f, which forms an infinite sequence of states called a trajectory.

Definition 2 (Trajectory of neural network controlled system with uncertain measurements). *A differentiable function $\phi : [0, T] \to \Psi$ is called a trajectory of a neural network controlled system $\mathcal{S}$ with uncertain measurements if it satisfies the following conditions*

$$\phi(0) \in I \tag{1}$$

$$\forall t \in [0, T]\, \exists \delta \in \mathbb{R}^n \left(\frac{d}{dt}\phi(t) = f(\phi(t), \mathcal{N}(\phi(t) + \delta)) \right) \tag{2}$$

Condition (2) stipulates that at any time, the trajectory of a neural network-controlled system may deviate from the vector $f(\phi(t), \mathcal{N}(\phi(t)))$ to the vector $f(\phi(t), \mathcal{N}(\phi(t) + \delta))$ as a result of the random measurement error δ.

The reachable set of a system consists of all its valid trajectories, which are formally defined as follows.

Definition 3 (Reachable set of neural network controlled systems with uncertain measurements). *A point $x \in \Psi$ is in the **reachable set** of system $\mathcal{S}$ if and only if there exists a trajectory ϕ of $\mathcal{S}$ such that $x = \phi(t), t \in [0, +\infty)$.*

A system $\mathcal{S}$ is considered to be safe concerning an unsafe region U if no trajectory starting from the initial set I invades the unsafe set U.

Definition 4 (Safety of neural network controlled systems with uncertain measurements). *A neural network controlled system $\mathcal{S}$ is called **safe** concerning the unsafe region U if and only if the intersection of its reachable set and unsafe region U is empty.*

Definition 2 states that in the presence of disturbances, at any time, the system trajectory can deviate in many directions, which makes predicting the system trajectory more difficult. Consequently, a barrier certificate can only guarantee safety against bounded measurement errors. We introduce ϵ-robust barrier certificates to formalize this observation.

Definition 5 (ϵ-Robust Barrier Certificates). *A differentiable function $B : \Psi \to \mathbb{R}$ is a ϵ - robust barrier certificates of a neural network controlled system $\langle V, I, \Psi, \mathcal{N}, \delta, f \rangle$, with respect to unsafe region U if it satisfies the following conditions:*

$$\forall x \in I \, (B(x) \geq 0) \tag{3}$$

$$\forall x \in \Psi \; \forall \delta \left(B(x) = 0 \land \|\delta\| < \epsilon \Rightarrow \frac{D}{dx} B(x) \cdot f(x, \mathcal{N}(x + \delta)) > 0 \right) \tag{4}$$

$$\forall x \in U \, (B(x) < 0), \tag{5}$$

Intuitively, in Definition 5, conditions (3) and (5) assert that the initial and unsafe regions are separated by the curve $B(x) = 0$. Furthermore, condition (4) requires that when any trajectory $\phi(t)$ intersects with the curve $B(\phi(t)) = 0$, the time derivative of B with respect to t, which is $\frac{D}{dx} B(\phi(t)) \cdot f(\phi(t) + \delta)$, must be strictly positive. Thus, trajectories starting from I are always evaluated to nonnegative by B, indicating that it never invades the unsafe region U, evaluated to negative by B. A formal proof is given below.

Theorem 1. *Given a neural network controlled system with uncertain measurements $\langle V, I, \Psi, \mathcal{N}, \delta, f \rangle$ and an unsafe set U, if there exists a ϵ-robust barrier certificate, then the system is safe concerning U.*

Proof. Proof by contradiction. Assume there exists a trajectory, and a time t_0, such that $\phi(t_0) \in U$, define $F(t) = B(\phi(t))$ and $A = \{t | F(t) \geq 0\}$. From $\phi(0) \in I$ and (3) we have $0 \in A$. Thus, $A \neq \emptyset$. Taking $a = \sup A$, from $F(t_0) < 0$, we get $a < t_0$. From B and the continuity of ϕ, we have $F(a) = 0$. Moreover,

$$\begin{aligned} F'(a) &= \lim_{t \to 0} \frac{F(a+t) - F(a)}{t} \\ &= \lim_{t \to 0} \frac{F(a+t)}{t} \\ &= \frac{D}{dx} B(\phi(a)) \cdot \frac{D}{dt} \phi(a) \end{aligned}$$

From (2) we know that there exists $\delta_a (\|\delta_a\| < \epsilon)$ satisfying $\frac{D}{dt}\phi(a) = f(x, \mathcal{N}(x + \delta_a)))$. Replacing it in the above equation, we have:

$$\lim_{t \to 0} \frac{F(a+t)}{t} = \frac{D}{dx} B(\phi(a)) \cdot f(x, \mathcal{N}(x + \delta_a)). \tag{6}$$

From (4) we get

$$\lim_{t \to 0} \frac{F(a+t)}{t} > 0. \tag{7}$$

so there exists $t' > 0$ such that $\frac{F(a+t')}{t'} > 0$. Let $b = a + t'$; we have $a < b < t_0$ and $F(b) > 0$, which contradicts the definition of a. ∎

The neural ϵ-robust barrier certificates used in this paper are defined as follows:

Definition 6 (Neural ϵ-Robust Barrier Certificates). *A Neural ϵ-robust barrier certificate $\mathcal{B}$ with $n + 1$ layers(from 0-th layer to n-th layer) is a tuple $\langle \mathcal{X}, W, b \rangle$, where*

- *$W : \{w_{1,1}, w_{1,2} \ldots, w_{n,1}, w_{n,2}\}$ is a set of weight matrices.*
- *$B : \{b_{1,1}, b_{1,2}, \ldots, b_{n,1}, b_{n,2}\}$ is a set of bias vectors where.*
- *$\mathcal{X} : \{x_0, \ldots, x_n\}$ is a set of layer value vectors. x_0 is the input of neural network and x_i consists of the neuron values on $i{-}th$ layer. $x_{i+1} = (w_{i+1,1}x_i + b_{i+1,1}) \otimes (w_{i+1,2}x_i + b_{i+1,2})$. Where $\otimes$ is the element-wise product.*

For neural network-controlled systems, at design time, ϵ-robust barrier certificates are employed to ensure that the controllers are robust to uncertain measurement errors; a conservative estimation of ϵ results in an expensive reconstruction of controllers. Thus, given a barrier certificate, it is necessary to infer the exact ϵ, as it provides the bound on measurement errors acceptable to controllers when maintaining the system in safe regions. Furthermore, when the given barrier certificate is associated with an overly conservative ϵ, it is worthwhile to study how to synthesize a barrier certificate with ϵ close to the actual robust bound of the controller. We study the problem of inferring ϵ in the next section and postpone the problem of synthesizing more robust barrier certificates to the section after next.

3   Infer the Robust Bound ϵ

The section focuses on how to infer the bound ϵ of a specific barrier certificate $\mathcal{B}$. Recall the definition of ϵ-robust barrier certificates. A measurement error can invalidate a barrier certificate by violating its time derivative condition. Thus, the bound ϵ is the minimal measurement error δ that damages the time derivative condition. An exhaustive search on δ constitutes the procedure of inferring ϵ. Theorem 2 presents a rigorous description.

Theorem 2. *Let $\mathcal{S}\langle V, I, \Psi, \mathcal{N}, \delta, f \rangle$ be a neural network-controlled system. If a barrier certificate $\mathcal{B}$ guarantees its safety concerning the unsafe region U, the robust bound ϵ of $\mathcal{B}$ satisfies:*

$$\epsilon = \inf \{\|\delta\| \,|\, \exists x_0(\mathcal{B}(x_0) = 0 \wedge L(x_0, \delta) \leq 0)\},$$

where $L(x, \delta) = \frac{D}{dx}\mathcal{B}(x) \cdot f(x, \mathcal{N}(x + \delta))$ is the Lie derivatives of $\mathcal{B}$.

Proof. For convenience, let $\Delta = \{\|\delta\| \,|\, \exists x_0(\mathcal{B}(x_0) = 0 \wedge L(x_0, \delta) \leq 0)\}$. We first prove that ϵ is a lower bound of Δ, i.e. $\forall \delta \in \Delta(\epsilon \leq \delta)$. Suppose there exists $\delta_0 \in \Delta$ such that $\epsilon > \delta_0$. Based on the definition of Δ, there exist x_0 and δ_0 satisfying $\mathcal{B}(x_0) = 0 \wedge \|\delta\| = \delta_0 \wedge L(x_0, \delta_0) \leq 0$, which concludes that δ_0 is not a tolerable error. It contradicts the definition that ϵ is the maximal tolerable error.

We then prove ϵ is the infimum, i.e. $\forall \epsilon' > \epsilon, \exists \delta \in \Delta(\epsilon \leq \delta \leq \epsilon')$. As ϵ is the maximal tolerable error, there exist x_0 and δ_0 such that $\mathcal{B}(x_0) = 0 \wedge \epsilon < \|\delta_0\| \leq \epsilon' \wedge L(x_0, \delta_0) \leq 0$ (otherwise it contradicts the definition that ϵ is the maximal tolerable error). Let $\delta = \delta_0$, the conclusion is reached. ∎

Theorem 3 provides an effective way of finding ϵ. The process involves exhaustively searching over all x such that $\mathcal{B}(x) = 0$ and simultaneously iterating over δ, searching for the δ with the smallest norm that can violate (4). After the δ is identified, its norm becomes ϵ. Fortunately, the constraint on the Lie derivative can be further tightened to narrow the search space, as shown in the following theorem.

Theorem 3. *Let $\mathcal{S}\langle V, I, \Psi, \mathcal{N}, \delta, f \rangle$ be a neural network controlled system, a barrier certificate $\mathcal{B}$ guarantees its safety with respect to the unsafe region U, the robust bound ϵ can be identified as:*

$$\epsilon = \inf \{\|\delta\| \,|\, \exists x_0(\mathcal{B}(x_0) = 0 \wedge L(x_0, \delta) = 0)\},$$

where $L(x, \delta) = \frac{D}{dx}\mathcal{B}(x) \cdot f(x, \mathcal{N}(x + \delta))$ is the Lie derivatives of $\mathcal{B}$.

Proof. Let $\tilde{\Delta} = \{\|\delta\| \,|\, \exists x_0(\mathcal{B}(x_0) = 0 \wedge L(x_0, \delta) = 0)\}$. Since $\tilde{\Delta} \subset \Delta$, by Theorem 2 we have $\forall \delta \in \tilde{\Delta}(\epsilon \leq \delta)$, that is ϵ is a lower bound of $\tilde{\Delta}$.

We then come to prove ϵ is the infimum, i.e. $\forall \epsilon' > \epsilon, \exists \delta_0 \in \tilde{\Delta}(\epsilon < \delta_0 < \epsilon')$. According to Theorem 2, there exist x' and δ' such that $\mathcal{B}(x') = 0 \wedge \epsilon < \|\delta'\| \leq \epsilon' \wedge L(x', \delta') \leq 0$. Then defining a auxiliary continuous function $G(\lambda) = L(x', \lambda \delta')$ by fixing x' and δ', we have $G(1) = L(x', \delta') \leq 0$. Meanwhile, as $\mathcal{B}$ is a barrier certificate for $\mathcal{S}$ without measurement errors, $G(0) = L(x', 0) > 0$. Using the continuity of $G(\lambda)$, the intermediate value theorem ensures there exists $0 < \lambda' \leq 1$ satisfying $G(\lambda') = L(x', \lambda'\delta') = 0$. Finally, we find $\lambda'\|\delta'\| \in \tilde{\Delta}$ which satisfies $\epsilon < \lambda'\|\delta'\| < \epsilon'$.

Let $\delta_0 \in \Delta$, from the definition, there exist x_0 such that $\mathcal{B}(x_0) = 0 \wedge L(x_0, \delta_0) \leq 0$. If $L(x_0, \delta_0) = 0$, we have $\delta_0 \in \tilde{\Delta}$. Otherwise, we have $G(1) = L(x_0, \delta_0) < 0$. As $\mathcal{B}$ is a barrier certificate with no measurement errors, $G(0) = L(x_0, 0) > 0$. Using the continuity of $G(\lambda)$, the intermediate value theorem ensures there exists $0 < \lambda_0 \leq 1$ such that $G(\lambda_0) = L(x_0, \lambda_0\delta_0) = 0$.

Therefore, it suffices to prove that $\forall \epsilon' > \epsilon, \exists a \in \tilde{\Delta}(a < \epsilon')$. According to Theorem 2, there exist x_0 and δ_0 such that $\mathcal{B}(x_0) = 0$, $\|\delta_0\| < \epsilon'$, and $L(x_0, \delta_0) \leq 0$. Moreover, since $\mathcal{B}$ is a barrier certificate, we have $L(x_0, 0) > 0$. Define the function $G(\lambda) = L(x_0, \lambda\delta_0)$. Then, G is continuous, and by the intermediate value theorem, there exists $0 < \lambda_0 \leq 1$ such that $G(\lambda_0) = L(x_0, \lambda_0\delta_0) = 0$. Let $a = \|\lambda_0\delta_0\|$. Then $a \in \tilde{\Delta}$ and $a = \lambda_0\|\delta_0\| < \epsilon'$, which is required. ∎

To facilitate the reconstruction of barrier certificates, the paper introduces neural networks as a potential solution, as they can be easily reshaped by tuning training data sets. Let the neural network $\mathcal{B}$ be of n-layers; the following quadratic optimization problem returns the desired ϵ.

$$
\begin{cases}
\epsilon = \mathbf{min}\|\delta\| \\
s.t. \ x_0 \in \Psi, \\
\quad x_k = (w_{k,1}x_{k-1} + b_{k,1}) \otimes (w_{k,2}x_{k-1} + b_{k,2}), k = 1, 2, \ldots, n \\
\quad x_n = 0, \\
\quad d_1 = diag[w_{1,1}x_0 + b_{1,1}] \cdot w_{1,2} + diag[w_{1,2}x_0 + b1, 2] \cdot w_{1,1}, \\
\quad d_k = (diag[w_{k,1}x_{k-1} + b_{k,1}] \cdot w_{k,2} + diag[w_{k,2}x_{k-1} + b_{k,2}] \cdot w_{k,1}) \cdot d_{k-1}, \\
\qquad\qquad\qquad\qquad\qquad k = 1, 2, \ldots, n \\
\quad d = d_n f(x_0, \mathcal{N}(x_0 + \delta)), \\
\quad d = 0,
\end{cases}
\tag{8}
$$

In the above programming, the first line represents the iteration over x in Ψ. Line 2 to line 3 encodes the $\mathcal{B}$ while the line 3 represents $\mathcal{B}(x) = 0$. Line 4 to line 6 encodes $L(x, \delta)$ while the last line represents $L(x, \delta) = 0$. The objective function guides the search of inf Δ'.

Note that, the solution x' to the problem (8) corresponds to a point locating on the curve $\mathcal{B} = 0$ that invalidates $\mathcal{B}$ by passing $x' + \delta$ ($\|\delta\| = \epsilon$) to the controller. Obviously, x' is the most vulnerable part of $\mathcal{B}$. In the next section, we try to make $\mathcal{B}$ more robust to measurement errors by repairing the region around x'.

4   Synthesize ϵ – Robust Neural Network Barrier Certificates

In this section, we study how to synthesize a more robust barrier certificate based on the exact estimation of the robust bound. Here, neural networks are employed as barrier certificates. Neural network training is a data-driven approach. Thus, it is possible to refine neural networks by fine-tuning the training dataset. The procedure of finding the robust bound ϵ reveals the most vulnerable region of neural networks; tuning the dataset may reshape the vulnerable region to be less sensitive to errors. We first present the algorithm for iterative training, verification, and refinement of neural networks, providing details of these steps in the following subsections.

4.1   Algorithm

Algorithm 1 presents an iterative approach to synthesizing an ϵ-robust neural network barrier certificate. Given a neural network system controlled system $\mathcal{S}$, and an unsafe set U, it adopts the precision threshold μ and the iteration threshold N to control the iteration. That is, either when the difference between the robust bounds of two successive barrier certificates is smaller than the specified threshold μ or when the iteration threshold N is reached, the iteration terminates.

In each iteration, a neural network $\mathcal{B}$ is trained as a candidate barrier certificate (line 6). Then, it is verified by solving optimization problems (line 7). If the verification fails, counterexamples found in problem-solving are added to the dataset to retrain the neural network (line 10). A verified neural network is passed to the next step to infer its robust bound ϵ while identifying its most vulnerable region (line 11). The dataset Ψ' is augmented with data around the most vulnerable region to support the tuning of the neural network in the next iteration (line 14). The verification iteration (lines 5–10) attempts to validate a candidate neural network up to M times.

4.2   Training Candidate Neural Network Barrier Certificates

For a neural network controlled system $\mathcal{S}\langle V, I, \Psi, \mathcal{N}, \delta, f \rangle$ associated with an unsafe set U, the training procedure tries to obtain a neural network conforming to the definition of ϵ-robust barrier certificates. It is achieved by designing a proper loss function that guides the training to converge with the objective.

The loss function adopted in our training consists of three parts, corresponding to conditions (3), (4), and (5), respectively. Accordingly, the training dataset is also divided into three groups: the first group is sampled from the initial region I, the second part is sampled from the invariant Ψ, and the third part is sampled from the unsafe region U. We denote the sets of training data as I', Ψ', and U', respectively. The loss function is defined as follows:

$$
\begin{aligned}
loss = {}& \alpha \sum\nolimits_{x \in I'} \max(\epsilon_1, -\mathcal{B}(x)) \\
& + \beta \sum\nolimits_{x \in \Psi'} \max\left(\epsilon_2, - \left(\tfrac{D}{dx}\mathcal{B}(x) \cdot f(x, \mathcal{N}(x)) - \lambda(x)\mathcal{B}(x)\right)\right) \\
& + \gamma \sum\nolimits_{x \in U'} \max(\epsilon_3, \mathcal{B}(x)),
\end{aligned}
\tag{9}
$$

where $\alpha + \beta + \gamma = 1, \lambda > 0, \epsilon_1, \epsilon_2, \epsilon_3 > 0$. The $\epsilon_i, 1 \leq i \leq 3$ is used to prevent $\mathcal{B}$ to become $\mathcal{B}(x) = 0$. Intuitively, the first term of the loss function penalizes the

---

Algorithm 1: Synthesize a ϵ - robust neural network barrier certificate

---

Input: Neural network controlled system $\mathcal{S}$, unsafe set U, precision threshold μ,
      iteration threshold N and M

Output: $<\mathcal{B}, \epsilon>$ or FAIL

1   Generate training datasets $I', \Psi', and\, U'$ from $\mathcal{S}$ and U;

2   $\epsilon = 0$, $LastB = null$;

3   **for** $i = 1, \ldots, N$ **do**

4      $\tilde{\epsilon} = \epsilon$;

5   **for** $j = 1, \ldots, M$ **do**

6   Train candidate neural network $\mathcal{B}$ using the loss function (13);

7   Verify $\mathcal{B}$ by solving the optimization problems (10), (11), and (12);

8   **if** *verified($\mathcal{B}$)* **then**

9             $LastB = \mathcal{B}$

10   Break;

11   Augment the dataset with counter-examples returned from (10), (11), and (12);

12   **if** *verified($\mathcal{B}$)* **then**

13   Compute the robust bound ϵ of $\mathcal{B}$ by solving the problem (8);

14   **else if** $LastB \neq null$ **then**

15   Return $<LastB, \tilde{\epsilon}>$;

16   **else**

17   Return FAIL;

18   Tune the dataset Ψ' using the solution of (8);

19   Return $<\mathcal{B}, \epsilon>$;

---

violation of (3), while the third term penalizes the violation of (5). The second term is more complex: when $\mathcal{B}(x) = 0$, it penalizes the violation of (4). It is a relaxation of (4); thus, a trainable neural network $\lambda(x)$ is used to increase the flexibility of $\mathcal{B}$.

When the training terminates, the loss function converges to zero, which ensures conditions (3)–(5) are satisfied by all samples in the dataset. It makes $\mathcal{B}$ a valid candidate as barrier certificates. To ensure that $\mathcal{B}$ conforms to the conditions (3)–(5) over the whole invariant, rigorous verification is required.

4.3   Verifying Candidate Neural Barrier Certificate

The verification procedure validates candidate neural networks as barrier certificates by examining their conformance to the definition of ϵ-robust barrier certificates. In this section, we settle the verification problems by encoding them as quadratic optimization problems. The global optimum of the problems offers sound guarantees.

For condition (3), it is equivalent to checking whether or not the global minimum value of $\mathcal{B}(x)$ over I is greater than or equal to 0. Therefore, the verification procedure solves the following optimization problem and requires its global optimum to be non-negative:

$$\begin{cases} p_1 = \mathbf{min}\ x_n \\ s.t.\quad x_0 \in I, \\ \qquad x_k = (w_{k,1}x_{k-1} + b_{k,1}) \otimes (w_{k,2}x_{k-1} + b_{k,2}),\ k = 1, 2, \ldots, n \end{cases} \tag{10}$$

In the above optimization problem, the first line indicates that the domain of $\mathcal{B}(x)$ is I. The remaining lines encode the process of computing the input x_0 through the $\mathcal{B}$ layer by layer, with x_n representing the output of $\mathcal{B}$. Based on the above discussion, when p_1 is non-negative, it indicates that condition (3) is satisfied.

Condition (5) has a similar structure to condition (3). It is equivalent to requiring that $\mathcal{B}(x)$ has a global maximum value less than zero over U. Using the same encoding while changing the domain in from I to U, the optimization problem corresponding to condition (5) is derived as:

$$\begin{cases} p_2 = \mathbf{max}\ x_n \\ s.t.\quad x_0 \in U, \\ \qquad x_k = (w_{k,1}x_{k-1} + b_{k,1}) \otimes (w_{k,2}x_{k-1} + b_{k,2}),\ k = 1, 2, \ldots, n \end{cases} \tag{11}$$

Similar to condition 3, p_2 in (11) being negative indicates that (5) is satisfied.

Condition (4) is equivalent to requiring that, when $x \in \Psi \wedge \mathcal{B}(x) = 0$, the minimum value of $\frac{D}{dx}\mathcal{B}(x) \cdot f(x)$ is greater than 0. To encode this optimization objective, it is necessary to encode $\frac{D}{dx}\mathcal{B}(x)$. According to the definition 6, $\frac{D}{dx}\mathcal{B}(x) = \frac{D}{dx}x_n(x) = (diag[w_{n,1}x_{n-1}+b_{n,1}] \cdot W_{n2} + diag[w_{n,2}x_{n-1}+b_{n,2}] \cdot W_{n,1}) \cdot \frac{D}{dx}x_{n-1}(x)$.

The above formula provides a method for calculating the gradient of the current layer using the gradient from the previous layer, with $\frac{D}{dx}x_1(x) = (diag[w_{1,1}x_0 + b_{11}] \cdot w_{1,2} + diag[w_{1,2}x_0 + b_{1,2}] \cdot w_{1,1})$. Thus, we have the following encoding for (4):

$$\begin{cases} x_0 \in \Psi, \\ x_k = (w_{k,1}x_{k-1} + b_{k,1}) \otimes (w_{k,2}x_{k-1} + b_{k,2}), k = 1, 2, \ldots, n \\ x_n = 0, \\ d_1 = diag[w_{1,1}x_0 + b1, 1] \cdot w_{1,2} + diag[w_{1,2}x_0 + b1, 2] \cdot w_{1,1}, \\ d_k = (diag[w_{k,1}x_{k-1} + b_{k,1}] \cdot w_{k,2} + diag[w_{k,2}x_{k-1} + b_{k,2}] \cdot w_{k,1}) \cdot d_{k-1}, \\ \qquad\qquad\qquad k = 1, 2, \ldots, n \\ d = d_n \cdot f(x_0, \mathcal{N}(x_0)), \\ d = 0 \end{cases} \tag{12}$$

In the above programming, the first three constraints represent the condition $x \in \Psi \wedge \mathcal{B}(x) = 0$, while the last four encode $d = \frac{D}{dx}\mathcal{B}(x) \cdot f(x)$, the optimization objective. $\mathcal{N}(x_0)$ can be encoded using the same way as in (10) or (11). When $p_3 > 0$, it indicates that condition (4) is satisfied.

Theorem 4 combines the inference of the robust bound ϵ and the verification of barrier certificates.

Theorem 4. *Given a neural network controlled system $\mathcal{S}\langle V, I, \Psi, \mathcal{N}, \delta, f \rangle$ with an unsafe set U, a feed-forward neural network $\mathcal{B}$ is a ϵ-robust barrier certificate* *for $\mathcal{S}$ with respect to U, if the global optimums of the optimization problems* (3),(5), (4),(8) *denoted as* $p_1, p_2, p_3, and\, \epsilon$ *satisfy:*

- $p_1 \geq 0$
- $p_2 < 0$
- $p_3 > 0$

When a counterexample is found by (10), (11), or (12), this counterexample and m points in its small neighborhood are added to the corresponding training dataset I', U', or Ψ', then restart the training process.

4.4   Iteratively Improve $\mathcal{B}$

After solving (8) for $\mathcal{B}$, we obtain solutions of x_0 as vulnerable points on $\mathcal{B}$, denoted as x'. And the global optimum ϵ of (8) is the robust bound of the current $\mathcal{B}$. The above information is then used in the iterative improvement of $\mathcal{B}$.

Enhancing the Reachable Set. The obtained ϵ can be used to improve the existing $\mathcal{B}$ through a data-driven approach, specifically: points are taken from the initial set I, and simulations are conducted, with the direction at each step of the simulation selected from $\{f(x, u(x + \delta)) | \|\delta\| \leq \epsilon\}$. Subsequently, the trajectories obtained from the simulation are added to the training dataset I'.

This method is based on the following observation: ϵ is the lower bound of the system's measurement robustness, so any trajectory obtained by simulating with a disturbance less than ϵ should not intersect with the unsafe region. Therefore, these trajectories should be added to I' in improvement training. The training process encourages $\mathcal{B}$ to take positive values at points in I'. Thus, the improved $\mathcal{B}'$ tolerates greater measurement uncertainty than $\mathcal{B}$.

Enhancing the Loss Function. ϵ can also be used in the loss function to improve the robustness of $\mathcal{B}$. The modified loss function is:

$$\begin{aligned} loss = \alpha \sum_{x \in I'} \max(\epsilon_1, -\mathcal{B}(x)) \\ + \beta \sum_{x \in \Psi'} \max(\epsilon_2, - (\tfrac{D}{dx}\mathcal{B}(x) \cdot f(x, \mathcal{N}(x + \delta)) - \lambda(x)\mathcal{B}(x))) \\ + \gamma \sum_{x \in U'} \max(\epsilon_3, \mathcal{B}(x)), \end{aligned} \tag{13}$$

where $\|\delta\| < \epsilon$ is a random measurement error added in every training epoch. Note that (13) is the same as (9) when $\epsilon = 0$. The second loss term makes $\mathcal{B}$ more robust to measurement errors on the whole invariant Ψ.

Enhancing Vulnerable Region. We define $\{x | \|x - x'\| < \epsilon\}$ as the vulnerable region and sample random points in this region to add them into Ψ'. The second term in the loss function (13) makes (4) less violated on the Vulnerable region, thereby making $\mathcal{B}$ more robust.

The improvement training may fail if the maximum training iteration is reached and the candidate NBC is still invalid. This suggests that the ϵ of the last iteration is likely the maximum and cannot be further improved by the data-driven method.

5   Experiments

In this section, we first illustrate our approach with one neural network-controlled system and then compare our *RobustNBC* with the state-of-the-art method [29] on several benchmarks [8].

5.1   Examples

Example 1 ([7]). Consider a NN-controlled system:

$$f(x, u) = \begin{bmatrix} x_1^3 - x_2 \\ x_3 \\ u \end{bmatrix} \tag{14}$$

With the invariant:

$$\Psi = \{\mathbf{x} \in \mathbb{R}^3 \mid -0.4 \le x_1 \le 1, -0.4 \le x_2 \le 1, -0.4 \le x_3 \le 1\}.$$

The initial condition is:

$$I = \{\mathbf{x} \in \mathbb{R}^3 \mid 0.38 \le x_1 \le 0.4, 0.45 \le x_2 \le 0.47, 0.25 \le x_3 \le 0.27\}.$$

The unsafe region is:

$$U = \{\mathbf{x} \in \mathbb{R}^3 \mid 0.8 \le x_1 \le 1, 0.8 \le x_2 \le 1, 0.8 \le x_3 \le 1\}.$$

A neural network controller with one hidden layer and 300 neurons is trained for the system to reach the region defined as:

$$\{\mathbf{x} \in \mathbb{R}^3 \mid 0.2 \le x_1 \le 0.3, -0.3 \le x_2 \le -0.05, -0.4 \le x_3 \le 1\}$$

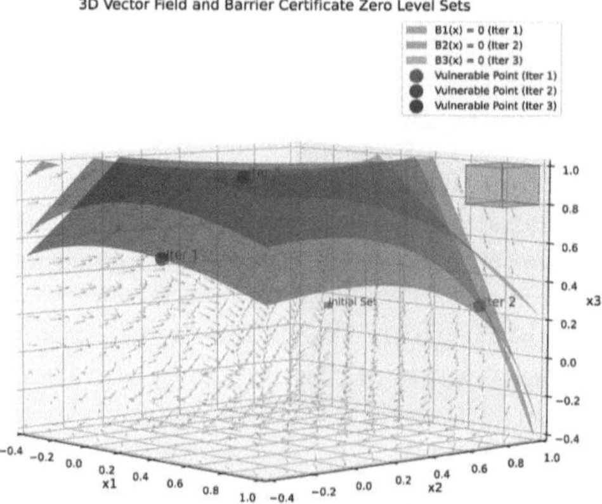

Fig. 2. Continuously enhanced robust barrier certificates in 3 dimensions.

As shown in Fig. 2, three barrier certificates are obtained after three iterations, represented by red, green, and purple surfaces, with robust bounds of 0.255, 0.427, and 0.580, respectively. Their vulnerable points are also shown in the figure with corresponding colors.

In this example, robustness enhancement is achieved by iteratively relocating the zero-level set of the barrier function to exclude previously identified vulnerable points. This mechanism is visually evidenced in Fig. 2, where substantial reshaping of barrier certificates is observed across the three iterations.

5.2 Benchmark Evaluation

We evaluated our method, *RobustNBC*, on the benchmarks proposed in [15] and compared it with the state-of-the-art method, *NBC* [29]. All experiments were conducted on a PC equipped with an Intel Core i7-12700 CPU, an NVIDIA RTX 2060 GPU, and 32 GB of RAM. The results represent the mean value obtained over 10 repetitions. The optimization problems were solved using the Gurobi 12.0 tool.

Different from us, *NBC* requires specifying the robust bound ϵ before synthesizing a neural network as a barrier certificate. To make a fair comparison, we incorporate *NBC* with the bisection method to find a good robust bound. To avoid endless searches, we set the time threshold to 2 h, which is approximately 5.5 times our worst-case scenario. Furthermore, for the NBC baseline, we exclusively measured computation time for successful bisection attempts, excluding computational overhead from timeout failures. For the example ACC, the bisection method searched a robust bound between 0 and 100, while for the rest of the examples, the search interval was set to [0,1]. Experimental results are summarized in Table 1, and better results are reported in bold.

Table 1. Performance Evaluation

Example	dim	C	RobustNBC							NBC		
			S	ϵ		epoch	time			S	ϵ	time
				I	F		train	verify	total			
B1	2	[2,100,1]	[2,20,1]	0.198	**0.955**	3	29.2	3.0	**32.2**	[2,100,1]	0.875	61.3
B2	2	[2,100,1]	[2,20,1]	0.001	**0.033**	2	38.3	1.2	**39.5**	[2,100,1]	0.031	72.1
B3	2	[2,100,1]	[2,100,1]	0.082	**0.125**	2	160.3	19.7	**180.0**	[2,100,1]	0.120	230.7
B5	3	[3,300,1]	[3,20,1]	0.268	0.492	3	25.0	71.7	**96.7**	[3,200,1]	**0.500**	112.3
MC	2	[2,300,1]	[2,20,20,1]	0.003	**0.017**	4	136.8	34.3	**171.1**	[2,100,20,1]	0.016	375.9
F1	4	[4,300,1]	[4,30,1]	0.112	**0.163**	3	232.4	24.6	**257.0**	[4,200,50,1]	0.125	1828.7
Tora	4	[4,300,1]	[4,10,5,1]	0.147	**0.534**	2	473.0	654.1	**1127.1**	[4,200,50,1]	0.313	3932.8
QMPC	6	[6,100,3]	[6,30,1]	0.002	**0.215**	5	524.7	101.2	**625.9**	[6,300,100,1]	0.063	5492.4
ACC	6	[6,300,1]	[6,100,1]	1.145	**32.024**	7	1297.6	499.1	**1796.7**	[6,300,100,1]	–	–

In Table 1, *dim* is the number of variables. C is the structure of neural network controllers. S under *RobustNBC* and *NBC* denote the structure of the corresponding neural network barrier certificate. ϵ is the robust bound. I records the robust bound of the initial barrier certificates, while F records the robust bound of the final barrier certificates. *epoch* represents the total number of enforcement iterations. All times are recorded in seconds. $'-'$ means that a barrier certificate was not found.

Experimental results show that our method achieved a larger robust bound for all nine examples while costing less time. Specifically, for the comparable 8 examples, our *RobustNBC* took 0.46 times the time of *NBC* to achieve a 1.46 times larger robust bound. Regarding the effectiveness of iterative refinement, the improvements from initial to final ranged from 45% to 10,000% with a mean of 1,981%. The bisection method has no idea of the vulnerable part of the barrier certificate; it relies on limited information to guide the search. Our *RobustNBC* has complete knowledge of the vulnerable region and keeps on repairing it. That is why our *RobustNBC* outperforms *NBC*.

6 Related Work

Safety verification of neural network controlled systems receives many attentions in recent years [7,10,11,15,16,18,19,28]. Most of them don't put the uncertainty into consideration, i.e. the controllers are assumed to always get the exact measurement of states. Existing work treating uncertainty devote to either stochastic systems with neural network controllers or neural network controllers against measurement perturbations.

The stochastic systems controlled by neural networks have been well studied. Sun et al. [17] propose the verification scheme for ReLU neural network controlled discrete-time LTI systems with Gaussian noise applied to dynamics. The verification goal is to estimate the tight upper bounds on the probability the system invade unsafe regions after a specified amount of steps. Zarei et al. [24] use statistical model checking (SMC) to verify complex neural network controlled cyber-physical systems. The SMC approach based on Clopper-Pearson confidence levels is able to tackle both reachability property and safety property. Wang et al. [21] extend the work to treat hyper probabilistic signal temporal logic formulating properties defined upon the relationship between multiple simultaneous executions in continuous time. For the cyber physical systems they studied, randomness is put on the initial conditions.

Markov Decision Processes (MDP) are also introduced to model neural network controlled systems. Bacci et al. [1,2] resort to abstract interpretation to represent the system as interval MDPs and evaluate the safety probabilities within in k-steps by probabilistic model checkers.

Carr et al. [3] verify Recurrent Neural Network (RNN) controlled system with respect to temporal logic specifications. By extracting a finite-state controller from the RNN, partially observable Markov decision processes are built as the system model, which induce Markov Chains for probabilistic model checkers. Failed verification may produce diagnostic information helping to adjust the extraction the finite-state controller.

Only a few works [4, 29] care for the robustness of neural network controllers against measurement perturbations. Dean et al. [5] present the Measurement-Robust Control Barrier Functions (MR-CBF) by augmenting the classic definition of Control Barrier Functions with component tolerating bounded measurement errors. MR-CBF synthesis is incorporated into a convex optimization-based controllers generation procedure so that they are produced as a whole. Data sampling methodology is proposed as well which ensures the measurement model yielding errors within the predefined bound.

Zhi et al. [29] propose a unified framework to tame the qualitative and quantitative safety verification of neural network controlled systems. Given the limit of state perturbations, the qualitative verification establishes almost-sure safety guarantees while quantitative verification provides precise lower and upper bounds on probabilistic safety if the former fails. They aim at the discrete-time systems and check the conditions of barrier certificates by interval bound propagation [6, 22].

Waite et al. [20] present a compositional model to accommodate the measurement noise. For autonomous systems, the perception model is decomposed into a canonical model derived from first principles and a noise model representing measurement noise coming from the real environment. Furthermore, two types of noise: benign and adversarial noise are represented as generative models and classifiers using data-driven approaches, respectively. They claim that the compositional noise-specific model can better satisfy the scalability requirement in safety verification, and employ the tool Verisig [9] to take verification tasks.

Unlike them, rather than giving the bound of measurement perturbations in advance and then synthesizing the corresponding barrier certificates, we firstly generate the barrier certificates and then compute their tolerable bounds of measurement errors. By continuously repairing the most vulnerable regions of the barrier certificate, we can produce barrier certificates more robust than existing methods.

7   Conclusion

This paper proposes a novel approach for verifying the safety of neural network-controlled systems under measurement uncertainty, utilizing neural networks as ϵ-robust barrier certificates. Unlike conventional methods that rely on predefined measurement error bounds, our approach iteratively improves robustness by computing the maximum allowable error bound supported by existing barrier certificates and progressively optimizing weak regions to tolerate larger uncertainty ranges. The verification process encodes the barrier certificate conditions and maximum error bound computation into quadratic programming problems, which are then solved through numerical optimization with guaranteed solutions. We implement our methodology as the tool RobustNBC and evaluate its performance against state-of-the-art methods on benchmark examples. Experimental results demonstrate that RobustNBC achieves larger error bounds within less computation time, confirming our approach's effectiveness and efficiency.

Acknowledgements. This work is supported by the National Natural Science Foundation of China under Grant 62172211, 62172210.

References

1. Bacci, E., Parker, D.: Probabilistic guarantees for safe deep reinforcement learning. In: Bertrand, N., Jansen, N. (eds.) FORMATS 2020. LNCS, vol. 12288, pp. 231–248. Springer, Cham (2020). https://doi.org/10.1007/978-3-030-57628-8_14
2. Bacci, E., Parker, D.: Verified probabilistic policies for deep reinforcement learning. In: Proceedings of 14th International Symposium on NASA Formal Methods. Lecture Notes in Computer Science, vol. 13260, pp. 193–212. Springer, Heidelberg (2022). https://doi.org/10.1007/978-3-031-06773-0_10
3. Carr, S., Jansen, N., Topcu, U.: Task-aware verifiable rnn-based policies for partially observable markov decision processes. J. Artif. Intell. Res. **72**, 819–847 (2021)
4. Dawson, C., Gao, S., Fan, C.: Safe control with learned certificates: a survey of neural lyapunov, barrier, and contraction methods for robotics and control. IEEE Trans. Rob. **39**(3), 1749–1767 (2023)
5. Dean, S., Taylor, A.J., Cosner, R.K., Recht, B., Ames, A.D.: Guaranteeing safety of learned perception modules via measurement-robust control barrier functions. In: Proceedings of 4th Conference on Robot Learning, CoRL 2020. Proceedings of Machine Learning Research, vol. 155, pp. 654–670. PMLR (2020)
6. Gowal, S., et al.: On the effectiveness of interval bound propagation for training verifiably robust models. CoRR arxiv:1810.12715 (2018)
7. Huang, C., Fan, J., Li, W., Chen, X., Zhu, Q.: Reachnn: reachability analysis of neural-network controlled systems. ACM Trans. Embed. Comput. Syst. (TECS) **18**(5s), 1–22 (2019)
8. Ivanov, R., Carpenter, T., Weimer, J., Alur, R., Pappas, G., Lee, I.: Verisig 2.0: verification of neural network controllers using taylor model preconditioning. In: Silva, A., Leino, K.R.M. (eds.) CAV 2021. LNCS, vol. 12759, pp. 249–262. Springer, Cham (2021). https://doi.org/10.1007/978-3-030-81685-8_11
9. Ivanov, R., Carpenter, T.J., Weimer, J., Alur, R., Pappas, G.J., Lee, I.: Verifying the safety of autonomous systems with neural network controllers. ACM Trans. Embed. Comput. Syst. (TECS) **20**(1), 1–26 (2020)
10. Julian, K.D., Kochenderfer, M.J.: A reachability method for verifying dynamical systems with deep neural network controllers (2019)
11. Katz, G., Barrett, C., Dill, D.L., Julian, K., Kochenderfer, M.J.: Reluplex: an efficient SMT solver for verifying deep neural networks. In: Majumdar, R., Kunčak, V. (eds.) CAV 2017. LNCS, vol. 10426, pp. 97–117. Springer, Cham (2017). https://doi.org/10.1007/978-3-319-63387-9_5
12. Kong, H., He, F., Song, X., Hung, W.N.N., Gu, M.: Exponential-condition-based barrier certificate generation for safety verification of hybrid systems. In: Sharygina, N., Veith, H. (eds.) CAV 2013. LNCS, vol. 8044, pp. 242–257. Springer, Heidelberg (2013). https://doi.org/10.1007/978-3-642-39799-8_17
13. Mitra, S., et al.: Formal verification techniques for vision-based autonomous systems – a survey, pp. 89–108. Springer, Cham (2025). https://doi.org/10.1007/978-3-031-75778-5_5
14. Prajna, S., Jadbabaie, A., Pappas, G.: A framework for worst-case and stochastic safety verification using barrier certificates. IEEE Trans. Autom. Control **52**(8), 1415–1429 (2007)

15. Sha, M., et al.: Synthesizing barrier certificates of neural network controlled continuous systems via approximations. In: Proceedings of 58th ACM/IEEE Design Automation Conference, pp. 631–636 (2021)
16. Singh, G., Gehr, T., Mirman, M., Püschel, M., Vechev, M.: Fast and effective robustness certification. In: Advances in Neural Information Processing Systems, pp. 10802–10813 (2018)
17. Sun, S., Zhang, Y., Luo, X., Vlantis, P., Pajic, M., Zavlanos, M.M.: Formal verification of stochastic systems with relu neural network controllers. In: Proceedings of 2022 International Conference on Robotics and Automation, ICRA 2022, pp. 6800–6806. IEEE (2022)
18. Sun, X., Khedr, H., Shoukry, Y.: Formal verification of neural network controlled autonomous systems. In: Proceedings of the 22nd ACM International Conference on Hybrid Systems: Computation and Control, pp. 147–156 (2019)
19. Tuncali, C.E., Kapinski, J., Ito, H., Deshmukh, J.V.: Reasoning about safety of learning-enabled components in autonomous cyber-physical systems. In: Proceedings of the 55th Annual Design Automation Conference, pp. 1–6 (2018)
20. Waite, T., Robey, A., Hassani, H., Pappas, G.J., Ivanov, R.: Data-driven modeling and verification of perception-based autonomous systems. CoRR arxiv:2312.06848 (2023)
21. Wang, Y., Zarei, M., Bonakdarpour, B., Pajic, M.: Statistical verification of hyperproperties for cyber-physical systems. ACM Trans. Embed. Comput. Syst. **18**(5s), 92:1–92:23 (2019)
22. Xu, K., et al.: Automatic perturbation analysis for scalable certified robustness and beyond. In: Proceedings of 33th Annual Conference on Neural Information Processing Systems, NeurIPS 2020 (2020)
23. Yang, Z., et al.: An iterative scheme of safe reinforcement learning for nonlinear systems via barrier certificate generation. In: Silva, A., Leino, K.R.M. (eds.) CAV 2021. LNCS, vol. 12759, pp. 467–490. Springer, Cham (2021). https://doi.org/10.1007/978-3-030-81685-8_22
24. Zarei, M., Wang, Y., Pajic, M.: Statistical verification of learning-based cyberphysical systems. In: Proceedings of 23rd ACM International Conference on Hybrid Systems: Computation and Control, pp. 12:1–12:7. ACM (2020)
25. Zeng, X., Yang, Z., Zhang, L., Tang, X., Zeng, Z., Liu, Z.: Safety verification of nonlinear systems with bayesian neural network controllers. In: Proceedings of the Thirty-Seventh AAAI Conference on Artificial Intelligence, AAAI 2023, pp. 15278–15286. AAAI Press (2023)
26. Zhang, H., et al.: Backdoor attacks against deep reinforcement learning based traffic signal control systems. Peer Peer Netw. Appl. **16**(1), 466–474 (2023)
27. Zhang, H., et al.: Robust deep reinforcement learning against adversarial perturbations on state observations. In: Proceedings of 33th Annual Conference on Neural Information Processing Systems (2020)
28. Zhao, Q., Chen, X., Zhao, Z., Zhang, Y., Tang, E., Li, X.: Verifying neural network controlled systems using neural networks. In: Proceedings of 25th ACM International Conference on Hybrid Systems: Computation and Control, pp. 3:1–3:11. ACM (2022)
29. Zhi, D., Wang, P., Liu, S., Ong, C.L., Zhang, M.: Unifying qualitative and quantitative safety verification of dnn-controlled systems. In: Proceedings of 36th International Conference on Computer Aided Verification, CAV 2024. Lecture Notes in Computer Science, vol. 14682, pp. 401–426. Springer, Heidelberg (2024). https://doi.org/10.1007/978-3-031-65630-9_20

Session Types

Compositional Interface Refinement Through Subtyping in Probabilistic Session Types

Paula Blechschmidt[1], Kirstin Peters[2]([✉]), and Uwe Nestmann[1]

[1] Technische Universität Berlin, Berlin, Germany
[2] Universität Augsburg, Augsburg, Germany
kirstin.peters@uni-a.de

Abstract. Multiparty session types (MPST) are a robust typing framework that ensures safe and deadlock-free communication within distributed protocols. As these protocols grow in complexity, compositional modeling becomes increasingly important for scalable verification. Therefore, we propose using refinement through subtyping to facilitate the modularity needed for compositional verification.

We present a probabilistic extension for MPST with a novel, flexible subtyping system which allows one channel (the interface) to be substituted by several channels (the refinement). Our subtyping is very expressive; any selection of well-typed channels as the refinement has a corresponding interface in a single channel type. To facilitate this generality, we base our system on a powerful variant of MPST, mixed choice multiparty session types, which offers greater flexibility in communication choices.

Keywords: multiparty session types · probabilistic · refinement

1 Introduction

In general, the term *interface* refers to the observable—or externally accessible—aspects of a component, module, or system; the exact representation of an interface inherently depends on the formalism at hand. In many cases, interfaces appear at various levels of abstraction and granularity, which may be developed through *stepwise refinement* starting from some high-level description and adding details with each refinement step; reasonable notions of refinement relations should obviously be transitive. Ideally, refinement can be done in a *compositional* manner, where single components may be refined independently, while yielding a refinement of the full system. There is a large body of research on notions of refinement and accompanying methods, as it is generally quite specific to the formalism at hand. Consequently, there is no real consensus on definitions and interpretations, not even on terminology.

State-based representations of systems are likely the class of formalisms with the most diverse contributions. There, refinement relations typically compare

Z. Liu et al. (Eds.): ICTAC 2025, LNCS 16237, pp. 145–163, 2026.
https://doi.org/10.1007/978-3-032-11176-0_10

behaviours (in its simplest form traces), often expressed as a mapping from the refined version back to its initial specification [1]. The concepts of (forward and/or backward) *simulation* [24], which roughly correspond to completeness and soundness requirements of an implementation w.r.t. its specification, are possibly even more wide-spread and come in many flavors.

In *multiparty session types* (MPST) [33], somewhat naturally, the interface of a process captures the type of the session it participates in, which describes the sequence of input/output actions (messages), along with their types, direction, and order of communication. Here, often enough, the notion of *channel* comprises a particular *session* of a protocol among several participants, including all of the roles that act within the respective protocol to achieve a common goal [16,17,31]. If an interface is represented as a type, then refinement is naturally and best realized as a subtyping relation.

In this paper, interfaces are (sets of) channels, which are themselves constructed from sessions and the roles used within them. As usual these channels are given as implementation in a session calculus and as specification in *local context*, where a local context Δ is a collection of channel names and their respective channel types. The type system provides rules to check the implementation against its specification and ensures safety and deadlock-freedom (among other properties that could be defined).

As part of our type system, we introduce a novel subtyping relation $\leq_\mathbb{P}$ that allows to also verify probabilities $\mathbb{P}$ and specifies a refinement relation on local contexts, where $\mathbb{P}$ is a real between 0 and 1. Cases $\mathbb{P} < 1$ are used to check single branches with probability $\mathbb{P}$. Ultimately, i.e., for an entire choice, we are interested in $\mathbb{P} = 1$. Starting from Δ, if $\Delta' \leq_1 \Delta$ then the *refinement* Δ' refines the *interface* Δ by distributing some behaviour (on single channels) on sets of interacting channels. Starting from Δ', if $\Delta' \leq_1 \Delta$ then the *interface* Δ provides an abstract specification of the *refinement* Δ', where abstract means from an external point of view abstracting from interactions within Δ'.

The advantages of refinement are well-known: e.g. modularity to reduce complexity, abstraction of unkown or untrusted parts, or the step-wise refinement allowing to reuse code and correctness proofs. A concrete example from security about refining access rights in authorisation can be found in [19]. Here we use a less technical toy-example to illustrate our approach.

Example 1 (Running Example). Consider a **plaintiff** bringing a lawsuit to **court**, which, after possibly taking **witness** testimony, announces a verdict. To initiate the protocol, the **plaintiff** sends a message to the **court**, announcing the lawsuit (`lws`). Upon receiving this, the **court** decides with a total 70% chance that it has enough information to announce the verdict to the **plaintiff**. Of those 70%, half of the time, i.e., with a probability of 35%, the **judge** will find the **defendant** *guilty* (`glt`) and else *not guilty*. Otherwise, with 30%, the **court** requests (`rqs`) a **witness** to testify. Upon receiving this request, the **witness** sends a message to the **court** representing the statement (`st`) after which the **court** announces the verdict *not guilty* to the **plaintiff**. In case no **witness** is called, the **court** will send them a message releasing (`rls`) them and the protocol terminates.

This protocol has an issue: The **defendant** is not represented as a participant. The **defendant** could implicitly be assumed part of the **court**, but then the **court** has a conflict of interest. Instead, we can consider the **court** to be an interface that must be refined into two separate participants: **defendant** and **judge**. The **plaintiff** is the same as before but interacts now with the **judge** instead of the **court**. This **judge**, after receiving the lawsuit, waits for a message from the **defendant**. The **defendant** will send a weak (`wk`) and strong (`str`) defence with a 50% and 20% likelihood, respectively. Otherwise, it requests to call upon a **witness**, in 30% of cases. If the defence is strong, the verdict is always *not guilty*. A weak defence results in *guilty* with 70% and in *not guilty* with 30%. If no defence is given and the **witness** is requested, the **judge** calls them, receives their testimony, and decides as before. ○

There is many related work on MPST (see [3,11,17,20,31,33] for some introductions and overviews). We heavily rely on mixed choice in MPST introduced in [28]. Probabilistic process calculi and session types are studied e.g. in [2,14,15,17,18,21,22]. Subtyping was studied e.g. in [5,7,9,12,13,23–25,27,29].

The only other approach that we found using subtyping to refine a single channel into a set of channels is [19]. Its main motivation is to capture compatibility in the multiparty setting (instead of refinement). Our subtyping is much more flexible, as any selection of well-typed, safe, and deadlock-free channels as the refinement has a corresponding interface in a single channel type. For instance, we do not exclude races, i.e., two senders that want to communicate with the same receiver at the same time. Moreover, [19] considers neither mixed choice nor probabilistic choice. There are other forms of refinement studied in the context of MPST, e.g. the reordering of actions using asynchronous subtyping (studied e.g. in [6]) or refinement types (studied e.g. in [10,34]).

After introducing the session calculus (Sect. 2), typing system (Sect. 3), and the novel subtyping rules (Sect. 4), we prove the standard properties such as safety, subject reduction, and deadlock-freedom (Sect. 5). We also prove that any selection of well-typed, safe, and deadlock-free channels has a corresponding interface in a single channel type. We conclude in Sect. 6. The paper is based on the Master thesis [4] that contains some additional material and the missing proofs.

Having a probabilistic system also opens the door to future work on imperfect refinement: Instead of requiring guaranteed deadlock-freedom in the subtypes, we could introduce probabilistic bounds on deadlocks, allowing an interface to be substituted by a refinement if the probability of deadlock is bounded.

2   A Probabilistic Session Calculus with Mixed Choice

We use a standard multiparty session calculus (as in [30,31]) without session initialisation and delegation extended by the mixed choices of [28] (based on [26]) and probabilities (as in [2,21]). Moreover, channels are defined on sets of roles and communication primitives indicate which of these roles are used.

Definition 1 (Process Syntax). *The processes of the* probabilistic mixed choice multiparty session π -calculus *are inductively given by:*

$$
\begin{array}{rll}
v ::= & x, y, z, .. \mid 1, 2, .. \mid \top, \bot & \text{(variables, numbers, booleans)} \\[4pt]
c ::= & s[\overline{\mathbf{r}}] & \text{(session with set of roles)} \\[4pt]
P, Q, P_i ::= & \mathbf{0} \mid P \mid Q \mid (\nu s)P & \text{(inaction, par. composition, restriction)} \\[4pt]
& \mid\ \mathtt{if}\ v\ \mathtt{then}\ P\ \mathtt{else}\ Q & \text{(conditional)} \\[4pt]
& \mid\ \mathtt{def}\ D\ \mathtt{in}\ P \mid X\langle \widetilde{v}, \widetilde{c}\rangle & \text{(process definition, process call)} \\[4pt]
& \mid\ c\sum_{i \in I} M_i & \text{(mixed choice on } c \text{ with finite } I \neq \emptyset) \\[12pt]
M_i ::= & \mathbf{p}\leftarrow\mathbf{q}\,?\,l(x).P & (\mathbf{p}\ \text{receives message } l(x) \text{ from } \mathbf{q}) \\[4pt]
& \mid\ \bigoplus_{i \in I} \mathbb{P}_i \blacktriangleright N_i.P_i & \text{(prob. choice with finite } I \neq \emptyset) \\[12pt]
N_i ::= & \mathbf{p}\rightarrow\mathbf{q}\,!\,l\langle v\rangle \mid \tau & (\mathbf{p}\ \text{sends message } l\langle v\rangle \text{ to } \mathbf{q}, \text{ int. action}) \\[4pt]
D ::= & X(\widetilde{x}; \widetilde{c}) \stackrel{\mathtt{def}}{=} P & \text{(declaration of process constant } X) \\
\end{array}
$$

A *channel* $c = s[\overline{\mathbf{r}}]$ specifies a session s being used as a communication endpoint by the roles $\overline{\mathbf{r}}$ to interact with other participants within that session. Either $\overline{\mathbf{r}}$ is a singleton (as for standard session types) or participant $s[\overline{\mathbf{r}}]$ is an interface that can be refined splitting $s[\overline{\mathbf{r}}]$ along the roles in $\overline{\mathbf{r}}$ by the multi-channel subtyping introduced later.

Inaction $\mathbf{0}$ represents a terminated process. We sometimes omit trailing $\mathbf{0}$. *Composition* $P \mid Q$ allows P and Q to run in parallel and possibly interact. *Restriction* $(\nu s)P$ encapsulates a *session s*. The *conditional* $\mathtt{if}\ v\ \mathtt{then}\ P\ \mathtt{else}\ Q$ behaves as P if v is true and else as Q. *Process definition* $\mathtt{def}\ D\ \mathtt{in}\ P$ introduces recursion. In contrast to [28], *mixed choices* $c\sum_{i\in I} M_i$ combine input guarded summands with probabilistic choices. In *probabilistic choices* $\bigoplus_{i\in I}\mathbb{P}_i \blacktriangleright N_i.P_i$, where the $\mathbb{P}_i \in \mathbb{R}$ are *probabilities*, summands are guarded by either output or internal actions. Accordingly, we follow e.g. [32] and allow non-deterministic choices over probability distributions. Moreover, it seems more natural to allow probability distributions only over outputs, e.g. to abstract from some unknown mechanism that guides this choice in the sender, whereas receivers as reacting part in communications cannot decide on a probability. *Declarations* D provide definitions of processes that may be invoked by a *process call* $X\langle\widetilde{v}, \widetilde{c}\rangle$ with some values $\widetilde{v}$, where $\widetilde{c}$ lists the channels used by the process that is declared by X.

Restriction $(\nu s)P$ binds session s in P. Declaration $X(\widetilde{x}; \widetilde{c}) \stackrel{\mathtt{def}}{=} P$ binds process constants X and variables $\widetilde{x}$ in P. The vector $\widetilde{c}$ lists the channels used in P. Message receiving $\mathbf{p}\leftarrow\mathbf{q}\,?\,l(x).P$ binds the variable x in P. All other occurrences of process constants, variables, and sessions are free. Let $\mathbf{fs}(P)$ and $\mathbf{fs}(D)$ denote the set of free sessions in P and D, respectively. Let $\mathbf{dpv}(D)$ be the set of process variables declared in D and let $\mathbf{fpv}(P)$ and $\mathbf{fpv}(D)$ denote the set of free process variables in P and D. Substitution $P[x_1, \ldots, x_n \mapsto v_1, \ldots, v_n]$

simultaneously replaces all free occurrences of x_i by v_i in P, possibly applying alpha-conversion to avoid capture. Substitution $P[\widetilde{x} \mapsto \widetilde{v}]$ is undefined if $|\widetilde{x}| \neq |\widetilde{v}|$.

We abbreviate singleton sums $c\sum_{i\in\{1\}} M$ as $c{\triangleright}M$ and $\bigoplus_{i\in\{1\}} \mathbb{P} \blacktriangleright N.P$ as $\mathbb{P} \blacktriangleright N.P$. We sometimes omit the probability 1, i.e., abbreviate outputs $1 \blacktriangleright N.P$ by $N.P$. Whenever $I \cap J = \emptyset$ and $I \cup J \neq \emptyset$, we allow to split a mixed choice $c\sum_{i\in I\cup J} M_i$ into $c{\triangleright}\sum_{i\in I} M_i + \sum_{j\in J} M_j$ and we allow to split a probabilistic choice $\bigoplus_{i\in I\cup J} \mathbb{P}_i \blacktriangleright N_i.P_i$ into $\bigoplus_{i\in I} \mathbb{P}_i \blacktriangleright N_i.P_i \oplus \bigoplus_{j\in J} \mathbb{P}_j \blacktriangleright N_j.P_j$. In particular, we often split sums into a single summand and the rest of the sum, i.e., $c\sum_{i\in I} M_i$ becomes $c{\triangleright}M_j + \mathsf{M}$ with $\mathsf{M} = c\sum_{i\in I\setminus\{j\}} M_i$ and $\bigoplus_{i\in I} \mathbb{P}_i \blacktriangleright N_i.P_i$ becomes $\mathbb{P}_j \blacktriangleright N_j.P_j \oplus \mathsf{N}$ with $\mathsf{N} = \bigoplus_{i\in I\setminus\{j\}} \mathbb{P}_i \blacktriangleright N_i.P_i$. To simplify the reduction rules in Fig. 1, we allow M and N to be empty mixed/probabilistic choices. We allow to unify and split similar summands of probabilistic choices, i.e., $\mathbb{P}_i \blacktriangleright N.P \oplus \mathbb{P}_j \blacktriangleright N.P = (\mathbb{P}_i + \mathbb{P}_j) \blacktriangleright N.P$. In outputs and inputs we sometimes use $\langle\rangle$ instead of $\langle\bot\rangle$ and $()$ instead of (z), if the respective argument is irrelevant.

Example 2 (Running Example—Syntax). The unrefined interface of the system in Example 1 can be implemented as a process $P_\mathcal{I} = (\nu s)(P_\mathbf{p} \mid P_\mathbf{c} \mid P_\mathbf{w})$, whose components represent the participants of the protocol: **plaintiff** $P_\mathbf{p}$, **court** $P_\mathbf{c}$, and **witness** $P_\mathbf{w}$. The implementations of these processes are given as

$$P_\mathbf{p} = s[\mathbf{p}]{\triangleright}\mathbf{p}{\to}\mathbf{j}\,!\,\mathtt{lws}\langle\rangle.s[\mathbf{p}]{\triangleright}\mathbf{p}{\leftarrow}\mathbf{j}\,?\,\mathtt{glt}(x)$$

$$P_\mathtt{rls} = s[\mathbf{j}]{\triangleright}\mathbf{j}{\to}\mathbf{w}\,!\,\mathtt{rls}\langle\rangle$$

$$P_\mathbf{c} = s[\overline{\mathbf{c}}]{\triangleright}\mathbf{j}{\leftarrow}\mathbf{p}\,?\,\mathtt{lws}().s[\overline{\mathbf{c}}]{\triangleright}\left\{\begin{array}{l} 0.35 \blacktriangleright \mathbf{j}{\to}\mathbf{p}\,!\,\mathtt{glt}\langle\top\rangle.P_\mathtt{rls} \\[4pt] \oplus\quad 0.35 \blacktriangleright \mathbf{j}{\to}\mathbf{p}\,!\,\mathtt{glt}\langle\bot\rangle.P_\mathtt{rls} \\[4pt] \oplus\quad 0.3 \blacktriangleright \mathbf{j}{\to}\mathbf{w}\,!\,\mathtt{rqs}\langle\rangle.s[\overline{\mathbf{c}}]{\triangleright}\mathbf{j}{\leftarrow}\mathbf{w}\,?\,\mathtt{st}(). \\[4pt] \hphantom{\oplus\quad 0.3 \blacktriangleright \mathbf{j}{\to}\mathbf{w}\,!\,\mathtt{rqs}} s[\overline{\mathbf{c}}]{\triangleright}\mathbf{j}{\to}\mathbf{p}\,!\,\mathtt{glt}\langle\bot\rangle \end{array}\right.$$

$$P_\mathbf{w} = s[\mathbf{w}]{\triangleright}\left\{\begin{array}{l} \mathbf{w}{\leftarrow}\mathbf{j}\,?\,\mathtt{mtg}().s[\mathbf{w}]{\triangleright}\mathbf{w}{\to}\mathbf{j}\,!\,\mathtt{st}\langle\rangle \\[4pt] +\quad \mathbf{w}{\leftarrow}\mathbf{j}\,?\,\mathtt{rls}() \end{array}\right.$$

where the role set of the channel $s[\overline{\mathbf{c}}]$ used by the **court** is $\overline{\mathbf{c}} = \{\mathbf{j}, \mathbf{d}\}$, as it embodies both the **judge** and the **defendant**. Note that $\mathbf{d}$ will only appear in the refinement below. Also the first role in outputs and inputs as $\mathbf{p}$ in $s[\mathbf{p}]{\triangleright}\mathbf{p}{\to}\mathbf{j}\,!\,\mathtt{lws}\langle\rangle.\,\ldots$ may seem redundant as it also appears as part of the channel. This information is used to simplify the subtyping rules introduced later (see also Remark 1).

$$s[\overline{\mathbf{r_2}}] \rhd (\mathbb{P} \blacktriangleright \mathbf{q}{\rightarrow}\mathbf{p}\,!\,l\langle v\rangle.Q \oplus \mathsf{N}) + \mathsf{M}_Q \mid s[\overline{\mathbf{r_1}}] \rhd \mathbf{p}{\leftarrow}\mathbf{q}\,?\,l(x).P + \mathsf{M}_P$$
$$\longrightarrow_\mathbb{P} Q \mid P[x \mapsto v] \quad \text{[R-Com]}$$

$$c \rhd (\mathbb{P} \blacktriangleright \tau.P \oplus \mathsf{N}) + \mathsf{M} \longrightarrow_\mathbb{P} P \quad \text{[R-}\tau\text{]} \qquad \mathtt{def}\ D\ \mathtt{in}\ 0 \longrightarrow_1 0 \quad \text{[R-Def-0]}$$

$$\mathtt{if}\ \top\ \mathtt{then}\ P\ \mathtt{else}\ Q \longrightarrow_1 P \quad \text{[R-Cond-}\top\text{]} \qquad \mathtt{if}\ \bot\ \mathtt{then}\ P\ \mathtt{else}\ Q \longrightarrow_1 Q \quad \text{[R-Cond-}\bot\text{]}$$

$$\frac{X(\widetilde{x};\widetilde{c}) \overset{\mathtt{def}}{=} P \in D}{\mathtt{def}\ D\ \mathtt{in}\ (X\langle\widetilde{v},\widetilde{c}\rangle \mid Q) \longrightarrow_1 \mathtt{def}\ D\ \mathtt{in}\ (P[\widetilde{x} \mapsto \widetilde{v}] \mid Q)} \quad \text{[R-Def]}$$

$$\frac{P \longrightarrow_\mathbb{P} P'}{P \mid Q \longrightarrow_\mathbb{P} P' \mid Q} \quad \text{[R-Par]} \qquad \frac{P \equiv P' \quad P' \longrightarrow_\mathbb{P} Q' \quad Q' \equiv Q}{P \longrightarrow_\mathbb{P} Q} \quad \text{[R-Struct]}$$

$$\frac{P \longrightarrow_\mathbb{P} P'}{(\nu s)P \longrightarrow_\mathbb{P} (\nu s)P'} \quad \text{[R-Res]} \qquad \frac{P \longrightarrow_\mathbb{P} P'}{\mathtt{def}\ D\ \mathtt{in}\ P \longrightarrow_\mathbb{P} \mathtt{def}\ D\ \mathtt{in}\ P'} \quad \text{[R-Def-In]}$$

Fig. 1. Probabilistic Reduction Semantics.

The refined system can be implemented as $P_\mathcal{R} = (\nu s)(P_\mathbf{p} \mid P_\mathbf{j} \mid P_\mathbf{d} \mid P_\mathbf{w})$. The processes $P_\mathbf{p}$ and $P_\mathbf{w}$ (and $P_\mathtt{rls}$) stay the same and we have:

$$P_\mathbf{d} = s[\mathbf{d}] \rhd \begin{cases} 0.5 \blacktriangleright \mathbf{d}{\rightarrow}\mathbf{j}\,!\,\mathtt{wk}\langle\rangle \\ \oplus\ 0.2 \blacktriangleright \mathbf{d}{\rightarrow}\mathbf{j}\,!\,\mathtt{str}\langle\rangle \\ \oplus\ 0.3 \blacktriangleright \mathbf{d}{\rightarrow}\mathbf{j}\,!\,\mathtt{wit}\langle\rangle \end{cases}$$

$$P_\mathbf{j} = s[\mathbf{j}] \rhd \mathbf{j}{\leftarrow}\mathbf{p}\,?\,\mathtt{lws}().s[\mathbf{j}] \rhd \begin{cases} \mathbf{j}{\leftarrow}\mathbf{d}\,?\,\mathtt{wk}().s[\mathbf{j}] \rhd \begin{cases} 0.7 \blacktriangleright \mathbf{j}{\rightarrow}\mathbf{p}\,!\,\mathtt{glt}\langle\top\rangle.P_\mathtt{rls} \\ \oplus\ 0.3 \blacktriangleright \mathbf{j}{\rightarrow}\mathbf{p}\,!\,\mathtt{glt}\langle\bot\rangle.P_\mathtt{rls} \end{cases} \\ +\ \mathbf{j}{\leftarrow}\mathbf{d}\,?\,\mathtt{str}().s[\mathbf{j}] \rhd \mathbf{j}{\rightarrow}\mathbf{p}\,!\,\mathtt{glt}\langle\bot\rangle.P_\mathtt{rls} \\ +\ \mathbf{j}{\leftarrow}\mathbf{d}\,?\,\mathtt{wit}().s[\mathbf{j}] \rhd \mathbf{j}{\rightarrow}\mathbf{w}\,!\,\mathtt{rqs}\langle\rangle. \\ \qquad s[\mathbf{j}] \rhd \mathbf{j}{\leftarrow}\mathbf{w}\,?\,\mathtt{st}().s[\mathbf{j}] \rhd \mathbf{j}{\rightarrow}\mathbf{p}\,!\,\mathtt{glt}\langle\bot\rangle \end{cases}$$

for the **d**efendant and **j**udge. ◯

Definition 2 (Structural Congruence $\equiv$). *Structural congruence $\equiv$ is the smallest congruence on processes that includes alpha conversion $\equiv_\alpha$ and:*

$$P \mid 0 \equiv P \qquad P \mid Q \equiv Q \mid P \qquad (P \mid Q) \mid R \equiv P \mid (Q \mid R) \qquad (\nu s)0 \equiv 0$$

$$(\nu s)(\nu s')P \equiv (\nu s')(\nu s)P \qquad P \mid (\nu s)Q \equiv (\nu s)(P \mid Q) \quad \textit{if } s \notin \mathtt{fs}(P)$$

$$\mathtt{def}\ D\ \mathtt{in}\ (\nu s)P \equiv (\nu s)\mathtt{def}\ D\ \mathtt{in}\ P \quad \textit{if } s \notin \mathtt{fs}(D)$$

$$(\mathtt{def}\ D\ \mathtt{in}\ P) \mid Q \equiv \mathtt{def}\ D\ \mathtt{in}\ (P \mid Q) \quad \textit{if } \mathtt{dpv}(D) \cap \mathtt{fpv}(Q) = \emptyset$$

$$\begin{aligned} \mathtt{def}\ D\ \mathtt{in}\ (\mathtt{def}\ D'\ \mathtt{in}\ P) \\ \equiv \mathtt{def}\ D \cup D'\ \mathtt{in}\ P \end{aligned} \quad \textit{if}\ \begin{aligned} \mathtt{dpv}(D) \cap \mathtt{dpv}(D') = \emptyset\ \textit{and} \\ \mathtt{fpv}(D) \cap \mathtt{dpv}(D') = \emptyset \end{aligned}$$

The reduction semantics is given as the relation $P \longrightarrow_\mathbb{P} P'$ in Fig. 1, meaning process P reduces to the continuation P' with probability $\mathbb{P}$. Rule [R-Com] allows communication between two parallel choices, one containing an input and the other an output with matching roles $\mathbf{p}, \mathbf{q}$ and label l, where the probability $\mathbb{P}$ of this step is determined by the sender. With $[\text{R-}\tau]$ an internal action is performed with the probability $\mathbb{P}$. Rule $[\text{R-Def-0}]$ allows to garbage collect disused declarations. The remaining rules are standard.

We write $P \longrightarrow_\mathbb{P}$ if $P \longrightarrow_\mathbb{P} P'$ for some P' and $P \nrightarrow$ if there is no $\mathbb{P}$ such that $P \longrightarrow_\mathbb{P}$. Let $\Longrightarrow_\mathbb{P}$ be inductively defined as (a) $P \Longrightarrow_1 P$ and (b) if $P \longrightarrow_{\mathbb{P}_1} P'$ and $P' \Longrightarrow_{\mathbb{P}_2} P''$ then $P \Longrightarrow_{\mathbb{P}_1\mathbb{P}_2} P''$.

Example 3 (Running Example—Semantics). The **plaintiff** of Example 2 sends the *lawsuit* to the **court**. With probability 35%, $\mathbf{c}$ sends the verdict *guilty* to the **plaintiff** and releases the **witness**.

$$P_\mathcal{I} \longrightarrow_1 (\nu s)\big(P'_\mathbf{p} \mid P'_\mathbf{c} \mid P_\mathbf{w}\big) \longrightarrow_{0.35} (\nu s)\big(P''_\mathbf{p} \mid P''_\mathbf{c} \mid P_\mathbf{w}\big) \longrightarrow_1 \mathbf{0}$$

$$P'_\mathbf{c} = s[\bar{\mathbf{c}}] \triangleright \begin{cases} & 0.35 \blacktriangleright \mathbf{j} \to \mathbf{p}\,!\,\mathtt{glt}\langle\top\rangle.s[\bar{\mathbf{c}}] \triangleright \mathbf{j} \to \mathbf{w}\,!\,\mathtt{rls}\langle\rangle \\ \oplus & 0.35 \blacktriangleright \mathbf{j} \to \mathbf{p}\,!\,\mathtt{glt}\langle\bot\rangle.s[\bar{\mathbf{c}}] \triangleright \mathbf{j} \to \mathbf{w}\,!\,\mathtt{rls}\langle\rangle \\ \oplus & 0.3 \blacktriangleright \mathbf{j} \to \mathbf{w}\,!\,\mathtt{rqs}\langle\rangle.s[\bar{\mathbf{c}}] \triangleright \mathbf{j} \leftarrow \mathbf{w}\,?\,\mathtt{st}().s[\bar{\mathbf{c}}] \triangleright \mathbf{j} \to \mathbf{p}\,!\,\mathtt{glt}\langle\bot\rangle \end{cases}$$

$$P'_\mathbf{p} = s[\mathbf{p}] \triangleright \mathbf{p} \leftarrow \mathbf{j}\,?\,\mathtt{glt}(x) \qquad P''_\mathbf{p} = \mathbf{0} \qquad P''_\mathbf{c} = s[\bar{\mathbf{c}}] \triangleright \mathbf{j} \to \mathbf{w}\,!\,\mathtt{rls}\langle\rangle$$

Hence, $P_\mathcal{I} \Longrightarrow_{0.35} \mathbf{0}$, where the **court** finds the **defendant** *guilty*. In the refined system the initial *lawsuit* message may be followed by the **defendant** delivering a *weak defense* to the **judge** with 50%.

$$P_\mathcal{R} \longrightarrow_1 (\nu s)\big(P'_\mathbf{p} \mid P'_\mathbf{j} \mid P_\mathbf{d} \mid P_\mathbf{w}\big) \longrightarrow_{0.5} (\nu s)\big(P'_\mathbf{p} \mid P''_\mathbf{j} \mid P'_\mathbf{d} \mid P_\mathbf{w}\big)$$

$$P'_\mathbf{p} = s[\mathbf{p}] \triangleright \mathbf{p} \leftarrow \mathbf{j}\,?\,\mathtt{glt}(x)$$

$$P'_\mathbf{d} = \mathbf{0} \qquad P''_\mathbf{j} = s[\mathbf{j}] \triangleright \begin{cases} 0.7 \blacktriangleright \mathbf{j} \to \mathbf{p}\,!\,\mathtt{glt}\langle\top\rangle.s[\mathbf{j}] \triangleright \mathbf{j} \to \mathbf{w}\,!\,\mathtt{rls}\langle\rangle \\ \oplus\ 0.3 \blacktriangleright \mathbf{j} \to \mathbf{p}\,!\,\mathtt{glt}\langle\bot\rangle.s[\mathbf{j}] \triangleright \mathbf{j} \to \mathbf{w}\,!\,\mathtt{rls}\langle\rangle \end{cases}$$

The **judge** then sends *guilty* to the **plaintiff** with 70% and releases the **witness**.

$$(\nu s)\big(P'_\mathbf{p} \mid P''_\mathbf{j} \mid P'_\mathbf{d} \mid P_\mathbf{w}\big) \longrightarrow_{0.7} (\nu s)\big(P''_\mathbf{p} \mid P'''_\mathbf{j} \mid P'_\mathbf{d} \mid P_\mathbf{w}\big) \longrightarrow_1 \mathbf{0}$$

$$P''_\mathbf{p} = \mathbf{0} \qquad P'''_\mathbf{j} = s[\mathbf{j}] \triangleright \mathbf{j} \to \mathbf{w}\,!\,\mathtt{rls}\langle\rangle$$

$$P_\mathbf{w} = s[\mathbf{w}] \triangleright \begin{cases} & \mathbf{w} \leftarrow \mathbf{j}\,?\,\mathtt{mtg}().s[\mathbf{w}] \triangleright \mathbf{w} \to \mathbf{j}\,!\,\mathtt{st}\langle\rangle \\ + & \mathbf{w} \leftarrow \mathbf{j}\,?\,\mathtt{rls}() \end{cases}$$

Again we have $P_\mathcal{R} \Longrightarrow_{0.35} \mathbf{0}$, where the **judge** finds the **defendant** *guilty*.   ○

Sometimes, *several* transition sequences of the refined system correspond to *one* sequence of the interface system. For instance the sequence of $P_\mathcal{I}$ that leads to *not guilty* without calling the **witness** with probability 0.35 is refined into two sequences with probabilities 0.15 and 0.2, respectively. We observe this in both processes and types, whenever probabilistic branches with the same continuations are summed up in the interface.

3   Probabilistic Mixed Choice Multiparty Session Types

Definition 3 (Type Syntax).

$$
\begin{array}{lll}
U ::= & \mathsf{nat} \mid \mathsf{bool} & \textit{(base types for numbers and booleans)} \\[4pt]
T, T_i ::= & \mathbf{end} \mid t \mid (\mu t)T & \textit{(inaction type, recursion variable, recursion)} \\[4pt]
& \mid \displaystyle\sum_{i \in I} L_i \mid L \mid H.T & \textit{(mixed choice type with a finite } I \neq \emptyset, \textit{ output)} \\[8pt]
L, L_i ::= & \mathsf{In} \mid \mathsf{Out} & \textit{(mixed choice modes)} \\[4pt]
\mathsf{In} ::= & \mathbf{p} \leftarrow \mathbf{q}\,?\,l(U).T & \textit{(}\mathbf{p}\textit{ receives msg. } l \textit{ with type } U \textit{ from } \mathbf{q}\textit{)} \\[4pt]
\mathsf{Out} ::= & \displaystyle\bigoplus_{i \in I} \mathbb{P}_i \blacktriangleright H_i.T_i & \textit{(prob. choice with finite } I \neq \emptyset \textit{ and } \displaystyle\sum_{i \in I} \mathbb{P}_i \leq 1\textit{)} \\[8pt]
H, H_i ::= & \mathbf{p} \rightarrow \mathbf{q}\,!\,l\langle U\rangle \mid \tau & \textit{(}\mathbf{p}\textit{ sends msg. } l \textit{ with type } U \textit{ to } \mathbf{q}, \textit{ internal action)} \\[4pt]
\Delta ::= & \emptyset \mid \Delta, c : T & \textit{(local context)} \\[4pt]
\Lambda ::= & \Delta \mid c \cdot \Delta & \textit{(local context with active channel, } c \in \Delta\textit{)}
\end{array}
$$

The syntax of types follows the syntax of processes. A local context Δ contains assignments $c:T$ of channels c to their type T. Let $c \in \Delta$ iff $c:T \in \Delta$ for some T. If $s[\overline{\mathbf{r}}] \in \Delta$ and $\mathbf{p} \in \overline{\mathbf{r}}$, we write $\mathbf{p} \in \Delta$ and $s \in \Delta$. Types in local contexts are treated equi-recursively, i.e., $\Delta, c:(\mu t)T = \Delta, c:T[t \mapsto (\mu t)T]$. Additionally, we consider a type assignment of a sum with empty index set to be inaction and abstract from inaction, i.e., $\Delta, s[\overline{\mathbf{r}}]:\sum_{i \in \emptyset} L_i = \Delta, s[\overline{\mathbf{r}}]:\mathbf{end} = \Delta$. Composition of local contexts is required to be linear, i.e., Δ_1, Δ_2 is defined iff $\overline{\mathbf{r}_1} \cap \overline{\mathbf{r}_2} = \emptyset$ for all $s[\overline{\mathbf{r}_1}] \in \Delta_1$ and $s[\overline{\mathbf{r}_2}] \in \Delta_2$. A Λ is a local context or a local context with an *active channel*. The latter is introduced by the subtyping rules and appears only within the derivation trees of subtyping (not in type judgements).

We inherit for choice types the abbreviations defined for choices in processes, except that we *do not* allow to omit the probability 1, i.e., $T = 1 \blacktriangleright H.T'$ is *not* the same as $H.T'$. This distinction is necessary for the subtyping rules. We overload the notations M and N to also use them on choices in types. We again allow to unify and split similar summands of probabilistic choices, i.e., $\mathbb{P}_i \blacktriangleright H.T \oplus \mathbb{P}_j \blacktriangleright H.T = (\mathbb{P}_i + \mathbb{P}_j) \blacktriangleright H.T$. Note that a refinement may split an output into several cases with smaller probabilities.

We sometimes abbreviate (bool) by $()$ and $\langle \mathsf{bool} \rangle$ by $\langle\rangle$ and omit trailing inaction types. Similar to [28], we allow for mixed and probabilistic choices to combine the same label with different messages and/or continuations, but require to combine the same label with the same types of message load and continuation. The subtyping rules decompose types in a stepwise manner. Hence, in subtyping trees we also have types such as probabilistic choices with $\sum_{i \in I} \mathbb{P}_i \leq 1$ or the output type $H.T$. A type T is *well-formed* if (a) all outputs H are part of a probabilistic choice, (b) if for all probabilistic choices $\sum_{i \in I} \mathbb{P}_i = 1$, and (c) for all $\mathbf{p} \leftarrow \mathbf{q}\,?\,l(U_i).T_i + \mathbf{p} \leftarrow \mathbf{q}\,?\,l(U_j).T_j$ and $\mathbb{P}_i \blacktriangleright \mathbf{p} \rightarrow \mathbf{q}\,!\,l\langle U_i\rangle.T_i \oplus \mathbb{P}_j \blacktriangleright \mathbf{p} \rightarrow \mathbf{q}\,!\,l\langle U_j\rangle.T_j$ we have $U_i = U_j$ and $T_i = T_j$.

$$\Gamma \vdash 1, 2, .. : \mathsf{nat}\ [\text{Nat}] \quad \Gamma \vdash \top, \bot : \mathsf{bool}\ [\text{Bool}] \quad \Gamma, x : U \vdash x : U\ [\text{Base}] \quad \Gamma \vdash \mathbf{0} \triangleright \emptyset\ [\text{T-0}]$$

$$\frac{\mathsf{safe}(\{s[\overline{\mathbf{r}_i}] : T_i\}_{i \in I}) \quad s \notin \Delta \quad \Gamma \vdash P \triangleright \Delta, \{s[\overline{\mathbf{r}_i}] : T_i\}_{i \in I}}{\Gamma \vdash (\nu s) P \triangleright \Delta}\ [\text{T-Res}]$$

$$\frac{\Gamma \vdash v : \mathsf{bool} \quad \Gamma \vdash P \triangleright \Delta \quad \Gamma \vdash Q \triangleright \Delta}{\Gamma \vdash \mathtt{if}\ v\ \mathtt{then}\ P\ \mathtt{else}\ Q \triangleright \Delta}\ [\text{T-If}] \qquad \frac{\Gamma \vdash P \triangleright \Delta_1 \quad \Gamma \vdash Q \triangleright \Delta_2}{\Gamma \vdash P \mid Q \triangleright \Delta_1, \Delta_2}\ [\text{T-Par}]$$

$$\frac{\Gamma, X : \left\langle \widetilde{U}, T_1, .., T_n \right\rangle, \widetilde{x} : \widetilde{U} \vdash P \triangleright c_1 : T_1, .., c_n : T_n \quad \Gamma, X : \left\langle \widetilde{U}, T_1, .., T_n \right\rangle \vdash Q \triangleright \Delta}{\Gamma \vdash \mathtt{def}\ X(\widetilde{x}; c_1, .., c_n) \stackrel{\mathtt{def}}{=} P\ \mathtt{in}\ Q \triangleright \Delta}\ [\text{T-Def}]$$

$$\frac{\Gamma \vdash \widetilde{v} : \widetilde{U}}{\Gamma, X : \left\langle \widetilde{U}, T_1, .., T_n \right\rangle \vdash X \langle \widetilde{v}, c_1, .., c_n \rangle \triangleright c_1 : T_1, .., c_n : T_n}\ [\text{T-Var}]$$

$$\frac{\forall i \in I.\ \Gamma \vdash c \triangleright M_i \triangleright \Delta, c : L_i}{\Gamma \vdash c \sum_{i \in I} M_i \triangleright \Delta, c : \sum_{i \in I} L_i}\ [\text{T-Sum}] \qquad \frac{\Gamma \vdash P \triangleright \Delta' \quad \Delta' \leq_1 \Delta}{\Gamma \vdash P \triangleright \Delta}\ [\text{T-Sub}]$$

$$\frac{\Gamma \vdash P \triangleright \Delta, c : T}{\Gamma \vdash c \triangleright \mathbb{P} \blacktriangleright \tau.P \triangleright \Delta, c : \mathbb{P} \blacktriangleright \tau.T}\ [\text{T-}\tau]$$

$$\frac{\mathbf{p} \in c \quad \Gamma, x : U \vdash P \triangleright \Delta, c : T}{\Gamma \vdash c \triangleright \mathbf{p} {\leftarrow} \mathbf{q}\,?\,l(x).P \triangleright \Delta, c : \mathbf{p} {\leftarrow} \mathbf{q}\,?\,l(U).T}\ [\text{T-Inp}]$$

$$\frac{\mathbf{p} \in c \quad \Gamma \vdash v : U \quad \Gamma \vdash P \triangleright \Delta, c : T}{\Gamma \vdash c \triangleright \mathbb{P} \blacktriangleright \mathbf{p} {\rightarrow} \mathbf{q}\,!\,l \langle v \rangle.P \triangleright \Delta, c : \mathbb{P} \blacktriangleright \mathbf{p} {\rightarrow} \mathbf{q}\,!\,l \langle U \rangle.T}\ [\text{T-Out}]$$

$$\frac{\forall i \in I.\ \Gamma \vdash c \triangleright \mathbb{P}_i \blacktriangleright N_i.P_i \triangleright \Delta, c : \mathbb{P}_i \blacktriangleright H_i.T_i}{\Gamma \vdash c \triangleright \bigoplus_{i \in I} \mathbb{P}_i \blacktriangleright N_i.P_i \triangleright \Delta, c : \bigoplus_{i \in I} \mathbb{P}_i \blacktriangleright H_i.T_i}\ [\text{T-Prob}]$$

Fig. 2. Typing Rules.

Definition 4 (Global Environment).

$$\Gamma ::= \emptyset \ \Big|\ \Gamma, x : U \ \Big|\ \Gamma, X : \langle \widetilde{U}, \widetilde{T} \rangle \qquad \textit{(empty set, variable, process variable)}$$

Global environments Γ contain assignments $x : U$ of variables to base types and $X : \langle \widetilde{U}, \widetilde{T} \rangle$ of process constants to base types and the types of the channels used in the respective declaration. A type judgement $\Gamma \vdash P \triangleright \Delta$ holds if it can be derived from the typing rules in Fig. 2, where we require that Δ contains only well-formed types.

The typing rules are mostly standard. Probabilistic choices are typed by [T-Prob] similarly to how sums are typed. [T-Out] and [T-τ] for outputs and τ additionally check that the probabilities used in the process coincide with those in the type. The predicate $\mathsf{safe}()$ used in [T-Res] is introduced with the properties of the type system in Sect. 5. Since the novel subtyping relation $\leq_{\mathbb{P}}$ (used in [T-Sub]) is our main contribution, we introduce it in its own Sect. 4.

Example 4 (Running Example—Types). The processes of Example 2 can be typed by the types $T_{\mathbf{p}}, T_{\mathbf{c}}, T_{\mathbf{w}}, T_{\mathbf{j}}$, and $T_{\mathbf{d}}$, such that $\emptyset \vdash P_{\mathcal{I}} \triangleright \Delta_{\mathcal{I}}$ with local context $\Delta_{\mathcal{I}} = s[\mathbf{p}] : T_{\mathbf{p}}, s[\overline{\mathbf{c}}] : T_{\mathbf{c}}, s[\mathbf{w}] : T_{\mathbf{w}}$ for the interface and $\emptyset \vdash P_{\mathcal{R}} \triangleright \Delta_{\mathcal{R}}$ with local context $\Delta_{\mathcal{R}} = s[\mathbf{p}] : T_{\mathbf{p}}, s[\mathbf{j}] : T_{\mathbf{j}}, s[\mathbf{d}] : T_{\mathbf{d}}, s[\mathbf{w}] : T_{\mathbf{w}}$ for the refinement.

$$s[\overline{\mathbf{r}}] : \mathbf{p} \leftarrow \mathbf{q}\,?\,l(U).T + \mathsf{M} \xrightarrow{\;s\,:\,\mathbf{p} \leftarrow \mathbf{q}\,?\,l(U)\;}_1 s[\overline{\mathbf{r}}] : T \quad [\text{TR-Inp}]$$

$$s[\overline{\mathbf{r}}] : (\mathbb{P} \blacktriangleright \mathbf{p} \rightarrow \mathbf{q}\,!\,l\langle U\rangle.T \oplus \mathsf{N}) + \mathsf{M} \xrightarrow{\;s\,:\,\mathbf{p} \rightarrow \mathbf{q}\,!\,l\langle U\rangle\;}_\mathbb{P} s[\overline{\mathbf{r}}] : T \quad [\text{TR-Out}]$$

$$s[\overline{\mathbf{r}}] : \mathbf{p} \rightarrow \mathbf{q}\,!\,l\langle U\rangle.T \xrightarrow{\;s\,:\,\mathbf{p} \rightarrow \mathbf{q}\,!\,l\langle U\rangle\;}_1 s[\overline{\mathbf{r}}] : T \quad [\text{TR}\Lambda\text{-Out}]$$

$$\Delta, s[\overline{\mathbf{r}}] : (\mathbb{P} \blacktriangleright \tau.T \oplus \mathsf{N}) + \mathsf{M} \xrightarrow{\;s\,:\,\tau\;}_\mathbb{P} \Delta, s[\overline{\mathbf{r}}] : T \quad [\text{TR-}\tau]$$

$$s[\overline{\mathbf{r}}] \cdot (\Delta, s[\overline{\mathbf{r}}] : (\mathbb{P} \blacktriangleright \tau.T \oplus \mathsf{N}) + \mathsf{M}) \xrightarrow{\;s\,:\,\tau\;}_\mathbb{P} \Delta, s[\overline{\mathbf{r}}] : T \quad [\text{TR}\Lambda\text{-}\tau]$$

$$s[\overline{\mathbf{r}}] \cdot (\Delta, s[\overline{\mathbf{r}}] : \tau.T) \xrightarrow{\;s\,:\,\tau\;}_1 \Delta, s[\overline{\mathbf{r}}] : T \quad [\text{TR}\Lambda\text{-}\tau\text{-2}]$$

$$\frac{c_1 : T_1 \xrightarrow{\;s\,:\,\mathbf{p} \rightarrow \mathbf{q}\,!\,l\langle U\rangle\;}_\mathbb{P} c_1 : T_1' \quad c_2 : T_2 \xrightarrow{\;s\,:\,\mathbf{q} \leftarrow \mathbf{p}\,?\,l(U)\;}_1 c_2 : T_2'}{\Delta, c_1 : T_1, c_2 : T_2 \xrightarrow{\;s\,:\,\mathbf{pq}\,:\,l\langle U\rangle\;}_\mathbb{P} \Delta, c_1 : T_1', c_2 : T_2'} \quad [\text{TR-Com}]$$

$$\frac{c_1 : T_1 \xrightarrow{\;s\,:\,\mathbf{p} \rightarrow \mathbf{q}\,!\,l\langle U\rangle\;}_\mathbb{P} c_1 : T_1' \quad c_2 : T_2 \xrightarrow{\;s\,:\,\mathbf{q} \leftarrow \mathbf{p}\,?\,l(U)\;}_1 c_2 : T_2'}{c_1 \cdot (\Delta, c_1 : T_1, c_2 : T_2) \xrightarrow{\;s\,:\,\mathbf{pq}\,:\,l\langle U\rangle\;}_\mathbb{P} \Delta, c_1 : T_1', c_2 : T_2'} \quad [\text{TR}\Lambda\text{-Com}]$$

Fig. 3. Labeled Transitions of Local Contexts (with an Active Channel).

$$T_\mathbf{p} = \mathbf{p} \rightarrow \mathbf{j}\,!\,\mathtt{lws}\langle\rangle.\mathbf{p} \leftarrow \mathbf{j}\,?\,\mathtt{glt}(\mathtt{bool})$$

$$T_\mathbf{c} = \mathbf{j} \leftarrow \mathbf{p}\,?\,\mathtt{lws}().\begin{cases} 0.7 \blacktriangleright \mathbf{j} \rightarrow \mathbf{p}\,!\,\mathtt{glt}\langle\mathtt{bool}\rangle.1 \blacktriangleright \mathbf{j} \rightarrow \mathbf{w}\,!\,\mathtt{rls}\langle\rangle \\ \oplus\;\; 0.3 \blacktriangleright \mathbf{j} \rightarrow \mathbf{w}\,!\,\mathtt{rqs}\langle\rangle.\mathbf{j} \leftarrow \mathbf{w}\,?\,\mathtt{st}().1 \blacktriangleright \mathbf{j} \rightarrow \mathbf{p}\,!\,\mathtt{glt}\langle\mathtt{bool}\rangle \end{cases}$$

$$T_\mathbf{w} = \begin{cases} \mathbf{w} \leftarrow \mathbf{j}\,?\,\mathtt{mtg}().\mathbf{w} \rightarrow \mathbf{j}\,!\,\mathtt{st}\langle\rangle \\ +\;\; \mathbf{w} \leftarrow \mathbf{j}\,?\,\mathtt{rls}() \end{cases} \qquad T_\mathbf{d} = \begin{cases} 0.5 \blacktriangleright \mathbf{d} \rightarrow \mathbf{j}\,!\,\mathtt{wk}\langle\rangle \\ \oplus\;\; 0.2 \blacktriangleright \mathbf{d} \rightarrow \mathbf{j}\,!\,\mathtt{str}\langle\rangle \\ \oplus\;\; 0.3 \blacktriangleright \mathbf{d} \rightarrow \mathbf{j}\,!\,\mathtt{wit}\langle\rangle \end{cases}$$

$$T_\mathbf{j} = \mathbf{j} \leftarrow \mathbf{p}\,?\,\mathtt{lws}().\begin{cases} \mathbf{j} \leftarrow \mathbf{d}\,?\,\mathtt{wk}().1 \blacktriangleright \mathbf{j} \rightarrow \mathbf{p}\,!\,\mathtt{glt}\langle\mathtt{bool}\rangle.1 \blacktriangleright \mathbf{j} \rightarrow \mathbf{w}\,!\,\mathtt{rls}\langle\rangle \\ +\;\; \mathbf{j} \leftarrow \mathbf{d}\,?\,\mathtt{str}().1 \blacktriangleright \mathbf{j} \rightarrow \mathbf{p}\,!\,\mathtt{glt}\langle\mathtt{bool}\rangle.1 \blacktriangleright \mathbf{j} \rightarrow \mathbf{w}\,!\,\mathtt{rls}\langle\rangle \\ +\;\; \mathbf{j} \leftarrow \mathbf{d}\,?\,\mathtt{wit}().1 \blacktriangleright \mathbf{j} \rightarrow \mathbf{w}\,!\,\mathtt{rqs}\langle\rangle. \\ \qquad\qquad \mathbf{j} \leftarrow \mathbf{w}\,?\,\mathtt{st}().1 \blacktriangleright \mathbf{j} \rightarrow \mathbf{p}\,!\,\mathtt{glt}\langle\mathtt{bool}\rangle \end{cases} \quad \bigcirc$$

Figure 3 presents rules for transitions of local contexts (the black rules without Λ in their name) and local contexts with an active channel (all rules). These rules map reductions of processes on their respective types, i.e., are similar to the reduction rules in Fig. 1. Labelled rules are used on types to highlight the main actors of a step. The labels α in these rules are of the form $s : \mathbf{p} \leftarrow \mathbf{q}\,?\,l(U)$ for inputs, $s : \mathbf{p} \rightarrow \mathbf{q}\,!\,l\langle U\rangle$ for outputs, $s : \tau$, or $s : \mathbf{pq} : l\langle U\rangle$ for communication (from $\mathbf{p}$ to $\mathbf{q}$). We write $\Lambda \xrightarrow{\alpha}_\mathbb{P}$ if $\Lambda \xrightarrow{\alpha}_\mathbb{P} \Lambda'$ for some Λ'. Moreover, we write $\Lambda \mapsto_\mathbb{P} \Lambda'$ if $\Lambda \xrightarrow{\;s\,:\,\mathbf{pq}\,:\,l\langle U\rangle\;}_\mathbb{P} \Lambda'$ or $\Lambda \xrightarrow{\;s\,:\,\tau\;}_\mathbb{P} \Lambda'$ and $\Lambda \not\mapsto$ if there are no Λ' and $\mathbb{P}$ such that $\Lambda \mapsto_\mathbb{P} \Lambda'$. Let $\mapsto_\mathbb{P}^*$ be inductively defined as (a) $\Lambda \mapsto_1^* \Lambda$ and (b) if $\Lambda \mapsto_{\mathbb{P}_1} \Lambda'$ and $\Lambda' \mapsto_{\mathbb{P}_2}^* \Lambda''$ then $\Lambda \mapsto_{\mathbb{P}_1\mathbb{P}_2}^* \Lambda''$.

4   Subtyping with Refinement and Probabilities

Our subtyping relation $\leq_\mathbb{P}$ is presented in the Figs. 4 and 5. The double lines indicate co-inductive rules. The rules in Fig. 4 split contexts and their choices

$$\frac{\bigcup_{k\in[1..n]} J_k \neq \emptyset \quad \forall k \in [1..n].\ s[\overline{\mathbf{r_k}}] \cdot \Delta \leq_{\mathbb{P}} s[\overline{\mathbf{r}}] : \sum_{j\in J_k} L_j}{\Delta = s[\overline{\mathbf{r_1}}] : T_1, \ldots, s[\overline{\mathbf{r_n}}] : T_n \leq_{\mathbb{P}} s[\overline{\mathbf{r}}] : \sum_{j\in J_1} L_j + \ldots + \sum_{j\in J_n} L_j} \ [\text{S-}\Sigma\text{-1}]$$

$$\frac{I \cup J \neq \emptyset \quad \begin{array}{c} s[\overline{\mathbf{r_1}}] \cdot \left(\Delta, s[\overline{\mathbf{r_1}}] : \sum_{i\in I'} \mathsf{In}_i\right) \leq_{\mathbb{P}} s[\overline{\mathbf{r_2}}] : \sum_{i\in I} L_i \\ s[\overline{\mathbf{r_1}}] \cdot \left(\Delta, s[\overline{\mathbf{r_1}}] : \sum_{j\in J'} \mathsf{Out}_j\right) \leq_{\mathbb{P}} s[\overline{\mathbf{r_2}}] : \sum_{j\in J} L_j \end{array}}{s[\overline{\mathbf{r_1}}] \cdot \left(\Delta, s[\overline{\mathbf{r_1}}] : \sum_{i\in I'} \mathsf{In}_i + \sum_{j\in J'} \mathsf{Out}_j\right) \leq_{\mathbb{P}} s[\overline{\mathbf{r_2}}] : \sum_{i\in I} L_i + \sum_{j\in J} L_j} \ [\text{S-}\Sigma\text{-2}]$$

$$\frac{\begin{array}{c} \bigcup_{i\in I'} I_i \neq \emptyset \\ \forall j \in J'.\ \exists i \in I'.\ \mathsf{pre}(\mathsf{In}'_j) = \mathsf{pre}(\mathsf{In}'_i) \end{array} \quad \forall i \in I'.\ \left(\begin{array}{c} s[\overline{\mathbf{r_1}}] \cdot (\Delta, s[\overline{\mathbf{r_1}}] : \mathsf{In}'_i) \\ \leq_{\mathbb{P}} s[\overline{\mathbf{r_2}}] : \sum_{k\in I_i} L_k \end{array}\right)}{s[\overline{\mathbf{r_1}}] \cdot (\Delta, s[\overline{\mathbf{r_1}}] : \sum_{i\in I'\cup J'} \mathsf{In}'_i) \leq_{\mathbb{P}} s[\overline{\mathbf{r_2}}] : \sum_{i\in I'} \left(\sum_{k\in I_i} L_k\right)} \ [\text{S-}\Sigma\text{-In}]$$

$$\frac{\begin{array}{c} \bigcup_{i\in I'} I_i \cup J \neq \emptyset \\ \forall j \in J.\ \exists i \in I'.\ \mathsf{pre}(\mathsf{Out}_j) = \mathsf{pre}(\mathsf{Out}'_i) \end{array} \quad \forall i \in I'.\ \left(\begin{array}{c} s[\overline{\mathbf{r_1}}] \cdot (\Delta, s[\overline{\mathbf{r_1}}] : \mathsf{Out}'_i) \\ \leq_{\mathbb{P}} s[\overline{\mathbf{r_2}}] : \sum_{k\in I_i} L_k \end{array}\right)}{s[\overline{\mathbf{r_1}}] \cdot (\Delta, s[\overline{\mathbf{r_1}}] : \sum_{i\in I'} \mathsf{Out}'_i) \leq_{\mathbb{P}} s[\overline{\mathbf{r_2}}] : \sum_{i\in I'} \left(\sum_{k\in I_i} L_k\right) + \sum_{j\in J} \mathsf{Out}_j} \ [\text{S-}\Sigma\text{-Out}]$$

$$\frac{\begin{array}{c} J = \bigcup_{i\in I} J_i \neq \emptyset \quad \sum_{j\in J} \mathbb{P}_j = \mathbb{P}^{\Sigma} \\ \forall i \neq j \in I.\ J_i \cap J_j = \emptyset \end{array} \quad \forall i \in I.\ \left(\begin{array}{c} s[\overline{\mathbf{r_1}}] \cdot (\Delta, s[\overline{\mathbf{r_1}}] : H'_i.T'_i) \\ \leq_{\mathbb{P}'_i\mathbb{P}^{\Sigma}} s[\overline{\mathbf{r_2}}] : \bigoplus_{j\in J_i} \mathbb{P}_j \blacktriangleright H_j.T_j \end{array}\right)}{s[\overline{\mathbf{r_1}}] \cdot (\Delta, s[\overline{\mathbf{r_1}}] : \bigoplus_{i\in I} \mathbb{P}'_i \blacktriangleright H'_i.T'_i) \leq_{\mathbb{P}^{\Sigma}} s[\overline{\mathbf{r_2}}] : \bigoplus_{j\in J} \mathbb{P}_j \blacktriangleright H_j.T_j} \ [\text{S-}\oplus]$$

Fig. 4. Subtyping Rules for Probabilistic and Compositional Sessions (Part 1).

into single actions. In the conclusions a single channel (the abstract interface) on the right is related to a set of channels (the refinement) on the left. We sometimes denote the single channel type on the right of such conclusions as supertype.

The five rules in Fig. 4 may be understood as one large rule, as the order of these rules within a derivation is fixed. Among these five rules and to split a single choice, $[\text{S-}\Sigma\text{-1}]$ is applied first (lowermost in the derivation tree) and $[\text{S-}\oplus]$ is last (uppermost). The already mentioned *active channels* in local contexts $\Lambda = c \cdot \Delta$ are crucial for our subtyping rules. They are introduced by $[\text{S-}\Sigma\text{-1}]$ (and only by $[\text{S-}\Sigma\text{-1}]$). We have $\Delta = s[\overline{\mathbf{r_1}}] : T_1, \ldots, s[\overline{\mathbf{r_n}}] : T_n \leq_{\mathbb{P}} s[\overline{\mathbf{r}}] : \sum_{j\in J_1} L_j + \ldots + \sum_{j\in J_n} L_j$ if there is a way to split the choice of the supertype along the n channels of the refinement. Therefore, $[\text{S-}\Sigma\text{-1}]$ creates n branches, where in each branch exactly one of the n channels is set active $s[\overline{\mathbf{r_1}}] \cdot \Delta$. Intuitively, $s[\overline{\mathbf{r_k}}] \cdot \Delta$ is used to identify the next possible action of $s[\overline{\mathbf{r_k}}]$ if it exists. Else $s[\overline{\mathbf{r_k}}]$ is pending (see below) and an empty choice $s[\overline{\mathbf{r}}] : \sum_{j\in J_k} L_j$ with $J_k = \emptyset$ is created. The side condition $\bigcup_{k\in[1..n]} J_k \neq \emptyset$ ensures that not all J_k are empty. For each (non-pending) channel in Δ, the derivation tree in the respective branch above $[\text{S-}\Sigma\text{-1}]$ creates the corresponding component of the mixed choice of $s[\overline{\mathbf{r}}]$. Using an active channel and branching in this way, allows us to separate the splitting of a choice onto several rules. Note that whether the sum was correctly split into the n parts of the refinement is checked by the remaining rules.

$$\frac{\overline{\mathbf{r_1}} \subseteq \overline{\mathbf{r_2}} \quad \mathbf{q} \in \overline{\mathbf{r_1}} \quad \mathbf{p} \notin \Delta \quad \Delta, s[\overline{\mathbf{r_1}}]:T' \leq_1 s[\overline{\mathbf{r_2}}]:T}{s[\overline{\mathbf{r_1}}] \cdot (\Delta, s[\overline{\mathbf{r_1}}]:\mathbf{q}{\leftarrow}\mathbf{p}\,?\,l(U).T') \leq_1 s[\overline{\mathbf{r_2}}]:\mathbf{q}{\leftarrow}\mathbf{p}\,?\,l(U).T} \quad \text{[S-In]}$$

$$\frac{\overline{\mathbf{r_1}} \subseteq \overline{\mathbf{r_2}} \quad \mathbf{p} \in \overline{\mathbf{r_1}} \quad \mathbf{q} \notin \Delta \quad \Delta, s[\overline{\mathbf{r_1}}]:T' \leq_1 s[\overline{\mathbf{r_2}}]:T}{s[\overline{\mathbf{r_1}}] \cdot (\Delta, s[\overline{\mathbf{r_1}}]:\mathbf{p}{\rightarrow}\mathbf{q}\,!\,l\langle U\rangle.T') \leq_{\mathbb{P}} s[\overline{\mathbf{r_2}}]:\mathbb{P} \blacktriangleright \mathbf{p}{\rightarrow}\mathbf{q}\,!\,l\langle U\rangle.T} \quad \text{[S-Out]}$$

$$\frac{\mathbf{p} \in \overline{\mathbf{r_1}} \quad \mathbf{q} \in \overline{\mathbf{r_2}} \quad \Delta, s[\overline{\mathbf{r_1}}]:T_1', s[\overline{\mathbf{r_2}}]:T_2' \leq_{\mathbb{P}} s[\overline{\mathbf{r}}]:T}{s[\overline{\mathbf{r_1}}] \cdot (\Delta, s[\overline{\mathbf{r_1}}]:\mathbf{p}{\rightarrow}\mathbf{q}\,!\,l\langle U\rangle.T_1', s[\overline{\mathbf{r_2}}]:\mathbf{q}{\leftarrow}\mathbf{p}\,?\,l(U).T_2' + \sum_{i\in I} L_i) \leq_{\mathbb{P}} s[\overline{\mathbf{r}}]:T} \quad \text{[S-Link]}$$

$$\frac{\Delta, s[\overline{\mathbf{r_1}}]:T' \leq_{\mathbb{P}} s[\overline{\mathbf{r_2}}]:T}{s[\overline{\mathbf{r_1}}] \cdot (\Delta, s[\overline{\mathbf{r_1}}]:\tau.T') \leq_{\mathbb{P}} s[\overline{\mathbf{r_2}}]:T} \quad \text{[S-}\tau\text{-L]} \qquad \frac{\Lambda \leq_1 s[\overline{\mathbf{r}}]:T}{\Lambda \leq_{\mathbb{P}} s[\overline{\mathbf{r}}]:\mathbb{P} \blacktriangleright \tau.T} \quad \text{[S-}\tau\text{-R]}$$

$$\frac{}{\emptyset \leq_1 \emptyset} \quad \text{[S-}\emptyset\text{-1]} \qquad \frac{\mathsf{pend}(c \cdot \Delta)}{c \cdot \Delta \leq_{\mathbb{P}} \emptyset} \quad \text{[S-}\emptyset\text{]} \qquad \frac{\Delta_1' \leq_1 \Delta \quad \Delta_2' \leq_1 c:T}{\Delta_1', \Delta_2' \leq_1 \Delta, c:T} \quad \text{[S-Split]}$$

Fig. 5. Subtyping Rules for Probabilistic and Compositional Sessions (Part 2).

The next splitting rule, [S-Σ-2], splits the mixed choice of the supertype into its inputs and probabilistic sums, while keeping the active channel on the left. Whether the right hand sides contain only inputs for the L_i's and only probabilistic choices for the L_j's is checked by the remaining rules.

Our subtyping is an extension of standard subtyping. As usual (see also [28,31]), choices on the left may have fewer outputs and more inputs. This is implemented by [S-Σ-In] and [S-Σ-Out]. Rule [S-Σ-In] splits an input choice into single summands. Thereby, it allows for additional inputs on left (via J') that are not matched on the right. It is ensured that no additional input In_j' introduces a prefix $\mathsf{pre}(\mathsf{In}_j') = \mathbf{p}{\leftarrow}\mathbf{q}\,?$ that is not matched. Similarly, [S-Σ-Out] splits a choice into probabilistic choices. Here, the right hand side may have additional probabilistic choices. [S-Σ-Out] ensures that no prefix of the supertype is lost.

Let $\mathsf{pre}(T)$ denote the set of unguarded prefixes of a type, where probabilities are summed up such that $\mathsf{pre}(\mathsf{N} \oplus \mathbb{P}_1 \blacktriangleright \mathbf{p}{\rightarrow}\mathbf{q}\,!\,l_1\langle U_1\rangle.T_1 \oplus \mathbb{P}_2 \blacktriangleright \mathbf{p}{\rightarrow}\mathbf{q}\,!\,l_2\langle U_2\rangle.T_2) = \mathsf{pre}(\mathsf{N}) \cup \{\mathbb{P}_1 \blacktriangleright \mathbf{p}{\rightarrow}\mathbf{q}\,!\} \cup \{\mathbb{P}_2 \blacktriangleright \mathbf{p}{\rightarrow}\mathbf{q}\,!\} = \mathsf{pre}(\mathsf{N}) \cup \{\mathbb{P}_1 + \mathbb{P}_2 \blacktriangleright \mathbf{p}{\rightarrow}\mathbf{q}\,!\}$ and $\mathsf{pre}(\mathsf{N} \oplus \mathbb{P}_1 \blacktriangleright \tau.T \oplus \mathbb{P}_2 \blacktriangleright \tau.T) = \mathsf{pre}(\mathsf{N}) \cup \{\mathbb{P}_1 \blacktriangleright \tau.T\} \cup \{\mathbb{P}_2 \blacktriangleright \tau.T\} = \mathsf{pre}(\mathsf{N}) \cup \{\mathbb{P}_1 + \mathbb{P}_2 \blacktriangleright \tau.T\}$.

[S-$\oplus$] splits a probabilistic choice into its summands and removes their probabilities $\mathbb{P}_i'$, by multiplying $\mathbb{P}_i'$ with the current probability in the index of the subtype relation $\leq_{\mathbb{P}}$. Hence, $\leq_{\mathbb{P}}$ identifies a branch in the subtyping derivation tree that considers a subterm of the supertype that occurs with probability $\mathbb{P}$.

Figure 5 contains the core of the actual subtyping behaviour; in most of these rules subtype contexts have an active channel whose type is a singular input/output action. Due to [S-In], a single input action is the supertype of a context if its active channel offers the same single action and the continuations are subtypes within the local context *without* an active channel. The communication partner $\mathbf{p}$ of this input must not be found within Δ. Both the acting role $\mathbf{q}$ and the subtype role set $\overline{\mathbf{r_1}}$ must be contained in the supertype role set $\overline{\mathbf{r_2}}$.

Rule [S-Out] is similar. Additionally it matches the probability on the relation $\leq_{\mathbb{P}}$ in the conclusion to the probability of the sending action of the supertype, $s[\overline{r_2}] : \mathbb{P} \blacktriangleright \mathbf{p} \rightarrow \mathbf{q}\,!\,l\langle U\rangle.T$. For the premise then $\leq_1$ is used.

[S-Link] unfolds internal communication in the left context, if the active channel offers the sending action. The respective communication is not visible in the supertype. As in [S-In] and [S-Out], there is no active channel in the premise.

Similarly, [S-τ-L] allows internal actions of the active channel of the subtype context to unfold. [S-τ-R] allows internal actions of the supertype to unfold. Sometimes a supertype is required to contain an internal action (see Example 5). [S-τ-R] matches the probabilities of the relation and the action similar to [S-Out].

[S-$\emptyset$-1] ensures that $\emptyset \leq_1 \emptyset$. As $\Delta, c\!:\!\mathbf{end} = \Delta$, this rule relates $\mathbf{end}$-typed channels. By [S-$\emptyset$], the $\mathbf{end}$ is also a supertype of a pending context. In [S-Σ-1], [S-Σ-2], [S-Σ-In], and [S-Σ-Out], some of the constructed parts of the choice in the supertype may be empty. This happens if the subtype context with its active channel is pending, $\mathsf{pend}(c \cdot \Delta)$. An action of $c_1 \cdot \Delta$ may be pending, because its communication partner on c_2 might need to first *link* with some c_3. Note that internal actions, treated by [S-Link] and [S-τ-L], are resolved only in branches, where the sender is the active channel. Hence, all internal inputs are pending, because they are handled in the branch of the sender. Sending actions may also be pending, if the corresponding receiving action is not available yet.

A local context with an active channel $\Lambda = s[\overline{\mathbf{p}}] \cdot \Delta$ is called pending, $\mathsf{pend}(\Lambda)$, if $s[\overline{\mathbf{p}}] : \sum_{i\in I} \mathsf{In}_i + \sum_{j\in J} \mathsf{Out}_j \in \Delta$ and for all $i \in I$ have $\mathsf{In}_i = \mathbf{p}_i{\leftarrow}\mathbf{q}_i\,?\,l_i(U_i).T_i$ for which exists $s[\overline{\mathbf{q}}] : T \in \Delta$ with $\mathbf{q}_i \in \overline{\mathbf{q}}$, and for all $j \in J$ have $\mathsf{Out}_j = \mathbf{p}_k{\rightarrow}\mathbf{q}_k\,!\,l_k\langle U_k\rangle.T_k \oplus \mathsf{N}_j$ for which exists $s[\overline{\mathbf{q}}] : T \in \Delta$ with $\mathbf{q}_k \in \overline{\mathbf{q}}$ and $T \neq \mathbf{q}_i{\leftarrow}\mathbf{p}_i\,?\,l_i(U_i).T_i' + \mathsf{M}$. In other words, $\mathsf{pend}(c \cdot \Delta)$ if the type of c is a mixed choice, where all inputs seek to communicate with a partner within Δ which are all not available, and all probabilistic choices containing an output seek to communicate with a partner within Δ which is not available.

Finally, [S-Split] splits contexts to obtain a single channel as supertype. This rule facilitates reflexivity and transitivity of $\leq_1$.

Remark 1 (Sets of Roles). The subtyping rules ensure that all roles used in actions in the refinement appear in the role set used in the interface—or role sets for more than one channel in the interface. This may appear as a limitation of our approach, since the interface needs to know about these roles even if it has no further knowledge about the inner structure of the refinement. However, this design decision simplifies the presentation of subtyping and is not crucial. Instead we may use a new role (for each channel) in the interface, let [S-Split] create a mapping between refinement roles and their interface role for the bookkeeping in the remaining subtyping rules, and replace in rules such as [S-In] each refinement role in actions on the left by the corresponding interface role in the actions on the right. Then channels can be defined as usual on a session and a single role and we can drop the first mentioned role in inputs and outputs. $\bigcirc$

Example 5 (Running Example—Subtyping). For the types from Example 4 with $\overline{\mathbf{c}} = \{\mathbf{j}, \mathbf{d}\}$ it holds that $s[\mathbf{j}] : T_{\mathbf{j}}, s[\mathbf{d}] : T_{\mathbf{d}} \leq_1 s[\overline{\mathbf{c}}] : T_{\mathbf{c}}$.

To further illustrate subtyping, consider a more complex version of the courthouse protocol. Here, the **defendant**, after notifying the **judge** about wanting a witness statement, seeks a meeting with the **witness**. With $T_\mathbf{p}$ and $T_\mathbf{w}$ untouched, we redefine only $T_\mathbf{c}, T_\mathbf{d}$, and $T_\mathbf{j}$ as follows.

$$T_\mathbf{c}^* = \mathbf{j}{\leftarrow}\mathbf{p}\,?\,\mathtt{lws}().\begin{cases} 0.7 \blacktriangleright \mathbf{j}{\rightarrow}\mathbf{p}\,!\,\mathtt{glt}\langle\mathsf{bool}\rangle.1 \blacktriangleright \mathbf{j}{\rightarrow}\mathbf{d}\,!\,\mathtt{rls}\langle\rangle \\ \oplus\ 0.3 \blacktriangleright \tau.\begin{cases} 1 \blacktriangleright \mathbf{d}{\rightarrow}\mathbf{w}\,!\,\mathtt{mtg}\langle\rangle.\mathbf{j}{\leftarrow}\mathbf{w}\,?\,\mathtt{st}().1 \blacktriangleright \mathbf{j}{\rightarrow}\mathbf{p}\,!\,\mathtt{glt}\langle\mathsf{bool}\rangle \\ +\ \mathbf{j}{\leftarrow}\mathbf{w}\,?\,\mathtt{st}().1 \blacktriangleright \mathbf{d}{\rightarrow}\mathbf{w}\,!\,\mathtt{mtg}\langle\rangle.1 \blacktriangleright \mathbf{j}{\rightarrow}\mathbf{p}\,!\,\mathtt{glt}\langle\mathsf{bool}\rangle \end{cases} \end{cases}$$

$$T_\mathbf{d}^* = \begin{cases} 0.5 \blacktriangleright \mathbf{d}{\rightarrow}\mathbf{j}\,!\,\mathtt{wk}\langle\rangle \\ \oplus\ 0.2 \blacktriangleright \mathbf{d}{\rightarrow}\mathbf{j}\,!\,\mathtt{str}\langle\rangle \\ \oplus\ 0.3 \blacktriangleright \mathbf{d}{\rightarrow}\mathbf{j}\,!\,\mathtt{wit}\langle\rangle.1 \blacktriangleright \mathbf{d}{\rightarrow}\mathbf{w}\,!\,\mathtt{mtg}\langle\rangle \end{cases}$$

$$T_\mathbf{j}^* = \mathbf{j}{\leftarrow}\mathbf{p}\,?\,\mathtt{lws}().\begin{cases} \mathbf{j}{\leftarrow}\mathbf{d}\,?\,\mathtt{wk}().1 \blacktriangleright \mathbf{j}{\rightarrow}\mathbf{p}\,!\,\mathtt{glt}\langle\mathsf{bool}\rangle.1 \blacktriangleright \mathbf{j}{\rightarrow}\mathbf{d}\,!\,\mathtt{rls}\langle\rangle \\ +\ \mathbf{j}{\leftarrow}\mathbf{d}\,?\,\mathtt{str}().1 \blacktriangleright \mathbf{j}{\rightarrow}\mathbf{p}\,!\,\mathtt{glt}\langle\mathsf{bool}\rangle.1 \blacktriangleright \mathbf{j}{\rightarrow}\mathbf{d}\,!\,\mathtt{rls}\langle\rangle \\ +\ \mathbf{j}{\leftarrow}\mathbf{d}\,?\,\mathtt{wit}().\mathbf{j}{\leftarrow}\mathbf{w}\,?\,\mathtt{st}().1 \blacktriangleright \mathbf{j}{\rightarrow}\mathbf{p}\,!\,\mathtt{glt}\langle\mathsf{bool}\rangle \end{cases}$$

Where, as before, for $\overline{\mathbf{c}} = \{\mathbf{j}, \mathbf{d}\}$ it holds that $s[\mathbf{j}] : T_\mathbf{j}^*, s[\mathbf{d}] : T_\mathbf{d}^* \leq_1 s[\overline{\mathbf{c}}] : T_\mathbf{c}^*$.

Notice how the interface now contains an *internal action* τ. The interface is created without knowledge of the specifics of the **witness** and therefore needs to accommodate for both the **defendant-witness** *meeting* coming before the **witness-judge** *statement* and vice versa. This leads in $T_\mathbf{c}^*$ to a probabilistic choice being followed in the case with probability 0.3 by a mixed choice containing receiving actions. A τ in between is necessary to connect these choices. Also note, that only the interface type $T_\mathbf{c}^*$ has mixed choice but not the refinement.
○

Example 6. In the subtyping derivation of $s[\mathbf{j}] : T_\mathbf{j}^*, s[\mathbf{d}] : T_\mathbf{d}^* \leq_1 s[\overline{\mathbf{c}}] : T_\mathbf{c}^*$ from Example 5, we highlight the following snippets to illustrate our subtyping rules. We reuse the identifiers $T_\mathbf{j}, T_\mathbf{d}, T_\mathbf{c}$ for legibility, they do not refer to the types from our previous examples. Moving bottom-up, we begin at the original statement to demonstrate how [S-Σ-1] handles cases in which channels are pending.

$$\cfrac{\cfrac{s[\mathbf{j}] : T_\mathbf{j}, s[\mathbf{d}] : T_\mathbf{d}^* \leq_1 s[\overline{\mathbf{c}}] : T_\mathbf{c}}{s[\mathbf{j}] \cdot \Delta \leq_1 s[\overline{\mathbf{c}}] : \mathbf{j}{\leftarrow}\mathbf{p}\,?\,\mathtt{lws}().T_\mathbf{c}}\ [\text{S-In}] \qquad \cfrac{\mathsf{pend}(s[\mathbf{d}] \cdot \Delta)}{s[\mathbf{d}] \cdot \Delta \leq_1 \emptyset}\ [\text{S-}\emptyset]}{\Delta = s[\mathbf{j}] : \mathbf{j}{\leftarrow}\mathbf{p}\,?\,\mathtt{lws}().T_\mathbf{j}, s[\mathbf{d}] : T_\mathbf{d}^* \leq_1 s[\overline{\mathbf{c}}] : \mathbf{j}{\leftarrow}\mathbf{p}\,?\,\mathtt{lws}().T_\mathbf{c}}\ [\text{S-}\Sigma\text{-1}]$$

Continuing upwards from the left-hand side of the previous tree, we have the following derivation. Note that in the probabilistic sum in the type of $s[\overline{\mathbf{c}}]$ the case guilty with 70% probability is split into a case of 50% and a case of 20%. [S-$\oplus$] splits the tree into three branches. We give the branch that leads to [S-τ].

$$\dfrac{\dfrac{\dfrac{s[\mathbf{j}]:\mathbf{j}{\leftarrow}\mathbf{w}\,?\,\mathtt{st}().T'_{\mathbf{j}},\,s[\mathbf{d}]:T'_{\mathbf{d}} \leq_1 s[\overline{\mathbf{c}}]:T'_{\mathbf{c}}}{s[\mathbf{j}]:\mathbf{j}{\leftarrow}\mathbf{w}\,?\,\mathtt{st}().T'_{\mathbf{j}},\,s[\mathbf{d}]:T'_{\mathbf{d}} \leq_{0.3} s[\overline{\mathbf{c}}]:0.3\blacktriangleright\tau.T'_{\mathbf{c}}}\;[\text{S-}\tau]}{\ldots\quad s[\mathbf{j}]\cdot(s[\mathbf{j}]:T_{\mathbf{j}},\,s[\mathbf{d}]:\mathbf{d}{\rightarrow}\mathbf{j}\,!\,\mathtt{wit}\langle\rangle.T'_{\mathbf{d}}) \leq_{0.3} s[\overline{\mathbf{c}}]:0.3\blacktriangleright\tau.T'_{\mathbf{c}}}\;[\text{S-Link}]}{s[\mathbf{j}]\cdot\left(s[\mathbf{j}]:T_{\mathbf{j}},\,s[\mathbf{d}]:\begin{cases}\ 0.5\blacktriangleright\mathbf{d}{\rightarrow}\mathbf{j}\,!\,\mathtt{wk}\langle\rangle\\ \oplus\ 0.2\blacktriangleright\mathbf{d}{\rightarrow}\mathbf{j}\,!\,\mathtt{str}\langle\rangle\\ \oplus\ 0.3\blacktriangleright\mathbf{d}{\rightarrow}\mathbf{j}\,!\,\mathtt{wit}\langle\rangle.T'_{\mathbf{d}}\end{cases}\right) \leq_1 s[\overline{\mathbf{c}}]:\begin{cases}\ 0.5\blacktriangleright H_{\mathtt{glt}}.T_{\mathtt{rls}}\\ \oplus\ 0.2\blacktriangleright H_{\mathtt{glt}}.T_{\mathtt{rls}}\\ \oplus\ 0.3\blacktriangleright\tau.T'_{\mathbf{c}}\end{cases}}\;[\text{S-}\oplus]$$

Finally, continuing on the previous branch, we see how [Sub-Σ-1] assembles a mixed choice in the supertype of a subtype context without any mixed choices.

$$\dfrac{\dfrac{\cdots}{s[\mathbf{d}]\cdot\Delta \leq_1 s[\overline{\mathbf{c}}]:1\blacktriangleright\mathbf{d}{\rightarrow}\mathbf{w}\,!\,\mathtt{mtg}\langle\rangle.T_1}\;[\text{S-}\oplus]\qquad \dfrac{\cdots}{s[\mathbf{j}]\cdot\Delta \leq_1 s[\overline{\mathbf{c}}]:\mathbf{j}{\leftarrow}\mathbf{w}\,?\,\mathtt{st}().T_2}\;[\text{S-In}]}{\Delta = \begin{array}{l}s[\mathbf{j}]:\mathbf{j}{\leftarrow}\mathbf{w}\,?\,\mathtt{st}().T'_{\mathbf{j}},\\ s[\mathbf{d}]:1\blacktriangleright\mathbf{d}{\rightarrow}\mathbf{w}\,!\,\mathtt{mtg}\langle\rangle\end{array} \leq_1 s[\overline{\mathbf{c}}]:\begin{cases}\ 1\blacktriangleright\mathbf{d}{\rightarrow}\mathbf{w}\,!\,\mathtt{mtg}\langle\rangle.T_1\\ +\ \mathbf{j}{\leftarrow}\mathbf{w}\,?\,\mathtt{st}().T_2\end{cases}\qquad\bigcirc}\;[\text{S-}\Sigma\text{-1}]$$

5 Properties

We inherit the predicates for *safety* and *deadlock-freedom* from [28,31]. A context is safe if it contains for every unguarded output for that there is an unguarded input on the same prefix also an unguarded matching input.

Definition 5 (Safety Property). *The co-inductive property φ is a safety property of local contexts Λ if and only if for all $\varphi(\Lambda)$*

1. *if $\Lambda = \Delta$ (without active channel), then*
   - *(a)* $\Delta \xrightarrow{\;s\,:\,\mathbf{p}\rightarrow\mathbf{q}\,!\,l\langle U\rangle\;}_{\mathbb{P}}$ *and* $\Delta \xrightarrow{\;s\,:\,\mathbf{q}\leftarrow\mathbf{p}\,?\,l'(U')\;}_1$ *imply* $\Delta \xrightarrow{\;s\,:\,\mathbf{pq}\,:\,l\langle U\rangle\;}_{\mathbb{P}} \Delta'$ *and $\varphi(\Delta')$, and*
   - *(b) the transition $\Delta \xrightarrow{\;s\,:\,\tau\;}_{\mathbb{P}} \Delta'$ implies $\varphi(\Delta')$.*
2. *if $\Lambda = s[\overline{\mathbf{r}}]\cdot\Delta$ (with active channel), then*
   - *(a) transitions* $\Delta \xrightarrow{\;s\,:\,\mathbf{p}\rightarrow\mathbf{q}\,!\,l\langle U\rangle\;}_{\mathbb{P}}$ *with $\mathbf{p}\in\overline{\mathbf{r}}$ and* $\Delta \xrightarrow{\;s\,:\,\mathbf{q}\leftarrow\mathbf{p}\,?\,l'(U')\;}_1$ *imply* $\Lambda \xrightarrow{\;s\,:\,\mathbf{pq}\,:\,l\langle U\rangle\;}_{\mathbb{P}} \Delta'$ *and $\varphi(\Delta')$, and*
   - *(b) the transition $\Lambda \xrightarrow{\;s\,:\,\tau\;}_{\mathbb{P}} \Delta'$ implies $\varphi(\Delta')$.*

We say that Λ is safe, $\mathsf{safe}(\Lambda)$, if $\varphi(\Lambda)$ for some safety property φ.

A context is deadlock-free if it can terminate only with $\emptyset$ and a process is deadlock-free if it can terminate modulo $\equiv$ only in $\mathbf{0}$. Also pending contexts are by definition deadlock-free, because their actions are supposed to be treated by another branch of the subtyping derivation. However, active channels and pending contexts can appear only in subtyping derivations and not type judgements.

Definition 6 (Deadlock-Freedom). *The local context (with active channel)* Λ *is* deadlock-free, dfree(Λ), *if* $\Lambda \mapsto^* \Lambda' \not\mapsto$ *implies* $\Lambda' = \emptyset$ *for all* Λ' *or if* pend(Λ). *A process* P *is* deadlock-free *if and only if for all* P' *such that* $P \Longrightarrow_{\mathbb{P}}$ P' *either (a) (b)* $P' \not\mapsto$ *and* $P \equiv \mathbf{0}$, *or (c) there are* $P'', \mathbb{P}'$ *such that* $P' \longrightarrow_{\mathbb{P}'} P''$.

Our subtyping is very flexible. Indeed for every safe and deadlock-free collection of channel types there exists their interface as a single channel type. Note that this is a major difference to [19]. For instance, we do not exclude races and allow to combine outputs and inputs into a mixed choice.

Theorem 1 (Interface Exists). *For all* $\Delta' = \{s[\overline{\mathbf{r}_i}] : T_i'\}_{i \in I}$ *with* safe(Δ') *and* dfree(Δ', Δ) *for some* Δ *there are* $\overline{\mathbf{r}}, T$ *such that* $\overline{\mathbf{r}} \subseteq \bigcup_{i \in I} \overline{\mathbf{r}_i}$ *and* $\Delta' \leq_1 s[\overline{\mathbf{r}}] : T$.

We do not prove the opposite direction, because it is much simpler. However, if safe$(s[\overline{\mathbf{r}}] : T)$ then there are $\overline{\mathbf{r}_1}, \ldots, \overline{\mathbf{r}_n}$ with $\overline{\mathbf{r}} \subseteq \bigcup_{i \in [1..n]} \overline{\mathbf{r}_i}$ and $T_1', \ldots, T_n'$ such that $\{s[\overline{\mathbf{r}_i}] : T_i'\}_{i \in [1..n]} \leq_1 s[\overline{\mathbf{r}}] : T$.

Similar to [28,31], we show that our type system satisfies the standard properties of subtyping, subject reduction, and ensures deadlock-freedom.

Theorem 2 (Subtyping and Properties).

1. *If* $\Lambda_1 \leq_{\mathbb{P}} \Lambda_2$ *and* safe(Λ_2), *then (a) (b)* safe(Λ_1) *and (c) if* $\Lambda_1 \mapsto_{\mathbb{P}_1} \Lambda_1'$ *then there exist* $\Lambda_2', \mathbb{P}_2, \mathbb{P}_3$ *such that* $\Lambda_2 \mapsto^*_{\mathbb{P}_1 \mathbb{P}_2} \Lambda_2'$ *and* $\Lambda_1' \leq_{\mathbb{P}_3} \Lambda_2'$ *with* $\mathbb{P} = \mathbb{P}_2 \mathbb{P}_3$ *and* safe(Λ_2').
2. *If* $\Lambda_1 \leq_{\mathbb{P}} \Lambda_2$, safe$(\Lambda_2)$, *and* dfree$(\Lambda_2)$, *then (a) (b)* dfree$(\Lambda_1)$ *and (c) if* $\Lambda_1 \mapsto_{\mathbb{P}_1} \Lambda_1'$ *then there exist* $\Lambda_2', \mathbb{P}_2, \mathbb{P}_3$ *such that* $\Lambda_2 \mapsto^*_{\mathbb{P}_1 \mathbb{P}_2} \Lambda_2'$ *and* $\Lambda_1' \leq_{\mathbb{P}_3} \Lambda_2'$ *with* $\mathbb{P} = \mathbb{P}_2 \mathbb{P}_3$ *and* dfree(Λ_2').
3. *Checking* safe(Δ) *and* dfree(Δ) *is decidable.*

The proof of subject reduction is straightforward by induction on $P \longrightarrow_{\mathbb{P}} P'$.

Theorem 3 (Subject Reduction). *If* $\Gamma \vdash P \triangleright \Delta$, safe$(\Delta)$, *and* $P \longrightarrow_{\mathbb{P}} P'$ *then there is some* Δ' *such that* $\Delta \mapsto^*_{\mathbb{P}} \Delta'$ *and* $\Gamma \vdash P' \triangleright \Delta'$.

Definition 7 (Error Process). *A process* P *has a communication error if*

$$P \equiv s[\overline{\mathbf{r}_1}] \triangleright (\mathbf{p} \rightarrow \mathbf{q}\,!\,l\langle U \rangle.Q \oplus \mathsf{N}) + \mathsf{M} \mid s[\overline{\mathbf{r}_2}] \triangleright \mathbf{q} \leftarrow \mathbf{p}\,?\,l_q(U_q).Q_q + \mathsf{M}^q \mid P'$$

where $l \neq l_q$ *and for all* $M_i^q = \mathbf{q} \leftarrow \mathbf{p}\,?\,l_i(U_i).Q_i \in \mathsf{M}^q$, *the labels do not match, i.e.,* $l \neq l_i$. *A process* P *has a value error if* $P \equiv \mathtt{if}\ v\ \mathtt{then}\ P\ \mathtt{else}\ Q \mid P'$ *with* $v \notin \{\top, \bot\}$. *P is an error process if it has a communication or value error.*

From Theorem 3 and the fact that error processes are untypable by a safe context it follows that:

Corollary 1 (Error Freedom). *If* $\Gamma \vdash P \triangleright \Delta$ *with* safe(Δ) *and* $P \Longrightarrow_{\mathbb{P}} P'$, *then* P' *is not an error process.*

The proof of Deadlock-Freedom is similar to the corresponding proof in [28]. However, similar to [31], we require two additional side conditions on the shape of these processes. For results on interleaved, interfering sessions, see [8].

Definition 8 (Canonical). *Assume $\vdash P \triangleright \Delta$, then P is canonical for Δ iff*

1. *there is no occurrence of restriction, $(\nu s')P'$, in P, and*
2. *$P \equiv p_1 \mid \ldots \mid P_n$ and $\Delta = c_1 : T_1, \ldots, c_n : T_n$ where for all $k \in [1..n]$ have $\vdash P_k \triangleright c_k : T_k$ and for all subterms of the form $c \sum_{i \in I} M_i$ occurring in P_k, have $c = c_k$.*

Theorem 4 (Deadlock-Freedom). *If $\vdash P \triangleright \Delta$, $\mathsf{safe}(\Delta)$, and $\mathsf{dfree}(\Delta)$, and P canonical for Δ, then P is deadlock-free.*

6   Conclusions

With the subtyping rules in the Figs. 4 and 5 we have presented a comprehensive and novel approach to refinement in multiparty session types that is very flexible and general. The system is based on a powerful calculus with mixed and probabilistic choices. Our flexible subtyping relation allows to unify any selection of well-typed, safe, and deadlock-free channels (the refinement) in an interface consisting of a single channel. Our subtyping enables robust stepwise refinement. A single channel within a protocol may be taken as interface and safely replaced by several channels that in turn can each be interfaces for another refinement. Moreover, by considering a refinement as the starting point, we can combine its channels into a single channel for whom the interactions within the refinement are concealed. Hence, our system facilitates strong compositional verifiability of protocols.

So far, we have been requiring deadlock-freedom to be preserved in 100% of all cases when constructing a refinement. As the system is probabilistic, we believe it would be very interesting to explore *imperfect refinement*, by allowing the refinement to deadlock with a bounded probability. We could extend the notion even further and allow bounded-probability safety, termination, or liveness.

References

1. Abadi, M., Lamport, L.: The existence of refinement mappings. In: Proceedings of LICS, pp. 165–175 (1988). https://doi.org/10.1109/LICS.1988.5115
2. Aman, B., Ciobanu, G.: Probabilities in session types. In: Proceedings of FROM. EPTCS, vol. 303, pp. 92–106 (2019). https://doi.org/10.4204/EPTCS.303.7
3. Bejleri, A., Yoshida, N.: Synchronous multiparty session types. In: Proceedings of PLACES. ENTCS, vol. 241, pp. 3–33 (2008). https://doi.org/10.1016/j.entcs.2009.06.002
4. Blechschmidt, P.: Compositional Interface Refinement Through Subtyping in Probabilistic Session Types. Master thesis, Technische Universität Berlin (2025). arXiv.org

5. Bocchi, L., King, A., Murgia, M., Thompson, S.: Abstract subtyping for asynchronous multiparty sessions. In: Proceediings of CONCUR. LIPIcs, vol. 348, pp. 10:1–10:19 (2025). https://doi.org/10.4230/LIPIcs.CONCUR.2025.10

6. Bravetti, M., Lange, J., Zavattaro, G.: Fair refinement for asynchronous session types. In: FOSSACS 2021. LNCS, vol. 12650, pp. 144–163. Springer, Cham (2021). https://doi.org/10.1007/978-3-030-71995-1_8

7. Chen, T., Dezani-Ciancaglini, M., Scalas, A., Yoshida, N.: On the preciseness of subtyping in session types. LMCS **13**(2) (2017). https://doi.org/10.23638/LMCS-13(2:12)2017

8. Coppo, M., Dezani-Ciancaglini, M., Yoshida, N., Padovani, L.: Global progress for dynamically interleaved multiparty sessions. MSCS **26**(2), 238–302 (2016). https://doi.org/10.1017/S0960129514000188

9. Dezani-Ciancaglini, M., Ghilezan, S., Jaksic, S., Pantovic, J., Yoshida, N.: Precise subtyping for synchronous multiparty sessions. In: Proceedings of PLACES. EPTCS, vol. 203, pp. 29–43 (2015). https://doi.org/10.4204/EPTCS.203.3

10. Fu, Q., Das, A., Gaboardi, M.: Probabilistic refinement session types. In: Proceedings of PLDI, pp. 1666–1691 (2025). https://doi.org/10.1145/3729317

11. Gay, S., Ravara, A.: Behavioural Types: From Theory to Tools. River Publishers (2017). https://doi.org/10.1145/2873052

12. Gay, S.J., Hole, M.: Subtyping for session types in the pi calculus. Acta Informatica **42**(2–3), 191–225 (2005). https://doi.org/10.1007/s00236-005-0177-z

13. Ghilezan, S., Pantović, J., Prokić, I., Scalas, A., Yoshida, N.: Precise subtyping for asynchronous multiparty sessions. ACM Trans. **24**(2), 1–73 (2023). https://doi.org/10.1145/3568422

14. Hansson, H.A.: Time and probability in formal design of distributed systems. Ph.D. thesis, University Uppsala, Sweden (1991)

15. Herescu, O.M., Palamidessi, C.: Probabilistic asynchronous pi-calculus. In: Tiuryn, J. (ed.) FoSSaCS 2000. LNCS, vol. 1784, pp. 146–160. Springer, Heidelberg (2000). https://doi.org/10.1007/3-540-46432-8_10

16. Honda, K., Vasconcelos, V.T., Kubo, M.: Language primitives and type discipline for structured communication-based programming. In: Hankin, C. (ed.) ESOP 1998. LNCS, vol. 1381, pp. 122–138. Springer, Heidelberg (1998). https://doi.org/10.1007/BFb0053567

17. Honda, K., Yoshida, N., Carbone, M.: Multiparty asynchronous session types. In: Proceedings of POPL, vol. 43, pp. 273–284. ACM (2008). https://doi.org/10.1145/1328438.1328472

18. Honda, K., Yoshida, N., Carbone, M.: Multiparty asynchronous session types. J. ACM **63**(1), 9:1–9:67 (2016). https://doi.org/10.1145/2827695

19. Horne, R.: Session subtyping and multiparty compatibility using circular sequents. In: Proceedings of CONCUR. LIPIcs, vol. 171, pp. 12:1–12:22 (2020). https://doi.org/10.4230/LIPICS.CONCUR.2020.12

20. Hüttel, H., et al.: Foundations of session types and behavioural contracts. ACM Comput. Surv. **49**(1), 3:1–3:36 (2016). https://doi.org/10.1145/2873052

21. Inverso, O., Melgratti, H., Padovani, L., Trubiani, C., Tuosto, E.: Probabilistic analysis of binary sessions. In: Proceedings of CONCUR. LIPIcs, vol. 171, pp. 14:1–14:21 (2020). https://doi.org/10.4230/LIPIcs.CONCUR.2020.14

22. Larsen, K.G., Skou, A.: Bisimulation through probabilistic testing. I&C **94**(1), 1–28 (1991). https://doi.org/10.1016/0890-5401(91)90030-6

23. Li, E., Stutz, F., Wies, T.: Deciding subtyping for asynchronous multiparty sessions. In: Proceedings of ESOP. LNCS, vol. 14576, pp. 176–205 (2024). https://doi.org/10.1007/978-3-031-57262-3_8

24. Lynch, N.A., Vaandrager, F.W.: Forward and backward simulations: I. Untimed systems. I&C **121**(2), 214–233 (1995). https://doi.org/10.1006/INCO.1995.1134
25. Milner, R. (ed.): A Calculus of Communicating Systems. LNCS, vol. 92. Springer, Heidelberg (1980). https://doi.org/10.1007/3-540-10235-3
26. Milner, R.: The polyadic π-calculus: a tutorial. In: Logic and Algebra of Specification, vol. 49, pp. 203–246 (1993). https://doi.org/10.1007/978-3-642-58041-3_6
27. Nicola, R.D., Hennessy, M.: Testing equivalences for processes. TCS **34**, 83–133 (1984). https://doi.org/10.1016/0304-3975(84)90113-0
28. Peters, K., Yoshida, N.: Separation and encodability in mixed choice multiparty sessions. In: Proceedings of LICS, no. 62, pp. 1–15. ACM (2024). https://doi.org/10.1145/3661814.3662085
29. Pierce, B.C., Sangiorgi, D.: Typing and Subtyping for Mobile Processes. MSCS **6**(5), 409–453 (1996). https://doi.org/10.1017/s096012950007002x
30. Scalas, A., Yoshida, N.: Less is More: Multiparty Session Types Revisited. Doc technical report dtrs-18-6. Imperial College London (2018)
31. Scalas, A., Yoshida, N.: Less is more: multiparty session types revisited. In: Proceedings of POPL, vol. 3, pp. 30:1–30:29 (2019). https://doi.org/10.1145/3290343
32. Segala, R., Lynch, N.: Probabilistic simulations for probabilistic processes. In: Jonsson, B., Parrow, J. (eds.) CONCUR 1994. LNCS, vol. 836, pp. 481–496. Springer, Heidelberg (1994). https://doi.org/10.1007/978-3-540-48654-1_35
33. Yoshida, N., Gheri, L.: A very gentle introduction to multiparty session types. In: Hung, D.V., D'Souza, M. (eds.) ICDCIT 2020. LNCS, vol. 11969, pp. 73–93. Springer, Cham (2020). https://doi.org/10.1007/978-3-030-36987-3_5
34. Zhou, F.: Refining Multiparty Session Types. Ph.D. thesis, Imperial College London (2024)

On Asynchronous Multiparty Session Types for Federated Learning

Ivan Prokić[1]([⊠]) [iD], Simona Prokić[1] [iD], Silvia Ghilezan[1,2] [iD], Alceste Scalas[3] [iD],
and Nobuko Yoshida[4] [iD]

[1] Faculty of Technical Sciences, University of Novi Sad, Novi Sad, Serbia
`{prokic,simona.k,gsilvia}@uns.ac.rs`
[2] Mathematical Institute of the Serbian Academy of Sciences and Arts,
Belgrade, Serbia
[3] Technical University of Denmark, Kongens Lyngby, Denmark
`alcsc@dtu.dk`
[4] University of Oxford, Oxford, UK
`nobuko.yoshida@cs.ox.ac.uk`

Abstract. This paper improves the session typing theory to support the modelling and verification of processes that implement federated learning protocols. To this end, we build upon the asynchronous "bottom-up" session typing approach by adding support for input/output operations directed towards multiple participants at the same time. We further enhance the flexibility of our typing discipline and allow for safe process replacements by introducing a session subtyping relation tailored for this setting. We formally prove safety, deadlock-freedom, liveness, and session fidelity properties for our session typing system. Moreover, we highlight the nuances of our session typing system, which (compared to previous work) reveals interesting interplays and trade-offs between safety, liveness, and the flexibility of the subtyping relation.

Keywords: Multiparty session types · Federated learning · π-calculus · Type systems

1 Introduction

Asynchronous multiparty session types [9] provide a formal approach to the verification of message-passing programs. The key idea is to express *protocols as types*, and use type checking to verify whether one or more communicating processes correctly implement some desired protocols. To enhance usability of session type theory in real-world applications, many extensions and variations of the approach have been proposed over the years [6,10,12,14,20,24,25]. However, these extensions remain insufficient for several important applications, including Federated learning (FL). FL is a distributed machine learning setting where clients train a model while keeping the training data decentralized [3,4,15,18,19, 27]. In FL, communication protocols follow key patterns that must be expressed

Z. Liu et al. (Eds.): ICTAC 2025, LNCS 16237, pp. 164–182, 2026.
https://doi.org/10.1007/978-3-032-11176-0_11

for proper modeling and verification. For instance, some initial investigations [18, 19] note that using existing session type theories to model and verify FL protocols can be challenging due to presence of "arbitrary order of message arrivals". We now explain the nature of these challenges.

Modelling an asynchronous centralised federated learning protocol. Originally, FL considered centralised approach [4,15,18,19], where, in *phase 1*, a central *server* distributes the learning model to the *clients*. In *phase 2*, the clients receive the model, train it locally, and send the updated version back to the server. Finally, the server aggregates the updates and obtains an improved model. As a concrete example, consider a single round of a *generic centralised one-shot federated learning algorithm (FLA)* [18,19] having one server and two clients. We may model the processes for server p and two clients q and r with a value passing labeled π-calculus as follows—where *ld* and *upd* are message labels meaning "local data" and "update," $\sum$ represents a choice, and and q!*ld*⟨...⟩ (resp. q?*ld*(...)) means "send (resp. receive) the message *ld* to (resp. from) participant q."

$$P = \mathsf{q}!ld\langle\mathsf{data}\rangle\,.\,\mathsf{r}!ld\langle\mathsf{data}\rangle.\sum\left\{\begin{matrix}\mathsf{q}?upd(x)\,.\,\mathsf{r}?upd(y)\\\mathsf{r}?upd(y)\,.\,\mathsf{q}?upd(x)\end{matrix}\right\}$$

$$Q = R = \mathsf{p}?ld(x).\mathsf{p}!upd\langle\mathsf{data}\rangle$$

In phase 1, p's process P above sends its local data (i.e., a machine learning model) to q and then to r. In phase 2, server p receives the update *upd* from q and also r; this can happen in two possible orders depending on whether the data is received from q or r first (i.e., arbitrary order of message arrivals), and this is represented by the two branches of the choice $\sum$. Clients q and r receive server's local data and reply with update.

Furthermore, suppose we have implemented the above process specifications and verified that they behave as intended. Now, we want to upgrade the participant q to support for *multi-model FL* [4], in which a client can train multiple models, but only one per round (due to computational constraints). Assuming q can train two models *ld* and *ld′*, we may model an updated process Q'.

$$Q' = \sum\left\{\begin{matrix}\mathsf{p}?ld(x).\mathsf{p}!upd\langle\mathsf{data}\rangle\\\mathsf{p}?ld'(y).\mathsf{p}!upd'\langle\mathsf{data}'\rangle\end{matrix}\right\}$$

This rises a question: *Can we safely substitute Q with Q' in the protocol without needing to re-verify the entire protocol?*

Modelling an Asynchronous Decentralised Federated Learning Protocol. Now let us consider a class of asynchronous decentralised federated learning (DFL) protocols that rely on a fully connected network topology (in which direct links exist between all pairs of nodes) [3,18,19,27]. Concretely, we consider a single round of a *generic decentralised one-shot federated learning algorithm (FLA)* [18,19] having three nodes, where there is no central point of control. Each participant in this algorithm follows the same behaviour divided in three phases. In *phase*

1, each participant sends its local data (i.e., a machine learning model) to all other participants. In *phase 2*, each participant receives the other participants' local data, trains the algorithm, and sends back the updated data. Finally, in *phase 3*, each participant receives the updated data from other participants and aggregates the updates.

Again, we may model the process for participant p with a value passing labeled π-calculus.

$$P_{12} = \mathsf{q}!ld\langle\mathsf{data}\rangle \,.\, \mathsf{r}!ld\langle\mathsf{data}\rangle. \sum \left\{ \begin{matrix} \mathsf{q}?ld(x)\,.\,\mathsf{q}!upd\langle\mathsf{data}\rangle\,.\,\mathsf{r}?ld(y)\,.\,\mathsf{r}!upd\langle\mathsf{data}\rangle.P_3 \\ \mathsf{r}?ld(y)\,.\,\mathsf{r}!upd\langle\mathsf{data}\rangle\,.\,\mathsf{q}?ld(x)\,.\,\mathsf{q}!upd\langle\mathsf{data}\rangle.P_3 \end{matrix} \right\}$$

$$P_3 = \sum \left\{ \begin{matrix} \mathsf{q}?upd(x)\,.\,\mathsf{r}?upd(y) \\ \mathsf{r}?upd(y)\,.\,\mathsf{q}?upd(x) \end{matrix} \right\}$$

In phase 1, p's process P_{12} above sends its local data to q and then to r. In phase 2 (starting with the sum), participant p receives local data and replies the update *upd* to q and also r; this can happen in two possible orders depending on whether the data is received from q or r first. Finally, in phase 3 (in process P_3), p receives update data from q and r in any order (again, this is represented with two choice branches).

Notice that each participant here exhibits an arbitrary order of message arrivals, and that no single participant guides the protocol. This can be challenging to model using session type theories that rely on global types.

Contributions and Outline of the Paper. We present a novel "bottom-up" asynchronous session typing theory (in the style of [20], i.e., that does not require global types) that supports input/output operations directed towards multiple participants. This enables the modeling of arbitrary message arrival orders. We demonstrate that our approach enables the modelling and enhances verification of processes implementing federated learning protocols (both centralized and decentralized) by abstracting protocol behavior to the level of types. We enhance flexibility of our typing discipline and allow for safe process replacements by introducing a session subtyping relation tailored for this setting. Furthermore, we formalise and prove safety, deadlock-freedom, liveness, and session fidelity properties for well-typed processes, revealing interesting dependencies between these properties in the presence of a subtyping relation.

The paper is organized as follows: Sect. 2 introduces the asynchronous session calculus; Sect. 3 presents the types and subtyping relation; Sect. 4 details the type system, our main results, and the implementation of federated learning protocols; and finally, Sect. 5 concludes with a discussion of related and future work.

2   The Calculus

In this section we present the syntax and operational semantics of the value-passing labeled π-calculus used in this work (we omit session creation and delegation). The syntax of the calculus is defined in Table 1. Values can be either variables (x, y, z) or constants (positive integers or booleans).

$$
\begin{aligned}
\mathsf{v} &::= x, y, z, \ldots \;\mid\; 1, 2, \ldots \;\mid\; \mathsf{true}, \mathsf{false} && \textit{(variables, values)} \\
\mathcal{M} &::= \mathsf{p} \triangleleft P \;\mid\; \mathsf{p} \triangleleft h \;\mid\; \mathcal{M} \mid \mathcal{M} && \textit{(participant, parallel)} \\
h &::= \varnothing \;\mid\; (\mathsf{q}, \ell(\mathsf{v})) \;\mid\; h \cdot h && \textit{(empty, message, concatenation)} \\
P, Q &::= \textstyle\sum_{i \in I} \mathsf{p}_i ? \ell_i(x_i).P_i \;\mid\; \sum_{i \in I} \mathsf{p}_i ! \ell_i \langle \mathsf{v}_i \rangle.P_i && \textit{(external choice, internal choice)} \\
&\quad\; \mathsf{if}\ e\ \mathsf{then}\ P\ \mathsf{else}\ Q && \textit{(conditional)} \\
&\quad\; X \;\mid\; \mu X.P \;\mid\; \mathbf{0} && \textit{(variable, recursion, inaction)}
\end{aligned}
$$

Fig. 1. Syntax of sessions, processes, and queues.

Our **asynchronous multiparty sessions** (ranged over by $\mathcal{M}, \mathcal{M}', \ldots$) represent a parallel composition of **participants** (ranged over by $\mathsf{p}, \mathsf{q}, \ldots$) assigned with their **process** P and **output message queue** h (notation: $\mathsf{p} \triangleleft P \mid \mathsf{p} \triangleleft h$). Here, $\mathsf{p} \triangleleft h$ denotes that h is the output message queue of participant p, and the **queued message** $(\mathsf{q}, \ell(\mathsf{v}))$ represents that participant p has sent message labeled ℓ with payload v to q. In the syntax of processes, the **external choice** $\sum_{i \in I} \mathsf{p}_i ? \ell_i(x_i).P_i$ denotes receiving from participant p_i a message labelled ℓ_i with a value that should replace variable x_i in P_i, for any $i \in I$. The **internal choice** $\sum_{i \in I} \mathsf{p}_i ! \ell_i \langle \mathsf{v}_i \rangle.P_i$ denotes sending to participant p_i a message labelled ℓ_i with value v_i, and then continuing as P_i, for any $i \in I$; we will see that, when the internal choice has more than one branch, then one of them is picked nondeterministically. In both external and internal choices, we assume $(\mathsf{p}_i, \ell_i) \neq (\mathsf{p}_j, \ell_j)$, for all $i, j \in I$, such that $i \neq j$. The **conditional** construct, process **variable**, **recursion**, and **inaction** $\mathbf{0}$ are standard; we will sometimes omit writing $\mathbf{0}$. As usual, we assume that recursion is guarded, i.e., in the process $\mu X.P$, the variable X can occur in P only under an internal or external choice.

We show how this syntax can be used to compactly model two federated learning protocols [18,19]: a centralized (Example 1) and a decentralized (Example 2). First, we set up some notation.

We define a **concurrent input** macro $\|R_j\|_{j \in I}.Q$ to represent a process that awaits a series of incoming messages arriving in arbitrary order:

$$
R ::= \mathsf{p}?l(x) \;\mid\; \mathsf{p}?l(x).R^{?!} \qquad R^{?!} ::= \mathsf{p}?l(x) \;\mid\; \mathsf{p}!l\langle \mathsf{v} \rangle \;\mid\; \mathsf{p}?l(x).R^{?!} \;\mid\; \mathsf{p}!l\langle \mathsf{v} \rangle.R^{?!}
$$

$$
\|R_i\|_{i \in I}.Q \;=\; \sum_{i \in I} R_i.\|R_j\|_{j \in I \setminus \{i\}}.Q \quad \text{and} \quad \|R_j\|_{j \in \{i\}}.Q \;=\; R_i.Q
$$

where R_i are all process prefixes starting with an input, possibly followed by other inputs or outputs. The concurrent input $\|R_i\|_{i \in I}.Q$ specifies an external choice of any input-prefixed R_i, for $i \in I$, followed by another choice of input-prefixed process with an index from $I \setminus \{i\}$; the composition continues until all $i \in I$ are covered, with process Q added at the end. In this way, concurrent input process $\|R_i\|_{i \in I}.Q$ can perform the actions specified by any R_i (for $i \in I$) in an arbitrary order, depending on which inputs become available first; afterwards, process Q is always executed. For instance, using our concurrent input macro, we may represent the FLA process P_3 from Sect. 1 as $P_3 = \|\mathsf{q}?upd(x),\ \mathsf{r}?upd(y)\|$.

$$[\text{R-SEND}] \quad \mathsf{p} \triangleleft \sum_{i \in I} \mathsf{q}_i!\ell_i\langle \mathsf{v}_i\rangle.P_i \mid \mathsf{p} \triangleleft h_\mathsf{p} \mid \mathcal{M}$$
$$\xrightarrow{\mathsf{p}:\mathsf{q}_k!\ell_k} \mathsf{p} \triangleleft P_k \mid \mathsf{p} \triangleleft h_\mathsf{p} \cdot (\mathsf{q}_k, \ell_k(\mathsf{v}_k)) \mid \mathcal{M} \qquad (k \in I)$$

$$[\text{R-RCV}] \quad \mathsf{p} \triangleleft \sum_{i \in I} \mathsf{q}_i?\ell_i(x_i).P_i \mid \mathsf{p} \triangleleft h_\mathsf{p} \mid \mathsf{q} \triangleleft Q \mid \mathsf{q} \triangleleft (\mathsf{p}, \ell(\mathsf{v})) \cdot h \mid \mathcal{M}$$
$$\xrightarrow{\mathsf{p}:\mathsf{q}?\ell} \mathsf{p} \triangleleft P_k\{\mathsf{v}/x_k\} \mid \mathsf{p} \triangleleft h_\mathsf{p} \mid \mathsf{q} \triangleleft Q \mid \mathsf{q} \triangleleft h \mid \mathcal{M} \quad (\exists k \in I : (\mathsf{q}, \ell) = (\mathsf{q}_k, \ell_k))$$

$$[\text{R-COND-T}] \; \mathsf{p} \triangleleft \text{if true then } P \text{ else } Q \mid \mathsf{p} \triangleleft h \mid \mathcal{M} \xrightarrow{\mathsf{p}:\text{if}} \mathsf{p} \triangleleft P \mid \mathsf{p} \triangleleft h \mid \mathcal{M}$$

$$[\text{R-COND-F}] \; \mathsf{p} \triangleleft \text{if false then } P \text{ else } Q \mid \mathsf{p} \triangleleft h \mid \mathcal{M} \xrightarrow{\mathsf{p}:\text{if}} \mathsf{p} \triangleleft Q \mid \mathsf{p} \triangleleft h \mid \mathcal{M}$$

$$[\text{R-STRUCT}] \; \mathcal{M}_1 \Rrightarrow \mathcal{M}_1' \; \text{ and } \; \mathcal{M}_1' \longrightarrow \mathcal{M}_2' \; \text{ and } \; \mathcal{M}_2' \Rrightarrow \mathcal{M}_2 \quad \implies \quad \mathcal{M}_1 \longrightarrow \mathcal{M}_2$$

Fig. 2. Reduction relation on sessions.

Example 1 (Modelling a centralised FL protocol implementation). As specified in [18,19], the *generic centralized one-shot federated learning protocol* is implemented with one server and $n-1$ clients (Sect. 1 presented the processes of the protocol for $n = 3$). We may model an implementation of this protocol as a session $\mathcal{M} = \prod_{i \in I}(\mathsf{p}_i \triangleleft P_i \mid \mathsf{p}_i \triangleleft \varnothing)$, where $I = \{1, 2 \ldots, n\}$, and where p_1 plays the role of the server, while the rest of participants are clients, defined with:

$$P_1 = \mathsf{p}_2!ld\langle \text{data}\rangle.\ldots.\mathsf{p}_n!ld\langle \text{data}\rangle.\|\mathsf{p}_2?upd(x_2),\ldots,\mathsf{p}_n?upd(x_n)\|$$
$$P_i = \mathsf{p}_1?ld(x).\mathsf{p}_1!upd\langle \text{data}\rangle \qquad \text{for } i = 2,\ldots,n$$

Notice that, after sending the data to all the clients, the server P_1 then receives the updates from all of them in an arbitrary order. The clients first receive the data and then reply the update back to the server.

Example 2 (Modelling a decentralised FL protocol implementation). As specified in [18,19], an implementation of the *generic decentralized one-shot federated learning protocol* comprises n participant processes acting both as servers and clients (Sect. 1 presented one process of the protocol for $n = 3$). We may model an implementation of this protocol with a session $\mathcal{M} = \prod_{i \in I}(\mathsf{p}_i \triangleleft P_i \mid \mathsf{p}_i \triangleleft \varnothing)$, where $I = \{1, 2 \ldots, n\}$, and where process P_1 is defined as follows: (the rest of the processes are defined analogously)

$$P_1 = \mathsf{p}_2!ld\langle \text{data}\rangle.\ldots.\mathsf{p}_n!ld\langle \text{data}\rangle.$$
$$\|\mathsf{p}_2?ld(x_2).\mathsf{p}_2!upd\langle \text{data}\rangle,\ldots,\mathsf{p}_n?ld(x_n).\mathsf{p}_n!upd\langle \text{data}\rangle\|.$$
$$\|\mathsf{p}_2?upd(y_2),\ldots,\mathsf{p}_n?upd(y_n)\|$$

Process P_1 specifies that participant p_1 first sends its local data to all other participants. Then, p_1 receives local data from all other participants and replies the update concurrently (i.e., in an arbitrary order). Finally, p_1 receives the updates from all other participants, again in an arbitrary order.

Session Reductions. The **reduction relation** for our process calculus is defined in Fig. 2. Rule [R-SEND] specifies sending one of the messages from the internal choice, while the other choices are discarded; the message ℓ_k with payload v_k sent to participant q_k is appended to the participant p's output queue, and p's process becomes the continuation P_k. Dually, rule [R-RCV] defines how a participant p can receive a message, directed towards p with a supported label, from the head of the output queue of the sender q; after the reduction, the message is removed from the queue and the received message then substitutes the placeholder variable x_k in the continuation process P_k. Observe that, by rules [R-SEND] and [R-RCV], output queues are used in FIFO order. Rules [R-COND-T] and [R-COND-F] define how to reduce a conditional process: the former when the condition is true, the latter when it is false. Rule [R-STRUCT] closes the reduction relation under a standard precongruence relation $\Rrightarrow$ (defined as expected) that allows reordering of messages in queues and unfolding recursive processes, combining the approach of [26] with [7].

Properties. In Definition 1 below we follow the approach of [7] and define how "good" sessions are expected to run by using behavioural properties. We define three behavioural properties. The first one is *safety*, ensuring that a session never has mismatches between the message labels supported by external choices and the labels of incoming messages. Since, in our sessions, one participant can choose to receive messages from multiple senders at once, our definition of safety requires external choices to support all possible message labels from all senders' queues. The *deadlock freedom* property requires that a session can get stuck (cannot reduce further) only in case it terminates. The *liveness* property ensures all pending inputs eventually receive a message and all queued messages are eventually received, if reduction steps are performed in a *fair* manner.

The fair path definition says that whenever a participant p is ready to perform an output in a session $\mathcal{M}_i$, then there is a session $\mathcal{M}_k$ (reached by reducing $\mathcal{M}_i$) where p actually performs an output. Dually, if a participant p in $\mathcal{M}_i$ is ready to receive a message which is already available at the top of the sender's output queue, then p will receive that message in $\mathcal{M}_k$. This avoids unfair paths, e.g., in which two participants recursively exchange messages, while a third participant forever waits to send a message. Our fair and live properties for session types with standard choices matches the liveness defined in [7, Definition 2.2]. Also, our fairness aligns with "fairness of components" according to [8] - where a "component" is a process in a session. Moreover, by the syntax and semantics of our processes, fairness of components coincides with justness [8].

Definition 1 (Session behavioral properties). *A **session path** is a (possibly infinite) sequence of sessions $(\mathcal{M}_i)_{i \in I}$, where $I = \{0, 1, 2, \ldots, n\}$ (or $I = \{0, 1, 2, \ldots\}$) is a set of consecutive natural numbers, and, $\forall i \in I \setminus \{n\}$ (or $\forall i \in I$), $\mathcal{M}_i \longrightarrow \mathcal{M}_{i+1}$. We say that a path $(\mathcal{M}_i)_{i \in I}$ is **safe** iff, $\forall i \in I$:*

(SS) *if $\mathcal{M}_i \Rrightarrow \mathsf{p} \triangleleft \sum_{j \in J} \mathsf{q}_j?\ell_j(x_j).P_j \mid \mathsf{p} \triangleleft h \mid \mathsf{q} \triangleleft Q \mid \mathsf{q} \triangleleft h_\mathsf{q} \mid \mathcal{M}'$ with $\mathsf{q} \in \{\mathsf{q}_j\}_{j \in J}$ and $h_\mathsf{q} \equiv (\mathsf{p}, \ell(\mathsf{v})) \cdot h'_\mathsf{q}$, then $(\mathsf{q}, \ell) = (\mathsf{q}_j, \ell_j)$, for some $j \in J$*

*We say that a path $(\mathcal{M}_i)_{i \in I}$ is **deadlock-free** iff:*

(SD) *if $I = \{0, 1, 2, \ldots, n\}$ and $\mathcal{M}_n \nrightarrow$ then $\mathcal{M}_n \Rrightarrow \mathsf{p} \triangleleft \mathbf{0} \mid \mathsf{p} \triangleleft \varnothing$*

*We say that a path $(\mathcal{M}_i)_{i \in I}$ is **fair** iff, $\forall i \in I$:*

(SF1) *if $\mathcal{M}_i \xrightarrow{\text{p:q!}\ell} \mathcal{M}'$, then $\exists k, j$ such that $I \ni k \geq i$ and $\mathcal{M}_k \xrightarrow{\text{p:q}_j!\ell_j} \mathcal{M}_{k+1}$*

(SF2) *if $\mathcal{M}_i \xrightarrow{\text{p:q?}\ell} \mathcal{M}'$, $\exists k, j$ such that $I \ni k \geq i$ and $\mathcal{M}_k \xrightarrow{\text{p:q}_j?\ell_j} \mathcal{M}_{k+1}$*

(SF3) *if $\mathcal{M}_i \xrightarrow{\text{p:if}} \mathcal{M}'$, $\exists k$ such that $I \ni k \geq i$ and $\mathcal{M}_k \xrightarrow{\text{p:if}} \mathcal{M}_{k+1}$*

*We say that a session path $(\mathcal{M}_i)_{i \in I}$ is **live** iff, $\forall i \in I$:*

(SL1) *if $\mathcal{M}_i \Rightarrow \mathsf{p} \triangleleft \text{if } \mathsf{v} \text{ then } P \text{ else } Q \mid \mathsf{p} \triangleleft h \mid \mathcal{M}'$, then $\exists k$ such that $I \ni k \geq i$ and, for some $\mathcal{M}''$, we have either $\mathcal{M}_k \Rightarrow \mathsf{p} \triangleleft P \mid \mathsf{p} \triangleleft h \mid \mathcal{M}''$ or $\mathcal{M}_k \Rightarrow \mathsf{p} \triangleleft Q \mid \mathsf{p} \triangleleft h \mid \mathcal{M}''$*

(SL2) *if $\mathcal{M}_i \Rightarrow \mathsf{p} \triangleleft \sum_{j \in J} \mathsf{q}_j!\ell_j\langle \mathsf{v}_j \rangle.P_j \mid \mathsf{p} \triangleleft h \mid \mathcal{M}'$, then $\exists k$ such that $I \ni k \geq i$ and $\mathcal{M}_k \xrightarrow{\text{p:q}_j!\ell_j} \mathcal{M}_{k+1}$, for some $j \in J$*

(SL3) *if $\mathcal{M}_i \Rightarrow \mathsf{p} \triangleleft P \mid \mathsf{p} \triangleleft (\mathsf{q}, \ell(\mathsf{v})) \cdot h \mid \mathcal{M}'$, then $\exists k$ such that $I \ni k \geq i$ and $\mathcal{M}_k \xrightarrow{\text{q:p?}\ell} \mathcal{M}_{k+1}$*

(SL4) *if $\mathcal{M}_i \Rightarrow \mathsf{p} \triangleleft \sum_{j \in J} \mathsf{q}_j?\ell_j(x_j).P_j \mid \mathsf{p} \triangleleft h \mid \mathcal{M}'$, then $\exists k$ such that $I \ni k \geq i$, and $\mathcal{M}_k \xrightarrow{\text{p:q?}\ell} \mathcal{M}_{k+1}$, where $(\mathsf{q}, \ell) \in \{(\mathsf{q}_j, \ell_j)\}_{j \in J}$*

*We say that a session $\mathcal{M}$ is **safe/deadlock-free** iff all paths beginning with $\mathcal{M}$ are safe/deadlock-free. We say that a session $\mathcal{M}$ is **live** iff all fair paths beginning with $\mathcal{M}$ are live.*

Like in standard session types [20], in our calculus safety does not imply liveness nor deadlock-freedom (Example 3). Also, liveness implies deadlock-freedom, since liveness requires that session cannot get stuck before all external choices are performed and queued messages are eventually received. The converse is not true: e.g., a session in which two participants recursively exchange messages is deadlock free (as it never gets stuck), even if a third participant waits forever to receive a message that nobody will send. This session is not live, since in any fair path the third participant never fires its actions.

However, *unlike* standard session types, in our calculus liveness does *not* imply safety: this is illustrated in Example 4 below.

Example 3 (A safe but non-live session). Consider session

$$\mathcal{M} = \mathsf{p} \triangleleft \sum \{\mathsf{q}?\ell_1(x).\mathsf{r}?\ell_2(y), \; \mathsf{r}?\ell_2(x), \; \mathsf{r}?\ell_3(x)\} \mid \mathsf{p} \triangleleft \varnothing$$
$$\mid \mathsf{q} \triangleleft \mathbf{0} \mid \mathsf{q} \triangleleft (\mathsf{p}, \ell_1(\mathsf{v}_1)) \mid \mathsf{r} \triangleleft \mathbf{0} \mid \mathsf{r} \triangleleft (\mathsf{p}, \ell_2(\mathsf{v}_2))$$

In the session, participant p is ready to receive an input either from q or r, which, in turn, both have enqueued messages for p. The labels of enqueued messages are safely supported in p's receive. Session $\mathcal{M}$ has two possible reductions, where p receives either from q, and $\mathcal{M} \longrightarrow \mathsf{p} \triangleleft \mathsf{r}?\ell_2(y) \mid \mathsf{p} \triangleleft \varnothing \mid \mathsf{r} \triangleleft \mathbf{0} \mid \mathsf{r} \triangleleft (\mathsf{p}, \ell_2(\mathsf{v}_2)) \longrightarrow \mathsf{p} \triangleleft \mathbf{0} \mid \mathsf{p} \triangleleft \varnothing$; or from r, in which case $\mathcal{M} \longrightarrow \mathsf{q} \triangleleft \mathbf{0} \mid \mathsf{q} \triangleleft (\mathsf{p}, \ell_1(\mathsf{v}_1))$.

Hence, session $\mathcal{M}$ is safe, since in all reductions inputs and matching enqueued messages have matching labels. However, $\mathcal{M}$ is not live, since the second path above starting with $\mathcal{M}$ is not live, for q's output queue contains an orphan message that cannot be received. Notice also that $\mathcal{M}$ is not deadlock-free since the final session in the second path cannot reduce further but is not equivalent to a terminated session.

Example 4 (A live but unsafe session). Consider the following session:

$$\mathcal{M}' = \mathsf{p} \triangleleft \sum \{\mathsf{q}?\ell_1(x).\mathsf{r}?\ell_2(y), \ \mathsf{r}?\ell_3(x)\} \ \mid \ \mathsf{p} \triangleleft \varnothing$$
$$\mid \ \mathsf{q} \triangleleft \mathbf{0} \ \mid \ \mathsf{q} \triangleleft (\mathsf{p}, \ell_1(\mathsf{v}_1)) \ \mid \ \mathsf{r} \triangleleft \mathbf{0} \ \mid \ \mathsf{r} \triangleleft (\mathsf{p}, \ell_2(\mathsf{v}_2))$$

The session $\mathcal{M}'$ is not safe since the message in r's output queue has label ℓ_2 which is not supported in p's external choice (that only supports label ℓ_3 for receiving from r). However, $\mathcal{M}'$ has a single reduction path where p receives from q, and then p receives from r; then, the session ends with all processes being $\mathbf{0}$ and all queues empty, which implies $\mathcal{M}'$ is live (and thus, also deadlock-free).

3   Types and Typing Environments

We now introduce our (local) session types, typing contexts and their properties, and subtyping. Our types are a blend of asynchronous multiparty session types [7] and the separated choice multiparty sessions (SCMP) types from [16].

Definition 2. *The **sorts** S are defined as* S $::=$ nat $|$ bool, *and **(local) session types** T are defined as:*

$$\mathsf{T} \ ::= \ \sum_{i \in I} \mathsf{p}_i!\ell_i\langle \mathsf{S}_i\rangle.\mathsf{T}_i \ \mid \ \sum_{i \in I} \mathsf{p}_i?\ell_i(\mathsf{S}_i).\mathsf{T}_i \ \mid \ \mathbf{end} \ \mid \ \mu t.\mathsf{T} \ \mid \ t$$

where $(\mathsf{p}_i, \ell_i) \neq (\mathsf{p}_j, \ell_j)$, *for all* $i, j \in I$ *such that* $i \neq j$. *The **queue types** σ and **typing environments** Γ are defined as:*

$$\sigma \ ::= \ \epsilon \ \mid \ \mathsf{p}!\ell\langle \mathsf{S}\rangle \ \mid \ \sigma \cdot \sigma \qquad\qquad \Gamma \ ::= \ \emptyset \ \mid \ \Gamma, \mathsf{p} : (\sigma, \mathsf{T})$$

Sorts are the types of values, which can be natural numbers (nat) or booleans (bool). The *internal choice* session type $\sum_{i \in I} \mathsf{p}_i!\ell_i\langle \mathsf{S}_i\rangle.\mathsf{T}_i$ describes an output of message ℓ_i with sort S_i towards participant p_i and then evolving to type T_i, for some $i \in I$. Similarly, $\sum_{i \in I} \mathsf{p}_i?\ell_i(\mathsf{S}_i).\mathsf{T}_i$ stands for *external choice*, i.e., receiving a message ℓ_i with sort S_i from participant p_i, for some $i \in I$. The type **end** denotes the terminated session type, $\mu t.\mathsf{T}$ is a recursive type, and t is a recursive type variable. We assume that all recursions are guarded and follow a form of Barendregt convention: every $\mu t.T$ binds a syntactically distinct t.

The *queue type* represents the type of the messages contained in an output queue; it can be empty (ϵ), or it can contain message ℓ with sort S for participant p ($\mathsf{p}!\ell\langle \mathsf{S}\rangle$), or it can be a concatenation of two queue types ($\sigma \cdot \sigma$). The *typing environment* assigns a pair of queue/session type to a participant ($\mathsf{p} : (\sigma, \mathsf{T})$). We use $\Gamma(\mathsf{p})$ to denote the type that Γ assigns to p.

Typing Environment Reductions. Now we define typing environment reductions, which relies on a structural congruence relation $\equiv$ over session types, queue types, and typing environments (defined as expected).

Definition 3. *The typing environment reduction* $\xrightarrow{\alpha}$, *with* α *being either* p:q?ℓ *or* p:q!ℓ *(for some* p, q, ℓ*), is inductively defined as follows:*

$$[\text{E-RCV}] \quad \mathsf{p}_k\colon(\mathsf{q}!\ell_k\langle\mathsf{S}_k\rangle\cdot\sigma,\mathsf{T}_\mathsf{p}),\mathsf{q}\colon(\sigma_\mathsf{q},\textstyle\sum_{i\in I}\mathsf{p}_i?\ell_i(\mathsf{S}_i).\mathsf{T}_i),\Gamma$$
$$\xrightarrow{\mathsf{q}:\mathsf{p}_k?\ell_k} \mathsf{p}_k\colon(\sigma,\mathsf{T}_\mathsf{p}),\mathsf{q}\colon(\sigma_\mathsf{q},\mathsf{T}_k),\Gamma \qquad (k\in I)$$

$$[\text{E-SEND}] \quad \mathsf{p}\colon(\sigma,\textstyle\sum_{i\in I}\mathsf{q}_i!\ell_i\langle\mathsf{S}_i\rangle.\mathsf{T}_i),\Gamma \xrightarrow{\mathsf{p}:\mathsf{q}_k!\ell_k} \mathsf{p}\colon(\sigma\cdot\mathsf{q}_k!\ell_k\langle\mathsf{S}_k\rangle,\mathsf{T}_k),\Gamma \qquad (k\in I)$$

$$[\text{E-STRUCT}] \quad \Gamma\equiv\Gamma_1\xrightarrow{\alpha}\Gamma_1'\equiv\Gamma' \implies \Gamma\xrightarrow{\alpha}\Gamma'$$

We use $\Gamma\longrightarrow\Gamma'$ *instead of* $\Gamma\xrightarrow{\alpha}\Gamma'$ *when* α *is not relevant, and* $\longrightarrow^*$ *for the reflexive and transitive closure of* $\longrightarrow$. $\Gamma\longrightarrow$ *denotes* $\Gamma\longrightarrow\Gamma'$, *for some* Γ'.

In rule [E-RCV] an environment has a reduction step labeled q:p_k?ℓ_k if participant p_k has at the head of its queue a message for q with label ℓ_k and payload sort S_k, and q has an external choice type that includes participant p_k with label ℓ_k and a corresponding sort S_k; the environment evolves by consuming p_k's message and activating the continuation T_k in q's type. Rule [E-SEND] specifies reduction if p has an internal choice type where p sends a message toward q_k, for some $k\in I$; the reduction is labelled p:q_k!ℓ_k and the message is placed at the end of p's queue. Rule [E-STRUCT] is standard closure of the reduction relation under structural congruence.

Properties. Similarly to [20], we define behavioral properties also for typing environments (and their reductions). As for processes, we use three properties for typing environments. *Safety* ensures that the typing environment never has label or sort mismatches. In our setting, where one participant can receive from more than one queue, this property ensures safe receptions of queued messages. The second property, *deadlock freedom*, ensures that typing environment which can not reduce further must be terminated. The third property is *liveness*, which, for the case of standard session types (as in [7]), matches the liveness defined in [7, Definition 4.7]: it ensures all pending inputs eventually receive a message and all queued messages are eventually received, if reduction steps are performed *fairly*.

Notably, our definition of deadlock-freedom and liveness also require safety. The reason for this is that liveness and deadlock-freedom properties for typing environments, if defined without assuming safety, are not preserved by the subtyping (introduced in the next section, see Example 9). We use the predicate over typing environments $\mathbf{end}(\Gamma)$ (read "Γ **is terminated**") that holds iff, for all $p\in dom(\Gamma)$, we have $\Gamma(\mathsf{p})\equiv(\epsilon,\mathbf{end})$.

Definition 4 (Typing environment properties). *A typing environment path is a (possibly infinite) sequence of typing environments* $(\Gamma_i)_{i\in I}$, *where* $I=\{0,1,2,\ldots,n\}$ *(or* $I=\{0,1,2,\ldots\}$*) is a set of consecutive natural numbers, and,* $\forall i\in I\backslash\{n\}$ *(or* $\forall i\in I$*),* $\Gamma_i\longrightarrow\Gamma_{i+1}$. *We say a path* $(\Gamma_i)_{i\in I}$ *is* ***safe*** *iff,* $\forall i\in I$:

(TS) *if* $\Gamma_i(\mathsf{p}) \equiv (\sigma_\mathsf{p}, \sum_{j \in J} \mathsf{q}_j?\ell_j(\mathsf{S}_j).\mathsf{T}_j)$ *and* $\Gamma_i(\mathsf{q}_k) \equiv (\mathsf{p}!\ell_k\langle \mathsf{S}_k\rangle \cdot \sigma_\mathsf{q}, \mathsf{T}_\mathsf{q})$, *with* $\mathsf{q}_k \in \{\mathsf{q}_j\}_{j \in J}$, *then* $\exists j \in J : (\mathsf{q}_j, \ell_j, \mathsf{S}_j) = (\mathsf{q}_k, \ell_k, \mathsf{S}_k)$

*We say that a path $(\Gamma_i)_{i \in I}$ is **deadlock-free** iff:*

(TD) *if* $I = \{0, 1, \ldots, n\}$ *and* $\Gamma_n \nrightarrow$ *then* $\mathsf{end}(\Gamma_n)$

*We say that a path $(\Gamma_i)_{i \in I}$ is **fair** iff, $\forall i \in I$:*

(TF1) *if* $\Gamma_i \xrightarrow{\mathsf{p:q}!\ell} \Gamma'$, *then* $\exists k, \mathsf{q}', \ell'$ *such that* $I \ni k \geq i$ *and* $\Gamma_k \xrightarrow{\mathsf{p:q}'!\ell'} \Gamma_{k+1}$

(TF2) *if* $\Gamma_i \xrightarrow{\mathsf{p:q}?\ell} \Gamma'$, *then* $\exists k, \mathsf{q}', \ell'$ *such that* $I \ni k \geq i$ *and* $\Gamma_k \xrightarrow{\mathsf{p:q}'?\ell'} \Gamma_{k+1}$

*We say that a path $(\Gamma_i)_{i \in I}$ is **live** iff, $\forall i \in I$:*

(TL1) *if* $\Gamma_i(\mathsf{p}) \equiv (\mathsf{q}!\ell\langle\mathsf{S}\rangle \cdot \sigma, \mathsf{T})$, *then* $\exists k$ *such that* $I \ni k \geq i$ *and* $\Gamma_k \xrightarrow{\mathsf{q:p}?\ell} \Gamma_{k+1}$

(TL2) *if* $\Gamma_i(\mathsf{p}) \equiv \left(\sigma_\mathsf{p}, \sum_{j \in J} \mathsf{q}_j?\ell_j(\mathsf{S}_j).\mathsf{T}_j\right)$, *then* $\exists k, \mathsf{q}, \ell$ *such that* $I \ni k \geq i$, $(\mathsf{q}, \ell) \in \{(\mathsf{q}_j, \ell_j)\}_{j \in J}$, *and* $\Gamma_k \xrightarrow{\mathsf{p:q}?\ell} \Gamma_{k+1}$

*A typing environment Γ is **safe** iff all paths starting with Γ are safe. A typing environment Γ is **deadlock-free** iff all paths starting with Γ are safe and deadlock-free. We say that a typing environment Γ is **live** iff it is safe and all fair paths beginning with Γ are live.*

Since our deadlock-freedom and liveness for typing environments subsumes safety, we do not have the situation in which typing environment is deadlock-free and/or live but not safe. Still, we can have typing environments that are safe but not deadlock-free or live.

Example 5. Consider typing environment

$$\Gamma = \{\mathsf{p} : (\epsilon, \sum\{\mathsf{q}?\ell_1(\mathsf{S}_1).\mathsf{r}?\ell_2(\mathsf{S}_2), \ \mathsf{r}?\ell_2(\mathsf{S}_2), \ \mathsf{r}?\ell_3(\mathsf{S}_3)\},$$
$$\mathsf{q} : (\mathsf{p}!\ell_1\langle\mathsf{S}_1\rangle, \mathsf{end}), \mathsf{r} : (\mathsf{p}!\ell_2\langle\mathsf{S}_2\rangle, \mathsf{end})\}$$

Here, Γ is safe by Definition 4, but is not live nor deadlock-free, because the path in which p receives from r message ℓ_2 leads to a typing environment that cannot reduce further but is not terminated. Now consider typing environment

$$\Gamma' = \{\mathsf{p} : (\epsilon, \sum\{\mathsf{q}?\ell_1(\mathsf{S}_1).\mathsf{r}?\ell_2(\mathsf{S}_2), \ \mathsf{r}?\ell_3(\mathsf{S}_3)\}, \mathsf{q} : (\mathsf{p}!\ell_1\langle\mathsf{S}_1\rangle, \mathsf{end}), \mathsf{r} : (\mathsf{p}!\ell_2\langle\mathsf{S}_2\rangle, \mathsf{end})\}$$

Γ' is not safe by Definition 4 (hence, also not deadlock-free nor live) since there is a mismatch between r sending ℓ_2 to p, while p can only receive ℓ_3 from r.

We now prove that all three behavioral properties are closed under structural congruence and reductions.

Proposition 1. *If Γ is safe/deadlock-free/live and $\Gamma \equiv \Gamma'$ or $\Gamma \longrightarrow \Gamma'$, then Γ' is safe/deadlock-free/live.*

3.1 Subtyping

In Definition 5 below we formalise a standard "synchronous" subtyping relation as in [16], not dealing with the possible reorderings of outputs and inputs allowed by asynchronous subtyping [7].

Definition 5. *The* subtyping $\leqslant$ *is coinductively defined as:*

$$\frac{\forall i \in I \quad T_i \leqslant T_i' \quad \{p_i\}_{i \in I} = \{p_i\}_{i \in I \cup J}}{\sum_{i \in I} p_i!\ell_i\langle S_i\rangle.T_i \leqslant \sum_{i \in I \cup J} p_i!\ell_i\langle S_i\rangle.T_i'} \; [\text{s-out}]$$

$$\frac{\forall i \in I \quad T_i \leqslant T_i' \quad \{p_i\}_{i \in I} = \{p_i\}_{i \in I \cup J}}{\sum_{i \in I \cup J} p_i?\ell_i(S_i).T_i \leqslant \sum_{i \in I} p_i?\ell_i(S_i).T_i'} \; [\text{s-in}]$$

$$\frac{T_1\{\mu t.T_1/t\} \leqslant T_2}{\mu t.T_1 \leqslant T_2} \; [\text{s-muL}] \qquad \frac{T_1 \leqslant T_2\{\mu t.T_2/t\}}{T_1 \leqslant \mu t.T_2} \; [\text{s-muR}] \qquad \frac{}{\text{end} \leqslant \text{end}} \; [\text{s-end}]$$

Pair of queue/session types are related via subtyping $(\sigma_1, T_1) \leqslant (\sigma_2, T_2)$ *iff* $\sigma_1 = \sigma_2$ *and* $T_1 \leqslant T_2$. *We define* $\Gamma \leqslant \Gamma'$ *iff* $dom(\Gamma) = dom(\Gamma')$ *and* $\forall p \in dom(\Gamma) : \Gamma(p) \leqslant \Gamma'(p)$.

The subtyping rules allow less branches for the subtype in the internal choice (in [s-out]), and more branches in the external choice (in [s-in]). The side condition in both rules ensures the set of participants specified in the subtype and supertype choices is the same. Hence, subtyping allows flexibility in the set of labels, not in the set of participants. Subtyping holds up to unfolding (by [s-muL] and [s-muR]), as usual for coinductive subtyping [17, Chapter 21]. By rule [s-end], end is related via subtyping to itself.

Example 6. Consider the typing environments Γ and Γ' from Example 5. Since $\sum\{q?\ell_1(S_1).r?\ell_2(S_2),\ r?\ell_2(S_2),\ r?\ell_3(S_3)\} \leqslant \sum\{q?\ell_1(S_1).r?\ell_2(S_2),\ r?\ell_3(S_3)\}$ holds by [s-in], we also have that $\Gamma \leqslant \Gamma'$ holds.

The following two lemmas show that subtyping of safe typing environments is a simulation and that subtyping preserves all typing environment properties.

Lemma 1. *If* $\Gamma' \leqslant \Gamma$, Γ *is safe, and* $\Gamma' \xrightarrow{\alpha} \Gamma_1'$, *then there is* Γ_1 *such that* $\Gamma_1' \leqslant \Gamma_1$ *and* $\Gamma \xrightarrow{\alpha} \Gamma_1$.

Lemma 2. *If* Γ *is safe/deadlock-free/live and* $\Gamma' \leqslant \Gamma$, *then* Γ' *is safe/deadlock-free/live.*

Remark 1. If in Definition 4 safety is not assumed in deadlock-freedom and liveness, then Lemma 2 does not hold (see Example 6). The same observation also holds for deadlock-freedom in the synchronous case [16, Remark 3.2].

$$\frac{}{\Theta \vdash 1, 2, \ldots : \mathsf{nat}}\;[\text{T-Nat}] \qquad \frac{}{\Theta \vdash \mathsf{true}, \mathsf{false} : \mathsf{bool}}\;[\text{T-Bool}] \qquad \frac{}{\Theta, x : \mathsf{S} \vdash x : \mathsf{S}}\;[\text{T-Var}]$$

$$\frac{}{\vdash \varnothing : \epsilon}\;[\text{T-Nul}] \qquad \frac{\vdash \mathsf{v} : \mathsf{S}}{\vdash (\mathsf{q}, \ell(\mathsf{v})) : \mathsf{q}!\ell\langle\mathsf{S}\rangle}\;[\text{T-Elm}] \qquad \frac{\vdash h_1 : \sigma_1 \quad \vdash h_2 : \sigma_2}{\vdash h_1 \cdot h_2 : \sigma_1 \cdot \sigma_2}\;[\text{T-Queue}]$$

$$\frac{}{\Theta \vdash \mathbf{0} : \mathsf{end}}\;[\text{T-0}] \qquad \frac{\forall i \in I \quad \Theta \vdash \mathsf{v}_i : \mathsf{S}_i \quad \Theta \vdash P_i : \mathsf{T}_i}{\Theta \vdash \sum_{i \in I} \mathsf{p}_i!\ell_i\langle\mathsf{v}_i\rangle.P_i : \sum_{i \in I} \mathsf{p}_i!\ell_i\langle\mathsf{S}_i\rangle.\mathsf{T}_i}\;[\text{T-Out}]$$

$$\frac{\forall i \in I \quad \Theta, x_i : \mathsf{S}_i \vdash P_i : \mathsf{T}_i}{\Theta \vdash \sum_{i \in I} \mathsf{p}_i?\ell_i(x_i).P_i : \sum_{i \in I} \mathsf{p}_i?\ell_i(\mathsf{S}_i).\mathsf{T}_i}\;[\text{T-In}]$$

$$\frac{\Theta \vdash \mathsf{v} : \mathsf{bool} \quad \Theta \vdash P_i : \mathsf{T} \;\;(i = 1, 2)}{\Theta \vdash \mathsf{if}\ \mathsf{v}\ \mathsf{then}\ P_1\ \mathsf{else}\ P_2 : \mathsf{T}}\;[\text{T-Cond}]$$

$$\frac{\Theta, X : \mathsf{T} \vdash P : \mathsf{T}}{\Theta \vdash \mu X.P : \mathsf{T}}\;[\text{T-Rec}] \qquad \frac{}{\Theta, X : \mathsf{T} \vdash X : \mathsf{T}}\;[\text{T-Var}] \qquad \frac{\Theta \vdash P : \mathsf{T} \quad \mathsf{T} \leqslant \mathsf{T}'}{\Theta \vdash P : \mathsf{T}'}\;[\text{T-Sub}]$$

$$\frac{\Gamma = \{\mathsf{p}_i : (\sigma_i, \mathsf{T}_i) \mid i \in I\} \quad \forall i \in I \quad \emptyset \vdash P_i : \mathsf{T}_i \quad \vdash h_i : \sigma_i}{\Gamma \vdash \prod_{i \in I}(\mathsf{p}_i \lhd P_i \mid \mathsf{p}_i \lhd h_i)}\;[\text{T-Sess}]$$

Fig. 3. Typing rules for values, queues, and for processes and sessions.

4 The Typing System and Its Properties

This section introduces the type system that assigns types to processes, queues, and sessions. Our typing system is an extension and adaptation of the one in [7].

Definition 6 (Typing system). *A **shared typing environment** Θ, which assigns sorts to expression variables, and (recursive) session types to process variables, is defined as $\Theta ::= \emptyset \mid \Theta, X : \mathsf{T} \mid \Theta, x : \mathsf{S}$.*

Our type system is inductively defined by the rules in Fig. 3, with 4 judgements—which cover respectively values and variables v, processes P, message queues h, and sessions $\mathcal{M}$:

$$\Theta \vdash \mathsf{v} : \mathsf{S} \qquad\qquad \Theta \vdash P : \mathsf{T} \qquad\qquad \vdash h : \sigma \qquad\qquad \Gamma \vdash \mathcal{M}$$

By Definition 6, the typing judgment $\Theta \vdash \mathsf{v} : \mathsf{S}$ means that value v is of sort S under environment Θ. The judgement $\Theta \vdash P : \mathsf{T}$ says that process P behaves as prescribed with type T and uses its variables as given in Θ. The judgement $\vdash h : \sigma$ says that the messages in the queue h correspond to the queue type σ. Finally, $\Gamma \vdash \mathcal{M}$ means that all participant processes in session $\mathcal{M}$ behave as prescribed by the session types in Γ.

We now illustrate the typing rules in Fig. 3. The first row gives rules for typing natural and boolean values and expression variables. The second row provides rules for typing message queues: an empty queue has the empty queue type (by [T-Nul]) while a queued message is typed if its payload has the correct sort (by [T-Elm]), and a queue obtained with concatenating two message queues is typed by concatenating their queue types (by [T-Queue]).

Rule [T-]**0** types a terminated process **0** with **end**. Rules [T-Out]/[T-In] type internal/external choice processes with the corresponding internal/external choice types: in each branch the payload v_i/x_i and the continuation process P_i have the corresponding sort S_i and continuation type T_i; observe that in [T-IN], each continuation process P_i is typed under environment Θ extended with the input-bound variable x_i having sort S_i. Rule [T-COND] types conditional: both branches must have the same type, and the condition must be boolean. Rule [T-REC] types a recursive process $\mu X.P$ with T if P has type T in an environment where that X has type T. Rule [T-VAR] types recursive process variables. Finally, [T-SUB] is the *subsumption rule*: a process P of type T can be typed with any supertype T'. This rule makes our type system equi-recursive [17], as $\leqslant$ relates types up-to unfolding (by Definition 5). Rule [T-SESS] types a session under environment Γ if each participant's queue and process have corresponding queue and process types in an empty Θ (which forces processes to be closed).

Example 7 (Types for a centralised FL protocol implementation). Consider session $\mathcal{M}$ from Example 1. Take that value data and variables $x, x_2, \ldots, x_n$ are of sort S. We may derive $\vdash P_1 : \mathsf{T}_1$ and $\vdash P_i : \mathsf{T}_2$ (for $i = 1, 2, \ldots, n$), where (with a slight abuse of notation using the concurrent input macro for types):

$$\mathsf{T}_1 = \mathsf{p}_2!ld\langle\mathsf{S}\rangle.\ldots.\mathsf{p}_n!ld\langle\mathsf{S}\rangle.\|\mathsf{p}_2?upd(\mathsf{S}), \ldots, \mathsf{p}_n?upd(\mathsf{S})\|$$
$$\mathsf{T}_2 = \mathsf{p}_1?ld(\mathsf{S}).\mathsf{p}_1!upd\langle\mathsf{S}\rangle$$

Hence, with $\Gamma = \{\mathsf{p}_1 : (\epsilon, \mathsf{T}_1)\} \cup \{\mathsf{p}_i : (\epsilon, \mathsf{T}_2) \,|\, i = 2, \ldots, n\}$ we obtain $\Gamma \vdash \mathcal{M}$. Observe that Γ is deadlock-free and live: after p_1 sends the data to all other participants, each participant receives and replies with an update, that p_1 finally receives in arbitrary order.

Furthermore, considering again the upgrade process Q' from Sect. 1 that allows multi-model FL. We may derive $\vdash Q' : \mathsf{T}'_2$, for

$$\mathsf{T}'_2 = \sum\{\mathsf{p}_1?ld(\mathsf{S}).\mathsf{p}_1!upd\langle\mathsf{S}\rangle, \ \mathsf{p}_1?ld'(\mathsf{S}).\mathsf{p}_1!upd'\langle\mathsf{S}\rangle\}$$

By our subtyping relation we have $\mathsf{T}'_2 \leqslant \mathsf{T}_2$. If we denote with Γ' typing environment where one of the clients has the upgraded type T'_2, and the rest is same as in Γ, we also have $\Gamma' \leqslant \Gamma$. Hence, by Lemma 2 we have that Γ' is also deadlock-free and live, confirming that Q can safely be replaced with Q' in this, but also in any other, session.

Example 8 (Types for a decentralised FL protocol implementation). Consider session $\mathcal{M}$ from Example 2. Take that value data and variables $x_2, \ldots, x_n, y_2, \ldots, y_n$ are of sort S. We may derive $\vdash P_1 : \mathsf{T}_1$ where (again with a slight abuse of notation using the concurrent input macro for types):

$$\mathsf{T}_1 = \mathsf{p}_2!ld\langle\mathsf{S}\rangle.\ldots.\mathsf{p}_n!ld\langle\mathsf{S}\rangle.\|\mathsf{p}_2?ld(\mathsf{S}).\mathsf{p}_2!upd\langle\mathsf{S}\rangle, \ldots, \mathsf{p}_n?ld(\mathsf{S}).\mathsf{p}_n!upd\langle\mathsf{S}\rangle\|.$$
$$\|\mathsf{p}_2?upd(\mathsf{S}), \ldots, \mathsf{p}_n?upd(\mathsf{S})\|$$

and similarly for other process we may derive the corresponding types so that $\vdash P_i : \mathsf{T}_i$, for $i = 1, 2, \ldots, n$. Thus, with $\Gamma = \{\mathsf{p}_i : (\epsilon, \mathsf{T}_i) \,|\, i = 1, \ldots, n\}$ we obtain $\Gamma \vdash \mathcal{M}$. Notice that Γ is safe, i.e., has no label or sort mismatches: participant p_i

always receives from p_j message *ld* before *up* (as they are enqueued in this order). This also implies Γ is deadlock-free and live: a participant first asynchronously sends all its *ld* messages (phase 1), then awaits to receive *ld* messages from queues of all other participants (phase 2), and only then awaits to receive *up* messages (phase 3). Hence, all $n(n-1)$ of *ld* and also of *up* messages are sent/received, and a reduction path always ends with a terminated typing environment.

Remark 2 (On the decidability of typing environment properties). Under the "bottom-up approach" to session typing, typing environment properties such as deadlock freedom and liveness are generally undecidable, since two session types with unbounded message queues are sufficient to encode a Turing machine [1, Theorem 2.5]. Still, many practical protocols have bounded buffer sizes—and in particular, the buffer sizes for the FL protocols in [19] are given in the same paper. Therefore, Examples 7 and 8 yield finite-state typing environment whose behavioural properties are decidable and easily verified, e.g., via model checking.

Properties of our Typing System. We now illustrate and prove the properties of our typing system in Definition 6. We aim to prove that if a session $\mathcal{M}$ is typed with safe/deadlock-free/live typing environment Γ, then so is $\mathcal{M}$. Along the way, we illustrate the subtle interplay between our deadlock freedom, liveness, and safety properties (Definition 4) and subtyping (Definition 5).

First, we introduce the subtyping-related Lemma 3 below, which holds directly by rule [T-SUB] and is important for proving Subject Reduction later on (Theorem 1). Based on this, in Example 9 we show why our definitions of deadlock-free and live typing environments (Definition 4) also require safety.

Lemma 3. *If $\Gamma \vdash \mathcal{M}$ and $\Gamma \leqslant \Gamma'$, then $\Gamma' \vdash \mathcal{M}$.*

Example 9. Consider the safe but not deadlock-free nor live session $\mathcal{M}$ from Example 3, and the typing environments Γ and Γ' from Example 5. It is straightforward to show that $\Gamma \vdash \mathcal{M}$, by Definition 6. Observe that, as shown in Example 6, we have $\Gamma \leqslant \Gamma'$; therefore, by Lemma 3 we also have $\Gamma' \vdash \mathcal{M}$. As noted in Example 5, the typing environment Γ' is not safe. Now, suppose that in Definition 4, deadlock-freedom and liveness of typing environments were defined without requiring safety (as for deadlock-freedom and liveness of sessions in Definition 1); also notice that Γ' has a single path that is deadlock-free and live, but not safe. Therefore, this change in Definition 4 would cause Γ', an unsafe but deadlock-free and live typing environment, to type $\mathcal{M}$, a session that is not deadlock-free nor live. This would hamper our goal of showing that if a session is typed by a deadlock-free/live typing environment, then the session is deadlock free/live.

Next we show our main theoretical results: subject reduction (a reduction of a typed session can be followed by its safe/deadlock-free/live typing environment); session fidelity (if the typing environemnt reduces so can the session); and type safety, deadlock-freedom, and liveness (if typing environment is safe/deadlock-free/live, then so is the session).

Theorem 1 (Subject Reduction). *Assume $\Gamma \vdash \mathcal{M}$ with Γ safe/deadlock-free/live and $\mathcal{M} \longrightarrow \mathcal{M}'$. Then, there is safe/deadlock-free/live type environment Γ' such that $\Gamma \longrightarrow^* \Gamma'$ and $\Gamma' \vdash \mathcal{M}'$.*

Theorem 2 (Type Safety). *If $\Gamma \vdash \mathcal{M}$ and Γ is safe, then $\mathcal{M}$ is safe.*

Theorem 3 (Session Fidelity). *Let $\Gamma \vdash \mathcal{M}$. If $\Gamma \longrightarrow$, then $\exists \Gamma', \mathcal{M}'$ such that $\Gamma \longrightarrow \Gamma'$ and $\mathcal{M} \longrightarrow^+ \mathcal{M}'$ and $\Gamma' \vdash \mathcal{M}'$.*

Theorem 4 (Deadlock freedom). *If $\Gamma \vdash \mathcal{M}$ and Γ is deadlock-free, then $\mathcal{M}$ is deadlock-free.*

Theorem 5 (Liveness). *If $\Gamma \vdash \mathcal{M}$ and Γ is live, then $\mathcal{M}$ is live.*

5   Related and Future Work

The original asynchronous multiparty session types [9] is "top-down," in the sense that it begins by specifying a *global type*, i.e., a choreographic formalisation of all the communications expected between the *participants* in the protocol; then, the global type is *projected* into a set of (local) session types, which can be used to type-check processes. There are many extensions to this "top-down" approach. [6,10] extend multiparty sessions to support protocols with optional and dynamic participants, allowing sender-driven choices directed toward multiple participants. This is used by other work [21–23] to express communication protocols utilized in distributed cloud and edge computing. The models in [12–14,24] generalize the notion of projection in asynchronous multiparty session types. Building on the global types of [10], they allow local types with internal and external choices directed at different participants, as we do in this paper. Nevertheless, these approaches are constrained by their reliance on global types and a projection function: the global type couples both sending and receiving in a single construct and enforces a protocol structure where a single participant drives the interaction. This results in at least one projected local type beginning with a receive action—unlike the local types for our decentralised FL protocol implementation (see Example 8).

An alternative "bottom-up" approach to session typing [20] removes the requirement of global types: instead, local session types are specified directly, and the properties of their composition (e.g. deadlock freedom and liveness) are checked and transferred to well-typed processes. The approach in [16] extends the "bottom-up" synchronous multiparty session model of [20], not only by introducing more flexible choices but also by supporting mixed choices—i.e., choices that combine inputs and outputs. In contrast to [16], which assumes synchronous communication, our theory supports asynchronous communication, which is essential for our motivating scenarios and running examples; moreover, [16] does not prove process liveness nor session fidelity.

The recent work [25] presents an automata-based approach for checking multiparty protocols. Unlike ours, [25] presents a top-down approach to session typing, providing a soundness and completeness result on its projection; moreover,

[25] shows that its typing system is also usable in "bottom-up" fashion, like ours. Their global types are specified as Protocol State Machines (PSMs), featuring decoupled send-receive operations, allowing for a wider range of protocols to be specified. Their local type specifications are specified as Communicating State Machines (CSMs), whereas ours are the extended session types. Their sessions are represented, as ours, as π-calculus processes (theirs with delegation), and the type system relates sessions to CSMs, and has the following distinguishing points w.r.t. our paper. First, we provide a coinductively defined subtyping relation with a standard subsumption rule [T-SUB], while [25] has no subtyping relation: specifically, it embeds output subtyping (i.e., the selection of one among multiple possible outputs) within the typing rules, but does not support input subtyping. [25] explicitly notes that "there are subtleties for subtyping as one cannot simply add receives". This makes the interplay of safety, deadlock-freedom/liveness, and subtyping we pointed out in our paper not reproducible in their setting. Second, [25] proves a safety property (no label mismatches and terminated sessions not leaving orphan messages) and the progress (deadlock-freedom) property (if the type of the session is not final, the process can take a step). Their progress property is proven for the processes containing only one session (like ours)—but their results do not include a proof of liveness, unlike ours. Finally, [25] specifies "...unsafe communication: a process is stuck because all the queues it is waiting to receive from are not empty, but the labels of the first messages do not match any of the cases the process is expecting"—while in our case it is sufficient for one queue to have an unmatching message. This is a reason why [25] does not allow for subtyping, unlike our paper.

The correctness of the decentralized FL algorithm has been formally verified for deadlock-freedom and termination in [5,19] by using the Communicating Sequential Processes calculus (CSP) and the Process Analysis Toolkit (PAT) model checker. Our asynchronous multiparty session typing model abstracts protocol behavior at the type level, paving the way for more scalable and efficient techniques—not only for model checking, but also for broader verification and analysis applications.

Conclusions and Future Work. We present the first "bottom-up" asynchronous multiparty session typing theory that supports internal and external choices targeting multiple distinct participants. We introduce a process and type calculus, which we relate through a type system. We formally prove safety, deadlock-freedom, liveness, and session fidelity, highlighting interesting dependencies between these properties in the presence of a subtyping relation. Finally, we demonstrate how our model can represent a wide range of communication protocols, including those used in asynchronous decentralized federated learning.

For future work, we identify two main research directions. The first focuses on the fundamental properties of our approach, including: verifying typing environment properties via model checking, in the style of [20]; investigating decidable approximations of deadlock freedom and liveness of typing contexts (see Remark 2), e.g. with the approach of [11]; and investigating the expressiveness of our model based on the framework in [16]. The second direction explores the application of our model as a foundation for reasoning about federated-learning-specific properties, e.g.: handling crashes of arbitrary participants [2]; supporting optional participation [6,10]; ensuring that participants only receive data they are able to process; statically enforcing that only model parameters—not raw data—are exchanged to preserve privacy; guaranteeing sufficiently large server buffers to receive messages from all clients; and ensuring that all clients contribute equally to the algorithm.

Acknowledgments. This work was supported by Horizon EU project 101093006 *TaRDIS*, MSTDI (Contract No. 451-03-137/2025-03/200156) and FTS-UNS through the project *Scientific and Artistic Research Work of Researchers in Teaching and Associate Positions at FTS-UNS 2025* (No. 01-50/295), COST CA20111 *EuroProofNet*, and EPSRC grants EP/T006544/2, EP/N027833/2,EP/T014709/2, EP/V000462/1, EP/X015955/1, EP/Y005244/1 and ARIA.

References

1. Bartoletti, M., Scalas, A., Tuosto, E., Zunino, R.: Honesty by typing. Log. Methods Comput. Sci. **12**(4) (2016)
2. Barwell, A.D., Hou, P., Yoshida, N., Zhou, F.: Designing asynchronous multiparty protocols with crash-stop failures. In: Ali, K., Salvaneschi, G. (eds.) 37th European Conference on Object-Oriented Programming, ECOOP 2023, Seattle, Washington, United States, 17–21 July 2023. LIPIcs, vol. 263, pp. 1:1–1:30. Schloss Dagstuhl - Leibniz-Zentrum für Informatik (2023). https://doi.org/10.4230/LIPIcs.ECOOP.2023.1
3. Beltrán, E.T.M., et al.: Decentralized federated learning: Fundamentals, state of the art, frameworks, trends, and challenges. IEEE Commun. Surv. Tutorials **25**(4), 2983–3013 (2023). https://doi.org/10.1109/COMST.2023.3315746
4. Bhuyan, N., Moharir, S.: Multi-model federated learning. In: 14th International Conference on COMmunication Systems & NETworkS, COMSNETS 2022, Bangalore, India, 4–8 January 2022, pp. 779–783. IEEE (2022). https://doi.org/10.1109/COMSNETS53615.2022.9668435
5. Djukic, M., Prokic, I., Popovic, M., Ghilezan, S., Popovic, M., Prokic, S.: Correct orchestration of federated learning generic algorithms: python translation to CSP and verification by PAT. Int. J. Softw. Tools Technol. Transf. **27**(1), 21–34 (2025). https://doi.org/10.1007/s10009-025-00795-0
6. Gheri, L., Lanese, I., Sayers, N., Tuosto, E., Yoshida, N.: Design-by-contract for flexible multiparty session protocols. In: Ali, K., Vitek, J. (eds.) 36th European Conference on Object-Oriented Programming, ECOOP 2022, Berlin, Germany, 6–10 June 2022. LIPIcs, vol. 222, pp. 8:1–8:28. Schloss Dagstuhl - Leibniz-Zentrum für Informatik (2022), https://doi.org/10.4230/LIPIcs.ECOOP.2022.8
7. Ghilezan, S., Pantovic, J., Prokic, I., Scalas, A., Yoshida, N.: Precise subtyping for asynchronous multiparty sessions. ACM Trans. Comput. Log. **24**(2), 14:1–14:73 (2023). https://doi.org/10.1145/3568422
8. van Glabbeek, R., Höfner, P.: Progress, justness, and fairness. ACM Comput. Surv. **52**(4), 69:1–69:38 (2019). https://doi.org/10.1145/3329125
9. Honda, K., Yoshida, N., Carbone, M.: Multiparty asynchronous session types. J. ACM **63**(1), 9:1–9:67 (2016). https://doi.org/10.1145/2827695

10. Hu, R., Yoshida, N.: Explicit connection actions in multiparty session types. In: Huisman, M., Rubin, J. (eds.) FASE 2017. LNCS, vol. 10202, pp. 116–133. Springer, Heidelberg (2017). https://doi.org/10.1007/978-3-662-54494-5_7

11. Lange, J., Yoshida, N.: Verifying asynchronous interactions via communicating session automata. In: Dillig, I., Tasiran, S. (eds.) CAV 2019. LNCS, vol. 11561, pp. 97–117. Springer, Cham (2019). https://doi.org/10.1007/978-3-030-25540-4_6

12. Li, E., Stutz, F., Wies, T., Zufferey, D.: Complete multiparty session type projection with automata. In: Enea, C., Lal, A. (eds.) Computer Aided Verification - 35th International Conference, CAV 2023, Paris, France, 17–22 July 2023, Proceedings, Part III. Lecture Notes in Computer Science, vol. 13966, pp. 350–373. Springer, Heidelberg (2023). https://doi.org/10.1007/978-3-031-37709-9_17

13. Li, E., Stutz, F., Wies, T., Zufferey, D.: Characterizing implementability of global protocols with infinite states and data. CoRR arxiv:2411.05722 (2024). https://doi.org/10.48550/arXiv.2411.05722

14. Majumdar, R., Mukund, M., Stutz, F., Zufferey, D.: Generalising projection in asynchronous multiparty session types. In: Haddad, S., Varacca, D. (eds.) 32nd International Conference on Concurrency Theory, CONCUR 2021, 24–27 August 2021, Virtual Conference. LIPIcs, vol. 203, pp. 35:1–35:24. Schloss Dagstuhl - Leibniz-Zentrum für Informatik (2021). https://doi.org/10.4230/LIPIcs.CONCUR.2021.35

15. McMahan, B., Moore, E., Ramage, D., Hampson, S., Arcas, B.A.: Communication-efficient learning of deep networks from decentralized data. In: Singh, A., Zhu, X.J. (eds.) Proceedings of the 20th International Conference on Artificial Intelligence and Statistics, AISTATS 2017, Fort Lauderdale, FL, USA, 20–22 April 2017. Proceedings of Machine Learning Research, vol. 54, pp. 1273–1282. PMLR (2017). http://proceedings.mlr.press/v54/mcmahan17a.html

16. Peters, K., Yoshida, N.: Separation and encodability in mixed choice multiparty sessions. In: Sobocinski, P., Lago, U.D., Esparza, J. (eds.) Proceedings of the 39th Annual ACM/IEEE Symposium on Logic in Computer Science, LICS 2024, Tallinn, Estonia, 8–11 July 2024, pp. 62:1–62:15. ACM (2024). https://doi.org/10.1145/3661814.3662085

17. Pierce, B.C.: Types and Programming Languages. MIT Press, Cambridge (2002)

18. Popovic, M., Popovic, M., Kastelan, I., Djukic, M., Ghilezan, S.: A simple Python testbed for federated learning algorithms. In: 2023 Zooming Innovation in Consumer Technologies Conference (ZINC), pp. 148–153. IEEE (2023)

19. Prokic, I., Ghilezan, S., Kasterovic, S., Popovic, M., Popovic, M., Kastelan, I.: Correct orchestration of federated learning generic algorithms: formalisation and verification in CSP. In: Kofron, J., Margaria, T., Seceleanu, C. (eds.) Engineering of Computer-Based Systems - 8th International Conference, ECBS 2023, Västerås, Sweden, 16–18 October 2023, Proceedings. Lecture Notes in Computer Science, vol. 14390, pp. 274–288. Springer, Heidelberg (2023). https://doi.org/10.1007/978-3-031-49252-5_25

20. Scalas, A., Yoshida, N.: Less is more: multiparty session types revisited. PACMPL 3(POPL), 30:1–30:29 (2019). https://doi.org/10.1145/3290343

21. Simic, M., Dedeic, J., Stojkov, M., Prokic, I.: A hierarchical namespace approach for multi-tenancy in distributed clouds. IEEE Access 12, 32597–32617 (2024). https://doi.org/10.1109/ACCESS.2024.3369031

22. Simic, M., Dedeic, J., Stojkov, M., Prokic, I.: Data overlay mesh in distributed clouds allowing collaborative applications. IEEE Access 13, 6180–6203 (2025). https://doi.org/10.1109/ACCESS.2024.3525336

23. Simic, M., Prokic, I., Dedeic, J., Sladic, G., Milosavljevic, B.: Towards edge computing as a service: dynamic formation of the micro data-centers. IEEE Access **9**, 114468–114484 (2021). https://doi.org/10.1109/ACCESS.2021.3104475
24. Stutz, F.: Asynchronous multiparty session type implementability is decidable - lessons learned from message sequence charts. In: Ali, K., Salvaneschi, G. (eds.) 37th European Conference on Object-Oriented Programming, ECOOP 2023, Seattle, Washington, United States, 17–21 July 2023. LIPIcs, vol. 263, pp. 32:1–32:31. Schloss Dagstuhl - Leibniz-Zentrum für Informatik (2023). https://doi.org/10.4230/LIPIcs.ECOOP.2023.32
25. Stutz, F., D'Osualdo, E.: An automata-theoretic basis for specification and type checking of multiparty protocols. In: Vafeiadis, V. (ed.) Programming Languages and Systems - 34th European Symposium on Programming, ESOP 2025, Hamilton, ON, Canada, 3–8 May 2025, Proceedings, Part II. Lecture Notes in Computer Science, vol. 15695, pp. 314–346. Springer, Heidelberg (2025). https://doi.org/10.1007/978-3-031-91121-7_13
26. Udomsrirungruang, T., Yoshida, N.: Top-down or bottom-up? Complexity analyses of synchronous multiparty session types. Proc. ACM Program. Lang. **9**(POPL), 1040–1071 (2025). https://doi.org/10.1145/3704872
27. Yuan, L., Wang, Z., Sun, L., Yu, P.S., Brinton, C.G.: Decentralized federated learning: a survey and perspective. IEEE Internet Things J. **11**(21), 34617–34638 (2024). https://doi.org/10.1109/JIOT.2024.3407584

Logic and Theorem Provers

Efficient Interpolation Beyond Cut-Free Proofs: Admissible Cuts and Optimized Extraction

Simon Corbard[1] and Anela Lolić[2(✉)]

[1] Université Paris-Saclay, ENS Paris-Saclay, Gif-sur-Yvette, France
`simon.corbard@ens-paris-saclay.fr`
[2] Institute of Logic and Computation, TU Wien, Vienna, Austria
`anela@logic.at`

Abstract. Craig interpolation is a foundational concept in logic with broad applications in formal verification, automated reasoning, and modular system design. While Maehara's lemma enables interpolant extraction from cut-free proofs, extending interpolation to proofs with cuts has remained challenging. In this paper, we propose a generalization of Maehara's lemma to admissible cuts – a class of cut-formulas satisfying structural constraints defined via end-sequent partitions. Our approach leverages the Ceres cut-elimination framework to identify cut-free components critical for interpolation. We show that this method not only generalizes previous results on atomic cuts but also reduces the asymptotic complexity of interpolant extraction from cubic to quadratic, thus enhancing the scalability of interpolation techniques in proof-theoretic reasoning.

Keywords: Interpolation · Proof Theory · Cut-Elimination

1 Introduction

Craig's interpolation theorem [8] has long been recognized as a key result in logic, with far-reaching applications in computer science and mathematics. Beyond its foundational importance, interpolation plays a practical role in areas such as model checking, program analysis, modular specification, and modular ontologies. Informally, interpolation states that if a formula $A \to B$ is valid in a logic L, then there exists an interpolant I such that $A \to I$ and $I \to B$ are valid in L, and I only contains the symbols common to both A and B. It demonstrates that only contradictory formulas A and valid formulas B admit the validity of $A \to B$ if A and B do not have anything in common.

In the realm of proof theory, interpolation is closely linked to *Maehara's lemma* [19], which establishes that interpolants can be directly constructed from

Recipient of an APART-MINT Fellowship of the Austrian Academy of Sciences at the Institute of Logic and Computation of TU Wien. This research was funded in part by the Austrian Science Fund (FWF) 10.55776/I5848.

Z. Liu et al. (Eds.): ICTAC 2025, LNCS 16237, pp. 185–201, 2026.
https://doi.org/10.1007/978-3-032-11176-0_12

cut-free proofs in the sequent calculus. This syntactic approach to interpolation is not only constructive but also offers complexity guarantees: the size and structure of the interpolant can be bounded in terms of the proof. However, requiring complete cut-elimination can be computationally expensive, and many practical proofs – especially those generated by automated reasoning tools – contain cuts.

To mitigate this, previous work has explored interpolation in the presence of restricted forms of cuts, such as atomic cut-formulas [3,11], for propositional proofs [4], or in [10], where the authors generalize Maehara's lemma to sequent calculi extended with singular geometric rules (rules involving at most one non-logical predicate), thus allowing for the construction of interpolants even in the presence of certain ineliminable cuts, such as those involving identity.

In this paper, we present a generalized form of Maehara's lemma that supports interpolant extraction from proofs containing *admissible cuts* – a novel class of cut-formulas identified via a partition-based structural criterion. This generalization strictly subsumes the atomic case, enabling interpolation from a wider range of proof structures.

Our method builds on the Ceres cut-elimination system [1,2], which uses resolution-based techniques to transform proofs. Crucially, we show how key transformation steps in Ceres can be exploited to isolate cut-free substructures, which are essential for interpolant computation. By focusing on these core regions of the proof, we devise an optimized interpolation procedure that outperforms the standard approach. For sequences of increasingly large proofs, we show that while interpolant extraction via full Ceres cut-elimination is at least cubic, our refined method is quadratic. This work advances the theoretical understanding of interpolation in proof systems with cuts and contributes practically relevant techniques for scalable reasoning in automated systems.

2   Cut-Free Proofs and Maehara's Lemma

In this section we will introduce a variant of Maehara's partition interpolation method. To this aim we extend Gentzen's system **LK** [9] by introducing the predicate symbol $\top$ with 0 argument places and the additional axiom $\vdash \top$. The obtained system is referred to as **LK#**.

In Maehara's partition interpolation method, the interpolant is constructed based on partitions of sequents $\Gamma \vdash \Delta$. These partitions are defined over permutation variants of the formulas occurring in Γ, Δ.

Definition 1. *Let Γ be a multiset of formulas $A_1, \ldots, A_n$, and π a permutation of $\{1, \ldots, n\}$. Then $A_{\pi(1)}, \ldots, A_{\pi(n)}$ is a permutation variant of Γ. This can be generalized to sequents $\Gamma \vdash \Delta$ by computing a permutation variant of Γ and a permutation variant of Δ.*

Definition 2. *Let $S : \Gamma \vdash \Delta$ be a sequent and let Γ_1, Γ_2 be a permutation variant of Γ, and Δ_1, Δ_2 a permutation variant of Δ. Then $[\{\Gamma_1; \Delta_1\}, \{\Gamma_2; \Delta_2\}]$ is called a partition of S, where $\{\Gamma_1; \Delta_1\}$ is the left and $\{\Gamma_2; \Delta_2\}$ the right part.*

In Sect. 4, we will introduce the cut-elimination method Ceres, which transforms a proof in Skolem form - derived from any non-Skolem proof - containing cuts into a proof with only atomic cuts. One of the central results of this work is that proofs produced by Ceres still admit interpolation, meaning interpolants can be extracted from proofs with so-called admissible cuts. To support this result, we will extend Maehara's partition method to proofs in Skolem form, which, by definition, lack strong quantifier inferences[1]. In this work, we will focus on the structural Skolem form of sequents and proofs.

Definition 3 (structural Skolem form). *Let A be a closed first-order formula. If A does not contain strong quantifiers, we define its structural Skolemization as $sk(A) = A$.*

Suppose now that A contains strong quantifiers and (Qy) is the first strong quantifier occurring in A. If (Qy) is not in the scope of weak quantifiers, then its structural Skolemization is

$$sk(A) = sk(A_{-(Qy)}\{y \leftarrow c\}),$$

where $A_{-(Qy)}$ is the formula A after omission of (Qy) and c is a constant symbol not occurring in A. If (Qy) is in the scope of the weak quantifiers $(Q_1 x_1) \dots (Q_n x_n)$, then its structural Skolemization is

$$sk(A) = sk(A_{-(Qy)}\{y \leftarrow f(x_1, \ldots, x_n)\}),$$

where f is a function symbol (Skolem function) not occurring in A.

If $F = \bigwedge \Gamma \to \bigvee \Delta$ and $sk(F) = \bigwedge \Pi \to \bigvee \Lambda$ we define the structural Skolemization of the sequent $\Gamma \vdash \Delta$ as

$$sk(\Gamma \vdash \Delta) = \Pi \vdash \Lambda.$$

A proof can be skolemized by computing the structural Skolem form of its end-sequent.

Since extracting interpolants directly from proofs with cuts is generally infeasible, we employ a simple workaround: rather than constructing interpolants I of skolemized end-sequents $A \vdash B$, we focus on extracting *weak interpolants*. The key distinction between the two is that, while interpolants must be entirely formulated in the common language of A and B, weak interpolants only require that the predicate symbols in I belong to this common language - function symbols, constants, and variables may differ.

Definition 4. *Let S be a skolemized sequent and $X : [\{\Gamma_1; \Delta_1\}, \{\Gamma_2; \Delta_2\}]$ a partition of S. Then the formula I is called a weak interpolant of S w.r.t. X if*

---

[1] Positive occurrences of universal quantifiers and negative occurrences of existential quantifiers are called strong quantifier occurrences. Thus, in a sequent calculus derivation, the inferences $\forall_r$ and $\exists_l$ are called strong quantifier inferences, $\forall_l$ and $\exists_r$ are called weak. Strong quantifier inferences are the ones that involve eigenvariable conditions.

*a) there are proofs φ_1 and φ_2, where φ_1 is an **LK#**-proof of $\Gamma_1 \vdash \Delta_1, I$ and φ_2 an **LK#**-proof of $I, \Gamma_2 \vdash \Delta_2$, and*

b) the predicate symbols in I are a subset of the predicate symbols occurring in both, Γ_1, Δ_1 and Γ_2, Δ_2.

A proof of the form

$$\frac{\begin{array}{cc} (\varphi_1) & (\varphi_2) \\ \Gamma_1 \vdash \Delta_1, I & I, \Gamma_2 \vdash \Delta_2 \end{array}}{\Gamma_1, \Gamma_2 \vdash \Delta_1, \Delta_2} \; cut$$

is called a weak interpolation derivation for S w.r.t. X.

Below, we adapt Maehara's lemma to accommodate weak interpolation and, in Sect. 3, demonstrate that weak interpolants can indeed be extracted from proofs containing not just atomic cuts but also more complex cut formulas, thus generalizing existing results as [3, 4, 11].

Lemma 1 (Maehara's lemma for weak interpolation). *Let $S\colon \Gamma \vdash \Delta$ be an **LK#**-provable skolemized sequent and $X\colon [\{\Gamma_1; \Delta_1\}, \{\Gamma_2; \Delta_2\}]$ be an arbitrary partition of S. Then there exists a weak interpolant I of S w.r.t. X.*

Proof. By induction on the number of inferences k in a cut-free skolemized proof of $\Gamma \vdash \Delta$. The cases different to the ones in [19] are:

1. The last rule is $\forall_l$. Then the derivation is of the form

$$\frac{\begin{array}{c} (\varphi) \\ A\{x \leftarrow t\}, \Gamma \vdash \Delta \end{array}}{\forall x A(x), \Gamma \vdash \Delta} \; \forall_l$$

Let $X\colon [\{\forall x A(x), \Gamma_1; \Delta_1\}, \{\Gamma_2; \Delta_2\}]$. We define $X'\colon [\{A\{x \leftarrow t\}, \Gamma_1; \Delta_1\}, \{\Gamma_2; \Delta_2\}]$ as the partition of $A\{x \leftarrow t\}, \Gamma \vdash \Delta$. By IH there is a weak interpolation derivation of the form

$$\frac{\begin{array}{cc} (\varphi_1) & (\varphi_2) \\ A\{x \leftarrow t\}, \Gamma_1 \vdash \Delta_1, I & I, \Gamma_2 \vdash \Delta_2 \end{array}}{A\{x \leftarrow t\}, \Gamma_1, \Gamma_2 \vdash \Delta_1, \Delta_2} \; cut$$

where the predicate symbols of I are in the intersection of the predicate symbols of $A\{x \leftarrow t\}, \Gamma_1, \Delta_1$ and Γ_2, Δ_2. We define $\psi =$

$$\frac{\dfrac{\begin{array}{c} (\varphi_1) \\ A\{x \leftarrow t\}, \Gamma_1 \vdash \Delta_1, I \end{array}}{\forall x A(x), \Gamma_1 \vdash \Delta_1, I} \; \forall_l \qquad \begin{array}{c} (\varphi_2) \\ I, \Gamma_2 \vdash \Delta_2 \end{array}}{\forall x A(x), \Gamma_1, \Gamma_2 \vdash \Delta_1, \Delta_2} \; cut$$

ψ is a weak interpolation derivation as the predicate symbols in $\forall x A(x)$ are equal to the ones in $A\{x \leftarrow t\}$. However, in general I is only a weak interpolant for $\forall x A(x), \Gamma \vdash \Delta$ w.r.t. X even if I is an interpolant for $A\{x \leftarrow t\}, \Gamma \vdash \Delta$ w.r.t. X', because by the rule $\forall_l$ some function symbols, constants, or variables can be removed from one side, but still occur in I.

The case of the partition $X : [\{\Gamma_1; \Delta_1\}, \{\forall x A(x), \Gamma_2; \Delta_2\}]$ is analogous.

2. The last rule is $\exists_r$. Analogous to the case above.

By inspecting the proof above, the following corollary follows directly.

Corollary 1. *The weak inteprolant of a skolemized proof constructed in Lemma 1 is quantifier-free.*

In Lemma 3 we will extend Maehara's lemma for weak interpolation to cuts. However, this result would be limited in scope if it was only working for weak interpolants, as in general we are interested in real interpolants. To address this, we present a method for translating weak interpolants into interpolants in the case of skolemized end-sequents.[2]

Lemma 2. *Let I be a weak interpolant of a skolemized sequent S w.r.t. a partition X. Then there exists an interpolant I^* of S w.r.t. X.*

Proof. Let $X : [\{\Gamma_1; \Delta_1\}, \{\Gamma_2; \Delta_2\}]$ be a partition of S, and let the corresponding weak interpolation derivation be $\psi =$

$$\frac{\begin{array}{cc} (\varphi_1) & (\varphi_2) \\ \Gamma_1 \vdash \Delta_1, I & I, \Gamma_2 \vdash \Delta_2 \end{array}}{\Gamma_1, \Gamma_2 \vdash \Delta_1, \Delta_2}\ cut$$

As long as there are terms t in the weak interpolant I that do not occur in both parts $\{\Gamma_1; \Delta_1\}$ and $\{\Gamma_2; \Delta_2\}$, we select a maximal such term (in size, which is given by counting the symbols of a term) and eliminate it by substitution: W.l.o.g. assume the maximal term is $t = f(t_1, \ldots, t_n)$ for some function symbol f not occurring as a function symbol in both parts. We distinguish

1. f occurs only in $\{\Gamma_1; \Delta_1\}$. Replace the term t in the proof φ_2 by a variable α to obtain the proof $\varphi_2' =$

$$\frac{\begin{array}{c} (\varphi_2\{t \leftarrow \alpha\}) \\ I\{t \leftarrow \alpha\}, \Gamma_2 \vdash \Delta_2 \end{array}}{\exists x I\{t \leftarrow x\}, \Gamma_2 \vdash \Delta_2}\ \exists_l$$

for a bound variable x not occurring in I. Note that f does not occur in Γ_2 and Δ_2, which are therefore not changed, and $\varphi_2\{t \leftarrow \alpha\}$ is indeed a proof (no quantifier introductions can be damaged by the replacement) and all contractions are preserved. The last inference $\exists_l$ is sound as α does not occur in the lower sequent. $\varphi_1' =$

$$\frac{\begin{array}{c} (\varphi_1) \\ \Gamma_1 \vdash \Delta_1, I \end{array}}{\Gamma_1 \vdash \Delta_1, \exists x I\{t \leftarrow x\}}\ \exists_r$$

The interpolant is $\exists x I\{t \leftarrow x\}$ and the interpolation derivation is defined by cut from the two derivations above.

---

[2] Note that in [3] a proof of the lemma below is given without addressing the problem of strong quantifier inferences in un-skolemized proofs. To the best of our knowledge, this proof however only works in the skolemized version.

2. f occurs only in $\{\Gamma_2; \Delta_2\}$. Analogously to above, except that the roles of the parts change and we introduce a $\forall$ quantifier. The interpolant is $\forall x I\{t \leftarrow x\}$.
3. f does not occur in the partitions. Then the interpolant can be constructed as in case 1 or in case 2, as both constructions work.

If the maximal term t is a variable or constant symbol, t can be used as an eigenvariable directly in the above constructions. Moreover, we can replace a constant symbol directly by an eigenvariable. By eliminating stepwise the maximal term still occurring in the weak interpolant but not in both partitions, we will eventually eliminate all of them and end up with an interpolant.

The crucial point for the soundness of Lemma 2 is that the weak interpolant extracted from a skolemized proof cannot contain quantifiers. Skolemization prior to the computation of interpolants is reasonable, as cut-elimination prior to the extraction of interpolants is necessary anyway. The cut-elimination method we will consider is Ceres, which does not eliminate all cuts and results in a proof with atomic cuts. The first step of Ceres is to skolemize the input proof.

Craig's interpolation theorem follows directly from Maehara's lemma (for the proof, see [19]).

Theorem 1. *Let A and B be formulas s.t. $A \to B$ is **LK**-provable. If A and B have at least one predicate in common, then there is a formula I, called the interpolant of A and B, s.t. I only contains free variables, predicates, and constants that occur in both A and B, and s.t. $A \to I$ and $I \to B$ are **LK**-provable. If A and B have no predicate constant in common, then either $A \to$ or $\to B$ is **LK**-provable.*

3   Maehara's Lemma and Proofs with Cuts

In this section, we show that an interpolant can be extracted from a proof that contains more complex cuts than atomic ones, thus generalizing Lemma 8.2.3 from [3]. The essence lies still in analyzing the occurrence of the predicate symbols of the cut: they may occur in the first, or the second part of the partition, or in none of them. Interpolants can be constructed as long as the predicate symbols of the cuts are not split between the two parts of the partition in such a way that some predicate symbols occur only in the first part and some other predicate symbols only in the second part.

Definition 5. *Let φ be an **LK#**-proof of the form*

$$\frac{\begin{array}{cc}(\varphi_1) & (\varphi_2)\\ \Gamma \vdash \Delta, F \qquad F, \Pi \vdash \Lambda\end{array}}{\Gamma, \Pi \vdash \Delta, \Lambda}\ cut$$

where φ_1, φ_2 are cut-free, and F is a formula containing predicate symbols $P_1, \ldots, P_n$. Consider an arbitrary partition

$$X \colon [\{\Gamma_1, \Pi_1; \Delta_1, \Lambda_1\}, \{\Gamma_2, \Pi_2; \Delta_2, \Lambda_2\}]$$

of $\Gamma, \Pi \vdash \Delta, \Lambda$. Then F is X-violating if at least one predicate symbol $P_i \in \{P_1, \ldots, P_n\}$ occurs only in $\{\Gamma_1, \Pi_1; \Delta_1, \Lambda_1\}$, and at least another predicate symbol $P_j \in \{P_1, \ldots, P_n\}$ (s.t. $i \neq j$) occurs only in $\{\Gamma_2, \Pi_2; \Delta_2, \Lambda_2\}$. F is X-admissible otherwise.

Many mathematical proofs have X-admissible cuts, see for instance the ordered infinitary pigeonhole principle (or ECS schema)[3] [6,7], or the NiA schema[4] [5]. In particular for proofs with induction, which can be represented as a proof schema and analyzed with the schematic Ceres method [13,14,16], X-admissability of cut-formulas will be vital for the extraction of interpolants, as the underlying schematic Ceres method does not produce proofs with at most atomic cuts, but quantifier-free cut-formulas (see Sect. 6).

Lemma 3. *Let φ be an* **LK#**-*proof of the form*

$$
\begin{array}{cc}
(\varphi_1) & (\varphi_2) \\
\Gamma \vdash \Delta, F \quad & F, \Pi \vdash \Lambda \\
\hline
\multicolumn{2}{c}{\Gamma, \Pi \vdash \Delta, \Lambda} \quad cut
\end{array}
$$

where φ_1 and φ_2 are cut-free. Let $X \colon [\{\Gamma_1, \Pi_1; \Delta_1, \Lambda_1\}, \{\Gamma_2, \Pi_2; \Delta_2, \Lambda_2\}]$ be a partition of the end-sequent $S \colon \ \Gamma, \Pi \vdash \Delta, \Lambda$ s.t. F is X-admissible. Then there exists an interpolant I of S w.r.t. X s.t. either $I = I^1 \wedge I^2$ or $I = I^1 \vee I^2$, where I^1 is an interpolant of $\Gamma \vdash \Delta, F$ and I^2 is an interpolant of $F, \Pi \vdash \Lambda$.

Proof. Assume $P_1, \ldots, P_n$ are all the predicate symbols in F. We distinguish:

1. Some of $P_1, \ldots, P_n$ occur as a predicate symbol in $\Gamma_2, \Pi_2, \Delta_2, \Lambda_2$ and a (possibly empty) subset $P_i, \ldots P_j$ thereof occurs also in $\Gamma_1, \Pi_1, \Delta_1, \Lambda_1$. Define the partitions

$$X_1 \colon [\{\Gamma_1; \Delta_1\}, \{\Gamma_2; \Delta_2, F\}]$$

   of $\Gamma \vdash \Delta, F$, and

$$X_2 \colon [\{\Pi_1; \Lambda_1\}, \{F, \Pi_2; \Lambda_2\}]$$

   of $F, \Pi \vdash \Lambda$. By Lemma 1 and Lemma 2 there are interpolation derivations ψ_1' w.r.t. X_1 and ψ_2' w.r.t. X_2 s.t. $\psi_1' =$

$$
\begin{array}{cc}
(\chi_{1,1}) & (\chi_{1,2}) \\
\Gamma_1 \vdash \Delta_1, I^1 \quad & I^1, \Gamma_2 \vdash \Delta_2, F \\
\hline
\multicolumn{2}{c}{\Gamma_1, \Gamma_2 \vdash \Delta_1, \Delta_2, F} \quad cut
\end{array}
$$

   s.t. the predicate symbols of I^1 are in the intersection of the predicate symbols in the sequents $\Gamma_1 \vdash \Delta_1$ and $\Gamma_2 \vdash \Delta_2, F$. By construction, I^1 can only contain predicate symbols that occur in F, if they also occur in Γ_1, Δ_1. More precisely, these may be predicate symbols among $P_i, \ldots, P_j$. We therefore conclude that

---

[3] (Eventually Constant Schema) Let f be a total monotonically decreasing function over the natural numbers, then f is eventually constant.

[4] (Non-injectivity Assertion) Let $f \colon \mathbb{N} \to [0, \ldots, n]$ where $n \in \mathbb{N}$ be total, then there exists $i, j \in \mathbb{N}$ s.t. $i < j$ and $f(i) = f(j)$.

the predicate symbols of I^1 are in the intersection of the predicate symbols of Γ_1, Δ_1 and Γ_2, Δ_2. In the special case where $P_i, \ldots, P_j$ is empty, I^1 does not contain any predicate symbols that occur in F.

On the other hand $\psi_2' =$

$$
\begin{array}{cc}
(\chi_{2,1}) & (\chi_{2,2}) \\
\Pi_1 \vdash \Lambda_1, I^2 & I^2, F, \Pi_2 \vdash \Lambda_2 \\
\hline
\multicolumn{2}{c}{\Pi_1, \Pi_2, F \vdash \Lambda_1, \Lambda_2} \; cut
\end{array}
$$

s.t. the predicate symbols of I^2 are in the intersection of the predicate symbols in the sequents $\Pi_1 \vdash \Lambda_1$ and $F, \Pi_2 \vdash \Lambda_2$. We face the same situation as above, as I^2 can only contain predicate symbols from F if they also occur in Π_1, Λ_1. This can only be the case for the subset $P_i, \ldots, P_j$ that occurs in both, $\Gamma_1, \Pi_1, \Delta_1, \Lambda_1$ and in $\Gamma_2, \Pi_2, \Delta_2, \Lambda_2$. So, all predicates symbols of I^2, whether or not they occur in F, occur in both sides of the partition: in Π_1, Λ_1 and in Π_2, Λ_2. Now we define an interpolation derivation ψ for S w.r.t. X:

$$
\begin{array}{c}
\begin{array}{cc}
(\chi_{1,1}) & (\chi_{2,1}) \\
\Gamma_1 \vdash \Delta_1, I^1 \quad \Pi_1 \vdash \Lambda_1, I^2 \\
\hline
\Gamma_1, \Pi_1 \vdash \Delta_1, \Lambda_1, I^1 \wedge I^2 \;\wedge_r
\end{array}
\quad
\begin{array}{c}
\begin{array}{cc}
(\chi_{1,2}) & (\chi_{2,2}) \\
I^1, \Gamma_2 \vdash \Delta_2, F \quad I^2, F, \Pi_2 \vdash \Lambda_2 \\
\hline
I^1, I^2, \Gamma_2, \Pi_2 \vdash \Delta_2, \Lambda_2 \; cut
\end{array} \\
\hline
I^1 \wedge I^2, \Gamma_2, \Pi_2 \vdash \Delta_2, \Lambda_2 \;\wedge_l
\end{array} \\
\hline
\Gamma_1, \Gamma_2, \Pi_1, \Pi_2 \vdash \Delta_1, \Delta_2, \Lambda_1, \Lambda_2 \; cut
\end{array}
$$

By construction the predicate symbols in $I^1 \wedge I^2$ are a subset of the ones in $\Gamma_1, \Pi_1, \vdash \Delta_1, \Lambda_1$ and $\Gamma_2, \Pi_2 \vdash \Delta_2, \Lambda_2$, i.e. $I^1 \wedge I^2$ is a valid interpolant.

2. Some of $P_1, \ldots, P_n$ occur as a predicate symbol in $\Gamma_1, \Pi_1, \Delta_1, \Lambda_1$ and a subset $P_i, \ldots P_j$ thereof occurs also in $\Gamma_2, \Pi_2, \Delta_2, \Lambda_2$. Define the partitions

$$
X_1 \colon [\{\Gamma_1; \Delta_1, F\}, \{\Gamma_2; \Delta_2\}]
$$

of $\Gamma \vdash \Delta, F$, and

$$
X_2 \colon [\{F, \Pi_1; \Lambda_1\}, \{\Pi_2; \Lambda_2\}]
$$

of $F, \Pi \vdash \Lambda$. By Lemma 1 and Lemma 2 there are interpolation derivations ψ_1' w.r.t. X_1 and ψ_2' w.r.t. X_2 s.t. $\psi_1' =$

$$
\begin{array}{cc}
(\chi_{1,1}) & (\chi_{1,2}) \\
\Gamma_1 \vdash \Delta_1, F, I^1 & I^1, \Gamma_2 \vdash \Delta_2 \\
\hline
\multicolumn{2}{c}{\Gamma_1, \Gamma_2 \vdash \Delta_1, \Delta_2, F} \; cut
\end{array}
$$

and $\psi_2' =$

$$
\begin{array}{cc}
(\chi_{2,1}) & (\chi_{2,2}) \\
F, \Pi_1 \vdash \Lambda_1, I^2 & I^2, \Pi_2 \vdash \Lambda_2 \\
\hline
\multicolumn{2}{c}{\Pi_1, \Pi_2, F \vdash \Lambda_1, \Lambda_2} \; cut
\end{array}
$$

Now we define an interpolation derivation ψ for S w.r.t. X:

$$
\cfrac{
  \cfrac{
    \cfrac{
      \begin{array}{cc}(\chi_{1,1}) & (\chi_{2,1})\\ \Gamma_1 \vdash \Delta_1, F, I^1 & F, \Pi_1 \vdash \Lambda_1, I^2\end{array}
    }{\Gamma_1, \Pi_1 \vdash \Delta_1, \Lambda_1, I^1, I^2} \ cut
  }{\Gamma_1, \Pi_1 \vdash \Delta_1, \Lambda_1, I^1 \vee I^2} \ \vee_r
  \qquad
  \cfrac{
    \begin{array}{cc}(\chi_{1,2}) & (\chi_{2,2})\\ I^1, \Gamma_2 \vdash \Delta_2 & I^2, \Pi_2 \vdash \Lambda_2\end{array}
  }{I^1 \vee I^2, \Gamma_2, \Pi_2 \vdash \Delta_2, \Lambda_2} \ \vee_l
}{\Gamma_1, \Gamma_2, \Pi_1, \Pi_2 \vdash \Delta_1, \Delta_2, \Lambda_1, \Lambda_2} \ cut
$$

The situation is similar as above: by construction the predicate symbols in $I^1 \vee I^2$ are a subset of the ones in $\Gamma_1, \Pi_1, \vdash \Delta_1, \Lambda_1$ and $\Gamma_2, \Pi_2 \vdash \Delta_2, \Lambda_2$.

3. None of the predicate symbols in F occur in $\Gamma, \Pi, \Delta, \Lambda$. Then both constructions from above work, as neither I^1 nor I^2 contains predicate symbols from F, thus $I^1 \wedge I^2$ and $I^1 \vee I^2$ do not contain predicate symbols from F.

4. All predicate symbols occur as a predicate symbol in $\Gamma_1, \Pi_1, \Delta_1, \Lambda_1$, and in $\Gamma_2, \Pi_2, \Delta_2, \Lambda_2$. Then any of the constructions from case 1 and case 2 above works. $I^1 \wedge I^2$ (and $I^1 \vee I^2$) might contain predicate symbols $P_1, \ldots, P_n$, but they also occur in $\Gamma_1, \Pi_1, \Delta_1, \Lambda_1$ and $\Gamma_2, \Pi_2, \Delta_2, \Lambda_2$.

Note that in Lemma 3 above, only proofs with one occurrence of an admissible cut inference are considered. However, this result can be easily extended to arbitrary many admissible cuts in a proof, by simply starting with a top-most cut in a derivation (which has cut-free sub-derivations), computing its interpolant, and going down to the end-sequent.

Example 1. Let us consider a simple example. Let $\varphi =$

$$
\cfrac{
  \cfrac{
    \cfrac{
      \cfrac{
        \cfrac{P(u) \vdash P(u) \quad Q(u) \vdash Q(u)}{P(u), P(u) \to Q(u) \vdash Q(u)} \ {\to}{:}\, l
      }{P(u) \to Q(u) \vdash P(u) \to Q(u)} \ {\to}{:}\, r
    }{P(u) \to Q(u) \vdash \exists y(P(u) \to Q(y))} \ \exists{:}\, r
  }{\forall x(P(x) \to Q(x)) \vdash \exists y(P(u) \to Q(y))} \ \forall{:}\, l
  }{\forall x(P(x) \to Q(x)) \vdash \forall x \exists y(P(x) \to Q(y))} \ \forall{:}\, r
  \qquad
  \cfrac{
    \cfrac{
      \cfrac{
        \cfrac{
          \cfrac{P(a) \vdash P(a) \quad Q(v) \vdash Q(v)}{P(a), P(a) \to Q(v) \vdash Q(v)} \ {\to}{:}\, l
        }{P(a) \to Q(v) \vdash P(a) \to Q(v)} \ {\to}{:}\, r
      }{P(a) \to Q(v) \vdash \exists y(P(a) \to Q(y))} \ \exists{:}\, r
    }{\exists y(P(a) \to Q(y)) \vdash \exists y(P(a) \to Q(y))} \ \exists{:}\, l
  }{\forall x \exists y(P(x) \to Q(y)) \vdash \exists y(P(a) \to Q(y))} \ \forall{:}\, l
}{\forall x(P(x) \to Q(x)) \vdash \exists y(P(a) \to Q(y))} \ cut
$$

with the partition $X\colon [(\forall x(P(x) \to Q(x));), (;\exists y(P(a) \to Q(y)))]$ of the end-sequent. The cut $\forall x \exists y(P(x) \to Q(y))$ is X-admissible, and as every predicate symbol occurs in each side of the partition, both constructions (case 1 and case 2) in the proof of Lemma 3 work. By choosing the second construction, we add the cut-formula to the left side of the partitions. We end up with the weak interpolant $I = (\bot \vee \bot) \vee (\neg P(a) \vee Q(v))$, equivalent to $P(a) \to Q(v)$. By transforming this weak interpolant to an interpolant, we end-up with an interpolant equivalent to the cut-formula.

4   Interpolation and Proofs with Atomic Cuts

The method Ceres [1,2] stands for cut-elimination by resolution and was specifically designed as an efficient cut-elimination method. It radically differs from reductive cut-elimination methods à la Gentzen or Tait as all cuts are eliminated simultaneously. In [2] it was shown that Ceres outperforms reductive methods of cut-elimination in computational complexity: There are infinite sequences of proofs where the computing time of Ceres is nonelementarily faster than that of the reductive methods. On the other hand a nonelementary speed-up of Ceres via reductive methods is shown impossible. The formal definitions of the method Ceres can be found in [12,17], and due to space restrictions we will only state the most important definition of the method, which is the characteristic clause set extraction, and explain the rest of the method informally on an example:

The structure of a proof φ of a skolemized end-sequent S containing cuts is encoded in an unsatisfiable set of clauses, which is referred to as the characteristic clause set. The construction of a characteristic clause set consists in collecting all atomic ancestors of the cuts which occur in the axioms of the proof. This means, that cut-formulas in a derivation are traced back in the proof tree until we reach the axioms, where ancestors of the cut-formulas occur as atomic formulas. The clause set is formed depending on how these atoms are related via binary inferences in the proof. The definition of the characteristic clause set is based on the cut-status of the formula occurrences in a proof, i.e. whether a given formula occurrence is a cut-ancestor or not. In the definition below we will use a set Ω describing the set of all cut-ancestors in a given proof φ.

Definition 6 (characteristic clause-set [1]). *Let φ be a proof of a skolemized sequent. The characteristic clause set is built recursively from the leaves of the proof to the end-sequent. Let ν be the occurrence of a sequent in this proof. Then:*

- *If ν is an axiom, then $\mathrm{CL}(\nu)$ contains the sub-sequent of ν composed only of cut-ancestors.*
- *If ν is the result of the application of a unary rule on a sequent μ, then $\mathrm{CL}(\nu) = \mathrm{CL}(\mu)$*
- *If ν is the result of the application of a binary rule on sequents μ_1 and μ_2, then we distinguish two cases:*
  - *If the rule is applied to ancestors of the cut formula, then $\mathrm{CL}(\nu) = \mathrm{CL}(\mu_1) \cup \mathrm{CL}(\mu_2)$*
  - *If the rule is applied to ancestors of the end-sequent, then $\mathrm{CL}(\nu) = \mathrm{CL}(\mu_1) \times \mathrm{CL}(\mu_2)$*

where[5]

$$\mathrm{CL}(\mu_1) \times \mathrm{CL}(\mu_2) = \{C \circ D \mid C \in \mathrm{CL}(\mu_1), D \in \mathrm{CL}(\mu_2)\}.$$

If ν_0 is the root node $\mathrm{CL}(\nu_0)$ is called the characteristic clause set of φ.

Consider the proof φ of Example 1 of the end-sequent S. The purpose of Ceres is to extract cut-related and cut-free fragments of φ. To this end, the input proof φ must be skolemized. The cut-related content defines the characteristic clause set. Following Definition 6 the characteristic clause set of our example is given as $\mathrm{CL}(\varphi) = \{P(u) \vdash Q(u); \vdash P(a); Q(v) \vdash\}$. It was shown in [1,2] that the characteristic clause set is always unsatisfiable, therefore it can be refuted by a resolution refutation [18]. This refutation will later serve as a skeleton for the

---

[5] Here $\circ$ denotes the composition of clauses, i.e. if $C_1 = A \vdash B$ and $C_2 = C \vdash D$, then the composition of C_1 and C_2 is defined as $C_1 \circ C_2 = A, C \vdash B, D$.

final result of Ceres, the so-called *Ceres normal form*, a new proof of S which still contains cuts, but only on atomic formulas. A possible resolution refutation of $\mathrm{CL}(\varphi)$ is

$$\frac{\dfrac{\vdash P(a) \quad P(u) \vdash Q(u)}{\vdash Q(a)} \; R\{u \leftarrow a\} \qquad Q(v) \vdash}{\vdash} \; R\{v \leftarrow a\}$$

This refutation, when grounded[6], forms the basis for the Ceres normal form, where the resolution rule becomes a cut:

$$\frac{\dfrac{(\varphi[\vdash P(a)]) \quad (\varphi[P(u) \vdash Q(u)]\{u \leftarrow a\})}{B \vdash C, P(a) \qquad P(a), B \vdash C, Q(a)}{B \vdash C, Q(a)} \; cut + c^* \qquad \dfrac{(\varphi[Q(v) \vdash]\{v \leftarrow a\})}{Q(a), B \vdash C}}{\forall x(P(x) \rightarrow Q(x)) \vdash \exists y(P(a) \rightarrow Q(y))} \; cut + c^*$$

with $B = \forall x(P(x) \rightarrow Q(x))$, $C = \exists y(P(a) \rightarrow Q(y))$.

What is still missing is to define the sub-derivations $\varphi[\vdash P(a)]$, $\varphi[P(u) \vdash Q(u)]$, and $\varphi[Q(v) \vdash]$. These derivations are so-called *proof projections*, which can be described as cut-free parts that can be extracted from the original input proof φ by omitting inferences operating on ancestors of cut-formulas: From each clause C_i in the characteristic clause set we construct a projection $\varphi[C_i]$ of the concatenation of the end-sequent with C_i by starting with the axioms from φ containing C_i and moving all ancestors of cut-formulas to the right side of the sequent by applying appropriate inference rules. All inferences on cut-formulas are omitted, and we end up with a *cut-free proof*. Therefore, by construction, all projections are cut-free. The projections in our example are $\varphi[P(u) \vdash Q(u)] =$

$$\frac{\dfrac{\dfrac{P(u) \vdash P(u) \quad Q(u) \vdash Q(u)}{P(u), P(u) \rightarrow Q(u) \vdash Q(u)} \; \rightarrow\!: l}{P(u), \forall x(P(x) \rightarrow Q(x)) \vdash Q(u)} \; \forall : l}{P(u), \forall x(P(x) \rightarrow Q(x)) \vdash \exists y(P(a) \rightarrow Q(y)), Q(u)} \; w : r$$

$\varphi[\vdash P(a)] =$

$$\frac{\dfrac{\dfrac{\dfrac{P(a) \vdash P(a)}{P(a) \vdash P(a), Q(v)} \; w : r}{\vdash P(a) \rightarrow Q(v), P(a)} \; \rightarrow\!: r}{\vdash \exists y(P(a) \rightarrow Q(y)), P(a)} \; \exists : r}{\forall x(P(x) \rightarrow Q(x)) \vdash \exists y(P(a) \rightarrow Q(y)), P(a)} \; w : l$$

$\varphi[Q(v) \vdash] =$

$$\frac{\dfrac{\dfrac{\dfrac{Q(v) \vdash Q(v)}{P(a), Q(v) \vdash Q(v)} \; w : l}{Q(v) \vdash P(a) \rightarrow Q(v)} \; \rightarrow\!: r}{Q(v) \vdash \exists y P(a) \rightarrow Q(y)} \; \exists : r}{Q(v), \forall x(P(x) \rightarrow Q(x)) \vdash \exists y(P(a) \rightarrow Q(y))} \; w : l$$

---

[6] Grounding a resolution refutation means applying the most general unifier.

Note that atomic cut-formulas are X-admissible by construction, as they contain only one predicate symbol. Therefore, we can apply Lemma 3 repeatedly and compute the interpolant directly from the Ceres normal form.

Theorem 2. *Let φ be a skolemized proof of an end-sequent $S\colon \Gamma \vdash \Delta$ and X a partition of S. Let φ^* be its Ceres normal form, where*

$$\varphi[C_1]\theta_1^1, \ldots, \varphi[C_1]\theta_1^j, \ldots, \varphi[C_n]\theta_n^1, \ldots, \varphi[C_n]\theta_n^j$$

are the cut-free parts, i.e. the substituted proof projections (and where the θ represent substitutions). Then there exists an interpolant of φ w.r.t. X of the form

$$I_1^1 \circ_1^1 \ldots \circ_1^{j-1} I_1^j \circ_1^j \ldots \circ_{n-1}^j I_n^1 \circ_n^1 \ldots \circ_n^{j-1} I_n^j$$

where the $\circ$ above are in $\{\wedge, \vee\}$, I_i^j the interpolant of $\varphi[C_i]\theta_i^j$.

Proof. By the number of cuts in φ^*. If there is only one cut in φ^*, the result follows directly by Lemma 3, as the cut-formula is atomic (thus X-admissible). Assume as IH that the result holds for n cuts, and consider $n+1$ cuts. Select an uppermost cut in φ^*. By construction of the Ceres normal form, the derivations above this cut are cut-free. As the cut-formula is atomic, we apply Lemma 3 to the sub-derivation ending in this uppermost cut, and compute its interpolant. But then we have only n cuts to consider, and the result holds by IH.

5   A Speed-Up Result Based on Ceres

In this section we show that we can improve the method for the computation of interpolants based on Ceres (which is already more efficient than the usual method based on Gentzen's cut-elimination [3]) in asymptotic complexity. The method presented in the previous section computes *interpolants from the cut-free parts* of the Ceres normal form and combines them by conjunctions or disjunctions to the final interpolant. The cut-free parts are given by the *instantiated projections*, where the instantiations are given by the substitutions obtained from grounding the refutation of the characteristic clause set. A clause may occur several times in the refutation, which leads to *several equal projections* that are later instantiated and become cut-free parts of the Ceres normal form. Our speed-up result is based on this fact, we show that instead of computing the Ceres normal form and the interpolants from the cut-free parts, we compute the *interpolants from the projections directly* and substitute these interpolants by the instantiations from the grounded refutation, rather than substituting the projections. We will call this method of computing interpolants *optimized-interpolation*, and the method based on first constructing the Ceres normal form as described in the previous section *Ceres-interpolation*. The speed-up result will follow from the fact that projections are computed only once, and not several times, thus reducing the size of the maximal expressions (proofs) constructed during the computation.

Theorem 3. *Let φ be a skolemized proof of an end-sequent $S: \Gamma \vdash \Delta$ and X a partition of S. Let $\mathrm{CL}(\varphi) = \{C_1, \ldots, C_n\}$ be the characteristic clause set of φ and ρ its refutation by resolution. Then there exists an interpolant of φ w.r.t. X of the form*

$$I_1\theta_1^1 \circ_1^1 \ldots \circ_1^{j-1} I_1\theta_1^j \circ_1^j \ldots \circ_{n-1}^j I_n\theta_n^1 \circ_n^1 \ldots \circ_n^{j-1} I_n\theta_n^j$$

where $\circ \in \{\wedge, \vee\}$, I_i an interpolant of $\varphi[C_i]$ for $i = \{1, \ldots, n\}$, and $\theta_i^1 \ldots \theta_i^j$ are the substitutions to the clauses given by grounding ρ.

To prove Theorem 3, we first have to show that interpolants are conservative over substitutions on projections.

Lemma 4. *Let φ be a cut-free proof of a skolemized end-sequent $S : (\Gamma \vdash \Delta) \circ (C \vdash C')$, where $\Gamma \vdash \Delta$ is a closed sequent and $C \vdash C'$ is an atomic one. Let I be an interpolant of S w.r.t. some partition X. Consider $S\theta : (\Gamma \vdash \Delta) \circ (C\theta \vdash C'\theta)$ for a substitution θ. Then $I\theta$ is an interpolant of $S\theta$ w.r.t. $X\theta$.*

Proof. Projection instances in the Ceres method are well defined because the proof contains only weak quantifiers, and thus no eigenvariable condition is violated. Here, for any substitution θ, $\varphi\theta$ is a derivation of $S\theta$. Take a partition

$$X: [\{\Gamma_1, C_1; \Delta_1, C_1'\}, \{\Gamma_2, C_2; \Delta_2, C_2'\}]$$

of S. Then $\Gamma_1, C_1 \vdash C_1', \Delta_1, I$ and $I, \Gamma_2, C_2 \vdash \Delta_2, C_2'$ are **LK#**-provable. But then so are $\Gamma_1, C_1\theta \vdash C_1'\theta, \Delta_1, I\theta$ and $I\theta, \Gamma_2, C_2\theta \vdash \Delta_2, C_2'\theta$ for any substitution θ. Hence, $I\theta$ is an interpolant for the partition

$$X\theta: [\{\Gamma_1, C_1\theta; \Delta_1, C_1'\theta\}, \{\Gamma_2, C_2\theta; \Delta_2, C_2'\theta\}]$$

of $S\theta$.

We are now ready to prove Theorem 3.

Proof (Proof of Theorem 3). I_i is an interpolant of $\varphi[C_i]$ for $i = \{1, \ldots, n\}$, thus, by Lemma 4, $I_i\theta_i^j$ is an interpolant of $\varphi[C_i]\theta_i^j$. By Theorem 2 there is an interpolant of φ of the form

$$J_1^1 \circ_1^1 \ldots \circ_1^{j-1} J_1^j \circ_1^j \ldots \circ_{n-1}^j J_n^1 \circ_n^1 \ldots \circ_n^{j-1} J_n^j,$$

where J_i^j is an interpolant of $\varphi[C_i]\theta_i^j$. As $I_i\theta_i^j$ is an interpolant of $\varphi[C_i]\theta_i^j$ we choose $J_i^j = I_i\theta_i^j$.

To measure the complexity of the two methods, we will measure the maximal sizes of the constructed expressions by counting symbols. Expressions might be formulas, sequents, or proofs. We want to show that the method *optimized-interpolation* outperforms the standard method *Ceres-interpolation*. It is important to note that the complexity of *optimized-interpolation* cannot be higher than that of *Ceres-interpolation*, as the steps of computing the characteristic clause set, its grounded resolution refutation, and the corresponding projections

198   S. Corbard and A. Lolić

are the same in both methods. The difference is only that in *Ceres-interpolation*, the Ceres normal form is computed (containing all instantiated projections) and then the interpolant is constructed. In *optimized-interpolation* this is not the case as all projections are computed only once. The interesting case is the other direction. We show that *optimized-interpolation* can be asymptotically better than *Ceres-interpolation* by inductively defining a sequence of proofs[7] $\varphi_n =$

$$
\cfrac{
  \cfrac{
    \cfrac{
      \cfrac{
        (\psi_n) \\
        Py, Py \to Pfy, \ldots, Pf^{n-1}y \to Pf^n y \vdash Pf^n y
      }{
        Py \to Pfy, \ldots, Pf^{n-1}y \to Pf^n y \vdash Py \to Pf^n y
      }\ {\to_r}
    }{
      \forall x(Px \to Pfx) \vdash Py \to Pf^n y
    }\ {\forall_l (n\times)}
  }{
    \forall x(Px \to Pfx) \vdash \forall x(Px \to Pf^n x)
  }\ {\forall_r}
  \qquad
  \cfrac{
    (\pi_n) \\
    \forall x(Px \to Pf^n x), Pa \vdash Pf^{n^2} a
  }{}
}{
  Pa, \forall x(Px \to Pfx) \vdash Pf^{n^2} a
}\ {cut}
$$

where $\pi_n =$

$$
\cfrac{
  (\chi_n) \\
  Pa \to Pf^n a, Pf^n a \to Pf^{2n}a, \ldots, Pf^{(n-1)n}a \to Pf^{n^2}a, Pa \vdash Pf^{n^2}a
}{
  \forall x(Px \to Pf^n x), Pa \vdash Pf^{n^2} a
}\ {\forall_l (n\times)}
$$

and ψ_n is defined recursively depending on n: $\psi_0 = Py \vdash Py$, and for $n > 0$ $\psi_n =$

$$
\cfrac{
  Py \vdash Py
  \qquad
  \cfrac{
    \psi_{n-1}\{y \leftarrow fy\} \\
    Pfy, Pfy \to Pf^2 y, \ldots, Pf^{n-1}y \to Pf^n y \vdash Pf^n y
  }{}
}{
  Py, Py \to Pfy, \ldots, Pf^{n-1}y \to Pf^n y \vdash Pf^n y
}\ {\to_l}
$$

For the complexity measure we obtain $\|\psi_n\| = 2 + 2(n+1) + \|\psi_{n-1}\|$. Note that $\|\psi_{n-1}\| = \|\psi_{n-1}\{y \leftarrow fy\}\|$. $\|\psi_0\| = 2$. Obviously, there are constants a_1, a_2, b_1, b_2 (all > 0) s.t. $a_1 * n^2 \leq \|\psi_n\| \leq a_2 * (n+1)^2$ and $b_1 * n^2 \leq \|\chi_n\| \leq b_2 * (n+1)^2$. Putting things together there are constants $c_1, c_2 > 0$ with $c_1 * n^2 \leq \|\varphi_n\| \leq c_2 * (n+1)^2$. Now we compute the characteristic clause sets of the φ_n:

$$
\mathrm{CL}(\varphi_n) = \{ C_{1,n} : Py \vdash Pf^n y;\ C_2 : \vdash Pa;\ C_{3,n} : Pf^{n^2} a \vdash \}.
$$

The next step is the resolution refutation. The recursive definition is given by $\gamma_1 =$

$$
\cfrac{
  \vdash Pa \qquad Pa \vdash Pf^n a
}{
  \vdash Pf^n a
}\ R
$$

and $\gamma_n =$

$$
\cfrac{
  \cfrac{(\gamma_{n-1})}{\vdash Pf^{(n-1)n}a}
  \qquad
  Pf^{(n-1)n}a \vdash Pf^{n^2}a
}{
  \vdash Pf^{n^2}a
}\ R
$$

---

[7] Note that we will omit the opening and closing parenthesis for predicate symbols in the examples below due to readability reasons.

We obtain $\|\gamma_n\| = \|\gamma_{n-1}\| + 3$. Thus, the resolution schema is $\delta_n =$

$$\frac{(\gamma_n)}{\dfrac{\vdash Pf^{n^2}a \qquad Pf^{n^2}a \vdash}{\vdash}}\;R$$

with substitutions $\{y \leftarrow a\}, \ldots, \{y \leftarrow f^{(n-1)n}a\}$. We then get $\|\delta_n\| = 3n + 2$. The projections are $\varphi_n[C_{1,n}] =$

$$\frac{(\psi_n)}{\dfrac{Py, Py \rightarrow Pfy, \ldots, Pf^{n-1}y \rightarrow Pf^n y \vdash Pf^n y}{Py, \forall x(Px \rightarrow Pfx) \vdash Pf^n y}}\;\forall_l(n\times) + c_l(n\times)$$

$\varphi_n[C_2] = Pa \vdash Pa$ and $\varphi_n[C_{3,n}] = Pf^{n^2}a \vdash Pf^{n^2}a$. The final step is the construction of the Ceres normal form $\varphi_n^* =$

$$\frac{\begin{array}{cc}\psi_n^* & (\varphi_n[C_{3,n}]) \\ Pa, \forall x(Px \rightarrow Pfx) \vdash Pf^{n^2}a & Pf^{n^2}a \vdash Pf^{n^2}a\end{array}}{Pa, \forall x(Px \rightarrow Pfx) \vdash Pf^{n^2}a}\;cut$$

Where ψ_n^* is given recursively by $\psi_1^* =$

$$\frac{\begin{array}{cc}(\varphi_n[C_2,n]) & (\varphi_n[C_{1,n}\{y \leftarrow a\}]) \\ Pa, \forall x(Px \rightarrow Pfx) \vdash Pa & Pa, \forall x(Px \rightarrow Pfx) \vdash Pf^n a\end{array}}{Pa, \forall x(Px \rightarrow Pfx) \vdash Pf^n a}\;cut$$

and $\psi_n^* =$

$$\frac{\begin{array}{cc}\begin{array}{c}(\psi_{n-1}^*) \\ \cdots \\ Pa, \forall x(Px \rightarrow Pfx) \vdash Pf^{(n-1)n}a\end{array} & \begin{array}{c}(\varphi_n[C_{1,n}\{y \leftarrow f^{(n-1)n}a\}]) \\ Pf^{(n-1)n}a, \forall x(Px \rightarrow Pfx) \vdash Pf^{n^2}a\end{array}\end{array}}{Pa, \forall x(Px \rightarrow Pfx) \vdash Pf^{n^2}a}\;cut + c^*$$

In φ_n^* there are n substitution instances of the proof ψ_n and therefore the size of the Ceres normal form is $\|\varphi_n^*\| \geq a_1 * n^3$. As the algorithm *Ceres-interpolation* contains the construction of φ_n^* we finally obtain that the complexity of *Ceres-interpolation* is at least cubic in n.

Now we consider the complexity of the method *optimized-interpolation*. We construct the projections first, here we have the complexity $O(n^2)$ (just for $\varphi_n[C_{1,n}]$, otherwise constant). The construction of the refutation δ_n is in $O(n)$. Then we compute the interpolants from the projections. The interpolant $I[C_{1,n}]$ of the first projection $\varphi_n[C_{1,n}]$ (with end-sequent $Py, \forall x(Px \rightarrow Pfx) \vdash Pf^n y$)) w.r.t. the partition

$$[\{\forall x(Px \rightarrow Pfx); \}, \{Py; Pf^n y\}]$$

is computed recursively, we get

$$I[C_{1,n}] = \neg Py \vee \bot \vee \ldots \vee \bot \vee Pf^n y$$

with $(n-1)$ times $\bot$, thus $\|I[C_{1,n}]\| = 2 + 2(n-1) + 1 = 2n + 1$. For the second projection $\varphi_n[C_2]$ (with end-sequent $Pa, \forall x(Px \to Pfx) \vdash Pa$), the interpolant $I[C_2]$ w.r.t. the partition

$$[\{Pa, \forall x(Px \to Pfx); \}, \{; Pa\}]$$

is $I[C_2] = Pa$, with $\|I[C_2]\| = 1$. The interpolant $I[C_{3,n}]$ of $\varphi_n[C_{3,n}]$ (with end-sequent $Pf^{n^2}a \vdash Pf^{n^2}a$) w.r.t. the partition

$$[\{; \}, \{Pf^{n^2}a; Pf^{n^2}a\}]$$

is $I[C_{3,n}] = \top$, with $\|I[C_{3,n}]\| = 1$. The next step is to substitute the interpolants $I[C_{1,n}]$, $I[C_2]$, and $I[C_{3,n}]$ with the corresponding substitutions given by the grounded resolution refutation and combine them with $\circ \in \{\wedge, \vee\}$ (where we always choose the first case, i.e. $\wedge$). Note that the substitutions are applied recursively on $I[C_{1,n}]$, and are given by $\{y \leftarrow a\}, \ldots, \{y \leftarrow f^{(n-1)n}a\}$. Thus, we obtain as final interpolant

$$\begin{aligned}
I &= I[C_{1,n}]\{y \leftarrow a\} \wedge \ldots \wedge I[C_{1,n}]\{y \leftarrow f^{(n-1)n}a\} \wedge I[C_2] \wedge I[C_{3,n}] \\
&= \neg(Py \vee Pf^n y)\{y \leftarrow a\} \wedge \ldots \wedge (Py \vee Pf^n y)\{y \leftarrow f^{(n-1)n}a\} \wedge Pa \wedge \top \\
&= \neg(Pa \vee Pf^n a) \wedge \ldots \wedge (Pf^{(n-1)n}a \vee Pf^{n^2}a) \wedge Pa
\end{aligned}$$

$O(n^2)$: concatenate sequents of complexity $2n + 1$ n-times. The total expense of *optimized-interpolation* is therefore quadratic.

6   Conclusion

The interpolant constructed by the method presented in this work cannot be obtained by the traditional method, i.e. by first eliminating cuts following Gentzen's reductive method and then constructing an interpolant following Maehara's lemma. The reason is that when applying reductive cut-elimination, the resulting cut-free proof may not contain any fragment of the original proof anymore, whereas in our method the original parts of the proof are preserved.

In future work we intend to extend the results of this work to *proof schemata*, a formalism for proofs with induction [13,14,16]. Roughly speaking, a proof schema is a finite description of an infinite sequence of proofs, indexed by an inductive parameter. A large class of arithmetic is representable as a proof schema (see [15] for primitive recursive arithmetic). Using the schematic Ceres method as defined in [17] (resulting in quantifier-free cut-formulas) together with the methodology developed in this work (X-admissability of non-atomic cut-formulas), we believe that it will be possible to extract schematic interpolants from proof schemata, which will be a considerable step towards the computation of interpolants for an interesting class of inductive proofs.

References

1. Baaz, M., Leitsch, A.: Cut-elimination and redundancy-elimination by resolution. J. Symb. Comput. **29**(2), 149–177 (2000)
2. Baaz, M., Leitsch, A.: Towards a clausal analysis of cut-elimination. J. Symb. Comput. **41**(3–4), 381–410 (2006)
3. Baaz, M., Leitsch, A.: Methods of Cut-Elimination, vol. 34. Springer (2011)
4. Carbone, A.: Interpolants, cut elimination and flow graphs for the propositional calculus. Ann. Pure Appl. Log. **83**(3), 249–299 (1997)
5. Cerna, D.: Advances in schematic cut elimination. Ph.D. thesis, TU Wien (2015)
6. Cerna, D.M., Leitsch, A.: Schematic cut elimination and the ordered pigeonhole principle. In: Olivetti, N., Tiwari, A. (eds.) IJCAR 2016. LNCS (LNAI), vol. 9706, pp. 241–256. Springer, Cham (2016). https://doi.org/10.1007/978-3-319-40229-1_17
7. Cerna, D.M., Leitsch, A., Lolic, A.: Schematic refutations of formula schemata. J. Autom. Reason. **65**(5), 599–645 (2021)
8. Craig, W.: Three uses of the Herbrand-Gentzen theorem in relating model theory and proof theory. J. Symb. Logic **22**(03), 269–285 (1957)
9. Gentzen, G.: Untersuchungen über das logische Schließen. Mathematische Zeitschrift 39, 176–210, 405–431 (1934-35)
10. Gherardi, G., Maffezioli, P., Orlandelli, E.: Interpolation in extensions of first-order logic. Stud. Logica. **108**(3), 619–648 (2020)
11. Krajíček, J.: Interpolation theorems, lower bounds for proof systems, and independence results for bounded arithmetic. J. Symb. Log. **62**(2), 457–486 (1997)
12. Leitsch, A., Lolic, A.: Extraction of expansion trees. J. Autom. Reason. **62**(3), 393–430 (2019)
13. Leitsch, A., Lolic, A.: Herbrand's theorem in inductive proofs. In: LPAR. EPiC Series in Computing, vol. 100, pp. 295–310. EasyChair (2024)
14. Leitsch, A., Lolic, A.: Extracting herbrand systems from refutation schemata. J. Logic Comput. **35**(7), exaf010 (2025)
15. Leitsch, A., Lolic, A., Mahler, S.: On proof schemata and primitive recursive arithmetic. In: LPAR 2024 Complementary Volume. Kalpa Publications in Computing, vol. 18, pp. 117–130. EasyChair (2024)
16. Leitsch, A., Peltier, N., Weller, D.: CERES for first-order schemata. J. Log. Comput. **27**(7), 1897–1954 (2017)
17. Lolic, A.: Automated Proof Analysis by CERES. Ph.D. thesis, TU Wien (2020)
18. Robinson, J.A.: A machine-oriented logic based on the resolution principle. J. ACM **12**(1), 23–41 (1965)
19. Takeuti, G.: Proof Theory, 2nd edn. North Holland (1987)

Lean4Less: Eliminating Definitional Equalities from Lean via an Extensional-to-Intensional Translation

Rishikesh Vaishnav[✉]

Université Paris-Saclay, INRIA Project Deducteam, Laboratoire Méthodes Formelles, ENS Paris-Saclay, Gif-sur-Yvette, France
`rishikesh-hirendu.vaishnav@inria.fr`

Abstract. The Lean proof assistant features a typechecker kernel that makes use of a set of "definitional equalities" for identifying terms under certain syntactic and typing conditions. While providing for convenient formalization, some definitional equalities in particular complicate meta-theoretical analyses and the export of Lean proofs to other proof assistants via logical frameworks such as Dedukti. In this paper, we describe a translation from Lean to a smaller theory "Lean$^-$" with fewer such definitional equalities, specifically eliminating uses of proof irrelevance and "K-like reduction" in the typing of Lean terms. We adapt a general translation from extensional to intensional type theory, making Lean's implicit use of these definitional equalities explicit through the use of type casts and a corresponding proof irrelevance axiom. The translation has been implemented in Lean itself in a tool called Lean4Less (https://github.com/rish987/Lean4Less), which is able to successfully translate certain libraries (e.g. the Lean standard library) to Lean$^-$. The methods developed for this translation may also be transferrable to other proof assistants based on dependent type theory.

Keywords: Lean · Dedukti · logical frameworks · extensional type theory · proof system interoperability · proof translation · dependent type theory · proof assistants

1 Introduction

Lean [11] is a proof assistant developed by the Lean FRO with type-theoretic foundations that are based on the Calculus of Inductive Constructions [13], sharing many similarities with the proof assistant Rocq [14]. It has become especially popular with mathematicians in recent years, being well-known for its "Mathlib" library [17,18], a large and quickly growing body of mathematics formalized in Lean. Lean features a small, fast kernel that attempts to be a "minimal" foundation for the sound typechecking of Lean proofs. Given Lean's popularity, it

Z. Liu et al. (Eds.): ICTAC 2025, LNCS 16237, pp. 202–219, 2026.
https://doi.org/10.1007/978-3-032-11176-0_13

is of high interest to export Lean proofs to other proof assistants (e.g. Rocq) in order to both allow for more confidence in their correctness by typechecking them with a separate kernel, and to provide other proof assistant communities with access to various formalizations developed in Lean.

However, this task is complicated by certain meta-theoretical aspects of Lean. Lean's kernel, while small, is not entirely minimal, as it enforces a number of additional definitional equalities[1], such as those of proof irrelevance and "K-like reduction" (and more recently, "struct eta" and "struct-like reduction"). Such equalities are not necessarily present in other proof assistants, so special consideration must be made during translation to ensure compatibility of these features at the kernel level. One promising approach to this may be to "eliminate" them entirely, namely by performing a "pre-translation" step on well-typed terms in the original theory so that they are able to type in a strictly smaller theory (possibly extended with some axioms). It is this approach of pre-translation to eliminate definitional equalities (prior to final proof export) that we have implemented with our tool "Lean4Less", which we describe in this paper.

The remainder of the paper is structured as follows: we start by describing proof irrelevance and K-like reduction, and bring up some meta-theoretical difficulties arising from their use in Lean's typing. This motivates the translation to our target theory of "Lean$^-$", where these definitional equalities have been eliminated. In Sect. 2, we describe the theory behind our approach, noting that this translation task can be interpreted as a special case of a translation from extensional to intensional type theory. In Sect. 3, we provide an overview of how we have implemented our tool as a modification of Lean4Lean [6], an external typechecker for Lean implemented in Lean. In Sect. 4, we provide more details on the implementation of the translation. In Sect. 5, we describe some translation results on specific libraries, providing data regarding translation overhead and runtime. We conclude by discussing future directions of our work, relating in particular to the possible addition of extensional typechecking to Lean and simplifications in the analyses of certain meta-theoretical properties.

1.1 Proof Irrelevance

Lean's type theory features a definitional equality known as "proof irrelevance", which enables it to ignore the computational content of proofs when typechecking terms, only concerning itself with the equality of their propositional types. It is represented by the following rule[2]:[3]

---

[1] In type theory, "definitional equalities" are rules describing "built-in" notions of equality between terms that are implemented by the typechecker kernel, often as a formalization convenience that allows the kernel to identify a larger class of terms without requiring explicit proof from the user.

[2] The full set of typing rules in Lean was first described by Carneiro [5].

[3] Lean features a universe hierarchy of "sorts", with `Sort 0`, a.k.a. `Prop`, being the bottommost universe of propositional types. Sort typing follows the relation `Sort u : Sort (u + 1)`.

$$\frac{\Gamma \vdash P : \texttt{Prop} \quad \Gamma \vdash h : P \quad \Gamma \vdash h' : P}{\Gamma \vdash h \equiv h'} \ \text{[PI]}$$

where $\Gamma \vdash t : T$ and $\Gamma \vdash t \equiv s$ denote Lean's typing and definitional equality judgments.

Proof irrelevance is useful, for example, in establishing the definitional equality of predicate subtype instances with equal values, but differing membership proofs. Subtypes in Lean can be defined as a parametric inductive type:

```
-- subtype inductive type parameterized by type `A` and predicate `p`
-- (curly brackets `{...}` denote auto-inferred implicit arguments)
inductive Subtype {A : Type} (p : A → Prop) where
-- we construct an instance of `Subtype A` with the constructor `mk`,
-- which takes a value `val` and proof `prf` that `val` satisfies `p`
| mk : (val : A) → (prf : p val) : Subtype p
```

Suppose that we define a subtype for natural numbers less than five:

```
def NatLT5 : Type := Subtype (fun n => n < 5)
def NatLT5.mk (n : Nat) (p : n < 5) : NatLT5 := -- pseudo-constructor
  @Subtype.mk Nat (fun n => n < 5) n p
```

Now, suppose we have two different proofs `p1 p2 : 3 < 5`. Proof irrelevance gives us a definitional equality between `NatLT5.mk 3 p1` and `NatLT5.mk 3 p2`, as one would expect, since when we consider the equality of these subtype constructions, all that we care about is the equality of their underlying values.

Forms of proof irrelevance are supported in a number of other proof assistants. Until recently, the use of proof irrelevance in Rocq had to be made explicit with an axiom[4]. However, optional support for definitional proof irrelevance has recently been added with the `SProp` type[5]. Agda supports user-annotated irrelevant function arguments and struct fields[6], in addition to a proof irrelevant type universe `Prop` (analogous to Rocq's `SProp`). F* erases the details of SMT solver-generated equality proofs [16]. The PVS proof assistant[7] features a special case of proof irrelevance in identifying predicate subtype constructions.

1.2   K-Like Reduction

Lean also features a related definitional equality rule known as "K-like reduction". It is based on the characterization of so-called "K-like" inductive types in Lean, which are defined as inductive types that live in `Prop` and have a single constructor without any (non-parametric) arguments. Lean's equality inductive type is an example of such a K-like inductive type:

---

[4] https://rocq-prover.org/doc/V9.0.0/stdlib/Stdlib.Logic.ProofIrrelevance.html.
[5] See https://rocq-prover.org/doc/V9.0.0/refman/addendum/sprop.html.
[6] See https://agda.readthedocs.io/en/v2.5.4/language/irrelevance.html.
[7] https://pvs.csl.sri.com/.

```
-- (we use 'u' and 'v' for level variables in universe-polymorphic
-- constants; Lean auto-infers their values when the constant is used)
inductive Eq {A : Sort u} (a : A) : A → Prop where
| refl : Eq a a
```

We will use the notation `a = b` for the equality type construction `Eq a b`. This inductive type has two parameters, found to the left of the colon in the inductive type signature: the polymorphic type `A` and the left hand-side element `a : A`. It also has an "index", which is a special kind of inductive type parameter that is determined by the constructor: in this case, this is the right hand-side element, which, as expressed in the output type of `Eq.refl`, must be the same as (i.e. definitionally equal to[8]) the left hand-side element. In the particular case of K-like inductive types, where constructors have no arguments, indices are effectively a function of the parameters.

In general, suppose we have a K-like type `K` with n parameters, m indices and the unique constructor `mk`. We can express K-like reduction as the rule:

$$\frac{\Gamma \vdash \mathtt{mk}\ p_1\ \ldots\ p_n : \mathtt{K}\ p_1\ \ldots\ p_n\ i_1\ \ldots\ i_m \qquad \Gamma \vdash t : \mathtt{K}\ p_1\ \ldots\ p_n\ i_1\ \ldots\ i_m}{\Gamma \vdash t \rightsquigarrow \mathtt{mk}\ p_1\ \ldots\ p_n} \ [\mathrm{KLR}]$$

For example, the above rule applies to the equality type with $n = 2$, $m = 1$, `K = Eq`, `mk = Eq.refl`, $p_1 = \mathtt{Nat}$, $p_2 = 0$, and $i_1 = 0$, allowing any term `t : 0 = 0` to be reduced[9] to `Eq.refl Nat 0`.

Note that K-like reduction is related to proof irrelevance, since t and `mk` $p_1 \ldots p_n$ are already definitionally equal in Lean by [PI] (as K-like inductive types must live in `Prop`). However, it represents a directed equality (i.e. "rewrite rule"), rather than an undirected one, which enables a more powerful elimination principle. For example, consider the K-like type `T` below. Lean automatically generates a reduction rule for `T.rec`, the recursor (a.k.a. eliminator[10]) of `T`:

```
inductive T : Prop where | mk : T
#check (T.rec : {m : T → Sort u} → m T.mk → (t : T) → m t)
-- ('rfl' is shorthand for 'Eq.refl _', where '_' is inferred;
-- it can be used as a quick check for whether the kernel considers
-- two terms to be definitionally equal)
example : T.rec true T.mk = true := rfl
```

---

[8] By type conversion and application congruence of definitional equality.

[9] With respect to a practical typechecker implementation, during reduction we must ensure that `t` is not already an application of `Eq.refl` before applying [KLR] in order to avoid non-termination.

[10] In proof assistants, recursors/eliminators are functions that enable the definition of general transformations on inductive types; they perform a function similar to that of "pattern matching" in many functional programming languages.

Normally, such reductions are limited to explicit well-typed constructions in the recursor's "major premise" argument that is eliminated upon (the `T.mk` argument above). However, K-like reduction also gives us the definitional equality:

```
example (t : T) : T.rec true t = true := rfl
```

That is, we are able to reduce on any well-typed major premise argument, without needing an explicit construction – here, it is simply the variable `t`. When reducing the recursor application, the kernel is able to "rewrite" `t` to `T.mk` using [KLR], allowing the left hand-side recursor application to reduce.

K-like reduction, in combination with Lean's impredicative `Prop` universe, results in non-termination of reduction, as shown by Abel and Coquand [1]. While its use in Lean has proven to be quite successful, such a theoretical lack of strong normalization may be part of the reason why very few other proof assistants support it. It does however exist to a limited extent in the Rocq proof assistant, where it can be enabled with the "Definitional UIP" flag[11] (this is not enabled by default to preserve certain theoretical properties, e.g. normalization).

1.3   Meta-theoretic Challenges

While proof irrelevance, K-like reduction, and other definitional equalities in Lean are crucial conveniences in scaling mathematical formalizations, they present difficulties at the meta-theoretic level, particularly when we want to reason about or perform transformations on Lean terms based on their typing derivations. Such definitional equalities also complicate the task of exporting Lean proofs to other proof assistants, which is important to enable greater proof system interoperability and avoid duplication of work in formalizing mathematical results. Existing work translating Lean to other proof assistants, such as that of Gilbert in translating Lean to Rocq,[12] rely on the presence of similar features in the target theory. When such features are not present, direct translation becomes more difficult. We may instead look into first translating to a more universal "intermediate theory" from which we can export to several different theories.

In light of this, one promising target for proof export is Dedukti [4], a logical framework featuring dependent types and rewrite rules to ease the translation of proofs between proof assistants by translating between various encodings of different type theories. Dedukti uses the $\lambda\Pi$-calculus modulo rewriting type theory, which is intentionally designed to be as "minimal" as possible to make it a good candidate for exporting proofs between different proof assistants with various different type theories. In particular, it does not feature proof irrelevance or K-like reduction. While proof irrelevance can be encoded in Dedukti in certain special cases, as was done for the case of predicate subtyping in the proof assistant PVS [10], an encoding of the general case of proof irrelevance

---

[11] https://rocq-prover.org/doc/V8.18.0/refman/addendum/sprop.html#definitional-uip.

[12] See https://github.com/SkySkimmer/rocq/tree/lean-import.

within Dedukti may not be possible without certain non-trivial extensions to its underlying theory.

Considering the above difficulties, one may wonder whether or not it is possible to "eliminate" certain (particularly problematic) definitional equalities to some extent, by translating Lean terms to typecheck in some smaller theory that does not use them. In some cases, terms may use certain definitional equalities in "non-essential" ways, and can be rewritten in such a way as to avoid them. However, there are cases where their use *is* essential in typing, enabling proofs that would not otherwise be possible. So, instead of eliminating definitional equalities entirely, we would like to retain them to some extent in our target theory, demoted to axiomatized/provable propositional equalities that are added to the typechecking environment, and translating terms to explicitly make use of them as needed to become typeable in the smaller theory.

2   Theoretical Background

2.1   Target Theory: Lean$^-$

To this end, we propose our target theory Lean$^-$, removing [PI] and [KLR] from our theory and adding the axiom:

```
-- proof irrelevance, represented as an axiom
axiom prfIrrel {P : Prop} (p q : P) : p = q
```

Using this axiom, we can also represent K-like reduction, which becomes a provable proposition in this smaller theory. For instance, in the case of T:

```
theorem T.KLR (t : T) : T.rec true t = true :=
  -- proof that 'T.rec true t = T.rec true T.mk'
  -- (without [KLR], the LHS cannot reduce to the RHS value of 'true')
  @congrArg _ _ t T.mk (T.rec true) (prfIrrel t T.mk)
```

To effect this translation, we can "inject" type casts (a.k.a. transports) around subterms in order for them to have the expected type that is imposed by a user-provided type annotation or the typing constraints of the surrounding term. For example, we can eliminate proof irrelevance when it is used directly:

```
variable (P : Prop) (p q : P) (T : P → Type)
-- 'T p' is defeq to 'T q' (due to proof irrelevance)
def ex (t : T p) : T q := t
theorem congrArg {A : Sort u} {B : Sort v} {x y : A}
  (f : A → B) (h : x = y) : f x = f y := ...
-- explicitly converts a term from type 'A' to provably equal type 'B'
def cast {A B : Sort u} (h : A = B) (a : A) : B := ...
def exTrans (t : T p) : T q := cast (congrArg T (prfIrrel p q)) t
```

and also when it is used indirectly via K-like reduction (as shown in T.KLR).

The Soundness Property. In our target theory Lean$^-$, we have removed [PI] and [KLR] from the type theory. We would like to define some translation $|\cdot|$ on Lean-typeable terms that satisfies a soundness criterion:

$$\Gamma \vdash t : A \implies (\texttt{prfIrrel} : \forall(P : \texttt{Prop}),\ (p, q : P).\ p = q) :: |\Gamma| \vdash^- |t| : |A|.$$

where $\Gamma \vdash^- t : T$ is the notation for Lean$^-$'s typing judgment, and $|\Gamma|$ applies the translation to every type in context Γ. In words, we want the translation of a well-typed Lean term to be well-typed in Lean$^-$ as the translation of its type, provided a proof irrelevance axiom in the typing context.

However, this property alone is not sufficient for our purposes. We would also like to ensure that type semantics are preserved by our translation. For instance, a translation that translates all types to the Lean proposition `True` and all terms to the constructor `True.intro` would be able to satisfy the above property. In particular, we would like to ensure that all translated terms are the same as the originals except possibly also having been "decorated" with type casts. We can capture this notion with the similarity relation "$\sim$" defined by Winterhalter et al. [19]. Specifically, we want our translation to satisfy the property that, for all Lean-typeable t, we have $t \sim |t|$. This also allows translated terms to easily be translated back to the original theory by simply removing the type casts.

2.2 A Middle-Ground Extensional Theory: Lean$_e^-$

The above suggests that translating from Lean to Lean$^-$ may be feasible using type casting. It is reminiscent of what one may do in Lean to align types that are provably, but not definitionally equal:

```
-- addition matches on the second operand, so this is not definitional
theorem addOneComm (n : Nat) : Nat.succ n = 1 + n := ...
inductive Vec : Nat → Type where
| nil : Vec 0
| cons {n : Nat} (v : Vec n) (x : Nat) : Vec (Nat.succ n)
def vecAppend1 (n : Nat) (v : Vec n) : Vec (1 + n) :=
  -- 'v.cons 1' has type 'Vec (Nat.succ n)', not 'Vec (1 + n)'
  cast (congr rfl (addOneComm n)) (v.cons 1)
```

The term `v.cons 1` has the inferred type `Vec (n + 1)`, which doesn't match the annotated expected type `Vec (1 + n)` (Lean's `Nat.add` function recurses on the second argument), so we have to apply a `cast` around it using an equality proof between these types, quite similarly to what we did in `exTrans` above. This may make us question whether our task is a special case of a translation from a more general theory. If Lean were to treat the equality of `addOneComm` as definitional in the same way that it does `prfIrrel`, we would not need to wrap `v.cons 1` in a cast. It could do so if we were to, for instance, add a rule that allows *all* propositional equalities to be promoted into definitional ones. This is exactly the rule of "equality reflection" from extensional type theory (ETT), which allows *any* provable propositional equality to be considered definitional[13].

To obtain such an extensional theory to translate from, we can add the "equality reflection" rule to Lean$^-$, obtaining the extensional theory "Lean$_e^-$":

$$\frac{\Gamma \vdash_e^- A : \texttt{Sort}\ u \quad \Gamma \vdash_e^- t, s : A \quad \Gamma \vdash_e^- \_ : t = s}{\Gamma \vdash_e^- t \equiv s}\ [\text{RFL}]$$

using the notation $\Gamma \vdash_e^- t : T$ and $\Gamma \vdash_e^- t \equiv s$ for Lean$_e^-$'s typing and definitional equality judgments. A translation from Lean to Lean$_e^-$ is simply the identity function, as we have via [RFL]:

$$\frac{\Gamma \vdash_e^- P : \texttt{Prop} \quad \Gamma \vdash_e^- p, q : P \quad \Gamma \vdash_e^- \texttt{prfIrrel}\ p\ q : p = q}{\Gamma \vdash_e^- p \equiv q}$$

which is equivalent to [PI]. We can derive a similar rule for [KLR]. In fact, because Lean$_e^-$'s theory is extensional, Lean's typing is a strict subset of Lean$_e^-$'s.

So, because for any t, $\Gamma \vdash t : A \implies \Gamma \vdash_e^- t : A$, we can reformulate our problem as finding a translation $|\cdot|$ to Lean$^-$ respecting soundness w.r.t. Lean$_e^-$:

$$\Gamma \vdash_e^- t : A \implies (\texttt{prfIrrel} : \forall (P : \texttt{Prop}),\ (p, q : P).\ p = q) :: |\Gamma| \vdash^- |t| : |A|.$$

This is an instance of the general problem of translating from extensional to intensional type theory (where any type theory lacking [RFL] is considered "intensional"). Such a translation is possible, with a formally verified implementation in Rocq by Winterhalter et al. in `ett-to-itt` [19,20], which builds on previous work by Oury [12] and Hofmann [9], with the first result showing conservativity of ETT over ITT demonstrated by Hofmann [8].

This translation places certain restrictions on the target intensional theory, namely that it exhibits propositional uniqueness of identity proofs (UIP) and function extensionality. Lean$^-$ satisfies UIP thanks to `prfIrrel`:

```
theorem UIP {A : Sort u} (x y : A) (p q : x = y) : p = q := prfIrrel p q
```

Lean$^-$ also satisfies function extensionality with the theorem `funext` from the Lean standard library, where it is proven through the use of quotient types:

```
-- (module 'Init.Core')
theorem funext {A : Sort u} {B : A → Sort v} {f g : (x : A) → B x}
    (h : (x : A) → f x = g x) : f = g := ...
```

---

[13] However, it should be noted that this comes at the cost of rendering typechecking undecidable – for instance, it is possible to encode the halting problem as a propositional equality, which we cannot hope to decide during typechecking. For this reason, practical systems employing extensionality such as Andromeda [3], F* [16], and Nuprl [2] restrict [RFL] to some subset of provable propositional equalities.

Restrictions are also placed on the source extensional theory by requiring an ETT syntax with domain- and codomain-annotated lambda and application constructors, which Lean does not have. We skirt this requirement through the use of an extra "hUV" premise in our application congruence lemma (see Sect. 4.1). Our theories can be summarized in the following table:

Theory	Rules	Axioms	$\subsetneq$
Lean^- $(\vdash^-)$		`prfIrrel`	Lean
Lean $(\vdash)$	[PI], [KLR]		Lean_e^-
Lean_e^- $(\vdash_e^-)$	[RFL]	`prfIrrel`	

Practically speaking, our translation does not need to implement a full ETT-to-ITT translation. We only care about translating terms that are already typeable in Lean, so proof irrelevance is the only definitional equality we need to make explicit. Nevertheless, this does not afford us any real simplifications in the translation algorithm. Proof irrelevance may be used during typechecking to the same extent as general extensional equalities, as there are no syntactic restrictions on where proofs can appear in terms. In particular, they can appear within types, leading to some fairly complex translations.

Such a translation must generalize the equality type `Eq` to the heterogeneous equality type `HEq`, which is able to take different left- and right-hand side types:

```
inductive HEq : {A : Sort u} → A → {B : Sort u} → B → Prop where
| refl (a : A) : HEq a a
```

We use the notation `a == b` for `HEq a b`. This is a different formulation of heterogeneous equality from the one used by Winterhalter et al. in [19], where the construction also carries a proof of equality of the left- and right-hand side's types. While such a formulation makes for more convenient correctness proofs, it is less convenient for an actual implementation, so we instead choose to return to the "John Major equality" used by Oury [12], which is a more compact and equivalent formulation already defined in the Lean standard library in the `HEq` type (`JMeq` in the Rocq standard library).

3   Implementation Overview

3.1   Adapting `ett-to-itt`?

Although a Rocq-verified translation from ETT to ITT already exists in the `ett-to-itt` repository [20], which could be extracted to an executable OCaml program [7] and possibly used in our translation, there would be a number of challenges associated with this approach, largely on account of its focus on the correctness of its translation, rather than its practicality. In particular, the extracted code would require as input some representation of Lean typing derivations, which Lean currently provides no way to obtain. Instead, we prefer to instead take the approach of modifying an existing typechecker to construct a translation in parallel to typechecking, where we have access to the typing derivation steps implicitly from the steps taken by the typechecker in deciding the well-typedness of Lean terms.

Such an approach would allow us to handle Lean's definitional equalities on a more modular basis, being able to choose which ones we eliminate at the level of the translation itself, rather than as a post-processing step. It will also allow us to retain some runtime optimizations in the Lean kernel that could translate into output optimizations, and, using utilities offered by the typechecker such as type inference and weak head normal form computation, more easily implement some output optimizations of our own (see Sect. 4.3). Also, by performing our translation in parallel to typechecking, we can implement a translation that only inserts type casts where necessary for the term to be well-typed in Lean$^-$ (see Sect. 4.2) – effecting, in this way, a kind of "patching" typechecker.

3.2   Modifying Lean4Lean

A promising Lean kernel implementation to modify to achieve our translation is Carneiro's "Lean4Lean" [6], a port of Lean's C++ kernel typechecker code into Lean, with the beginnings of the formalization of certain meta-theoretical properties in the direction of the MetaRocq project [15]. Modifying a typechecker that is implemented in Lean itself provides us with several benefits. As Lean is a partly bootstrapped language, many of its higher-level features are implemented exclusively in Lean, which use a number of helper functions for traversing and constructing expressions, manipulating free/bound variables, modifying the typechecking environment, etc., that will be useful in our own implementation. Also, Lean's orientation towards formal proof and typechecking afford us certain "soft" guarantees in the correctness of our implementation, and leaves the door open to an eventually fully verified translation on account of Lean's capabilities as a general theorem prover.

Lean4Lean's typechecker implements a bidirectional typechecking algorithm using three primary mutually recursive functions (found in `TypeChecker.lean`):

```
-- type inference
def inferType (e : Expr) : RecM Expr := ...
-- definitional equality check
def isDefEq (t s : Expr) : RecM Bool := ...
-- weak-head normalization
def whnf (e : Expr) : RecM Expr := ...
```

- `inferType` is a type inference function that checks that `e` is well-typed (throwing an error if it is not), returning its inferred type.
- `isDefEq` returns whether or not the well-typed terms `t` and `s` are definitionally equal according to Lean's definitional equality judgment.
- `whnf` reduces an expression to its weak-head normal form (WHNF). It is a subroutine of `isDefEq`, where terms must sometimes be (partly) reduced to determine if they are definitionally equal.

In "Lean4Less", our translation implementation adapted from Lean4Lean, we modify the return values of these functions as follows:

```
def inferType (e : Expr) : RecM (PExpr × Option PExpr) := ...
                                    -- ^ "patched" `e`
def isDefEq (t s : PExpr) : RecM (Bool × Option EExpr) := ...
                                    -- ^ proof of `t == s`
def whnf (e : PExpr) : RecM (PExpr × Option EExpr) := ...
                                    -- ^ proof of `e == (whnf e)`
```

(`PExpr` and `EExpr` are Lean4Less-specific types for representing translated terms and equality proof, respectively). All three functions *optionally* return a patched expression/equality proof depending on whether proof irrelevance was used in typing/definitional equality checking. If it was not, then we return `Option.none`, indicating that no equality proof/translation was required.

The `inferType` function may now also return a translated version of the input expression injected with transports where required by typing constraints (see Sect. 4.2) – note that the first return value is the original inferred type return value, and we maintain that this inferred type is Lean^--typeable (that is, it is a translation to Lean^- of the type that would have normally been inferred by Lean4Lean's `inferType` function). The `isDefEq` function now also possibly returns a generated proof of equality between the input terms, and the `whnf` function may also return a proof of equality between the input term and its weak head normal form. Both functions return *heterogeneous* equality proofs with the type `HEq` (in particular, `whnf` must also return a heterogeneous equality proof because the type of the input term may change during reduction).

A returned proof from `isDefEq` or `whnf` can be interpreted as a "trace" of the typechecker's steps in deciding definitional equality/performing WHNF reduction. For instance, if the typechecker determines that the applications `f a` and `f b` are definitionally equal, where proof irrelevance was used at some point when comparing `a` and `b` to produce a proof term `p : a = b`, Lean4Less will construct a proof using Lean's `congrArg` lemma in order to produce the proof term `congrArg f a b p : f a = f b`.

3.3 Verification

Once we have our translated output from Lean4Less, we can verify that it is well-typed in Lean^-. Specifically, for some output environment E^P translated from an input environment E, we typecheck E^P using a modified fork of Lean4Lean with proof irrelevance and K-like reduction disabled. We must also verify that our translation did not change the semantics of annotated constant types as a result of translation – as explained in Sect. 2.1, the output of our translation should only "decorate" the input with casts between types that are already Lean-defeq. For this, we generate a verification environment E^T containing equality theorems between the original and translated types of every defined constant, proven by reflection. We then typecheck E^T with the normal Lean kernel. Our translation and verification workflow is summarized in the diagram below:

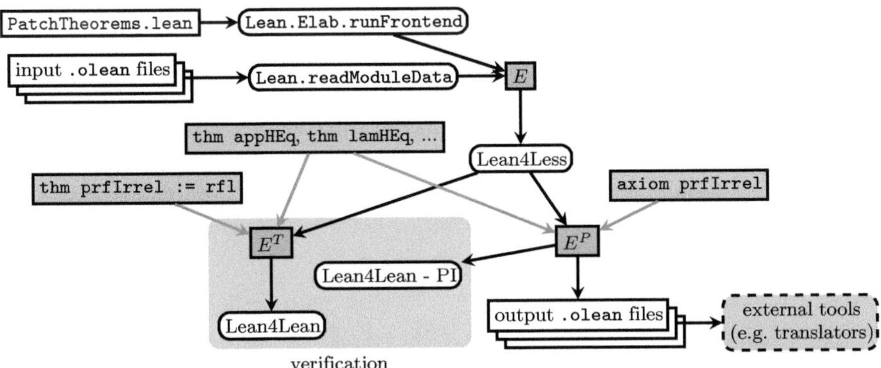

verification

4   Implementation Details

4.1   Congruence Lemmas

In the process of translating from Lean to Lean$^-$, we use a number of specialized definitions to cast terms and build the needed type equality proofs[14]. In particular, we need a set of "congruence lemmas" to compose equality proofs from the proofs of equality of corresponding subterms, for the forall, lambda, and application cases:

```
theorem forallHEqABUV' {A B : Sort u} {U : A → Sort v} {V : B → Sort v}
  (hAB : A == B) (hUV : (a : A) → (b : B) → a == b → U a == V b)
  : ((a : A) → U a) ((b : B) → V b) := ...
theorem lambdaHEqABUV' {A B : Sort u} {U : A → Sort v} {V : B → Sort v}
  (f : (a : A) → U a) (g : (b : B) → V b)
  (hAB : A == B) (hfg : (a : A) → (b : B) → a == b → f a == g b)
  : (fun a => f a) == (fun b => g b) := ...  -- (uses funext)
theorem appHEqABUV' {A B : Sort u} {U : A → Sort v} {V : B → Sort v}
  (hAB : A == B) (hUV : (a : A) → (b : B) → a == b → U a == V b)
  {f : (a : A) → U a} {g : (b : B) → V b} {a : A} {b : B}
  (hfg : f == g) (hab : a == b)
  : f a == g b := ...
```

appHEqABUV' contains the additional hypothesis hUV that allows us to equate U and V in its proof. This enables us to prove the lemma without the presence of domain- and codomain-annotated lambda and application constructors, which was a requirement on the source ETT syntax imposed by [19] in order to be able to prove a version of this lemma that does not carry this hypothesis[15]. While it may seem feasible to derive this hypothesis from the equality of the types of f and g implied by hfg, this is not possible in Lean without the addition of a "forall η" axiom with the signature:

---

[14] The full list of translation-specific constants can be found here: https://github.com/rish987/Lean4Less/blob/main/patch/PatchTheorems.lean.

[15] For a verified translation, using this hypothesis requires a proof that it can always be inhabited, which has not been shown by Winterhalter et al. [20]. However, we have not had any problems proving this hypothesis on-the-fly as a part of our translation.

```
-- (not used by our translation)
axiom forallEta : ((a : A) → U a) = ((a : A) → V a) → U = V
```

Assuming such an axiom breaks some theoretical properties of Lean, in particular its interpretation under a cardinality model where all types of equal size are considered equal[16].

We also need the proof irrelevance axiom and its extension to provably equal proof types. For convenience, we also add a heterogeneous cast function:

```
axiom prfIrrel {P : Prop} (p q : P) : p = q
theorem prfIrrelHEq {P : Prop} (p q : P) : p == q := ...
theorem prfIrrelHEqPQ {P Q : Prop} (hPQ : P == Q)
  (p : P) (q : Q) : p == q := ...
def castHEq {A B : Sort u} (h : A == B) (a : A) : B :=
  cast (eq_of_heq h) a
```

These constants, along with all of their dependencies, need to be enumerated to Lean4Less to be added to the environment first, since any later definitions may reference them as a result of translation. Importantly, they must already be well-typed in Lean⁻ and should not require translation themselves, since this could result in cyclic self-references.

4.2 Producing Patched Terms

During translation, the output is obtained by "injecting" type casts into the terms around subterms whose expected and inferred types are not Lean⁻-defeq. Expected type requirements can arise either from user-provided annotations or from typing restrictions imposed by certain typing rules. The type casts require a proof of equality between these expected and inferred types, which is computed with a call to `isDefEq`.

User-provided type annotations can come from constant signatures or let bindings (a.k.a. local definitions). In the case that the annotated types do not match, we cast the entirety of the constant/let body. Checking that constant type signatures and inferred body types are equal is performed at the highest level of translation/typechecking, that is, when adding constants to the typing environment. Checking let bindings, on the other hand, occurs as a subroutine of type inference.

---

[16] If we assume this axiom, we can show a counterexample to the cardinality model as follows: Let `A := Fin 2`, and let `U := fun x => if x = 0 then Bool else Unit` and `V := fun x => if x = 0 then Unit else Bool`. Then, we have the function type cardinalities $|(a : A) → U\ a| = |(a : A) → V\ a| = 2$, allowing us to derive `U = V` from `forallEta`. By application congruence `U 0 = V 0`, which contradicts that $|U\ 0| = 2 \neq |V\ 0| = 1$

Type casts may also be inserted due to the following typing rules:

$$\frac{\Gamma \vdash A : \texttt{Sort u} \quad \Gamma, x : A \vdash e : B}{\Gamma, x : A \vdash \lambda x : A.\ e : \forall x : A.\ B} \ \text{[LAM]} \qquad \frac{\Gamma \vdash A : \texttt{Sort u} \quad \Gamma, x : A \vdash B : \texttt{Sort v}}{\Gamma \vdash \forall x : A.\ B : \texttt{Sort (imax u v)}} \ \text{[ALL]}$$

$$\frac{\Gamma \vdash e : \forall x : A.\ B \quad \Gamma \vdash e' : A}{\Gamma \vdash e\ e' : B[e'/x]} \ \text{[APP]} \qquad \frac{\Gamma \vdash A : \texttt{Sort u} \quad \Gamma \vdash e : A \quad \Gamma, x : A \vdash b : B}{\Gamma \vdash \texttt{let}\ (x : A)\ \texttt{:=}\ e\ \texttt{in}\ b : B[e/x]} \ \text{[LET]}$$

The rules [LAM], [ALL], and [LET] require the binder types (and output type, in the case of [ALL]) to be sorts, so these types may be cast if their inferred types are not Lean$^-$-defeq to some $\texttt{Sort u}$. Typing restrictions are also enforced by [APP], where the domain type of the function must definitionally match the inferred type of the argument, with the argument being cast if this is not the case. The function itself may also be cast, if its inferred type is not Lean$^-$-defeq to some function type.

The translation of a Lean constant is identical to the original, save for the fact that various subterms may have been "decorated" by casts (that is, they are related by the "$\sim$" similarity relation described in [19]). It is easy to recover the input Lean term from its Lean$^-$ translation: one must simply remove all type casts introduced by the translation, which are easy to identify as they use the translation-specific $\texttt{castHEq}$ cast function.

4.3   Output/Runtime Optimizations

Output and runtime optimizations are particularly important for a tool like Lean4Less, to be able to scale up the translation to large libraries and to have a reasonably sized output that avoids redundancy. Additionally, it is important to have an efficient implementation that enables the translation to complete within a reasonable amount of time without excessive memory requirements. By virtue of being based on an efficient typechecker implementation, Lean4Less already enjoys many output and runtime optimizations that transfer over from the kernel. For instance:

- Lean uses "lazy δ-reduction" in its $\texttt{isDefEq}$ check, avoiding the expansion of equal δ-expandable constant function application heads where possible, opting to first perform a comparison on each pair of arguments. This translates to an output optimization in which we can also avoid expanding these constants in the output when generating equality proofs.
- Lean's proof irrelevance check is placed very early on in the $\texttt{isDefEq}$ check, ensuring that we do not needlessly compare proof subterms if we already know that the proof types are equal (thus making the proofs definitionally equal by proof irrelevance). This also becomes an output optimization, because we can immediately output an equality proof using the $\texttt{prfIrrel}$ axiom, rather than possibly producing a larger proof resulting from a more detailed comparison of subterms (in the case that the proofs can be shown equal without applying [PI]).

– Lean's kernel makes use of a cache for recording previously computed weak-head normal forms. Lean4Less adapts this cache to store an equality proof in addition to the weak-head normal form itself, and can be queried to avoid unnecessary computations. This translates into an output optimization since these redundant proofs will also share object pointers in the `.olean` output.

Lean4Less also implements some optimizations of its own, not described here.

5   Results

We have tested our translation on the Lean standard library and various lower-level Mathlib modules, verifying our output in the manner described in Sect. 3.3. We have already had success in translating significant subsets of Mathlib to Lean⁻, for instance Lean's real numbers library `Mathlib.Data.Real.Basic`, containing several thousands of lines of code and thousands of uses of proof irrelevance and K-like reduction.

We benchmark our translation on `Std`, the Lean core standard library, and on the mathlib library `Mathlib.Algebra.Order.Field.Rat`, with the versions of both libraries using Lean toolchain `v4.16.0-rc2`. We report below on some measures relating to the translation of these modules on a machine with an Intel Xeon 8-core CPU @ 2.20GHz and 32 GB RAM:

Module	Total Constants	Constants Using [PI]/[KLR] (% of total)	Input/Output Environment Size (Overhead)	Translation Runtime	Input/Output Typechecking Runtime (Overhead)[17]
Std	29859	1736/134 (6.3%)	226MB/261MB (15.5%)	18m02s	2m19s/3m9s (36.0%)
Algebra.Order.Field.Rat	113899	2965/237 (2.8%)	1485MB/1501MB (1.1%)	32m16s	5m11s/5m44s (10.6%)

The standard library translation overhead of 15.5% is not very excessive relative to the 6% of total constants using proof irrelevance/K-like reduction, and we observe an even more modest translation overhead when translating an actual `Mathlib` module. In both cases, however, this is somewhat disproportionate to the amount of extra typechecking runtime overhead translation incurs. It is not clear how much of this overhead is truly unavoidable, but more work can certainly to be done to optimize the output size.

We can see above that translation takes significantly longer than typechecking, and we have found that the translation tends to get "stuck" for significant amounts of time translating certain constants, sometimes taking longer than ten minutes to translate a single definition. Such long-running translations also consume significant amounts of memory, which has proven to be a prohibitive factor in attempting to translate larger mathlib libraries. Further investigation is needed here. Such slowdowns may be related to general scaling problems that are closely tied to output inefficiencies, and may be resolved through the implementation of further output optimizations – for instance, the generation of auxiliary helper definitions and the more efficient use of caching.

---

[17] When run with the Lean and Lean⁻ kernels, respectively (i.e. Lean4Lean with and without PI/K-like reduction)

6   Prospects and Conclusion

Because Lean4Less implements a special case of the ETT-to-ITT translation, an immediate interest is the possible adaptation of its translation framework for use in a general extensional-to-intensional translation. This could enable the adoption of new, possibly user-specified definitional equalities in Lean, while maintaining the ability to translate back to Lean's core type theory, producing terms that are checkable with the same small, trusted kernel. Such a development could take Lean in the direction of being an extensional proof assistant, which could significantly simplify many reasoning tasks where equality goals and hypotheses feature prominently.

Another potential benefit of having a translation from Lean to Lean$^-$ is that it can simplify meta-theoretical analyses of Lean's type theory by enabling us to use Lean$^-$ as a "proxy theory" for Lean itself. Specifically, some important meta-theoretical results, such as consistency, could be shown for Lean$^-$ and automatically transfer to Lean, provided the correctness of the translation implementation.

Additionally, while this work primarily concerns a particular implementation of an extensional-to-intensional translation applied specifically to eliminating the use of proof irrelevance in the typing of Lean terms, the framework developed for Lean4Less should be general enough to extend to eliminate other definitional equalities present in the Lean kernel, for instance the "struct eta" rule (and its reduction counterpart), and Lean's special reduction rules for quotient type eliminators. In addition, the techniques and optimizations developed here could be transferrable to similar translations implemented for other proof assistants, either for the purpose of proof export or for extending them to have extensional-like features of their own.

Conclusion. In this paper, we describe the theory, design, and implementation of a tool that is capable of translating Lean to smaller theories through the implementation of a more general translation framework from extensional to intensional type theory. We have described how we have adapted our translation from an independent typechecker kernel implementation for Lean called "Lean4Lean" [6]. Our tool, "Lean4Less", has been successfully able to translate certain medium-sized libraries, and we hope to scale up our translation to handle larger formalizations. We believe that this work sets the foundation for the first practical translation from extensional to intensional type theory that has been implemented for a proof assistant. Such a translation may enable future extensions to the Lean kernel, allowing for more convenient mathematical formalization while retaining the ability to translate terms back to the original theory to typecheck with the same small, trusted kernel. Additionally, while this work primarily concerns a particular implementation of an extensional-to-intensional translation applied specifically to eliminating the use of proof irrelevance in the typing of Lean terms, the general techniques and optimizations developed here could be transferrable to similar translations that may be implemented for other proof assistants.

Acknowledgments. This publication is based upon work completed under COST Action EuroProofNet, CA20111, supported by COST (European Cooperation in Science and Technology).

Disclosure of Interests. The author claims no competing interests.

References

1. Abel, A., Coquand, T.: Failure of normalization in impredicative type theory with proof-irrelevant propositional equality. Log. Methods Comput. Sci. **16**(2), 14 (2020). https://doi.org/10.23638/LMCS-16(2:14)2020
2. Allen, S.F., Constable, R.L., Eaton, R., Kreitz, C., Lorigo, L.: The Nuprl open logical environment. In: McAllester, D. (ed.) CADE 2000. LNCS (LNAI), vol. 1831, pp. 170–176. Springer, Heidelberg (2000). https://doi.org/10.1007/10721959_12
3. Bauer, A., Gilbert, G., Haselwarter, P.G., Pretnar, M., Stone, C.A.: Design and implementation of the andromeda proof assistant. In: Ghilezan, S., Geuvers, H., Ivetic, J. (eds.) 22nd International Conference on Types for Proofs and Programs (TYPES 2016). Leibniz International Proceedings in Informatics (LIPIcs), vol. 97, pp. 5:1–5:31. Schloss Dagstuhl – Leibniz-Zentrum für Informatik, Dagstuhl, Germany (2018). https://doi.org/10.4230/LIPIcs.TYPES.2016.5
4. Blanqui, F., Dowek, G., Grienenberger, E., Hondet, G., Thiré, F.: A modular construction of type theories. Log. Methods Comput. Sci. **19**(1), 12 (2023). https://doi.org/10.46298/lmcs-19(1:12)2023
5. Carneiro, M.: The Type Theory of Lean. Master's thesis (2019). https://github.com/digama0/lean-type-theory/releases/tag/v1.0
6. Carneiro, M.: Lean4lean: towards a formalized metatheory for the lean theorem prover (2024). https://arxiv.org/abs/2403.14064
7. Forster, Y., Sozeau, M., Tabareau, N.: Verified extraction from Coq to OCaml (2024). https://doi.org/10.1145/3656379
8. Hofmann, M.: Conservativity of equality reflection over intensional type theory. In: Selected Papers from the International Workshop on Types for Proofs and Programs, TYPES 1995, pp. 153–164. Springer, Heidelberg (1995)
9. Hofmann, M., Rijsbergen, C.J.: Extensional Constructs in Intensional Type Theory. Springer, Heidelberg (1997)
10. Hondet, G., Blanqui, F.: Encoding of predicate subtyping with proof irrelevance in the λΠ-calculus modulo theory. In: de'Liguoro, U., Berardi, S., Altenkirch, T. (eds.) 26th International Conference on Types for Proofs and Programs (TYPES 2020). Leibniz International Proceedings in Informatics (LIPIcs), vol. 188, pp. 6:1–6:18. Schloss Dagstuhl – Leibniz-Zentrum für Informatik, Dagstuhl, Germany (2021). https://doi.org/10.4230/LIPIcs.TYPES.2020.6
11. Moura, L., Ullrich, S.: The lean 4 theorem prover and programming language. In: Platzer, A., Sutcliffe, G. (eds.) CADE 2021. LNCS (LNAI), vol. 12699, pp. 625–635. Springer, Cham (2021). https://doi.org/10.1007/978-3-030-79876-5_37
12. Oury, N.: Extensionality in the calculus of constructions. In: Hurd, J., Melham, T. (eds.) TPHOLs 2005. LNCS, vol. 3603, pp. 278–293. Springer, Heidelberg (2005). https://doi.org/10.1007/11541868_18
13. Paulin-Mohring, C.: Introduction to the calculus of inductive constructions. In: Paleo, B.W., Delahaye, D. (eds.) All about Proofs, Proofs for All, Studies in Logic (Mathematical logic and foundations), vol. 55. College Publications (2015). https://inria.hal.science/hal-01094195

14. Rocq Community: The Rocq theorem prover. https://rocq-prover.org/
15. Sozeau, M., Boulier, S., Forster, Y., Tabareau, N., Winterhalter, T.: Coq coq correct! Verification of type checking and erasure for coq, in coq. Proc. ACM Program. Lang. **4**(POPL) (2019). https://doi.org/10.1145/3371076
16. Swamy, N., et al.: Dependent types and multi-monadic effects in F*. SIGPLAN Not. **51**(1), 256–270 (2016). https://doi.org/10.1145/2914770.2837655
17. The mathlib community: mathlib4 (Github). https://github.com/leanprover-community/mathlib4
18. The mathlib community: The lean mathematical library. In: Proceedings of the 9th ACM SIGPLAN International Conference on Certified Programs and Proofs, CPP 2020, pp. 367–381. Association for Computing Machinery, New York (2020). https://doi.org/10.1145/3372885.3373824
19. Winterhalter, T., Sozeau, M., Tabareau, N.: Eliminating reflection from type theory. In: Proceedings of the 8th ACM SIGPLAN International Conference on Certified Programs and Proofs (2019). https://api.semanticscholar.org/CorpusID:57379755
20. Winterhalter, T., Tabareau, N.: ett-to-itt (Github). https://github.com/TheoWinterhalter/ett-to-itt

From Program Logics Towards Language Logics

Matteo Cimini[✉]

University of Massachusetts Lowell, Lowell, MA 01854, USA
`matteo_cimini@uml.edu`

Abstract. Program logics are a powerful formal method in the context of program verification. Can we develop a counterpart of program logics in the context of language verification?

This paper proposes *language logics*, which allow for statements of the form $\{P\}\ \mathcal{X}\ \{Q\}$ where $\mathcal{X}$, the subject of analysis, can be a language component such as a piece of grammar, a typing rule, a reduction rule, or other parts of a language definition. To demonstrate our approach, we develop a number of language logics for analyzing various aspects of programming languages.

We illustrate our language logics to the analysis of a faulty programming language. We have also implemented LANG-N-ASSERT, an automated prover for our logics, and we report on our experiments with the tool, which include the above-mentioned analysis on the faulty language.

Ultimately, our language logics do not fully verify languages. Nonetheless, we believe that this paper provides a strong step towards adopting the methods of program logics for the analysis of languages.

Keywords: Language verification · Functional languages · Program logics

1 Introduction

Once we have created a programming language, there are many questions that are important to investigate about it. Language verification strives to establish whether the metatheoretic properties that are intended for a language actually hold. These properties vary greatly and they concern both *all-encompassing properties* of a language such as type soundness and strong normalization as well as *selected aspects* of operators, grammar rules, and reduction rules, for example to determine whether the behaviour of our elimination forms is defined for all the expected values, whether we have defined all the necessary evaluation contexts, or whether the variance (covariant, contravariant, invariant) of arguments of type constructors is sound, to make a few examples.

In the context of program verification, program logics stand out as a powerful formal method with decades of development and myriads of success stories. Various program logics have been proposed. The seminal Floyd-Hoare logic has been

© The Author(s), under exclusive license to Springer Nature Switzerland AG 2026
Z. Liu et al. (Eds.): ICTAC 2025, LNCS 16237, pp. 220–238, 2026.
https://doi.org/10.1007/978-3-032-11176-0_14

applied to the verification of imperative programs [11,16]. Pointer-manipulating programs are better analyzed with separation logics [19,23], while thread-based concurrent programs with concurrent separation logics [2,20]. The literature also offers works on program logics for higher-order functional programs [3], weak memory models [25,26], as well as many other domains.

Our question: *Can we develop a counterpart of program logics for the verification of languages?*

Language Logics. In this paper, we take a first step towards developing such a counterpart. We propose *language logics*. In language logics, the subject of analysis is a language definition rather than a program. Statements have the form $\{P\}\ \mathcal{X}\ \{Q\}$ where $\mathcal{X}$ can be the entire language at hand or some of its components such as a piece of grammar, a typing rule, a reduction rule, or other parts of the language definition. Analogously to program logics, P is a precondition and Q is a postcondition. To make an example, given an inference rule r, $\{P\}\ r\ \{Q\}$ can be read "when P holds, Q holds after having added the inference rule r to the language definition".

To demonstrate our approach, we have developed three language logics: $\mathbb{L}(\mathcal{T}_{dupEf})$, $\mathbb{L}(\mathcal{T}_{eh})$, and $\mathbb{L}(\mathcal{T}_{mut})$. Each language logic is formed by a base logic $\mathbb{L}$ that is parametrized by the *theories* $\mathcal{T}_{dupEf}$, $\mathcal{T}_{eh}$, and $\mathcal{T}_{mut}$, respectively. (The logic $\mathbb{L}$, as well as the three theories, are contributions of this paper.) Intuitively, each theory is tailored to reason about a specific aspect of programming languages. For example, $\mathcal{T}_{dupEf}$ reasons about the duplication of effects and can express assertions `effectful`, which means that the language is effectful, i.e., operations can modify a state, and assertions `no-dupli-ef`(rn), which means that the reduction rule with name rn does not lead to the duplication of effects. The theory $\mathcal{T}_{mut}$ reasons about the variance of types for mutable data and can express assertions `mutable`(c), which means that the type constructor c is for mutable data, and assertions `sound-variance`(c), which can be derived only when the type constructor c for mutable data is invariant (for type soundness). Section 4 will describe the three theories $\mathcal{T}_{dupEf}$, $\mathcal{T}_{eh}$, and $\mathcal{T}_{mut}$ in detail.

Evaluation: Language Logics at Work. To demonstrate our language logics, we embark on a journey towards debugging the definition of a faulty language, which we call λ_{err}^{ref}. This language has a few issues, for example it duplicates effects due to a call-by-name strategy and adopts covariant mutable references, which are unsound (see [22, §15.5]). We use our language logics to reason about these issues and, for each issue, we show that we cannot derive the assertion that states the absence of the issue. We show, then, that after we modify the language and fix the issue we now can provide such proof derivation. For example, after we replace the subtyping rule for the reference type `Ref` of our faulty λ_{err}^{ref} with the standard rule for invariance `Ref` T <: `Ref` T, we now can derive $\{$`mutable(Ref)`$\}\ \lambda_{err}^{ref}\ \{$`sound-variance(Ref)`$\}$.

As further contribution of this paper, we have implemented an automated prover for our language logics called LANG-N-ASSERT [9]. Users can specify the theories to be used and a statement $\{P\}\ \mathcal{L}\ \{Q\}$. The output of the tool is a proof derivation or an error message based on the proof rule that could not be satisfied. We confirm that our tool replicates our debugging journey of the faulty language, failing to derive sought for assertions and succeeding upon fixing the issues. We also report on using the tool in other experiments (Sect. 6).

In this paper, we do not provide a soundness theorem for our language logics, they therefore cannot be used to formally establish a property, hence the word "towards" in our title. We believe that a soundness theorem deserves its own study and paper, and we offer a discussion of this matter in Sect. 8. Nonetheless, we believe that this paper provides a strong step towards adopting the methods of program logics for the analysis of languages.

The paper is organized as follows. Section 2 reviews how languages are defined in operational semantics through our running example language λ_{err}^{ref}. Section 3 provides the base logic $\mathbb{L}$. Section 4 presents our theories $\mathcal{T}_{dupEf}$, $\mathcal{T}_{eh}$, and $\mathcal{T}_{mut}$, which populate the base logic $\mathbb{L}$ with assertions and proof rules for reasoning about certain specific aspects. Section 5 applies the language logics so constructed to the analysis of (the faulty) λ_{err}^{ref} and its fixes. Section 6 describes our LANG-N-ASSERT tool. Section 7 offers a comparison between program logics and language logics. Section 8 discusses the limitations of language logics. Section 9 discusses related work and Sect. 10 concludes the paper.

2   Operational Semantics (Review)

Figure 1 shows the language definition of our running example λ_{err}^{ref}, a λ-calculus with integers, floating points, subtyping, a simple **try** error handler, and references (with heap allocation **ref**, dereference operator !, assignment :=, and sequential composition ;). To briefly review, a language has a grammar, which consists of a series of *grammar rules*, each of which defines a *syntactic category*, such as Type and Expression. Each syntactic category has a metavariable, such as T and e, and *grammar productions*. A language also has inference rules that define relations such as a typing, a subtyping, and a reduction relation. Each inference rule has a series of formulae called *premises* and one formula called *conclusion*. For example, $\Sigma \mid \Gamma \vdash e : \text{Ref } T$ is a premise of rule [T-DEREF], and $\Sigma \mid \Gamma \vdash !e : T$ is its conclusion. Inference rules whose conclusion can derive a $\vdash$-formula are called *typing rules*. The $\vdash$-formulae rely on a type environment Γ (map from variables to types) and a location environment Σ (map from labels of heap locations to types). Inference rules that derive a $<:$-formula are called *subtyping rules*, and those that derive a $\longrightarrow$-formula are called *reduction rules*. The $\longrightarrow$-formulae include a state μ (map from labels to values), i.e., the heap. Reduction rules make use of auxiliary notation such as $\text{dom}(\mu)$ for the domain of the heap and $[\ell \mapsto v]\mu$ for updates to μ (see [22, §13]). (Typing rules are many for λ_{err}^{ref}, and also include store typing [22, §13.4] and the typing of configurations e, μ. Figure 1 becomes too big with all of them, and so we show a selection.)

Evaluation contexts declare which arguments of an expression constructor can be evaluated (and in which order). *Error contexts* define which contexts are allowed to detect the occurrence of an error and fail the overall computation.

Disclaimer: There are a few issues, highlighted below and discussed in Section 2.

$$n \in \mathbb{N}, f \in \mathbb{R}, \ell \in \text{LABEL}, \oplus \in \{+, -, \times, \div\}$$

Type	$T ::= \text{Int} \mid \text{Float} \mid T \to T \mid \text{Ref } T \mid \text{Unit}$
Expression	$e ::= v \mid e \oplus e \mid x \mid e\, e \mid \text{ref } e \mid\; !e \mid e := e \mid e; e \mid \text{error} \mid \text{try } e \text{ with } e$
Value	$v ::= n \mid f \mid \lambda x : T.e \mid \ell \mid \text{unit}$
Error	$er ::= \text{error}$
EvalCtx	$E ::= \square \mid E \oplus e \mid v \oplus E \mid E\, e \mid \text{ref } E \mid\; !E$
	$\mid E := e \mid v := E \mid E; e \mid \text{try } E \text{ with } e$
ErrorCtx	$F ::= \square \mid F \oplus e \mid v \oplus F \mid F\, e \mid \text{ref } F \mid\; !F$
	$\mid F := e \mid v := F \mid F; e \mid \boxed{\text{try } F \text{ with } e}$
TypeEnv	$\Gamma ::= \emptyset \mid \Gamma, x : T$
Heap	$\mu ::= \emptyset \mid \mu, (l \mapsto v)$
LocEnv	$\Sigma ::= \emptyset \mid \Sigma, (l \mapsto T)$

Type System $\boxed{\Sigma \mid \Gamma \vdash e : T}$

$$\Sigma \mid \Gamma \vdash n : \text{Int}$$

$$\Sigma \mid \Gamma \vdash f : \text{Float}$$

$$\Sigma \mid \Gamma \vdash \text{unit} : \text{Unit}$$

$$\frac{\Sigma \mid \Gamma \vdash e_1 : \text{Float} \qquad \Sigma \mid \Gamma \vdash e_2 : \text{Float}}{\Sigma \mid \Gamma \vdash e_1 \oplus e_2 : \text{Float}}$$

$$\frac{\Sigma \mid \Gamma \vdash e_1 : \text{Ref } T \qquad \Sigma \mid \Gamma \vdash e_2 : T}{\Sigma \mid \Gamma \vdash e_1 := e_2 : \text{Unit}} \quad \cdots$$

[T-DEREF]
$$\frac{\Sigma \mid \Gamma \vdash e : \text{Ref } T}{\Sigma \mid \Gamma \vdash\; !e : T}$$

$$\frac{\Sigma \mid \Gamma \vdash e_1 : T \qquad \Sigma \mid \Gamma \vdash e_2 : T}{\Sigma \mid \Gamma \vdash \text{try } e_1 \text{ with } e_2 : T}$$

[SUBSUMPTION]
$$\frac{\Sigma \mid \Gamma \vdash e : T_1 \qquad T1 <: T_2}{\Sigma \mid \Gamma \vdash e : T_2} \quad \cdots$$

Subtyping $\boxed{T <: T}$

$$\text{Int} <: \text{Float}$$

$$\text{Int} <: \text{Int}$$
$$\text{Float} <: \text{Float}$$
$$\text{Unit} <: \text{Unit}$$

$$\frac{T_1' <: T_1 \qquad T_2 <: T_2'}{T_1 \to T_2 <: T_1' \to T_2'}$$

[S-REF-BAD]
$$\frac{\boxed{T <: T'}}{\text{Ref } T <: \text{Ref } T'}$$

Reduction Semantics $\boxed{e, \mu \longrightarrow e, \mu}$

$$\begin{aligned}
f_1 \oplus f_2, \mu &\longrightarrow f_3, \mu \quad (when \oplus = \div,\; f_2 \neq 0) \\
f_1 \div 0, \mu &\longrightarrow \text{error}, \mu \\
(\lambda x : T.e_1)\; \boxed{e_2}, \mu &\longrightarrow e_1[\,\boxed{e_2}\,/x], \mu && \text{[CBN-BETA]} \\
!\ell, \mu &\longrightarrow \mu(\ell); \mu \\
\ell := v, \mu &\longrightarrow \text{unit}; [\ell \mapsto v]\mu && \text{[R-ASSIGN]} \\
v; e, \mu &\longrightarrow e, \mu \\
\text{try } v \text{ with } e, \mu &\longrightarrow v, \mu \\
\text{try error with } e, \mu &\longrightarrow e, \mu && \text{[ERR]}
\end{aligned}$$

where f_3 is the result of operation $\oplus$ between f_1 and f_2.

$$\frac{\ell \notin \text{dom}(\mu)}{\text{ref } v, \mu \longrightarrow \ell; \mu, (\ell \mapsto v)} \qquad \frac{e, \mu \longrightarrow e', \mu'}{E[e], \mu \longrightarrow E[e'], \mu'}$$

[ERR-CTX]
$$F[er], \mu \longrightarrow er, \mu$$

Fig. 1. Language definition of $\lambda_{\text{err}}^{\text{ref}}$.

There are issues with $\lambda_{\mathtt{err}}^{\mathtt{ref}}$. The language definition of $\lambda_{\mathtt{err}}^{\mathtt{ref}}$ contains a few issues. (None of these issues nor their fixes in Sect. 5 are new in this paper.) *Issue 1:* [CBN-BETA] adopts a call-by-name strategy in the presence of effects. This may lead to the unpredictable duplication of effects. *Issue 2:* The error context $\mathtt{try}\ F\ \mathtt{with}\ e$ entails that the evaluator may "steal" the error from the error handler and terminate the computation rather than letting $\mathtt{try}$ handle the error. *Issue 3:* [S-REF-BAD] defines the reference type to be covariant. However, it is well-known that covariant mutable references are unsound [22, §15.5].

It would be desirable to reason about these issues using proof derivations in the style of program logics.

A Syntax for Language Definitions. Language logics analyze a language $\mathcal{L}$. We adopt the following syntax for language definitions $\mathcal{L}$ from prior work [5], which is simply a grammar for operational semantics definitions.

$cname \in \textsc{CatName},\ X \in \textsc{MetaVar}, pn \in \textsc{PredName},\ rn \in \textsc{RuleName}$
$c, op \in \textsc{ConstrName}$

Language	$\mathcal{L}$	$::= (G, I)$
Grammar	G	$::= g_1 \cdots g_n$
Grammar Rule	g	$::= cname\ X ::= t_1 \mid \cdots \mid t_n$
Inference System	I	$::= r_1 \cdots r_n$
Rule	r	$::= rn : \dfrac{f_1 \cdots f_n}{f}$
Formula	f	$::= (pn\ t_1 \cdots t_n)$
Term	t	$::= X \mid (c\ t_1 \cdots t_n) \mid (X)t \mid t[t/X]$

where $\textsc{CatName}$ contains syntactic category names, $\textsc{MetaVar}$ contains metavariables, $\textsc{ConstrName}$ contains constructor names, $\textsc{PredName}$ contains predicate names (names of relations), and $\textsc{RuleName}$ contains names of inference rules such as [CBN-BETA]. Terms and formulae are in abstract syntax style (top-level name applied to arguments). For readability, we will use familiar syntax such as formulae $e_1, \mu_1 \longrightarrow e_2, \mu_2$ and terms $T_1 \rightarrow T_2$. Terms can also use unary binding $(X)t$ and capture-avoiding substitution $t[t/X]$.

Prior works [5,7] have shown examples of operational semantics definitions in this syntax. Our language $\lambda_{\mathtt{err}}^{\mathtt{ref}}$, too, can be accommodated as a language $\mathcal{L}$.

Given a language $\mathcal{L}$, [5] defines a semantics for it with a translation $[\![\mathcal{L}]\!]^{lp}$ into higher-order logic programs [17].

3   Language Logics for Analyzing Languages

A language logic $\mathbb{L}(\mathcal{T}_1, \ldots, \mathcal{T}_n)$ is parameterized by *theories* $\mathcal{T}_1, \ldots, \mathcal{T}_n$. Although we discuss theories $\mathcal{T}$ in the next section, we say here that they have a grammar $\mathcal{T}.\mathtt{grammar}$ and proof rules $\mathcal{T}.\mathtt{rules}$. The syntax of $\mathbb{L}(\mathcal{T}_1, \ldots, \mathcal{T}_n)$ is

$P, Q ::= \mathtt{true} \mid P \wedge Q \mid \neg P$
$stmt ::= \{P\}\ \mathcal{L}\ \{Q\} \mid \{P\}\ G\ \{Q\} \mid \{P\}\ I\ \{Q\} \mid \{P\}\ g\ \{Q\} \mid \{P\}\ r\ \{Q\}$

$\qquad \cup\ \mathcal{T}_1.\mathtt{grammar} \cdots \cup\ \mathcal{T}_n.\mathtt{grammar}.$

$$\text{(LANG)}\quad \frac{\{P\}\ G\ \{Q\}\quad \{Q\}\ I\ \{R\}}{\{P\}\ (G,I)\ \{R\}}$$

$$\text{(GRAM)}\quad \frac{\{P_0\}\ g_1\ \{P_1\}\quad \{P_1\}\ g_2\ \{P_2\}\quad \cdots\quad \{P_{n-1}\}\ g_n\ \{P_n\}}{\{P_0\}\ g_1\ \cdots\ g_n\ \{P_n\}}$$

$$\text{(INF)}\quad \frac{\{P_0\}\ r_1\ \{P_1\}\quad \{P_1\}\ r_2\ \{P_2\}\quad \cdots\quad \{P_{n-1}\}\ r_n\ \{P_n\}}{\{P_0\}\ r_1\ \cdots\ r_n\ \{r_n\}}$$

$$\text{(PERM-G)}\quad \frac{\pi\ \text{is a permutation of } g_1\ \cdots\ g_n \qquad \{P\}\ \pi\ \{Q\}}{\{P\}\ g_1\ \cdots\ g_n\ \{Q\}}$$

$$\text{(PERM-R)}\quad \frac{\pi\ \text{is a permutation of } r_1\ \cdots\ r_n \qquad \{P\}\ \pi\ \{Q\}}{\{P\}\ r_1\ \cdots\ r_n\ \{Q\}}$$

$$(\mathcal{X}\text{-NEUTRAL})\quad \{P\}\ \mathcal{X}\ \{P\}$$

$$\text{(ITERATE)}\quad \frac{\{P\}\ \mathcal{X}\ \{Q\}\quad \{Q\}\ \mathcal{X}\ \{R\}}{\{P\}\ \mathcal{X}\ \{R\}}$$

$$\text{(CONSEQUENCE)}\quad \frac{P \Rightarrow P' \quad \{P'\}\ \mathcal{X}\ \{Q'\} \quad Q' \Rightarrow Q}{\{P\}\ \mathcal{X}\ \{Q\}}$$

$$\cup\ \mathcal{T}_1.\mathtt{rules}\ \cdots\ \cup\ \mathcal{T}_n.\mathtt{rules}$$

Fig. 2. Proof rules of $\mathbb{L}$. In this figure, $\mathcal{X} \in \{\mathcal{L}, G, I, g, r\}$.

Intuitively, we start with an "empty" logic which we refer to as our *base logic* $\mathbb{L}$. This logic only contains the most common connectives. Then, the grammar unions above add the grammar of the parameterized theories, which populates the assertions of $\mathbb{L}(\mathcal{T}_1, \ldots, \mathcal{T}_n)$. We employ the standard grammar union $\cup$.

A statement *stmt* can be a language with a pre- and postcondition: $\{P\}\ \mathcal{L}\ \{Q\}$ means that "when P holds, Q holds after having analyzed the language $\mathcal{L}$". Similarly, we have statements with a grammar, grammar rule, inference system, and inference rule. The meaning of these is analogous to statements with languages. For example, $\{P\}\ r\ \{Q\}$ means that "when P holds, Q holds after having added the inference rule r". We write $\{\}$ in lieu of $\{\mathtt{true}\}$.

Proof Rules of $\mathbb{L}(\mathcal{T}_1, \ldots, \mathcal{T}_n)$. Figure 2 shows the proof rules of $\mathbb{L}(\mathcal{T}_1, \ldots, \mathcal{T}_n)$. The design principle that they follow is that they govern the traversing of a language definition at hand. Proof rule (LANG) analyzes the grammar of the language and, starting from the assertions so derived, analyzes the inference system. Proof rule (GRAM) analyzes the grammar rules, one by one, in the order they are encountered. Each time, the assertions derived from a grammar rule are used as preconditions in the analysis of the next grammar rule. Proof rule (INF) is analogous to (GRAM) and analyzes the inference rules in the order they are encountered. Proof rules (PERM-G) and (PERM-R) allow to reorder grammar rules and inference rules, respectively. Proof rule ($\mathcal{X}$-NEUTRAL) propagates the precondition as postcondition. Rule (ITERATE) analyzes a language component to derive Q. Then, it analyzes again the same language component using Q as precondition. (CONSEQUENCE), as in program logics, allows for the strengthening of preconditions and the weakening of postconditions. Finally, $\mathbb{L}(\mathcal{T}_1, \ldots, \mathcal{T}_n)$ includes the proof rules of the parameterized theories.

4   Theories

A theory consists of two components. The first component is a grammar that defines assertions P. The second component is a set of proof rules.

In the following paragraphs, we define three theories: $\mathcal{T}_{dupEf}$, $\mathcal{T}_{eh}$, and $\mathcal{T}_{mut}$. The design idea behind their assertions is that they state a specific property regarding that aspect. We have selected a handful of formulae. They are by no means all that it would be interesting to detect of a language.

As for the proof rules of our theories, their design principle is the following: For each of the assertions in the grammar of P of the theory, we provide one or more proof rules that can derive that assertion. (We make an exception with $\mathtt{mutable}(c)$ of $\mathcal{T}_{mut}$, which we leave with no proof rules to demonstrate a point.)

Theory $\mathcal{T}_{dupEf}$. This theory reasons about the possibility of duplicating effects. Figure 3 shows the grammar of assertions and the proof rules of the theory $\mathcal{T}_{dupEf}$.

The assertion $\mathtt{effectful}$ holds whenever the language has a state and reductions that can modify the state. Proof rule (EFFECTFUL) derives $\mathtt{effectful}$. The conclusion of (EFFECTFUL) is of the form $\{P\}\ r\ \{Q\}$ where r is a reduction rule. To avoid the confusion that may arise with inference rules that analyze inference rules, we frame the rules in the conclusion within a box. (We omit such a box in our examples when they are clear without.) Here, (EFFECTFUL) detects whether one of the states is modified after the step.

The assertion $\mathtt{no\text{-}dupli\text{-}ef}(rn)$ holds whenever the step of the reduction rule rn does not duplicate arguments that may produce effects. (NO-DUPLI-EF) derives assertions $\mathtt{no\text{-}dupli\text{-}ef}(rn)$. This rule analyzes a reduction rule of op with name rn. The precondition is that the language is effectful (with $\mathtt{effectful} \in P$). We assume that the language designer knows which syntactic categories do not produce effects. We assume that the set INEFFECTUAL contains the metavariables of these categories. For $\lambda_{\mathtt{err}}^{\mathtt{ref}}$, we have INEFFECTUAL $= \{v, er\}$. The rule focuses on the arguments that cannot be derived by any of the categories of INEFFECTUAL (with $\nexists X \in$ INEFFECTUAL$, X \Rightarrow_G^* t$). These arguments may produce effects which may be duplicated. For each, we check that the target of the step does not replicate it nor use it in a substitution operation. (The rule makes use of context-like notation $C[t, t, \ldots]$ to denote a term that contains t two or more times, and $C[t''[t/x]]$ to denote a term that contains a substitution that involves t.) Notice that (NO-DUPLI-EF) expects that some reduction rule has been previously analyzed for deriving $\mathtt{effectful}$. This motivates the permutation rules of Fig. 2.

Theory $\mathcal{T}_{eh}$. This theory reasons about error handlers and their interaction with the evaluation contexts of the language. Figure 4 shows $\mathcal{T}_{eh}$. The assertion $\mathtt{inductive}(X, c, \{n_1, \ldots, n_k\})$ holds whenever c is a top-level constructor of a grammar production of the category with metavariable X and its arguments at

$$\mathcal{T}_{dupEf}.\textbf{grammar} \triangleq \quad P ::= \textbf{effectful} \mid \textbf{no-dupli-ef}(op)$$

$$\mathcal{T}_{dupEf}.\textbf{rules} \triangleq$$

(EFFECTFUL)

$$\{P\} \; rn : \dfrac{\begin{array}{c} s_i \neq s'_i \\[2pt] \widetilde{f} \\[2pt] \hline (op\,\widetilde{t}), s_1, \ldots, s_m \longrightarrow t, s'_1, \ldots, s'_m \end{array}}{} \; \{P \wedge \textbf{effectful}\}$$

(NO-DUPLI-EF)

$$\textbf{effectful} \in P$$
$$\forall t \in \widetilde{t}, (\not\exists X \in \text{INEFFECTUAL}, X \Rightarrow^*_G t) \; \textit{implies}$$
$$(\; \neg(t' \textit{ is of the form } C[t, t, \ldots]) \quad \wedge \quad \neg(t' \textit{ is of the form } C[t''[t/x]]) \;)$$

$$\{P\} \; rn : \dfrac{\widetilde{f}}{(op\,\widetilde{t}), \widetilde{s} \longrightarrow t', \widetilde{s'}} \; \{P \wedge \textbf{no-dupli-ef}(rn)\}$$

Fig. 3. Theory $\mathcal{T}_{dupEf}$ (assertions and proof rules). Notation $\widetilde{}$ denotes finite sequences.

positions $n_1, \ldots, n_k$ are *inductive* in that they are X also. To make an example, $\texttt{inductive}(T, \to, \{1,2\})$ holds because the two arguments of the function type in Type $T := \ldots \mid T \to T$ are inductive. Proof rule (INDUCTIVE) derives assertions $\texttt{inductive}(X, c, n_1, \ldots, n_k)$. This rule analyzes a grammar rule. In (INDUCTIVE), $t.constr$ returns the top-level constructor of t, e.g., $(T \to T).constr = \to$. Also, $t.argsIdx(X)$ returns the positions of the arguments of t that are equal to X, e.g., $(T \to T).argsIdx(T) = \{1,2\}$. The terms $t_1, \ldots, t_n$ are the grammar productions. The rule focuses on those terms whose top-level constructor is c (with $t_i.constr = c$). The premise $\forall i \in (\{1, \ldots, n\} - I), t_i.constr \neq c$ makes sure that we select all of them. For each, we extract the position of their arguments that are X with $t_i.argsIdx(X)$. These positions are combined together in I'.

The assertion $\texttt{ctx-compliant}(rn)$ means that if the reduction rule with name rn needs some arguments to be values (or errors) in order to fire, then the corresponding evaluation contexts are in place for those arguments. To see what $\texttt{ctx-compliant}$ tells us, consider rule [R-ASSIGN], which requires $\ell := v$ for values ℓ and v to fire. Given an assignment $e_1 := e_2$, the existence of evaluation contexts $E := e$ and $v := E$ means that $\texttt{ctx-compliant}([\text{R-ASSIGN}])$ holds and that e_1 and e_2 may have a chance to evaluate to some ℓ and v for [R-ASSIGN] to apply. Proof rule (CTX-COMPLIANT) derives $\texttt{ctx-compliant}(rn)$. This rule analyzes a reduction rule of op with name rn. Its precondition is the assertion $\texttt{inductive}(E, op, I)$, that is, the arguments of op at positions I are subject to an evaluation context. For example, $\texttt{inductive}(E, \div, \{1,2\})$. The rule checks whether any argument of op is required to be a value or an error for the rule to fire. This is checked with the standard grammar derivation $\Rightarrow^*_G$ to see if those

$$\mathcal{T}_{eh}.\textbf{grammar} \triangleq \ P ::= \texttt{inductive}(X, c, \{n_1, \ldots, n_k\}) \mid \texttt{ctx-compliant}(rn)$$
$$\mid \texttt{handles-error}(op, n)$$

$$\mathcal{T}_{eh}.\textbf{rules} \triangleq$$

(INDUCTIVE)
$$\dfrac{I \subseteq \{1 \ldots n\} \quad\quad}{\{P\} \ cname \ X ::= t_1 \ \mid \cdots \mid \ t_n \ \{P \wedge \texttt{inductive}(X, c, I')\}}$$

$$\forall i \in I, t_i.constr = c \qquad \forall i \in (\{1, \ldots, n\} - I), t_i.constr \neq c \qquad I' = \bigcup_{i \in I} t_i.argsIdx(X)$$

(CTX-COMPLIANT)
$$\dfrac{\texttt{inductive}(E, op, I) \in P \qquad \forall i, 1 \leq i \leq n, (v \Rightarrow_G^* t_i \vee er \Rightarrow_G^* t_i) \ implies \ i \in I}{\{P\} \ \left\lvert\ rn : \dfrac{\widetilde{f}}{(op \ t_1, \ldots, t_n), \widetilde{s} \longrightarrow t, \widetilde{s'}} \ \right\rvert \ \{P \wedge \texttt{ctx-compliant}(rn)\}}$$

(HANDLES-ERROR)
$$\dfrac{\texttt{ctx-compliant}(rn) \in P \qquad \texttt{inductive}(F, op, I) \in P \qquad er \Rightarrow_G^* t_i \qquad i \notin I}{\{P\} \ \left\lvert\ rn : \dfrac{\widetilde{f}}{(op \ t_1, \ldots, t_n), \widetilde{s} \longrightarrow t, \widetilde{s'}} \ \right\rvert \ \{P \wedge \texttt{handles-error}(op, i)\}}$$

Fig. 4. Theory $\mathcal{T}_{eh}$ (assertions and proof rules)

arguments are derived from the metavariable of values v or errors er. For each, we check that an evaluation context has been declared for them. Notice that this does not mean that a reduction is sure to occur using rn. For example, rule rn may require the state to unify with a state that does not occur at runtime.

The assertion $\texttt{handles-error}(op, n)$ holds whenever a reduction rule for op exists that is "ctx-compliant", handles an error as n-th argument of op, and error contexts are unable to detect the error at that position. Proof rule (HANDLES-ERROR) derives assertions $\texttt{handles-error}(op, i)$. The preconditions are $\texttt{ctx-compliant}(rn)$ and $\texttt{inductive}(F, op, I)$. The latter informs about the error contexts for op. If the rule requires an argument to be an error to fire, then we check that such argument is *not* subject to an error context (with $i \notin I$).

Theory $\mathcal{T}_{mut}$. This theory reasons about the variance of types of mutable data. Figure 5 shows $\mathcal{T}_{mut}$. The assertion $\texttt{mutable}(c)$ says that the type constructor c is for mutable data (as in $\texttt{mutable}(\texttt{Ref})$). We purposely do not provide any proof rules for $\texttt{mutable}(c)$. Rather, we illustrate an aspect of the flexibility of language logics. Designing proof rules for detecting whether a type is for mutable data may be nontrivial and cumbersome. At the same time, it is well-understood that references are mutable in a language such as $\lambda_{\texttt{err}}^{\texttt{ref}}$. Language designers can use language logics to derive their sought for assertions starting with the *assumption* $\texttt{mutable}(\texttt{Ref})$ as precondition, as they know it to be true.

$$\mathcal{T}_{mut}.\textbf{grammar} \triangleq \quad P ::= \texttt{mutable}(c) \mid \texttt{sound-variance}(c)$$

$$\mathcal{T}_{mut}.\textbf{rules} \triangleq$$

(SOUND-VARIANCE)
$$\cfrac{\texttt{mutable}(c) \in P \qquad \forall i,\, (T_i = T_i') \in \widetilde{f} \vee T_i = T_i'}{\{P\} \; rn : \cfrac{\widetilde{f}}{(c\ T_1\ \dots\ T_n) <: (c\ T_1'\ \dots\ T_n')} \; \{P \wedge \texttt{sound-variance}(c)\}}$$

Fig. 5. Theory $\mathcal{T}_{mut}$ (assertions and proof rules)

The assertion $\texttt{sound-variance}(c)$ holds when the variance adopted by the arguments of type constructor c is sound. Theory $\mathcal{T}_{mut}$ offers only one way to derive that: Types of mutable data must be invariant. Other theories in the future may latch on the assertion $\texttt{sound-variance}(c)$ and provide proof rules for deriving such assertion according to other ways, as indeed the variance of types can be sound for a variety of reasons. Proof rule (SOUND-VARIANCE) analyzes the subtyping rule of a type constructor c and says that if we previously established that c is for mutable data and all the arguments of c of the type at the left of $<:$ and of the type at the right of $<:$ are pairwise equal then variance is sound for c. To detect that these two arguments are equal, (SOUND-VARIANCE) checks that a premise of the rule specifically says so (with $(T_i = T_i') \in \widetilde{f}$) or that the very same metavariable is used (with $T_i = T_i'$). The former case applies for a subtyping rule with conclusion $\texttt{Ref}\ T <: \texttt{Ref}\ T'$ and a premise $T = T'$, for example, and the latter applies for a subtyping rule with conclusion $\texttt{Ref}\ T <: \texttt{Ref}\ T$, for example.

5   Evaluation: Language Logics at Work

Issue 1a: Duplicating Effects. The following $\lambda_{\text{err}}^{\text{ref}}$ program stores the number of parameter passings at location ℓ. The program increments the counter before passing 4 to a function, and then returns the counter.

$$prg_1 = ((\lambda x : \texttt{Float}.\ x + x)\ (\ell := !\ell + 1\ ;\ 4))\ ;\ !\ell, \{\ell \mapsto 0\}$$

$$prg_1 \longrightarrow^* 4 + 4\ ;\ !\ell, \{\ell \mapsto 2\} \longrightarrow^* 2, \{\ell \mapsto 2\}$$

However, the increment effect has been duplicated with [CBN-BETA]. Let us try to derive $\texttt{no-dupli-ef}([\text{CBN-BETA}])$ with $\mathbb{L}(\mathcal{T}_{dupEf})$. We start with the precondition $\texttt{effectful}$, which we assume for now but we derive later. When we try to use (NO-DUPLI-EF), however, there are premises that we cannot satisfy.

230   M. Cimini

$$\{\} \ [\text{R-ASSIGN}] \ \{\texttt{effectful}\}$$
$$\{\texttt{effectful}\} \ [\text{BETA}] \ \{\texttt{no-dupli-ef}([\text{BETA}])\}$$
$$\{\texttt{no-dupli-ef}([\text{BETA}])\} \ r_1 \ \{\texttt{no-dupli-ef}([\text{BETA}])\}$$
$$\cdots$$
$$\{\texttt{no-dupli-ef}([\text{BETA}])\} \ r_n \ \{\texttt{no-dupli-ef}([\text{BETA}])\}$$

$$\frac{\{\} \ [\text{R-ASSIGN}] \ [\text{BETA}] \ r_1 \cdots \cdots r_n \ \{\texttt{no-dupli-ef}([\text{BETA}])\}}{}\ \text{INF}$$

$$\{\} \ G \ \{\} \qquad \frac{\{\} \ r_1 \cdots [\text{R-ASSIGN}] \cdots [\text{BETA}] \cdots r_n \ \{\texttt{no-dupli-ef}([\text{BETA}])\}}{\{\} \ (G, I) \ \{\texttt{no-dupli-ef}([\text{BETA}])\}} \ \begin{matrix}\text{PERM-R}\\[4pt]\text{LANG}\end{matrix}$$

(EFFECT)

$$\frac{\mu \neq ([\ell \mapsto v]\mu)}{\{\} \ [\text{R-ASSIGN}] : \ell := v, \mu \longrightarrow \texttt{unit}, [\ell \mapsto v]\mu \ \{\texttt{effectful}\}}$$

(NO-DUPLI-EF & CONSEQUENCE)

$$\frac{\texttt{effectful} \in \texttt{effectful} \qquad v \in \text{INEFFECTUAL} \ \wedge \ v \Rightarrow^*_G (\lambda x : T.e)}{v \in \text{INEFFECTUAL} \ \wedge \ v \Rightarrow^*_G v}$$

$$\{\texttt{effectful}\} \ (\lambda x : T.e) \ v, s \longrightarrow e[v/x], s \ \{\texttt{no-dupli-ef}([\text{BETA}])\}$$

Fig. 6. Proof derivation of $\{\} \ (G, I) \ \{\texttt{no-dupli-ef}([\text{BETA}])\}$

Below, the premise that is not satisfied is indicated with a box around it.

(NO-DUPLI-EF)

$$\texttt{effectful} \in \texttt{effectful}$$
$$v \in \text{INEFFECTUAL} \ \wedge \ v \Rightarrow^*_G (\lambda x : T.e_1) \qquad (\text{* 1st arg of } (\lambda x : T.e_1) \ e_2 \ \text{*})$$
$$(\nexists X \in \text{INEFFECTUAL}, X \Rightarrow^*_G e_2) \ \textit{implies}$$

$$\frac{(\neg(e_1[e_2/x] \ \textit{is of form} \ C[e_2, e_2, \ldots]) \ \wedge \ \boxed{\neg(e_1[e_2/x] \ \textit{is of form} \ C[t''[e_2/x]])}\ )}{\{\texttt{effectful}\} \ (\lambda x : T.e_1) \ e_2, s \longrightarrow e_1[e_2/x], s \ \{ \ \ldots \ \}}$$

The premise in the box cannot be satisfied because $e_1[e_2/x]$ *is* of the form $C[t''[e_2/x]]$ for an empty context C and $t'' = e_1$. In other words, we cannot apply (NO-DUPLI-EF) because e_2 cannot be classified as ineffectual, and the target of the step does use e_2 in a substitution. We debug our language by replacing [CBN-BETA] with (call-by-value) [BETA] : $(\lambda x : T.e) \ v, s \longrightarrow e[v/x], s$. (Another solution could make the language pure and introduce monads but we did not go that route.) Figure 6 shows a derivation of $\texttt{no-dupli-ef}([\text{BETA}])$.

Convention: Formulae that do not mention the name of the proof rule being applied are derived with ($\mathcal{X}$-NEUTRAL) unless they have a color. The derivation of colored formulae is shown afterwards using the same color. Notice that (CONSEQUENCE) can "forget" assertions due to $P \wedge Q \Rightarrow Q$. In the remainder of the paper, when our proof derivations forget assertions, it is understood that we applied (CONSEQUENCE).

Issue 1b: [BETA] is Not Ctx-compliant. With [BETA], we have $prg_1 \not\longrightarrow$ because the argument $(\ell := !\ell + 1 \ ; \ 4))$ does not evaluate. Indeed, $\lambda^{\text{ref}}_{\text{err}}$ declares the only

$$\{ctxOfApp\}\ [\textsc{beta}]\ \{ctxCmplBeta\}$$
$$\{ctxCmplBeta\}\ r_1\ \{ctxCmplBeta\}$$
$$\cdots$$
$$\{ctxCmplBeta\}\ r_n\ \{ctxCmplBeta\}$$

$$\frac{\{ctxOfApp\}\ [\textsc{beta}]\ r_1 \cdots r_n\ \{ctxCmplBeta\}}{\{ctxOfApp\}\ r_1 \cdots [\textsc{beta}] \cdots r_n\ \{ctxCmplBeta\}}\ \begin{matrix}\textsc{inf}\\[2pt]\textsc{perm}\\[2pt]\textsc{lang}\end{matrix}$$

$$\{\}\ G\ \{ctxOfApp\}$$

$$\{\}\ (G, I)\ \{ctxCmplBeta\}$$

$$(E\ e).argsIdx(E) \cup (v\ E).argsIdx(E) = \{1\} \cup \{2\} = \{1, 2\}$$

$$\{\}\ (\mathsf{EvalCtx}\ E ::= \cdots \mid E\ e \mid v\ E \cdots)\ \{ctxOfApp\}$$
$$\{ctxOfApp\}\ g_1\ \{ctxOfApp\}\ \cdots\ \{ctxOfApp\}\ g_n\ \{ctxOfApp\}$$

$$\frac{\{\}\ (\mathsf{EvalCtx}\ E ::= \cdots)\ g_1\ \cdots\ g_n\ \{ctxOfApp\}}{\{\}\ g_1 \cdots (\mathsf{EvalCtx}\ E ::= \cdots) \cdots g_n\ \{ctxOfApp\}}\ \begin{matrix}\textsc{gram}\\[2pt]\textsc{perm-g}\end{matrix}$$

(CTX-COMPLIANT & CONSEQUENCE)

$$\frac{\begin{array}{c}\mathtt{inductive}(E, app, \{1, 2\}) \in \mathtt{inductive}(E, app, \{1, 2\}) \\ v \Rightarrow^*_G (\lambda x : T.e)\ implies\ 1 \in \{1, 2\} \qquad v \Rightarrow^*_G v\ implies\ 2 \in \{1, 2\}\end{array}}{\{\mathtt{inductive}(E, app, \{1, 2\})\}\ [\textsc{beta}] : (\lambda x : T.e)\ v, s \longrightarrow e[v/x], s\ \{ctxCmplBeta\}}$$

Fig. 7. Proof derivation of $\{\}\ (G, I)\ \{ctxCmplBeta\}$

evaluation context $(E\ e)$ for (call-by-name) application. When we use $\mathbb{L}(\mathcal{T}_{eh})$, (CTX-COMPLIANT) cannot be applied for [BETA] with $\mathtt{inductive}(E, app, \{1\})$:

(CTX-COMPLIANT)

$$\frac{\begin{array}{c}\mathtt{inductive}(E, app, \{1\}) \in \mathtt{inductive}(E, app, \{1\}) \\ v \Rightarrow^*_G (\lambda x : T.e)\ implies\ 1 \in \{1\}\ \text{(* 1st arg of } (\lambda x : T.e)\ v\ \text{*)} \\ v \Rightarrow^*_G v\ implies\ \boxed{2 \in \{1\}}\ \text{(* 2nd arg of } (\lambda x : T.e)\ v\ \text{*)}\end{array}}{\{\mathtt{inductive}(E, app, \{1\})\}\ (\lambda x : T.e)\ v, s \longrightarrow e[v/x], s\ \{\dots\}}$$

We debug our language by adding the evaluation context $(v\ E)$ (and error context $(v\ F)$ for completeness). After this fix, $prg_1 \longrightarrow^* 1, \{\ell \mapsto 1\}$ as expected. Figure 7 shows our derivation, where $ctxOfApp = \mathtt{inductive}(E, app, \{1, 2\})$, and $ctxCmplBeta = \mathtt{ctx\text{-}compliant}([\textsc{beta}])$.

Issue 2: Error Handler May Be Ignored. The following program prg_2 should increment the counter at location ℓ when we meet a division by zero. However, $prg_2 = \mathtt{try}\ 2 \div 0\ \mathtt{with}\ \ell := !\ell + 1\ ;\ !\ell, \{\ell \mapsto 0\}$

$\longrightarrow^* \mathtt{try\ error\ with}\ \ell := !\ell + 1\ ;\ !\ell, \{\ell \mapsto 0\} \longrightarrow \mathtt{error}, \{\ell \mapsto 0\}$.

The last step disregarded the **with**-clause of **try** because of the error context **try** F **with** e, and failed the computation. If we apply the proof rule (HANDLES-ERROR) of $\mathbb{L}(\mathcal{T}_{eh})$ after having derived the error contexts of **try**, i.e., $\mathtt{inductive}(F, try, \{1\})$, and also $\mathtt{ctx\text{-}compliant}([\textsc{err}])$, we would fail:

$$\dfrac{\dfrac{\{ctxOfTry \wedge errCtxTry\}\ [\text{ERR}]\ \{handlesTry\} \quad \{handlesTry\}\ r_1\ \{handlesTry\} \quad \cdots \quad \{handlesTry\}\ r_n\ \{handlesTry\}}{\{ctxOfTry \wedge errCtxTry\}\ [\text{ERR}]\ r_1 \ldots r_n\ \{handlesTry\}}\ \text{INF}}{\{ctxOfTry \wedge errCtxTry\}\ r_1 \ldots [\text{ERR}] \ldots r_n\ \{handlesTry\}}\ \text{PERM}$$

$$\dfrac{\{\} \ G\ \{{}^{ctxOfTry}_{\wedge\, errCtxTry}\} \qquad \cdots}{\{\}\ (G, I)\ \{handlesTry\}}\ \text{LANG}$$

(INDUCTIVE)
$$\dfrac{\{\} \subseteq \{1 \ldots n\} \quad (\text{*}\ I = \{\}\ \text{because}\ \mathtt{try}\ \text{is not in any}\ t_i\ \text{*}) \qquad I' = \{\} \quad (\text{*}\ \text{as}\ \bigcup\ \text{for}\ j \in \{\}\ \text{is vacuously}\ \{\}\ \text{*})}{\{ctxOfTry\}\ (\text{ErrorCtx}\ F ::= t_1 \mid \cdots \mid t_n)\ \{ctxOfTry \wedge errCtxTry\}}$$

(ITERATE)
$$\dfrac{\{ctxOfTry \wedge errCtxTry\}\ [\text{ERR}]\ \{ctxOfTry \wedge errCtxTry \wedge ctxCmplTry\} \qquad \{ctxOfTry \wedge errCtxTry \wedge ctxCmplTry\}\ [\text{ERR}]\ \{handlesTry\}}{\{ctxOfTry \wedge errCtxTry\}\ [\text{ERR}]\ \{handlesTry\}}$$

Fig. 8. Proof derivation of $\{\}\ (G, I)\ \{handlesTry\}$

(HANDLES-ERROR)
$$\dfrac{\begin{array}{c}P = \mathtt{ctx\text{-}compliant}([\text{ERR}]) \wedge \mathtt{inductive}(F, try, \{1\}) \\ \mathtt{ctx\text{-}compliant}([\text{ERR}]) \in P \qquad \mathtt{inductive}(F, try, \{1\}) \in P \\ er \Rightarrow^{*}_{G} \mathtt{error} \qquad \boxed{1 \notin \{1\}}\end{array}}{\{P\}\ [\text{ERR}] : \mathtt{try\ error\ with}\ e, s \longrightarrow e, s\ \{\ \ldots\ \}}$$

Indeed, that argument should *not* be the subject of an error context. We can fix this by removing that error context. After this fix, we have $prg_2 \longrightarrow^{*} 1, \{\ell \mapsto 1\}$. Figure 8 shows our derivation, where $ctxOfTry = \mathtt{inductive}(E, try, \{1\})$, $errCtxTry = \mathtt{inductive}(F, try, \{\})$, $handlesTry = \mathtt{handles\text{-}error}(try, 1)$, and $ctxCmplTry = \mathtt{ctx\text{-}compliant}([\text{ERR}])$. To show the main point, we start with $ctxOfTry$ already derived. The derivation of $ctxCmplTry$ (first premise of (ITER-ATE)) follows the same lines of $ctxCmplBeta$ for application, and we do not show it. The second premise of (ITERATE) is derived as follows.

(HANDLES-ERROR & CONSEQUENCE)
$$\dfrac{\begin{array}{c}P = ctxOfTry \wedge errCtxTry \wedge \mathtt{ctx\text{-}compliant}([\text{ERR}]) \\ \mathtt{ctx\text{-}compliant}([\text{ERR}]) \in P \qquad \mathtt{inductive}(F, try, \{\}) \in P \\ er \Rightarrow^{*}_{G} \mathtt{error} \qquad 1 \notin \{\}\end{array}}{\{P\}\ [\text{ERR}] : \mathtt{try\ error\ with}\ e, s \longrightarrow e, s\ \{handlesTry\}}$$

Issue 3: Covariant Mutable References are Unsound. It is well-known that *(a)* the reference type handles mutable data in a language such as $\lambda^{\mathtt{ref}}_{\mathtt{err}}$ and that covariant mutable references are unsound (see [22, §15.5]). As *(a)* is well-known, we simply launch our analysis with the assumption `mutable(Ref)` as precondition. However, (SOUND-VARIANCE) of $\mathbb{L}(\mathcal{T}_{mut})$ does not apply to [S-REF-BAD]:

(SOUND-VARIANCE)

$$\frac{\texttt{mutable(Ref)} \in \texttt{mutable(Ref)} \qquad \boxed{\forall i, (T_i = T_i') \in \widetilde{f} \vee T_i = T_i'}}{\{\texttt{mutable(Ref)}\}\ [\text{S-REF-BAD}] : \dfrac{T <: T'}{\text{Ref } T <: \text{Ref } T'}\ \{\dots\}}$$

To fix this, we replace [S-REF-BAD] with [S-REF] : Ref T <: Ref T and derive: (We do not show it, but this can be used in the derivation for the overall $\lambda_{\text{err}}^{\text{ref}}$.)

(SOUND-VARIANCE)

$$\frac{\texttt{mutable(Ref)} \in \texttt{mutable(Ref)} \qquad T = T \quad (\text{* 1st arg of Ref *})}{\{\texttt{mutable(Ref)}\}\ [\text{S-REF}] : \text{Ref } T <: \text{Ref } T\ \{\texttt{sound-variance(Ref)}\}}$$

6   Implementation

We have implemented an automated prover for our language logics in OCaml. The tool is called LANG-N-ASSERT [9]. The tool takes the name of the theories to "load" as input, and the elements of a statement: a precondition assertion, a language definition, and a postcondition. Language definitions are given in a textual representation. (Examples can be found in the repo [9].) The output is a proof derivation or an error message (more details are below).

LANG-N-ASSERT is a *forward reasoner*. It starts from the input precondition and analyzes all the grammar and inference rules. For each, LANG-N-ASSERT tries all the proof rules, once, of the theories that have been specified, and strives to derive their corresponding assertions. These are a finite number of attempts. After having analyzed the language, LANG-N-ASSERT has accumulated all the assertions derived. To avoid non-determinism, we use (CONSEQUENCE) only at the end to single out the goal assertion. Since (HANDLES-ERROR) needs `ctx-compliant` *of the same rule*, we always apply (CTX-COMPLIANT) first.

We have applied LANG-N-ASSERT to $\lambda_{\text{err}}^{\text{ref}}$ and we confirm that we can repeat the debugging journey of Sect. 5. (*Issue 1a*): LANG-N-ASSERT fails to derive `no-dupli-ef([CBN-BETA])` but `no-dupli-ef([BETA])` succeeds. (*Issue 1b*): Then, `ctx-compliant([BETA])` fails, but it succeeds when $(v\ E)$ is added. (*Issue 2*): Then, `handles-error(try, 1)` fails, but it succeeds when we remove the error context. (*Issue 3*): `sound-variance(Ref)` fails but succeeds with [S-REF].

The tools' proofs differ from those in this paper, as they accumulate all assertions, for example. When the tool fails in finding a proof derivation, it provides an error message based on the premise that failed. For example, the output of the tool on *Issue 1a* for $\lambda_{\text{err}}^{\text{ref}}$ is "*Proof not found. The target of the reduction rule* [CBN-BETA] *is* E1[E2/x] *and performs a substitution of a possibly effectful term, which may lead to a duplication of effects"*.

Additionally, we have analyzed the same issues of $\lambda_{\mathrm{err}}^{\mathrm{ref}}$ on a different language where the state is a string buffer and the effect appends strings to this buffer, except for Issue 3 because that language does not have mutable data. In lieu of Issue 3, we checked that the typing rule for function application makes sure that the type of the argument is subtype of the domain of the function. Also, we have used LANG-N-ASSERT on other languages to detect whether they use lazy lists/pairs, have inductive types, check that other reduction rules are ctx-compliant, and that errors can be typed at any type (for type preservation).

7   Comparison with Program Logics

Program logics define the proof rules of $\{P\}\ c\ \{Q\}$ by induction on c. That is, there is a proof rule for `if`, assignment, `while`, and so on. These proof rules are based on the invariants that we learn after executing a command. In language logics: What do we learn from adding the inference rule $f_1 \wedge f_2 \cdots f_n \implies f$ (here in implicational notation) into a language? Akin to adding a formula to a theory, we learn the formula itself. The same program logics' perspective does not seem to be helpful in language logics. Therefore, our proof rules are based on the structure of $\mathcal{L}$ only to traverse the language and reach grammar rules g and inference rules r. For g and r, then, our proof rules are defined by cases on the grammar of assertions. This means that 1) language logics focus on one aspect at a time, and therefore we added (ITERATE) to remain on an inference rule and possibly derive more assertions. It also means that 2) there may be inference rules from which we do not derive any assertions, and therefore we have added ($\mathcal{X}$-NEUTRAL) to continue the rest of the analysis.

8   Limitations of Language Logics

As for a soundness theorem, we do not provide it in this paper. Soundness means that if we derive, say, `no-dupli-ef`(rn), then it *is* the case that rule rn cannot lead to effect duplication. It is generally undecidable to establish whether a language duplicates effects because it is an extensional property (Rice theorem). Our proof rules necessarily are approximations. (NO-DUPLI-EF), for example, only considers explicit duplication or substitution. If a reduction rule makes use of a term linearly (one time) but in the context of a user-defined operation that *acts* like substitution, the rule unsoundly derives a `no-dupli-ef` assertion. A way to obtain soundness would be to enforce restrictions on the language in input. A challenge is that other assertions may simultaneously require their own restrictions. This exploration and a metatheoretic proof are rather involved. We believe that they belong to a subsequent paper or a journal version of this paper.

As for a completeness theorem, it is impossible to provide it because our logics contain assertions that are, in general, undecidable.

As for all-encompassing properties, it is unclear how to capture properties such as type soundness and strong normalization. Our logics must be extended. For the progress theorem, for example, a well-typed application (e_1 e_2) derives the "progress" of e_1 and e_2 by induction before finding a reduction for all cases. Therefore, our logics need inductive reasoning, at least, which is now missing.

9   Related Work

Much work has been done on testing random programs that are automatically generated from language definitions [1,12,24]. This is the approach of many semantics engineering tools such as the $\mathbb{K}$ framework, PLT Redex, and MPS, among others. These works differ from our approach in that 1) they adopt testing and 2) they execute programs. Our approach, instead, is akin to a static analysis in that we analyze the language definition (without executing programs).

Intrinsic typing [4] leverages the meta-theoretic properties of a type theory to derive type soundness from a well-typed evaluator. LANG-N-ASSERT is part of a series that also comprises LANG-N-CHECK, LANG-N-PROVE, and LANG-SQL (and other systems that do not analyze languages.) LANG-N-CHECK [10] classifies parts of a language definition and applies a meta type system for ensuring the type soundness of certain functional languages. LANG-N-PROVE [6,13] expresses the proof of type soundness in a way that applies to all languages in a certain class of functional languages. These works (including intrinsic typing) target an all-encompassing property like type soundness. On the contrary, language logics can analyze various "smaller" aspects such as those addressed in this paper. LANG-SQL [8] can flexibly interrogate languages over various aspects with customizable queries. However, these queries do not provide a proof derivation.

Veritas [15] and Twelf [21] use automated theorem proving to establish facts about languages. Proof assistants such as Rocq, Isabelle, Agda, and others, can reason about several aspects of languages. In these tools, whether proofs are interactive or automated, the formulae for aspects such as `ctx-compliant` and `sound-variance` must be provided manually while they are built-in in our work. Also, our proof rules are specific to the domain of language design and the output proofs may make for more readable explanations for why a property holds.

The way language logics use syntactic means to analyze inference rules is inspired by rule formats [18]. Language logics provide a flexible way to analyze a rule when we must simultaneously consider other elements of the language.

10   Conclusion

We have proposed *language logics* as a counterpart of program logics in the context of language verification. We have developed language logics based on three example theories for reasoning over certain aspects of programming languages. We have applied our logics to the analysis of a faulty language and its debugging fixes. We have implemented an automated prover, LANG-N-ASSERT, and we confirm that it replicates the analyses that we performed on the faulty language.

We believe that our results offer a convincing first step towards adopting the methods of program logics for the analysis of languages. In the future, we would like to address the limitations in Sect. 8, especially those concerning providing a soundness theorem, which is challenging and deserves its own investigation. As of now, language definitions must be manually fixed after LANG-N-ASSERT has detected an error but we would like to explore their automatic repair. It would be interesting to explore connections with unified approaches such as [14] and [27].

References

1. Berghofer, S., Nipkow, T.: Random testing in Isabelle/HOL. In: Proceedings of the 2nd International Conference on Software Engineering and Formal Methods, SEFM 2004, pp. 230–239. IEEE Computer Society, USA (2004). https://doi.org/10.1109/SEFM.2004.10049
2. Brookes, S.: A semantics for concurrent separation logic. Theor. Comput. Sci. **375**(1), 227–270 (2007). https://doi.org/10.1016/j.tcs.2006.12.034
3. Charguéraud, A.: Program verification through characteristic formulae. In: Proceedings of the 15th ACM SIGPLAN International Conference on Functional Programming, ICFP 2010, pp. 321–332. ACM, New York (2010). https://doi.org/10.1145/1863543.1863590
4. Church, A.: A formulation of the simple theory of types. J. Symb. Log. **5**, 56–68 (1940). https://doi.org/10.2307/2266170
5. Cimini, M.: A calculus for multi-language operational semantics. In: Software Verification: 13th International Conference, VSTTE 2021, New Haven, CT, USA, 18–19 October 2021, and 14th International Workshop, NSV 2021, Los Angeles, CA, USA, 18–19 July 2021, pp. 25–42. Springer, Heidelberg (2021). https://doi.org/10.1007/978-3-030-95561-8_3
6. Cimini, M.: Lang-n-prove: A DSL for language proofs. In: Proceedings of the 15th ACM SIGPLAN International Conference on Software Language Engineering, SLE 2022, pp. 16–29. ACM, New York (2022). https://doi.org/10.1145/3567512.3567514
7. Cimini, M.: Lang-n-send: processes that send languages. In: Carbone, M., Neykova, R. (eds.) Proceedings of the 13th International Workshop on Programming Language Approaches to Concurrency and Communication-cEntric Software, PLACES 2022, Munich, Germany, 3rd April 2022. EPTCS, vol. 356, pp. 46–56 (2022). https://doi.org/10.4204/EPTCS.356.5
8. Cimini, M.: A query language for language analysis. In: Schlingloff, B., Chai, M. (eds.) Software Engineering and Formal Methods - 20th International Conference, SEFM 2022, Berlin, Germany, 26–30 September 2022, Proceedings. Lecture Notes in Computer Science, vol. 13550, pp. 57–73. Springer, Cham (2022). https://doi.org/10.1007/978-3-031-17108-6_4
9. Cimini, M.: Lang-n-assert (2024). https://github.com/mcimini/lang-n-assert
10. Cimini, M., Miller, D., Siek, J.G.: Extrinsically typed operational semantics for functional languages. In: Proceedings of the 13th ACM SIGPLAN International Conference on Software Language Engineering, SLE 2020, Virtual Event, USA, 16–17 November 2020, pp. 108–125 (2020). https://doi.org/10.1145/3426425.3426936

11. Dijkstra, E.W.: Guarded commands, nondeterminacy and formal derivation of programs. Commun. ACM **18**(8), 453–457 (1975). https://doi.org/10.1145/360933.360975
12. Fetscher, B., Claessen, K., Pałka, M., Hughes, J., Findler, R.B.: Making random judgments: automatically generating well-typed terms from the definition of a type-system. In: Vitek, J. (ed.) ESOP 2015. LNCS, vol. 9032, pp. 383–405. Springer, Heidelberg (2015). https://doi.org/10.1007/978-3-662-46669-8_16
13. Galasso, S., Cimini, M.: Language-parameterized proofs for functional languages with subtyping. In: Gibbons, J., Miller, D. (eds.) Functional and Logic Programming - 17th International Symposium, FLOPS 2024, Proceedings. pp. 291–310 (2024). https://doi.org/10.1007/978-981-97-2300-3_15
14. Goguen, J.A., Burstall, R.M.: Institutions: abstract model theory for specification and programming. J. ACM (JACM) **39**(1), 95–146 (1992). https://doi.org/10.1145/147508.147524
15. Grewe, S., Erdweg, S., Wittmann, P., Mezini, M.: Type systems for the masses: deriving soundness proofs and efficient checkers. In: 2015 ACM International Symposium on New Ideas, New Paradigms, and Reflections on Programming and Software (Onward!), Onward! 2015, pp. 137–150. ACM, New York (2015). https://doi.org/10.1145/2814228.2814239
16. Hoare, C.A.R.: An axiomatic basis for computer programming. Commun. ACM **12**(10), 576–580 (1969). https://doi.org/10.1145/363235.363259
17. Miller, D., Nadathur, G.: Programming with Higher-Order Logic, 1st edn. Cambridge University Press, New York (2012)
18. Mousavi, M.R., Reniers, M.A., Groote, J.F.: SOS formats and meta-theory: 20 years after. Theoret. Comput. Sci. **373**(3), 238–272 (2007). https://doi.org/10.1016/j.tcs.2006.12.019
19. O'Hearn, P., Reynolds, J., Yang, H.: Local reasoning about programs that alter data structures. In: Fribourg, L. (ed.) CSL 2001. LNCS, vol. 2142, pp. 1–19. Springer, Heidelberg (2001). https://doi.org/10.1007/3-540-44802-0_1
20. O'Hearn, P.W.: Resources, concurrency, and local reasoning. Theor. Comput. Sci. **375**(1), 271–307 (2007). https://doi.org/10.1016/j.tcs.2006.12.035
21. Pfenning, F., Schürmann, C.: System description: twelf — a meta-logical framework for deductive systems. In: CADE 1999. LNCS (LNAI), vol. 1632, pp. 202–206. Springer, Heidelberg (1999). https://doi.org/10.1007/3-540-48660-7_14
22. Pierce, B.C.: Types and Programming Languages. MIT Press (2002)
23. Reynolds, J.C.: Separation logic: a logic for shared mutable data structures. In: Proceedings of the 17th Annual IEEE Symposium on Logic in Computer Science, LICS 2002, pp. 55–74. IEEE Computer Society, USA (2002). https://doi.org/10.1109/LICS.2002.1029817
24. Roberson, M., Harries, M., Darga, P.T., Boyapati, C.: Efficient software model checking of soundness of type systems. In: Harris, G.E. (ed.) Proceedings of the 23rd ACM SIGPLAN Conference on Object-Oriented Programming Systems Languages and Applications, OOPSLA 2008, pp. 493–504. ACM, New York (2008). https://doi.org/10.1145/1449764.1449803
25. Svendsen, K., Pichon-Pharabod, J., Doko, M., Lahav, O., Vafeiadis, V.: A separation logic for a promising semantics. In: Ahmed, A. (ed.) ESOP 2018. LNCS, vol. 10801, pp. 357–384. Springer, Cham (2018). https://doi.org/10.1007/978-3-319-89884-1_13

26. Vafeiadis, V., Narayan, C.: Relaxed separation logic: a program logic for c11 concurrency. ACM SIGPLAN Not. **48**(10), 867–884 (2013). https://doi.org/10.1145/2544173.2509532
27. Woodcock, J.: Hoare and He's Unifying Theories of Programming, 1 edn, pp. 285–316. Association for Computing Machinery, New York (2021). https://doi.org/10.1145/3477355.3477369

A Variety of Request-Response Specifications

Daichi Aiba[1]([✉]), Masaki Waga[1,2]([✉]), Hiroya Fujinami[1,5]([✉]), Koko Muroya[3]([✉]),
Shutaro Ouchi[4], Naoki Ueda[4], Yosuke Yokoyama[4], Yuta Wada[4],
and Ichiro Hasuo[1,5,6]([✉])

[1] National Institute of Informatics, Tokyo, Japan
{daichi-aiba,makenowjust}@nii.ac.jp
[2] Kyoto University, Kyoto, Japan
[3] Ochanomizu University, Tokyo, Japan
kmuroya@is.ocha.ac.jp
[4] Mitsubishi Electric Corporation, Kamakura, Japan
{Ouchi.Shutaro,Wada.Yuta}@ab.mitsubishielectric.co.jp,
Ueda.Naoki@cw.mitsubishielectric.co.jp,
Yokoyama.Yosuke@ea.mitsubishielectric.co.jp
[5] SOKENDAI, Tokyo, Japan
hasuo@nii.ac.jp
[6] Imiron Co., Ltd., Tokyo, Japan

Abstract. We find, motivated by real-world applications, that the well-known *request-response specification* comes with multiple variations, and that these variations should be distinguished. As the first main contribution, we introduce a classification of those variations into six types, and present it as a decision tree, where a user is led to the type that is suited for their application by answering a couple of questions. Our second main contribution is the formalization of those six types in various formalisms such as grammars, temporal logics, and automata; here, two types out of the six are non-regular specifications and their formalization requires extended formalisms. We also present an overview of tools for monitoring these specifications to cater for practitioners' needs. Through these contributions, we address an issue in formal specification that is practically important but has been scientifically somewhat overlooked.

1 Introduction

Formal specification refers to the process of pinning down requirements for a target system in a rigorous, mathematical and formal language. It is a prerequisite of *formal verification*, where one aims to prove $\mathcal{M} \models \varphi$ ($\mathcal{M}$ *satisfies* φ), given a formal model $\mathcal{M}$ of a system and a formal specification φ.

The authors are partially supported by the ASPIRE grant (No. JPMJAP2301) & CREST ZT-IoT Project (No. JPMJCR21M3), JST.

Z. Liu et al. (Eds.): ICTAC 2025, LNCS 16237, pp. 239–257, 2026.
https://doi.org/10.1007/978-3-032-11176-0_15

However, with the recent rise of diverse computing paradigms that make white-box models M expensive or impossible to get, the importance of formal specification itself is increasingly recognized. Examples of such paradigms include cyber-physical systems (whose physical components are hard to model) and machine learning systems (where neural networks are large numerical objects and hard to model logically). For those systems, formal verification is often too expensive, and one would turn to *modelless, spec-only* techniques such as monitoring and property-based testing. Although these techniques do not give the guarantee level of formal verification, they can automate various quality assurance tasks on a solid basis of mathematical representations of requirements, and thus attract attention both from academia and industry. See e.g., [9,16,21].

One class of formal specifications that appear often in many application domains is *request-response specifications* (*req-resp specs*). They require that, whenever a request *req* is issued, it has to be responded by *resp*. Examples include error/anomaly handling, server-client interaction, commercial transactions, communication protocols, etc. (some concrete examples are in Sect. 3.3). Req-resp specs are often expressed by LTL formulas of the form $\mathbf{G}(req \to \mathbf{F}\ resp)$—at any moment ($\mathbf{G}$), if *req* occurs, then eventually ($\mathbf{F}$), *resp* should occur.

This work is motivated by the observation that the simple spec $\mathbf{G}(req \to \mathbf{F}\ resp)$ *may not adequately express the designer's intention.* Consider, for example, a word *req req resp* of *req*'s and *resp*'s. It does satisfy the formula $\mathbf{G}(req \to \mathbf{F}\ resp)$, but in case we count the number of pending *req*'s (e.g., when *req* stands for a coin put in a vending machine), one *resp* is not enough to resolve two *req*'s. Therefore we have to consider multiple types of req-resp specs, and moreover, to clarify the criteria for choosing a type that is suited for each specific application.

In this paper, we make the following contributions, through which we address a problem that has often discouraged industrial adoption of formal technologies.

- We present a classification of req-resp specs into six types (RR1–6, Sect. 3). The classification is organized in a decision tree (Fig. 1), where a user is led to a suitable type by answering a couple of questions (criteria C1–C3).
- We formalize the six types in three formalisms, namely grammars, temporal logic formulas, and automata (Sect. 4). Two types are non-regular (RR3,4); for them, we show which extensions of the common formalisms can be used. There are some non-trivial observations here, too, such as Theorem 4.1.
- We evaluate our classification (Sect. 5), assessing if its level of distinction is appropriate and if its decision tree presentation is sensible. The examples we present for the six types in Sect. 3.3 help our case, too.
- We present an overview of monitoring tools for req-resp specs. This will cater for practitioners' needs of monitoring data at their hand.

2   Preliminaries

We introduce some formalisms for temporal specifications. Many of them are standard; for them, our purpose here is to fix notations. Others are less known; for them, we provide a brief introduction.

Notations. Fix a finite alphabet Σ. For a finite word $w = w_0 w_1 \ldots w_{n-1} \in \Sigma^*$, the i-th element is denoted by $w_i \in \Sigma$. The suffix $w_i w_{i+1} \ldots w_{n-1}$ of w is $w_{i\leq}$; the prefix $w_0 w_1 \ldots w_i$ is $w_{\leq i}$. $\#a$ is the number of occurrences of $a \in \Sigma$ in a given word. The empty word is ε. AP is a set of *atomic propositions*. A partial function is denoted by $f \colon X \rightharpoonup Y$ with $\rightharpoonup$, where $f(x) = \bot$ denotes $f(x)$ is undefined.

2.1 Regular Expressions and Context-Free Grammars

Regular expressions over an alphabet Σ, as usual, are defined by the following abstract grammar: $r \ ::= \ 0 \mid \sigma \mid 1 \mid (r|r) \mid r \cdot r \mid r^*$. Here 0 is for the empty language $\emptyset$, σ denotes the singleton language $\{\sigma\}$ (with $\sigma \in \Sigma$), 1 denotes $\{\varepsilon\}$, $r|r$ denotes alternation, $r \cdot r$ denotes concatenation, and r^* denotes repetition. We often drop $\cdot$ in $r \cdot r$, and r^+ is short for $r \cdot r^*$.

A *context-free grammar* is a quadruple (N, Σ, P, S), where N is a finite set of nonterminals, Σ is a finite set of terminals, P is a set of production rules, and $S \in N$ is a start variable. A production rule is of the form $\alpha \to \beta$, where $\alpha \in N$ is a nonterminal and $\beta \in (N|\Sigma)^*$ is a word over nonterminals and terminals.

2.2 Linear Temporal Logic (LTL)

The (usual, future-time) *LTL* has propositional formulas extended with temporal operators $\mathbf{X}$ (next), $\mathbf{F}$ (future), $\mathbf{G}$ (globally), $\mathbf{U}$ (until), and $\mathbf{R}$ (release). We use LTL extended with *past-time* temporal operators, namely $\mathbf{Y}$ (yesterday), $\mathbf{O}$ (once), $\mathbf{H}$ (historically), $\mathbf{S}$ (since), and $\mathbf{T}$ (trigger). Past-time operators have been found useful for expressing some specs—also in the current paper, see Sect. 4.2.

Definition 2.1 (syntax of LTL). We define LTL formulas as follows:
$$\varphi \ ::= \ \bot \mid p \mid \neg\varphi \mid \varphi \wedge \varphi \mid \mathbf{X}\,\varphi \mid \mathbf{Y}\,\varphi \mid \varphi\,\mathbf{U}\,\varphi \mid \varphi\,\mathbf{S}\,\varphi \ \text{(here } p \in \text{AP)}.$$
In addition, we use some abbreviations: $\top = \neg\bot$, $\varphi \vee \psi = \neg(\neg\varphi \wedge \neg\psi)$, $\varphi\,\mathbf{R}\,\psi = \neg(\neg\varphi\,\mathbf{U}\,\neg\psi)$, $\varphi\,\mathbf{T}\,\psi = \neg(\neg\varphi\,\mathbf{S}\,\neg\psi)$, $\mathbf{F}\,\varphi = \top\,\mathbf{U}\,\varphi$, $\mathbf{G}\,\varphi = \bot\,\mathbf{R}\,\varphi$, $\mathbf{O}\,\varphi = \top\,\mathbf{S}\,\varphi$, $\mathbf{H}\,\varphi = \bot\,\mathbf{T}\,\varphi$.

The semantics is defined as usual over finite words. See [1, Appendix A.1].

2.3 CaRet

As announced in Sect. 1, two types of req-resp specs (namely RR3,4) are not regular, and thus are not expressible in LTL. We use an extension of LTL, namely the *temporal logic of calls and returns (CaRet)* [4]. Here we introduce CaRet as originally presented in [4]; later in Sect. 4.2 we introduce and use its slight variation.

In CaRet, they consider two kinds of correspondences between *calls* and *returns*: the *matching-return* correspondence R, and *innermost-call* Q. Intuitively, R maps i to *the first unmatched return* after i, and Q maps i to *the most recent pending call* before i. Using them, three successor functions are introduced.

Definition 2.2. Let $\widehat{\Sigma} = \Sigma \times \{call, int, ret\}$. For $\alpha \in \Sigma$, we call the symbols of the form $(\alpha, call), (\alpha, int), (\alpha, ret) \in \widehat{\Sigma}$, *calls*, *internals*, and *returns*, respectively. We thus have three disjoint finite alphabets: Σ_c is a finite set of calls, Σ_{int} is a finite set of internals, and Σ_r is a finite set of returns, with $\widehat{\Sigma} = \Sigma_c \cup \Sigma_{int} \cup \Sigma_r$.

Let σ be a finite word on $\widehat{\Sigma}$. The *matching-return* correspondence $R_\sigma : \mathbb{N} \rightharpoonup \mathbb{N}$ on σ is a partial function defined as follows. (Case 1) If there is j such that 1) $j > i$, 2) σ_j is a return, and 3) the numbers of calls and returns from $i+1$ to $j-1$ are equal, then $R_\sigma(i)$ is the smallest such j. (Case 2) Otherwise, $R_\sigma(i) = \bot$.

The *innermost-call* $Q_\sigma : \mathbb{N} \rightharpoonup \mathbb{N}$ on σ is a partial function defined as follows. (Case 1) If there is j such that 1) $j < i$, 2) σ_j is a call, and 3) $R_\sigma(j) > i$ or $R_\sigma(j) = \bot$, then $Q_\sigma(i)$ is the greatest such j. (Case 2) Otherwise, $Q_\sigma(i) = \bot$.

If σ_i is a call, σ_j is a return, and $R_\sigma(i) = j$, then we say that σ_j is *the matching return* for σ_i. Similarly, if σ_i is a return, σ_j is a call, and $Q_\sigma(i) = j$, then we say that σ_j is *the innermost call* for σ_i. For a quick intuition, see Fig. 3.

Definition 2.3. Let σ be a finite word on $\widehat{\Sigma}$. Three *successor functions* $\mathrm{succ}^g, \mathrm{succ}^a, \mathrm{succ}^- : \mathbb{N} \rightharpoonup \mathbb{N}$ are defined as follows.

The *global-successor* function succ^g_σ is defined by $\mathrm{succ}^g_\sigma(i) = i + 1$.

The *abstract-successor* function succ^a_σ is defined as follows: $\mathrm{succ}^a_\sigma(i) = R_\sigma(i)$ if σ_i is a call; $\mathrm{succ}^a_\sigma(i) = i + 1$ if σ_i is not a call and σ_{i+1} is not a return; and $\mathrm{succ}^a_\sigma(i) = \bot$ otherwise.

The *past-successor* function succ^-_σ is defined by $\mathrm{succ}^-_\sigma(i) = Q_\sigma(i)$.

Definition 2.4. The *formulas* of CaRet are defined as follows:
$$\varphi ::= p \mid \neg\varphi \mid \varphi \wedge \varphi \mid \mathbf{X}^g\, \varphi \mid \varphi\, \mathbf{U}^g\, \varphi \mid \mathbf{X}^a\, \varphi \mid \varphi\, \mathbf{U}^a\, \varphi \mid \mathbf{X}^-\, \varphi \mid \varphi\, \mathbf{U}^-\, \varphi.$$
The superscript "g" comes from global, "a" from abstract, and "p" from past.

Definition 2.5 (semantics of CaRet). Let σ be a finite word on $\widehat{2^{AP}} = 2^{AP} \times \{call, int, ret\}$ and $i \in \mathbb{N}$ be such that $0 \leq i < |\sigma|$. We define the satisfaction relation $\models$ of CaRet formulas inductively as follows.

$$
\begin{aligned}
\sigma, i \models p &\iff \sigma_i = (\tau, \_) \text{ for some } \tau \text{ such that } p \in \tau \\
\sigma, i \models \neg\varphi &\iff \sigma, i \not\models \varphi \\
\sigma, i \models \varphi \wedge \psi &\iff \sigma, i \models \varphi \text{ and } \sigma, i \models \psi \\
\sigma, i \models \mathbf{X}^g\, \varphi &\iff \sigma, \mathrm{succ}^g_\sigma(i) \models \varphi, \text{ i.e., } \sigma, i+1 \models \varphi \\
\sigma, i \models \mathbf{X}^a\, \varphi &\iff \mathrm{succ}^a_\sigma(i) \neq \bot \text{ and } \sigma, \mathrm{succ}^a_\sigma(n) \models \varphi \\
\sigma, i \models \mathbf{X}^-\, \varphi &\iff \mathrm{succ}^-_\sigma(i) \neq \bot \text{ and } \sigma, \mathrm{succ}^-_\sigma(n) \models \varphi \\
\sigma, i \models \varphi\, \mathbf{U}^g\, \psi &\iff \text{there is a sequence } i_0, i_1, \ldots, i_k \text{ (where } i_0 = i) \text{ such that} \\
&\qquad \sigma, i_k \models \psi \text{ and } \forall j \in [0, k).\ (i_{j+1} = \mathrm{succ}^g_\sigma(i_j) \text{ and } \sigma, i_j \models \varphi) \\
\sigma, i \models \varphi\, \mathbf{U}^a\, \psi &\iff \text{there is a sequence } i_0, i_1, \ldots, i_k \text{ (where } i_0 = i) \text{ such that} \\
&\qquad \sigma, i_k \models \psi \text{ and } \forall j \in [0, k).\ (i_{j+1} = \mathrm{succ}^a_\sigma(i_j) \text{ and } \sigma, i_j \models \varphi) \\
\sigma, i \models \varphi\, \mathbf{U}^-\, \psi &\iff \text{there is a sequence } i_0, i_1, \ldots, i_k \text{ (where } i_0 = i) \text{ such that} \\
&\qquad \sigma, i_k \models \psi \text{ and } \forall j \in [0, k).\ (i_{j+1} = \mathrm{succ}^-_\sigma(i_j) \text{ and } \sigma, i_j \models \varphi)
\end{aligned}
$$

2.4   Automata, Regular and (Visibly) One-Counter

Definition 2.6 ((regular) automata). A *nondeterministic finite automaton* is a tuple $(Q, \Sigma, q_0, F, \Delta)$, where Q is a finite set of states, Σ is a finite alphabet, $q_0 \in Q$ is an initial state, $F \subseteq Q$ is a set of final states, and Δ is a finite set of rules of the form $p \xrightarrow{a} q$, where $p, q \in Q$ and $a \in \Sigma$.

For the two types of non-regular req-resp specs (RR3,4), we will use the following non-regular extensions of automata. These notions are proposed originally in [7]; here we follow the notations in [23].

Definition 2.7 (pushdown automata). A *pushdown automaton* is a tuple $(Q, \Sigma, \Gamma, q_0, F, \Delta)$, where Q is a finite set of states, Σ is a finite alphabet, Γ is a stack alphabet, $q_0 \in Q$ is an initial state, $F \subseteq Q$ is a set of final states, and Δ is a finite set of rules of the form $pX \xrightarrow{a} q\alpha$, where $p, q \in Q$, $a \in \Sigma$, $X \in \Gamma$, and $\alpha \in \Gamma^*$. We assume that Q, Σ, Γ are pairwise disjoint.

Pushdown automata manipulate the stack (by pushing and popping) as part of transition. For example, $pX \to qXY$ means pushing Y to the stack, and $pX \to q\varepsilon$ means popping X from the stack. The top of the stack is used to decide which transition to take.

Definition 2.8 (one-counter automata, cf. [23]). A pushdown automaton is called *one-counter* if the stack alphabet consists of two symbols, $\Gamma = \{I, Z\}$, and every rule is of the form $pI \xrightarrow{a} q\alpha$ or $pZ \xrightarrow{a} q\alpha Z$ with $\alpha \in \{I\}^*$.

In this definition, every configuration reachable from pZ is of the form $pI^n Z$. The symbol I means adding one to the counter value, and Z denotes the bottom of the stack, which means the counter value is zero.

In depicting one-counter automata (cf. Fig. 4), we express stack/counter manipulation accordingly: we write c for a counter value, and transition rules $pI \to qII$ and $pI \to q\varepsilon$ are expressed as $p \xrightarrow{c := c+1} q$ and $p \xrightarrow{c := c-1} q$. A transition rule $pZ \to qZ$ means that if the counter value is zero, it is unchanged.

Pushdown automata are an expressive formalism that correspond to context-free languages, but this expressivity comes with increased complexity. The *visible* restriction of pushdown automata [7]—and thus that of one-counter automata— aim to strike a middle-ground. In this restriction, each character $a \in \Sigma$ is either *call* (pushing one symbol to the stack), *return* (popping one symbol from the stack), or *internal* (not changing the stack size). Therefore the effect of $a \in \Sigma$ on the stack size is fixed and independent of the current (control) state $p \in Q$ or the stack content. This restriction makes the class of recognized languages intersection-closed—unlike general context-free languages—and it has shown to be useful for various program verification problems (see e.g., [2,17]).

In the following formal definition, note that the effect of $a \in \Sigma$ on the stack size can also depend on whether the stack is empty (i.e., whether $X = Z$). This is allowed in visible restrictions; see [7, §2.1] and [23, Rem. 2.2].

Definition 2.9 (visibly one-counter automata). Assume a partition $\widehat{\Sigma} = \Sigma_c \cup \Sigma_{int} \cup \Sigma_r$ of the alphabet $\widehat{\Sigma}$, much like Definition 2.2. A *visibly one-counter automaton* is a one-counter automaton $(Q, \widehat{\Sigma}, \Gamma, q_0, F, \Delta)$ that satisfies the following additional condition: for each rule $pX \xrightarrow{a} q\alpha$, 1) $|\alpha| = 2$ for each $a \in \Sigma_c$, 2) $|\alpha| = 1$ for each $a \in \Sigma_{int}$, and 3) $|\alpha| = 0$ or $X = \alpha = Z$ for each $a \in \Sigma_r$.

3   A Decision Tree for Classifying Req-Resp Specs

We propose a decision tree for classifying request-response specifications. We assume the satisfaction of $\mathbf{G}(req \rightarrow \mathbf{F}\, resp)$ as a baseline.

Our proposal is presented in Fig. 1. The tree has three classification criteria (C1–C3), and they yield six types (RR1–RR6) of req-resp specifications. We explain and illustrate these types of specifications in this section, and we will provide mathematical formalizations of the six types in Sect. 4.

3.1   Three Classification Criteria

We identify three criteria (C1–C3) for classifying request-response specifications. Each criterion is expressed as a simple yes-no question. By answering them, users can specify which type of specification is of interest to them.

(C1) Do you allow multiple pending requests?
- Yes: requests can occur in succession (e.g., *req req resp* is accepted).
- No: there is no succession of requests (e.g., *req req resp* is rejected).

(C2) (Request-redundancy) When there are multiple pending requests, is it the same as there is only one pending request? (If yes, it means that those requests in the presence of a pending request are redundant.)
- Yes: one response resolves all pending requests at that moment (e.g., *req req resp* is identified with *req resp*).
- No: one response resolves only one pending request (e.g., when *req req resp*, the last *resp* only resolves one of the two *req*'s, and the remaining *req* is considered still pending).

(C3) (Response-redundancy) Do you allow unrequested responses?
- Yes: extra responses may occur for a single request (e.g., *req resp resp* is accepted).
- No: all responses must be requested in advance (e.g., *req resp resp* is rejected, because the last *resp* is not requested).

3.2   Our Decision Tree and Six Types of Req-Resp Specifications

These three criteria C1–C3 are combined to form a decision tree, shown in Fig. 1. The tree first asks C1. If the answer is yes, it then asks C2. If not, there are only zero or one pending requests at any time—therefore there is no need to ask C2. The tree asks C3, at the end. As a result, the tree yields six types (RR1–RR6) of request-response specifications. Here are brief explanations of these six types. Their formalizations will be given in Sect. 4; the classification is evaluated in Sect. 5.

RR1 is the most liberal out of the six types of req-resp specs, meaning that each of RR2–6 implies RR1. It also coincides with the *baseline* specification "every time *req* occurs, *resp* will eventually follow," a spec that is commonly

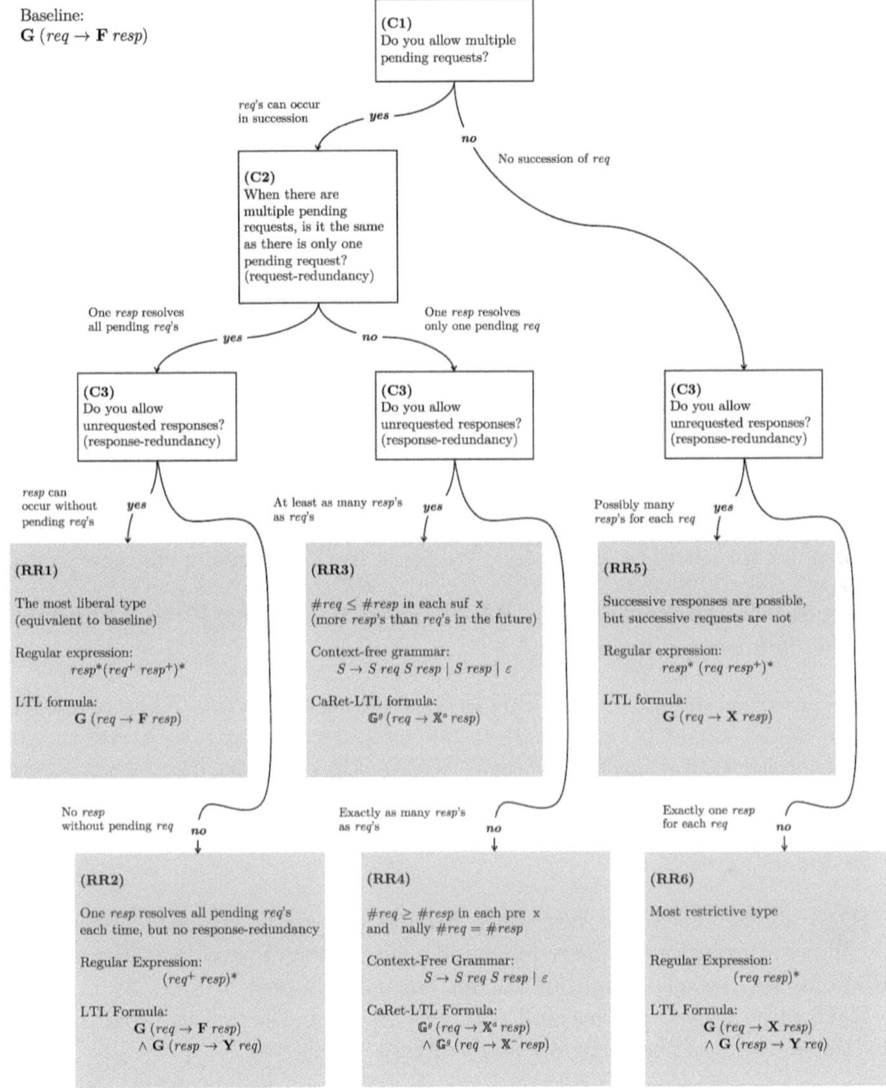

Fig. 1. our proposed decision tree

called *the* request-response specification. RR1 allows both request-redundancy (C2) and response-redundancy (C3).

RR2 restricts RR1 by removing response-redundancy: no *resp* allowed unless there is pending *req*. For example, RR1 holds for *req resp resp* but not RR2.

RR3–4 are the counterparts of RR1–2, respectively, where request-redundancy is disallowed. The latter means that, in presence of pending *req*'s, additional *req*'s are no longer redundant; in other words, each *resp* resolves only one pending *req* (unlike in RR1–2 where *resp* resolves all pending *req*'s). For RR3–4, therefore, we have to count the number of pending *req*'s, making the specs non-regular.

RR3 is the version with response-redundancy, meaning that *resp*'s are allowed even when there is no pending *req*. We present the following mathematical characterization of RR3. Its proof is deferred to [1, Appendix A].

Theorem 3.1 (characterizing RR3). *Let $\sigma \in \{req, resp\}^*$ be a finite word. Then the following are equivalent.*

1. *The word σ satisfies RR3. Precisely, there is an injective correspondence ρ from the index set $\{i \mid \sigma_i = req\}$ to the set $\{j \mid \sigma_j = resp\}$ such that $i < \rho(i)$.*
2. *In each suffix of σ, we have $\#req \le \#resp$ (i.e., the number of req's is no bigger than that of resp's).* □

RR4 does not allow response-redundancy; accordingly, there must be a 1-1 correspondence ρ from *req*'s to *resp*'s. Due to the baseline $\mathbf{G}(req \to \mathbf{F}\, resp)$, ρ should point forward ($i < \rho(i)$), too. We come to the following characterization.

Theorem 3.2 (characterizing RR4). *Let $\sigma \in \{req, resp\}^*$ be a finite word. Then the following are equivalent.*

1. *The word σ satisfies RR4. Precisely, there is a bijective correspondence ρ from the index set $\{i \mid \sigma_i = req\}$ to the set $\{j \mid \sigma_j = resp\}$ such that $i < \rho(i)$.*
2. *In each prefix of σ, we have $\#req \ge \#resp$. Moreover, we have $\#req = \#resp$ for the whole word.*
3. *In each suffix of σ, we have $\#req \le \#resp$. Moreover, we have $\#req = \#resp$ for the whole word.* □

RR5 allows successive responses, but no successive requests. Therefore it only allows alternation of one request and a succession of responses. For example, RR5 holds for *req resp resp*, but not for *req req resp resp*.

RR6 only allows one *req* and one *resp* to come alternately. RR6 holds for only those words of the form *req resp req resp . . . req resp*.

3.3   Examples of the Six Req-Resp Spec Types

We present realistic examples of the six types RR1–6. There should be a vast variety of examples and we show only a fraction; they should nevertheless serve the illustration purposes. They also show that all of RR1–6 have practical relevance.

RR1: Waiter. Imagine calling a waiter at a restaurant. Here *req* is a call—by a hand sign, a bell, etc.—and *resp* is a waiter's attendance. It is possible (if not appreciated) to make multiple calls before being served (so C1 is yes); when a waiter comes then it resolves all the calls (C2 is yes; here we focus on a single table). Sometimes a waiter can come, too, without calls (thus C3 is yes).

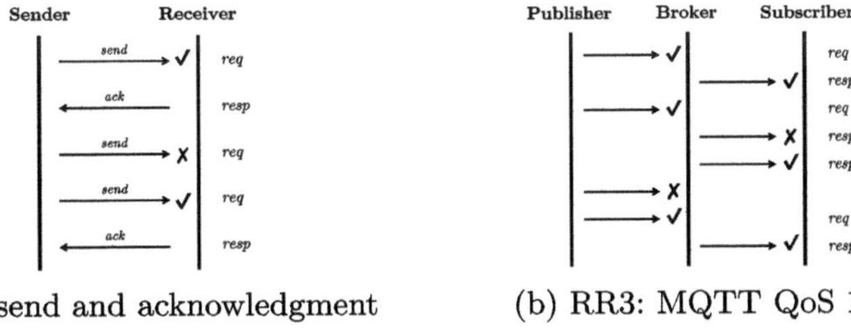

(a) RR2: send and acknowledgment   (b) RR3: MQTT QoS 1

Fig. 2. network communication examples. ✔ is successful; ✘ is not

RR2: Send-Ack in Communication. Consider the relationship between *send* and *acknowledgment* (Ack) in network communication (see Fig. 2a). Many communication protocols require explicit Acks for reliability. Here *req* is a message sent, and *resp* is an Ack of successful delivery. A message can be sent many times before the sender gets Ack (so C1 is yes). Here we focus on single-threaded communication (no parallel sending of different messages), so one *req* resolves all *resp*'s so far (C2 is yes). Acks should not occur without sending (C3 is no).

RR3: Broker in MQTT QoS 1. *MQTT* (message queuing telemetry transport) is a lightweight publish-subscribe network protocol used e.g., in IoT applications. MQTT features a network entity called a *broker*; when an agent A_1 communicates a message to A_2, A_1 (the *publisher*) sends it to a broker, which sends it to A_2 (the *subscriber*). Hence all messages get relayed by a broker.

MQTT offers three *QoS levels* (quality of service) that give different guarantees. Among them, *QoS 1* guarantees successful delivery of each message from a publisher to a subscriber. An example run of the protocol is in Fig. 2b, where both the publisher and the broker sends a message repeatedly before its receipt is confirmed (by suitable ack messages, which we ignore in the current discussion).

We take the broker's view. Let *req* stand for the broker receiving a message from the publisher, and *resp* for the broker sending a message to the subscriber (Fig. 2b). This is where use of RR3 is suitable: the broker can receive multiple messages before relaying them (C1 is yes); each received message (*req*) must be relayed separately (C2 is no); and one *req* can trigger multiple *resp*'s, when some messages sent from the broker do not reach the subscriber (C3 is yes).

RR4: Vending Machine. Consider a vending machine. We let *req* stand for accepting a coin (we assume that each item is one coin worth), and *resp* stand for dispensing a purchased item. This is a req-resp situation where we must have $\#req = \#resp$ in the end, so RR4 is suitable. Indeed, C1 is yes (here we assume that the machine allows pending purchases—otherwise we should use RR6), C2 is no (we must count the number of coins), and C3 is no (no free items).

RR5: Reception with Numbered Tickets. Consider a reception desk— or a bakery as in Lamport's bakery algorithm—that issues numbered tickets to clients. Here we take a client's viewpoint, and let *req* stand for the client taking a ticket, and *resp* stand for the client called by the desk. When the client has a ticket they will not take another (so C1 is no); the desk can call the client even if a ticket is not taken—e.g., when there are no other clients or an emergent situation is obvious)—so C2 is yes. Therefore RR5 is a suitable spec type.

Note that, if we take a reception desk's viewpoint, RR3 is a suitable type, since the desk can issue multiple tickets to different clients. This example points to the following general principle: different agents in the same system have different viewpoints that make different spec types suited.

RR6: Toggle Light Switch. Consider a toggle light switch, where *req* is to turn on an electric light and and *resp* is to turn off. It is a req-resp situation—once a light is turned on, we want it to be off eventually. Since it is a toggle switch, *req* and *resp* must strictly alternate.

4   Formalization

We formalize the six types of req-resp specifications (RR1–RR6) introduced in Sect. 3. We do so in three formalisms: 1) as formal grammars, such as regular expressions and context-free grammars; 2) as logical formulas, in LTL or its variation; and 3) as automata, regular or visibly one-counter.

4.1   Formalization as Grammars

Here we formalize each spec type as a formal grammar G. Then the monitoring problem—deciding a given word w satisfies the spec or not—becomes the *membership problem* in formal language theory, that is, to decide if $w \in L(G)$.

Let $\Sigma = \{req, resp\}$, and $w \in \Sigma^*$ be a finite word of *req*'s and *resp*'s. Among the six types, the regular ones (RR1, RR2, RR5 and RR6) can be formalized as the following regular expressions. These should be intuitive.

$$\begin{aligned} &\textbf{RR1}: \quad resp^* \, (req^+ \, resp^+)^* \qquad\qquad \textbf{RR2}: \quad (req^+ \, resp)^* \\ &\textbf{RR5}: \quad resp^* \, (req \, resp^+)^* \qquad\qquad \textbf{RR6}: \quad (req \, resp)^* \end{aligned} \qquad (1)$$

The remaining two (RR3–4) require counting pending *req*'s and thus are not regular. We thus use context-free grammars. They have only one nonterminal S.

$$\textbf{RR3}: S \to S \, req \, S \, resp \mid S \, resp \mid \varepsilon \qquad\qquad \textbf{RR4}: S \to S \, req \, S \, resp \mid \varepsilon \qquad (2)$$

Their correctness proofs, based on Theorems 3.1 and 3.2, are not entirely trivial. Proofs for RR3 (Theorem 4.1) and RR4 (Theorem 4.2) are deferred to [1, Appendix A].

Theorem 4.1 (RR3 as a CFG). *The language* $L_{\mathrm{RR3}} = \{w \in \{a, b\}^* \mid \#a \leq \#b$ *in each suffix of* $w\}$ *is produced by the rules* $S \to SaSb \mid Sb \mid \varepsilon$. $\qquad\square$

Theorem 4.2 (RR4 as a CFG). $L_{\mathrm{RR4}} = \{w \in \{a, b\}^* \mid \#a \geq \#b$ *in each prefix of* w, *and* $\#a = \#b$ *in the whole* $w\}$ *is produced by* $S \to SaSb \mid \varepsilon$. $\qquad\square$

The grammar characterization in (2) trivially shows that RR4 implies RR3—the grammar for RR3 extends that for RR4 by an additional rule $S \to S \, resp$. This implication is not trivial in the characterization in Theorems 3.1 and 3.2.

4.2   Formalization as Logical Formulas

Here we use another common formalism, namely temporal logics (specifically LTL (Sect. 2.2) and CaRet (Sect. 2.3)). Formalization in LTL makes specs amenable to many tools, such as model checkers (e.g., Spin and NuSMV) and monitoring tools (e.g., MonPoly). See Sect. 6 for further discussion on monitoring tools.

Assumption 4.3 (req,$resp$ as atomic propositions). Throughout the current Sect. 4.2, we set that $req, resp \in \mathrm{AP}$ are propositions. Moreover, we assume that *exactly one of req and $resp$ is true at each moment*. This removes such anomalies as req and $resp$ occurring together, making the formalization compatible with the grammatical one in Sect. 4.1 (where $req, resp \in \Sigma$ are characters).

This assumption is posed mostly for the simplicity of presentation; see [1, Appendix A.6] for technical justification. Lifting it should be strarightforward; doing so is future work.

As we discussed in Sect. 3, we assume the LTL formula $\varphi_{\mathsf{baseRR}} = \mathbf{G}(req \to \mathbf{F}\, resp)$ as a baseline requirement for all of RR1–6. Therefore we are interested in what additional requirement ψ_i is needed to express each of RR1–6, which leads to a formalization $\varphi_{\mathsf{RR}i} = \varphi_{\mathsf{baseRR}} \wedge \psi_i$ of each type. Sometimes the additional requirement ψ_i itself implies the baseline $\varphi_{\mathsf{baseRR}}$, in which case we do not see $\varphi_{\mathsf{baseRR}}$ explicitly in the formalization $\varphi_{\mathsf{RR}i}$.

Regular Spec Types We start with regular spec types. They are all expressible in LTL. Non-regular spec types (RR3–4) are formalized later in (4).

$$
\begin{aligned}
\underline{\mathbf{RR1}}:\ &\varphi_{\mathsf{RR1}} = \mathbf{G}(req \to \mathbf{F}\, resp) \\
\underline{\mathbf{RR2}}:\ &\varphi_{\mathsf{RR2}} = \mathbf{G}(req \to \mathbf{F}\, resp) \wedge \mathbf{G}(resp \to \mathbf{Y}\, req) \\
\underline{\mathbf{RR5}}:\ &\varphi_{\mathsf{RR5}} = \mathbf{G}(req \to \mathbf{X}\, resp) \\
\underline{\mathbf{RR6}}:\ &\varphi_{\mathsf{RR6}} = \mathbf{G}(req \to \mathbf{X}\, resp) \wedge \mathbf{G}(resp \to \mathbf{Y}\, req)
\end{aligned}
\tag{3}
$$

RR1 is the most liberal type, and it is equivalent to the baseline $\varphi_{\mathsf{baseRR}}$.

RR2 poses an additional constraint that $resp$ must not occur when there is no pending req. In the current setting where 1) req and $resp$ do not occur simultaneously and 2) either req or $resp$ occurs at each moment (Assumption 4.3), this translates to a simpler condition that "each $resp$ must be preceded by req," that is, $\mathbf{G}(resp \to \mathbf{Y}\, req)$. Indeed, (Case 1) if $\mathbf{G}(resp \to \mathbf{Y}\, req)$ is true, then every $resp$ is preceded by req that is pending, satisfying RR2; (Case 2) if $\mathbf{G}(resp \to \mathbf{Y}\, req)$ is false, then there must be two consecutive $resp$'s, violating RR2 (this contradicts with "C3 is no"). This additional constraint $\psi_2 = \mathbf{G}(resp \to \mathbf{Y}\, req)$ does not imply the baseline ($req\ resp\ req$ is a counterexample); so the formalization is $\varphi_{\mathsf{RR2}} = \varphi_{\mathsf{baseRR}} \wedge \psi_2$.

Remark 4.4 (RR2 without Assumption 4.3**).** The above argument does not work in the general setting where Assumption 4.3 is not true. We discuss alternatives.

The formula $\psi = \mathbf{F}\,resp \rightarrow ((\neg resp)\,\mathbf{U}\,req)$ is suggested in [14, p.85] for an intention similar to RR2. It does not coincide with RR2, however, with a counterexample *req resp resp* (the formula is true but RR2 is false).

Its modification $\mathbf{G}\,\psi$ does not coincide with RR2 either. Consider the word *req $\emptyset$ resp*, where $\emptyset$ means neither *req* or *resp* is true. RR2 holds for this word, but ψ is false at time 2, making $\mathbf{G}\,\psi$ false for the whole word.

Another candidate is $\mathbf{G}(resp \rightarrow \mathbf{Y}((\neg resp)\,\mathbf{S}\,req))$ suggested in [11], and this seems to work. A proof of the coincidence with RR2 is left as future work.

RR5 adds, to the baseline $\varphi_{\mathsf{baseRR}}$, the constraint that *req*'s cannot come in succession. Under Assumption 4.3, this is the LTL formula $\mathbf{G}(req \rightarrow \mathbf{X}\,resp)$. Since this implies $\varphi_{\mathsf{baseRR}}$, we obtain the formalization $\varphi_{\mathsf{RR5}} = \mathbf{G}(req \rightarrow \mathbf{X}\,resp)$ in (3).

Remark 4.5 (RR5 without Assumption 4.3). We discuss, much like in Remark 4.4, a formula for RR5 in the general setting where Assumption 4.3 is not true.

A good candidate is $\mathbf{G}(req \rightarrow \mathbf{X}((\neg req)\,\mathbf{U}\,resp))$, and one can show that this coincides with RR5, under its interpretation that *resp* occurring simultaneously with *req* does *not* address *req*. Further investigation is future work.

RR6 is understood as the conjunction of RR2 and RR5. See (3). Since RR5 implies the baseline $\mathbf{G}(req \rightarrow \mathbf{F}\,resp)$, we come to the formalization $\varphi_{\mathsf{RR6}} = \mathbf{G}(req \rightarrow \mathbf{X}\,resp) \wedge \mathbf{G}(resp \rightarrow \mathbf{Y}\,req)$. Note that requiring $\mathbf{G}(resp \rightarrow \mathbf{X}\,req)$ is too strong—combined with $\mathbf{G}(req \rightarrow \mathbf{X}\,resp)$, it does not allow a word to end.

Non-Regular Spec Types For the non-regular spec types RR3–4, LTL is not enough, since all specs expressible in LTL are regular. We use a variant of CaRet (Sect. 2.3), a minimal extension of LTL that accommodates the necessary kind of counting we need. In other words, using CaRet, we can track injective/bijective correspondences between *req*'s and *resp*'s (cf. Theorems 3.1 and 3.2).

We first introduce the variant of CaRet we use; this is required since there is a subtle difference between the call-return correspondence that CaRet aims to capture, and the req-resp correspondence that we aim to capture. For distinction, we use symbols $\mathbb{X}$, $\mathbb{G}$, $\mathbb{F}$, etc. for the temporal operators in our variant of CaRet.

This variant differs from the original CaRet (Sect. 2.3) only in the definition of the innermost-call correspondence $Q_\sigma : \mathbb{N} \rightharpoonup \mathbb{N}$. Here, it is defined to be a partial function that satisfies the following.

- If there is j such that 1) $j < i$, 2) σ_j is a call, and 3) $R_\sigma(j) \geq i$ or $R_\sigma(j) = \bot$, then $Q_\sigma(i)$ is the greatest such j.
- Otherwise, $Q_\sigma(i) = \bot$.

The precise difference is in the condition 3) of the first item: here we have $R_\sigma(j) \geq i$; in the original CaRet (Sect. 2.3), we had $R_\sigma(j) > i$. This difference leads to the following property, making the logic suited for req-resp correspondence.

Proposition 4.6. *In the above variant of CaRet, we have the following. 1) If σ_i is a return and $Q_\sigma(i)$ is defined, $R_\sigma(Q_\sigma(i)) = i$ holds. 2) If σ_i is a call and and $R_\sigma(i)$ is defined, $Q_\sigma(R_\sigma(i)) = i$ holds.* □

In this variant of CaRet, we also identify *req* with *call* and *resp* with *return*. Concretely, this means that in the extended alphabet $\widehat{\Sigma} = \Sigma \times \{call, int, ret\}$, *req* is interpreted as $(req, call)$ and *resp* is $(resp, ret)$.

Using this variant of CaRet, RR3–4 are naturally expressed as follows.

$$
\begin{aligned}
\textbf{RR3:} \quad &\varphi_{\mathsf{RR3}} = \mathbb{G}^g(req \to \mathbb{X}^a\, resp) \\
\textbf{RR4:} \quad &\varphi_{\mathsf{RR4}} = \mathbb{G}^g(req \to \mathbb{X}^a\, resp) \wedge \mathbb{G}^g(resp \to \mathbb{X}^-\, req)
\end{aligned}
\tag{4}
$$

In φ_{RR3}, by the definition of the semantics of $\mathbb{X}^a$, one easily sees that $\mathbb{X}^a\, resp$ is equivalent to $\mathbb{X}^a\, \top$. We prefer the former presentation that is more intuitive. In φ_{RR4}, the additional conjunct mandates a corresponding *req* to each *resp*.

Some (positive and negative) examples, with relevant links that indicate R_σ and Q_σ (that are mutually inverse in the sense of Proposition 4.6), are shown in Fig. 3.

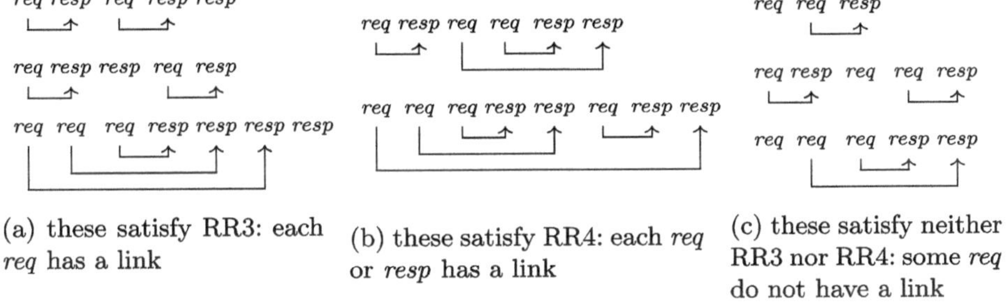

(a) these satisfy RR3: each *req* has a link

(b) these satisfy RR4: each *req* or *resp* has a link

(c) these satisfy neither RR3 nor RR4: some *req* do not have a link

Fig. 3. examples for RR3–4. The links indicate R_σ (forward) and Q_σ (backward)

4.3 Formalization as Automata

Here we present formalization of the six req-resp spec types as automata. Such representations as *state machines* are amenable to efficient algorithms: indeed, in the formal methods community and elsewhere, grammars and logical formulas commonly get translated to automata for algorithmic processing.

The automata presentations are in Fig. 4. Those for regular types (RR1,2,5,6) are usual automata (Definition 2.6); they happen to be deterministic as well. They can be easily obtained, e.g., by translating the regular expressions in Sect. 4.1.

For non-regular types (RR3–4), we use visibly one-counter automata (Sect. 2.4). They are indeed *visibly* one-counter, since each of *req* and *resp* has a fixed effect on the counter c (incrementing and decrementing, respectively). The occurrence of max in RR3 is allowed; see Definition 2.9 and the discussion before it.

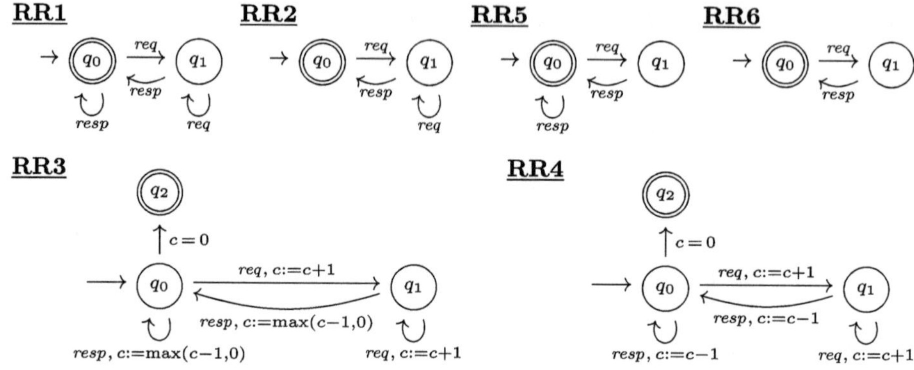

Fig. 4. automata representation of the six types of req-resp specifications

5   Assessment

We assess the validity of the classification in Fig. 1. We do so by addressing three research questions: whether it is fine-grained enough (RQ1), not overly fine-grained (RQ2), and whether its organization as a tree is sensible (RQ3).

RQ1: Is the Proposed Classification Sufficiently Discriminative?. We argue it is. One reason is that the four regular types (RR1,2,5,6) cover all four possible patterns of singularity/plurality of req's and $resp$'s. Specifically, we look at their regular expression presentations (1) and find, as patterns therein,

$$req^+\, resp^+ \text{ in RR1,} \quad req^+\, resp \text{ in RR2,} \quad req\, resp^+ \text{ in RR5,} \quad \text{and } req\, resp \text{ in RR6.}$$

These cover all four combinations of whether to put $+$ or not for req and $resp$.

In RR3–4 where we count the number of req's, the question is not about singularity/plurality, but more specifically about the numbers of req's and $resp$'s. Because of the baseline spec $\mathbf{G}(req \to \mathbf{F}\, resp)$, we must have $\#req \le \#resp$ for each suffix of a word w; this is RR3. RR4 imposes another condition, that is, $\#req = \#resp$ should hold for the whole w. Besides this, we have not found any reasonable additional condition so far. Therefore the classification of this "counting" case into RR3 and RR4 is the best we can come up with now.

RQ2: Is the Proposed Classification Not Overly Discriminative?. The above arguments for RQ1 also show that our six types are distinguished for fundamental reasons (e.g., plurality of req's and $resp$'s). The realistic examples in Sect. 3.3 demonstrate the need of this distinction, too: each of these examples demands the use of a specific type out of the six.

One can also see that the three criteria C1–C3 in Fig. 1 are natural questions to ask when one fixes a req-resp specification. They do not seem overly detailed.

RQ3: Is the Decision Tree Sensible?. The three criteria C1–C3 are tightly coupled with the classification into RR1–6; so we can say that their validity, individually and collectively, has been addressed by the above discussion. Therefore, here we focus on the specific *order* of C1–C3 in Fig. 1: is there any better order of C1–C3 when we ask them?

We argue, in fact, that the order in Fig. 1 is one that is *logically derived.*

Firstly, we need to ask C2 before we ask C3. This is because the meaning of C3 depends on the answer of C2. More specifically, the meaning of "unrequested responses" changes depending on whether C2 is yes or no. For example, with the same word *req req resp resp*, if C2 is yes, then the last *resp* is considered to be unrequested; but if C2 is no, it should not be considered unrequested.

Secondly, we need to ask C1 before we ask C2. This is because, if C1 is no, then there is no need to ask C2.

These two points requires the order C1-C2-C3, one that we have in Fig. 1.

6   Monitoring Tool Support, an Overview

In this section, we give an overview of available tools for monitoring the six types of req-resp specifications, with an emphasis different ways of formalization (Sect. 4). Here *monitoring* of a spec means deciding if the spec is true in a given word w.

Monitoring: What It Is and Why It Is Important. When it comes to industrial usages of formal specs, monitoring is probably the most common task. Theoretically, monitoring can be seen as a special case of model checking: in monitoring, a system model is restricted to a single execution trace that is moreover finite; in contrast, in model checking, a system model is typically a state machine that can generate infinitely many execution traces each of which can be infinitely long. Consequently, *fixed point reasoning*—that reduces infinitary to finitary—is a central theme in model checking, making it a theoretically intriguing topic.

While fixed point reasoning is not much an issue in monitoring, monitoring does come with its own theoretical challenges, especially about (time and space) complexity. Specifically, an input word w for monitoring can be very long (e.g., GBs of data), and monitoring such w is only realistic if a monitoring algorithm has time complexity $O(|w|)$ and space complexity $O(1)$. Demand of practical speed is stronger in monitoring, too, since time constraints for monitoring tasks are often strict (especially when one conducts *online* monitoring). Because of these differences, monitoring tools and model checking tools are usually separate.

In practice, deployment of monitoring is considered easier than that of model checking. This is because the former requires only an execution trace w of a target system—w can be easily collected, e.g., from a log file—while the latter requires a white-box system model, building which can cost many person-months. Certainly, monitoring does not establish that every behavior of a system is correct— it examines only one execution trace—but its result often gives useful insights.

Therefore we focus on monitoring here, and present a current landscape of different tools available for different formalizations of req-resp specs. One can think of this overview as an evaluation of different formalisms: some come with sophisticated tools; others do not.

6.1 Tools Based on Grammars

Regular Expressions. "Monitoring" regular expression specs is a special case of *pattern matching* [24]. (Monitoring asks if the whole word matches a spec, while pattern matching usually answers all subwords that match.)

There are many pattern matching tools; one is the `grep` command of Unix. Use of `grep` for monitoring requires some care, however, such as the gap between characters and lines (`grep` is line-based) and the use of the `-o` option.

Another class of tools is regex-matching engines, often offered as libraries in programming languages and frameworks. Examples are ones that come with Ruby, Google's RE2 (https://github.com/google/re2), to name a couple.

We also discuss *timed* extensions, i.e., formalisms that accommodate real-time constraints such as "*resp* must come within 2.1 s," although this is outside the current paper's scope. *Timed regular expressions* [8] are a well-known such extension; monitoring tools for them include MONAA [29] and Montre [26].

Context-Free Grammars (CFGs). "Monitoring" CFGs largely amounts to *parsing* (although the tree structure given by parsing is not needed). Parsing is a classic topic with a number of research works as well as tools. Examples of parsers are Lex/Yacc (available as Menhir in OCaml and flex/bison in C/C++), Antlr, and PEG-based parsers (such as Pyparsing in Python and Parsec in Haskell).

We tried Menhir, Antlr, and Pyparsing for our CFG formalization of RR3–4 (see (2)). Menhir and Antlr worked well with both RR3–4. Pyparsing did not; this seems to be attributed to the absence of look-ahead in Pyparsing.

A timed extension of CFGs is proposed in [20]. At this moment, its practical relevance in monitoring is unclear.

6.2 Tools Based on Temporal Logics

LTL. LTL is probably the most common formalism for temporal specs. Its notable advantage is readability: unlike grammars and automata, LTL formulas allow natural language-like human interpretation (to a certain extent).

Monitoring LTL specs is an active topic of research, with the work [12] being one of the earliest. There are many tools for that, such as DejaVu [15].

Among those tools, MonPoly [10] stands out in its suitability to our current purpose. Firstly, it supports both future- and past-time operators in LTL, and we need both of them in our formalization (Sect. 4.2). DejaVu, in contrast, supports only past-time operators. Secondly, it has a track record of scalable real-world applications [18]. Thirdly, it is an expressive tool and can accommodate real-time constraints as well as first-order specs.

One possible disadvantage of MonPoly is that it is "too expressive" in a certain sense: sometimes a spec is deemed *not monitorable* due to some theoretical constraints, and it is not easy to figure out what exactly is a problem. With our simple req-resp specs RR1,2,5,6, however, we did not encounter this problem.

CaRet. CaRet seems to be a largely theoretical language, without much tool support or practical case studies. It is introduced in [4], and further theoretical studies are in [13,19]. A monitor implementation is mentioned in [19] but it does not seem to be available now. A timed extension of CaRet is not known, either.

6.3 Tools Based on Automata

(Regular) Automata. Automata are a fundamental model of computation. "Monitoring" an automaton spec amounts to executing the automaton under a given word w; if w is accepted, the spec is true for w. Executing an automaton is such a basic task that there are numerous implementations.

Automata are used in the backend of many tools which take specs in another formalism. For example, the work [12] assumes a translation of LTL formulas to Büchi automata (e.g., [27]). Most regex-matching engines (Sect. 6.1), too, first translate regular expressions to automata.

Timed automata are introduced in [3] as an extension of (regular) automata with real-time constraints. Monitoring timed automata specs is studied, e.g., in [6,28]; MONAA [29] is a tool for monitoring timed automata (and timed regular expressions, too, via translation).

Visibly Pushdown/One-Counter Automata. Visibly one-counter/ pushdown automata, after their introduction in [7], have been actively studied from the viewpoint of formal language theory [5,23] as well as for application [2,17,22]. However, their use for monitoring is rare.

Regarding the timed extension, *synchronized recursive timed automata* (SRTA) [25] seem to be the closest. An SRTA extends a timed automaton with a stack.

7   Conclusions and Future Work

We studied a variety of request-response specifications, classifying them into six types organized in a decision tree, and formalizing them in three different formalisms. The decision tree can be used for a practitioner to decide which type is suited for their application; they can do so by answering three questions (criteria C1–C3). Moreover, focusing on the monitoring task that is one of the most industry-relevant, we presented an overview of tool support. We believe all these will help practitioners when they use req-resp specs.

As theoretical future work, we will investigate the general setting where Assumption 4.3 is lifted (see Remarks 4.4 and 4.5). An applicational direction is to develop further monitoring tools. For example, for non-regular RR3–4, the only tools available for practical use seem to be parsers (Sect. 6); dedicated monitoring tools for the current limited class of CFGs can be of practical interest.

References

1. Aiba, D., et al.: A variety of request-response specifications (extended version) (2025). https://arxiv.org/abs/2509.13078
2. Alur, R., Bouajjani, A., Esparza, J.: Model checking procedural programs. In: Clarke, E.M., Henzinger, T.A., Veith, H., Bloem, R. (eds.) Handbook of Model Checking, pp. 541–572. Springer, Cham (2018). https://doi.org/10.1007/978-3-319-10575-8_17
3. Alur, R., Dill, D.L.: A theory of timed automata. Theor. Comput. Sci. **126**(2), 183–235 (1994)
4. Alur, R., Etessami, K., Madhusudan, P.: A temporal logic of nested calls and returns. In: Jensen, K., Podelski, A. (eds.) Tools and Algorithms for the Construction and Analysis of Systems, pp. 467–481. Springer, Heidelberg (2004)
5. Alur, R., Kumar, V., Madhusudan, P., Viswanathan, M.: Congruences for visibly pushdown languages. In: Caires, L., Italiano, G.F., Monteiro, L., Palamidessi, C., Yung, M. (eds.) ICALP 2005. LNCS, vol. 3580, pp. 1102–1114. Springer, Heidelberg (2005). https://doi.org/10.1007/11523468_89
6. Alur, R., Kurshan, R.P., Viswanathan, M.: Membership questions for timed and hybrid automata. In: Proceedings of the 19th IEEE Real-Time Systems Symposium, Madrid, Spain, 2–4 December 1998, pp. 254–263. IEEE Computer Society (1998). https://doi.org/10.1109/REAL.1998.739751
7. Alur, R., Madhusudan, P.: Visibly pushdown languages. In: Proceedings of the Thirty-Sixth Annual ACM Symposium on Theory of Computing, pp. 202–211 (2004)
8. Asarin, E., Caspi, P., Maler, O.: Timed regular expressions. J. ACM **49**(2), 172–206 (2002). https://doi.org/10.1145/506147.506151
9. Bartocci, E., et al.: Specification-based monitoring of cyber-physical systems: a survey on theory, tools and applications. In: Bartocci, E., Falcone, Y. (eds.) Lectures on Runtime Verification. LNCS, vol. 10457, pp. 135–175. Springer, Cham (2018). https://doi.org/10.1007/978-3-319-75632-5_5
10. Basin, D.A., Klaedtke, F., Zalinescu, E.: The monpoly monitoring tool. RV-CuBES **3**, 19–28 (2017)
11. Cimatti, A., Roveri, M., Sheridan, D.: Bounded verification of past LTL. In: Hu, A.J., Martin, A.K. (eds.) Formal Methods in Computer-Aided Design, pp. 245–259. Springer, Heidelberg (2004)
12. d'Amorim, M., Roşu, G.: Efficient monitoring of ω-languages. In: Etessami, K., Rajamani, S.K. (eds.) CAV 2005. LNCS, vol. 3576, pp. 364–378. Springer, Heidelberg (2005). https://doi.org/10.1007/11513988_36
13. Decker, N., Leucker, M., Thoma, D.: Impartiality and anticipation for monitoring of visibly context-free properties. In: Legay, A., Bensalem, S. (eds.) Runtime Verification, pp. 183–200. Springer, Heidelberg (2013)
14. Goldblatt, R.: Logics of time and computation. CSLI lecture notes; no. 7, Center for the Study of Language and Information, Stanford, CA (1987)
15. Havelund, K., Peled, D., Ulus, D.: First-order temporal logic monitoring with BDDs. Formal Methods Syst. Des. **56**(1), 1–21 (2020)
16. Menghi, C., et al.: ARCH-COMP23 category report: falsification. In: Frehse, G., Althoff, M. (eds.) Proceedings of 10th International Workshop on Applied Verification of Continuous and Hybrid Systems (ARCH 2023), San Antonio, Texas, USA, 9 May 2023. EPiC Series in Computing, vol. 96, pp. 151–169. EasyChair (2023). https://doi.org/10.29007/6nqs

17. Murawski, A.S., Walukiewicz, I.: Third-order idealized algol with iteration is decidable. Theor. Comput. Sci. **390**(2-3), 214–229 (2008). https://doi.org/10.1016/j.tcs.2007.09.022
18. Reger, G.: A report of RV-cubes 2017. In: Reger, G., Havelund, K. (eds.) RV-CuBES 2017. An International Workshop on Competitions, Usability, Benchmarks, Evaluation, and Standardisation for Runtime Verification Tools. Kalpa Publications in Computing, vol. 3, pp. 1–9. EasyChair (2017). https://doi.org/10.29007/2496
19. Roşu, G., Chen, F., Ball, T.: Synthesizing monitors for safety properties: this time with calls and returns. In: Leucker, M. (ed.) Runtime Verification, pp. 51–68. Springer, Heidelberg (2008)
20. Saeedloei, N., Gupta, G.: Timed definite clause omega-grammars. In: Technical Communications of the 26th International Conference on Logic Programming, pp. 212–221 (2010). Schloss Dagstuhl–Leibniz-Zentrum für Informatik (2010)
21. Sánchez, C., et al.: A survey of challenges for runtime verification from advanced application domains (beyond software). Formal Methods Syst. Des. **54**(3), 279–335 (2019). https://doi.org/10.1007/s10703-019-00337-w
22. Schwentick, T.: Automata for XML - a survey. J. Comput. Syst. Sci. **73**(3), 289–315 (2007). https://doi.org/10.1016/j.jcss.2006.10.003
23. Srba, J.: Beyond language equivalence on visibly pushdown automata. Logical Methods Comput. Sci. **5** (2009)
24. Thompson, K.: Regular expression search algorithm. Commun. ACM **11**(6), 419–422 (1968). https://doi.org/10.1145/363347.363387
25. Uezato, Y., Minamide, Y.: Synchronized recursive timed automata. In: Davis, M., Fehnker, A., McIver, A., Voronkov, A. (eds.) Logic for Programming, Artificial Intelligence, and Reasoning, pp. 249–265. Springer, Heidelberg (2015)
26. Ulus, D.: MONTRE: a tool for monitoring timed regular expressions. In: Majumdar, R., Kunčak, V. (eds.) CAV 2017. LNCS, vol. 10426, pp. 329–335. Springer, Cham (2017). https://doi.org/10.1007/978-3-319-63387-9_16
27. Vardi, M.Y.: An automata-theoretic approach to linear temporal logic. In: Moller, F., Birtwistle, G. (eds.) Logics for Concurrency. LNCS, vol. 1043, pp. 238–266. Springer, Heidelberg (1996). https://doi.org/10.1007/3-540-60915-6_6
28. Waga, M.: Empowering runtime verification with polyhedra. Ph.D. thesis, Graduate University for Advanced Studies, Japan (2020). https://ci.nii.ac.jp/naid/500001483041
29. Waga, M., Hasuo, I., Suenaga, K.: MONAA: a tool for timed pattern matching with automata-based acceleration. In: 3rd Workshop on Monitoring and Testing of Cyber-Physical Systems, MT@CPSWeek 2018, 10 April 2018, pp. 14–15. IEEE (2018). https://doi.org/10.1109/MT-CPS.2018.00014

Probabilistic Systems

Weighted Automata for Exact Inference in Discrete Probabilistic Programs

Dominik Geißler[1]([envelope]) [iD] and Tobias Winkler[2] [iD]

[1] Technische Universität Berlin, Berlin, Germany
dominik.geissler@tu-berlin.de
[2] RWTH Aachen University, Aachen, Germany

Abstract. In probabilistic programming, the *inference problem* asks to determine a program's posterior distribution conditioned on its "observe" instructions. Inference is challenging, especially when exact rather than approximate results are required. Inspired by recent work on probability generating functions (PGFs), we propose encoding distributions on $\mathbb{N}^k$ as weighted automata over a commutative alphabet with k symbols. Based on this, we map the semantics of various imperative programming statements to automata-theoretic constructions. For a rich class of programs, this results in an effective translation from prior to posterior distribution, both encoded as automata. We prove that our approach is sound with respect to a standard operational program semantics.

Keywords: Weighted Automata · Probabilistic Programming · Posterior Inference · Program Semantics · Probability Generating Functions

1 Introduction

Probabilistic programming languages extend traditional programming languages by capabilities for *sampling* numbers from pre-defined distributions, and *conditioning* the current program state on observations [11]. Probabilistic programs have numerous applications, including machine learning [25], cognitive science [10], and autonomous systems [21]. Semantically, probabilistic programs can be seen as *transformers of probability distributions*: From an initial distribution over inputs, also called *prior*, to a final distribution over outputs, also called *posterior* [11,17]. *Inference* means characterizing the posterior resulting from a given prior.

In this paper, we study the imperative language `ReDiP` [5,15], short for *rectangular discrete probabilistic programming language*. This language imposes some syntactical restrictions (see Sect. 3 for details), while preserving decidability of many (inference) tasks: For instance, for loop-free programs, the moments of the posterior distributions can be computed exactly, and program equivalence is decidable [5]. We only consider the *loop-free* fragment of `ReDiP` in this paper; adding general `while` loops renders the language Turing-complete.

The original version of the chapter has been revised. A correction to this chapter can be found at https://doi.org/10.1007/978-3-032-11176-0_29

Z. Liu et al. (Eds.): ICTAC 2025, LNCS 16237, pp. 261–278, 2026.
https://doi.org/10.1007/978-3-032-11176-0_16

```
// all variables initially 0
{R := 0} [⁹/₁₀] {R := 1} ;
if (R = 0) {
    X += NegBin(1,1/2)
} else {
    X += NegBin(2,1/2)
} ;
observe (X ≥ 2)
```

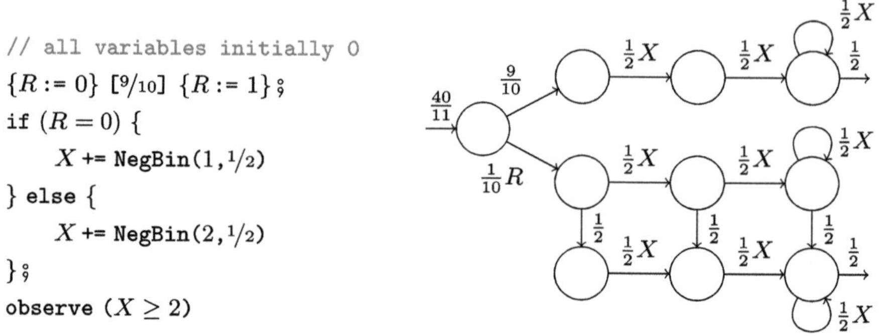

Fig. 1. *Left:* High-risk policyholder model in ReDiP. *Right:* Illustration of the PGA construction for the posterior distribution (defined in detail in Sect. 4). $\frac{40}{11}$ is the normalization factor resulting from the observe-operation as described in Sect. 4.7.

A key challenge related to ReDiP is its support for some *infinite-support* distributions. Implementing the distribution transformer semantics directly thus requires manipulating such distributions in an effective manner. In [5,14,15], symbolic closed-form expressions of *probability generating functions* (PGFs) were employed for this purpose. In this paper, we propose an automata-theoretic alternative to the PGF approach. Our main idea is to encode distributions over the $\mathbb{N}$-valued variables of a ReDiP program by means of *weighted automata* over a commutative alphabet. This automaton model, which we call *probability generating automata* (PGA), is a restricted form of a weighted multi-counter system: Intuitively, each time a PGA takes an X-transition, the program variable represented by X is incremented. The probability that $X = n$ in the distribution described by a PGA is thus the sum of the weights of all paths containing exactly n many X-transitions; this extends naturally to joint distributions.

Motivating Example: Inferring High-Risk Policyholders. Suppose that an insurance company models the number X of claims filed by each individual policyholder as a Poisson-Gamma model $\theta \sim \text{Gamma}(\alpha,\beta); X \sim \text{Poisson}(\theta)$, which is equivalent to a negative binomial model $X \sim \text{NegBin}(\alpha, \frac{\beta}{1+\beta})$ [26].[1] For simplicity, we further assume a Bernoulli prior on α ($\alpha = 1$ with prior probability 0.9; $\alpha = 2$ with prior probability 0.1) and fix $\beta = 1$; these choices imply that low-risk customers ($\alpha = 1$) file one claim on average, whereas high-risk policyholders ($\alpha = 2$) file two claims. Now consider the following scenario: An employee of the insurance notices that she is processing, for the second time, a claim of the same policyholder—hence she knows that this individual has filed *at least* two claims. A typical inference problem is to determine the probability of the customer being in the high-risk category. This situation can be modeled in ReDiP as shown in Fig. 1, and solved[2] by analyzing the resulting automaton (see Example 3).

---

[1] Poisson and gamma distributions are not supported directly by our language.
[2] The posterior probability of being high-risk is exactly $2/11 \approx 0.182$.

Contributions. In summary, the contributions of this paper are as follows:

- We propose encoding joint distributions—possibly with infinite support—over non-negative integer variables as certain weighted automata (Sect. 2).
- We provide an effective translation from programs to automata transformations, enabling posterior inference via common automata-theoretic constructions (Sects. 3 and 4).
- We prove our approach sound with regards to an existing *operational* program semantics in terms of Markov chains [23] (Sect. 5).

An extended version of this paper is available online [8].

2   Background on Weighted Automata

We define $\mathbb{R}_+ = \{r \in \mathbb{R} \mid r \geq 0\}$, $\mathbb{R}_+^\infty = \mathbb{R}_+ \cup \{\infty\}$, and $\mathbb{B} = \{0, 1\}$.

Semirings and Formal Power Series. The following definitions closely follow [19]. A *semiring* is a 5-tuple $(\mathbb{S}, +, \cdot, 0, 1)$ where $(\mathbb{S}, +, 0)$ is a commutative monoid, $(\mathbb{S}, \cdot, 1)$ is a monoid, $\cdot$ distributes over $+$, and $a \cdot 0 = 0 \cdot a = 0$ for all $a \in \mathbb{S}$. If the operations and neutral elements are clear from the context, we only use $\mathbb{S}$ to refer to the semiring. We call a semiring $\mathbb{S}$ *naturally ordered* if the binary relation $a \sqsubseteq b \overset{\text{def}}{\iff} \exists c \in \mathbb{S} : a + c = b$ forms a partial order on $\mathbb{S}$. A semiring together with a sum operator $\sum_{i \in I} a_i$ defined for arbitrary—possibly infinite—families $(a_i)_{i \in I}$ is called *complete* if $\sum_{i \in I} a_i$ behaves as usual finite sums for finite I, and is commutative as well as distributive (see [19] for the formal definitions). A naturally ordered, complete semiring $\mathbb{S}$ is called ω-*continuous* if the following condition holds for all *countable* families $(a_i)_{i \in \mathbb{N}}$: $\forall c \in \mathbb{S} : \forall n \in \mathbb{N} : \sum_{i \leq n} a_i \sqsubseteq c \implies \sum_{i \in \mathbb{N}} a_i \sqsubseteq c$.

Two ω-continuous semirings of interest are the *Boolean semiring* $(\mathbb{B}, \vee, \wedge, 0, 1)$ and the *non-negative extended real semiring* $(\mathbb{R}_+^\infty, +, \cdot, 0, 1)$. In the latter, the sum operator is defined via $\sum_{i \in I} a_i = \sup\{\sum_{i \in E} a_i \mid E \subseteq I, E \text{ finite}\}$, which possibly evaluates to the ∞ element.

Given an ω-continuous semiring $(\mathbb{S}, +, \cdot, 0, 1)$ and a monoid $(\mathbb{M}, \circ, e)$, we define the set $\mathbb{S}\langle\!\langle \mathbb{M} \rangle\!\rangle$ of *formal power series* (FPS) as the set of maps $\{f : \mathbb{M} \to \mathbb{S}\}$. As usual, FPS are denoted as "formal infinite sums" $f = \sum_{m \in \mathbb{M}} f(m)\ m$. We call $f(m)$ the *coefficient* of $m \in \mathbb{M}$ and define the *support* of f as $\mathrm{supp}(f) = \{m \in \mathbb{M} \mid f(m) \neq 0\}$. $\mathbb{S}\langle\!\langle \mathbb{M} \rangle\!\rangle$ is a semiring with the following operations: For all $f_1, f_2 \in \mathbb{S}\langle\!\langle \mathbb{M} \rangle\!\rangle$ and $m \in \mathbb{M}$, $(f_1 + f_2)(m) = f_1(m) + f_2(m)$ and $(f_1 \cdot f_2)(m) = \sum_{m = m_1 \circ m_2} f_1(m_1) \cdot f_2(m_2)$. The neutral elements are 0 and $1e = e$. If $\mathbb{S}$ is ω-continuous, then so is $\mathbb{S}\langle\!\langle \mathbb{M} \rangle\!\rangle$ [19].

Example 1 (Formal Power Series). We illustrate FPS by means of the instances relevant to this paper. The overall idea is that FPS generalize the concept of (weighted) formal languages. Let V be a finite alphabet.

- V^* is a monoid with concatenation and neutral element ε, and $\mathbb{B}\langle\!\langle V^* \rangle\!\rangle$ is isomorphic to the *semiring of formal languages* 2^{V^*} over V. In this semiring, addition is union and multiplication is word-wise concatenation of languages.

– Languages over *commutative* symbols can be modeled using the monoid $\mathbb{N}^V = \{\sigma\colon V \to \mathbb{N}\} \cong \mathbb{N}^{|V|}$ with pointwise addition. In this paper, we employ FPS from $\mathbb{R}_+^\infty \langle\!\langle \mathbb{N}^V \rangle\!\rangle$ to encode distributions over $\mathbb{N}^V$. For instance,

$$\tfrac{1}{2}Y \;+\; \tfrac{1}{4}XY^2 \;+\; \tfrac{1}{8}X^2Y^3 \;+\; \ldots \quad \in \mathbb{R}_+^\infty \langle\!\langle \mathbb{N}^V \rangle\!\rangle$$

describes a joint distribution over the variables $V = \{X, Y, \ldots\}$ where X is geometrically distributed and, with probability 1, $Y = X + 1$ and $Z = 0$ for all $Z \in V \setminus \{X, Y\}$. Note that we use *monomial notation*[3] for the variable valuations $\mathbb{N}^V$.

Weighted Automata over Semirings. We adopt the following automaton model:

Definition 1 (Weighted Automaton [19]). *Let $\mathbb{S}$ be an ω-continuous semiring and let $\emptyset \neq \mathbb{S}' \subseteq \mathbb{S}$. An $\mathbb{S}'$-automaton over $\mathbb{S}$ is a 4-tuple $\mathcal{A} = (Q, M, I, F)$ where $Q \neq \emptyset$ is a finite set of* states, *$M \in \mathbb{S}'^{Q \times Q}$ is a transition matrix, and $I \in \mathbb{S}'^{1 \times Q}$ and $F \in \mathbb{S}'^{Q \times 1}$ are vectors of initial and* final weights, *respectively.*

Notice that only the elements in $\mathbb{S}'$ are allowed as transition labels and initial/final weights. A state $s \in Q$ is called *initial (final)* if $I_s \neq 0$ ($F_s \neq 0$), where 0 refers to the semiring zero. The *behavior* (or semantics) of $\mathcal{A}$ is defined as

$$\|\mathcal{A}\| \;=\; IM^*F \;\in\; \mathbb{S}\,, \qquad \text{where} \quad M^* = \sum_{n \in \mathbb{N}} M^n\,.$$

The infinite sum M^* is well-defined because $\mathbb{S}$ is complete by assumption. Intuitively, $\|\mathcal{A}\|$ is the semiring-sum of the weights of all finite-length paths in $\mathcal{A}$, where the weight of a path is the semiring-product of the initial weight of its first state, the weights of its transitions, and the weight of the final state. As usual, we often represent automata graphically; we use *unlabeled* dangling arrows for initial and final states with weight 1, and *labeled* dangling arrows for initial and final states with a weight other than 1.

We only consider automata over FPS semirings $\mathbb{S}\langle\!\langle \mathbb{M} \rangle\!\rangle$ in this paper. Let $\mathcal{A} = (Q, M, I, F)$ be such an automaton. We write $\mathcal{A}\colon s \xrightarrow{a\,m} t$ iff $M_{s,t}(m) = a$, where $s, t, \in Q$, $a \in \mathbb{S}$, $m \in \mathbb{M}$; $\mathcal{A}$ may be omitted if clear from context. Further, we say that $\mathcal{A}$ is *normalized*[4] if $\bigcup_{s \in Q} \mathrm{supp}(I_s) \cup \mathrm{supp}(F_s)$ is either $\emptyset$ or $\{e\}$, where e is the unit of $\mathbb{M}$. For $\mathbb{B}\langle\!\langle V^* \rangle\!\rangle$ and $\mathbb{R}_+^\infty \langle\!\langle \mathbb{N}^V \rangle\!\rangle$ (see Example 1), this condition means that the initial and final weights are elements from $\mathbb{B}$ and $\mathbb{R}_+^\infty$, respectively.

Example 2 (Relevant Automata in this Paper). Let V be a finite alphabet.

– Define the following subset of $\mathbb{R}_+^\infty \langle\!\langle \mathbb{N}^V \rangle\!\rangle$:

$$\mathbb{R}_+ V \;=\; \{rX \mid r \in \mathbb{R}_+, X \in V\} \cup \mathbb{R}_+$$

---

[3] Formally, assuming $V = \{X_1, \ldots, X_k\}$, $\sigma \in \mathbb{N}^V$ is written as $X_1^{\sigma(X_1)} \ldots X_k^{\sigma(X_k)}$ where variables with an exponent of 0 are omitted.

[4] The notion of normalization in [19] is slightly stronger than ours.

The protagonists of our method are $\mathbb{R}_+ V$-automata over the semiring $\mathbb{R}_+^\infty\langle\!\langle\mathbb{N}^V\rangle\!\rangle$ (see Fig. 1 for an example). The behavior of such an automaton is an FPS where the coefficient of $\sigma \in \mathbb{N}^V$ equals the sum of the weights of all paths in which every $X \in V$ appears exactly $\sigma(X)$ many times. An $\mathbb{R}_+ V$-automaton is thus similar to a weighted multi-counter system with $|V|$ counters admitting increment operations only.

- A *nondeterministic finite automaton* (NFA) over alphabet V is a normalized 2^V-automaton over the *semiring of formal languages* $\mathbb{B}\langle\!\langle V^*\rangle\!\rangle \cong 2^{V^*}$. A *deterministic* finite automaton (DFA) is an NFA with the additional restrictions that (i) there exists exactly one initial state, and (ii) for all $s \in Q$ and $X \in V$ there exists exactly one $t \in Q$ such that $s \xrightarrow{X} t$.

Probability Generating Functions and Automata. A *probability generating function* (PGF) is an FPS $f \in \mathbb{R}_+\langle\!\langle\mathbb{N}^V\rangle\!\rangle$ with *mass* $\sum_{\sigma\in\mathbb{N}^V} f(\sigma) \leq 1$. A PGF thus describes a probability (sub-)distribution on $\mathbb{N}^V$, see Example 1.

Definition 2 (PGA: Probability Generating Automaton). *A PGA is an $\mathbb{R}_+ V$-automaton $\mathcal{A}$ over $\mathbb{R}_+^\infty\langle\!\langle\mathbb{N}^V\rangle\!\rangle$ s.t. $\|\mathcal{A}\|$ is a PGF, i.e. $\sum_{\sigma\in\mathbb{N}^V}\|\mathcal{A}\|(\sigma) \leq 1$.*

Although all coefficients are included in $[0,1]$, $[0,1]$ alone is not sufficient as we need elements from $\mathbb{R}_{>1}$ for normalization (see Fig. 1).

Figure 2 provides examples of PGA for basic distributions; it can be checked that $\|\mathcal{A}_{\mathtt{Geom}_X(\mathtt{p})}\| = \sum_{i\geq 0}(1-p)^i p X^i$, $\|\mathcal{A}_{\mathtt{Bern}_X(\mathtt{p})}\| = 1-p+pX$, $\|\mathcal{A}_{\mathtt{Dirac}_X(\mathtt{n})}\| = X^n$, and $\|\mathcal{A}_{\mathtt{Unif}_X(\mathtt{m})}\| = \sum_{i=0}^{m-1}\frac{1}{m}X^i$. More generally, we say that a distribution is *PGA-definable* if its PGF is the behavior of some PGA. It follows from the definitions that the class of PGA-definable distributions includes the so-called *discrete-phase distributions* (see, e.g., [3]); a more thorough characterization of PGA-definable distributions is left for future work.

It may not always be obvious if a given automaton is a PGA, i.e. if the sum of the weights of its finite paths is at most 1. However, the following lemma asserts that this can be tested in polynomial time:

Lemma 1. *For every given[5] $\mathbb{R}_+ V$-automaton $\mathcal{A}$ over $\mathbb{R}_+^\infty\langle\!\langle\mathbb{N}^V\rangle\!\rangle$, the exact mass $\sum_{\sigma\in\mathbb{N}^V}\|\mathcal{A}\|(\sigma) \in \mathbb{R}_+^\infty$ can be computed in polynomial time in the size of $\mathcal{A}$.*

Proof. We construct an $\mathbb{R}_+$-automaton $\mathcal{A}' = (Q, M, I, F)$ from $\mathcal{A}$ by removing the symbols V from the transitions of $\mathcal{A}$ (see "transition label substitution" in Sect. 4.1), as well as from its initial and final weights. It can be verified that $\|\mathcal{A}'\| = \sum_{\sigma\in\mathbb{N}^V}\|\mathcal{A}\|(\sigma)$. Next, we use that $\|\mathcal{A}'\| = IB$, where B is the componentwise least solution of the linear equation system $B = MB + F$ over $\mathbb{R}_+^\infty$, see [19, Thm. 4.1]. Consequently, $\|\mathcal{A}'\|$ is either the optimal value of the linear program "minimize IB s.t. $B = MB + F \wedge B \geq 0$," or ∞ if the linear program is infeasible. In either case, the outcome can be determined in polynomial time.

---

[5] This statement assumes binary-encoded *rational* numbers as transition weights.

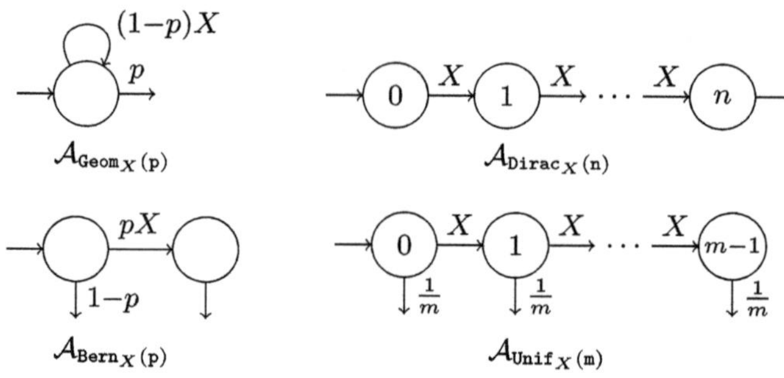

Fig. 2. PGA for basic distributions ($X \in V, p \in [0,1], n \in \mathbb{N}, m \in \mathbb{N}_{>0}$ are constants).

3   Probabilistic Programs

Let V be a finite alphabet of *program variables*, fixed throughout the rest of the paper. The following is a slight extension[6] of (loop-free) `ReDiP` from [5,15]:

Definition 3 (Syntax of `ReDiP`). *`ReDiP` programs $\mathcal{P}$ adhere to the following grammar (where $X, Y \in V$, and D is a PGA-definable distribution):*

$$
\begin{array}{lll}
\mathcal{P} & ::= & X := 0 \qquad\qquad\qquad\qquad\qquad \text{Set variable } X \text{ to } 0 \\
& \mid & X \mathrel{+}= n \qquad\qquad\qquad \text{Increment by constant } n \in \mathbb{N} \\
& \mid & X \mathrel{+}= D \qquad\qquad \text{Increment by random sample from } D \\
& \mid & X \mathrel{+}= Y \qquad\qquad\qquad\quad \text{Increment by variable} \\
& \mid & X \mathrel{+}= \texttt{iid}(D,Y) \quad \text{Increment by sum of } Y \text{ i.i.d. samples from } D \\
& \mid & \{\mathcal{P}\}\ [p]\ \{\mathcal{P}\} \qquad\qquad \text{Random branching } (p \in [0,1]) \\
& \mid & \texttt{if } (\varphi)\ \{\mathcal{P}\}\ \texttt{else }\{\mathcal{P}\} \qquad\quad \text{Conditional branching} \\
& \mid & X\texttt{--} \qquad\qquad \text{Decrement (``monus'' semantics)} \\
& \mid & \texttt{observe } (\varphi) \qquad\qquad\qquad\qquad \text{Conditioning} \\
& \mid & \mathcal{P}\,\mathbin{;}\mathcal{P} \qquad\qquad\qquad \text{Sequential composition} \\
\varphi & ::= & X < n \ \mid\ X \equiv_m n \ \mid\ \varphi \wedge \varphi \ \mid\ \neg\varphi \qquad \text{Guards } (n, m \in \mathbb{N}, m > n)
\end{array}
$$

The particular instruction set of `ReDiP` is chosen so that each instruction roughly corresponds to an elementary automata-theoretic construction, see Sect. 4. The intended effect of each statement should be sufficiently clear, perhaps with the exception of $X \mathrel{+}= \texttt{iid}(D,Y)$ and `observe` (φ), which we explain in Sects. 4.3 and 4.7, respectively. Notice that the instructions 1–2 and 4 together allow assigning linear expressions with coefficients in $\mathbb{N}$ to variables. For instance,

---

[6] Specifically, we allow $\equiv_m$ (congruence modulo m) in guards, and explicitly incorporate some statements that are only available as syntactic sugar in [5,15].

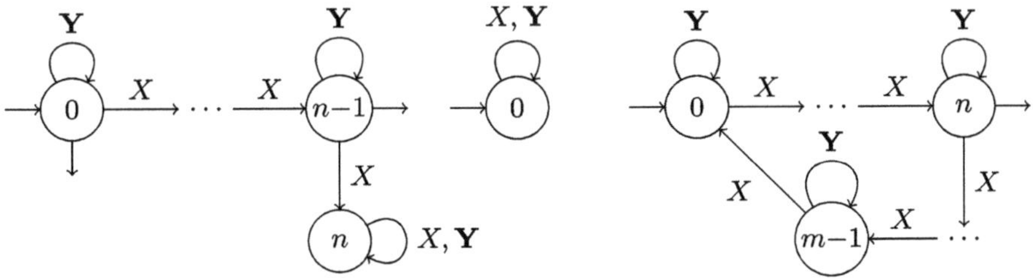

Fig. 3. DFA for guards $\mathcal{B}_{X<n}$ $(n > 0)$, $\mathcal{B}_{X<0}$ $(= \mathcal{B}_{\texttt{false}})$ and $\mathcal{B}_{X\equiv_m n}$ $(m > n)$ (with $\mathbf{Y} = V \setminus \{X\}$).

$X := 1 + X + 2Y$ can be expressed as $X := 0 \,\hbox{\fontsize{6pt}{6pt}\selectfont\raisebox{0pt}{\textbf{\textsc{;}}}}\, X \mathrel{+}= 1 \,\hbox{;}\, X \mathrel{+}= Y \,\hbox{;}\, X \mathrel{+}= Y$. We use
$\texttt{skip}$ as a shorthand for the effectless program $X \mathrel{+}= 0$.

An important syntactic restriction of $\texttt{ReDiP}$ is that guards can only compare
variables to *constants*, but not to other variables—hence the name "rectangular".
Other common comparison operators (e.g., $\geq$, $=$) and Boolean connectives (e.g.,
$\vee$, $\rightarrow$) are included as syntactic sugar. The semantics $[\![\varphi]\!]$ of guards is standard
and defined in Table 1. For $\sigma \in \mathbb{N}^V$ we often write $\sigma \models \varphi$ instead of $\sigma \in [\![\varphi]\!]$.

As a first step towards our automata-theoretic interpretation of $\texttt{ReDiP}$ in the
upcoming Sect. 4, we encode the rectangular guards φ from Definition 3 as DFA.
For $w \in V^*$ we define its *Parikh image* $\Psi(w) = \lambda X.|w|_X \in \mathbb{N}^V$; that is, for every
$X \in V$, $\Psi(w)(X)$ is the number of occurrences of X in w.

Table 1. Guard semantics and translation to automata.

Guard φ	Semantics $[\![\varphi]\!]$	Guard DFA $\mathcal{B}_\varphi$
$X < n$	$\{\sigma \in \mathbb{N}^V \mid \sigma(X) < n\}$	see Fig. 3
$X \equiv_m n$	$\{\sigma \in \mathbb{N}^V \mid \sigma(X) = n \mod m\}$	see Fig. 3
$\varphi \wedge \varphi'$	$[\![\varphi]\!] \cap [\![\varphi']\!]$	$\mathcal{B}_\varphi \times \mathcal{B}_{\varphi'}$ (standard DFA product)
$\neg\varphi$	$\mathbb{N}^V \setminus [\![\varphi]\!]$	$\overline{\mathcal{B}_\varphi}$ (standard DFA complement)

Definition 4 (Automaton Modeling a Guard). *We say that an NFA $\mathcal{B}$ over
alphabet V models a guard φ if*

$$\forall w \in V^*: \qquad \mathcal{B} \text{ accepts } w \quad \text{if and only if} \quad \Psi(w) \models \varphi \,.$$

It follows that the language accepted by an NFA modeling some guard is
closed under permutations.

Lemma 2 (Properties of the Automata $\mathcal{B}_\varphi$). *For every guard φ, the
automaton $\mathcal{B}_\varphi$ (defined inductively in Table 1) is a DFA which models φ in the
sense of Definition 4.*

Proof The base automata in Fig. 3 are deterministic and model the corresponding atomic guards. The statement then follows by induction on the structure of φ, using the standard constructions for DFA intersection and complement.

4   Interpreting ReDiP with Weighted Automata

As explained in Sect. 1, we view ReDiP programs semantically as *transformers of probability distributions*: from initial (prior) distributions to final (posterior) distributions. Our philosophy is to represent such distributions with PGA.

In this section, we implement the distribution transformer semantics of ReDiP by means of effective automata-theoretic constructions. More precisely, given a PGA $\mathcal{A}$ (fixed throughout the rest of this section) encoding an initial distribution and a ReDiP program $\mathcal{P}$, we outline an algorithm to construct a PGA $[\![\mathcal{P}]\!](\mathcal{A})$ for the resulting (unnormalized[7]) posterior distribution. The overall construction, which is recursive, is summarized in Table 2.

Lemma 3. *For every ReDiP program $\mathcal{P}$, the automata transformer $[\![\mathcal{P}]\!]$ defined in Table 2 is an endofunction on the set of normalized PGA over variables V.*

Proof (sketch). Follows by induction on the structure of $\mathcal{P}$ since all constructions in Table 2 preserve normalized PGA, which we detail in the following.

Table 2. Inductive definition of the translation from a prior distribution automaton $\mathcal{A}$ to an automaton $[\![\mathcal{P}]\!](\mathcal{A})$ for the (unnormalized) posterior distribution.

$\mathcal{P}$	$[\![\mathcal{P}]\!](\mathcal{A})$	*Construction*
$X := 0$	$\mathcal{A}[X/1]$	Label substitution
$X \mathrel{+}= n$	$\mathcal{A} \cdot \mathcal{A}_{\mathrm{Dirac}_X(n)}$	Concatenation
$X \mathrel{+}= D$	$\mathcal{A} \cdot \mathcal{A}_{D_X}$	Concatenation
$X \mathrel{+}= Y$	$\mathcal{A}[Y/\bigcirc \xrightarrow{Y} \bigcirc \xrightarrow{X} \bigcirc]$	Transition substitution
$X \mathrel{+}= \mathtt{iid}(D,Y)$	$\mathcal{A}[Y/\bigcirc \xrightarrow{Y} \bigcirc \cdot \mathcal{A}_{D_X}]$	Transition substitution
$\{\mathcal{P}_1\}\ [p]\ \{\mathcal{P}_2\}$	$[\![\mathcal{P}_1]\!](\mathcal{A})\,{}^p{\oplus}^{1-p}\,[\![\mathcal{P}_2]\!](\mathcal{A})$	Disjoint union
$\mathtt{if}\ (\varphi)\ \{\mathcal{P}_1\}\ \mathtt{else}\ \{\mathcal{P}_2\}$	$[\![\mathcal{P}_1]\!](\mathcal{A} \times \mathcal{B}_\varphi) \oplus [\![\mathcal{P}_2]\!](\mathcal{A} \times \mathcal{B}_{\neg\varphi})$	Products & disjoint union
$X\mathtt{-\!-}$	$\mathcal{A}^{X\mathtt{-\!-}}$	Special construction (Def. 7)
$\mathtt{observe}\ (\varphi)$	$\mathcal{A} \times \mathcal{B}_\varphi$	Product
$\mathcal{P}_1 \mathbin{;} \mathcal{P}_2$	$[\![\mathcal{P}_2]\!]([\![\mathcal{P}_1]\!](\mathcal{A}))$	(None required)

---

[7] $[\![\mathcal{P}]\!](\mathcal{A})$ may describe a *sub*-distribution even if $\|\mathcal{A}\|$ is a proper distribution, i.e. has mass one. Section 4.7 describes how to obtain a PGA for the *normalized* posterior.

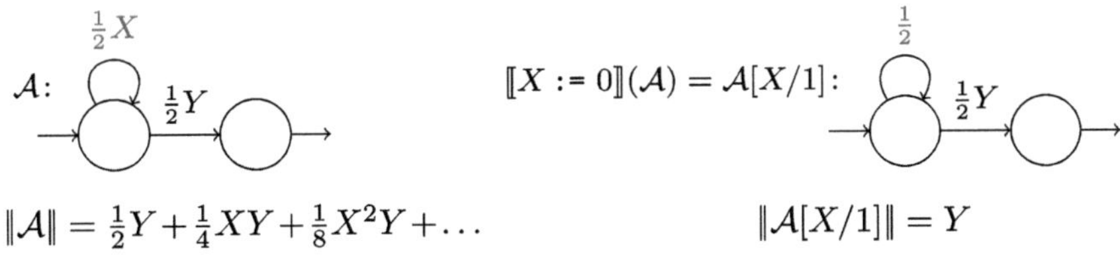

$$\|\mathcal{A}\| = \tfrac{1}{2}Y + \tfrac{1}{4}XY + \tfrac{1}{8}X^2Y + \dots \qquad\qquad \|\mathcal{A}[X/1]\| = Y$$

Fig. 4. Transition label substitution $\mathcal{A}[X/1]$ for implementing the instruction $X := 0$.

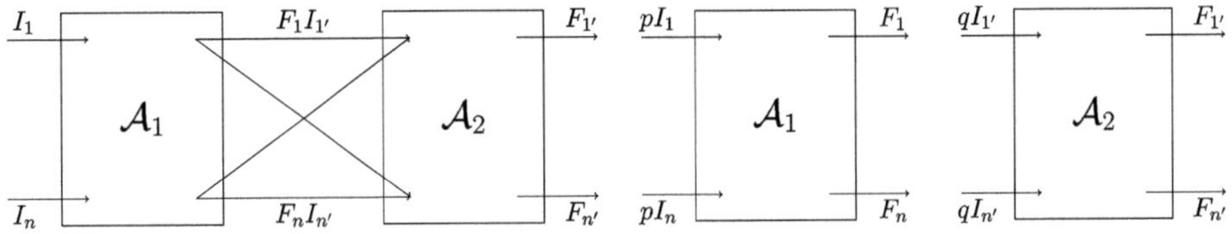

Fig. 5. Concatenation $\mathcal{A}_1 \cdot \mathcal{A}_2$ (left) and weighted disjoint union $\mathcal{A}_1 \,^p\!\oplus^q \mathcal{A}_2$ (right) of weighted automata $\mathcal{A}_1$ and $\mathcal{A}_2$ with disjoint sets of states $\{1, \dots, n\}$ and $\{1', \dots, n'\}$, respectively. We write $\mathcal{A}_1 \oplus \mathcal{A}_2$ instead of $\mathcal{A}_1 \,^1\!\oplus^1 \mathcal{A}_2$.

4.1 Setting a Variable to Zero: Transition Label Substitution

The idea for applying $X := 0$ to the distribution $\|\mathcal{A}\|$ is as follows. Each time $\mathcal{A}$ takes an X-transition, i.e. "increases the X-counter", the updated automaton $[\![X := 0]\!](\mathcal{A})$ must not increase that counter. More formally, we define the automaton $\mathcal{A}[X/1]$ which is almost identical to $\mathcal{A}$, except that all transitions of the form $\bigcirc \xrightarrow{rX} \bigcirc$ in $\mathcal{A}$ (recall $r \in \mathbb{R}_+$) become "ε-transitions" $\bigcirc \xrightarrow{r} \bigcirc$ in $\mathcal{A}[X/1]$. For a normalized $\mathcal{A}$, the effect of this construction on the PGF $\|\mathcal{A}\|$ is a substitution of X by 1; that is, X is marginalized out. See Fig. 4 for an example.

4.2 Incrementing a Variable I: Automata Concatenation

We now consider the statement $X \mathrel{+}= n$ and its generalization $X \mathrel{+}= D$ for incrementing X by a constant and a random sample, respectively.

First, the automaton $[\![X \mathrel{+}= n]\!](\mathcal{A})$ must increment the X-counter an additional n times compared to $\mathcal{A}$. To achieve this, we append a gadget—in fact, the PGA $\mathcal{A}_{\mathrm{Dirac}_X(n)}$ from Fig. 2—to the final states of $\mathcal{A}$. Formally, this construction is the standard *concatenation* $\mathcal{A} \cdot \mathcal{A}_{\mathrm{Dirac}_n(X)}$, defined visually in Fig. 5. For general $\mathbb{S}$-automata $\mathcal{A}_1, \mathcal{A}_2$ ($\mathbb{S}$ an ω-continuous semiring), their concatenation satisfies $\|\mathcal{A}_1 \cdot \mathcal{A}_2\| = \|\mathcal{A}_1\| \cdot \|\mathcal{A}_2\|$; see, e.g., [19, Thm. 4.6].

Second, and more generally, to construct $[\![X \mathrel{+}= D]\!](\mathcal{A})$ we take the concatenation of $\mathcal{A}$ and $\mathcal{A}_{D_X}$, a PGA for distribution D w.r.t. X. Thus, after reaching a final state of $\mathcal{A}$, the automaton $\mathcal{A} \cdot \mathcal{A}_{D_X}$ additionally traverses $\mathcal{A}_{D_X}$, which has the desired effect of incrementing the sample from $\|\mathcal{A}\|$ by a sample from D. We require the PGA for distribution D to also be normalized and have a probability mass of 1.

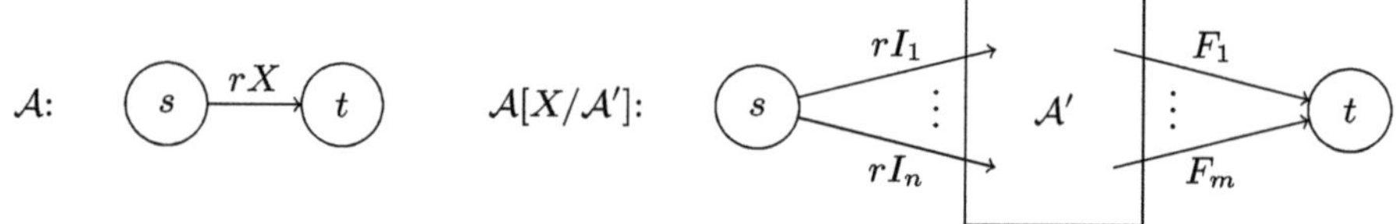

Fig. 6. Transition substitution. The automaton $\mathcal{A}[X/\mathcal{A}']$ arises from $\mathcal{A}$ by replacing *all* transitions $\bigcirc\xrightarrow{rX}\bigcirc$ in $\mathcal{A}$ (left) by the gadget depicted on the right.

4.3   Incrementing a Variable II: Transition Substitution

Next, we consider X += Y. The idea for implementing this statement is a refined variant of transition label substitution. Intuitively, the automaton $[\![X$ += $Y]\!](\mathcal{A})$ should be similar to $\mathcal{A}$, but every time $\mathcal{A}$ increments Y, the new automaton increments both Y *and* X. We thus replace every transition of the form $\bigcirc\xrightarrow{rY}\bigcirc$ in $\mathcal{A}$ by the sub-automaton[8] $\bigcirc\xrightarrow{rY}\bigcirc\xrightarrow{X}\bigcirc$. Notice that this is also meaningful if $X = Y$. We call this operation *transition substitution*:

Definition 5 (Transition Substitution). *For $\mathbb{R}_+V$-automata $\mathcal{A}, \mathcal{A}'$, we define the $\mathbb{R}_+V$-automaton $\mathcal{A}[X/\mathcal{A}']$ as in Fig. 6.*

Observe that label substitution $\mathcal{A}[X/1]$ from Sect. 4.1 is just a shorthand for the transition substitution $\mathcal{A}[X/\bigcirc]$.

We now consider the special statement X += $\mathtt{iid}(D,Y)$. Its intended semantics is that of the program "$\mathtt{for}\ i = 1..Y\ \{\ X$ += $D\ \}$", i.e. X is incremented by a sum of Y many i.i.d. samples from the distribution D. Notice that X += Y is equivalent to X += $\mathtt{iid}(\mathtt{Dirac(1)},Y)$. The motivation for including the rather specialized $\mathtt{iid}$ statement as a primitive in $\mathtt{ReDiP}$ is that it is naturally supported on PGFs in closed form [5] and, as we show here, on PGA. Indeed, we can construct an automaton $[\![X$ += $\mathtt{iid}(D,Y)]\!](\mathcal{A})$ which is again similar to $\mathcal{A}$, except that every time $\mathcal{A}$ traverses a Y-transition, the new automaton additionally traverses $\mathcal{A}_{D_X}$ as a sub-automaton. This amounts to the following transition substitution: $[\![X$ += $\mathtt{iid}(D,Y)]\!](\mathcal{A}) = \mathcal{A}[Y/\bigcirc\xrightarrow{Y}\bigcirc\cdot\mathcal{A}_{D_X}]$.

The $\mathtt{iid}$ statement is also of practical interest: For example, it holds that $\mathtt{Binom}(N,p) = \mathtt{iid}(\mathtt{Bern(p)}, N)$, $\mathtt{NegBin}(N,p) = \mathtt{iid}(\mathtt{Geom(p)}, N)$, etc. Therefore, $\mathtt{ReDiP}$ allows sampling from these distributions even if their parameter N is a program variable, which may itself be non-trivially distributed.

4.4   Random Branching: Disjoint Union

To implement the random branching instruction $\{\mathcal{P}_1\}\ [p]\ \{\mathcal{P}_2\}$, we construct an automaton that, intuitively speaking, behaves like $[\![\mathcal{P}_1]\!](\mathcal{A})$ with probability p and like $[\![\mathcal{P}_2]\!](\mathcal{A})$ with probability $1 - p$. This is achieved by multi-

---

[8] We omit initial and final weights here and assume implicitly, that the left-most state is initial and the right-most state is final (with a weight of 1).

plying each initial weight of $[\![\mathcal{P}_1]\!](\mathcal{A})$ and $[\![\mathcal{P}_2]\!](\mathcal{A})$ by p and $1 - p$, respectively, and taking the *disjoint union* of the resulting two automata (in symbols: $[\![\mathcal{P}_1]\!](\mathcal{A})\,{}^p{\oplus}^{1-p}\,[\![\mathcal{P}_2]\!](\mathcal{A})$; see Fig. 5). The automata $[\![\mathcal{P}_1]\!](\mathcal{A})$ and $[\![\mathcal{P}_2]\!](\mathcal{A})$ themselves are obtained recursively.

4.5 Conditional Branching: Product with Guard Automata

We now consider the statement `if (`φ`) {`$\mathcal{P}_1$`} else {`$\mathcal{P}_2$`}`. The basic idea is to "partition" the distribution $\|\mathcal{A}\|$ relative to φ and $\neg\varphi$, recursively transform the resulting (sub-)distributions—the first by $[\![\mathcal{P}_1]\!]$ and the second by $[\![\mathcal{P}_2]\!]$—and finally sum up the results [17]. To realize the partitioning on automaton-level, we employ the DFA $\mathcal{B}_\varphi$ and $\mathcal{B}_{\neg\varphi}$ from Sect. 3, and take the products $\mathcal{A} \times \mathcal{B}_\varphi$ and $\mathcal{A} \times \mathcal{B}_{\neg\varphi}$. To this end, we rely on the following product construction, a weighted variant of the standard product of an ε-NFA with a (non-ε) NFA:

Definition 6 (Product). *Let $\mathcal{A} = (Q, M, I, F)$ be a $\mathbb{R}_+V$-automaton and let $\mathcal{B} = (Q', M', I', F')$ be an NFA with alphabet V. We define the product $\mathcal{A} \times \mathcal{B}$ as the $\mathbb{R}_+V$-automaton with states $Q \times Q'$ and transitions according to the following rules:*

$$(X\text{-TRANS.})\ \frac{\mathcal{A}\colon q \xrightarrow{aX} r \qquad \mathcal{B}\colon s \xrightarrow{X} t}{\mathcal{A} \times \mathcal{B}\colon (q,s) \xrightarrow{aX} (r,t)} \qquad (\varepsilon\text{-TRANS.})\ \frac{\mathcal{A}\colon q \xrightarrow{a} r \qquad s \in Q'}{\mathcal{A} \times \mathcal{B}\colon (q,s) \xrightarrow{a} (r,s)}$$

The initial and final weight of $(q,s) \in Q \times Q'$ is $I_q \cdot I_s$ and $F_q \cdot F_s$, respectively.

If $\mathcal{A}$ is normalized, then so is $\mathcal{A} \times \mathcal{B}$. The next lemma asserts that the products $\mathcal{A} \times \mathcal{B}_\varphi$ and $\mathcal{A} \times \mathcal{B}_{\neg\varphi}$ have the desired effect (recall that $\mathcal{B}_\varphi$ and $\mathcal{B}_{\neg\varphi}$ are closed under permutations by definition):

Lemma 4. *Let $\mathcal{A}$ be a normalized $\mathbb{R}_+V$-automaton over $\mathbb{R}_+^\infty\langle\!\langle\mathbb{N}^V\rangle\!\rangle$ and let $\mathcal{B}$ be a DFA[9] over alphabet V. Assume that the language accepted by $\mathcal{B}$ is closed under permutations. Then, for all $\sigma \in \mathbb{N}^V$, it holds that*

$$\|\mathcal{A} \times \mathcal{B}\|(\sigma) \;=\; \begin{cases} \|\mathcal{A}\|(\sigma) & \text{if } \mathcal{B} \text{ accepts some } w \in V^* \text{ with } \Psi(w) = \sigma, \\ 0 & \text{else.} \end{cases}$$

To complete the construction for `if (`φ`) {`$\mathcal{P}_1$`} else {`$\mathcal{P}_2$`}`, we obtain $[\![\mathcal{P}_1]\!](\mathcal{A} \times \mathcal{B}_\varphi)$ and $[\![\mathcal{P}_2]\!](\mathcal{A} \times \mathcal{B}_{\neg\varphi})$ recursively and recombine them via disjoint union (see Table 2).

4.6 Decrementing a Variable: Specialized Construction

The decrement statement $X\,\texttt{-{}-}$ is somewhat involved since our program variables are non-negative. Following [5], we adopt the convention that decrementing 0 has no effect, i.e. $X\,\texttt{-{}-}$ is equivalent to `if (`$X > 0$`) {`$X\texttt{-{}-}$`} else {skip}`. Based on

---

[9] Lemma 4 holds more generally if $\mathcal{B}$ is only unambiguous instead of deterministic.

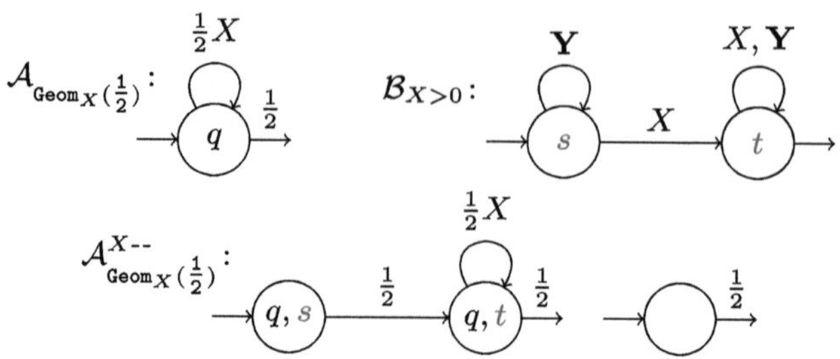

Fig. 7. Example for the decrement construction from Definition 7 (with $\mathbf{Y} = V \setminus \{X\}$).

this, we propose to implement X-- similar to `if-else` from Sect. 4.5 as follows: We first filter $\mathcal{A}$ w.r.t. $X > 0$; that is, we take the product $\mathcal{A} \times \mathcal{B}_{X>0}$. Afterwards, we convert *the first* X-transition on any path of this product to an ε-transition. This is achieved by a transition label substitution, which is, however, only applied to the transitions of the form $(\dots, s) \xrightarrow{rX} (\dots, t)$, where $s \neq t$ are the two states of $\mathcal{B}_{X>0}$. Finally, we take the disjoint union with $\mathcal{A} \times \mathcal{B}_{X=0}$, which has the same behavior as $\mathcal{A}[X/0]$. See Fig. 7 for an example. Formally:

Definition 7 (Decrement Automaton). *Let $\mathcal{A}$ be a normalized PGA and let s, t be the two states of $\mathcal{B}_{X>0}$. Consider the PGA $\mathcal{A}' = (\mathcal{A} \times \mathcal{B}_{X>0}) \oplus \mathcal{A}[X/0]$. The decrement PGA $\mathcal{A}^{X\text{--}}$ is obtained from $\mathcal{A}'$ via replacing every transition $(q, s) \xrightarrow{rX} (u, t)$ by $(q, s) \xrightarrow{r} (u, t)$, where q, u are arbitrary states of $\mathcal{A}$, and $r \in \mathbb{R}_+$.*

4.7   Conditioning (`observe`): Product

The purpose of the `observe` (φ) statement is to discard the portion of the input distribution $\|\mathcal{A}\|$ violating φ. This may yield a proper sub-distribution, the *unnormalized posterior*. Implementing `observe` (φ) on PGA-level works similarly to conditional branching (Sect. 4.5): We define $[\![\text{observe } (\varphi)]\!](\mathcal{A}) = \mathcal{A} \times \mathcal{B}_\varphi$, i.e. we filter the distribution $\|\mathcal{A}\|$ according to φ.

A PGA norm($\mathcal{A}$) for the *normalized* distribution of any arbitrary PGA $\mathcal{A}$— this applies in particular to the unnormalized posterior PGA $[\![\mathcal{P}]\!](\mathcal{A})$ resulting from a program $\mathcal{P}$—can be effectively constructed as follows: Let $M_\mathcal{A}$ be the probability mass of the (sub-)distribution $\|\mathcal{A}\|$, which can be determined using Lemma 1, and let

$$\text{norm}(\mathcal{A}) = \begin{cases} \mathcal{A} \text{ with initial weights multiplied by } \frac{1}{M_\mathcal{A}} & \text{if } M_\mathcal{A} > 0 \,, \\ \text{undefined} & \text{if } M_\mathcal{A} = 0 \,. \end{cases}$$

If defined, it follows that $\|\text{norm}(\mathcal{A})\| = \frac{1}{M_\mathcal{A}}\|\mathcal{A}\|$, as desired. Notice that we could have defined norm($\cdot$) equivalently by scaling up the final instead of the initial weights.

Example 3. Figure 1 shows a program and the resulting normalized posterior PGA^{10} with respect to a prior Dirac distribution where all variables are 0 with probability 1. The normalizing constant $\frac{11}{40}$ can be computed "by hand" (i.e. without solving an explicit LP) as follows: We consider the upper and the lower branch of the automaton in Fig. 1 separately. The upper branch has a mass of

$$\tfrac{9}{10} \cdot \tfrac{1}{2} \cdot \tfrac{1}{2} \cdot \left(\tfrac{1}{2}\right)^* \cdot \tfrac{1}{2} \;=\; \tfrac{9}{40}$$

whereas the lower branch has mass

$$\tfrac{1}{10} \cdot \left(\tfrac{1}{2} \cdot \tfrac{1}{2} \cdot \left(\tfrac{1}{2}\right)^* \cdot \tfrac{1}{2} \cdot \left(\tfrac{1}{2}\right)^* \cdot \tfrac{1}{2} + 2 \cdot \left(\tfrac{1}{2} \cdot \tfrac{1}{2} \cdot \tfrac{1}{2} \cdot \left(\tfrac{1}{2}\right)^* \cdot \tfrac{1}{2}\right)\right) \;=\; \tfrac{1}{20} \cdot$$

Here, we have used that $\left(\tfrac{1}{2}\right)^* = \sum_{n=0}^{\infty}\left(\tfrac{1}{2}\right)^n = 2$. The mass of the unnormalized posterior PGA, i.e. the normalizing constant, is therefore $\frac{9}{40} + \frac{1}{20} = \frac{11}{40}$.

4.8   Complexity

We conclude this section by examining the overall complexity of the construction resulting from Table 2. We define the *size* $|\mathcal{A}|$ of a PGA $\mathcal{A}$ as the number of transitions with non-zero weight, and the size of a guard φ (see Table 1) recursively as $|\varphi_1 \wedge \varphi_2| = |\varphi_1| + |\varphi_2|$, $|\neg\varphi| = |\varphi|$, and $|\varphi| = 1$ for the other two atomic cases. Similarly, the size $|\mathcal{P}|$ of a ReDiP program $\mathcal{P}$ is defined recursively as $|\mathcal{P}_1 \,\mathring{,}\, \mathcal{P}_2| = |\mathcal{P}_1| + |\mathcal{P}_2|$, $|\text{if } (\varphi) \{\mathcal{P}_1\} \text{ else } \{\mathcal{P}_2\}| = |\{\mathcal{P}_1\} \, [p] \, \{\mathcal{P}_2\}| = 1 + |\mathcal{P}_1| + |\mathcal{P}_2|$, and $|\mathcal{P}| = 1$ for all base cases. Intuitively, the size of a program is roughly proportional to the length of the program text.

Theorem 1 (Complexity). *For every ReDiP program $\mathcal{P}$ and PGA $\mathcal{A}$ we have*

$$|[\![\mathcal{P}]\!](\mathcal{A})| \;\in\; \mathcal{O}\big(|\mathcal{A}| \cdot |\mathcal{A}_D|^{|\mathcal{P}|} \cdot n^{|\mathcal{P}|\eta}\big)$$

where $|\mathcal{A}_D|$ is the size of the largest distribution automaton in $\mathcal{P}$, $n \in \mathbb{N}$ is the largest constant[11] in $\mathcal{P}$, and $\eta = \max\{|\varphi|, 1\}$ where $|\varphi|$ is the size of the largest guard in $\mathcal{P}$.

Mitigating the exponential worst-case complexity by minimising the intermediate PGA is a promising direction for future work.

5   Soundness Relative to Operational Semantics

In this section, we prove that our PGA transformations from Table 2 are sound with respect to an existing (small-step) operational semantics for imperative probabilistic programs as presented in [23]. This semantics is defined in terms of a (discrete-time) *Markov chain*, where the states are tuples $\langle \mathcal{P}, \sigma \rangle$, containing the program statement to be executed next and the current variable valuation.

---

[10] Unreachable states have been removed and some transitions are slightly simplified.

[11] Recall from Definition 3 that integer constants can occur on the right hand side of increment instructions and in guards.

Additionally, there are some special states, which are detailed below. The transitions of the Markov chain model individual execution steps. An excerpt of the rules defining this Markov chain is given in Fig. 8. We remark that the straightforward rule (SAMPLE) was not included in [23]; we have incorporated it to model the `ReDiP` statement $x \mathrel{+}= D$, which increments the variable x by a random sample from a distribution D over $\mathbb{N}$. In the subsequent discussion, we disregard programs containing the special `iid` instruction because its operational semantics is somewhat involved. In fact, the `iid` statement has not been discussed in prior work on operational semantics [23]. A complete construction is left for future work.

Formally, a *Markov chain* can be defined as a $[0,1]$-weighted automaton $\mathcal{M} = (S, P, I)$ without final weights where the initial weights I sum to at most one, and where the matrix P is (row-)stochastic.

Definition 8 (Markov Chain Semantics). *Let $\mathcal{A}$ be a PGA (for the initial distribution) and let $\mathcal{P}$ be a `ReDiP` program without `iid` statements. We define the operational Markov chain $\mathcal{M}_{\mathcal{A}}[\![\mathcal{P}]\!] = (S, P, I)$ as follows:*

- $S = \big(\texttt{ReDiP} \cup \{\downarrow\}\big) \times \mathbb{N}^V \cup \{\langle \lightning \rangle\}$
- $I(s) = \begin{cases} \|\mathcal{A}\|(\sigma) & \text{if } s = \langle \mathcal{P}, \sigma \rangle, \\ 0 & \text{else} \end{cases}$
- $P(s,t) = \begin{cases} p & \text{if } s \xrightarrow{p} t \text{ is derivable from the rules in Fig. 8,} \\ 0 & \text{else} \end{cases}$

States of the form $\langle \downarrow, \sigma \rangle$ indicate that the program has *terminated* in state σ; the special absorbing state $\langle \lightning \rangle$ is entered once an observation violation occurs. We can now state our soundness theorem formally.

Theorem 2 (Soundness w.r.t. Operational Semantics). *Let $\mathcal{A}$ be a PGA and let $\mathcal{P}$ be a `ReDiP` program (without `iid` statements) such that $\mathrm{norm}([\![\mathcal{P}]\!](\mathcal{A}))$ is defined. Then, for all $\sigma \in \mathbb{N}^V$, it holds that*

$$\|\mathrm{norm}([\![\mathcal{P}]\!](\mathcal{A}))\|(\sigma) = \mathrm{Pr}^{\mathcal{M}_{\mathcal{A}}[\![\mathcal{P}]\!]}(\lozenge\langle \downarrow, \sigma \rangle \mid \neg\lozenge\langle \lightning \rangle),$$

where the right hand side is the conditional probability of reaching state $\langle \downarrow, \sigma \rangle$ in $\mathcal{M}_{\mathcal{A}}[\![\mathcal{P}]\!]$ given that $\langle \lightning \rangle$ is not reached (see [23] for the formal definition).

Example 4 (Operational Markov Chain). Consider the program

$$\mathcal{P} = \overbrace{\underbrace{\{X \mathrel{+}= Y\}}_{\mathcal{P}_{11}} [^1\!/_2] \underbrace{\{\texttt{skip}\}}_{\mathcal{P}_{12}}}^{\mathcal{P}_1} \; \fatsemi \; \underbrace{\texttt{observe } (X = 0)}_{\mathcal{P}_2}.$$

Assuming an initial PGA $\mathcal{A}$ with $\|\mathcal{A}\| = \frac{1}{2} + \frac{1}{2}Y^2$, the reachable fragment of the resulting operational Markov chain $\mathcal{M}_{\mathcal{A}}[\![\mathcal{P}]\!]$ is depicted in Fig. 9. We have:

$$- \ \Pr^{\mathcal{M}_{\mathcal{A}}[\![\mathcal{P}]\!]}(\Diamond\langle\downarrow, \sigma_{00}\rangle) = \tfrac{1}{2} = \|[\![\mathcal{P}]\!](\mathcal{A})\|(\sigma_{00})$$
$$- \ \Pr^{\mathcal{M}_{\mathcal{A}}[\![\mathcal{P}]\!]}(\Diamond\langle\downarrow, \sigma_{02}\rangle) = \tfrac{1}{4} = \|[\![\mathcal{P}]\!](\mathcal{A})\|(\sigma_{02})$$
$$- \ \Pr^{\mathcal{M}_{\mathcal{A}}[\![\mathcal{P}]\!]}(\Diamond\langle\lightning\rangle) = \tfrac{1}{4} = 1 - \tfrac{3}{4} = \sum_{\sigma\in\mathbb{N}^V}\|\mathcal{A}\|(\sigma) - \sum_{\sigma\in\mathbb{N}^V}\|[\![\mathcal{P}]\!](\mathcal{A})\|(\sigma)$$
$$- \ \Pr^{\mathcal{M}_{\mathcal{A}}[\![\mathcal{P}]\!]}(\Diamond\langle\downarrow, \sigma_{00}\rangle \mid \neg\Diamond\langle\lightning\rangle) = \tfrac{1/2}{3/4} = \tfrac{2}{3} = \|\mathrm{norm}([\![\mathcal{P}]\!](\mathcal{A}))\|(\sigma_{00})$$
$$- \ \Pr^{\mathcal{M}_{\mathcal{A}}[\![\mathcal{P}]\!]}(\Diamond\langle\downarrow, \sigma_{02}\rangle \mid \neg\Diamond\langle\lightning\rangle) = \tfrac{1/4}{3/4} = \tfrac{1}{3} = \|\mathrm{norm}([\![\mathcal{P}]\!](\mathcal{A}))\|(\sigma_{02})$$

$$(\textsc{Sample})\ \frac{D \in \mathit{Distr}(\mathbb{N}) \qquad D(n) = p}{\langle X \mathrel{+}= D, \sigma\rangle \xrightarrow{p} \langle\downarrow, \sigma[X \leftarrow \sigma(X) + n]\rangle} \qquad (\textsc{Obs-f})\ \frac{\sigma \not\models \varphi}{\langle\mathbf{observe}\ (\varphi), \sigma\rangle \rightarrow \langle\lightning\rangle}$$

$$(\textsc{Choice-l})\ \frac{}{\langle\{\mathcal{P}_1\}\ [p]\ \{\mathcal{P}_2\}, \sigma\rangle \xrightarrow{p} \langle\mathcal{P}_1, \sigma\rangle} \qquad \ldots$$

Fig. 8. Excerpt of the operational Markov chain semantics (see [8, Appendix A.4] for full details). Sample is a new rule added for this paper.

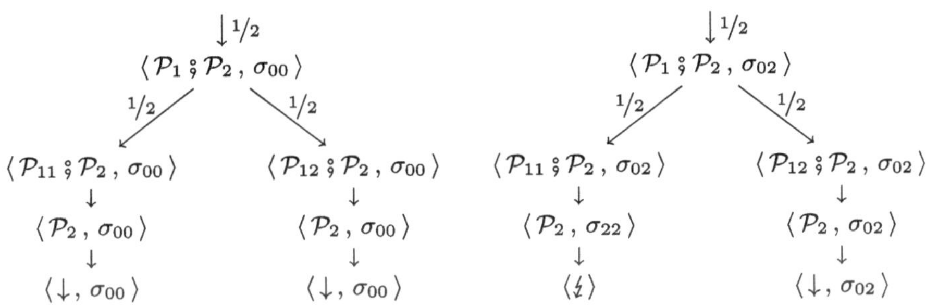

Fig. 9. Operational Markov chain of the program $\mathcal{P}$ from Example 4. σ_{ij} refers to a variable valuation σ satisfying $\sigma(X) = i$ and $\sigma(Y) = j$.

6   Related Work

The general idea of probabilistic programming as an engineer-friendly paradigm for encoding statistical inference problems goes back to at least [16]. As mentioned in Sect. 1, our work is primarily inspired by more recent research focused on the analysis of probabilistic programs and exact inference using probability generating functions (PGFs) [5,14,15,27]. Our approach can be seen as an automata-theoretic counterpart to these methods.

Several alternative techniques for exact inference have been proposed. The tool Dice [13] leverages weighted model counting, but it is not directly applicable to programs that sample from distributions with infinite support. The

`PSI` tool [7] employs symbolic representations of probability density functions to perform inference. In [24], sum-product expressions are used to compactly represent complex distributions. *Weakest pre-expectations* [18,22], a probabilistic generalization of classic weakest preconditions, were amended to conditioning and inference in [23]. The more recent paper [6] focuses on exact inference in programs with recursion by compiling them to systems of polynomial equations. Probabilistic model checking techniques for computing exact conditional probabilities exist as well [1], but these methods are generally restricted to programs unwinding to *finite* Markov chains.

Finally, we mention that there exist mature probabilistic programming systems such as `Stan` [4], `WebPPL` [9], and others. These tools typically focus on *approximate* inference using Monte-Carlo sampling methods.

7   Conclusion and Future Work

We have introduced a method for performing exact inference within a class of syntactically restricted discrete probabilistic programs with infinite support distributions. The core idea is to represent a program's posterior distribution as a weighted automaton derivable from the program text via standard automata-theoretic constructions.

For future work, we aim to explore the possibility of relaxing some of the syntactic restrictions imposed by the `ReDiP` language. Notably, [27] has recently extended the PGF-based approach from [5,15] to support certain *continuous* distributions. Investigating how such extensions could be integrated into our PGA encoding presents an intriguing direction. Another promising avenue is to enrich the PGA model with more expressive automata-theoretic features, such as stacks or registers. Given the extensive body of work in automata theory, we believe this framework is well-suited for characterizing broader classes of probabilistic programs where inference—and possibly other analysis problems—remain decidable.

We also plan to implement our approach, potentially building on existing probabilistic model checkers such as `Storm` [12] or `PRISM` [20]. After all, the PGA resulting from our construction often resembles finite-state Markov chains, a class of models on which these tools perform very well [2].

References

1. Baier, C., Klein, J., Klüppelholz, S., Märcker, S.: Computing conditional probabilities in Markovian models efficiently. In: Ábrahám, E., Havelund, K. (eds.) TACAS 2014. LNCS, vol. 8413, pp. 515–530. Springer, Heidelberg (2014). https://doi.org/10.1007/978-3-642-54862-8_43
2. Budde, C.E., et al.: On correctness, precision, and performance in quantitative verification. In: Margaria, T., Steffen, B. (eds.) ISoLA 2020. LNCS, vol. 12479, pp. 216–241. Springer, Cham (2021). https://doi.org/10.1007/978-3-030-83723-5_15

3. Campillo Navarro, A.: Order statistics and multivariate discrete phase-type distributions. Ph.D. thesis (2019). https://orbit.dtu.dk/files/177528739/PHD_2018_492.pdf
4. Carpenter, B., et al.: Stan: a probabilistic programming language. J. Stat. Softw. **76**(1), 1–32 (2017). https://doi.org/10.18637/jss.v076.i01. https://www.jstatsoft.org/index.php/jss/article/view/v076i01
5. Chen, M., Katoen, J.P., Klinkenberg, L., Winkler, T.: Does a program yield the right distribution? Verifying probabilistic programs via generating functions. In: International Conference on Computer Aided Verification, pp. 79–101. Springer (2022)
6. Chiang, D., McDonald, C., Shan, C.C.: Exact recursive probabilistic programming. Proc. ACM Program. Lang. **7**(OOPSLA1) (2023). https://doi.org/10.1145/3586050
7. Gehr, T., Misailovic, S., Vechev, M.: PSI: exact symbolic inference for probabilistic programs. In: Chaudhuri, S., Farzan, A. (eds.) CAV 2016. LNCS, vol. 9779, pp. 62–83. Springer, Cham (2016). https://doi.org/10.1007/978-3-319-41528-4_4
8. Geißler, D., Winkler, T.: Weighted automata for exact inference in discrete probabilistic programs (2025). https://arxiv.org/abs/2509.15074
9. Goodman, N.D., Stuhlmüller, A.: The Design and Implementation of Probabilistic Programming Languages (2014). http://dippl.org. Accessed 16 June 2025
10. Goodman, N.D., Tenenbaum, J.B., Contributors, T.P.: Probabilistic Models of Cognition (2016). http://probmods.org/. Accessed 03 May 2025
11. Gordon, A.D., Henzinger, T.A., Nori, A.V., Rajamani, S.K.: Probabilistic programming. In: Future of Software Engineering Proceedings, FOSE 2014, pp. 167–181. Association for Computing Machinery, New York (2014). https://doi.org/10.1145/2593882.2593900
12. Hensel, C., Junges, S., Katoen, J., Quatmann, T., Volk, M.: The probabilistic model checker storm. Int. J. Softw. Tools Technol. Transf. **24**(4), 589–610 (2022). https://doi.org/10.1007/S10009-021-00633-Z
13. Holtzen, S., Van den Broeck, G., Millstein, T.: Scaling exact inference for discrete probabilistic programs. Proc. ACM Program. Lang. **4**(OOPSLA) (2020). https://doi.org/10.1145/3428208
14. Klinkenberg, L., Batz, K., Kaminski, B.L., Katoen, J.-P., Moerman, J., Winkler, T.: Generating functions for probabilistic programs. In: Fernandez, M. (ed.) LOPSTR 2020. LNCS, vol. 12561, pp. 231–248. Springer, Cham (2021). https://doi.org/10.1007/978-3-030-68446-4_12
15. Klinkenberg, L., Blumenthal, C., Chen, M., Haase, D., Katoen, J.P.: Exact Bayesian inference for loopy probabilistic programs using generating functions. Proc. ACM Program. Lang. **8**(OOPSLA1), 923–953 (2024)
16. Koller, D., McAllester, D.A., Pfeffer, A.: Effective Bayesian inference for stochastic programs. In: AAAI/IAAI, pp. 740–747. AAAI Press/The MIT Press (1997). http://www.aaai.org/Library/AAAI/1997/aaai97-115.php
17. Kozen, D.: Semantics of probabilistic programs. J. Comput. Syst. Sci. **22**(3), 328–350 (1981). https://doi.org/10.1016/0022-0000(81)90036-2
18. Kozen, D.: A probabilistic PDL. In: STOC, pp. 291–297. ACM (1983). https://doi.org/10.1145/800061.808758
19. Kuich, W.: Semirings and Formal Power Series: Their Relevance to Formal Languages and Automata. In: Rozenberg, G., Salomaa, A. (eds.) Handbook of Formal Languages, pp. 609–677. Springer, Heidelberg (1997). https://doi.org/10.1007/978-3-642-59136-5_9

20. Kwiatkowska, M., Norman, G., Parker, D.: PRISM 4.0: verification of probabilistic real-time systems. In: Gopalakrishnan, G., Qadeer, S. (eds.) CAV 2011. LNCS, vol. 6806, pp. 585–591. Springer, Heidelberg (2011). https://doi.org/10.1007/978-3-642-22110-1_47

21. Mahdi Shamsi, S., Pietro Farina, G., Gaboardi, M., Napp, N.: Probabilistic programming languages for modeling autonomous systems. In: 2020 IEEE International Conference on Multisensor Fusion and Integration for Intelligent Systems (MFI), pp. 32–39 (2020). https://doi.org/10.1109/MFI49285.2020.9235230

22. McIver, A., Morgan, C.: Abstraction, Refinement and Proof for Probabilistic Systems. Monographs in Computer Science. Springer (2005). https://doi.org/10.1007/B138392

23. Olmedo, F., Gretz, F., Jansen, N., Kaminski, B.L., Katoen, J., McIver, A.: Conditioning in probabilistic programming. ACM Trans. Program. Lang. Syst. **40**(1), 4:1–4:50 (2018). https://doi.org/10.1145/3156018

24. Saad, F.A., Rinard, M.C., Mansinghka, V.K.: SPPL: probabilistic programming with fast exact symbolic inference. In: Proceedings of the 42nd ACM SIGPLAN International Conference on Programming Language Design and Implementation, PLDI 2021, pp. 804–819. Association for Computing Machinery, New York (2021). https://doi.org/10.1145/3453483.3454078

25. Tran, D., Hoffman, M.D., Saurous, R.A., Brevdo, E., Murphy, K., Blei, D.M.: Deep Probabilistic Programming (2017). https://arxiv.org/abs/1701.03757

26. Willmot, G.: Mixed compound poisson distributions. ASTIN Bull. **16**(S1), S59–S79 (1986). https://doi.org/10.1017/S051503610001165X

27. Zaiser, F., Murawski, A., Ong, C.H.L.: Exact Bayesian inference on discrete models via probability generating functions: a probabilistic programming approach. In: Oh, A., Naumann, T., Globerson, A., Saenko, K., Hardt, M., Levine, S. (eds.) Advances in Neural Information Processing Systems, vol. 36, pp. 2427–2462. Curran Associates, Inc. (2023). https://proceedings.neurips.cc/paper_files/paper/2023/file/0747af6f877c0cb555fea595f01b0e83-Paper-Conference.pdf

Forward and Backward Simulations
for Partially Observable Probability

Chris Chen[1]([✉])(iD), Annabelle McIver[1](iD), and Carroll Morgan[2](iD)

[1] School of Computing, Macquarie University, Sydney, Australia
`chris@openendings.net`, `annabelle.mciver@mq.edu.au`
[2] University of New South Wales and Trustworthy Systems, Sydney, Australia
`carroll.morgan@unsw.edu.au`

Abstract. Data refinement is the standard extension of a refinement relation from programs to datatypes (i.e. a behavioural subtyping relation). Forward/backward simulations provide a tractable method for establishing data refinement, and have been thoroughly studied for nondeterministic programs. However, for standard models of mixed probability and nondeterminism, ordinary assignment statements may not commute with (variable-disjoint) program fragments. This (1) invalidates a key assumption underlying the soundness of simulations, and (2) prevents modelling probabilistic datatypes with encapsulated state.

We introduce a weakest precondition semantics for Kuifje$_\sqcap$, a language for partially observable Markov decision processes, using so-called *loss (function) transformers*. We prove soundness of forward/backward simulations in this richer setting, modulo healthiness conditions with a remarkable duality: forward simulations *cannot leak* information, and backward simulations *cannot exploit* leaked information.

Keywords: Forward and backward simulations · Abstract datatypes · Data refinement · Probabilistic nondeterminism · Weakest precondition · Quantitative information flow · Probabilistic predicates

1 Introduction

Datatype encapsulation [1,19,20,28] is a long-established organising principle for datatypes that encourages defining a datatype's representation and logic separately from a surrounding program ("program context") $\mathscr{P}$ that uses the datatype for its own purposes. A *data refinement* relation [37] from e.g., an "abstract" datatype D_A to a "concrete" one D_C indicates that "the behavior of $\mathscr{P}$ is unchanged when $[D_C]$ is substituted for $[D_A]$" [27]—that is, replacing abstract with concrete preserves all "safety/correctness properties" of the surrounding program (a notion that varies with the model of computation).

A *forward(/backward) simulation* [19,29] from D_A to D_C is a transformation between their internal states that (informally) witnesses a data refinement. This allows a programmer to avoid a full inductive proof by providing a few small program refinements instead.

Z. Liu et al. (Eds.): ICTAC 2025, LNCS 16237, pp. 279–297, 2026.
https://doi.org/10.1007/978-3-032-11176-0_17

The probabilistic programming language pGCL [30,33] combines probabilistic choice [25] with (demonic) nondeterminism. However, in the Markov decision process (MDP) model underlying pGCL, nondeterminism may depend on the program state.[1] This means nondeterminism and probabilistic choice do not necessarily commute, invalidating a key assumption underlying the soundness of forward/backward simulations [9]. Furthermore, MDPs are unable to model datatypes with encapsulated state (inaccessible to the programmer)—see e.g. the cached random bit generator (Fig. 1).

Partially observable MDPs (POMDPs) [24,31] model internal state as *hidden* from the $\sqcap$-resolver. [9] proposed using POMDPs and techniques from *quantitative information flow* (QIF) [3,40]—which deals with refinement distinguishing hidden/visible state—as a basis to study datatype encapsulation for mixed probability and nondeterminism. POMDPs provide a reasonable model for e.g. one-sided abstraction and client-server situations—though this requires a conflation of *hidden* vs. *encapsulated* (from the $\sqcap$-resolver vs. the programmer) which prevents full generality. Our aim is to provide a <u>full theoretical basis</u> for [9].

Contributions. We provide a weakest precondition semantics [11,12] for Kuifje$_\sqcap$, a language for POMDPs, using *loss functions* as our predicates. This *weakest pre-loss* (wpl) semantics is similar to the leakage logic of [10] but additionally supports nontermination, nondeterminism, and (type) context extension.

Our <u>first</u> main results are sound *healthiness conditions* for our semantics [14,34]—i.e. equational properties of the "loss transformer" functions in the image of wpl that enable axiomatic reasoning in our proofs. Notably, we find that each loss transformer is superlinear, partial, and Scott-continuous (Lemma 1). Furthermore, under context extension, healthy loss transformers commute with *partial* hidden assignment on disjoint state (Lemma 2). The former resembles healthiness for probabilistic predicate transformers [34, §7]. The latter is a stronger version of "correlation transformers" [36] that commutes with assertions.

For our <u>second</u> main results we obtain sound forward and backward simulation rules for Kuifje$_\sqcap$ (Theorem 1, Theorem 2). We require additional healthiness conditions on simulations, which we justify with counterexamples. These conditions reveal a remarkable duality: forward simulations *must not leak* information, whereas backward simulations *must not exploit* leaked information.

Section 2 reviews data refinement for typed languages. Section 3 reviews MDPs and probabilistic predicate transformers, and demonstrates how non-commutativity of probability and nondeterminism in pGCL (9) complicates data encapsulation (Example 4). Section 4 introduces Kuifje$_\sqcap$ (our POMDP language), loss functions, and our "weakest pre-loss" (wpl) semantics. Section 5 gives our healthiness properties for wpl and relates them to 'hidden' and 'choiceless' Kuifje$_\sqcap$ programs. Finally, Sect. 6 gives our forward+backward simulation rules,

---

[1] This behaviour is inherited from GCL, where the absence of probability mitigates any issues.

and in Sect. 7 we apply our results to a number of positive and negative examples that pGCL alone cannot model.

An extended version of this paper containing proofs and other supporting material is available at https://arxiv.org/abs/2506.08437?

Related Work. [31] gave a covariant "state transformer" semantics for POMDPs involving powerdomains over *hyperdistributions*—distributions of distributions. Unfortunately, in the hyperdistribution model our soundness conditions prove cumbersome to characterise and reason with; this motivates our dual (by construction) contravariant "weakest pre-loss" semantics.

Much of the early work on simulations for (demonic) nondeterminism takes the relational view [19,20,29], ordering programs by trace inclusion. This is opposite to refinement [5,12].[2] A note, then, regarding nomenclature. With respect to nondeterminism, what we call forward (backward) simulations are similar to the downward (upward) simulations of [20], the encodings (decodings) of [6], the simulations (cosimulations) of [14], and the forward (backward) simulations of [18,29]; they are 2-dual to the lax (oplax) morphisms of [18,22].[3]

2   Preliminaries

We occasionally refer to the Scott topology on posets, in which open sets are open under directed joins (see e.g. [2]). Functions between posets are *Scott-continuous* ("Scott-cts.") if they preserve (existing) directed joins; they are necessarily monotone.

By "state spaces" we always mean (discrete) sets. We write $P\colon \mathcal{X} \to \mathcal{Y}$ to denote a program with initial and final state space $\mathcal{X}$ and $\mathcal{Y}$ respectively.

We write $\mathbb{P}_+\mathcal{X}$ for the nonempty powerset. We write $\mathbb{D}_\perp\mathcal{X}$ for the *partial probability distributions* over $\mathcal{X}$ ($\sum_x \delta(x) \leq 1$), and $\mathbb{D}\mathcal{X}$ for the (total) probability distributions. Supports are countable but need not be finite.

2.1   Refinement and Nondeterminism

A *(program) refinement relation* ($\sqsubseteq$) formalises the notion of behavioural subtyping [13,43]. Given compatibly-typed programs $P, Q\colon \mathcal{X} \to \mathcal{Y}$ (or their denotations), $P \sqsubseteq Q$ ("P is refined by Q") denotes that replacing P with Q "preserves safety/correctness properties". We require that ($\sqsubseteq$) is a partial order giving a poset-enriched category (1). *(Demonic) nondeterministic choice* ($\sqcap$) is defined as the meet for this order (2).

$$P_1 \sqsubseteq Q_1 \wedge P_2 \sqsubseteq Q_2 \implies P_1; P_2 \sqsubseteq Q_1; Q_2 \tag{1}$$

$$Q \sqsubseteq P_1 \wedge Q \sqsubseteq P_2 \iff Q \sqsubseteq P_1 \sqcap P_2 \tag{2}$$

---

[2] This is a "may-must" duality: possible executions/traces vs. necessary properties.

[3] For partial probability our terminology disagrees with [18], whose orders on $\mathbb{P}$ and $\mathbb{D}_\perp$ inconsistently take $\sqcap$-identity (**magic** [5]) vs. divergence (**abort**) as least element.

There are two common interpretations of $P_1 \sqcap P_2$. The first, emphasising abstraction, is *programmer's choice:* during development, the programmer may choose between P_1 and P_2 however she pleases. The second, emphasising small-step semantics, is *runtime choice.* In this view there is some "$\sqcap$-resolver" that chooses between P_1 and P_2 at runtime according to some unknown strategy which may depend on program state. These interpretations are consistent in ordinary pGCL but will diverge as we impose encapsulation boundaries.

2.2   Datatypes

Our datatypes are explicitly typed [7, 19]. Datatype operations are interpreted via the copy rule [8, 26] (i.e. inlining); parameters and return values are passed using some (unencapsulated) *shared state* $\mathcal{S}$.[4]

Definition 1. *A* <u>datatype signature</u> $(\mathcal{S}, J)$ *is given by a shared state space* $\mathcal{S}$ *and an indexing set* J.

Definition 2 (Datatypes [14, 19]). *A* <u>datatype</u> *with signature* $(\mathcal{S}, J)$ *is a tuple* $D = (I, OP, F, \mathcal{A})$, *where the set* $\mathcal{A}$ *is called the* <u>encapsulated state space</u>, $I: \mathcal{S} \rightarrowtail \mathcal{S} \times \mathcal{A}$ *and* $F: \mathcal{S} \times \mathcal{A} \rightarrowtail \mathcal{S}$ *are programs called respectively the* <u>initialisation</u> *and* <u>finalisation</u>, *and* $OP = \{OP_j: \mathcal{S} \times \mathcal{A} \rightarrowtail \mathcal{S} \times \mathcal{A}\}_{j:J}$ *is an indexed set of programs.*

Collectively, I, F, *and the members of* OP *are called the* <u>operations</u> *of the datatype.*

A *program context* $\mathscr{P}$ for signature $(\mathcal{S}, J)$ is "a program with OP_j-shaped holes": a syntactic program defined with programs $\{OP_j: \mathcal{S} \rightarrowtail \mathcal{S}\}_{j:J}$ in scope. Write $\mathscr{P}(OP)$ for the result of inlining OP; the types enforce state encapsulation.

Definition 3 (Data refinement). *Fix signature* $(\mathcal{S}, J)$. *Let* $D_{\mathcal{A}} := (I, OP, F, \mathcal{A})$ *and* $D_{\mathcal{C}} := (I', OP', F', \mathcal{C})$. *We say* $D_{\mathcal{C}}$ <u>(data) refines</u> $D_{\mathcal{A}}$ *whenever*

$$I; \mathscr{P}(OP); F \ \sqsubseteq \ I'; \mathscr{P}(OP'); F' \tag{3}$$

for all program contexts $\mathscr{P}$. *Overloading notation, we write* $D_{\mathcal{A}} \sqsubseteq D_{\mathcal{C}}$.

2.3   Forward and Backward Simulations

Simulations are the standard generalisation of bisimulations from equivalence to refinement.[5] Recall that a denotational semantics maps syntactic programs to a category of so-called *abstract programs* (e.g. predicate transformers). A forward or backward simulation is then an abstract program as follows:

---

[4] Coalgebraic models [18] might instead encode $\mathcal{S}$ in the endofunctor.
[5] When the squares (4–5) are equalities we may speak of *functional bisimulation* [38].

Definition 4. *Let $D_{\mathcal{A}} = (I, OP, F, \mathcal{A})$ and $D_{\mathcal{C}} = (I', OP', F', \mathcal{C})$ be datatypes with shared signature $(\mathcal{S}, J)$. A <u>forward simulation</u> from $D_{\mathcal{A}}$ to $D_{\mathcal{C}}$ is an abstract program $\mathrm{rep}_F \colon \mathcal{A} \to \mathcal{C}$ such that the refinements (4) hold:*

$$
\begin{array}{ccc}
\begin{array}{ccc}
\mathcal{S} & \xrightarrow{I} & \mathcal{S} \times \mathcal{A} \\
 & \sqsupseteq & \downarrow \mathrm{rep}_F \\
I' & \searrow & \mathcal{S} \times \mathcal{C}
\end{array}
&
\begin{array}{ccc}
\mathcal{S} \times \mathcal{A} & \xrightarrow{OP_j} & \mathcal{S} \times \mathcal{A} \\
\mathrm{rep}_F \downarrow & \sqsupseteq & \downarrow \mathrm{rep}_F \\
\mathcal{S} \times \mathcal{C} & \xrightarrow[OP'_j]{} & \mathcal{S} \times \mathcal{C}
\end{array}
&
\begin{array}{ccc}
\mathcal{S} \times \mathcal{A} & \searrow & F \\
\mathrm{rep}_F \downarrow & \sqsupseteq & \searrow \\
\mathcal{S} \times \mathcal{C} & \xrightarrow[F']{} & \mathcal{S}
\end{array}
\end{array}
\tag{4}
$$

and a <u>backward simulation</u> from $D_{\mathcal{A}}$ to $D_{\mathcal{C}}$ is an abstract program $\mathrm{rep}_B \colon \mathcal{C} \to \mathcal{A}$ such that the refinements (5) hold.

$$
\begin{array}{ccc}
\begin{array}{ccc}
I & \nearrow & \mathcal{S} \times \mathcal{A} \\
 & \sqsubseteq & \uparrow \mathrm{rep}_B \\
\mathcal{S} & \xrightarrow[I']{} & \mathcal{S} \times \mathcal{C}
\end{array}
&
\begin{array}{ccc}
\mathcal{S} \times \mathcal{A} & \xrightarrow{OP_j} & \mathcal{S} \times \mathcal{A} \\
\mathrm{rep}_B \uparrow & \sqsubseteq & \uparrow \mathrm{rep}_B \\
\mathcal{S} \times \mathcal{C} & \xrightarrow[OP'_j]{} & \mathcal{S} \times \mathcal{C}
\end{array}
&
\begin{array}{ccc}
\mathcal{S} \times \mathcal{A} & \xrightarrow{F} & \mathcal{S} \\
\mathrm{rep}_B \uparrow & \sqsubseteq & \uparrow \\
\mathcal{S} \times \mathcal{C} & \nearrow & F'
\end{array}
\end{array}
\tag{5}
$$

Note that, according to the types, rep can *only* act on encapsulated state, not on shared state. The rep arrows above represent (type-)context extensions of rep to a state space including $\mathsf{s} \colon \mathcal{S}$.

As Eqs. (4–5) hint, soundness of simulation is often shown by induction over $\mathscr{P}$. This requires a property for interleaving independent programs $P \colon \mathcal{X} \to \mathcal{Y}$:

$$
\begin{array}{cc}
\begin{array}{ccc}
\mathcal{X} \times \mathcal{A} & \xrightarrow{P} & \mathcal{Y} \times \mathcal{A} \\
\mathrm{rep}_F \downarrow & \sqsupseteq & \downarrow \mathrm{rep}_F \\
\mathcal{X} \times \mathcal{C} & \xrightarrow[P]{} & \mathcal{Y} \times \mathcal{C}
\end{array}
&
\begin{array}{ccc}
\mathcal{X} \times \mathcal{A} & \xrightarrow{P} & \mathcal{Y} \times \mathcal{A} \\
\mathrm{rep}_B \uparrow & \sqsubseteq & \uparrow \mathrm{rep}_B \\
\mathcal{X} \times \mathcal{C} & \xrightarrow[P]{} & \mathcal{Y} \times \mathcal{C}
\end{array}
\end{array}
\tag{6}
$$

Example 1. It is well-known that for guarded nondeterminism, e.g. $\mathrm{Kl}(\mathbb{P})$ [29] and $\mathrm{Kl}(\mathbb{P}+\perp)$ [19,20], (6) holds. In these settings, certain forward and backward simulations are sound, and composition of backward-then-forward simulations is complete. For $\mathrm{Kl}(\mathbb{P}_+ + \perp)$, under reasonable assumptions about finalisations, backward simulations are complete [14].

3   MDPs

We briefly review pGCL, a language for Markov decision processes (MDPs) mixing nondeterminism and probability [30,33]. Assignment ($:=$) takes probabilistic expressions on the right. As syntactic sugar we write nondeterministic choice between *expressions* (instead of programs), e.g. "$\mathsf{x} := 0 \sqcap 1$" is *shorthand* for $(\mathsf{x} := 0) \sqcap (\mathsf{x} := 1)$.

Per "programmer's choice", the $\sqcap$-resolver may employ a "mixed" (probabilistic) strategy (7), or depend on the state (8). (Below, $\mathsf{b} \colon \{0, 1\}$, and pGCL refinement ($\sqsubseteq_{\mathrm{MDP}}$) and equivalence ($\equiv_{\mathrm{MDP}}$) are to be defined.)

$$
\mathsf{x} := 0 \sqcap 1 \quad \sqsubseteq_{\mathrm{MDP}} \quad \mathsf{x} := 0 \tfrac{2}{3} \oplus 1
\tag{7}
$$

$$
\mathsf{x} := 0 \sqcap 1 \quad \equiv_{\mathrm{MDP}} \quad \mathsf{x} := \mathsf{b} \sqcap \neg \mathsf{b} \quad \sqsubseteq_{\mathrm{MDP}} \quad \mathsf{x} := \mathsf{b}
\tag{8}
$$

Operationally, pGCL programs of type $\mathcal{X} \to \mathcal{Y}$ are modellable as $\mathcal{X} \to \mathbb{P}_+\mathbb{D}_\perp\mathcal{Y}$ functions, normalised by upper convex closure.

3.1 Probabilistic Predicates and pGCL Semantics

Preliminaries. The *extended (non-negative) reals* are $\bar{\mathbb{R}}_+ := [0, \infty]$. They form a semiring ("rig") under the usual addition/multiplication, with all operations monotone (indeed, Scott-cts.). Recall a *d-cone* [41] is a directed-complete '$\bar{\mathbb{R}}_+$-semimodule' $(C, \leq, +, 0, \cdot)$ equipped with Scott-cts. $\bar{\mathbb{R}}_+$-scalar multiplication and a Scott-cts. addition monoid, that obey various distributivity laws.

The *probabilistic predicates* over state space $\mathcal{X}$ are the "extended random variables" $\mathbb{L}\mathcal{X} := (\mathcal{X} \to \bar{\mathbb{R}}_+)$. They form a d-cone with all operations pointwise. We write $\mathrm{id}_\mathcal{X}$ for the identity function on $\mathbb{L}\mathcal{X}$.

Given a Boolean expression $\mathcal{B}$ with $\mathbf{x}\colon \mathcal{X}$ free, the *indicator function* $[\![\mathcal{B}]\!]_\mathcal{X}\colon \mathbb{L}\mathcal{X}$ takes $x \mapsto 1$ if $\mathcal{B}[x/x]$ is true, and $x \mapsto 0$ otherwise. (We generally omit the subscript.) As a special case, let $1_\mathcal{X} = [\![\mathbf{true}]\!]_\mathcal{X}$ and $1_x = [\![\mathbf{x} = x]\!]_\mathcal{X}$. When $e \leq 1_\mathcal{X}$, write $\neg e$ for the unique solution to $e + \neg e = 1_\mathcal{X}$. The *conjunction* monoid $(\mathbb{L}\mathcal{X}, \boxtimes, 1_\mathcal{X})$ is given by $(e_1 \boxtimes e_2)(x) = e_1(x)e_2(x)$.

Given $e\colon \mathbb{L}\mathcal{X}$, its *context extension* $e^\mathcal{Z}\colon \mathbb{L}(\mathcal{X} \times \mathcal{Z})$ is $e^\mathcal{Z}(x, z) = e(x)$. Given linear, Scott-cts. functions $f\colon \mathbb{L}\mathcal{Z} \to \mathbb{L}\mathcal{X}, f'\colon \mathbb{L}\mathcal{W} \to \mathbb{L}\mathcal{Y}$, their *tensor* $f \otimes f'\colon \mathbb{L}(\mathcal{Z} \times \mathcal{W}) \to \mathbb{L}(\mathcal{X} \times \mathcal{Y})$ is the unique linear, Scott-cts. function s.t. $(f \otimes f')(1_{(z,w)})(x, y) = f(1_z)(x) \times f'(1_w)(y)$.

Every function $f\colon \mathcal{X} \to \mathbb{D}_\perp\mathcal{Y}$ has a *dual* $f^\intercal\colon \mathbb{L}\mathcal{Y} \to \mathbb{L}\mathcal{X}$ given by $f^\intercal(e)(x) = \sum_y e(y) \times f(x)(y)$. The dual is linear, Scott-cts., and *partial* $(f^\intercal(1_\mathcal{Y}) \leq 1_\mathcal{X})$; if $f\colon \mathcal{X} \to \mathbb{D}\mathcal{Y}$ is *total*, then so is its dual $(f^\intercal(1_\mathcal{Y}) = 1_\mathcal{X})$.

Let $\mathsf{copy}_\mathcal{Y}\colon \mathcal{Y} \to \mathbb{D}\mathcal{Y}^2$ be zero everywhere except $\mathsf{copy}_\mathcal{Y}(y)(y, y) = 1$.

Given a weight $p \in [0, 1]$, we write $\delta_p \oplus \delta'$ for the "convex combination" of two compatible probability distributions, $(\delta_p \oplus \delta')(x) = p\delta(x) + (1 - p)\delta'(x)$.

Weakest preexpectation (wp). Just as Dijkstra gave the semantics of GCL in terms of weakest precondition Boolean "predicate transformers" [11,12], the semantics of pGCL can be given in terms of *probabilistic predicate transformers* [23,34] —for our purposes, with mutable state [44].

For each pGCL program $P\colon \mathcal{X} \to \mathcal{Y}$ there is a *weakest preexpectation* function $\mathsf{wp}.P\colon \mathbb{L}\mathcal{Y} \to \mathbb{L}\mathcal{X}$ [34, §4, Fig. 2]. The *refinement relation* $(\sqsubseteq_{\mathrm{MDP}})$ over two pGCL programs is defined as $P \sqsubseteq_{\mathrm{MDP}} Q$ whenever $\mathsf{wp}.P \leq \mathsf{wp}.Q$ pointwise.

Remark 1 (Interpreting wp*).* Informally, the expected value ("EV") of e after executing P is $\geq r$ for all $\sqcap$-resolvers *iff* the initial EV of $\mathsf{wp}.P.e$ is $\geq r$.

If P doesn't terminate, we say the EV of e is zero. Hence $\mathsf{wp}.\mathbf{abort}.e = 0_\mathcal{X}$, and $\mathsf{wp}.P.1_\mathcal{Y}$ is the vector of *termination probabilities* $\Pr(\top \mid \mathbf{x} = x)$.

Example 2. Given $r\colon \bar{\mathbb{R}}_+$, $e_\mathcal{Y}\colon \mathbb{L}\mathcal{Y}$, $\mathcal{B}\colon \mathcal{X} \to \mathsf{Bool}$, we have $r[\![\mathcal{B}]\!] \leq \mathsf{wp}.P.e_\mathcal{Y}$ iff the final EV of $e_\mathcal{Y}$ is at least r whenever $\mathcal{B}$ initially holds.

3.2 pGCL, Hidden State, and Noncommutativity

pGCL has only *visible* state: the nondeterminism may always depend directly on the state. We have the following *strict* inequality:

$$(\mathsf{y} := 0\ _p\!\oplus 1;\ \mathsf{x} := 0 \sqcap 1) \quad \sqsubsetneq_{\mathrm{MDP}} \quad (\mathsf{x} := 0 \sqcap 1;\ \mathsf{y} := 0\ _p\!\oplus 1) \tag{9}$$

Since probabilistic and nondeterministic choice do not commute, Eq. (6) doesn't hold in general: simulations are not sound for pGCL.

Example 3 (Strictness of(9)). Write P and Q for the left/right programs of (9) respectively. After running Q, we are guaranteed that $\Pr(\mathsf{x} = \mathsf{y}) = \frac{1}{2}$ (as any $\sqcap$-resolver for Q is independent of the final value of y). However, for the left program we cannot guarantee that $\Pr(\mathsf{x} = \mathsf{y}) > 0$ as a $\sqcap$-resolver may potentially always choose $\mathsf{x} := \neg\mathsf{y}$. Then $\mathsf{wp}.P.[\![\mathsf{x} = \mathsf{y}]\!] \not\geq \mathsf{wp}.Q.[\![\mathsf{x} = \mathsf{y}]\!]$, and therefore $P \not\sqsupseteq_{\mathrm{MDP}} Q$.

On the other hand, a simple strategy stealing argument between $\sqcap$-resolvers gives $P \sqsubseteq_{\mathrm{MDP}} Q$.

Remark 2. Strictness of (9) reduces algebraically to the asymmetry in pGCL of

$$P;(Q \sqcap R) \sqsubseteq_{\mathrm{MDP}} (P;Q) \sqcap (P;R) \tag{10}$$

when P contains probabilistic choice. In other words, the problem is that (;) fails to left-distribute over ($\sqcap$). This amounts to the well-known nonexistence of a distributive law $\mathbb{D}\mathbb{P} \to \mathbb{P}\mathbb{D}$. [6] [7]

Visible state also poses a problem for modelling forms of encapsulation which *ought* to hide information from the resolver.

Example 4. In Fig. 1, the datatype $D_{\mathcal{A}} := (I_{\mathcal{A}}, OP_{\mathcal{A}}, F_{\mathcal{A}}, \{*\})$ specifies a random bit generator ($\{*\}$ being the trivial 1-element state space), while $D_{\mathcal{C}} := (I_{\mathcal{C}}, OP_{\mathcal{C}}, F_{\mathcal{C}}, \mathsf{Bool})$ is a potential implementation that precomputes random bits ahead of time. We wish to model "programmer's choice" with encapsulated state, so the cached bit b should *hidden* from the $\sqcap$-resolver such that the precomputation has no effect on functionality, i.e. $D_{\mathcal{A}} \sqsubseteq D_{\mathcal{C}}$.

However, pGCL does not provide a way to model b as hidden. Let $\mathscr{P}(OP) = (\mathsf{x}:=0\sqcap1;\ OP;\mathsf{y}:=\mathsf{s})$. The same argument as for Eq. (9) shows that $I_{\mathcal{A}};\ \mathscr{P}(OP_{\mathcal{A}}); F_{\mathcal{A}} \not\sqsubseteq I_{\mathcal{C}};\ \mathscr{P}(OP_{\mathcal{C}}); F_{\mathcal{C}}$. Hence pGCL alone is insufficient to model datatypes with hidden precomputation.

---

[6] We thank the anonymous referee #3 for pointing out this connection.

[7] Indeed, it turns out the $(\not\sqsupseteq_{\mathrm{MDP}})$ argument in Example 3 is isomorphic to the nonexistence proof given in Varacca's thesis [42]'s thesis [42]. (There the construction corresponding to the left of (9) is attributed to Plotkin.).

Shared state: s: $\{0, 1\}$.

$D_{\mathcal{A}}$	$D_{\mathcal{C}}$
$I_{\mathcal{A}}$: **skip**;	$I_{\mathcal{C}}$: **var** b $:= 0\,{}_{\frac{1}{2}}\!\oplus 1$;
$OP_{\mathcal{A}}$: s $:= 0\,{}_{\frac{1}{2}}\!\oplus 1$;	$OP_{\mathcal{C}}$: s $:=$ b;
$F_{\mathcal{A}}$: **skip**;	b $:= 0\,{}_{\frac{1}{2}}\!\oplus 1$;
	$F_{\mathcal{C}}$: **unvar** b;

Fig. 1. An abstract "random bit generator" $D_{\mathcal{A}}$, and a concrete implementation $D_{\mathcal{C}}$ precomputed with hidden variables. Under the copy rule, $D_{\mathcal{C}}$'s encapsulated state is visible in pGCL, but can be modelled as hidden in Kuifje$_\sqcap$ (Example 11).

4   POMDPs

Ideally, we want to model a mix of visible and *hidden* variables in our datatypes. (When a variable is *hidden* then the $\sqcap$-resolver can at best infer its value based on probabilistic inference and side channel information.)[8]

Partially observable MDPs (POMDPs) are traditionally MDPs that probabilistically emit *observations* with every state transition [24]; the $\sqcap$-resolver only knows the observation history, not the underlying state. We use POMDPs to model mixed nondeterminism and probability with partially visible state.

Hereon we interpret nondeterminism as *runtime choice*: the $\sqcap$-resolver may condition on the "program trace" in a way a programmer cannot (except at the expense of modularity and encapsulation).

$$\frac{}{\textbf{skip}: \mathcal{X} \twoheadrightarrow \mathcal{X}} \quad \frac{}{\textbf{abort}: \mathcal{X} \twoheadrightarrow \mathcal{Y}} \quad \frac{P: \mathcal{X} \twoheadrightarrow \mathcal{Y} \quad Q: \mathcal{Y} \twoheadrightarrow \mathcal{Z}}{P; Q: \mathcal{X} \twoheadrightarrow \mathcal{Z}}$$

$$\frac{f: \mathcal{X} \to \mathbb{D}_\perp \mathcal{X}}{\textbf{x} := f(\textbf{x}): \mathcal{X} \twoheadrightarrow \mathcal{X}} \quad \frac{f: \mathcal{Y} \to \mathbb{D}_\perp \mathcal{X}}{\textbf{hid var x} := f(\textbf{y}): \mathcal{Y} \twoheadrightarrow \mathcal{Y} \times \mathcal{X}} \quad \frac{}{\textbf{unvar x}: \mathcal{Y} \times \mathcal{X} \twoheadrightarrow \mathcal{Y}}$$

$$\frac{P_1: \mathcal{X} \twoheadrightarrow \mathcal{Y} \quad P_2: \mathcal{X} \twoheadrightarrow \mathcal{Y}}{P_1 \sqcap P_2: \mathcal{X} \twoheadrightarrow \mathcal{Y}} \quad \frac{g: \mathbb{L}\mathcal{X} \wedge g \leq 1_{\mathcal{X}} \quad P: \mathcal{X} \twoheadrightarrow \mathcal{Y} \quad Q: \mathcal{X} \twoheadrightarrow \mathcal{Y}}{\textbf{if } g(\textbf{x}) \textbf{ then } P \textbf{ else } Q: \mathcal{X} \twoheadrightarrow \mathcal{Y}}$$

$$\frac{g: \mathbb{L}\mathcal{X} \wedge g \leq 1_{\mathcal{X}} \quad P: \mathcal{X} \twoheadrightarrow \mathcal{X}}{\textbf{while } g(\textbf{x}) \, \{P\}: \mathcal{X} \twoheadrightarrow \mathcal{X}} \quad \frac{f: \mathcal{X} \to \mathbb{D}_\perp \Omega}{\textbf{print } f(\textbf{x}): \mathcal{X} \twoheadrightarrow \mathcal{X}}$$

Fig. 2. Simplified program syntax for Kuifje$_\sqcap$. We elide (standard) type contexts: it is assumed that x: $\mathcal{X}$, y: $\mathcal{Y}$, etc., and that x: $\mathcal{X}$ may stand for multiple variables $(\textbf{x}_i)_{i \in I}: \prod_i \mathcal{X}_i$. We equivocate betwen functions $f(\textbf{x})$ and expressions with x: $\mathcal{X}$ free.

"Kuifje$_\sqcap$", our language for POMDPs, extends the Kuifje language for HMMs [3, 16, 32, §8.3–4, §14.4] with *(i)* nondeterminism, *(ii)* explicit syntax for declaring

---

[8] Although we conflate them in our datatypes and examples (Sect. 6–7), the *visible vs. hidden* distinction is orthogonal to *global vs. encapsulated*. The former relates to runtime choice (the $\sqcap$-resolver's knowledge); the latter, to programmer's choice.

and freeing variables, and *(iii)* context extension. Kuifje$_\sqcap$ looks similar to, but is not an extension of, pGCL: all variables are intrinsically *hidden*.

Operationally, Kuifje$_\sqcap$ programs $P\colon \mathcal{X} \to \mathcal{Y}$ may be considered $\mathbb{D}\mathcal{X} \to \mathbb{P}_+\mathbb{D}_\perp\mathbb{D}\mathcal{Y}$ functions [31,32]. Loosely speaking, P carries an implicit *observation space* Ω (in the automata model, the observable traces). The worst-case $\sqcap$-resolver begins with prior belief $\delta\colon \mathbb{D}\mathcal{X}$. Then, provided that P terminates, it performs Bayesian inference, combining the observation $\omega \in \Omega$ (the outer $\mathbb{D}_\perp$) with knowledge of source code to obtain a posterior belief (the inner $\mathbb{D}\mathcal{Y}$). (See also Remark 4.)

Figure 2 gives our syntax. Per convention, **skip**$\colon \mathcal{X} \to \mathcal{X}$ is the identity for composition, and **abort**$\colon \mathcal{X} \to \mathcal{Y}$ is the nonterminating program, alt. "undefined behaviour" (hence the bottom element for refinement). Sequential composition (;) and nondeterminism ($\sqcap$) are standard.

As with pGCL, assignment is probabilistic; e.g. $(\mathbf{x} := \mathbf{y}{+}1 \,{}_{\frac{4}{5}}{\oplus}\, \mathbf{z})$ sets $\mathbf{x}$ to $\mathbf{z}$ with $\frac{1}{5}$ probability. If f is not total ($f^\intercal 1_\mathcal{Y} \neq 1_\mathcal{X}$) then $\mathbf{x} := f(\mathbf{x})$ '**abort**'s with the remaining probability. **hid var** and **unvar** are variations mutating the state space (/type context).

The **print** instruction makes information available to the $\sqcap$-resolver. Control flow (**if** and **while**) is also considered *visible*: only thus can we avoid merging observation types between different branches (a failure of modularity).

As syntactic sugar, we introduce an **assert** statement (11). Here, given $g \leq 1_\mathcal{X}$ we define $\ulcorner g_\lrcorner\colon \mathcal{X} \to \mathbb{D}_\perp\mathcal{X}$ as $\ulcorner g_\lrcorner(x)(x) = g(x)$ and $x \neq x' \Rightarrow \ulcorner g_\lrcorner(x)(x') = 0$.

$$\textbf{assert } g(\mathbf{x}) \;=\; (\mathbf{x} := \ulcorner g_\lrcorner(\mathbf{x})) \tag{11}$$

Example 5. In Kuifje$_\sqcap$, *"it is safer to reveal nothing than something"* (12), *"***print** *is seldom idempotent"* (13), and isomorphic but syntactically distinct leaks (e.g. of a variable b: $\{0, 1\}$) are equivalent (14).

$$\textbf{print } f(\mathbf{x}) \sqsubseteq \textbf{skip} \tag{12}$$
$$\textbf{print } f(\mathbf{x}); \textbf{print } f(\mathbf{x}) \sqsubseteq \textbf{print } f(\mathbf{x}) \tag{13}$$
$$\textbf{print } \mathbf{b} \equiv \textbf{print } \neg\mathbf{b} \tag{14}$$

When f is *total* (terminates with $\Pr = 1$), inequality (12) is strict unless f is a constant function, and (13) is strict unless f is deterministic.

We remark that the refinements above compare programs with incompatible "observation spaces": the observations are not part of the type signature.

Remark 3. Kuifje$_\sqcap$ is not quite a conservative extension of pGCL. A pGCL program can be transformed into a Kuifje$_\sqcap$ program by **print**-ing the entire state before and after every statement. This transformation is sound (reflects refinement) but is either incomplete (failing to preserve the refinement **skip** $\sqsubseteq_{\mathrm{MDP}}$ v := v) or non-functorial (does not preserve **skip**).

4.1   Loss Functions

What is the analogue of the probabilistic predicates $\mathbb{L}\mathcal{X}$ for POMDPs?

Example 6. Let $P\colon \mathbb{Z}_4 \dashrightarrow \mathbb{Z}_4 \times \mathbb{Z}_2 := \big(\mathbf{print}\ 2\lfloor \mathbf{n}\div 2\rfloor; \mathbf{var}\ \mathbf{b}{:=}0\sqcap 1\big)$. The $\sqcap$-resolver chooses $\mathbf{b}$ depending on the observed higher-order bit of $\mathbf{n}$: write $f\colon \{0,2\} \to \mathbb{D}\mathbb{Z}_2$ for its (unknown) strategy.

Following Remark 1 we consider necessary and sufficient conditions for $\Pr(\mathbf{n}+\mathbf{b}$ even$) \geq r$. Let $\delta\colon \mathbb{D}\mathbb{Z}_4$ be the initial distribution of $\mathbf{n}$. Suppose $\delta(0) \leq \delta(1)$ and $\delta(3) \leq \delta(2)$. If the $\sqcap$-resolver chooses $f(0) = \eta\,0$ (the point distribution on 0) and $f(2) = \eta\,1$, this minimises $\Pr(\mathbf{n}+\mathbf{b}$ even$)$. Hence if $\Pr(\mathbf{n} = 0) + \Pr(\mathbf{n} = 3) < r$, then in the worst case $\Pr(\mathbf{n}+\mathbf{b}$ even$) < r$ also.

By similar reasoning, $\Pr(\mathbf{n}+\mathbf{b}$ even$) \geq r$ for all resolver strategies f if and only if *four* 'pre-'predicates have $\mathrm{EV} \geq r$: these are $[\![\mathbf{n} = 0]\!] + [\![\mathbf{n} = 2]\!]$, $[\![\mathbf{n} = 0]\!] + [\![\mathbf{n} = 3]\!]$, $[\![\mathbf{n} = 1]\!] + [\![\mathbf{n} = 2]\!]$, and $[\![\mathbf{n} = 1]\!] + [\![\mathbf{n} = 3]\!]$.

Example 6 motivates using (nonempty) *sets* of predicates $E \in \mathbb{P}_{+}\mathbb{L}\mathcal{X}$ for Kuifje$_\sqcap$'s "predicate transformer" semantics. By analogy with Remark 1 we evaluate these against priors/posteriors via judgements "$r \leq \inf_{e \in E}(\mathrm{EV}\ \text{of}\ e)$". But since we *only* evaluate such sets by taking minimum EVs, there is some redundancy here. (E.g. $\{[\![\mathbf{x}{=}1]\!], [\![\mathbf{x}{=}2]\!]\}$ and $\{[\![\mathbf{x}{=}1]\!], [\![\mathbf{x}{=}2]\!], \frac{1}{2}[\![\mathbf{x} = 1]\!] + \frac{1}{2}[\![\mathbf{x}{=}2]\!], [\![\mathbf{x} \geq 2]\!]\}$ have the same minimum EV against all distributions.) An appropriate *normal form* for $\mathbb{P}_{+}\mathbb{L}\mathcal{X}$ would give a partial order based on min. EVs, allowing e.g. least fixed points for **while** (alongside other tools from domain theory).

Algebraically, we want to equip $\mathbb{L}\mathcal{X}$ with a *formal meet* ($\square$) that is indifferent to convex combinations, while preserving d-cone structure. The "Smyth powercone" [41, Thm. 4.23] provides this construction, which we use to define our (normalised) *loss functions* (Definition 5).

Definition 5 (Loss functions).   *The "loss functions" over $\mathcal{X}$, written $\mathbb{SL}\mathcal{X}$, are the nonempty, Scott-compact, convex, upper subsets of $\mathbb{L}\mathcal{X}$. Their canonical refinement order ($\sqsubseteq$) is given by* <u>reverse</u> *set inclusion.*

Remark 4. These are named after the loss functions of Bayesian decision theory [45], which [4,39] first applied to QIF. Given $E\colon \mathbb{SL}\mathcal{X}$, the score of an (optimal) Bayes estimator for the Bayesian loss function with actions E is $\inf_{e:E}(\mathrm{EV}\ \text{of}\ e)$. We interpret the worst-case $\sqcap$-resolver as such an estimator.

This gives a bijection of $\mathbb{SL}\mathcal{X}$ with the superlinear Scott-cts. functionals $\mathbb{D}_{\perp}\mathcal{X} \to \bar{\mathbb{R}}_{+}$ (see e.g. [41]).[9] Refinement is equivalent to the pointwise ordering, and addition and infima can be interpreted pointwise on these functionals.

Remark 5. The predicates of [10] are *gain* functions (evaluated via *max* EV). Under their model nontermination is angelic: e.g. "$\mathbf{print\ b} \sqsubseteq \mathbf{skip} \sqsubseteq \mathbf{assert\ b}$" whereas "**assert**" should be least. Using loss functions resolves this, and our semantics agrees with existing accounts of nontermination in QIF [32, Def. 7.4].

---

[9] Taking Bayes risk for a "hyperdistribution" $\mathbb{D}_{\perp}\mathbb{D}\mathcal{X}$ gives a unique linear Scott-cts. $U\colon \mathbb{D}_{\perp}\mathbb{D}\mathcal{X} \to \bar{\mathbb{R}}_{+}$ satisfying $\forall\nabla\colon \mathbb{D}_{\perp}\mathbb{D}^2\mathcal{X} \cdot U(\mu\nabla) \leq U((\mathbb{D}_{\perp}\mu)\nabla)$: this is the *data processing inequality* [3,31]. [35, §4.4] studies duality for such "affine extensions".

We have a linear Scott-cts. injection of $\mathbb{L}\mathcal{X} \hookrightarrow \mathbb{SL}\mathcal{X}$ given by principal filters: $e \mapsto \uparrow\{e\}$, which we treat as an *embedding*, e.g. writing $[\![\mathcal{B}]\!]$ as shorthand for $\uparrow\{[\![\mathcal{B}]\!]\}$. The embedding does not preserve meets; to avoid ambiguity we write meets of loss functions as $\boxdot$.

Given a nonempty $E \subseteq \mathbb{L}\mathcal{X}$, write $\uparrow\mathrm{conv}\,E \in \mathbb{SL}\mathcal{X}$ for its upper convex closure. The d-cone structure of $\mathbb{SL}\mathcal{X}$ and its finite meets are as follows [41]:

$$r \cdot E_1 + E_2 = \uparrow\mathrm{conv}\{r \cdot e_1 + e_2 \mid e_1 \in E_1, e_2 \in E_2\} \tag{15}$$

$$E_1 \boxdot E_2 = \uparrow\mathrm{conv}(E_1 \cup E_2) \tag{16}$$

$$\bigvee_{i \in I}^{\uparrow} E_i = \bigcap_{i \in I}^{\downarrow} E_i \tag{17}$$

Given a linear, Scott-cts. probabilistic predicate transformer $f\colon \mathbb{L}\mathcal{Y} \to \mathbb{L}\mathcal{X}$, it extends to a loss transformer $\mathsf{map}(f)\colon \mathbb{SL}\mathcal{Y} \to \mathbb{SL}\mathcal{X}$, with $\mathsf{map}(f)(E) = \uparrow\, \mathrm{f}(\mathrm{E})$.

Proposition 1 ([41, Prop. 4.19]). *Suppose $f\colon \mathbb{L}\mathcal{Y} \to \mathbb{L}\mathcal{X}$ is linear and Scott-cts. Then $\mathsf{map}(f)$ is linear, Scott-cts., and $\boxdot$-preserving, i.e. $\mathsf{map}(f)(E_1 \boxdot E_2) = \mathsf{map}(f)(E_1) \boxdot \mathsf{map}(f)(E_2)$.*

Following [10] we also extend the *conjunction* operator $\boxtimes$ pointwise to an action on $\mathbb{SL}\mathcal{X}$: let $e \boxtimes E = \mathsf{map}(e \boxtimes -)(E)$.

4.2   Weakest Pre-loss Semantics

Definition 6 gives a loss transformer semantics in terms of a family of "weakest pre-loss" functions $\mathsf{wpl}^{\mathcal{Z}}.P\colon \mathbb{SL}(\mathcal{Y}\times\mathcal{Z}) \to \mathbb{SL}(\mathcal{X}\times\mathcal{Z})$. The parameter $\mathcal{Z}$ provides the *context extension* needed for e.g. evaluating $\mathscr{P}(OP)$.

Definition 6 (Weakest pre-loss). *The weakest pre-loss for Kuifje$_{\sqcap}$ program $P\colon \mathcal{X} \to \mathcal{Y}$ and correlated state space $\mathcal{Z}$, $\mathsf{wpl}^{\mathcal{Z}}.P\colon \mathbb{SL}(\mathcal{Y}\times\mathcal{Z}) \to \mathbb{SL}(\mathcal{X}\times\mathcal{Z})$, is*

$$\mathsf{wpl}^{\mathcal{Z}}.\mathbf{skip}\,.E = E \tag{18a}$$

$$\mathsf{wpl}^{\mathcal{Z}}.\mathbf{abort}\,.E = [\![\mathtt{false}]\!] \tag{18b}$$

$$\mathsf{wpl}^{\mathcal{Z}}.(P\,;Q).E = \mathsf{wpl}^{\mathcal{Z}}.P.(\mathsf{wpl}^{\mathcal{Z}}.Q.E) \tag{18c}$$

$$\mathsf{wpl}^{\mathcal{Z}}.\mathtt{x} := f(\mathtt{x}).E = \mathsf{map}(f^{\mathsf{T}} \otimes \mathsf{id}_{\mathcal{Z}})E \tag{18d}$$

$$\mathsf{wpl}^{\mathcal{Z}}.\mathbf{hid\,var}\,\mathtt{x} := f(\mathtt{y}).E = \mathsf{map}((\mathsf{copy}_{\mathcal{Y}}^{\mathsf{T}} \circ (\mathsf{id}_{\mathcal{Y}} \otimes f^{\mathsf{T}})) \otimes \mathsf{id}_{\mathcal{Z}})E \tag{18e}$$

$$\mathsf{wpl}^{\mathcal{Z}}.\mathbf{unvar}\,\mathtt{x}.E = \mathsf{map}(\mathsf{id}_{\mathcal{Y}} \otimes 1_{\mathcal{X}} \otimes \mathsf{id}_{\mathcal{Z}})E \tag{18f}$$

$$\mathsf{wpl}^{\mathcal{Z}}.\mathbf{if}\,g(\mathtt{x})\,\mathbf{then}\,P\,\mathbf{else}\,Q.E = g^{\mathcal{Z}} \boxtimes \mathsf{wpl}^{\mathcal{Z}}.P.E + (\neg g)^{\mathcal{Z}} \boxtimes \mathsf{wpl}^{\mathcal{Z}}.Q.E \tag{18g}$$

$$\mathsf{wpl}^{\mathcal{Z}}.\mathbf{while}\,g(\mathtt{x})\{P\}.E = \sum_{n \in \mathbb{N}} ((g^{\mathcal{Z}} \boxtimes -) \circ \mathsf{wpl}^{\mathcal{Z}}.P)^{n}((\neg g)^{\mathcal{Z}} \boxtimes E) \tag{18h}$$

$$\mathsf{wpl}^{\mathcal{Z}}.\mathbf{print}\,f(\mathtt{x}).E = \sum_{\omega \in \Omega} (f^{\mathsf{T}} 1_{\omega} \otimes 1_{\mathcal{Z}}) \boxtimes E \tag{18i}$$

$$\mathsf{wpl}^{\mathcal{Z}}.P_1 \sqcap P_2.E = \mathsf{wpl}^{\mathcal{Z}}.P_1.E \boxdot \mathsf{wpl}^{\mathcal{Z}}.P_2.E \tag{18j}$$

When $\mathcal{Z}$ is a singleton set we write wpl.

Remark 6. Assignment (18d) applies wp.f pointwise to E, and (18e) and (18f) are analogues that "copy/discard" parts of the state. Nondeterministic choice (18j) is exactly the meet of its constituent programs.

For **print**, applying (15) to (18i) we find that the post-loss E is evaluated against all possible *choice functions* $h\colon \Omega \to E$ to give the expected minimum EV of its conjuncts *conditioned* on ω. The sums for (18g–18h) are similarly "visible". For **if** we "condition" (sum) over each branch; for **while**, over each iteration count.

As with Example 2, let $\mathcal{B}$ be a Boolean predicate over $\mathcal{X}$. Then $r[\![\mathcal{B}]\!] \sqsubseteq \mathsf{wpl}^{\mathcal{Z}}.P.E_{\mathcal{Y}}$ iff $\forall e_{\mathcal{Y}} \in E_{\mathcal{Y}}$ the final EVof $e_{\mathcal{Y}}$ is at least r whenever $\mathcal{B}$ initially holds.

Proposition 2 (Loops (least fixed point)). *Fix $P\colon \mathcal{X} \twoheadrightarrow \mathcal{X}$. Given a loss transformer $\alpha\colon \mathbb{SL}(\mathcal{X} \times \mathcal{Z}) \to \mathbb{SL}(\mathcal{X} \times \mathcal{Z})$, let $\mathsf{step}(\alpha)(E) = g^{\mathcal{Z}} \boxtimes \mathsf{wpl}^{\mathcal{Z}}.P.\alpha(E) + (\neg g)^{\mathcal{Z}} \boxtimes E$. Then (18h) matches the standard least fixed point definition (19):*

$$\mathsf{wpl}^{\mathcal{Z}}.\mathbf{while}\, g\{P\} = \big(\mathsf{LFP}\,\alpha\colon \big(\mathbb{SL}(\mathcal{X}\times\mathcal{Z}) \to \mathbb{SL}(\mathcal{X}\times\mathcal{Z})\big) \cdot \mathsf{step}(\alpha)\big) \qquad (19)$$

Example 7. We have that $\mathsf{wpl}^{\mathcal{Z}}.\mathbf{assert}\, g(\mathrm{x}).E = g^{\mathcal{Z}} \boxtimes E = \mathsf{wpl}^{\mathcal{Z}}.(\mathbf{if}\, g(\mathrm{x})\,\mathbf{then}\,\mathbf{skip}\,\mathbf{else}\,\mathbf{abort}).E$. So assertions can be interpreted either as hidden assignment or visible control flow.

Example 8. We reprise Example 6 using wpl.

$\mathsf{wpl}.(\mathbf{print}\, 2\lfloor \mathrm{n} \div 2 \rfloor; \mathbf{var}\, \mathrm{b} := 0 \sqcap 1).[\![\mathrm{n}+\mathrm{b}\ \text{even}]\!]$

$\quad = \mathsf{wpl}.\mathbf{print}\, 2\lfloor \mathrm{n} \div 2 \rfloor.([\![\mathrm{n}\ \text{even}]\!]\ \Box\ [\![\mathrm{n}\ \text{odd}]\!])$

$\quad = [\![\mathrm{n} \in \{0,1\}]\!] \boxtimes ([\![\mathrm{n}\ \text{even}]\!]\ \Box\ [\![\mathrm{n}\ \text{odd}]\!]) + [\![\mathrm{n} \in \{2,3\}]\!] \boxtimes ([\![\mathrm{n}\ \text{even}]\!]\ \Box\ [\![\mathrm{n}\ \text{odd}]\!])$

$\quad = ([\![\mathrm{n} = 0]\!]\ \Box\ [\![\mathrm{n} = 1]\!]) + ([\![\mathrm{n} = 2]\!]\ \Box\ [\![\mathrm{n} = 3]\!])$

$\quad = ([\![\mathrm{n}{=}0]\!]+[\![\mathrm{n}{=}2]\!])\ \Box\ ([\![\mathrm{n}{=}0]\!]+[\![\mathrm{n}{=}3]\!])\ \Box\ ([\![\mathrm{n}{=}1]\!]+[\![\mathrm{n}{=}2]\!])\ \Box\ ([\![\mathrm{n}{=}1]\!]+[\![\mathrm{n}{=}3]\!])$

Definition 7 (Refinement, *Kuifje*$_\sqcap$ programs). *Given $P, Q\colon \mathcal{X} \twoheadrightarrow \mathcal{Y}$, we say P is <u>refined by</u> Q ("$P \sqsubseteq Q$") whenever $\mathsf{wpl}^{\mathcal{Z}}.P.E \sqsubseteq \mathsf{wpl}^{\mathcal{Z}}.Q.E$ for all E.*

5   Healthiness for **wpl**

For our simulations we will allow abstract programs, i.e. loss transformers that may not arise as some $\mathsf{wpl}.P$. Lemmas 1 and 2 give "healthiness" (well-formedness) properties [5,11,34] that are obeyed by wpl, which we subsequently require for our simulations.

A loss transformer (i.e. function) $f\colon \mathbb{SL}\mathcal{Y} \to \mathbb{SL}\mathcal{X}$ is *partial* if $f(1_{\mathcal{Y}}) \leq 1_{\mathcal{X}}$; it is *total* if $f(1_{\mathcal{Y}}) = 1_{\mathcal{X}}$. It is *homogenous* if $\forall r\colon \bar{\mathbb{R}}_+,\ rf(E) = f(rE)$. It is *superlinear* (resp. *linear*) if it is homogenous and $f(E_1 + E_2) \geq f(E_1) + f(E_2)$ (resp. $=$).

Definition 8. *A Kuifje$_\sqcap$ program $P\colon \mathcal{X} \to \mathcal{Y}$ is* <u>hidden</u> *if it has no* if, while *or* print *instructions. It is* <u>choiceless</u> *if it has no $\sqcap$ instructions.*

Lemma 1. *Let $P\colon \mathcal{X} \to \mathcal{Y}$ be a Kuifje$_\sqcap$ program. Then $\mathsf{wpl}^{\mathcal{Z}}.P\colon \mathbb{SL}(\mathcal{Y}\times\mathcal{Z}) \to \mathbb{SL}(\mathcal{X}\times\mathcal{Z})$ is superlinear, partial, and Scott-cts. Additionally, if P is* hidden *then $\mathsf{wpl}^{\mathcal{Z}}.P$ is $\square$ -preserving; if P is choiceless then $\mathsf{wpl}^{\mathcal{Z}}.P$ is linear.*

Remark 7. Given a superlinear, Scott-cts. loss transformer f, finite meets (resp. infinite sums) such as in (18j) (resp. (18g–18i)) *oplaxly distribute* (resp. *laxly distribute*) over f, so $\square \circ f \sqsupseteq f \circ \square$ and $\sum \circ f \sqsubseteq f \circ \sum$ respectively.

We have distributivity exactly when f is $\square$-preserving (resp. linear), hence setting $\mathsf{rep} = f$ we satisfy the left (resp. right) side of (6), minding the contravariance of wpl (21). This foreshadows the role played by hidden (resp. choiceless) programs in our forward (resp. backward) simulation rule.

Because our datatypes and program contexts may operate on separate parts of the state space, we require a characterisation of *context extension*. From [10, §5.3] we derive a *"weak frame rule"*:

$$\mathsf{wpl}^{\mathcal{Z}}.P.(e_{\mathcal{Z}} \boxtimes E_{\mathcal{Y}}) = e_{\mathcal{Z}} \boxtimes \mathsf{wpl}.P.E_{\mathcal{Y}} \tag{20}$$

Unfortunately, analogously to (10), $(\mathbf{print}\ \mathsf{y}; \mathsf{x} := 0 \sqcap 1) \not\sqsubseteq (\mathsf{x} := 0 \sqcap 1; \mathbf{print}\ \mathsf{y})$, so extending $\boxtimes$ to a monoid on $\mathbb{SL}\mathcal{X}$ would not give a true frame rule. Instead, Lemma 2 gives "weak independence" in terms of *correlation transformers* [36].

Definition 9. *A* <u>correlation transformer</u> *$f\colon \mathcal{X} \to \mathcal{Y}$ is a family of loss transformers $f^{\mathcal{Z}}\colon \mathbb{SL}(\mathcal{Y}\times\mathcal{Z}) \to \mathbb{SL}(\mathcal{X}\times\mathcal{Z})$ (for all state spaces $\mathcal{Z}$) such that $\mathsf{map}(\mathrm{id}_{\mathcal{X}} \otimes g) \circ f^{\mathcal{Z}} = f^{\mathcal{W}} \circ \mathsf{map}(\mathrm{id}_{\mathcal{Y}} \otimes g)$ for all linear, partial, Scott-cts. $g\colon \mathbb{L}\mathcal{Z} \to \mathbb{L}\mathcal{W}$.*

Remark 8. Our correlation transformers are defined more restrictively than those of [36], which only requires commutativity with *total* hidden assignment. We claim ours is a *strictly* stronger notion, ruling out unhealthy abstract programs well known in QIF [3, Ex. 4.15].

Lemma 2. *Given a Kuifje$_\sqcap$ program $P\colon \mathcal{X} \to \mathcal{Y}$, its various context extensions $\mathsf{wpl}^{\mathcal{Z}}.P\colon \mathbb{SL}(\mathcal{Y}\times\mathcal{Z}) \to \mathbb{SL}(\mathcal{X}\times\mathcal{Z})$ form a correlation transformer.*

6   Simulations for Kuifje$_\sqcap$

For our simulations (Definition 4), we must mind that wpl is contravariant. E.g. the center squares of (4–5) now become (21), and so on.

$$
\begin{array}{ccc}
\mathcal{A}\times\mathcal{S} \xleftarrow{\ \mathsf{wpl}.OP_j\ } \mathcal{A}\times\mathcal{S} & \qquad & \mathcal{A}\times\mathcal{S} \xleftarrow{\ \mathsf{wpl}^{\mathcal{A}}.OP_j\ } \mathcal{A}\times\mathcal{S} \\
\mathsf{rep}^{\mathcal{S}}_{\mathrm{F}}\uparrow \quad \sqsupseteq \quad \uparrow\mathsf{rep}^{\mathcal{S}}_{\mathrm{F}} & & \mathsf{rep}^{\mathcal{S}}_{\mathrm{B}}\downarrow \quad \sqsubseteq \quad \downarrow\mathsf{rep}^{\mathcal{S}}_{\mathrm{B}} \\
\mathcal{C}\times\mathcal{S} \xleftarrow[\ \mathsf{wpl}.OP'_j\ ]{} \mathcal{C}\times\mathcal{S} & & \mathcal{C}\times\mathcal{S} \xleftarrow[\ \mathsf{wpl}^{\mathcal{C}}.OP'_j\ ]{} \mathcal{C}\times\mathcal{S}
\end{array}
\tag{21}
$$

$D_\mathcal{A}$	$D_\mathcal{C}$
$I_\mathcal{A}$: **hid var** b $:= 0 \, _\frac{1}{2}\oplus \, 1$;	$I_\mathcal{C}$: **hid var** b $:= 0 \, _\frac{1}{2}\oplus \, 1$;
$OP_\mathcal{A}$: **s** $:=$ **b**;	$OP_\mathcal{C}$: **s** $:=$ **b**;
$F_\mathcal{A}$: **print** b;	**print** b;
unvar b;	$F_\mathcal{C}$: **unvar** b;

Fig. 3. Nonrefinement from Example 9. Shared state is **hid var s**: $\{0, 1\}$.

6.1 Forward Simulations

Example 9. Forward simulations that leak can be unsound.

Consider the datatypes in Fig. 3. Setting $\mathscr{P}(OP) = (OP; (\mathsf{s} := \neg \mathsf{s}) \sqcap \mathbf{skip})$ demonstrates that $D_\mathcal{A} \not\sqsubseteq D_\mathcal{C}$. Yet there is a forward simulation rep $=$ **print** b satisfying (4). In a sense, the **print** in rep "masks" the **print** in $OP_\mathcal{C}$.

Theorem 1. *Let correlation transformer* rep: $\mathcal{A} \to \mathcal{C}$ *be a forward simulation from* $D_\mathcal{A}$ *to* $D_\mathcal{C}$. *If* rep *is superlinear, partial, Scott-cts., and* $\square$*-preserving, then* $D_\mathcal{A} \sqsubseteq D_\mathcal{C}$.

Corollary 1. *Let* $R: \mathcal{A} \to \mathcal{C}$ *be a* <u>hidden</u> *Kuifje$_\sqcap$ program such that* wpl.R *is a forward simulation from* $D_\mathcal{A}$ *to* $D_\mathcal{C}$. *Then* $D_\mathcal{A} \sqsubseteq D_\mathcal{C}$.

6.2 Backward Simulations

$D_\mathcal{A}$	$D_\mathcal{C}$
$I_\mathcal{A}$: **hid var** b $:= 0 \sqcap 1$;	$I_\mathcal{C}$: **hid var** b $:= 0 \sqcap 1$;
$OP_\mathcal{A}$: **s** $:=$ **b**;	$OP_\mathcal{C}$: **b** $:= 0 \sqcap 1$;
b $:= 0 \sqcap 1$;	**s** $:=$ **b**;
$F_\mathcal{A}$: **unvar** b;	$F_\mathcal{C}$: **unvar** b;

Fig. 4. Nonrefinement from Example 10. Shared state is **hid var s**: $\{0, 1\}$.

Example 10. Nondeterministic backward simulations can be unsound.

Consider the datatypes in Fig. 4. Setting $\mathscr{P}(OP) = (\mathbf{print}\,\mathsf{a}; OP; \mathsf{a} := \mathsf{s} \mathbf{\,xor\,} \mathsf{a})$ demonstrates that $D_\mathcal{A} \not\sqsubseteq D_\mathcal{C}$. Yet there is a backward simulation rep $= (\mathsf{b} := 0 \sqcap 1)$ satisfying (5). In a sense, the $(\sqcap)$ in rep "masks" the $(\sqcap)$ in $OP_\mathcal{C}$.

Theorem 2. *Let correlation transformer* rep: $\mathcal{C} \to \mathcal{A}$ *be a backward simulation from* $D_\mathcal{A}$ *to* $D_\mathcal{C}$. *If* rep *is* <u>linear</u>, *partial, and Scott-cts., then* $D_\mathcal{A} \sqsubseteq D_\mathcal{C}$.

Corollary 2. *Let* $R: \mathcal{C} \to \mathcal{A}$ *be a* <u>choiceless</u> *Kuifje$_\sqcap$ program such that* wpl.R *is a backward simulation from* $D_\mathcal{A}$ *to* $D_\mathcal{C}$. *Then* $D_\mathcal{A} \sqsubseteq D_\mathcal{C}$.

7 Examples

7.1 Example: Random Bit Generator/"fork+spade"

Example 11. Recall the random bit generator example (Fig. 1, Example 4). In Kuifje$_\sqcap$ we interpret the encapsulated state as hidden, replacing "**var**" with "**hid var**" to get $I_C = (\mathbf{hid\,var}\,b := 0 \,{}_{\frac{1}{2}}{\oplus}\, 1)$.

Defining a forward simulation $\mathsf{rep} = (\mathbf{hid\,var}\,b := 0 \,{}_{\frac{1}{2}}{\oplus}\, 1)$, we verify (4):

$$\mathbf{skip}; \mathsf{rep} \sqsubseteq \mathsf{rep}$$

$$\begin{pmatrix} \mathbf{s} := 0 \,{}_{\frac{1}{2}}{\oplus}\, 1; \\ \mathbf{hid\,var}\,b := 0 \,{}_{\frac{1}{2}}{\oplus}\, 1; \end{pmatrix} \sqsubseteq \begin{pmatrix} \mathbf{hid\,var}\,b := 0 \,{}_{\frac{1}{2}}{\oplus}\, 1; \\ \mathbf{s} := \mathbf{b};\ \mathbf{b} := 0 \,{}_{\frac{1}{2}}{\oplus}\, 1; \end{pmatrix}$$

$$\mathbf{skip} \sqsubseteq (\mathbf{hid\,var}\,b := 0 \,{}_{\frac{1}{2}}{\oplus}\, 1; \mathbf{unvar}\,b)$$

and so Corollary 1 gives $D_\mathcal{A} \sqsubseteq D_\mathcal{C}$ as expected.

In fact, these are all refinement-equalities, so $\mathsf{rep} \colon \mathcal{A} \to \mathcal{C}$ also serves as a backward simulation from $D_\mathcal{C}$ to $D_\mathcal{A}$. By Corollary 2, $D_\mathcal{C} \sqsubseteq D_\mathcal{A}$, and so the datatypes are equivalent.

Remark 9. We are not aware of a linear backward simulation showing $D_\mathcal{A} \sqsubseteq D_\mathcal{C}$. The difficulty is that any $OP_\mathcal{C}; \mathsf{rep}$ reveals information about the initial value of b which, though irrelevant, causes (5) to fail.

7.2 Example: Encrypted Database

Shared state: $\mathbf{hid\,var}\,\mathbf{x}\colon \mathcal{X},\ \mathtt{U}\colon \mathcal{X}[N],\ \mathbf{r}\colon \{0,1\}.$

$D_\mathcal{A}$		
$I_\mathcal{A}\colon \mathbf{hid\,var}\,\mathtt{H} := \mathtt{U};$	$OP_\mathcal{A}\colon \mathbf{r} := (\mathbf{x} \in \mathtt{H});$	$F_\mathcal{A}\colon \mathbf{unvar}\,\mathtt{H};$

$D_\mathcal{C}$	$D_\mathcal{C}'$
$I_\mathcal{C}\colon \mathbf{hid\,var}\,\mathtt{H} := \mathtt{U};$	$I_\mathcal{C}'\colon \mathbf{hid\,var}\,\mathtt{H} := \mathtt{U};$
$OP_\mathcal{C}\colon \mathbf{hid\,var}\,\mathbf{n} := 0;$	$OP_\mathcal{C}'\colon \mathbf{hid\,var}\,\mathbf{n} := 0;$
$\quad$ **while** $(\mathbf{n} \neq N \wedge \mathtt{H}[\mathbf{n}] \neq \mathbf{x})\,\{$	$\quad \mathbf{hid\,var}\,\mathbf{m} := 0 \,{}_{\frac{1}{N}}{\oplus}\, 1 \,{}_{\frac{1}{N}}{\oplus}\, \ldots \,{}_{\frac{1}{N}}{\oplus}\, N-1;$
$\quad\quad \mathbf{n} := \mathbf{n}+1;$	$\quad$ **while** $(\mathbf{n} \neq N \wedge \mathtt{H}[(\mathbf{n}+\mathbf{m})\%N] \neq \mathbf{x})\,\{$
$\quad\};$	$\quad\quad \mathbf{n} := \mathbf{n}+1;$
$\quad \mathbf{r} := (\mathbf{n} < N);$	$\quad\};$
$\quad \mathbf{unvar}\,\mathbf{n};$	$\quad \mathbf{r} := (\mathbf{n} < N);$
$F_\mathcal{C}\colon \mathbf{unvar}\,\mathtt{H};$	$\quad \mathbf{unvar}\,\mathbf{n};\ \mathbf{unvar}\,\mathbf{m};$
	$F_\mathcal{C}'\colon \mathbf{unvar}\,\mathtt{H};$

Fig. 5. An "encrypted database" $D_\mathcal{A}$ [9, Fig. 6], and flawed implementations $D_\mathcal{C}$ [9, Fig. 7] and $D_\mathcal{C}'$ that leak side channel information. In $OP_\mathcal{C}'$, $\mathbf{m}$ is initialised uniformly over the first N naturals.

Figure 5 builds upon an "encrypted database" example from [9, §4]. $D_{\mathcal{A}}$ provides membership testing for a secret array, and $D_{\mathcal{C}}$ performs linear search with short-circuiting. $D_{\mathcal{C}}$ is vulnerable to a *timing attack* leaking the index at which x was found, hence $D_{\mathcal{A}} \not\sqsubseteq D_{\mathcal{C}}$ [9, Eqns. 6–7].

We might consider the alternative implementation $D'_{\mathcal{C}}$ (Fig. 5), which uses a (hidden) random offset to obfuscate which index is checked at each iteration of the loop. But in fact this is insufficient to fully hide the database contents.

Let $\mathcal{X} = \{a, b, c\}$, $\mathscr{P}(OP) = (\mathtt{x} := a;\ OP;\ \mathbf{var}\ \mathtt{v} := 2 \sqcap 3)$. Suppose the array U is initialised uniformly from $\delta \colon \mathbb{D}(\mathcal{X}[4]) = [a, b, c, a]\, {}_{\frac{1}{2}}\oplus\, [a, b, a, c]$. As $OP_{\mathcal{A}}$ leaks nothing about the position of c, we have $\mathsf{wpl}.\big(\mathtt{U} := \delta;\ I_{\mathcal{A}};\ \mathscr{P}(OP_{\mathcal{A}})\big).\llbracket \mathtt{U}[\mathtt{v}] \neq \mathtt{c} \rrbracket \geq \frac{1}{2}$. However, this is not the case for $D'_{\mathcal{C}}$. Let $e_n = \llbracket \forall 0 \leq i \leq n \cdot (\mathtt{H}[(\mathtt{m} + i)\%N] = a \Longleftrightarrow i = n) \rrbracket$. Then

$$
\begin{aligned}
&\mathsf{wpl}.(\mathtt{U} := [a, b, c, a]\, {}_{\frac{1}{2}}\oplus\, [a, b, a, c];\ I'_{\mathcal{C}};\ \mathscr{P}(OP'_{\mathcal{C}})).\llbracket \mathtt{U}[\mathtt{v}] \neq c \rrbracket \\
&\quad = \mathsf{wpl}.(\mathtt{U} := \delta;\ I'_{\mathcal{C}};\ \mathtt{x} := a;\ OP'_{\mathcal{C}}).(\llbracket \mathtt{U}[2] \neq c \rrbracket \ \Box\ \llbracket \mathtt{U}[3] \neq c \rrbracket) \\
&\quad = \mathsf{wpl}.\left(\begin{array}{c}\mathtt{U} := \delta;\ \mathbf{var}\ \mathtt{m} := \\ 0\, {}_{\frac{1}{N}}\oplus \ldots {}_{\frac{1}{N}}\oplus\, N{-}1\end{array}\right) \cdot \sum_{n=0}^{N-1} \left(e_n\ \boxtimes\ (\llbracket \mathtt{U}[2] \neq c \rrbracket \ \Box\ \llbracket \mathtt{U}[3] \neq c \rrbracket\,)\right) \\
&\quad = \mathsf{wpl}.\left(\begin{array}{c}\mathbf{var}\ \mathtt{m} := \\ 0\, {}_{\frac{1}{N}}\oplus \ldots {}_{\frac{1}{N}}\oplus\, N{-}1\end{array}\right) \cdot \sum_{n=0}^{N-1} e_n\ \boxtimes\ \left(\begin{array}{c}\frac{1}{2}\big(\sum_{U \in \mathrm{supp}\, \delta}\llbracket U[2] \neq c \rrbracket\big)\ \Box \\ \frac{1}{2}\big(\sum_{U \in \mathrm{supp}\, \delta}\llbracket U[3] \neq c \rrbracket\big)\end{array}\right) \\
&\quad \leq \tfrac{1}{4}\big((1 \sqcap 1) + (\tfrac{1}{2} \sqcap 1) + (\tfrac{1}{2} \sqcap 0) + (0 \sqcap 0)\big) = \tfrac{3}{8}
\end{aligned}
$$

and so by (1), $D_{\mathcal{A}} \not\sqsubseteq D'_{\mathcal{C}}$.

This issue can be resolved with further restrictions on U. Let e_{uniq} evaluate to 1 when all elements of U are distinct, and 0 otherwise. Let $D'_{\mathcal{A}} := ((I_{\mathcal{A}};\ \mathbf{assert}\ e_{\mathrm{uniq}}),\ OP_{\mathcal{A}},\ F_{\mathcal{A}},\ \mathcal{A})$. In other words, its behaviour is undefined when there are duplicate elements. Then $\mathsf{rep} := \mathbf{assert}\ e_{\mathrm{uniq}}$ is a backward simulation satisfying the conditions of Theorem 2, and so $D'_{\mathcal{A}} \sqsubseteq D'_{\mathcal{C}}$.

8   Conclusions and Future Work

We introduced a "loss transformer" semantics for POMDPs. These POMDPs have a single $\sqcap$-resolver: leaks on one side of the encapsulation barrier affect nondeterminism on the other side. This is too restrictive to model e.g. true "programmer's choice" or secure multi-party computation—this may require extending loss functions to multiple resolvers with *independent knowledge* [17].

Kuifje$_{\sqcap}$ is not a conservative extension of pGCL (Remark 3), in part because all state is hidden. In future work we intend to model "first-class" visible variables via *exponentiation* ("$(\mathbb{S}\mathcal{L}\mathcal{H})^{\mathcal{V}}$"), and study the semantics of 'promoting' hidden state to visible ("hypernormalisation" [15,21]).

Our *healthiness conditions* for Kuifje$_{\sqcap}$ (Lemma 1–2) are strong enough to give our forward (resp. backward) simulation rules modulo $\Box$-preserving (resp. linearity) conditions. They resemble those for pGCL [34, §7]. However pGCL's are *complete* for (the image of) wp, whereas ours may be incomplete for wpl's (even after "dcpo-closure"/sobrification).

Our forward and backward simulations for Kuifje$_\sqcap$ data refinement are *sound* modulo "hidden/choiceless" restrictions (Theorems 1–2). We leave *completeness* to future work. Forward simulation is incomplete, even for GCL [14]. We suspect backward simulation is also incomplete for Kuifje$_\sqcap$ (Remark 9).

Backward simulation composed with forward is *jointly* complete for GCL [19, 20, 29]. But it is unclear how to perform standard constructions such as limits of Kan extensions [14, 19] or final coalgebras [18, 29] while preserving superlinearity, Scott-cty., or (as required) linearity or $\Box$-preservation.

Additionally, the requirement that a family of rep$^\mathcal{Z}$ be a correlation transformer (Definition 9) is difficult to establish in the absence of a corresponding syntactic Kuifje$_\sqcap$ program. It is an open question under what circumstances a function $\mathbb{SL}\mathcal{Y} \to \mathbb{SL}\mathcal{X}$ "extends" to a correlation transformer.

Disclosure of Interests. The authors have no competing interests to declare that are relevant to the content of this article.

References

1. Abadi, M., Lamport, L.: The existence of refinement mappings. In: LICS, pp. 165–175 (1988)
2. Abramsky, S., Jung, A.: Domain Theory. In: Handbook of Logic and Computer Science, pp. 1–168. Oxford Science Publications (1994)
3. Alvim, M.S., Chatzikokolakis, K., McIver, A., Morgan, C., Smith, G., Palamidessi, C.: The Science of Quantitative Information Flow. Springer (2020)
4. Alvim, M.S., Chatzikokolakis, K., Palamidessi, C., Smith, G.: Measuring information leakage using generalized gain functions. In: Proceedings of 25th IEEE Computer Security Foundations Symposium (CSF 2012), pp. 265–279 (2012)
5. Back, R.-J., von Wright, J.: Refinement Calculus: A Systematic Introduction. Springer (1998)
6. Back, R.-J., Wright, J.: Encoding, decoding and data refinement. Formal Aspects Comput. **12**(5), 313–349 (2000)
7. Bolton, C., Davies, J., Woodcock, J.: On the refinement and simulation of data types and processes. In: Proceedings of iFM, pp. 273–292 (1999)
8. Bottenbruch, H.: Structure and use of ALGOL 60. J. ACM **9**(2), 161–221 (1962). https://doi.org/10.1145/321119.321120
9. Chen, C., McIver, A., Morgan, C.: Probabilistic datatypes. In: Proceedings of ICTAC. LNCS, pp. 3–16. Springer, Heidelberg (2024)
10. Chen, C., McIver, A., Morgan, C.: Source-level reasoning for quantifying information leaks. In: Jansen, N., et al. (eds.) Principles of Verification: Cycling the Probabilistic Landscape. LNCS, pp. 98–127. Springer, Cham (2025)
11. Dijkstra, E.: A Discipline of Programming. Prentice-Hall (1976)
12. Dijkstra, E., Scholten, C.: Predicate Calculus and Program Semantics. Springer (1990)
13. Floyd, R.: Assigning meanings to programs. In: Schwartz, J. (ed.) Mathematical Aspects of Computer Science, pp. 19–32. American Mathematical Society (1967)

14. Gardiner, P., Morgan, C.: A single complete rule for data refinement. Formal Aspects Comput. **5**(4), 367–82 (1993)
15. Garner, R.: Hypernormalisation in an abstract setting. Inf. Comput. **293**, 105044 (2023)
16. Gibbons, J., McIver, A., Morgan, C., Schrijvers, T.: Quantitative information flow with monads in haskell. In: Barthe, G., Katoen, J.-P., Silva, A. (eds.) Foundations of Probabilistic Programming. CUP (2019)
17. Giro, S., D'Argenio, P.: On the expressive power of schedulers in distributed probabilistic systems. ENTCS **253**(3), 45–71 (2009)
18. Hasuo, I.: Generic forward and backward simulations. In: Baier, C., Hermanns, H. (eds.) CONCUR 2006. LNCS, vol. 4137, pp. 406–420. Springer, Heidelberg (2006). https://doi.org/10.1007/11817949_27
19. Hoare, C.A., Sanders, J.W.: Data refinement refined. In: ESOP 1986: European Symposium on Programming, pp. 187–196 (1986)
20. Hoare, C., He, J., Sanders, J.: Prespecification in data refinement. Inf. Proc. Lett. **25**(2), 71–6 (1987)
21. Jacobs, B.: Hyper normalisation and conditioning for discrete probability distributions. Log. Methods Comput. Sci. **13** (2017)
22. Johnson, M., Naumann, D., Power, J.: Category theoretic models of data refinement. Electron. Notes Theor. Comput. Sci. **225**, 21–38 (2009)
23. Jones, C., Plotkin, G.: A probabilistic powerdomain of evaluations. In: LICS 1989, pp. 186–95. Computer Society Press, Los Alamitos (1989)
24. Kaebling, L.P., Littman, M.L., Cassandra, A.R.: Planning and acting in partially observable stochastic domains. Artif. Intell. **101**, 99–134 (1998)
25. Kozen, D.: Semantics of probabilistic programs. J. Comput. Syst. Sci. **22**, 328–50 (1981)
26. Langmaack, H., Olderog, E.-R.: Present-day Hoare-like systems for programming languages with procedures: power, limits and most likely extensions. In: De Bakker, J., van Leeuwen, J. (eds.) ICALP, pp. 363–373. Springer, Heidelberg (1988)
27. Liskov, B.: Data abstraction and hierarchy. In: Addendum to Proceedings of OOPSLA, pp. 17–34 (1987)
28. Liskov, B., Zilles, S.: Programming with abstract data types. ACM Sigplan Not. **9**(4), 50–59 (1974)
29. Lynch, N., Vaandrager, F.: Forward and backward simulations. Inf. Comput. **121**(2), 214–233 (1995)
30. McIver, A., Morgan, C.: Abstraction, Refinement and Proof for Probabilistic Systems. Springer, New York (2005)
31. McIver, A., Meinicke, L., Morgan, C.: A Kantorovich-monadic powerdomain for information hiding, with probability and nondeterminism. In: Proceedings of LICS 2012 (2012)
32. McIver, A., Meinicke, L., Morgan, C.: Hidden-Markov program algebra with iteration. Math. Struct. Comput. Sci. **24** (2014). https://doi.org/10.1017/S0960129513000625
33. Morgan, C., McIver, A.: pGCL: formal reasoning for random algorithms. South Afr. Comput. J. **22**, 14–27 (1999)
34. Morgan, C., McIver, A., Seidel, K.: Probabilistic predicate transformers. ACM Trans. Prog. Lang. Syst. **18**(3), 325–53 (1996)
35. Perrone, P.: Categorical probability and stochastic dominance in metric spaces. Ph.D. thesis, Dissertation, Leipzig, Universität Leipzig (2018)

36. Rabehaja, T., McIver, A., Morgan, C., Struth, G.: Categorical information flow. In: Alvim, M.S., Chatzikokolakis, K., Olarte, C., Valencia, F. (eds.) The Art of Modelling Computational Systems: A Journey from Logic and Concurrency to Security and Privacy. LNCS, vol. 11760, pp. 329–343. Springer, Cham (2019). https://doi.org/10.1007/978-3-030-31175-9_19
37. de Roever, W.-P., Engelhardt, K.: Data Refinement: Model-Oriented Proof Methods and their Comparison. Cambridge University Press (1998)
38. Rutten, J.J.M.M.: Universal coalgebra: a theory of systems. TCS **249**(1), 3–80 (2000)
39. Smith, G.: On the foundations of quantitative information flow. In: de Alfaro, L. (ed.) FoSSaCS 2009. LNCS, vol. 5504, pp. 288–302. Springer, Heidelberg (2009). https://doi.org/10.1007/978-3-642-00596-1_21
40. Smith, G.: Quantifying information flow using min-entropy. In: Proceedings of QEST 2011, pp. 159–167 (2011)
41. Tix, R., Keimel, K., Plotkin, G.: Semantic domains for combining probability and non-determinism. ENTCS **222**, 3–99 (2009)
42. Varacca, D.: Probability, nondeterminism and concurrency: two denotational models for probabilistic computation. Ph.D. thesis (2003)
43. Wirth, N.: Program development by stepwise refinement. Commun. ACM **14**(4), 221–227 (1971). http://www.acm.org/classics/doc96/
44. Ye, K., Foster, S., Woodcock, J.: Automated reasoning for probabilistic sequential programs with theorem proving. In: RAMiCS, pp. 465–482. Springer (2021)
45. Zellner, A.: Bayesian estimation and prediction using asymmetric loss functions. J. Am. Stat. Assoc. **81**(394), 446–451 (1986)

Graphical Quadratic Algebra

Dario Stein[1]([✉]), Fabio Zanasi[2]([✉]), Robin Piedeleu[2]([✉]),
and Richard Samuelson[3]([✉])

[1] Radboud University Nijmegen, Nijmegen, Netherlands
`dario.stein@ru.nl`
[2] University College London, London, UK
`{f.zanasi,r.piedeleu}@ucl.ac.uk`
[3] University of Florida, Gainesville, USA
`rsamuelson@ufl.edu`

Abstract. Convex analysis and Gaussian probability are tightly connected, as mostly evident in the theory of linear regression. Our work introduces an algebraic perspective on such relationships, in the form of a diagrammatic calculus of string diagrams, called Graphical Quadratic Algebra (GQA). We show that GQA is a complete axiomatisation for the category of quadratic relations, a compositional formulation of quadratic problems. Moreover, we identify a sub-theory of GQA which is complete for the category of Gaussian probabilistic processes. We show how GQA may be used to study linear regression and probabilistic programming.

Keywords: string diagrams · categorical semantics · linear algebra · linear regression · categorical probability

1 Introduction

Gaussian probability theory studies phenomena governed by *normal* distributions—bell-shaped curves fully determined by mean and variance. Quadratic optimisation, on the other hand, is concerned with minimising quadratic functions—those expressible as polynomials of degree at most 2. Though they arise in different contexts, these two areas are deeply related. A clear instance of this connection appears in linear regression, where one seeks the best-fitting solution to a linear system $Ax = b$, with A a matrix and b a vector representing observed data. If the error term ϵ is assumed to follow a Gaussian distribution, then finding the most likely solution to the model $Ax + \epsilon = b$ is equivalent to minimising the quadratic loss function $f(x) = ||Ax - b||^2$, which measures the sum of squared residuals. The relationship goes further: the log-density of a Gaussian distribution is itself a quadratic function, and computing conditional distributions in Gaussian models often reduces to solving least-squares problems.

In this paper, we introduce a fresh perspective on Gaussian probability, quadratic optimisation, and their web of connections, by presenting them as

Z. Liu et al. (Eds.): ICTAC 2025, LNCS 16237, pp. 298–316, 2026.
https://doi.org/10.1007/978-3-032-11176-0_18

categorical structures. Our main results are *complete axiomatisations* for these categories, via an axiomatic calculus called *graphical quadratic algebra.*

Our approach unfolds as follows. First, we study how quadratic problems *compose*, so that they can be organised into a category. To this aim, we view a partial quadratic function $F\colon \mathbb{R}^m \times \mathbb{R}^n \to [0,\infty]$ as a $[0,\infty]$-weighted relation on $\mathbb{R}^m \times \mathbb{R}^n$, called *quadratic relation.* This perspective has three major appeals. First, quadratic relations characterise the solutions of constrained least-square problems [9]. Second, their composition is naturally defined via constrained minimisation (see (8) below). Third, quadratic relations extend affine relations [6], linking our work with the theory of *Graphical Affine Algebra* [6] and offering a clear pathway towards a complete axiomatic calculus.

The resulting category **QuadRel**, with morphisms the quadratic relations, provides an algebraic setting to study quadratic optimisation. Gaussian probability enters the picture as a subcategory **Gauss** of **QuadRel**. The category **Gauss** has been previously studied as a *Markov category*, in the context of a more general framework for categorical probability theory [14]. Morphisms of **Gauss**, called Gaussian stochastic maps, generalise Gaussian distributions in the same way as linear maps generalise vectors. The study of **Gauss** is of independent interest because of its use as a semantics for Gaussian probabilistic programming [29].

Once the 'semantic' structures **QuadRel** and **Gauss** are in place, we introduce their 'syntactic' presentation. Our language adopts the graphical notation of *string diagrams* (see eg. [23,25] for recent introductions). As a two-dimensional formalism, string diagrams can be flexibly treated both as syntax and as combinatorial objects. They are now widely adopted in axiomatic reasoning on resource-sensitive models, eg. in linear algebra [2,7,11,12] and probabilistic reasoning [14,17,18,21], making it a natural choice for our approach.

The language we introduce, called **GQA** ('Graphical Quadratic Algebra'), consists of the string diagrams obtained by sequential and parallel composition of the following generators, for $k \in \mathbb{R}$:

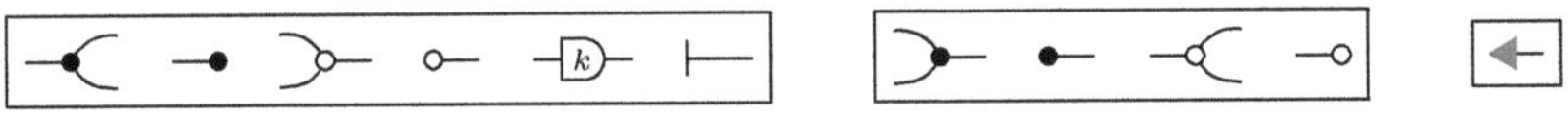

(1)

As the name suggests, **GQA** directly extends *Graphical Affine Algebra* (**GAA**, [6]), which is given by the generators of the first two blocks in (1). Semantically, the generators in the first block model basic linear algebraic operations of copying ( ), discarding ( ) addition ( ), scaling ( ), and the constants zero ( ) and one ( ). With the equational theory of Hopf bimonoids (Fig. 1, first block), string diagrams built with these generators are known to axiomatise the category **AffVect** of affine maps [6]. If we add the generators of the second block of (1), namely , , , , with behaviour symmetric to their mirrored version and extra equations (third block in Fig. 1, notably including two Frobenius monoid structures), we obtain the full **GAA**, which axiomatises the category **AffRel** of affine relations, i.e. affine subspaces that compose relationally [6].

The surprising discovery of our work is that, in order to extend the axiomatisation of the category **AffRel** of affine relations to one of the category **QuadRel** of *quadratic* relations, it suffices to add just one extra generator, ◄— (and three equations as in Fig. 1, second block): this yields **GQA**. Moreover, we axiomatise **Gauss** by restricting **GQA** to generators in the first and third block in (1).

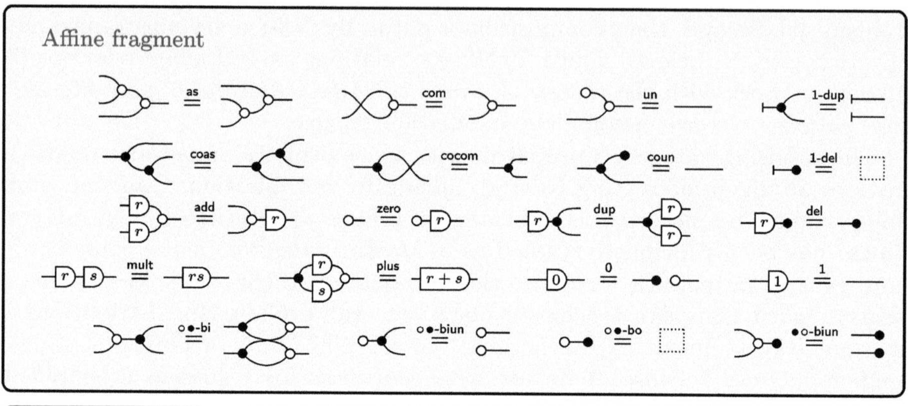

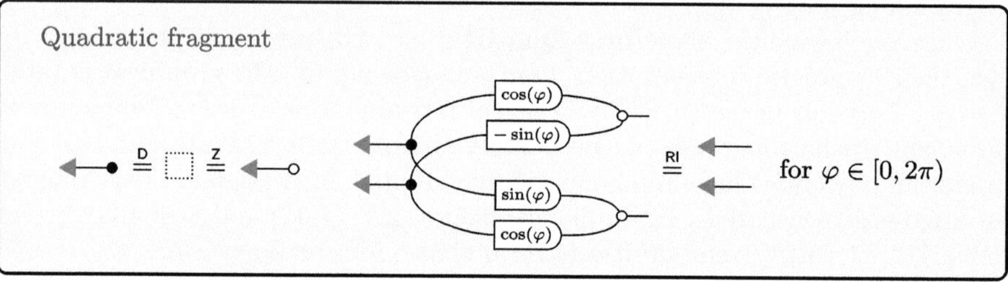

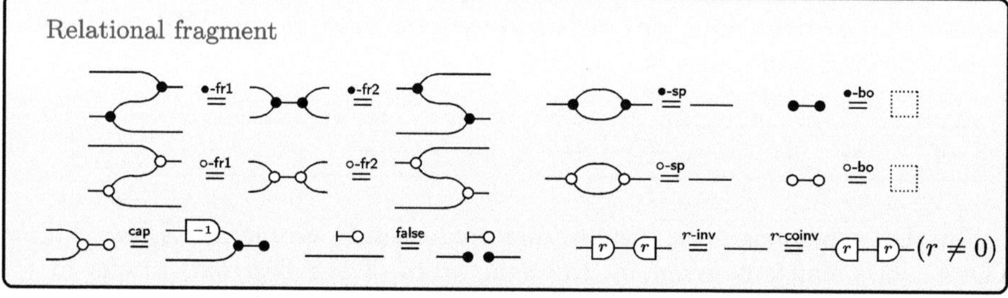

Fig. 1. Axioms of Graphical Quadratic Algebra.

In **Gauss**, ◄— is interpreted as the standard normal distribution $\mathcal{N}(0,1)$, and in **QuadRel** as the quadratic function $f(x) = \frac{1}{2}x^2$ (ie., a unary quadratic relation on $\mathbb{R}$). We illustrate this dual interpretation via an example.

Example 1. The semantics of the string diagram ⟩◦— in **QuadRel**, built up from two instances of ◄— and ⟩◦—, is the constrained minimisation problem on the left below, whose solution can be found on the right-hand side, with its corresponding diagram:

$$\left[\!\!\left[\; \rightthreetimes \!\!- \right]\!\!\right] = \left(y \mapsto \inf\left\{ \frac{1}{2}x_1^2 + \frac{1}{2}x_2^2 : x_1 + x_2 = y \right\} \right) = \left(y \mapsto \frac{1}{4}y^2 \right) = \left[\!\!\left[\; \leftharpoonup\!\!-\boxed{\sqrt{2}}\!\!- \right]\!\!\right] \tag{2}$$

In **Gauss**, (2) means that if $X_1, X_2 \sim \mathcal{N}(0,1)$ are independent variables, then $Y = X_1 + X_2$ has distribution $\mathcal{N}(0,2)$.

We can now use the axioms of GQA (Fig. 1) to derive (2). The notable step involves the axiom scheme RI, expressing that the function $f(x,y) = \frac{1}{2}(x^2 + y^2)$ is *invariant under rotations*. When interpreted in **Gauss**, RI is evocative of the Herschel-Maxwell theorem, which states that the normal distribution is uniquely characterised by its rotation invariance (e.g. [15]). Because $\cos(\pi/4) = \sin(\pi/2 - \pi/4) = \sin(\pi/4) = 1/\sqrt{2}$, we can apply RI with $\varphi = \pi/4$ as below. We then simplify the resulting string diagram via linear algebraic manipulations in the fragment GAA, obtaining the desired outcome $\leftharpoonup\!\!-\boxed{\sqrt{2}}\!\!-$.

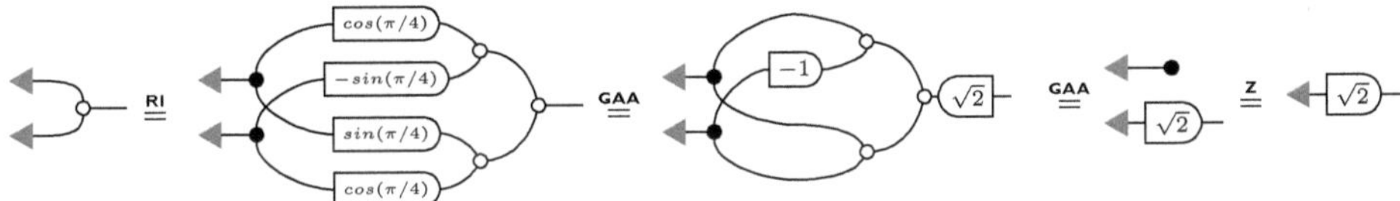

Completeness of **GQA** for **QuadRel** and **Gauss** ensures that any semantic equality as in Example 1 can in principle be derived. More broadly, this algebraic characterisation sheds light on the connections between quadratic optimisation and Gaussian probability theory, revealing their relative expressive power. Notably, the equational theory of **Gauss** is a fragment of the one of **QuadRel**, without the ability to model relational behaviours using Frobenius monoids. Moreover, the presentation of **Gauss** omits the generator $-\!\circ$, which we may regard as conditioning of Gaussians. From this perspective, we may view quadratic relations as generalised Gaussian distributions, which combine probability and conditioning.

There are a few more interesting ramifications of our work. As noted, there are transformations relating Gaussian distributions, quadratic problems, and affine spaces. However, turning them into functors is technically challenging, as studied in [28]. Thanks to our axiomatic presentations, it suffices to define these mappings on the generators of **GQA** to obtain functoriality as a simple corollary. We explore this in Sect. 5.1.

Our characterisations also enable a new methodology, based on equational diagrammatic reasoning, to study domains modelled by quadratic relations or Gaussian distributions, such as linear regression and probabilistic program semantics. We explore these examples in Sect. 5. As a preview, the program below left is written in a language with support for Gaussian distributions and a conditioning operator ($=:=$), and computes inference of a latent variable from a noisy observation. The corresponding **GQA**-diagram is below right.

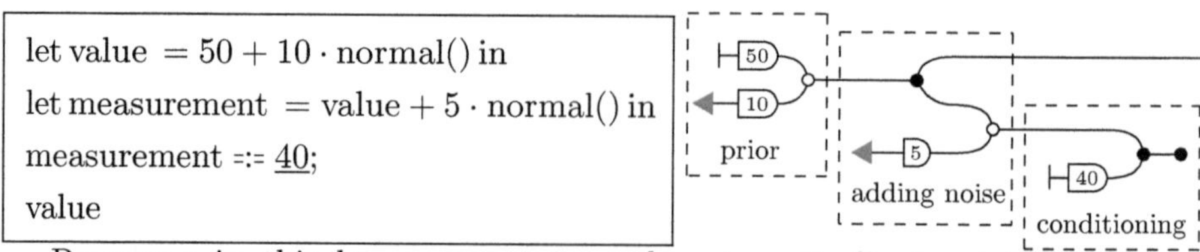

Programs in this language correspond systematically to string diagrams. Moreover, the axioms of **GQA** suffice to reduce such a diagram to one representing the posterior distribution, effectively mirroring the program's execution.

Synopsis: After preliminaries (Sect. 2), we present our work in two steps: first we introduce the simpler theory **Gauss**, and show how the fragment $\overrightarrow{\mathbf{GQA}}$ axiomatises it (Sect. 3). Next, we introduce **QuadRel** and its axiomatic calculus, the full **GQA** (Sect. 4). We then conclude with some applications (Sect. 5) and future work (Sect. 6). For further details and proofs we refer to the extended version of this paper [31].

2   Background: Graphical Affine Algebra

We recall background on string diagrams and Graphical Affine Algebra, referring to [6] for more details. A symmetric strict monoidal category with set of objects the natural numbers, and monoidal product on objects given by addition, is called a *prop* [22]. Prop morphisms are identity-on-objects symmetric monoidal functors between props. Props play a role akin to algebraic clones, in a monoidal setting. Various linear algebraic transformations may be organised into props.

Definition 1.   *The prop* **AffVect** *has affine maps of type* $\mathbb{R}^m \to \mathbb{R}^n$ *as morphisms* $m \to n$, *with composition given by matrix multiplication and monoidal product given by direct sum. The prop* **AffRel** *has affine subspaces of* $\mathbb{R}^{m+n}$ *as morphisms* $m \to n$, *with relational composition* $R; S = \{(\mathbf{v}, \mathbf{w}) \mid \exists \mathbf{u}.(\mathbf{v}, \mathbf{u}) \in R \wedge (\mathbf{u}, \mathbf{w}) \in S\}$, *and monoidal product given by direct sum.*

Because of the way they compose, **AffRel**-morphisms are called *affine relations*. Complete axiomatisations for these categories are provided by string diagrammatic calculi, which we now introduce. A *symmetric monoidal theory* (SMT) is a pair (Σ, E), where Σ is a signature of operations $o\colon m \to n$ with an arity m and coarity n, and E is a set of equations between Σ-terms. A Σ-term c of type $m \to n$ will be represented graphically as *a string diagram* [23,25] with m dangling wires on the left and n on the right, also written $\overset{m}{}\boxed{c}\overset{n}{}$. Formally, Σ-terms are freely obtained by sequential and parallel compositions of the operations in Σ together with the identity $-\!\!-\colon 1 \to 1$, the symmetry $\asymp\colon 2 \to 2$, and the 'empty' diagram $\square\colon 0 \to 0$. Sequential composition of Σ-terms $\overset{m}{}\boxed{c}\overset{n}{}$ and $\overset{v}{}\boxed{d}\overset{n}{}$ is depicted as $\overset{m}{}\!-\!\boxed{c}\!-\!\boxed{d}\!-\!\overset{n}{}$, of type $m \to n$. Parallel composition of Σ-terms $\overset{m_1}{}\boxed{c_1}\overset{n_1}{}$ and $\overset{m_2}{}\boxed{c_2}\overset{n_2}{}$ is depicted as $\begin{smallmatrix} m_1 \boxed{c_1} n_1 \\ m_2 \boxed{c_2} n_2 \end{smallmatrix}$, of type $m_1 + m_2 \to n_1 + n_2$. We refer to Σ-terms quotiented by the laws of symmetric strict monoidal categories [31, Appendix A] as *string diagrams*.[1]

Given an SMT (Σ, E), the prop $\mathsf{FreeP}_{(\Sigma,E)}$ freely generated by (Σ, E) has morphisms $m \to n$ the string diagrams of type $m \to n$ quotiented by E, with sequential and parallel composition defined as on the corresponding Σ-terms. We will typically regard $\mathsf{FreeP}_{(\Sigma,E)}$ as a *string diagrammatic calculus*, with the string diagrams being its (graphical) *syntax*. The props defined 'directly', as **AffVect** and **AffRel**, are regarded as *semantic models* for diagrammatic calculi. When there is an isomorphism of props $[\![\cdot]\!]$ between $\mathsf{FreeP}_{(\Sigma,E)}$ and another prop $\mathbf{C}$, we say that $\mathbf{C}$ is *presented* (or axiomatised) by (Σ, E). Because prop morphisms are identity-on-objects, to prove such result it suffices to prove that $[\![\cdot]\!]$ is full and faithful. In logical terms, we can phrase these requirements as *soundness* (if $s = t$ in $\mathsf{FreeP}_{(\Sigma,E)}$, then $[\![s]\!] = [\![t]\!]$), *completeness* (if $[\![s]\!] = [\![t]\!]$ in $\mathbf{C}$, then $s = t$ in $\mathsf{FreeP}_{(\Sigma,E)}$) and *definability* (for every $f : m \to n$ in $\mathbf{C}$, there exists a Σ-term $s : m \to n$ with $[\![s]\!] = f$).

Graphical Affine Algebra is based on the following operations:

$$\text{(3)} \qquad\qquad\qquad\qquad \text{(4)}$$

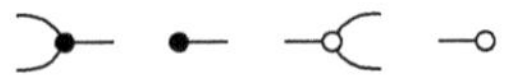

Row (3) denotes basic linear transformations such as copying ($\prec$), discarding ($\rightarrow\bullet$) addition ($\succ\!\!-$), the constant zero ($\circ\!\!-$), multiplication by scalar k ($-\!\boxed{k}\!-$), and the constant one ($\vdash\!\!-$). Row (4) expresses the converse of these maps, regarded as relations (subspaces), with the 'mirror' of $-\!\boxed{k}\!-$ and $\vdash\!\!-$ derivable as follows: $-\!\boxed{k}\!- :=$ and $-\!\dashv :=$.

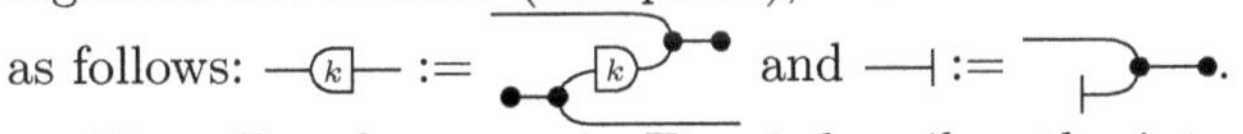

The affine fragment in Fig. 1 describes the interaction between operations in (3): $\succ\!\!-$, $\circ\!\!-$ form a commutative monoid, $-\!\prec$, $\rightarrow\bullet$ form a commutative comonoid, distributing over each other according to the laws of bimonoids. Furthermore, scalars and $\vdash\!\!-$ distribute over the bimonoid, and there are laws expressing the field structure on $\mathbb{R}$.

The relational fragment in Fig. 1 describes additional laws involving operations in (4) and $-\!\boxed{k}\!-$, $-\!\dashv$ defined above: black and white special Frobenius monoids, the equivalence between the black and the white compact closed structure arising from the Frobenius algebras (cap), the fact that scalars have inverses (*r*-inv, *r*-coinv), and an "ex-falso quodlibet" principle (false, where $\vdash\!\!\circ$ expressed the 'impossible' condition that $1 = 0$). Note at this stage we may also prove that $-\!\prec$, $-\!\circ$ form a commutative comonoid and $\succ\!\!-$, $\bullet\!\!-$ form a commutative monoid. We write $\overrightarrow{\mathbf{GAA}}$ for the prop freely generated by operations (3) and equations in the affine fragment. Similarly, we write $\mathbf{GAA}$ for the prop freely generated by operations (3)–(4), and equations in the causal and relational fragments. These props present affine maps and affine relations respectively.

---

[1] We adopt a 'syntactic' definition of string diagrams, which follows eg. [6,7,23] and is more convenient for our axiomatic perspective. The reader may be familiar with the combinatorial [5] and topological [19] view on string diagrams: the three are ultimately equivalent. Additional details may be found eg. in [23].

Proposition 1 ([6]). $\overrightarrow{\textbf{GAA}}$ *presents* **AffVect** *and* **GAA** *presents* **AffRel**.

Importantly, Proposition 1 implies that, whenever we reason in the aforementioned calculi, any equivalence of matrices or subspaces represented by string diagrams are provable in the corresponding equational theory. This will allow us to use freely known facts of linear algebra (e.g. those recalled in [31, Appendix B]) in diagrammatic reasoning whenever needed, allowing us to focus on the quadratic extension that is the topic of this paper.

In preparation for our completeness theorems, we recall standard notation to represent matrices and subspaces as string diagrams of **GAA**. First, for readability, we use thick wires for an arbitrary number of ingoing/outgoing wires in a string diagrams, as in $-\boxed{c}- := {}^{m}\boxed{c}{}^{n}$. We use a similar convention to represent multiple instances of the same generator, e.g. $-\!\!\prec\; :=\; \vdots\;\rlap{$\times$}{\prec}\;\vdots\;,\; -\!\!\prec\; :=\; \vdots\;\rlap{$\times$}{\prec}\;\vdots\;,$ and 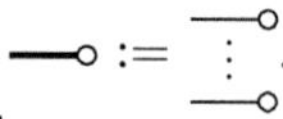 $-\!\!-\!\circ := \vdots\;{}^{\circ}_{\circ}.$ An $n \times m$ matrix A may be represented by a string diagram $-\boxed{A}- : m \to n$, as follows: the wires on the left of $-\boxed{A}-$ stand for the columns of A, the wires on the right stand for the rows, and the left j-th wire is connected to the i-th wire on the right through a scalar $-\boxed{k}-$ if the coefficient A_{ij} is k (see [33] for details). In particular, up to the axioms of **GAA**, two wires are disconnected when $A_{ij} = 0$, and are just a plain wire when $A_{ij} = 1$. For instance,

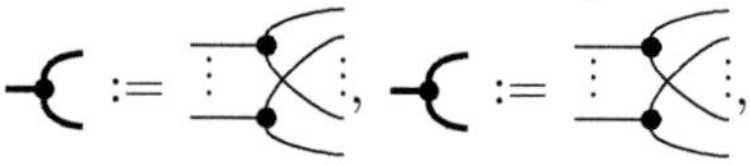

$$\text{if } A = \begin{pmatrix} k_1 & 0 & 0 \\ k_2 & 0 & 1 \\ 1 & 0 & 0 \\ 0 & 0 & 0 \end{pmatrix} \text{ then } -\boxed{A}- := \qquad\qquad . \tag{5}$$

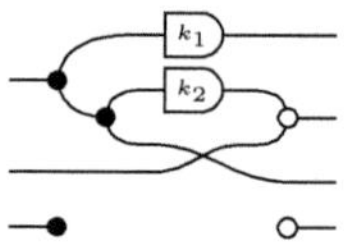

Here , $-\boxed{A}-$ represents A in the sense that it is interpreted as $A \colon n \to m$ via the isomorphism $\overrightarrow{\textbf{GAA}} \to$ **AffVect**, and as $\{(\mathbf{v}, \mathbf{w}) \mid \mathbf{w} = A\mathbf{v}\}$ via the isomorphism **GAA** $\to$ **AffRel**. Similarly, a subspace $S \subseteq \mathbb{R}^{m+n}$ may be represented by the string diagram $\bullet\!-\boxed{A}-$ in **GAA**, for any A such that $\mathrm{im}(A) = S$. We will also write this as $\boxed{S}\!-\!\!-$. Well-definedness of this encoding is justified by [31, Proposition 8, Appendix B]. For a scalar $c \in \mathbb{R}$, we sometimes abbreviate $\vdash\!\boxed{c}- $ with $\boxed{c}\!-\!\!-$.

3   Axiomatising Gaussian Probability

3.1   Gaussian Probability

Gaussian probability is an expressive self-contained fragment of probability theory. We recall what is strictly necessary here, referring to e.g. [3] for further background. A random variable X is called *normally distributed* or *Gaussian* with mean $\mu \in \mathbb{R}^n$ and variance σ^2 for $\sigma \in [0, \infty)$, if it has density function $f(x) = \frac{1}{\sqrt{2\pi\sigma^2}} \exp\left(-\frac{(x-\mu)^2}{2\sigma^2}\right)$ with respect to the Lebesgue measure. This is typically written $X \sim \mathcal{N}(\mu, \sigma^2)$, meaning the distribution $\mathcal{N}(\mu, \sigma^2)$, also called Gaussian distribution, is the law of X. The *standard normal distribution* $\mathcal{N}(0, 1)$ is particularly significant, as it generates any other normal distribution, in the following sense: a random vector $\mathbf{X}$ is *multivariate normal* if its distribution arises as $\mathbf{X} = A \cdot (Z_1, \ldots, Z_k) + \mu$, where $Z_1, \ldots, Z_k \sim \mathcal{N}(0, 1)$ are independent variables and $A \in \mathbb{R}^{n \times k}$ is a matrix and $\mu \in \mathbb{R}^n$. In other words, multivariable normal distributions arise as the pushforwards of standard normal distributions under affine maps. The distribution of $\mathbf{X}$ is fully characterised by its mean μ and its covariance matrix $\Sigma = AA^T \in \mathbb{R}^{n \times n}$, for $A \in \mathbb{R}^{n \times k}$. Conversely, every positive semidefinite matrix Σ is the covariance matrix of a unique Gaussian distribution $\mathcal{N}(\mu, \Sigma)$, supported on the affine subspace $\mu + \mathrm{im}(\Sigma)$. A convenient way of building up complicated Gaussian distributions is by pushing forward existing distributions under affine maps: if $\mathcal{N}(\mu, \Sigma)$ is a Gaussian distribution and A is a matrix, then the pushforward distribution $A_* \mathcal{N}(\mu, \Sigma)$ is $\mathcal{N}(A\mu, A\Sigma A^T)$.

If we aim to include Gaussian distributions and affine maps in the same categorical structure, it is natural to study *Gaussian maps*, which are a simple kind of stochastic map consisting of an affine function with Gaussian noise, informally written $f(x) = Ax + \mathcal{N}(b, \Sigma)$, with $A \in \mathbb{R}^{n \times m}$, $b \in \mathbb{R}^n$ and $\Sigma \in \mathbb{R}^{n \times n}$.

To compose this with another Gaussian map $g(y) = Cy + \mathcal{N}(d, \Xi)$, we combine their Gaussian noise independently using the transformation rule $g(f(x)) = CAx + \mathcal{N}(Cb + d, C\Sigma C^T + \Xi)$.

Definition 2 ([14, § 6]). *The prop* **Gauss** *has as morphisms* $m \to n$ *the tuples* (A, b, Σ) *with* $A \in \mathbb{R}^{n \times m}$, $b \in \mathbb{R}^n$ *and positive semidefinite* $\Sigma \in \mathbb{R}^{n \times n}$. *Composition and monoidal product are given by*

$$(A, b, \Sigma); (C, d, \Xi) = (CA, Cb + d, C\Sigma C^T + \Xi)$$

$$(A_1, b_1, \Sigma_1) \oplus (A_2, b_2, \Sigma_2) = \left(\begin{pmatrix} A_1 & 0 \\ 0 & A_2 \end{pmatrix}, \begin{pmatrix} b_1 \\ b_2 \end{pmatrix}, \begin{pmatrix} \Sigma_1 & 0 \\ 0 & \Sigma_2 \end{pmatrix} \right)$$

Gaussian distributions are the 'states' $0 \to n$ in **Gauss**. There is a prop morphism **Vect** $\to$ **Gauss** representing an affine map $x \mapsto Ax + b$ as the Gaussian map $(A, b, 0)$.

3.2   Causal Graphical Quadratic Algebra and Completeness

We now turn our attention to the axiomatic theory of **Gauss**. The prop $\overrightarrow{\mathbf{GQA}}$, which stands for *causal* Graphical Quadratic Algebra, is freely generated by the following operations

$$\dashv\mathord{\bullet} \quad \mathord{\to}\mathord{\bullet} \quad \mathord{>}\!\mathord{\circ}\!\mathord{-} \quad \mathord{\circ}\!\mathord{-} \quad \dashv\boxed{k}\mathord{-} \quad \vdash\!\mathord{-} \quad \leftarrow \tag{6}$$

where k ranges over $\mathbb{R}$, and equations as in the first two blocks of Fig. 1 (linear and quadratic fragments), *except* for axiom Z (where the generator $\mathord{\to}\mathord{\circ}$ appears, which is not among those in (6)). As in related work [10,14], the term 'causal' indicates that the operations in (6) should be read as processing values from left-to-right, without constraining the values of inputs. Note we may regard $\overrightarrow{\mathbf{GQA}}$ as an extension of $\overrightarrow{\mathbf{GAA}}$ from Sect. 2. The extension is simply given by adding the operation $\leftarrow$ and the associated equations. It is also a fragment of full **GQA**,

306   D. Stein et al.

which we will introduce later. We now define an interpretation $\langle\cdot\rangle$ of $\overrightarrow{\mathbf{GQA}}$-generators as morphisms of **Gauss**. We use the notation $f(x) = Ax + \mathcal{N}(b, \Sigma)$ for such a morphism of type $m \rightarrow n$.

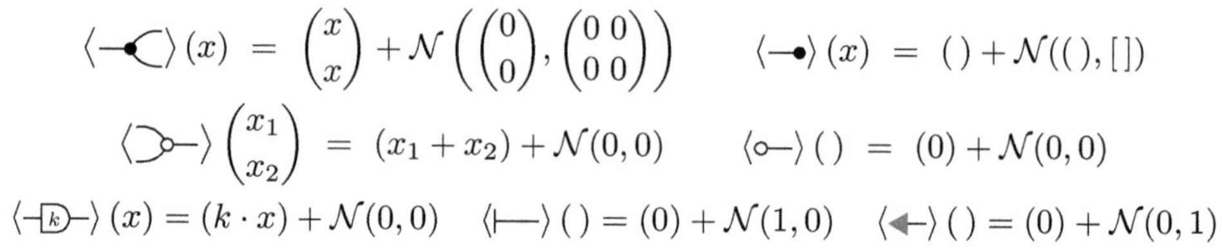

$$\langle -\!\!\!\blacktriangleleft\rangle (x) = \begin{pmatrix} x \\ x \end{pmatrix} + \mathcal{N}\left(\begin{pmatrix} 0 \\ 0 \end{pmatrix}, \begin{pmatrix} 0 & 0 \\ 0 & 0 \end{pmatrix} \right) \qquad \langle -\!\!\bullet\rangle (x) = () + \mathcal{N}((), [])$$

$$\langle \!\!\triangleright\!\!-\rangle \begin{pmatrix} x_1 \\ x_2 \end{pmatrix} = (x_1 + x_2) + \mathcal{N}(0,0) \qquad \langle \circ\!\!-\rangle () = (0) + \mathcal{N}(0,0)$$

$$\langle -\!\!\boxed{k}\!\!-\rangle (x) = (k \cdot x) + \mathcal{N}(0,0) \qquad \langle \vdash\!\!-\rangle () = (0) + \mathcal{N}(1,0) \qquad \langle \!\!\blacktriangleleft\!\!-\rangle () = (0) + \mathcal{N}(0,1)$$

Note that the newly added operation $\blacktriangleleft$ is the only one with a non-trivial probabilistic component. The assignment extends[2] to a prop morphism $\langle\cdot\rangle :$ $\overrightarrow{\mathbf{GQA}} \rightarrow \mathbf{Gauss}$, by interpreting sequential and parallel compositions of string diagrams as the corresponding operations in **Gauss**. In fact, we can show that the equational theory of Fig. 1 makes $\langle\cdot\rangle$ an isomorphism.

Theorem 1. Gauss *is presented by the fragment* $\overrightarrow{\mathbf{GQA}}$.

Proof. For definability, let $f \in \mathbf{Gauss}(m, n)$ be given by $f(x) = Ax + \mathcal{N}(\mu, \Sigma)$. Then, for $\Sigma = LL^T$, where L is lower triangular,

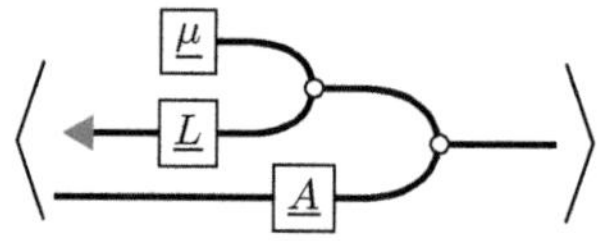

$$\left\langle \vcenter{\hbox{\includegraphics{diagram}}} \right\rangle = f. \tag{7}$$

For completeness, we may transform any string diagram of $\overrightarrow{\mathbf{GQA}}$ into the form (7), see [31, Proposition 15]. This is a normal form, because we can read off the values of (A, μ, Σ) unambiguously from it [31, Proposition 14]. Note a key part in uniqueness is played by the property that $\blacktriangleleft$ is invariant under arbitrary orthogonal matrices, a generalisation of RI [31, Proposition 13]. Finally, $\langle(A, \mu, \Sigma)\rangle = \langle(A', \mu', \Sigma')\rangle$ implies $(A, \mu, \Sigma) = (A', \mu', \Sigma')$, yielding completeness.

4   Axiomatising Quadratic Problems

As mentioned in the introduction, Gaussian probability and quadratic problems are tightly related. We will now introduce *quadratic relations* as a categorical formalism to express quadratic problems in a compositional way. We then give a presentation $\mathbf{GQA}$ for this category, and use this presentation to study the relationship with Gaussian probability in an algebraic fashion.

---

[2] This holds provided that $\langle\cdot\rangle$ is sound, namely $c = d$ in GQA implies $\langle c\rangle = \langle d\rangle$. This can be readily verified on the axioms of Fig. 1, see [31, Appendix C]. For a comprehensive explanation of the universal property of freely generated props, which is used both here and in Sect. 5.1, see [1].

4.1 Quadratic Problems as Quadratic Relations

We justify the introduction of quadratic relations in steps. The basic setup of an optimisation problem is: given a weight (or cost) function $f(x_1, \dots, x_{m+n})$, compute the parameterised infimum $(x_1, \dots, x_m) \mapsto \inf\{f(x_1, \dots, x_{m+n}) : (x_{m+1}, \dots, x_{m+n}) \in \mathbb{R}^n\}$ over some variables. We can type such a weight function as $F : \mathbb{R}^m \times \mathbb{R}^n \to [0, +\infty]$, thereby formally specifying the 'input' and 'output' variables. How to compose such functions? We can see $F : \mathbb{R}^m \times \mathbb{R}^n \to [0, +\infty]$ as a *weighted relation* the same way that an ordinary relation can be seen as $R : \mathbb{R}^m \times \mathbb{R}^n \to \{0, 1\}$. This suggests a notion of composition: while relations compose as on the left below, weighted relations compose by adding the weights and minimising over the shared variable[3], as on the right below:

$$(R; S)(x, z) = \bigvee_y R(x, y) \cdot S(y, z) \qquad (F; G)(x, z) = \inf_y \left\{ F(x, y) + G(y, z) \right\} \quad (8)$$

This way of building up optimisation problems is well-established, see e.g. [16] for model-predictive control, [24] for convex analysis (where weighted relations are called *bifunctions*), [32] for control theory, and [28] for a categorical perspective. In our developments, it is convenient to introduce the following notation, reminiscent of Iverson brackets [24], associating a weighted relation $\{\!|\,\phi\,|\!\}$ to a formula ϕ, denoting a linear equation between its free variables:

$$\{\!|\,\phi\,|\!\} \stackrel{\text{def.}}{=} 0 \quad \text{if } \phi \text{ is true,} \quad \infty \quad \text{otherwise} \quad (9)$$

Note that 0 denotes truth and ∞ falsity in this context! The indicator function of a set A is given by $1_A(x) = \{\!|\, x \in A \,|\!\}$.

Example 2. Consider the weighted relation $F : \mathbb{R} \times \mathbb{R}^2 \to [0, \infty]$ given by the constraint $F(c, (x, y)) = \{\!|\, c = x + y \,|\!\}$, and let $G : \mathbb{R}^2 \times \mathbb{R}^0 \to [0, \infty]$ be $G((x, y), ()) = \frac{1}{2}(x^2 + y^2)$. Then the composite $F; G$ computes the parameterised quadratic problem $(F; G)(c, ()) = \inf\{\frac{1}{2}(x^2 + y^2) : x + y = c\} = \frac{1}{4}c^2$. We will render this composition diagrammatically in **GQA**, *cf.* Example 4.

We now focus on the class of weighted relations, called *quadratic relations*, which correspond to quadratic problems: this is a type of optimisation problem involving quadratic objective functions and affine constraints. First, a *quadratic function* $f : \mathbb{R}^n \to \mathbb{R}$ is a function that can be written as a multivariate polynomial of degree at most 2. Examples of quadratic functions are the squared euclidean distance $||\mathbf{x}||^2$, $(x_1 - 1)x_2$, and $x_1^2 - x_2$. A *partial quadratic function* is allowed to assume the value $+\infty$ (indicating falsity/partiality) outside an affine subspace M.

Definition 3 ([24, p.109]). *A partial quadratic function $f : \mathbb{R}^n \to [-\infty, \infty]$ is a function that can be written in form $f(x) = \langle x, \Sigma x \rangle + \langle b, x \rangle + c + \{\!|\, x \in M \,|\!\}$ where $M \subseteq \mathbb{R}^n$ is an affine subspace, $\Sigma \in \mathbb{R}^{n \times n}$ is a symmetric matrix, $b \in \mathbb{R}^n$, $c \in \mathbb{R}$, and $\langle -, - \rangle$ denotes the standard inner product on $\mathbb{R}^n$.*

---

[3] This analogy can be made rigorous with quantales [20]. Our weighted relations are parametrised over the quantale $([0, +\infty], \geq, +)$.

Recall that a function $f : \mathbb{R}^n \to [-\infty, \infty]$ is *convex* if its epigraph $\{(x, y) : y \geq f(x)\}$ is a convex subset of $\mathbb{R}^{n+1}$. An *elementary convex partial quadratic function* is one in diagonal form $h(x) = \sum_i \lambda_i x_i^2$ with $\lambda_i \in [0, +\infty]$. The function h is partial, because $h(x) = \infty$ whenever $\lambda_i = \infty$ and $x_i \neq 0$.

Example 3. The negative log-density function of a Gaussian distribution on $\mathbb{R}^n$ is a partial convex quadratic function on $\mathbb{R}^n$. It is partial because it takes the value $+\infty$ (corresponding to density 0) outside of its support subspace S.

It turns out that nonnegative partial quadratic functions are automatically convex. Also, they are closed under the composition formula (8). We state a slightly more general proposition, namely closure under arbitrary constrained infima [31, Appendix E].

Proposition 2. *If $M \subseteq \mathbb{R}^n \times \mathbb{R}^m$ is an affine subspace, and g is a nonnegative partial quadratic function, then so is $f(x) = \inf\{g(y) \mid (x, y) \in M\}$.*

Definition 4 (Quadratic Relations). *The prop **QuadRel** of quadratic relations has:*

- *morphisms $m \to n$ are non-negative partial quadratic functions $F : \mathbb{R}^m \times \mathbb{R}^n \to [0, \infty]$, called* quadratic relations
- *identities are indicator functions $\mathrm{id}_n(x, y) = \{\!|\, x = y\,|\!\}$*
- *composition is by minimisation: for $F \colon m \to n$ and $G \colon n \to p$, define $F; G \colon m \to p$ as $(F; G)(x, z) := \inf_y \{F(x, y) + G(y, z)\}$.*
- *the monoidal product is addition. Given $F_i \colon m_i \to n_i$ for $i = 1, 2$, then $F_1 \oplus F_2 \colon m_1 + m_2 \to n_1 + n_2$ is defined by $(F_1 \oplus F_2)((x_1, x_2), (y_1, y_2)) = F_1(x_1, y_1) + F_2(x_2, y_2)$.*

Composition in **QuadRel** is well-defined by Proposition 2, since we can write $(F; G)(x, z) = \inf\{H(\mathbf{y}) : (x, z, \mathbf{y}) \in M\}$ where $H(y_1, y_2, y_3, y_4) = F(y_1, y_2) + G(y_3, y_4)$ and $M = \{(x, z, y_1, y_2, y_3, y_3) : x = y_1, y_2 = y_3, z = y_4\}$.

To every affine relation $M \subseteq \mathbb{R}^m \times \mathbb{R}^n$, we can associate the quadratic relation 1_M given by its indicator function. This assignment respects composition, i.e. yields a prop morphism **AffRel** $\to$ **QuadRel**.

4.2   Graphical Quadratic Algebra

We now introduce the diagrammatic calculus presenting **QuadRel**. The prop **GQA** is freely generated by the following operations and the equations in Fig. 1, for $k \in \mathbb{R}$.

We may regard **GQA** as an extension of **GAA** from Sect. 2, where we add $\twoheadleftarrow$, and the associated equations. As we did for $-\!\boxed{k}\!-$ and $-\!\!\dashv$ we can define the 'mirror image' of ⭠ as ⭢ := ⟍⟋•. We now define an interpretation of $\overrightarrow{\mathbf{GQA}}$-generators as morphisms of **QuadRel**. To each operation c of type $m \to n$ we assign a quadratic relation $[\![c]\!]$ of the same type, i.e. a nonnegative partial quadratic function $\mathbb{R}^{m+n} \to [0, \infty]$. We make use of the notation $\{\!|\, \phi \,|\!\}$ introduced in (9).

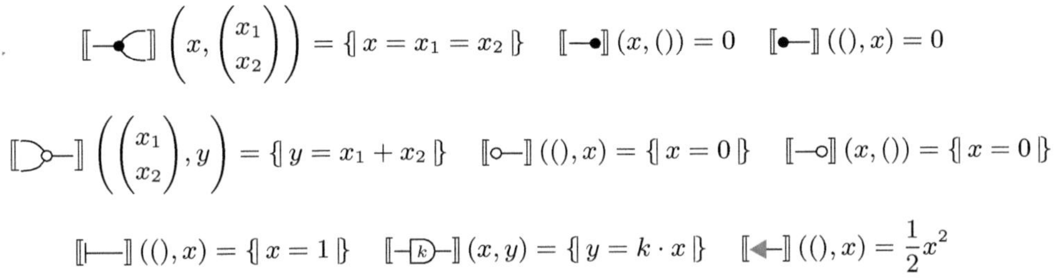

$$[\!\!-\!\!\vartriangleleft]\!\!\left(x, \binom{x_1}{x_2}\right) = \{\!|\, x = x_1 = x_2 \,|\!\} \qquad [\!\!\rightarrow\!\!\bullet]\!(x, ()) = 0 \qquad [\!\bullet\!\!-\!\!]((), x) = 0$$

$$[\!\vartriangleright\!\!-\!\!]\!\!\left(\binom{x_1}{x_2}, y\right) = \{\!|\, y = x_1 + x_2 \,|\!\} \qquad [\!\circ\!\!-\!\!]((), x) = \{\!|\, x = 0 \,|\!\} \qquad [\!\!-\!\!\circ]\!(x, ()) = \{\!|\, x = 0 \,|\!\}$$

$$[\!|\!\!-\!\!]((), x) = \{\!|\, x = 1 \,|\!\} \qquad [\!\!-\!\boxed{k}\!\!-\!\!]\!(x, y) = \{\!|\, y = k \cdot x \,|\!\} \qquad [\!\blacktriangleleft\!\!-\!\!]((), x) = \frac{1}{2}x^2$$

The interpretation for $\vartriangleright\!\!-$, $\bullet\!\!-$, $-\!\!\vartriangleleft$, and $-\!\!\circ$ is defined symmetrically, e.g. $[\!\vartriangleright\!\!-\!\!]\!\!\left(\binom{x_1}{x_2}, x\right) = \{\!|\, x = x_1 = x_2 \,|\!\}$. Also, except for the new generator ⭠, it extends conservatively the interpretation of these operations in **AffRel** given in [6] (see Proposition 4 below). As for $\overrightarrow{\mathbf{GQA}}$, by freeness of **GQA** the interpretation yields a prop morphism $[\![\cdot]\!] : \mathbf{GQA} \to \mathbf{QuadRel}$.

Example 4. Returning to Example 2, $F = [\!\!-\!\!\vartriangleleft]\!]$, $G = [\!\boxed{\Rightarrow}]\!]$, and $[\!\!-\!\!\circ\!\!\vartriangleleft\!\boxed{\Rightarrow}]\!] = F; G$. We can solve $(F; G)(c, ()) = \inf\left\{\frac{1}{2}(x^2 + y^2) : x + y = c\right\} = \frac{1}{4}c^2$ by equational reasoning in **GQA**. The derivation, which is the mirror image of the one given for ⟍⟋⭢$-$ = ⭠$\boxed{\sqrt{2}}-$ in Sect. 1, proves $-\!\!\circ\!\!\langle$ = $-\!\boxed{\sqrt{2}}\!\!\rightarrow$ (observe that $[\!\!-\!\boxed{\sqrt{2}}\!\!\rightarrow]\!]\,(c, ()) = \frac{1}{4}c^2$).

4.3 Completeness of GQA for QuadRel

In this section we establish that **GQA** presents **QuadRel**. For this, we need to prove soundness, completeness and definability.

Soundness is a routine check on the axioms [31, Proposition 11]. We focus on definability and completeness.

First, in a category where objects are equipped with Frobenius monoids, questions about arbitrary morphisms can be reduced to questions about states, i.e. morphisms $0 \to n$, as follows: for a morphism $f : m \to n$, its 'name' $\lceil f \rceil :$ $0 \to m \oplus n$ is defined as

$$\boxed{\lceil f \rceil}\!=\quad = \quad \bullet\!\!-\!\!\langle\!\boxed{f}\!\!- \tag{10}$$

The assignment $f \mapsto \lceil f \rceil$ is bijective – every morphism can be recovered from its name by bending back the top wire, composing with $\vartriangleright\!\!-\!\!\bullet$ and using axiom •-fr and coun.

It will be useful to introduce a subprop $\overrightarrow{\mathbf{GQA}}_E$ of **GQA**, defined as follows.

310   D. Stein et al.

Definition 5. *The prop $\overrightarrow{\mathbf{GQA}}_E$ is freely generated as $\overrightarrow{\mathbf{GQA}}$ with the addition of the generator $\bullet\!\!-$ and equations, for $k \in \mathbb{R}\setminus\{0\}$*

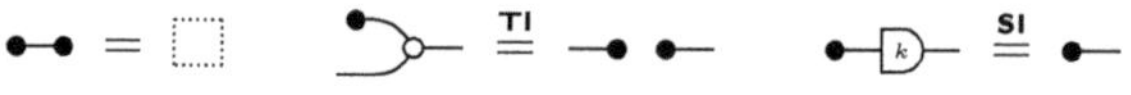

$$\bullet\!\!-\!\!\bullet \;=\; \Box \qquad \stackrel{\text{TI}}{=} \qquad \stackrel{\text{SI}}{=}$$

Diagrams in $\overrightarrow{\mathbf{GQA}}_E$ are not only a useful intermediary step in the proof of completeness; it turns out they axiomatise the *extended Gaussians* of [27,28], which can be thought of intuitively as Gaussian maps that incorporate a form of (non-probabilistic) nondeterminism, modelled by the extra generator $\bullet\!\!-$ (see [31, Appendix F] for details). In this paper, we focus on $\mathbf{GQA}$, and leave further exploration of $\overrightarrow{\mathbf{GQA}}_E$ to future work.

A fundamental piece of the completeness proof involves showing that any quadratic problem, represented as a string diagram of $\mathbf{GQA}$ with no inputs, can be turned into a string diagram of the fragment $\overrightarrow{\mathbf{GQA}}_E$. This crucial step is Theorem 2 below, an elimination procedure which, given a state in $\mathbf{GQA}$, iteratively removes all occurrences of conditioning on some variable being zero ($-\!\circ$).

The elimination procedure can therefore be understood as symbolically conditioning an (extended) Gaussian to obtain an explicit posterior, or as solving a quadratic problem via QR decomposition.

Theorem 2. *Let $M : 0 \to n$ be a string diagram in $\mathbf{GQA}$. Then there exists a string diagram M' in $\overrightarrow{\mathbf{GQA}}_E$, and a 'scalar' $\alpha : 0 \to 0$, such that $M = M' \oplus \alpha$ is derivable in $\mathbf{GQA}$. The scalar is of the form $\boxed{c}\!\!\to$ with $c \in [0, \infty)$, or $\vdash\!\!-\!\!\circ$.*

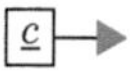

Theorem 3. *The prop $\mathbf{QuadRel}$ is presented by $\mathbf{GQA}$.*

Proof (Sketch). This proof relies on combining various normalisation steps for different fragments of $\mathbf{GQA}$ in a modular way. The steps are detailed in the appendix of [31]. For definability, note that by taking names (10), it suffices to show that all states $M : 0 \to n$ (i.e. nonnegative partial quadratic functions) are definable. We can then always apply an affine change of coordinate, *i.e.*, some invertible affine map g, such that $g(\llbracket M \rrbracket (\mathbf{x_1}, \mathbf{x_2}, \mathbf{x_3})) = \frac{1}{2}\|\mathbf{x_1}\|^2 + \{\!| \mathbf{x_3} = 0 |\!\}$, which is definable as the state $\quad$. Hence, $\llbracket M \rrbracket = \quad\boxed{g^{-1}}\!\!-$.

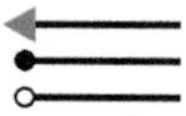

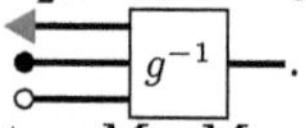

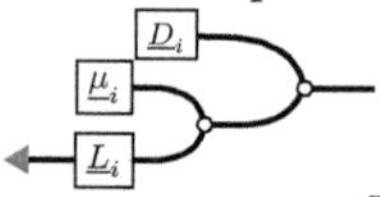

For completeness, it suffices to show that for all states $M_1, M_2 : 0 \to n$ of $\mathbf{GQA}$, if $\llbracket M_1 \rrbracket = \llbracket M_2 \rrbracket$ in $\mathbf{QuadRel}$, then $M_1 = M_2$ is derivable in $\mathbf{GQA}$. The steps of the proof are as follows: First, using Theorem 2 we transform each M_i (for $i = 1, 2$) into the form $\boxed{c_i}\!\!\to \boxed{M_i'}\!\!-$, where M_i' lies in $\overrightarrow{\mathbf{GQA}}_E$. Then, to each M_i', we apply a normalisation procedure for states in $\overrightarrow{\mathbf{GQA}}_E$, which brings them to the form $N_i := \quad$, where D_i is a vector subspace, $\mu_i \in D_i^\perp$, L_i is lower triangular, and $\text{im}(L_i L_i^T) \subseteq D_i^\perp$. This is a normal form in the sense that $\llbracket N_1 \rrbracket = \llbracket N_2 \rrbracket$ if and only if $D_1 = D_2$, $\mu_1 = \mu_2$, and $L_1 L_1^T = L_2 L_2^T$. We can thus reduce the two diagrams to the case of $L_1 = L_2$. Then, by appealing to the completeness of **GAA**, we can show that $N_1 = N_2$. Finally, since $M_i = N_i$, we can conclude $M_1 = M_2$ as desired.

5   Applications

5.1   Functorial Transformations

A powerful application of our presentations for **Gauss** and **QuadRel** is the ease with which we can now define functors on these categories, as mappings on generators preserving the relevant equations. By the universal property of a presentation, such an assignment extends uniquely to a morphism of props. The first functor we consider clarifies the connection between Gaussian probability and quadratic problems. Relying on the isomorphisms **Gauss** $\cong \overrightarrow{\textbf{GQA}}$ and **QuadRel** $\cong$ **GQA**, we can define a functor $L :$ **Gauss** $\to$ **QuadRel** simply by mapping the generators of $\overrightarrow{\textbf{GQA}}$ to the same generators in **GQA**. Note that L is functorial by construction, even though composition operations in **Gauss** (integration/pushforward) and composition in **QuadRel** (infimisation) are at first glance very different. It remains to compute how the functor L acts concretely on a Gaussian map (see [31, Appendix H] for details).

Proposition 3. *The functor L sends a Gaussian map $f(x) = Ax + \mathcal{N}(\mu, \Sigma)$ to the quadratic relation given by its negative conditional log-density. That is, $Lf(x, y)$ is defined as $\frac{1}{2}\langle (y - Ax - \mu), \Omega(y - Ax - \mu)\rangle + \{\!\!\{ (y - Ax - \mu) \in \mathrm{im}(\Sigma) \}\!\!\}$, where Ω is a generalised inverse of Σ, i.e. satisfies $\Sigma\Omega\Sigma = \Sigma$.*

Proposition 4. *The functor $L :$ **Gauss** $\to$ **QuadRel** is faithful and **GQA** is conservative over $\overrightarrow{\textbf{GQA}}$, meaning that $s = t$ in **GQA** implies $s = t$ in $\overrightarrow{\textbf{GQA}}$.*

These results provide an elegant and precise connection between the world of Gaussians and of convex optimisation problems. Functoriality of the log-density was laboriously proved in [28] by explicit means. Here, we obtain the result "for free" from our use of presentations, from which it also easily follows faithfulness and conservativity of **GQA** over $\overrightarrow{\textbf{GQA}}$.

Another functor of interest, $S :$ **Gauss** $\to$ **AffRel** can be defined by mapping every generator except $\leftarrow$ to the same generator in **AffRel**, and mapping $\leftarrow$ to $\bullet\!\!-$. This functor takes a Gaussian map to the affine relation given by its support; if $f(x) = Ax + \mathcal{N}(b, \Sigma)$, then $S(f) := \{(x, y) : y \in Ax + b + \mathrm{im}(\Sigma)\}$. Again, functoriality of this assignment is an immediate consequence of our presentation results. A similar definition yields a functor **QuadRel** $\to$ **AffRel**, mapping $f : \mathbb{R}^{m+n} \to [0, \infty]$ to its effective domain dom $f = \{(x, y) \mid f(x, y) < \infty\}$.

5.2   Ordinary Least-Squares

We now demonstrate how to apply our theory of **GQA** to the method of ordinary least squares in linear regression. The aim of linear regression is simple:

to find a linear model that best fits a set of observations. In its usual vectorial formulation, all available observations of the regressors form the columns of a single matrix A and all observations of the dependent variable form a single vector y; then, a linear model with parameters x is expressed concisely as the system $Ax = y$. Typically, for consistency, we also assume that the regressors are linearly independent, $i.e.$, that A is injective. If A is not invertible–as it usually is not–this system does not admit an exact solution. We can nevertheless look for parameters x such that Ax best approximates the observed values y. Here, 'best' is interpreted in such a way that the sum of squared errors, $||y - Ax||^2$, is minimised. This function can be translated directly into the following diagram:

$$\left[\!\!\left[\begin{array}{c} \boxed{A}\!-\!\boxed{-1} \end{array} \right]\!\!\right] = \begin{pmatrix} x \\ y \end{pmatrix} \mapsto \frac{1}{2}||y - Ax||^2$$

The formula for the optimal $\hat{x}$ is the familiar ordinary least squares (OLS) estimator $\hat{x} = (A^T A)^{-1} A^T y = A^+ y$. This can be derived by applying equational reasoning in **GQA** (as detailed in [31, Appendix I]), showing that

$$\boxed{A}\!-\!\boxed{-1} \quad = \quad \boxed{A^+}\;\boxed{-1}\;\boxed{A} \;\; \boxed{A^+}\!-\!\boxed{A}\!-\!\boxed{-1}$$

The   semantics   of   the   last   diagram   is $\begin{pmatrix} x \\ y \end{pmatrix} \mapsto \frac{1}{2}\left(||AA^+ y - Ax||^2 + ||y - AA^+ y||^2\right)$. Its infimum is clearly reached at $\hat{x} = A^+ y$, as wished: in this case $||AA^+ y - A\hat{x}||^2 = 0$ and the remaining term $||y - AA^+ y||^2 = ||y - A\hat{x}||^2$ indicates the distance between $A\hat{x}$ and y, $i.e.$, how far we are from having successfully inverted A.

5.3 Gaussian Probabilistic Programming

In [29,30] the authors study a simple first-order probabilistic programming language for Gaussian probability, which we name GPL. The core probabilistic constructs are sampling from a standard-normal distribution normal() and an operator (=:=) for conditioning two random variables to be equal. Terms of GPL are, for $\alpha, \beta \in \mathbb{R}$, $i \in \{0, 1\}$,

$$s, t :: = x \mid s + t \mid \alpha \cdot s \mid \underline{\beta} \mid (s, t) \mid () \mid \text{let } x = s \text{ in } t \mid s; t \mid \pi_i s \mid \text{normal}() \mid s =:= t$$

For the typing judgements of this language see [31, Appendix J]. In GPL we can express an inference problem such as a noisy measurement as follows:

$$\text{let } x = 10 \cdot \text{normal}() \text{ in let } y = x + 5 \cdot \text{normal}() \text{ in } (y =:= \underline{40}); x \qquad (11)$$

This expresses the following mathematical problem: If $X \sim \mathcal{N}(0, 100)$ and $Y|X \sim \mathcal{N}(X, 25)$, what is $X|(Y = 40)$? The answer turns out to be $\mathcal{N}(32, 20)$, which can be found by factorising the joint negative log-density: $f(x, 40) \propto$

$\frac{1}{2}\frac{x^2}{100} + \frac{1}{2}\frac{(x-40)^2}{25} = \frac{1}{2}\frac{(x-32)^2}{20} + 6.4$. The constant $c = 6.4$ at the end corresponds to the *score* of the problem, i.e. the negative logarithm of the *normalisation constant* or *model evidence*. The higher c, the less likely was the observation.

It is possible to associate any GPL term to a **GQA**-string diagram. This translation is rigorously definable as a functor, by understanding GPL as the internal language of a suitable monoidal category, as discussed in [13, 26, 29]. Given the focus of the present work, we do not pursue this systematically here, and confine ourselves to showing how the constructs of GPL map into **GQA**:

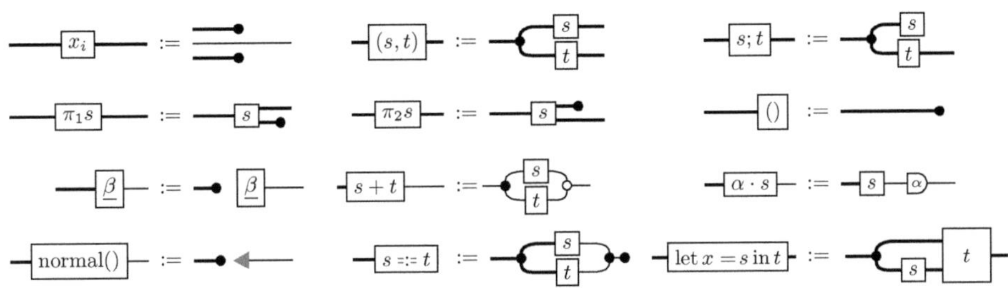

For instance, the program (11) translates to the leftmost diagram, and normalises modulo **GQA** to the posterior distribution and normalisation constant expressed by the rightmost diagram.

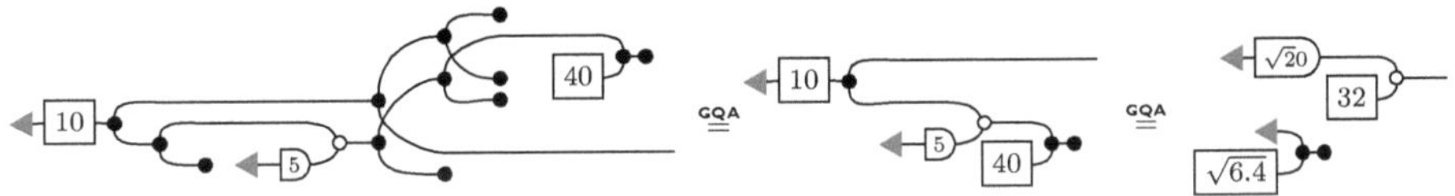

Via this translation, GPL receives denotational semantics in **QuadRel**, which is comparable to existing GPL semantics in interesting ways: First, the elimination procedure of Theorem 2 mirrors the operational semantics of [30] by reducing conditioning statements whenever they occur. Second, the normal form argument of Theorem 3 can be also employed to compare two GPL terms once understood as **GQA** diagrams. This may yield a decidability procedure for contextual equivalence, and thus a fully abstract (and completely axiomatised) denotational semantics for GPL, which unlike the one in [29] does not rely on an equivalence relation that is hard to decide. A complete account of this conjecture is outside of the scope of this paper; we leave it for future work.

6   Conclusions

We gave a compositional account of quadratic optimisation via a category of quadratic relations called **QuadRel**, and provided a complete calculus **GQA** to reason algebraically about this class of problems. We also showed that a fragment $\overrightarrow{\textbf{GQA}}$ of **GQA** axiomatises Gaussian probabilistic maps, thus highlighting the relationship between Gaussian probability and convex analysis. We illustrated our approach by discussing functorial tranlations between the Gaussian, quadratic, and affine domain, by modelling the method of ordinary least-squares in linear regression as diagrammatic reasoning, and by giving semantics to probabilistic programming. The last two applications are by no means intended to be the final word on the subject, but rather a starting point for a more systematic treatment. In particular, we plan to give a complete account of full abstraction for Gaussian probabilistic programming, as outlined at the end of Sect. 5. Also, we will further investigate the fragment $\overrightarrow{\mathbf{GQA}}_E$ and its relationship with extended Gaussian relations. This semantic model is connected with the notion of open stochastic system in Willems' approach to control theory [32], which we should be able to account for similarly to how $\mathbf{GAA}$ interprets electrical circuits [4,6].

From an algebraic viewpoint, we would like to explore whether the symmetries present in Graphical Affine Algebra extend to Graphical Quadratic Algebra. In particular, we conjecture the 'colour-swap' symmetry, mapping eg. ─◖ to ─◗ and ○─ to ●─, extends to $\mathbf{GQA}$ by mapping ◄─ to itself.

The semantics of this functor should correspond to convex conjugation (Legendre transformation). Indeed, in convex analysis terminology, every quadratic relation is a so-called convex bifunction [24], which have been studied in categorical terms in [28]. Independently and at the same time as a preprint [31] of our work, the authors of [8] introduced a notion of 'Gaussian relation' in the context of quantum computation; their semantics is very different, but their axiomatisation is highly reminiscent of $\mathbf{GQA}$. Their presentation exhibits the colour-swap symmetry discussed earlier, which is interpreted by the Fourier transform. The precise relationship between these approaches remains to be explored.

Acknowledgements. F. Zanasi acknowledges support from EPSRC grant EP/V002376/1, MIUR PRIN P2022HXNSC, and ARIA Safeguarded AI programme.

References

1. Baez, J.C., Coya, B., Rebro, F.: Props in network theory. arXiv:1707.08321 (2018)
2. Baez, J.C., Erbele, J.: Categories in control. Theory Appl. Categ. **30**, 836–881 (2015)
3. Billingsley, P.: Probability and Measure, 3 edn. Wiley (1995)
4. Boisseau, G., Sobocinski, P.: String diagrammatic electrical circuit theory. In: ACT. EPTCS, vol. 372, pp. 178–191 (2021)
5. Bonchi, F., Gadducci, F., Kissinger, A., Sobocinski, P., Zanasi, F.: String diagram rewrite theory II: rewriting with symmetric monoidal structure. Math. Struct. Comput. Sci. **32**(4), 511–541 (2022). https://doi.org/10.1017/S0960129522000317
6. Bonchi, F., Piedeleu, R., Sobocinski, P., Zanasi, F.: Graphical affine algebra. In: 34th Annual ACM/IEEE Symposium on Logic in Computer Science (LICS) (2019)
7. Bonchi, F., Sobociński, P., Zanasi, F.: Interacting Hopf algebras. J. Pure Appl. Algebra **221**(1), 144–184 (2017)

8. Booth, R.I., Carette, T., Comfort, C.: Complete equational theories for classical and quantum Gaussian relations. arXiv abs/2403.10479 (2024)

9. Boyd, S., Vandenberghe, L.: Convex Optimization. Cambridge University Press (2004)

10. Cho, K., Jacobs, B.: Disintegration and Bayesian inversion via string diagrams. Math. Struct. Comput. Sci. **29**, 938–971 (2019)

11. Coecke, B., Genovese, F., Lewis, M., Marsden, D., Toumi, A.: Generalized relations in linguistics & cognition. Theoret. Comput. Sci. **752**, 104–115 (2018). https://doi.org/10.1016/j.tcs.2018.03.008

12. Coecke, B., Kissinger, A.: Picturing quantum processes. In: Chapman, P., Stapleton, G., Moktefi, A., Perez-Kriz, S., Bellucci, F. (eds.) Diagrams 2018. LNCS (LNAI), vol. 10871, pp. 28–31. Springer, Cham (2018). https://doi.org/10.1007/978-3-319-91376-6_6

13. Di Lavore, E., Jacobs, B., Román, M.: A simple formal language for probabilistic decision problems. arXiv preprint arXiv:2410.10643 (2024)

14. Fritz, T.: A synthetic approach to Markov kernels, conditional independence and theorems on sufficient statistics. Adv. Math. **370**, 107239 (2020). https://doi.org/10.1016/j.aim.2020.107239

15. Gyenis, B.: Maxwell and the normal distribution: a colored story of probability, independence, and tendency toward equilibrium. Stud. Hist. Philos. Sci. Part B Stud. Hist. Philos. Mod. Phys. **57**, 53–65 (2017)

16. Hanks, T., She, B., Patterson, E., Hale, M., Klawonn, M., Fairbanks, J.: Modeling model predictive control: a category theoretic framework for multistage control problems. In: 2024 American Control Conference (ACC), pp. 4850–4857. IEEE (2024)

17. Jacobs, B., Kissinger, A., Zanasi, F.: Causal inference via string diagram surgery: a diagrammatic approach to interventions and counterfactuals. Math. Struct. Comput. Sci. **31**(5), 553–574 (2021). https://doi.org/10.1017/S096012952100027X

18. Jacobs, B., Zanasi, F.: The logical essentials of Bayesian reasoning. In: Barthe, G., Katoen, J., Silva, A. (eds.) Foundations of Probabilistic Programming, pp. 295–332. Cambridge University Press (2020). https://doi.org/10.1017/9781108770750.010

19. Joyal, A., Street, R.: The geometry of tensor calculus. I. Adv. Math. **88**(1), 55–112 (1991). https://doi.org/10.1016/0001-8708(91)90003-P

20. Lawvere, F.W.: Metric spaces, generalized logic, and closed categories. Rendiconti Del Seminario Matematico E Fisico Di Milano **43**(1), 135–166 (1973). https://doi.org/10.1007/BF02924844

21. Lorenz, R., Tull, S.: Causal models in string diagrams. CoRR abs/2304.07638 (2023). https://doi.org/10.48550/ARXIV.2304.07638

22. MacLane, S.: Categorical algebra. Bull. Am. Math. Soc. **71**(1), 40–106 (1965). https://doi.org/10.1090/S0002-9904-1965-11234-4

23. Piedeleu, R., Zanasi, F.: An Introduction to String Diagrams for Computer Scientists. Elements in Applied Category Theory, Cambridge University Press (2025)

24. Rockafellar, R.T.: Convex Analysis. Princeton University Press (1997)

25. Selinger, P.: A Survey of Graphical Languages for Monoidal Categories, Lecture Notes in Physics, vol. 813, pp. 289–355. Springer, Heidelberg (2011). https://doi.org/10.1007/978-3-642-12821-9_4

26. Stein, D.: Structural foundations for probabilistic programming languages. DPhil thesis, University of Oxford (2021)

27. Stein, D., Samuelson, R.: A category for unifying Gaussian probability and non-determinism. In: 10th Conference on Algebra and Coalgebra in Computer Science (CALCO 2023). Schloss Dagstuhl-Leibniz-Zentrum für Informatik (2023)
28. Stein, D., Samuelson, R.: Towards a compositional framework for convex analysis (with applications to probability theory). In: International Conference on Foundations of Software Science and Computation Structures, pp. 166–187. Springer (2024)
29. Stein, D., Staton, S.: Compositional semantics for probabilistic programs with exact conditioning. In: 2021 36th Annual ACM/IEEE Symposium on Logic in Computer Science (LICS), pp. 1–13. IEEE (2021)
30. Stein, D., Staton, S.: Probabilistic programming with exact conditions. J. ACM **71**(1) (2024). https://doi.org/10.1145/3632170
31. Stein, D., Zanasi, F., Piedeleu, R., Samuelson, R.: Graphical Quadratic Algebra (extended version). arXiv:2403.02284 (2024)
32. Willems, J.C.: Open stochastic systems. IEEE Trans. Autom. Control **58**(2), 406–421 (2013). https://doi.org/10.1109/TAC.2012.2210836
33. Zanasi, F.: Interacting Hopf Algebras- the Theory of Linear Systems. (Interacting Hopf Algebras - la théorie des systèmes linéaires). Ph.D. thesis, École normale supérieure de Lyon, France (2015)

Automata

Active Learning of Symbolic Mealy Automata

Kengo Irie[1], Masaki Waga[1,2](✉) (iD), and Kohei Suenaga[1] (iD)

[1] Graduate School of Informatics, Kyoto University, Kyoto, Japan
mwaga@fos.kuis.kyoto-u.ac.jp
[2] National Institute of Informatics, Tokyo, Japan

Abstract. We propose Λ_M^*—an active learning algorithm that learns symbolic Mealy automata, which support infinite input alphabets and multiple output characters. Each of these two features has been addressed separately in prior work. Combining these two features poses a challenge in learning the outputs corresponding to potentially infinite sets of input characters at each state. To address this challenge, we introduce the notion of *essential input characters*, a finite set of input characters that is sufficient to learn the output function of a symbolic Mealy automaton. Λ_M^* maintains an underapproximation of the essential input characters and refines this set during learning. We prove that Λ_M^* terminates under certain assumptions. Moreover, we provide upper and lower bounds for the query complexity. Their similarity suggests the tightness of the bounds. We empirically demonstrate that Λ_M^* is *i)* efficient regarding the number of queries on practical benchmarks and *ii)* scalable according to evaluations with randomly generated benchmarks.

Keywords: Automata learning · Symbolic automata · Mealy automata

1 Introduction

Active automata learning [2] is the problem of exactly identifying an unknown automaton via a finite number of queries. Since the seminal work of Angluin [2], it has received much attention from both the machine learning theory and system verification communities. In the context of verification, for example, it is used to identify an automaton representing the behavior of an unknown system for testing [12,15,22] or controller synthesis [23].

The L* algorithm [2], the best-known active DFA learning algorithm, infers the minimum DFA recognizing the target regular language $\mathcal{L}_{\mathrm{tgt}}$ using *membership* and *equivalence* queries: In a membership query, the learner asks if a word belongs to $\mathcal{L}_{\mathrm{tgt}}$; in an equivalence query, the learner asks if the DFA built by the learner—called a *hypothesis DFA*—recognizes $\mathcal{L}_{\mathrm{tgt}}$. L* is proved to infer the minimum DFA that recognizes $\mathcal{L}_{\mathrm{tgt}}$ within a polynomial number of queries.

Although active automata learning is known to be theoretically interesting and practically useful, classical algorithms are restrictive for real-world systems

Z. Liu et al. (Eds.): ICTAC 2025, LNCS 16237, pp. 319–337, 2026.
https://doi.org/10.1007/978-3-032-11176-0_19

due to the following gaps: *i)* real-world systems usually take inputs of infinite values (e. g., numbers), and modeling them as state machines typically requires manual or automatic identification of alphabet abstraction (e. g., guard predicates), and *ii)* real-world systems usually produce multi-valued outputs, and we need to learn a state machine representing a *function* rather than a *language*.

On the one hand, Drews and D'Antoni proposed Λ^* [6] to address the first challenge by extending L*. Λ^* learns a *symbolic finite automaton (s-FA)*, an automaton with predicate-labeled transitions to handle *large* or even *infinite* input alphabets. The learner in Λ^* constructs a hypothesis automaton by *i)* learning an automaton (called an *evidence automaton*) over a finite subset of the alphabet using a variant of L* and *ii)* learning predicates from concrete characters to generalize the evidence automaton into a symbolic finite automaton.

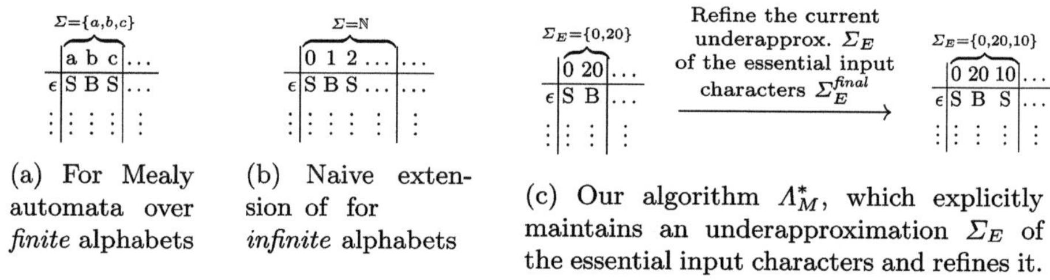

(a) For Mealy automata over *finite* alphabets

(b) Naive extension of for *infinite* alphabets

(c) Our algorithm Λ_M^*, which explicitly maintains an underapproximation Σ_E of the essential input characters and refines it.

Fig. 1. Observation tables for learning Mealy-style automata. The cell indexed by (s, e) contains the output for the input $s \cdot e$. The algorithm in [14] identifies the output function by recording the output for each input character (Fig. 1a), which does not work for infinite alphabets (Fig. 1b). Instead, we learn the output function focusing on the essential characters Σ_E (Fig. 1c).

On the other hand, Niese [14] extended L* to learn a *deterministic Mealy automaton* to address the second challenge. Figure 1a shows the idea of learning Mealy-style outputs with a data structure called an *observation table*. Each cell in the observation table is indexed by a row–column pair $(s, e) \in \Sigma^* \times \Sigma^*$ of words, and the cell indexed by (s, e) contains the output of the target Mealy automaton after processing $s \cdot e$. The row indexed by s corresponds to the state reached by consuming s, and by recording the output after processing $s \cdot a$ for each $a \in \Sigma$, Niese's algorithm identifies a Mealy-style output function.

Contribution: Active Learning of Symbolic Mealy Automata. We propose an active learning algorithm Λ_M^*—an extension of Λ^*—that learns *symbolic Mealy automata (s-MAs)*. An s-MA is a special case of a *symbolic finite transducer* [21] with predicate-labeled transitions, like s-FAs, and outputs associated with transitions, like Mealy automata. To the best of our knowledge, this is the first active learning algorithm for automata that supports general Boolean algebras for input predicates and Mealy-style multiple outputs with the minimality guarantee.

Λ_M^* is based on the automata learning algorithms mentioned above. However, it is more than a naive combination of them. In particular, the major challenge is that Niese's algorithm requires recording output characters for every input character, which is infeasible when dealing with an infinite input alphabet (Fig. 1b).

Our central observation is that, for learnable symbolic automata, tracking only a finite subset of the input alphabet, which we call *essential input characters* Σ_E^{final}, is sufficient for learning. Furthermore, we found that tracking Σ_E^{final} alone is enough to learn the output function of an s-MA. Following this observation, Λ_M^*, refines an underapproximation Σ_E to identify Σ_E^{final} and learns the output function by focusing on Σ_E (Fig. 1c).

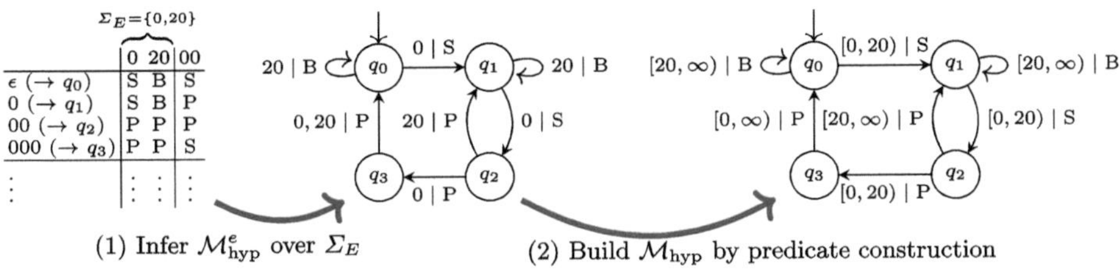

(1) Infer $\mathcal{M}_{\mathrm{hyp}}^e$ over Σ_E (2) Build $\mathcal{M}_{\mathrm{hyp}}$ by predicate construction

Fig. 2. Outline of Λ_M^*. A Mealy automaton $\mathcal{M}_{\mathrm{hyp}}^e$ is constructed from the observation table (1), and the input character on each transition of $\mathcal{M}_{\mathrm{hyp}}^e$ is generalized into a predicate, such as an interval (2).

Figure 2 outlines Λ_M^*. First, we use a variant of Niese's algorithm to infer a Mealy automaton $\mathcal{M}_{\mathrm{hyp}}^e$ over Σ_E. Then, following the idea of Λ^*, we generalize $\mathcal{M}_{\mathrm{hyp}}^e$ into an s-MA $\mathcal{M}_{\mathrm{hyp}}$, which is a hypothesis automaton in Λ_M^*. The refinement of Σ_E occurs through equivalence queries.

We prove the termination of the Λ_M^* algorithm and provide a detailed analysis of its query complexity. By explicitly formulating the essential characters Σ_E^{final}, we give a detailed analysis of the number of explored inputs and improve the complexity analysis of the query compared to [6]. In [6], the upper bound of the number of equivalence queries is quadratic in the number of states, whereas we provide a linear bound. We also give a theoretical *lower* bound of the number of equivalence queries. To the best of our knowledge, this is the first lower bound in the context of active learning of symbolic automata. Our lower bound supports the tightness of our complexity analysis.

We implemented the Λ_M^* algorithm and conducted experiments to evaluate its efficiency. Our experiments suggest that the practical query complexity is significantly lower than the theoretical upper bound because the discovery of states and essential characters usually occurs in parallel.

Overall, our contributions are summarized as follows.

- We propose the Λ_M^* algorithm for active learning of symbolic Mealy automata. The central idea is to explicitly maintain a set of essential inputs.
- We give upper and lower bounds of the number of queries required in Λ_M^*.

– Our experiments show that, despite the theoretical lower bound for a specific case, Λ_M^* typically requires much fewer queries than the theoretical bounds.

Table 1. Active learning algorithms for automata with an infinite input alphabet.

	Outputs	Learned Predicates	Learnable Boolean Algebra	Minimal?
Ours	Multiple Constants (Mealy-style)	Concrete	General	Yes
[3,6]	Only Boolean (Moore-style)	Concrete	General	Yes
[7]	Multiple Constants (Mealy-style)	Abstract	Fixed	Yes
[11]	Constants and Identity Function (Mealy-style)	Concrete	Fixed	No
[1]	Any Handcrafted Functions (Mealy-style)	N/A (No Learning)	N/A (No Learning)	Yes
[13]	Only Boolean (Moore-style)	Concrete	Fixed	Yes

Related Work. Several algorithms have been proposed for actively learning finite-state automata with an infinite input alphabet. Table 1 summarizes some of these algorithms. In [6], Drews and D'Antoni presented the Λ^* algorithm to learn symbolic finite automata. Λ^* is a combination of L* [2] and predicate learning with a *partitioning function*. Our algorithm is an extension of Λ^* [6] for Mealy-style multiple outputs. For the complexity analysis of Λ^*, they introduced the notion of learnability of a Boolean algebra and classified the Boolean algebras with respect to the learning complexity. Compared with their query complexity analysis, ours is finer thanks to the theoretical gadgets (e. g., Σ_E^{final}) we introduce.

In [3], Argyros and D'Antoni presented another algorithm, called MAT*, to learn symbolic finite automata. MAT* is a combination of TTT [9] and *active* predicate learning, unlike the *passive* predicate learning in Λ^* and our algorithm Λ_M^*. Extending Λ_M^* to active predicate learning is a viable future direction.

In [7], Howar et al. proposed alphabet abstraction to extend existing automata learning algorithms to handle infinite input alphabets. However, the learned predicates are defined in terms of the target automaton's evaluation, making them abstract. Additionally, their algorithm can only handle abstract predicates over a Boolean algebra defined by the target automaton.

In [11], Lathouwers et al. proposed a learning algorithm for symbolic finite transducers. Their algorithm supports both constant outputs, like those in Λ_M^*, and identity functions as outputs. However, their algorithm is limited to a specific Boolean algebra known as *equality algebra*. Therefore, it cannot handle, for example, the benchmarks in Sect. 4.1. Moreover, their learning algorithm uses *Moore*-style criteria to identify the state space, while the learned transducer has *Mealy*-style outputs. As a result, it essentially learns an automaton with Moore-style outputs, and the learned transducer may not be minimal.

In [1], Aarts et al. proposed a learning algorithm for symbolic Mealy machines, finite automata with abstraction to handle infinite or large alphabets. Their method relies on externally provided abstractions, which presumably must be handcrafted. In contrast, our method automatically learns abstractions through queries to an oracle.

In [13], a learning algorithm for symbolic finite automata over ordered domains was proposed. In contrast, our algorithm and its termination proof apply to more general Boolean algebras, e.g., the equality algebra.

2 Preliminaries

Let $\mathbb{N}$ be the set of naturals. For a set X, we let $\mathcal{P}(X)$ be the powerset of X and $\mathcal{P}_{\mathrm{fin}}(X)$ be the finite powerset of X. For a set X, we denote its size by $|X|$. For a set X of *characters*, we let X^* be the set of *words* over X, i.e., $X^* = \bigcup_{n=0}^{\infty} X^n$, where X^n is the set of length-n sequences over X ($n \in \mathbb{N}$). The word of length 0 (i.e., the empty word) is denoted by ϵ. We write X^+ for $X^* \setminus \{\epsilon\}$. For words $w, w' \in X^*$, we denote the concatenation of w and w' by $w \cdot w'$. For a set X and for a finite sequence $L = l_1 l_2 \ldots l_n \in (\mathcal{P}(X))^*$ of subsets of X, we write $\mathrm{elem}(L)$ for $\bigcup_{i=1}^{n} l_i$. For sets X, Y, we write $X \triangle Y$ for their symmetric difference, i.e., $X \triangle Y = (X \setminus Y) \cup (Y \setminus X)$.

2.1 Symbolic Finite Automata and Symbolic Mealy Automata

A *deterministic Mealy automaton* is a 6-tuple $\mathcal{M} = (\Sigma, Q, q_{init}, \Gamma, \delta_t, \delta_o)$, where Σ is a finite set of *input characters*, Q is a non-empty finite set of *states*, $q_{init} \in Q$ is the *initial state*, Γ is a finite set of *output characters*, $\delta_t \colon Q \times \Sigma \to Q$ is the *transition function*, and $\delta_o \colon Q \times \Sigma \to \Gamma$ is the *output function*. By abuse of notation, we extend δ_t and δ_o for words in the standard manner. We also define the function $\mathcal{M} \colon \Sigma^+ \to \Gamma$ by $\mathcal{M}(w) := \delta_o(q_{init}, w)$.

In *symbolic* finite automata [5], transitions are labeled by predicates over an *effective Boolean algebra*[1].

Definition 1 (Effective Boolean Algebra). A *Boolean algebra* $\mathcal{B}$ is a tuple $\mathcal{B} = (\mathfrak{D}_{\mathcal{B}}, \Psi_{\mathcal{B}}, \bot, \top, \vee, \wedge, \neg, \llbracket \_ \rrbracket)$, where $\mathfrak{D}_{\mathcal{B}}$ is the domain, $\Psi_{\mathcal{B}}$ is a set of predicates closed under Boolean connectives, $\bot \in \Psi_{\mathcal{B}}$ is the bottom predicate, $\top \in \Psi_{\mathcal{B}}$ is the top predicate, and $\llbracket \_ \rrbracket \colon \Psi_{\mathcal{B}} \to \mathcal{P}(\mathfrak{D}_{\mathcal{B}})$ is a denotation function. It satisfies the following conditions: *i)* $\llbracket \bot \rrbracket = \emptyset$; *ii)* $\llbracket \top \rrbracket = \mathfrak{D}_{\mathcal{B}}$; and *iii)* For all $\varphi, \psi \in \Psi_{\mathcal{B}}$, $\llbracket \varphi \vee \psi \rrbracket = \llbracket \varphi \rrbracket \cup \llbracket \psi \rrbracket$, $\llbracket \varphi \wedge \psi \rrbracket = \llbracket \varphi \rrbracket \cap \llbracket \psi \rrbracket$, $\llbracket \neg \varphi \rrbracket = \mathfrak{D}_{\mathcal{B}} \setminus \llbracket \varphi \rrbracket$. A Boolean algebra $\mathcal{B}$ is *effective* if the denotation function is computable.

---

[1] We use the definition of Boolean algebras used in the context of symbolic automata, e.g., [6], for clear comparison with existing results. In a lattice-theoretic definition, this is often formulated as a Boolean algebra $\Psi_{\mathcal{B}}$ together with a homomorphism $\llbracket \_ \rrbracket$.

324   K. Irie et al.

Example 2 (Equality algebra). For any set $\mathfrak{D}_\mathcal{B}$, the *equality algebra* over $\mathfrak{D}_\mathcal{B}$ is defined as follows. The set of predicates is the Boolean closure of $\{\lambda x.x = i \mid i \in \mathfrak{D}_\mathcal{B}\}$. The denotation function is such that $[\![\lambda x.x = i]\!] = \{i\}$.

Example 3 (Interval algebra). The *interval algebra* over naturals is defined as follows. The domain is $\mathfrak{D}_\mathcal{B} = \mathbb{N}$. The set of predicates is the Boolean closure of $\{[i,j) \mid i,j \in \mathfrak{D}_\mathcal{B}\} \cup \{[i,+\infty) \mid i \in \mathfrak{D}_\mathcal{B}\}$. The denotation function is such that $[\![[i,j)]\!] = \{k \in \mathfrak{D}_\mathcal{B} \mid i \le k < j\}$ and $[\![[i,+\infty)]\!] = \{k \in \mathfrak{D}_\mathcal{B} \mid i \le k\}$.

Definition 4 (s-FA). A *symbolic finite automaton (s-FA)* $\mathcal{A}$ is a tuple $\mathcal{A} = (\mathcal{B}, Q, q_{init}, F, \delta)$, where $\mathcal{B}$ is an effective Boolean algebra, Q is a non-empty finite set of states, $q_{init} \in Q$ is the initial state, $F \subseteq Q$ is the set of accepting states, and $\delta \subseteq Q \times \Psi_\mathcal{B} \times Q$ is the transition relation.

For $a \in \mathfrak{D}_\mathcal{B}$ and $q_1, q_2 \in Q$, we write $q_1 \xrightarrow{a} q_2$ if there is φ such that $a \in [\![\varphi]\!]$ and $(q_1, \varphi, q_2) \in \delta$. A word $w = a_1 a_2 \ldots a_k$ is *accepted* by an s-FA $\mathcal{A}$ if there are $q_1, q_2, \ldots, q_k$ such that $q_0 = q_{init}$, $q_{i-1} \xrightarrow{a_i} q_i$ for each $i \in \{1, 2 \ldots, k\}$, and $q_k \in F$. The language $\mathcal{L}(\mathcal{A})$ of an s-FA $\mathcal{A}$ is the set of words accepted by $\mathcal{A}$. An s-FA $\mathcal{A}$ is *deterministic* if $q_1 \ne q_2$ implies $[\![\varphi_1 \wedge \varphi_2]\!] = \emptyset$ for any $(q, \varphi_1, q_1), (q, \varphi_2, q_2) \in \delta$. An s-FA $\mathcal{A}$ is *complete* if $[\![\bigvee_{(q,\varphi_i,q_i)\in\delta} \varphi_i]\!] = \mathfrak{D}_\mathcal{B}$ for all $q \in Q$. A list $\pi = \varphi_1 \ldots \varphi_k \in \Psi_\mathcal{B}^*$ of predicates is called a *partition* if for any $i, j \in \{1, 2, \ldots, k\}$, $i \ne j$ implies $[\![\varphi_i \wedge \varphi_j]\!] = \emptyset$ and $[\![\bigvee_{i=1}^k \varphi_i]\!] = \mathfrak{D}_\mathcal{B}$. We write $\Pi_\mathcal{B}$ for the set of partitions. For any deterministic and complete s-FA $\mathcal{A}$ and for any state q of $\mathcal{A}$, the list of the predicates associated with the transitions leaving from q constitutes a partition.

In this paper, we study *symbolic Mealy automata (s-MAs)*, which is a special case of *symbolic finite transducers* [21]. Intuitively, an s-MA is a Mealy automaton over a possibly infinite input alphabet, where the transitions are labeled by predicates over a Boolean algebra.

Definition 5 (s-MA) A *symbolic Mealy automaton (s-MA)* $\mathcal{M}$ is a tuple $\mathcal{M} = (\mathcal{B}, Q, q_{init}, \Gamma, \delta)$, where $\mathcal{B}$ is an effective Boolean algebra, Q is a non-empty finite set of states, $q_{init} \in Q$ is the initial state, Γ is a finite set of output characters, and $\delta \subseteq Q \times \Psi_\mathcal{B} \times Q \times \Gamma$ is the transition-output relation. We write $q_1 \xrightarrow{a|o} q_2$ for $(q_1, \varphi, q_2, o) \in \delta$ and $a \in [\![\varphi]\!]$.

An s-MA $\mathcal{M}$ is *deterministic* if $q_1 \ne q_2$ or $o_1 \ne o_2$ implies $[\![\varphi_1 \wedge \varphi_2]\!] = \emptyset$ for any $(q, \varphi_1, q_1, o_1), (q, \varphi_2, q_2, o_2) \in \delta$. An s-MA $\mathcal{M}$ is *complete* if $[\![\bigvee_{(q,\varphi_i,q_i,o_i)\in\delta} \varphi_i]\!] = \mathfrak{D}_\mathcal{B}$ for any $q \in Q$. If $\mathcal{M}$ is deterministic and complete, we define the *transition function* $\delta_t \colon Q \times \mathfrak{D}_\mathcal{B} \to Q$ and the *output function* $\delta_o \colon Q \times \mathfrak{D}_\mathcal{B} \to \Gamma$ of $\mathcal{M}$ as follows: $\delta_t(q, a) = q'$ and $\delta_o(q, a) = o$ if there exists φ such that $(q, \varphi, q', o) \in \delta$ and $a \in [\![\varphi]\!]$. We extend δ_t and δ_o to words $w \in \mathfrak{D}_\mathcal{B}^+$ as follows: $\delta_t \colon Q \times \mathfrak{D}_\mathcal{B}^* \to Q$ is defined by $\delta_t(q, \epsilon) = q$ and $\delta_t(q, wa) = \delta_t(\delta_t(q, w), a)$; $\delta_o \colon Q \times \mathfrak{D}_\mathcal{B}^+ \to \Gamma$ is defined by $\delta_o(q, aw) = \delta_o(\delta_t(q, a), w)$. For any word $w \in \mathfrak{D}_\mathcal{B}^+$, we write $\mathcal{M}(w)$ for $\delta_o(q_{init}, w)$. In this paper, we consider only deterministic and complete s-MAs.

2.2   The Λ^* Algorithm for Learning S-FAs

Λ^* [6] is an algorithm for active learning of s-FAs. Given an effective Boolean algebra $\mathcal{B}$, Λ^* learns an s-FA recognizing the target language $\mathcal{L}_{\text{tgt}}$ using two kinds of queries to an oracle: *membership* and *equivalence* queries. In a membership query, the learner submits a word $w \in \mathfrak{D}_{\mathcal{B}}^*$ to the oracle; the oracle then answers whether $w \in \mathcal{L}_{\text{tgt}}$ or not. In an equivalence query, the learner submits a hypothesis s-FA $\mathcal{A}_{\text{hyp}}$ to the oracle; the oracle returns either *"true"* indicating $\mathcal{L}(\mathcal{A}_{\text{hyp}}) = \mathcal{L}_{\text{tgt}}$ or a counterexample $cex \in \mathfrak{D}_{\mathcal{B}}^*$ satisfying $cex \in \mathcal{L}(\mathcal{A}_{\text{hyp}}) \triangle \mathcal{L}_{\text{tgt}}$.

To construct a hypothesis s-FA, Λ^* first learns an *evidence automaton* $\mathcal{A}^e$, whose transitions are labeled with some elements of $a \in \mathfrak{D}_{\mathcal{B}}$. Λ^* uses a variant of L* to learn an evidence automaton. Then, Λ^* applies a *partitioning function* to convert the characters appearing in $\mathcal{A}^e$ into predicates.

Λ^* uses a data structure called *observation tables* to learn an evidence automaton. An observation table consists of a finite set of prefixes, a finite set of suffixes, and a 2-D array that keeps information on the acceptance of the words obtained by concatenating each prefix and each suffix. The acceptance is checked by asking membership queries.

Definition 6 (Observation Table for Λ^*). An *observation table* T is a tuple $T = (\mathfrak{D}_{\mathcal{B}}, S, R, E, f)$, where $\mathfrak{D}_{\mathcal{B}}$ is the domain of the Boolean algebra $\mathcal{B}$, $S, R, E \subseteq \mathfrak{D}_{\mathcal{B}}^*$, and $f \colon (S \cup R) \times E \to \{0, 1\}$ is a function where $f(w, e) = 1$ if $w \cdot e \in \mathcal{L}_{\text{tgt}}$, and $f(w, e) = 0$ otherwise. In addition, the following conditions hold: *i)* $S \cup R$ is prefix-closed; *ii)* $\epsilon \in S$; *iii)* E is suffix-closed (thus, we have $\epsilon \in E$); *iv)* For all $s \in S$, there exists a character $a \in \mathfrak{D}_{\mathcal{B}}$ such that $s \cdot a \in S \cup R$.

For $w \in S \cup R$, we let $row(w) = \{e \in E \mid f(w, e) = 1\}$. Λ^* increases S, R, and E until the observation table becomes *cohesive*, which is the condition necessary for constructing an evidence automaton[2].

Definition 7 (Cohesiveness). Let $T = (\mathfrak{D}_{\mathcal{B}}, S, R, E, f)$ be an observation table. T is *closed* if for any $r \in R$, there exists $s \in S$ satisfying $row(s) = row(r)$. T is *consistent* if for any $w_1, w_2 \in S \cup R$ satisfying $row(w_1) = row(w_2)$ and for any $a \in \mathfrak{D}_{\mathcal{B}}$, $w_1 \cdot a, w_2 \cdot a \in S \cup R$ implies $row(w_1 \cdot a) = row(w_2 \cdot a)$. T is *evidence-closed* if for any $s \in S$ and $e \in E$, $s \cdot e \in S \cup R$ holds. T is *cohesive* if it is closed, consistent and evidence-closed.

From a cohesive observation table, one can construct a (possibly incomplete) DFA called an *evidence automaton*. Then, a *partitioning function* P is used to construct an s-FA from an evidence automaton. Given a list of pairwise disjoint sets of characters, P returns a partition consistent with the list.

Definition 8 (Partitioning Function). For an effective Boolean algebra $\mathcal{B}$, a *partitioning function* over $\mathcal{B}$ is a function $P \colon (\mathcal{P}_{\text{fin}}(\mathfrak{D}_{\mathcal{B}}))^* \to \Pi_{\mathcal{B}}$ that satisfies the following: Let $L_{\mathfrak{D}_{\mathcal{B}}} = l_1 \ldots l_k \in (\mathcal{P}_{\text{fin}}(\mathfrak{D}_{\mathcal{B}}))^*$ satisfying $l_i \cap l_j = \emptyset$ for any $i, j \in$

---

[2] Evidence-closedness is not necessary for constructing a well-defined hypothesis but is necessary for Theorem 14, which can also reduce the number of equivalence queries.

Algorithm 1: A partitioning function for the interval algebra over $\mathbb{N}$

Input: A list $l_1 \ldots l_k$ of pairwise disjoint finite sets $l_i \subseteq \mathbb{N}$

1 $\varphi_1, \varphi_2, \ldots, \varphi_k \leftarrow \bot, \bot, \ldots, \bot;\ b \leftarrow +\infty$

2 **while** $\exists i \in \{1, 2, \ldots, k\}.\, l_i \neq \emptyset$ **do**

3 $\quad$ **pop** the maximum $a \in l_i$ in $l_1 \ldots l_k$ **from** l_i

4 $\quad$ $\varphi_i \leftarrow \varphi_i \vee [a, b);\ b \leftarrow a;\ i' \leftarrow i$

5 $\varphi_{i'} \leftarrow \varphi_{i'} \vee [0, a)$

6 **return** $\varphi_1 \varphi_2 \ldots \varphi_k$

$\{1, \ldots, k\}$ with $i \neq j$; We have $|L_{\mathfrak{D}_\mathcal{B}}| = |P(L_{\mathfrak{D}_\mathcal{B}})|$; For $\varphi_1 \ldots \varphi_k = P(L_{\mathfrak{D}_\mathcal{B}})$, we have *i)* $a \in [\![\varphi_i]\!]$ for any $i \in \{1, 2, \ldots, k\}$ and $a \in l_i$ and *ii)* for any $L'_{\mathfrak{D}_\mathcal{B}} = l'_1 \ldots l'_k$, if $l_i \subseteq l'_i \subseteq [\![\varphi_i]\!]$ for all $i \in \{1, 2, \ldots, k\}$, then $P(L_{\mathfrak{D}_\mathcal{B}}) = P(L'_{\mathfrak{D}_\mathcal{B}})$.

For example, the function outlined in Algorithm 1 is a partitioning function for the interval algebra over naturals introduced in Algorithm 3. For $l_1 = \{2, 7, 10\}$ and $l_2 = \{5\}$, Algorithm 1 returns $\varphi_1 = [0, 5) \cup [7, \infty)$ and $\varphi_2 = [5, 7)$.

Λ^* constructs a s-FA from an evidence automaton $\mathcal{A}^e = (\mathfrak{D}_\mathcal{B}, Q, q_{init}, F, \delta^e)$ by the following algorithm, which we call `sepPred`. Let P be a partitioning function over $\mathcal{B}$. For each $q \in Q$, let $l_q \colon Q \to \mathcal{P}_{\mathrm{fin}}(\mathfrak{D}_\mathcal{B})$ be $l_q(q') = \{a \in \mathfrak{D}_\mathcal{B} \mid q' = \delta^e(q, a)\}$. Then, we give the list of sets $L_q = l_q(q_1) l_q(q_2) \ldots l_q(q_n)$, where $Q = \{q_1, q_2, \ldots, q_n\}$, to the partitioning function P. Let $\varphi_q^{q_1} \ldots \varphi_q^{q_n} = P(L_q)$. Finally, we add each $(q, \varphi_q^{q_i}, q_i)$ to δ unless $\varphi_q^{q_i} = \bot$.

2.3 Learnability of Boolean Algebras

In [6], Drews and D'Antoni discussed the learnability of s-FA using a mathematical notion called a *generator*, which was used to capture the learnability of a Boolean algebra. They formulated the learnability of Boolean algebras with respect to the generator g as s_g-*learnability* and used it to discuss the termination and complexity of the entire algorithm. A generator g is a function that models one-step refinement of the sampled data $L = l_1 \ldots l_h$ to be given to a partitioning function to learn a partition. Intuitively, $L' = g(L, P(L), \pi_{\mathrm{tgt}})$ represents a part of the learning behavior of Λ^*, where L corresponds to L_q in `sepPred`: the learner constructs the predicates in a hypothesis automaton using $P(L)$ and refines L via queries to the oracle, which has the knowledge of the target partition π_{tgt}. The definition of generators captures this behavior: if a hypothesis partition $P(L)$ generated from L is different from the target partition π_{tgt}, the returned L' refines L with a witness of $P(L) \neq \pi_{\mathrm{tgt}}$.

Definition 9 (Generator [6]). For a Boolean algebra $\mathcal{B}$ and a partitioning function P, a *generator* is a function $g \colon (\mathcal{P}_{\mathrm{fin}}(\mathfrak{D}_\mathcal{B}))^* \times \Pi_\mathcal{B} \times \Pi_\mathcal{B} \to (\mathcal{P}_{\mathrm{fin}}(\mathfrak{D}_\mathcal{B}))^*$ s.t., for any $L = l_1 \ldots l_h \in (\mathcal{P}_{\mathrm{fin}}(\mathfrak{D}_\mathcal{B}))^*$, $\pi_{\mathrm{tgt}} \in \Pi_\mathcal{B}$, and $L' = g(L, P(L), \pi_{\mathrm{tgt}}) = l_1 \ldots l_{h'}$:

- if $l_1, l_2 \ldots l_h$ are pairwise disjoint, then $l'_1, l'_2 \ldots l'_{h'}$ are also pairwise disjoint;

- $\bigcup_{i \in \{1,2,\ldots,h\}} l_i \subseteq \bigcup_{i' \in \{1,2,\ldots,h'\}} l'_{i'}$;
- L' is a refined partition with respect to L, i.e., for any $a, a' \in \mathfrak{D}_\mathcal{B}$ satisfying $a \in l_i$ and $a' \in l_j$ for some $i, j \in \{1, 2, \ldots, h\}$ satisfying $i \neq j$, there is no $i' \in \{1, 2, \ldots, h'\}$ satisfying $a \in l'_{i'}$ and $a' \in l'_{i'}$; and
- Exactly one of the following conditions holds:
  - $P(L) \neq \pi_{\mathrm{tgt}}$, $\bigcup_{i \in \{1,2,\ldots,h\}} l_i \subsetneq \bigcup_{i' \in \{1,2,\ldots,h'\}} l'_{i'}$, and $h = h'$;
  - $P(L) \neq \pi_{\mathrm{tgt}}$, $\bigcup_{i \in \{1,2,\ldots,h\}} l_i \subseteq \bigcup_{i' \in \{1,2,\ldots,h'\}} l'_{i'}$, and $h < h'$; or
  - $P(L) = \pi_{\mathrm{tgt}}$, $\bigcup_{i \in \{1,2,\ldots,h\}} l_i \subseteq \bigcup_{i' \in \{1,2,\ldots,h'\}} l'_{i'}$, and $h = h'$.

For a Boolean algebra $\mathcal{B}$, its partitioning function P, and a partition $\pi_{\mathrm{tgt}} \in \Pi_\mathcal{B}$, we inductively define $L_0^{\pi_{\mathrm{tgt}}}, L_1^{\pi_{\mathrm{tgt}}}, \ldots$ as $L_0^{\pi_{\mathrm{tgt}}} = \emptyset$ and $L_i^{\pi_{\mathrm{tgt}}} = g(L_{i-1}^{\pi_{\mathrm{tgt}}}, P(L_{i-1}^{\pi_{\mathrm{tgt}}}), \pi_{\mathrm{tgt}})$. A generator g for $\mathcal{B}$ and P is *finitely exhaustive* for $\pi_{\mathrm{tgt}} \in \Pi_\mathcal{B}$ if, for the above sequence $L_0^{\pi_{\mathrm{tgt}}}, L_1^{\pi_{\mathrm{tgt}}}, \ldots$, there is $i \in \mathbb{N}$ such that $L_i^{\pi_{\mathrm{tgt}}} = L_j^{\pi_{\mathrm{tgt}}}$ for any $j \geq i$; we write $L_\infty^{\pi_{\mathrm{tgt}}}$ for such $L_i^{\pi_{\mathrm{tgt}}}$. By the definition of generators, $P(L_\infty^{\pi_{\mathrm{tgt}}}) = \pi_{\mathrm{tgt}}$ holds.

Finally, we present s_g-*learnability*, which defines the difficulty of learning partitions consisting of the predicates in the Boolean algebra $\mathcal{B}$ using a generator g and a partitioning function P. Intuitively, for $\pi_{\mathrm{tgt}} \in \Pi_\mathcal{B}$, s_g is an upper bound of the number of samples required to learn π_{tgt} with g.

Definition 10 (s_g-learnability [6]). Let $\mathcal{B}$ be a Boolean algebra, P be a partitioning function, and g be a generator. $\mathcal{B}$ is s_g-*learnable* with P if for any $\pi_{\mathrm{tgt}} \in \Pi_\mathcal{B}$, g is finitely exhaustive for π_{tgt}.

For instance, the equality algebra (Example 2) for any finite alphabet and interval algebra (Example 3) for integers are s_g-learnable for any generator g for some partitioning functions. Moreover, for any s_g learnable Boolean algebras, their product is also s_g learnable. See [6] for other examples.

3 Active Learning of Symbolic Mealy Automata

We present our algorithm, Λ_M^*, for learning s-MAs. Our algorithm is based on Λ^* with an extension to learn an output function that maps a pair of a state and an input character to an output character.

In the learning algorithm [14] for (non-symbolic) Mealy automata, an output function is learned by recording the output for *all* the elements of the input alphabet for each state in an observation table. However, since the input alphabet of an s-MA may be infinite, this technique does not work.

To overcome this issue, we maintain a finite subset Σ_E of the input alphabet to learn an output function and refine it as learning progresses. Concretely, we introduce a new condition *output-closedness* of an observation table and introduce a set Σ_E to record the essential characters.

3.1   Observation Table and Algorithm Description

Given a Boolean algebra $\mathcal{B}$, Λ_M^* learns an s-MA that returns the same output for all inputs as the target $\mathcal{M}_{\mathrm{tgt}}$ using two kinds of queries to an oracle: In an *output query*, the learner submits a word $w \in \mathfrak{D}_{\mathcal{B}}^+$ to the oracle and obtains an output character $\mathcal{M}_{\mathrm{tgt}}(w)$. In an *equivalence query*, the learner submits a hypothesis s-MA $\mathcal{M}_{\mathrm{hyp}}$ to the oracle, and the oracle returns either *"true"* indicating that for all $w \in \mathfrak{D}_{\mathcal{B}}^+$, we have $\mathcal{M}_{\mathrm{hyp}}(w) = \mathcal{M}_{\mathrm{tgt}}(w)$, or there is a counterexample $cex \in \mathfrak{D}_{\mathcal{B}}^+$ such that $\mathcal{M}_{\mathrm{hyp}}(cex) \neq \mathcal{M}_{\mathrm{tgt}}(cex)$.

Λ_M^* also uses an observation table. Unlike Λ^*, an observation table keeps information on an output character of target $\mathcal{M}_{\mathrm{tgt}}$ instead of acceptance and non-acceptance. Moreover, the column index is changed from E to $\Sigma_E \cup E$.

Definition 11 (Observation Table for Λ_M^*). An *observation table* T is a tuple $T = (\mathfrak{D}_{\mathcal{B}}, S, R, \Sigma_E, E, f)$, where $\mathfrak{D}_{\mathcal{B}}$ is the domain of the Boolean algebra, $S, R, E \subseteq \mathfrak{D}_{\mathcal{B}}^*$, $\Sigma_E \subseteq \mathfrak{D}_{\mathcal{B}}$, and $f \colon (S \cup R) \times (\Sigma_E \cup E) \to \Gamma$ is such that $f(w, e) = \mathcal{M}_{\mathrm{tgt}}(w \cdot e)$. In addition, the following conditions hold: *i)* $S \cup R$ is prefix-closed; *ii)* $\Sigma_E \cup E$ is suffix-closed; *iii)* $\epsilon \in S$ and Σ_E is non-empty.

Λ_M^* updates the observation table and constructs an s-MA. For this, the table must satisfy certain properties. We call such a table *cohesive*. For $w \in S \cup R$, we let $row(w) \colon \Sigma_E \cup E \to \Gamma$ be $row(w)(e) = f(w, e)$.

Definition 12 (Cohesiveness). Let $T = (\mathfrak{D}_{\mathcal{B}}, S, R, E, f)$ be an observation table. T is *closed* if for any $r \in R$, there is $s \in S$ such that $row(s) = row(r)$. T is *consistent* if for any $w_1, w_2 \in S \cup R$ satisfying $row(w_1) = row(w_2)$, for all $a \in \mathfrak{D}_{\mathcal{B}}$, $w_1 \cdot a, w_2 \cdot a \in S \cup R$ implies $row(w_1 \cdot a) = row(w_2 \cdot a)$. T is *evidence-closed* if for any $s \in S$ and $e \in \Sigma_E$, $s \cdot e \in S \cup R$ holds. T is *output-closed* if for any $w \in S \cup R$ and for any $a \in \mathfrak{D}_{\mathcal{B}}$, $w \cdot a \in S \cup R$ implies $a \in \Sigma_E$. T is *cohesive* if it is closed, consistent, evidence-closed, and output-closed.

Together with prefix-closedness of $S \cup R$, output-closedness guarantees that all characters appearing in the observation table are in Σ_E. Unlike Λ^*, evidence-closedness focuses on Σ_E rather than on the entire column indices.

From a cohesive observation table, we construct a deterministic Mealy automaton called *evidence Mealy automaton*. The input alphabet of an evidence Mealy automaton in Λ_M^* is *not* $\mathfrak{D}_{\mathcal{B}}$ but Σ_E. Since the observation table is evidence-closed, $row(s \cdot a)$ and $f(s, a)$ are defined for all $s \in S$ and for all $a \in \Sigma_E$, and thus, an evidence Mealy automaton is *complete*.

Definition 13 (Evidence Mealy Automata). For a cohesive observation table $T = (\mathfrak{D}_{\mathcal{B}}, S, R, \Sigma_E, E, f)$, the *evidence Mealy automaton* $\mathcal{M}_{\mathrm{hyp}}^e$ is $\mathcal{M}_{\mathrm{hyp}}^e = (\Sigma_E, Q, q_{init}, \Gamma, \delta_t^e, \delta_o^e)$, where $Q = \{row(s) \mid s \in S\}$, $q_{init} = row(\epsilon)$, $\delta_t^e(row(s), a) = row(s \cdot a)$ for all $s \in S$, $a \in \Sigma_E$, and $\delta_o^e(row(s), a) = f(s, a)$ for all $s \in S$, $a \in \Sigma_E$.

Let $\mathcal{M}_{\mathrm{hyp}}^e = (\Sigma_E, Q, q_{init}, \Gamma, \delta_t^e, \delta_o^e)$ be an evidence Mealy automaton and P be a partitioning function. An s-MA $\mathcal{M}_{\mathrm{hyp}} = (\mathcal{B}, Q, q_{init}, \Gamma, \delta)$ is defined by generating partitions using P. The following algorithm constructs the transition-output relation. For each $q \in Q$, let $l_q \colon Q \times \Gamma \to \mathcal{P}_{\mathrm{fin}}(\mathfrak{D}_\mathcal{B})$ be the function mapping the target state $q' \in Q$ and $o \in \Gamma$ to the set of characters to transit and output from q, i.e., $l_q(q', o) = \{a \in \mathfrak{D}_\mathcal{B} \mid q' = \delta_t^e(q, a) \text{ and } o = \delta_o^e(q, a)\}$. Then, the list of the set $L_q = l_q(q_1, o_1) l_q(q_1, o_2) \ldots l_q(q_1, o_m) l_q(q_2, o_1) \ldots l_q(q_n, o_m)$, where $Q = \{q_1, q_2, \ldots, q_n\}$ and $\Gamma = \{o_1, o_2, \ldots, o_m\}$, is given to the partitioning function. For the list of predicates $\varphi_{q,o_1}^{q_1} \ldots \varphi_{q,o_m}^{q_1} \varphi_{q,o_1}^{q_2} \ldots \varphi_{q,o_m}^{q_n} = P(L_q)$, we add each $(q, \varphi_{q,o_j}^{q_i}, q_i, o_j)$ to δ unless $\varphi_{q,o_j}^{q_i} = \bot$.

Finally, we confirm that an s-MA constructed from a cohesive observation table has the minimum number of states. These results are natural and similar to well-known properties in a classical setting. However, they are not immediately obtained from standard results, e. g., due to the subtleties related to the use of the partitioning function to construct an s-MA from an evidence Mealy automaton.

Theorem 14 (Symbolic Compatibility). *Let $T = (\mathfrak{D}_\mathcal{B}, S, R, \Sigma_E, E, f)$ be a cohesive observation table, and P be a partitioning function. The s-MA $\mathcal{M}_{\mathrm{hyp}}$ constructed from T and P is* symbolic compatible *with T, i. e., for all $s \in S \cup R$, for all $e \in \Sigma_E \cup E$, we have $\mathcal{M}_{\mathrm{hyp}}(s \cdot e) = f(s, e)$.* $\square$

Theorem 15 (Minimality). *Let T be a cohesive observation table, and P be a partitioning function. The s-MA $\mathcal{M}_{\mathrm{hyp}}$ constructed from T and P has the minimum number of states among s-MAs symbolic compatible with T.* $\square$

Algorithm 2 outlines Λ_M^*. Given a Boolean algebra $\mathcal{B}$ and a partitioning function P, it initializes S to $\{\epsilon\}$, R to $\{a\}$, Σ_E to $\{a\}$ and E to $\emptyset$ where a is an arbitrary character in $\mathfrak{D}_\mathcal{B}$ (line 1) and constructs the initial observation table $T = (\mathfrak{D}_\mathcal{B}, S, R, \Sigma_E, E, f)$ (line 2). In contrast to the initialization in Λ^*, Σ_E is initialized by $\{a\}$ for some $a \in \mathfrak{D}_\mathcal{B}$, and E is initialized by $\emptyset$. This is because Λ_M^* learns Mealy-style outputs.

Until the observation table becomes cohesive, the operations `makeClosed`, `makeConsistent`, `makeEvidenceClosed`, and `makeOutputClosed` are repeatedly applied (line 4-8). Each of the operations works as follows.

- `makeClosed` picks $r \in R$ satisfying $row(r) \neq row(s)$ for any $s \in S$ and moves r from R to S.
- `makeConsistent` picks $w_1, w_2 \in S \cup R$, $a \in \mathfrak{D}_\mathcal{B}$, and $e \in \Sigma_E \cup E$ satisfying $row(w_1) = row(w_2)$, $w_1 \cdot a, w_2 \cdot a \in S \cup R$, and $f(w_1 \cdot a, e) \neq f(w_2 \cdot a, e)$. Then, it adds $a \cdot e$ to E.
- `makeEvidenceClosed` picks $s \in S$ and $e \in \Sigma_E$ such that $s \cdot e \notin S \cup R$ and adds it to R.
- `makeOutputClosed` picks $w \in S \cup R$ and $a \in \mathfrak{D}_\mathcal{B}$ satisfying $w \cdot a \in S \cup R$ and $a \notin \Sigma_E$. Then it adds a to Σ_E.

Once the observation table becomes cohesive, Λ_M^* constructs an s-MA $\mathcal{M}_{\mathrm{hyp}}$ from the observation table by *i)* building an evidence Mealy automaton and *ii)* applying `sepPred` to form an s-MA. Then, Λ_M^* makes an equivalence query with $\mathcal{M}_{\mathrm{hyp}}$ (line 9). If the oracle returns *"true"*, Λ_M^* returns $\mathcal{M}_{\mathrm{hyp}}$ and terminates

---

Algorithm 2: Λ_M^* for active learning of s-MAs

Input: A Boolean algebra $\mathcal{B}$ with domain $\mathfrak{D}_\mathcal{B}$ and a partitioning function P
Output: An s-MA $\mathcal{M}_{\mathrm{hyp}}$ satisfying for all $w \in \mathfrak{D}_\mathcal{B}^+$, $\mathcal{M}_{\mathrm{hyp}}(w) = \mathcal{M}_{\mathrm{tgt}}(w)$

1 $S \leftarrow \{\epsilon\};\ R \leftarrow \{a\};\ \Sigma_E \leftarrow \{a\}$ for some $a \in \mathfrak{D}_\mathcal{B};\ E \leftarrow \emptyset$
2 **Construct the initial observation table** $T = (\mathfrak{D}_\mathcal{B}, S, R, \Sigma_E, E, f)$
3 **while** *true* **do**
4   **while** T *is not cohesive* **do**
5   **if** T *is not closed* **then** $T \leftarrow \mathtt{makeClosed}T$
6   **else if** T *is not consistent* **then** $T \leftarrow \mathtt{makeConsistent}T$
7   **else if** T *is not evidence-closed* **then** $T \leftarrow \mathtt{makeEvidenceClosed}T$
8   **else if** T *is not output-closed* **then** $T \leftarrow \mathtt{makeOutputClosed}T$
9      $\mathcal{M}_{\mathrm{hyp}} \leftarrow \mathtt{enerateHypothesis}T, P$ // Predicates are inferred by P
10   **switch** $\mathtt{eq}_{\mathcal{M}_{\mathrm{tgt}}}(\mathcal{M}_{\mathrm{hyp}})$ **do**
11   **case** *true* **do return** $\mathcal{M}_{\mathrm{hyp}}$
12   **case** $cex \in \mathfrak{D}_\mathcal{B}^+$ **do add** $\mathrm{prefixes}(cex) \setminus (S \cup R)$ **to** R

(line 11). Otherwise, the oracle returns a counterexample $cex \in \mathfrak{D}_\mathcal{B}^+$, and Λ_M^* adds all prefixes of $cex \in \mathfrak{D}_\mathcal{B}^+$ to R, except those that are already in $S \cup R$ (line 12) and goes back to line 3.

3.2   Termination and Complexity of Λ_M^*

We prove the termination of Λ_M^* using generators and s_g-learnability defined in Sect. 2.3. For the proof, we formulate the behavior of the oracle using the generator to learn the partition on the transitions from each state. Namely, we assume that by fixing an oracle, a generator for learning each partition is implicitly fixed, and the oracle returns counterexamples following the generator. Thus, for each equivalence query, the oracle returns a counterexample only using the characters returned by the generators. Formally, we assume that an equivalence oracle, together with the target Mealy automaton, induces a mapping from its state $q_i \in Q$ to a generator g_i, which determines the generator for each partition.

The following formulates the set of characters for learning the partitions in the target s-MA. Notice that Σ_E^{final} captures how the counterexamples returned by the oracle are helpful, as well as the difficulty of the learning itself: Σ_E^{final} blows up if the counterexample returned by the oracle is not helpful or uses redundant characters when answering equivalence queries.

Definition 16 (l_g, Σ_E^{final})**.** For a generator g of $\mathcal{B}$ and P such that $\mathcal{B}$ is s_g-learnable with P, we let $l_g \colon \Pi_\mathcal{B} \to \mathcal{P}_{\mathrm{fin}}(\mathfrak{D}_\mathcal{B})$ be such that $l_g(\pi) = \mathrm{elem}(L_\infty^\pi)$. For an s-MA $\mathcal{M}_{\mathrm{tgt}}$ with states Q, we let $\Sigma_E^{final} = \bigcup_{q_i \in Q} l_{g_i}(\pi_i)$, where π_i is the partition at state q_i of $\mathcal{M}_{\mathrm{tgt}}$ and g_i is the generator to learn π_i.

We formulate the behavior of an oracle as follows. Our formulation is permissive in the sense that we focus only on L_∞^π rather than on each L_j^π.

Definition 17 (Follow). Let $\mathcal{M}_{\mathrm{tgt}}$ be the target s-MA, with states $Q = \{q_1, \ldots, q_n\}$. An oracle *follows* generators $g_1, \ldots, g_n$ at $q_1, \ldots, q_n$ if any counterexample *cex* returned in equivalence queries satisfies $cex \in (\Sigma_E^{final})^+$.

Theorem 18 (Termination). *Let $\mathcal{M}_{\mathrm{tgt}} = (\mathcal{B}, Q, q_{init}, \Gamma, \delta)$ be the target s-MA, with $Q = \{q_1, q_2, \ldots, q_n\}$. If the oracle follows $g_1, g_2, \ldots, g_n$ at $q_1, q_2, \ldots, q_n$ and for any $q_i \in Q$, $\mathcal{B}$ is s_{g_i}-learnable with P, the Λ_M^* algorithm terminates with a finite number of output and equivalence queries.*

Proof (Sketch). Let $T = (\mathfrak{D}_\mathcal{B}, S, R, \Sigma_E, E, f)$ be an observation table. By symbolic compatibility and minimality, we have $|S| \leq |Q|$. Since for any $q_i \in Q$, $\mathcal{B}$ is s_{g_i}-learnable with P, Σ_E^{final} is finite. Since the oracle follows the generators, we have $\Sigma_E \subseteq \Sigma_E^{final}$. In Algorithm 2, the loop from line 4 terminates due to $|S| \leq |Q|$ and $\Sigma_E \subseteq \Sigma_E^{final}$. The loop from line 3 terminates because: *i)* each iteration strictly increases either $|S|$ or $|\Sigma_E|$ and *ii)* if $|S| = |Q|$ and $\Sigma_E = \Sigma_E^{final}$, the learner can identify the correct s-MA by symbolic compatibility, minimality, and the condition ii) in Definition 8. $\qquad\square$

We show the query complexity of the Λ_M^* algorithm with respect to $|\Sigma_E^{final}|$.

Theorem 19 (Query Complexity of Λ_M^*). *Let $\mathcal{M}_{\mathrm{tgt}}$ be the target s-MA, n be the number of states of $\mathcal{M}_{\mathrm{tgt}}$, and m be the maximum length of counterexamples returned from the oracle for equivalence queries. If the oracle follows $g_1, \ldots, g_n$ at $q_1, \ldots, q_n$, and for all $q_i \in Q$, $\mathcal{B}$ is s_{g_i}-learnable with P, the number of output and equivalence queries used by the Λ_M^* algorithm is bounded by $(|\Sigma_E^{final}| + m + 1) \times n^2 + (2m + |\Sigma_E^{final}| + 1) \times |\Sigma_E^{final}| \times n + m \times |\Sigma_E^{final}|^2$ and $n + |\Sigma_E^{final}|$, respectively.* $\qquad\square$

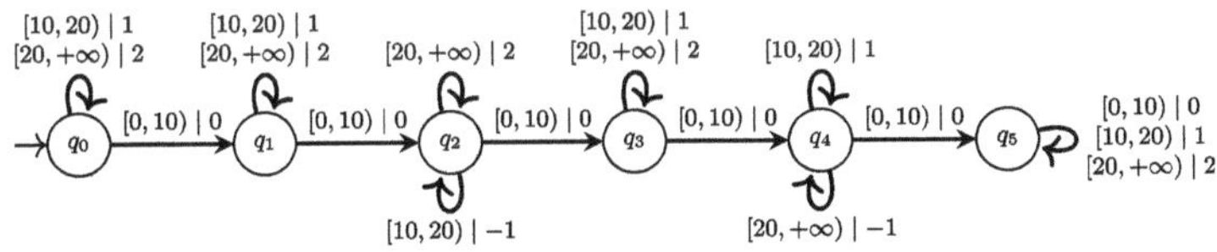

Fig. 3. s-MA illustrating the independent discovery of the state space and Σ_E^{final}.

Theorem 19 suggests that the number of states of $\mathcal{M}_{\mathrm{tgt}}$ and the complexity of identifying the predicates in $\mathcal{M}_{\mathrm{tgt}}$ independently increase the number of equivalence queries in Λ_M^*. This independent influence indeed occurs for the oracle returning the lexicographically minimum counterexample for each equivalence query, which is reasonably smart. Consider s-MAs $\mathcal{M}_{n,k}$ with $2n$ states and $|\Sigma_E^{final}| = k$, where *i)* the state space has a sequential shape, *ii)* at the $2i$-th state, $\mathcal{M}_{n,k}$ returns a different output character only for the i-th input character in Σ_E^{final}, and *iii)* at the initial state, $\mathcal{M}_{n,k}$ returns a different output character for each $a \in \Sigma_E^{final}$. Figure 3 illustrates one of the instances. For equivalence queries, since each $a \in \Sigma_E^{final} \setminus \Sigma_E$ is a counterexample, the oracle initially uses each of them as a counterexample; the oracle then uses words to discover new states as counterexamples. Proposition 20 formally states this independent behavior.

Proposition 20 (Lower Bound). *Let $\mathcal{B}$ be the interval algebra over naturals (Example 3) and P be the partitioning function in Algorithm 1 for $\mathcal{B}$. For the oracle returning the lexicographically minimum counterexample for each equivalence query, for any $n, k \in \mathbb{N}$ satisfying $n \geq 2$ and $k \geq n$, there is an s-MA $\mathcal{M}_{tgt}$ with $2n$ states such that $|\Sigma_E^{final}| = k$ and Λ_M^* requires at least $n + k$ equivalence queries to learn $\mathcal{M}_{tgt}$.* $\square$

4   Experiments

We implemented our algorithm in Java[3]. More specifically, we implemented *i)* a learner that executes the Λ_M^* algorithm and *ii)* an oracle that answers the learner's queries based on the target s-MA given as input. Our implementation is based on the library [4], which implements various algorithms for s-FA. We implemented the oracle based on the following design decisions: *i)* the oracle answers an equivalence query by exhaustively comparing the target and hypothesis s-MAs, *ii)* the returned counterexample may vary even if the same hypothesis is given, and *iii)* the oracle constructs counterexamples only using the essential characters Σ_E^{final}. Throughout this section, we denote the number of states of the target s-MA by n, and the maximum length of counterexamples returned by the oracle for equivalence queries by m.

Environments. All experiments were performed on a server with Intel(R) Xeon(R) CPU E5-2687W v3 @ 3.10GHz, 251GiB RAM running Ubuntu 22.04.4 LTS. For each example, we executed each experiment for 10 times.

4.1   Efficiency for Practical Examples

To observe the efficiency for practical examples, we took two benchmarks from MATLAB/Simulink demonstrations: MH (Mars Helicopter) [18] and ATGS (Automatic Transmission Gear System) [19]. Table 2 summarizes them. MH takes inputs consisting of both Boolean and numeric values. ATGS takes purely numeric inputs. We use the equality algebra (Example 2) over $\{0, 1\}$ for Boolean values and the interval algebra (Example 3) for numeric values. We use the product algebra in [6] for their products. We report the number of queries, total runtime including the time to answer queries, the size of the final observation table, and the length of the longest counterexamples returned for equivalence queries.

---

[3] Our implementation is distributed under Apache 2.0 License at https://github.com/ SoftwareFoundationGroupAtKyotoU/learningsma.

Table 2. Summary of the benchmarks and the experimental results for RQ1. The columns "$|\Gamma|$", "n", and "$|\delta|$" show the size of the output alphabet, the number of states, and the number of transitions. The columns "# Bool. " and "# Num. " show the number of Boolean and numeric values in each input character. The columns "# of eq.", "# of oq.", and "runtime" show the average number of equivalence and output queries made during learning and the average runtime. The columns "$|\Sigma_E^{final}|$", "$|R|$", and "$|E|$" show their size in the final observation table. The column "m" shows the average of the maximum length of the counterexamples returned for equivalence queries during learning.

	$|\Gamma|$	n	$|\delta|$	# Bool.	# Num.	# of eq.	# of oq.	runtime [s.]	$|\Sigma_E^{final}|$	$|R|$	$|E|$	m
MH	4	5	12	1	3	36.0	6516.0	10.9	36.0	176.0	0.0	4
ATGS	4	16	34	0	2	66.0	86446.8	2481.2	68.0	1152.2	6.0	12

Table 2 summarizes the experimental results. In Table 2, we observe that the number of equivalence queries is at most $|\Sigma_E^{final}|$. This is in contrast to the theoretical upper bound $(n + |\Sigma_E^{final}|)$ in Theorem 19 and the lower bound $(n/2 + |\Sigma_E^{final}|)$ in Proposition 20 for an extreme case.[4] This is because Λ_M^* usually identifies the state space and the essential characters Σ_E^{final} simultaneously. Moreover, for the target s-MA of MH, any pair of states can be distinguished with a suffix of length 1. For such an automaton, Λ_M^* identifies the state space only using membership queries once the essential characters Σ_E^{final} are identified. Thus, the number of equivalence queries was equal to $|\Sigma_E^{final}|$ for MH. In ATGS, there are pairs of states requiring a suffix of length 2 to be distinguished. Although the number of equivalence queries can be more than $|\Sigma_E^{final}|$ for such an automaton, it was less than $|\Sigma_E^{final}|$. This is likely because multiple essential characters are identified by one equivalence query.

In Table 2, we observe that the number of output queries is also smaller than their theoretical upper bound, which is 14,309 and 168,592, for MH and ATGS, respectively. In particular, $|R|$ and $|E|$ are smaller than their upper bounds. $|R|$ is smaller than the upper bound because: *i)* Λ_M^* made fewer equivalence queries than the upper bound and processed fewer counterexamples, and *ii)* not all counterexamples are of length m. $|E|$ is smaller than the upper bound because not all pairs of states require suffixes of length longer than 1 to be distinguished.

Furthermore, we believe that in practice, the number of equivalence queries is usually linear to Σ_E^{final} and $|R|$ and $|E|$ tend to be smaller than their theoretical upper bounds. For instance, [10] reports that in many practical non-symbolic examples, any pair of states can be distinguished by suffixes of length 1, in which case the number of equivalence queries is at most $|\Sigma_E^{final}|$ and $|E| = 0$.

In Table 2, we observe that ATGS was learned in 41.353 min. Although our implementation requires an oracle to have a model of a target system as an s-MA

---

[4] The fact that the numbers of equivalence queries in Table 2 are less than $n/2 + |\Sigma_E^{final}|$ does not contradict with Proposition 20; this proposition asserts the *existence* of an s-MA that requires at least $n/2 + |\Sigma_E^{final}|$ equivalence queries.

to answer equivalence queries, which itself is not a very realistic assumption, this computational cost is not excessive. This suggests that our learning algorithm has the potential to be used in realistic scenarios, at least for learning the behavior of a system with reasonable execution time.

4.2 Scalability for Random Symbolic Mealy Automata

To observe the experimental scalability of our algorithm, we used randomly generated benchmarks. We used the interval algebra over naturals in Example 3. The size of the output alphabet is fixed to 3. The values specified in the random generation are the number of states of the automaton and Σ_E^{final} for the current oracle. The number of states is 10, 20, 40, 80, and $|\Sigma_E^{final}|$ is 10, 20, 30, 40; Thus, we have 16 configurations in total. For each configuration, we randomly generated 10 s-MAs. See Appendix C.3 of [8] for the details of the random generation. We measured the number of output and equivalence queries and $|R|$ and $|E|$ of the final observation table.

Table 3. Summary of the experimental setting and the results. The columns "n" and "$|\Sigma_E^{final}|$" show the number of states and the size of Σ_E^{final} of the s-MAs. The columns "# of eq." and "# of oq." show the average number of equivalence and output queries made during learning. The columns "$|R|$" and "$|E|$" show the size of R and E in the final observation table.

n	$|\Sigma_E^{final}|$	# of eq.	# of oq.	$|R|$	$|E|$
10	10	10.00	1015.60	91.56	0.0
10	20	20.00	4075.60	193.78	0.0
10	30	29.99	9104.70	293.49	0.0
10	40	40.00	16161.60	394.04	0.0
20	10	10.10	2035.95	181.57	0.1
20	20	20.00	8030.80	381.54	0.0
20	30	30.00	18080.70	582.69	0.0
20	40	40.00	32110.80	782.77	0.0

n	$|\Sigma_E^{final}|$	# of eq.	# of oq.	$|R|$	$|E|$
40	10	10.00	4010.90	361.09	0.0
40	20	20.00	16036.20	761.81	0.0
40	30	30.00	36079.20	1162.64	0.0
40	40	40.00	64175.60	1564.39	0.0
80	10	10.18	8186.59	722.55	0.2
80	20	20.00	32031.80	1521.59	0.0
80	30	30.00	72072.00	2322.40	0.0
80	40	40.00	128100.80	3122.52	0.0

Table 3 summarizes the experimental results for random s-MAs, and Fig. 4 plots the number of output queries w.r.t. the generation parameters. Similarly to the results for RQ1 in Table 2, Table 3 shows that the number of equivalence queries is almost $|\Sigma_E^{final}|$. This is for the same reason as discussed in Sect. 4.1.

In Fig. 4, we observe that the number of output queries is linear to the number of states. This is in contrast to the theoretical upper bound, which is quadratic to the number of states. This is because, as shown in Table 3, $|E|$ is almost 0, and the number of equivalence queries is almost $|\Sigma_E^{final}|$. Thus, $|R|$ is almost $m \times |\Sigma_E^{final}|$, in which case the n^2 term in the upper bound disappears.

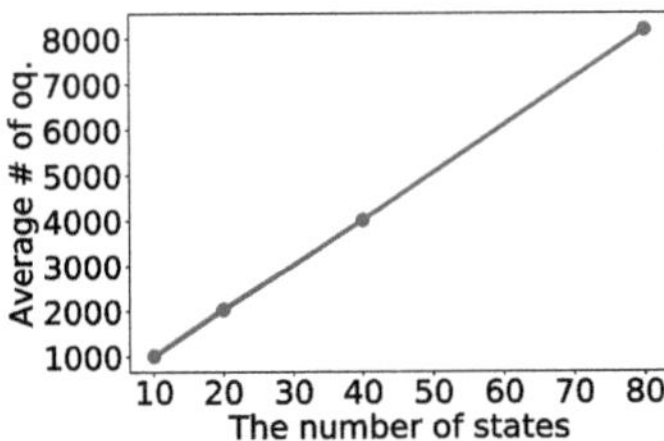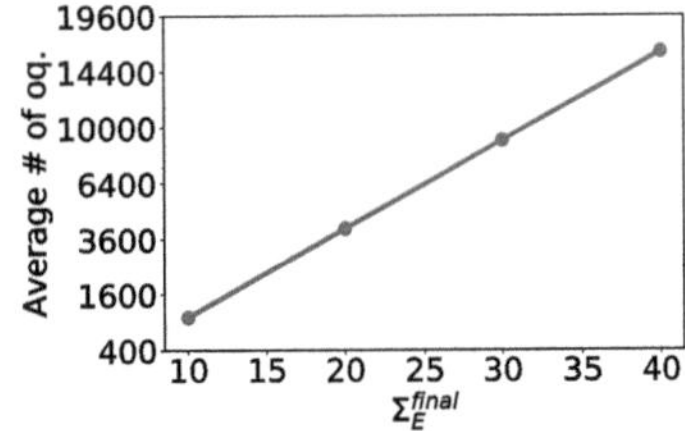

Fig. 4. The number of output queries, where the size of Σ_E^{final} is fixed to 10 (left) and the number of states is fixed to 10 (right). The y-axis of the figure right is on a quadratic scale.

5 Conclusions and Future Work

We propose the Λ_M^* algorithm for active learning of s-MAs. The central idea is to explicitly maintain and revise the set Σ_E of essential inputs during learning. In general, the discovery of the state space and the essential inputs can occur independently, and the number of states and the number of essential inputs can independently affect the number of queries. In contrast, our experimental results show that identification typically occurs simultaneously and that query complexity is typically much better.

One future direction is to improve the query complexity with the counterexample analysis in [16], as in [17] for Mealy automata. Extending recent algorithms for automata learning, e. g., [3,20], to the current setting is also future work.

Acknowledgements. This work was partially supported by JST PRESTO Grant No. JPMJPR22CA, JST CREST Grant No. JPMJCR2012, JSPS KAKENHI Grant No. 22K17873, JSPS KAKENHI Grant No. 25H01113, and JST BOOST Grant No. JPMJBY24H8.

References

1. Aarts, F., Jonsson, B., Uijen, J.: Generating models of infinite-state communication protocols using regular inference with abstraction. In: Petrenko, A., Simão, A., Maldonado, J.C. (eds.) ICTSS 2010. LNCS, vol. 6435, pp. 188–204. Springer, Heidelberg (2010). https://doi.org/10.1007/978-3-642-16573-3_14

2. Angluin, D.: Learning regular sets from queries and counterexamples. Inf. Comput. **75**(2), 87–106 (1987). https://doi.org/10.1016/0890-5401(87)90052-6

3. Argyros, G., D'Antoni, L.: The learnability of symbolic automata. In: Chockler, H., Weissenbacher, G. (eds.) CAV 2018. LNCS, vol. 10981, pp. 427–445. Springer, Cham (2018). https://doi.org/10.1007/978-3-319-96145-3_23

4. D'Antoni, L.: Library for symbolic automata and symbolic visibly pushdown automata. https://github.com/lorisdanto/symbolicautomata/. Accessed 14 Oct 2024

5. D'Antoni, L., Veanes, M.: Minimization of symbolic automata. In: Jagannathan, S., Sewell, P. (eds.) The 41st Annual ACM SIGPLAN-SIGACT Symposium on Principles of Programming Languages, POPL 2014, pp. 541–554. ACM (2014). https://doi.org/10.1145/2535838.2535849
6. Drews, S., D'Antoni, L.: Learning symbolic automata. In: Legay, A., Margaria, T. (eds.) TACAS 2017. LNCS, vol. 10205, pp. 173–189. Springer, Heidelberg (2017). https://doi.org/10.1007/978-3-662-54577-5_10
7. Howar, F., Steffen, B., Merten, M.: Automata learning with automated alphabet abstraction refinement. In: Jhala, R., Schmidt, D. (eds.) VMCAI 2011. LNCS, vol. 6538, pp. 263–277. Springer, Heidelberg (2011). https://doi.org/10.1007/978-3-642-18275-4_19
8. Irie, K., Waga, M., Suenaga, K.: Active learning of symbolic mealy automata. CoRR abs/2509.14694 (2025)
9. Isberner, M., Howar, F., Steffen, B.: The TTT algorithm: a redundancy-free approach to active automata learning. In: Bonakdarpour, B., Smolka, S.A. (eds.) RV 2014. LNCS, vol. 8734, pp. 307–322. Springer, Cham (2014). https://doi.org/10.1007/978-3-319-11164-3_26
10. Kruger, L., Garhewal, B., Vaandrager, F.W.: Lower bounds for active automata learning. In: ICGI. Proceedings of Machine Learning Research, vol. 217, pp. 157–180. PMLR (2023)
11. Lathouwers, S., Everts, M.H., Huisman, M.: Verifying sanitizer correctness through black-box learning: A symbolic finite transducer approach. In: Furnell, S., Mori, P., Weippl, E.R., Camp, O. (eds.) Proceedings of the 6th International Conference on Information Systems Security and Privacy, ICISSP 2020, pp. 784–795. SCITEPRESS (2020). https://doi.org/10.5220/0009371207840795
12. Meinke, K.: Learning-based testing: recent progress and future prospects. In: Bennaceur, A., Hähnle, R., Meinke, K. (eds.) Machine Learning for Dynamic Software Analysis: Potentials and Limits. LNCS, vol. 11026, pp. 53–73. Springer, Cham (2018). https://doi.org/10.1007/978-3-319-96562-8_2
13. Mens, I., Maler, O.: Learning regular languages over large ordered alphabets. Log. Methods Comput. Sci. 11(3) (2015). https://doi.org/10.2168/LMCS-11(3:13)2015
14. Niese, O.: An integrated approach to testing complex systems. Ph.D. thesis, Technical University of Dortmund, Germany (2003)
15. Peled, D.A., Vardi, M.Y., Yannakakis, M.: Black box checking. In: Wu, J., Chanson, S.T., Gao, Q. (eds.) Formal Methods for Protocol Engineering and Distributed Systems, FORTE XII / PSTV XIX'99, IFIP TC6 WG6.1 Joint International Conference on Formal Description Techniques for Distributed Systems and Communication Protocols (FORTE XII) and Protocol Specification, Testing and Verification (PSTV XIX). IFIP Conference Proceedings, vol. 156, pp. 225–240. Kluwer (1999)
16. Rivest, R.L., Schapire, R.E.: Inference of finite automata using homing sequences. In: Hanson, S.J., Remmele, W., Rivest, R.L. (eds.) Machine Learning: From Theory to Applications. LNCS, vol. 661, pp. 51–73. Springer, Heidelberg (1993). https://doi.org/10.1007/3-540-56483-7_22
17. Shahbaz, M., Groz, R.: Inferring mealy machines. In: Cavalcanti, A., Dams, D.R. (eds.) FM 2009. LNCS, vol. 5850, pp. 207–222. Springer, Heidelberg (2009). https://doi.org/10.1007/978-3-642-05089-3_14
18. The MathWorks Inc.: Mars helicopter system-level design. https://www.mathworks.com/help/sps/ug/mars-helicopter-system.html
19. The MathWorks Inc.: Simplify stateflow charts by incorporating active state output. https://www.mathworks.com/help/stateflow/ug/use-active-state-output.html

20. Vaandrager, F., Garhewal, B., Rot, J., Wißmann, T.: A new approach for active automata learning based on apartness. In: TACAS 2022. LNCS, vol. 13243, pp. 223–243. Springer, Cham (2022). https://doi.org/10.1007/978-3-030-99524-9_12
21. Veanes, M., Hooimeijer, P., Livshits, B., Molnar, D., Bjørner, N.S.: Symbolic finite state transducers: algorithms and applications. In: Field, J., Hicks, M. (eds.) Proceedings of the 39th ACM SIGPLAN-SIGACT Symposium on Principles of Programming Languages, POPL 2012, pp. 137–150. ACM (2012). https://doi.org/10.1145/2103656.2103674
22. Waga, M.: Falsification of cyber-physical systems with robustness-guided black-box checking. In: HSCC, pp. 11:1–11:13. ACM (2020)
23. Zhang, H., Feng, L., Li, Z.: Control of black-box embedded systems by integrating automaton learning and supervisory control theory of discrete-event systems. IEEE Trans. Autom. Sci. Eng. $\mathbf{17}$(1), 361–374 (2020)

AP-Observation Automata
for Abstraction-Based Verification
of Continuous-Time Systems

Sasinee Pruekprasert[1]([✉]) [iD] and Clovis Eberhart[2] [iD]

[1] The University of Tokyo, Tokyo, Japan
`spruekprasert@g.ecc.u-tokyo.ac.jp`
[2] Tohoku University, Sendai, Japan
`eberhart.clovis.d1@tohoku.ac.jp`

Abstract. A key challenge in abstraction-based verification and control under complex specifications such as Linear Temporal Logic (LTL) is that abstract models retain significantly less information than their original systems. This issue is especially true for continuous-time systems, where the system state trajectories are split into intervals of discrete actions, and satisfaction of atomic propositions is abstracted to a whole time interval. To tackle this challenge, this work introduces a novel translation from LTL specifications to *AP*-observation automata, a particular type of Büchi automata specifically designed for abstraction-based verification. Based on this automaton, we present a game-based verification algorithm played between the system and the environment, and an illustrative example for abstraction-based system verification under several LTL specifications.

Keywords: Linear temporal logic · Verification · Automata · Abstraction · Continuous-time system · Symbolic control

1 Introduction

The growing complexity of engineered physical systems has increased the need for formal methods that can specify and verify their desired behaviors. Many such properties can only be specified in temporal logics, a powerful framework for formalizing complex specifications of timed systems. In particular, *Linear Temporal Logic* (LTL) [1] strikes a good balance between expressivity and complexity of verification. Indeed, LTL is widely used for describing temporal specifications

S. Pruekprasert is supported by JSPS KAKENHI Grant Numbers JP21K14191 and JP22KK0155 and C. Eberhart is supported by JSPS KAKENHI Grant Number JP25H00446. This work was partly done while S. Pruekprasert was with the National Institute of Advanced Industrial Science and Technology, Tokyo, Japan, and C. Eberhart was with the National Institute of Informatics, Tokyo, Japan.
S. Pruekprasert and C. Eberhart—Both authors have contributed equally.

in many fields, such as verification [2–4] and control theory [5–7], thanks to its expressivity. Verification of LTL properties can be reduced to language emptiness of Büchi automata [8–10], which gives rise to efficient verification algorithms. However, these techniques are developed for discrete-time, discrete-state systems, while physical systems evolve in continuous space and time.

On the other hand, traditional control theory provides a wealth of methods for analyzing and designing controllers for continuous-time, continuous-state systems [11,12]. However, they focus primarily on specifications such as stability [13], robustness [14], and safety constraints [15]. Meanwhile, modern applications, such as autonomous systems, require temporal and logic-based properties [16–18], which conventional control methods are not designed for.

Abstraction-based control, or *symbolic control* [19–21], offers a framework to handle complex specifications by constructing a discrete abstraction, called a *symbolic model*, of the original continuous system. This approach allows us to leverage automata-theoretic techniques to prove properties of continuous systems. Recent studies on abstraction-based frameworks [22–25] have primarily addressed computational complexity and adaptability, key challenges in this domain. This work focuses on another fundamental issue in abstraction-based approaches: the substantial loss of information in abstract models relative to their concrete counterparts. This is especially true for continuous-time systems, where trajectories are partitioned into discrete intervals and atomic proposition satisfaction is abstracted over these intervals, complicating verification under complex specifications like LTL.

Contribution. We introduce a novel approach for abstraction-based system verification for LTL specifications called *AP-observation automata*. They encode the abstract properties of *atomic propositions (APs)* along system trajectories through their transition labels, classifying them into four values. We define a new construction called *AP*-observation automaton, which is a translation from an LTL specification for continuous-time systems to a generalized Büchi automaton.

Building on this structure, we propose a verification framework that soundly approximates the satisfiability of atomic propositions along system trajectories. It relies on a game played by the system and the environment, represented by angelic and demonic nondeterminism, respectively. Our approach is highly general, supporting nondeterministic, continuous-state, continuous-time systems without global stability assumptions. To the best of our knowledge, no existing technique provides formal verification for this broad class of systems under LTL specifications. Prior work has instead focused on discrete-time systems [5–7], imposed more restrictive dynamics or assumptions [19,21,22,25], or addressed smaller classes of specifications [23,26–28]. Hybrid automata [29] can also be used for verification [30], but most of their problems remain undecidable in general. To achieve this level of generality, we impose a constraint on the satisfaction zones of atomic propositions, a condition met by many systems in practice.

Outline. The rest of the paper proceeds as follows. Section 2 introduces systems, specifications, and the verification problem. Section 3 shows how to soundly abstract a dynamical system into a finite symbolic model. Section 4 presents AP-observation automata as an abstraction of the specification. Section 5 proposes the verification algorithm. Section 6 provides an illustrative application example. The omitted proofs can be found in the appendix [31].

Notations. We write $\mathbb{R}$, $\mathbb{R}_{>0}$, $\mathbb{R}_{\geqslant 0}$, $\mathbb{Z}$, and $\mathbb{Z}_{\geqslant 0}$ for the sets of real, positive real, nonnegative real, integer, and nonnegative integer numbers. The infinity norm is $\|x\|_\infty = \max_{i=0}^{n-1} \|x_i\|$ for $x \in \mathbb{R}^n$. Let $2 = \{\top, \bot\}$ be the set of booleans, and Y^X the space of functions from X to Y. We use X^* (*resp.* X^ω) for the set of finite (*resp.* infinite) sequences of elements of X. We use "iff" for "if and only if".

2   Dynamical Systems and LTL Specifications

In this section, we formally introduce dynamical systems, LTL specifications, and the verification problem for the system.

2.1   Nondeterministic Dynamical Systems

We consider dynamical systems $\Sigma = (X, \xi, x_{\text{in}})$ where $X \subseteq \mathbb{R}^n$ is the set of considered n-dimensional system states, $\xi : (2^X \backslash \{\varnothing\}) \times \mathbb{R}_{\geqslant 0} \to 2^X \backslash \{\varnothing\}$ is the system evolution function, and $x_{\text{in}} \in X$ is the initial state. For a set $\mathfrak{x} \in 2^X \backslash \{\varnothing\}$ of states and a time instant $t \in \mathbb{R}_{\geqslant 0}$, the set $\xi(\mathfrak{x}, t) \in 2^X \backslash \{\varnothing\}$ contains all possible states reachable from some state in the set $\mathfrak{x}$ at time t. We require that ξ satisfy the following properties: $\xi(\mathfrak{x}, 0) = \mathfrak{x}$ and $\xi(\mathfrak{x}, t_1 + t_2) = \xi(\xi(\mathfrak{x}, t_1), t_2)$. Note that, unlike symbolic control approaches such as [23,26], we do not take control signals as inputs to the system's evolution function. Nevertheless, the results presented in this paper are applicable to controlled systems with fixed control strategies, as these systems can be modeled as dynamical systems Σ given above. For $x \in X$, by abuse of notation, we write $\xi(x, t)$ for $\xi(\{x\}, t)$.

A trajectory (*resp.* finite trajectory) of Σ from x is a function $\sigma : \mathbb{R}_{\geqslant 0} \to X$ (*resp.* $\sigma : [0, T] \to X$, where $T \in \mathbb{R}_{\geqslant 0}$) such that $\sigma(0) = x$ and $\sigma(t) \in \xi(\sigma(0), t)$ for all time $t \in \mathbb{R}_{\geqslant 0}$ (*resp.* $t \in [0, T]$). Let $Traj(\Sigma)$ denote all possible (infinite) trajectories of Σ starting from x_{in}.

2.2   Atomic Propositions and Assumptions on Trajectories

Atomic propositions (AP), statements about a state of the system, are the basic building blocks of temporal logic formulas for specifications in this paper. Examples of atomic propositions include properties such as whether the system is colliding with an obstacle or whether its position is in a desirable region. Let AP denote the finite set of considered atomic propositions, and $P : X \to 2^{\text{AP}}$ represent the set of atomic propositions that hold at each system state: if $a \in$ AP represents the property that the system is safe, then $P(x)(a) = \top$ means that the system is safe at state $x \in X$. In other words, $\{x \in X \mid P(x)(p) = \top\}$ is the region of states that satisfies the atomic proposition $p \in$ AP.

2.3   Classic LTL with Signal Semantics

Linear Temporal Logic (LTL) formulas are generated by the following grammar:

$$\varphi ::= \top \mid p \mid \neg\varphi \mid \varphi \vee \varphi \mid \bigcirc\varphi \mid \varphi\,\mathsf{U}\,\varphi,$$

where $\top$ is syntax for *truth* (not to be confused with the semantic boolean $\top \in 2$) and $p \in \mathrm{AP}$ is an atomic proposition.

Conventionally, the semantics of LTL is defined on words, i.e., in discrete time. For example, a classic LTL formula may contain $\bigcirc\varphi$ (*next* φ), which holds for $x_i x_{i+1}\ldots$ if φ holds at the *next* discrete step $x_{i+1}x_{i+2}\ldots$ (see [1] for a formal definition). However, we are interested in the property of a system trajectory $\sigma :$ $\mathbb{R}_{\geq 0} \to X$ defined on the continuous timeline. We consider *AP-signal* $\varsigma : \mathbb{R}_{\geq 0} \to 2^{\mathrm{AP}}$ where $\varsigma(t) = P(\sigma(t))$, i.e., ς indicates the atomic propositions that hold along σ. Note that trajectories $\sigma : \mathbb{R}_{\geq 0} \to X$ and AP-signals $\varsigma : \mathbb{R}_{\geq 0} \to 2^{\mathrm{AP}}$ have slightly different types. We say that a formula is *continuous-time* if it contains no subformulas of the form $\bigcirc\varphi$. Then, the *signal semantics* of continuous-time LTL is the relation $\vDash$ defined on ς as follows:

- $\varsigma, t \vDash \top$ always,
- $\varsigma, t \vDash p$ iff $\varsigma(t)(p) = \top$,
- $\varsigma, t \vDash \neg\varphi$ iff $\varsigma, t \vDash \varphi$ does not hold,
- $\varsigma, t \vDash \varphi \vee \psi$ iff $\varsigma, t \vDash \varphi$ or $\varsigma, t \vDash \psi$,
- $\varsigma, t \vDash \varphi\,\mathsf{U}\,\psi$ iff $\exists t' \geq t$ such that $\varsigma, t' \vDash \psi$ and for all $t'' \in [t, t')$, $\varsigma, t'' \vDash \varphi$.

The formula $\varphi\,\mathsf{U}\,\psi$ (φ *until* ψ) means that φ must remain true until ψ becomes true, and ψ must become true at some point. We also use the usual shorthands: $\varphi \wedge \psi = \neg(\neg\varphi \vee \neg\psi)$, $\varphi\,\mathsf{R}\,\psi = \neg(\neg\varphi\,\mathsf{U}\,\neg\psi)$, $\Diamond\varphi = \top\,\mathsf{U}\,\varphi$, and $\Box\varphi = \neg\Diamond\neg\varphi$. The formula $\varphi\,\mathsf{R}\,\psi$ (φ *release* ψ) means that ψ must remain true until φ becomes true, and ψ must remain true forever if φ never becomes true. The formula $\Diamond\varphi$ (*eventually* φ) means that φ will hold at some point, while $\Box\varphi$ (*globally* φ) means that φ holds all the time. LTL is a very expressive logic. For example, a reach-avoid specification can be represented as $\Box\neg a \wedge \Diamond r$, where a is an atomic proposition that holds on the zone to avoid and r is the one that holds on the zone to reach.

2.4   System Verification for LTL Specifications

This work considers system verification under LTL specifications, i.e., checking whether the system only produces trajectories that satisfy a given specification. Formally, we consider the following problem.

Problem 1. Given system Σ, $P \colon X \to 2^{\mathrm{AP}}$, and a continuous-time LTL specification φ, our goal is to verify whether $P \circ \sigma, 0 \vDash \varphi$ for all $\sigma \in \mathit{Traj}(\Sigma)$.

A standard approach to verification is to construct a Büchi automaton corresponding to the LTL formula, as it is well-known [8,10] that LTL formulas can be translated to Büchi automata in the following sense.

Proposition 1. ([8, Theorem 2.1]). *For all LTL formulas φ, there exists a Büchi automaton $\mathcal{B}$ such that for all words $w \colon \mathbb{Z}_{\geq 0} \to 2^{\mathrm{AP}}$, $w, 0 \vDash \varphi$ iff $w \in \mathcal{L}(\mathcal{B})$.*

We refer interested readers to [8,10] for the translation algorithm of Proposition 1. However, we briefly explain the key concepts here. The translation heavily relies on the fact that $\varphi \, \mathrm{U} \, \psi$ is equivalent to $\psi \vee (\varphi \wedge \bigcirc(\varphi \, \mathrm{U} \, \psi))$, and similarly $\varphi \, \mathrm{R} \, \psi$ is equivalent to $\psi \wedge (\varphi \vee \bigcirc(\varphi \, \mathrm{R} \, \psi))$. For example, if p and $p \, \mathrm{U} \, p'$ hold at time k, but p' does not, then necessarily $p \, \mathrm{U} \, p'$ must hold at time $k+1$. Using this fact, it is possible to build a generalized Büchi automaton for φ whose action labels are valuations of atomic propositions and whose states are valuations of sub-formulas of φ. The Büchi automaton's transitions reflect behaviors as described above: in a state where p and $p \, \mathrm{U} \, p'$ hold but p' does not, it can only transition to a state where $p \, \mathrm{U} \, p'$ holds. Its accepting sets ensure that if $\varphi_1 \, \mathrm{U} \, \varphi_2$ holds at some point, then φ_2 must hold at some later point. The accepting states are the states that capture a property of the operator U that cannot be verified by comparing two consecutive states in a run. In this case, in the accepting states, either p' holds or $p \, \mathrm{U} \, p'$ does not, due to the fact that if $p \, \mathrm{U} \, p'$ holds in some state x_i, then eventually p' later holds at some state x_j where $j \geqslant i$.

3   System Abstraction and Information Loss

A dynamical system, as described in the previous section, is a continuous-state, continuous-time system. In order to verify a system under an LTL specification by checking the system with the corresponding Büchi automaton, we need to abstract the system into a finite-state, discrete-time *symbolic model* that approximates the behavior of the dynamical system.

3.1   Time-Abstraction and Signal Chopping

When abstracting a system, one of the most important losses of information comes from discretizing time. Indeed, since we are interested in complex temporal specifications, where the order in which atomic propositions are satisfied matters, discretizing time loses information about whether an LTL formula holds between two time instants. This information can be arbitrarily complex, and any abstraction into a finite number of patterns necessarily induces a loss of precision.

We discretize time by chopping an AP-signal $\varsigma \colon \mathbb{R}_{\geqslant 0} \to 2^{\mathrm{AP}}$ into slices of a fixed length $\tau \in \mathbb{R}_{>0}$. We abstract the satisfaction of each $p \in \mathrm{AP}$ within each of these slices into one of four possible patterns $\mathbb{O} = \{A, Z, E, N\}$, referred to as an *observation*. Conceptually, A means that the p holds at **A**ll time throughout the interval, Z means that p holds only at the beginning of the interval (time **Z**ero), E means that p holds only at the **E**nd of the interval, and N means that p holds at **N**one of the interval time points. Formally, we define the *signal chopping* of ς along τ, denoted $[\varsigma]_\tau \colon \mathbb{Z}_{\geqslant 0} \to \mathbb{O}^{\mathrm{AP}}$, as follows: for all $n \in \mathbb{Z}_{\geqslant 0}$,

- $[\varsigma]_\tau(n)(p) = A$ if for all $t \in [n\tau, (n+1)\tau]$, $\varsigma(t)(p) = \top$,
- $[\varsigma]_\tau(n)(p) = Z$ if there exists $t' \in [n\tau, (n+1)\tau)$ such that $\varsigma(t)(p) = \top$ for all $t \leqslant t'$ and $\varsigma(t)(p) = \bot$ for all $t > t'$.
- $[\varsigma]_\tau(n)(p) = E$ if there exists $t' \in [n\tau, (n+1)\tau)$ such that $\varsigma(t)(p) = \bot$ for all $t \leqslant t'$ and $\varsigma(t)(p) = \top$ for all $t > t'$.

- $[\varsigma]_\tau(n)(p) = N$ if for all $t \in [n\tau, (n+1)\tau]$, $\varsigma(t)(p) = \bot$.

The slice $[\varsigma]_\tau(n)(p)$ is undefined if $[\varsigma]_\tau(n)(p) \notin \{A, Z, E, N\}$. To ensure that $[\varsigma]_\tau(n)$ is well-defined for all $p \in \mathrm{AP}$, we impose the following assumptions.

Assumption 1. *For all trajectories σ, all $p \in \mathrm{AP}$, all $t \in \mathbb{R}_{\geqslant 0}$, and all $t' \in [0, \tau]$,*

$$P(\sigma(t))(p) = P(\sigma(t + t'))(p) \Rightarrow \forall t'' \in [0, t'], \; P(\sigma(t))(p) = P(\sigma(t + t''))(p). \quad (1)$$
$$P(\sigma(t))(p) \neq P(\sigma(t + \tau))(p) \; and \; P(\sigma(t))(p') \neq P(\sigma(t + \tau))(p') \Rightarrow p = p'. \quad (2)$$

The property in (1) restricts that, within time τ, a system trajectory cannot cross the border of each AP region twice. It is possible to ensure that the system trajectories have this property by appropriately designing or selecting a Lyapunov-like barrier function (see, e.g., [32,33]) to enforce that any deviation of $\sigma(t)$ from the initial AP region results in a monotonic decrease in a certificate function over $[0, \tau]$, thus preventing the system from returning to its initial AP region within the time horizon. The property in (2) implies that a system trajectory can cross at most one AP region boundary within a time interval of length τ. To enforce this property, one may take τ small enough so that the minimum distance between the boundaries of any two AP regions is greater than the distance the system can travel in time τ. This is made formal by the following lemma, whose proof is provided in [31, Appendix A.1].

Lemma 1. *System Σ has* bounded speed *if there exists $\Delta \colon \mathbb{R}_{>0} \to \mathbb{R}_{>0}$ such that for all $t \in \mathbb{R}_{>0}$, $x \in X$, $t' \leqslant t$, and $y \in \xi(x, t')$, $\|y - x\|_\infty \leqslant \Delta(t)$. It is* AP-separated *if for all $p \neq p' \in \mathrm{AP}$, there exists $d_{p,p'} > 0$ such that the distance from the (topological) boundary of $\{x \in X \mid p \in P(x)\}$ to that of $\{x \in X \mid p' \in P(x)\}$ is at least $d_{p,p'}$. If Σ is speed-bounded and AP-separated, then for any choice of $\tau \leqslant \inf_{p \in \mathrm{AP}} \inf_{p' \in \mathrm{AP}, p' \neq p} \inf \Delta^{-1}(d_{p,p'})$, (2) holds.*

The two properties in Assumption 1 are necessary because we want to prevent different subformulas from changing truth value at different times in the same time interval of length τ and also to prevent two subformulas from having Z and E as observations during the same time interval of length τ. Otherwise, we need to introduce new observations: B (if a formula holds at **B**oth ends of the interval, but not on the whole interval) and S (if it holds **S**omewhere but not at the ends). In this paper, we show that it is possible to deduce the observation of all subformulas from those of atomic propositions (see Lemma 4). If we allow these new observations, the result no longer holds, and it is unclear how to construct a sound translation. From Assumption 1, we get the following lemma.

Lemma 2. *Assume both properties in Assumption 1. Given a trajectory σ, let $[\varsigma]_\tau \colon \mathbb{Z}_{\geqslant 0} \to \mathbb{O}^{\mathrm{AP}}$ be the chopped AP-signal of $\varsigma = P \circ \sigma$. For all $n \in \mathbb{Z}_{\geqslant 0}$,*

1. For all $p \in \mathrm{AP}$, we have its observation $[\varsigma]_\tau(n)(p) \in \{A, Z, E, N\}$.
2. For all $p, p' \in \mathrm{AP}$, if $[\varsigma]_\tau(n)(p) \in \{Z, E\}$ and $[\varsigma]_\tau(n)(p') \in \{Z, E\}$, then $p = p'$.

Lemma 2 indicates that at any time step $n \in \mathbb{Z}_{\geq 0}$: *1.* $[\varsigma]_\tau(n) \in \mathbb{O}$ for all $p \in$ AP, and *2.* the system trajectory crosses at most one AP-region border during the time interval $[n\tau, (n+1)\tau]$. By this lemma and the definition of signal slicing, we also have the following corollary.

Corollary 1. *Assume both properties in Assumption 1. Given a trajectory σ, let $[\varsigma]_\tau$ be the chopped AP-signal of $\varsigma = P \circ \sigma$. For all $n \in \mathbb{Z}_{\geq 0}$ and $p \in$ AP,*

$$[\varsigma]_\tau(n)(p) \in \{A, E\} \iff [\varsigma]_\tau(n+1)(p) \in \{A, Z\}.$$

Corollary 1 follows from Lemma 2. Indeed, because we use closed intervals, an atomic proposition holds at the end of an interval (A or E) iff it holds at the beginning of the next one (A or Z).

3.2   Symbolic Models

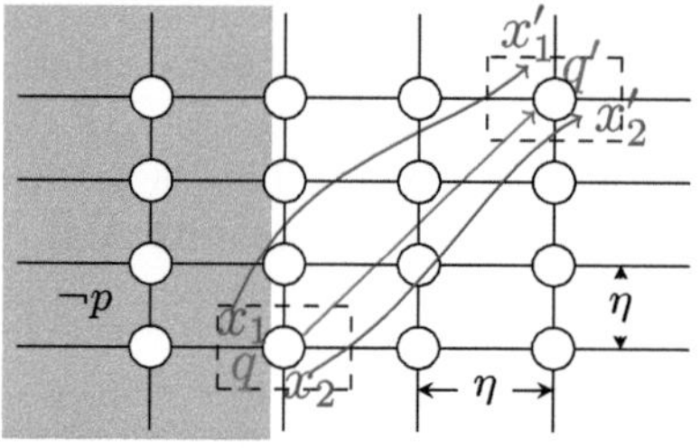

Fig. 1. A quantized state space using a quantization parameter $\eta \in \mathbb{R}_{>0}$. The circles symbolize discrete states. Each discrete state represents (e.g., q and q') a corresponding state region of the size $\eta \times \eta$ (e.g., the dashed boxes around q and q' circles, respectively). The atomic proposition p holds at all states, except those in the left gray half space.

We consider a symbolic model that serves as an abstraction of the dynamical system Σ, not only with respect to the time interval τ discussed in the previous section, but also by abstracting the continuous state space into a discrete set of states. A symbolic model is a labeled transition system [34] $\mathcal{S} = (Q, \delta, q_{\mathrm{in}})$, where Q is a discrete set of states, $\delta \subseteq Q \times \mathbb{O}^{\mathrm{AP}} \times Q$ is a transition relation, and $q_{\mathrm{in}} \in Q$ is the initial state. If a transition $(q, o, q') \in \delta$ exists, this means that the system may move from state q to q' in exactly time τ, provided that the observations of atomic propositions are those given by the function $o \colon \mathrm{AP} \to \mathbb{O}$. The transition system is nondeterministic in the sense that there may exist two transitions $(q, o, q'), (q, o, q'') \in \delta$ with $q' \neq q''$, meaning that the system may transition from q to q' or q''. Moreover, there may exist two transitions $(q, o, q'), (q, o', q') \in \delta$ with $o \neq o'$, meaning that the observation of an atomic proposition $p \in$ AP may be $o(p)$ or $o'(p)$.

Symbolic models have discrete executions defined in terms of runs, whereas dynamical systems have continuous executions defined in terms of trajectories.

Namely, an *infinite* (resp. *finite) run* of the symbolic model $\mathcal{S}$ is a sequence $r_s = q_0 o_0 q_1 \ldots \in Q(\mathbb{O}^{\mathrm{AP}} Q)^\omega$ (*resp.* $r_s = q_0 o_0 q_1 \ldots o_{n-1} q_n \in Q(\mathbb{O}^{\mathrm{AP}} Q)^*$ with $n \in \mathbb{Z}_{\geqslant 0}$) such that $(q_i, o_i, q_{i+1}) \in \delta$ for all $i \in \mathbb{Z}_{\geqslant 0}$ (*resp.* $i \in \{0, \ldots, n-1\}$). In what follows, we refer to infinite runs simply as *runs*, and specify *finite runs* explicitly when needed.

A symbolic state $q \in Q$ may represent an infinite number of actual system states. We are interested in when a symbolic model soundly represents a dynamical system, i.e., when all behaviors of the dynamical system are modeled by those of the symbolic model. In Fig. 1, state q represents all states in the dashed square centered around it, including x_1 and x_2. In this example, both trajectories from x_1 to x_1' and x_2 to x_2' are abstracted to the transition from q to q'. However, the atomic proposition p holds throughout the entire trajectory from x_2, but not at the beginning of the trajectory from x_1. Therefore, there must exist two transitions, (q, o, q') and (q, o', q'), where $o(p) = E$ and $o'(p) = A$, reflecting the fact that the atomic proposition p may hold either only at the end or throughout the entire trajectory.

We consider symbolic models constructed by any method as long as they provide the following information.

1. An abstraction map $\gamma : X \to Q$ that maps each system state to its corresponding symbolic state. For the example in Fig. 1, the states in the dashed boxes around q and q' are mapped to q and q', respectively.
2. It must be so that,

$$\text{For all } x \in X \text{ and all } x' \in \xi(x, \tau), \text{ there exists } (\gamma(x), o, \gamma(x')) \in \delta. \qquad (3)$$

Namely, there always exists a transition $(\gamma(x), o, \gamma(x')) \in \delta$ representing a trajectory from x to x'. This property is known as *approximate simulation* and can be ensured by constructing symbolic models using the methods in [23, 26–28]. Note that a transition $(q, o, q') \in \delta$ may represent infinitely many trajectories from $\gamma^{-1}(q)$ to $\gamma^{-1}(q')$ under observations given by o.

3. Functions $\rho_Z, \rho_E : Q \times Q \times \mathrm{AP} \to \{+, -, ?\}$ from which we define P_Z, and P_E as follows:

$$P_Z(q, q', p) = \begin{cases} \{A, Z\} & \text{if } \rho_Z(q, q', p) = + \\ \{E, N\} & \text{if } \rho_Z(q, q', p) = - \\ \mathbb{O} & \text{otherwise} \end{cases}$$

$$P_E(q, q', p) = \begin{cases} \{A, E\} & \text{if } \rho_E(q, q', p) = + \\ \{Z, N\} & \text{if } \rho_E(q, q', p) = - \\ \mathbb{O} & \text{otherwise.} \end{cases}$$

They must be such that, for all trajectories σ from $x \in \gamma^{-1}(q)$ to $x' \in \gamma^{-1}(q')$, the observation of p along σ must belong to $P_Z \cap P_E$. Formally, for all $(x, x') \in \gamma^{-1}(q) \times \gamma^{-1}(q')$,

$$x' \in \xi(x, \tau) \implies \forall p \in \mathrm{AP}, [\varsigma]_\tau(0)(p) \in P_Z(q, q', p) \cap P_E(q, q', p), \qquad (4)$$

where $[\varsigma]_\tau$ is the chopped AP-signal of $\varsigma = P \circ \sigma$, and $\sigma \colon [0,\tau] \to X$ is the finite trajectory from x to x'. Then, for all $o \colon \mathrm{AP} \to \mathbb{O}$, we require that there exists a transition $(q, o, q') \in \delta$ if

$$o(p) \in P_Z(q, q', p) \cap P_E(q, q', p), \text{ for all } p \in \mathrm{AP}. \tag{5}$$

An intuitive explanation of the two functions is as follows. The function ρ_Z under-approximates the set of atomic propositions that hold and do not hold along the system trajectory at the beginning (at time **Zero**). We have that $\rho_Z(q, q', p) = +$ if we know p holds at the beginning of any trajectory from q to q' and $\rho_Z(p) = -$ if we know it never holds at the beginning. It returns ? if the approximation is too imprecise to give an answer or there exist a trajectory where p holds at the beginning and another where it does not. The function ρ_E is ρ_Z's counterpart for the **End** of trajectories (at time τ). We show example methods to construct these functions in Sect. 3.3.

The following theorem states soundness of the reduction to symbolic models.

Theorem 1. *Given a dynamical system Σ, let $\mathcal{S}$ be a symbolic model constructed as above. For a trajectory $\sigma \colon \mathbb{R}_{\geqslant 0} \to X$ of Σ, there exists a run $q_0 o_0 q_1 \ldots$ such that, for all $k \in \mathbb{Z}_{\geqslant 0}$, $q_k = \gamma(\sigma(k\tau))$ and $o_k = [\varsigma]_\tau(k)$, where $[\varsigma]_\tau$ is the chopped AP-signal of $\varsigma = P \circ \sigma \colon \mathbb{R}_{\geqslant 0} \to 2^{\mathrm{AP}}$.*

Proof. By induction, there exists a run $q_0 o_0 q_1 \ldots$ such that, for all $k \in \mathbb{Z}_{\geqslant 0}$, we have $q_k = \gamma(\sigma(k\tau))$ by (3), and $o_k = [\varsigma]_\tau(k)$ by (4) and (5). $\qquad\square$

3.3   System Discretization

The most common way to construct $\mathcal{S}$ from Σ is to quantize the system state space X into a discrete finite state set Q using fixed-length grid cells. The quantization of space is illustrated in Fig. 1. Formally, $Q = \{(k_1\eta, \ldots, k_n\eta) \in X \mid k_i \in \mathbb{Z}\}$, and γ maps each state X to the closest state in Q (with an arbitrary choice for states at equal distance from several points in Q). Using this abstraction process, the following ρ_Z and ρ_E satisfy the requirements in Sect. 3.2:

$$\rho_Z(q, q', p) = \begin{cases} + & \text{if for all } x \in \mathcal{B}_{\eta/2}(q), P(x)(p) = \top \\ - & \text{if for all } x \in \mathcal{B}_{\eta/2}(q), P(x)(p) = \bot \\ ? & \text{otherwise} \end{cases}$$

where $\mathcal{B}_{\eta/2}(q) = \{x \in \mathbb{R}^n \mid \|q - x\|_\infty \leqslant \eta/2\}$, and $\rho_E(q, q', p)$ is defined similarly, replacing $\mathcal{B}_{\eta/2}(q)$ by $\mathcal{B}_{\eta/2}(q')$. The intuition is that $\rho_Z(q, q', p)$ (*resp.* $\rho_E(q, q', p)$) should be $+$ if for all trajectories from $x \in \mathcal{B}_{\eta/2}(q)$ to $x' \in \mathcal{B}_{\eta/2}(q')$, p holds at the beginning (*resp.* the end) of the trajectory, i.e., exactly when for all $x \in \mathcal{B}_{\eta/2}(q)$, $P(x)(p) = \top$. By Lemma 2 and (3), these functions ρ_Z and ρ_E can be used to construct P_Z and P_E satisfying (4), and δ satisfying (5).

4 *AP*-Observation Automata

We introduce *AP-observation automata*, where the transitions are labeled by observations of atomic propositions. For a given LTL formula, we construct a generalized *AP*-observation automaton that approximates all observations of the subformulas. This construction is inspired by Vardi and Wolper's translation of LTL formulas to generalized Büchi automata [8], but is specifically adapted to our setting for continuous-time LTL, as we need to consider four observations in $\mathbb{O} = \{A, Z, E, N\}$, instead of the two values $\top$ and $\bot$.

4.1 Signal Word and *AP*-Observation Automata

A *signal word* is a function $w\colon \mathbb{Z}_{\geq 0} \to \mathbb{O}^{\mathrm{AP}}$ such that for all $k \in \mathbb{Z}_{\geq 0}$ and $p \in \mathrm{AP}$, $w_k(p) \in \{A, E\}$ iff $w_{k+1}(p) \in \{A, Z\}$ (thus $w_k(p) \in \{Z, N\}$ iff $w_{k+1}(p) \in \{E, N\}$), where w_k is a shorthand for $w(k)$. Notice that a chopped AP-signal $[\varsigma]_\tau$, defined in Sect. 3.1, is a signal word. The intuition is that a signal word is an abstraction of all possible signals mapped to it through signal chopping.

In this section, we assume some given LTL formula φ, and we want to construct an automaton $\mathcal{B}_\varphi$ that is sound for φ, i.e., it only accepts words that represent signals that satisfy φ. Formally, we want to build $\mathcal{B}_\varphi$ such that, if w is in its recognized language, then for all signals ς and durations τ, if $[\varsigma]_\tau = w$, then $\varsigma, 0 \vDash \varphi$.

Hence, we introduce *AP*-observation automata, which we use to verify that dynamical systems satisfy continuous-time LTL properties. They are very similar to classic Büchi automata used for verification of LTL, but one crucial difference is that they work on signal words on the alphabet $\mathbb{O}^{\mathrm{AP}}$, rather than words on the alphabet 2^{AP}. Formally, a *nondeterministic AP-observation automaton* (or simply *AP-observation automaton*) is a tuple $\mathcal{B} = (B, \delta_b, b_{\mathrm{in}}, F)$, where B is a finite set of states, $\delta_b \subseteq B \times \mathbb{O}^{\mathrm{AP}} \times B$ is the transition relation, $b_{\mathrm{in}} \in B$ is the initial state, and $F \subseteq B$ is the set of accepting states. A *run* of a signal word w through $\mathcal{B}$ is an infinite sequence of states $b_0 b_1 \ldots$ such that $b_0 = b_{\mathrm{in}}$ and for all $k \in \mathbb{Z}_{\geq 0}$, $(b_k, w_k, b_{k+1}) \in \delta$. A run is accepting if it visits F infinitely many times. The *recognized language* of $\mathcal{B}$ is the set of signal words that induce at least one accepting run.

Like the original LTL-to-Büchi-automaton construction [8], we start by first building a generalized *AP*-observation automaton $\mathcal{A}_\varphi$, then turn it into a (nondeterministic) *AP*-observation automaton $\mathcal{B}_\varphi$. The following construction is the counterpart of generalized Büchi automata. A *generalized AP-observation automaton* is a tuple $\mathcal{A} = (A, \delta_a, a_{\mathrm{in}}, \mathcal{F})$, where $\mathcal{F} \subseteq \mathcal{P}(A)$ is a set of accepting sets. All definitions are similar to those of *AP*-observation automata, except that a run is accepting if it visits all $F \in \mathcal{F}$ infinitely often. Figure 2 shows an example of a generalized Büchi automaton $(\{q_0, q_1, q_2, q_3\}, \delta_b, q_0, \{\{q_2, q_3\}, \{q_1, q_2, q_3\}\})$, where δ_b can be derived from the picture. For example, $(q_0, g^N, q_1) \in \delta_b$, where g^N denotes the observation function that maps g to N.

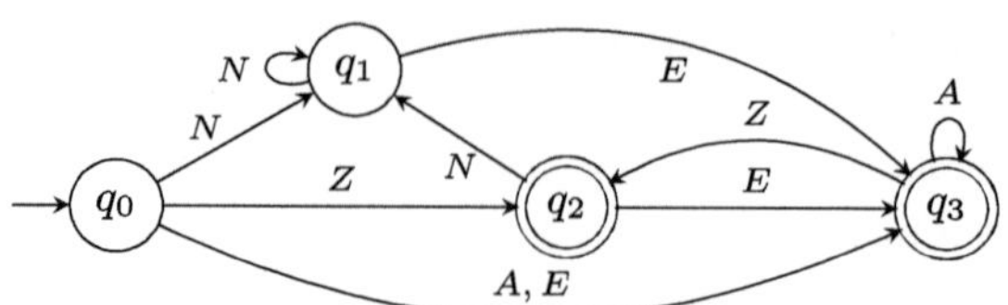

Fig. 2. The generalized AP-observation automaton for verifying the LTL formula $\square \lozenge g$ ($\equiv \bot \, R(\top \, U \, g)$) in Sect. 6, but minimized by merging equivalent states (q_3 is a merged state). The subformulas are g, $\lozenge g$, and $\square \lozenge g$, and the accepting state sets are $\mathcal{F} = \{F_{\lozenge g} = \{q_2, q_3\}, F_{\square \lozenge g} = \{q_1, q_2, q_3\}\}$. Apart from q_0, the only non-accepting state (for $\lozenge g$) is q_1. This reflects the fact that the system violates the specification only if its trajectory never visits a region satisfying g after some point, i.e., the observation along the transitions is always N (g is never satisfied) after that point.

4.2   Translation to Generalized AP-Observation Automaton

Given an LTL formula φ, the construction of the corresponding generalized AP-observation automaton $\mathcal{A}_\varphi$ relies on the set $\mathrm{cs}(\varphi)$ of *consistent subformula valuations* $\nu \colon \mathrm{sub}(\varphi) \to \mathbb{O}$ of φ, where $\mathrm{sub}(\varphi)$ is the set of subformulas of φ. We first present the construction of the automaton and define $\mathrm{cs}(\varphi)$ later. $\mathcal{A}_\varphi = (A_\varphi = \mathrm{cs}(\varphi) \cup \{q_0\}, \delta_\varphi, q_0, \mathcal{F}_\varphi)$ is constructed as follows.

– For all states $\nu \in \mathrm{cs}(\varphi)$, $(\nu, o, \nu') \in \delta_\varphi$ iff (A1) for all $p \in \mathrm{AP}$, $\nu'(p) = o(p)$, and (A2) for all subformulas $\psi \in \mathrm{sub}(\varphi)$, $\nu(\psi) \in \{A, E\}$ iff $\nu'(\psi) \in \{A, Z\}$.
– There exists $(q_0, o, \nu') \in \delta_\varphi$ from the initial state q_0 iff (B1) for all $p \in \mathrm{AP}$, $\nu'(p) = o(p)$, and (B2) $\nu'(\varphi) \in \{A, Z\}$.
– $\mathcal{F}_\varphi = \{F_{\psi_1 \, U \, \psi_2} \mid \psi_1 \, U \, \psi_2 \in \mathrm{sub}(\varphi)\} \cup \{F_{\psi_1 \, R \, \psi_2} \mid \psi_1 \, R \, \psi_2 \in \mathrm{sub}(\varphi)\}$ is the set of accepting states, where $F_{\psi_1 \, U \, \psi_2} = \{\nu \in \mathrm{cs}(\varphi) \mid \nu(\psi_2) \neq N \text{ or } \nu(\psi_1 \, U \, \psi_2) \neq A\}$ and $F_{\psi_1 \, R \, \psi_2} = \{\nu \in \mathrm{cs}(\varphi) \mid \nu(\psi_2) \neq A \text{ or } \nu(\psi_1 \, R \, \psi_2) \neq N\}$.

ψ_1	ψ_2	$\psi_1 \wedge \psi_2$	$\psi_1 \vee \psi_2$	$\psi_1 \, U \, \psi_2$	$\psi_1 \, R \, \psi_2$
A	A	A	A	A	A
	Z	Z	A	AZ	Z
	E	E	A	A	E
	N	N	A	AN	N
Z	A	Z	A	A	AZ
	Z	Z	Z	Z	Z
	E	N	A	A	EN
	N	N	Z	N	N

ψ_1	ψ_2	$\psi_1 \wedge \psi_2$	$\psi_1 \vee \psi_2$	$\psi_1 \, U \, \psi_2$	$\psi_1 \, R \, \psi_2$
E	A	E	A	A	A
	Z	N	A	AZ	N
	E	E	E	E	E
	N	N	E	EN	N
N	A	N	A	A	AN
	Z	N	Z	Z	N
	E	N	E	E	EN
	N	N	N	N	N

Fig. 3. The consistency rules for generalized AP-observation automata.

Next, we define $\mathrm{cs}(\varphi)$. A *subformula valuation* is a function $\nu \colon \mathrm{sub}(\varphi) \to \mathbb{O}$. For example, in Fig. 2, the valuations of all states map $\lozenge g (\equiv \top \, U \, g)$ and $\square \lozenge g (\equiv$

$\perp \mathrm{R} \Diamond g)$ to A, state q_1 maps g to N, q_2 maps it to Z, and q_3 (which is a merge of two states) maps it either to A or E. The valuation ν is *consistent* if ν follows the rules given by Fig. 3. Then, $\mathrm{cs}(\varphi)$ is the set of consistent subformula valuations of φ. The size of the automaton is exponential in the number of subformulas.

The way to read the table in Fig. 3 is as follows: given observations for subformulas ψ_1 and ψ_2, the consistent observations of $\psi_1 \wedge \psi_2$, $\psi_1 \vee \psi_2$, $\psi_1 \mathrm{U} \psi_2$, and $\psi_1 \mathrm{R} \psi_2$ are given in the table. The intuition is that a valuation ν represents the current state of all subformulas. For example, let us consider the second row of the table (the one with underlined text). It states in particular that, if $\nu(\psi_1) = A$ and $\nu(\psi_2) = Z$, then $\nu(\psi_1 \wedge \psi_2) = Z$ and $\nu(\psi_1 \mathrm{U} \psi_2) \in \{A, Z\}$. Indeed, if ψ_1 holds on a whole time interval and ψ_2 holds at its beginning but not at the end, then $\psi_1 \wedge \psi_2$ also holds at the beginning and not at the end, and $\psi_1 \mathrm{U} \psi_2$ either holds only at the beginning (if ψ_2 never holds again, or ψ_1 stops holding before ψ_2 holds again) or on the whole interval (if ψ_1 keeps holding until ψ_2 holds again).

A noteworthy case is in the fourth row of the table (in bold blue text): $\nu(\psi_1) = A$, $\nu(\psi_2) = N$, and $\nu(\psi_1 \mathrm{U} \psi_2) \in \{A, N\}$. If ψ_1 holds at all times and ψ_2 holds at none of the interval, then $\psi_1 \mathrm{U} \psi_2$ either holds for the whole interval (if ψ_1 keeps holding until ψ_2 holds) or does not hold on the interval (if ψ_1 stops holding before ψ_2 holds). Notice that a run $\nu_1 \nu_2 \ldots$ that assigns $\nu_k(\psi_1 \mathrm{U} \psi_2) = A$ and $\nu_k(\psi_2) = N$ at all time steps k is not an accepting run thanks to $F_{\psi_1 \mathrm{U} \psi_2}$. The reasoning is the same for R when $\nu(\psi_1) = N$ and $\nu(\psi_2) = A$.

We remark that the two rows $(\nu(\psi_1) = Z, \nu(\psi_2) = E)$ and $(\nu(\psi_1) = E, \nu(\psi_2) = Z)$ use the fact that only one atomic proposition may change during a time interval of length τ by Assumption 1, so if the satisfaction of two subformulas change during that interval, they must change exactly at the same point in time.

Formally, the connector $\wedge$ comes equipped with a function $c_\wedge : \mathbb{O} \times \mathbb{O} \to 2^\mathbb{O}$ described by the third column of Fig. 3 (and similarly for connectors $\vee$, U, and R). A subformula valuation $\nu : \mathrm{sub}(\varphi) \to \mathbb{O}$ is *consistent* if for all $\psi_1, \psi_2 \in \mathrm{sub}(\varphi)$ such that $\psi_1 \odot \psi_2 \in \mathrm{sub}(\varphi)$, $\nu(\psi_1 \odot \psi_2) \in c_\odot(\nu(\psi_1), \nu(\psi_2))$ for all connectors $\odot \in \{\wedge, \vee, \mathrm{U}, \mathrm{R}\}$.

The following lemma states that the table in Fig. 3 is sound and complete. Note that the AP-signals ς referred to in this lemma are general, and not necessarily those generated by Σ.

Lemma 3. *For all connectors $\odot \in \{\wedge, \vee, \mathrm{U}, \mathrm{R}\}$, formulas $\psi = \psi_1 \odot \psi_2$, and signals $\varsigma : \mathbb{R}_{\geq 0} \to 2^{\mathrm{AP}}$ and $\tau \in \mathbb{R}_{>0}$ that satisfy Assumption 1, $[\varsigma]_\tau(k)(\psi) \in c_\odot([\varsigma]_\tau(k)(\psi_1), [\varsigma]_\tau(k)(\psi_2))$ for all $k \in \mathbb{Z}_{\geq 0}$.*

Moreover, for all $\psi = \psi_1 \odot \psi_2$, $o_1, o_2 \in \mathbb{O}$ and $o \in c_\odot(o_1, o_2)$, there exists a signal $\varsigma : \mathbb{R}_{\geq 0} \to 2^{\mathrm{AP}}$ and $\tau \in \mathbb{R}_{>0}$ that satisfy Assumption 1 and such that, for all $k \in \mathbb{Z}_{\geq 0}$, $[\varsigma]_\tau(k)(\psi_i) = o_i$ for $i \in \{1, 2\}$ and $[\varsigma]_\tau(k)(\psi) = o$.

The proof can be found in [31, Appendix A.2]. The following theorem proves that the generalized *AP*-observation automaton construction of $\mathcal{A}_\varphi$ is sound.

Theorem 2. *For all continuous-time LTL formulas φ, AP-signals $\varsigma : \mathbb{R}_{\geq 0} \to 2^{\mathrm{AP}}$, and durations τ, if $[\varsigma]_\tau$ is in the recognized language of $\mathcal{A}_\varphi$, then $\varsigma, 0 \models \varphi$.*

We relegate the full proof to the appendix [31, Appendix A.3] and only state a few crucial lemmas. Lemma 4 gives a fundamental property of $\mathcal{A}_\varphi$: given a word, there exists exactly one non-initial state and one accepting run along that word from that state. Its proof heavily relies on Lemma 3 in order to show by induction on subformulas ψ that there is a unique possible value for $\nu_k(\psi)$.

Lemma 4. *For all words* $w\colon \mathbb{Z}_{\geqslant 0} \to \mathbb{O}^{\mathrm{AP}}$ *such that*

$$\forall k \in \mathbb{Z}_{\geqslant 0}.\ \forall p \in \mathrm{AP}.\ w_k(p) \in \{A, E\} \iff w_{k+1}(p) \in \{A, Z\}, \tag{6}$$
$$\forall k \in \mathbb{Z}_{\geqslant 0}.\ \forall p, p' \in \mathrm{AP}.\ w_k(p), w_k(p') \in \{Z, E\} \Rightarrow p = p', \tag{7}$$

there exists a unique accepting run $\nu_0\nu_1 \ldots$ *such that for all* $k \in \mathbb{Z}_{\geqslant 0}$ *and* $p \in \mathrm{AP}$, $\nu_k(p) = w_k(p)$.

The following corollary demonstrates that accepting runs are, in fact, exactly valuations of signal choppings. Its proof is relegated to [31, Appendix A.4], but it crucially uses Assumption 1 to show that signal choppings have the same shape as the accepting runs exhibited in Lemma 4.

Corollary 2. *Given* $\varsigma\colon \mathbb{R}_{\geqslant 0} \to 2^{\mathrm{AP}}$ *and* $\tau \in \mathbb{R}_{>0}$, *a run* $\nu_0\nu_1 \ldots$ *such that* $\nu_k(p) = [\varsigma]_\tau(k)(p)$, *for all* $k \in \mathbb{Z}_{\geqslant 0}$ *and* $p \in \mathrm{AP}$, *is an accepting run iff* $[\varsigma]_\tau(k)(\psi) = \nu_k(\psi)$, *for all* $k \in \mathbb{Z}_{\geqslant 0}$ *and* $\psi \in \mathrm{sub}(\varphi)$.

Theorem 2 follows directly from Corollary 2, using the shape of transitions from the initial state, as we only have transitions from q_0 to ν with $\nu(\varphi) \in \{A, Z\}$.

As a side result, Corollary 2 and the proof of Lemma 4 can be used to show that, given a word of observations w_k for atomic propositions, there exists a unique word of observations ν_k for all formulas compatible with w_k (regardless of the AP-observation automaton considered). This can in turn be used to define whether a symbolic model satisfies a formula and prove that the construction is sound and complete *for symbolic models*. However, due to the loss of information during discretization, the construction is not complete for dynamical systems.

Theorem 2 ensures that the construction of $\mathcal{A}_\varphi$ is sound. This construction is inspired by the LTL-to-Büchi-automaton construction by Vardi and Wolper [8], which we briefly discussed in Sect. 2.4. However, there is a fundamental difference in that there are no explicit constraints on transitions. Indeed, in the original construction, where states are consistent valuations $\nu\colon \mathrm{sub}(\varphi) \to 2$, there can be a transition from ν to ν' only if they "agree" on the value of all formulas $\psi_1 \,\mathrm{U}\, \psi_2$ and $\psi_1 \,\mathrm{R}\, \psi_2$. This uses the fact that, in discrete time, $\psi_1 \,\mathrm{U}\, \psi_2 \iff \psi_2 \vee (\psi_1 \wedge \bigcirc(\psi_1 \,\mathrm{U}\, \psi_2))$, so for example if $\psi_1 \,\mathrm{U}\, \psi_2$ holds in ν, then either ψ_2 should hold in ν, or ψ_1 should hold in ν and $\psi_1 \,\mathrm{U}\, \psi_2$ in ν'. Similarly, for Release, using the fact that $\psi_1 \,\mathrm{R}\, \psi_2 \iff \psi_2 \wedge (\psi_1 \vee \bigcirc(\psi_1 \,\mathrm{R}\, \psi_2))$.

In our translation, this constraint comes from the fact that the consistency rules in Fig. 3 also contain constraints on Until and Release, while the original translation only has constraints on conjunction and disjunction. This, coupled with a generalization of (6) to all subformulas, gives constraints between valuations in ν and ν'. However, we need to add another constraint to only retain good behaviors. Indeed, while the original construction only has accepting sets for Until subformulas, here we also need to add accepting sets for the Release subformulas to make up for the constraints in the original construction.

Following the translation from generalized Büchi automata to nondeterministic Büchi automata [10], we can translate the generalized *AP*-observation automata $\mathcal{A}_\varphi$ to their *nondeterministic AP-observation automata* counterpart $\mathcal{B}_\varphi$, from which it is easier to build a game-based verification algorithm. In our implementation for the example in Sect. 6, before applying this translation, we prune the generalized *AP*-observation automaton $\mathcal{A}_\varphi$ by removing states that cannot lead to any accepting run (i.e., that fail to reach at least one state in each $F \in \mathcal{F}(\mathcal{A}_\varphi)$), and merge states that are equivalent with respect to acceptance conditions and outgoing transitions. The generalized *AP*-observation automaton shown in Fig. 2 reflects the outcome of this pruning and minimization.

5   System Verification

We can build a symbolic model $\mathcal{S} = (Q, \delta_s, q_{\mathrm{in}})$ that over-approximates the behaviors of the dynamical system Σ in the sense of Theorem 1 and a nondeterministic *AP*-observation automaton $\mathcal{B}_\varphi = (B, \delta_b, b_{\mathrm{in}}, F)$ whose language is that of φ in the sense of Theorem 2. Both $\mathcal{S}$ and $\mathcal{B}_\varphi$ are nondeterministic. The nondeterminism in $\mathcal{S}$ is demonic and comes from that of Σ: if $(q, o_1, q_1), (q, o_2, q_2) \in \delta_s$, then we cannot choose whether the system goes to q_1 by reading o_1 and to q_2 by reading o_2. The nondeterminism in $\mathcal{B}_\varphi$ is angelic: a word is recognized if there exists an accepting run. We mix these two forms of nondeterminism using a Büchi game [35], a particular type of parity game [36] (with parities 1 and 2).

A *Büchi game* is a tuple $\mathcal{G} = (G, G_0, \delta_g, F_g, g_{\mathrm{in}})$, where G is a set of *vertices*, $G_0 \subseteq G$ is the set of *Player* vertices, $G_1 = G \backslash G_0$ is that of *Opponent* vertices, $\delta_g \subseteq G \times G$ is a set of *edges*, and $F_g \subseteq G$ is the set of *Büchi vertices*. A *play* is a sequence $g_0 g_1 \ldots$ of states such that $(g_i, g_{i+1}) \in \delta_g$ for all $i \in \mathbb{Z}_{\geqslant 0}$. A play is *accepting* if it reaches F_g infinitely often. A *Player strategy* is a function $\pi_0 \colon G_0 \to G$ such that for all $g \in G_0$, $(g, \pi_0(g)) \in \delta_g$. An *Opponent strategy* $\pi_1 \colon G_1 \to G$ is defined similarly. The play *induced* by a Player strategy π_0 and an Opponent strategy π_1 from a state g_0 is the sequence $g_0 g_1 \ldots$ such that for all $i \in \mathbb{Z}_{\geqslant 0}$, if $g_i \in G_k$, then $\pi_k(g_i) = g_{i+1}$. A Player strategy π_0 is *winning* from g if for all Opponent strategies π_1, the play induced by π_0 and π_1 from g is accepting. A state g is winning if there exists a winning Player strategy from g, and $\mathcal{G}$ is winning if g_{in} is winning.

Given a nondeterministic *AP*-observation automaton $\mathcal{B}$ and a symbolic model $\mathcal{S}$, we build $\mathcal{G}_{\mathcal{S} \times \mathcal{B}} = (G, G_0, \delta_g, F_g = \{(q, b) \mid b \in F\}, g_{\mathrm{in}} = (q_{\mathrm{in}}, b_{\mathrm{in}}))$ as follows:

- $G = \{(q, b) \mid q \in Q, b \in B\} \cup \{(q, o, b) \mid q \in Q, o \in \mathbb{O}, b \in B\}$,
- $G_0 = \{(q, o, b) \mid q \in Q, o \in \mathbb{O}, b \in B\}$,
- $((q, b), (q', o, b)) \in \delta_g$ if and only if $(q, o, q') \in \delta_s$, and $((q, o, b), (q, b')) \in \delta_g$ if and only if $(b, o, b') \in \delta_b$.

Theorem 3. *Given a symbolic model $\mathcal{S}$ an AP-observation automaton $\mathcal{B}$, $\mathcal{G}_{\mathcal{S} \times \mathcal{B}}$ is winning iff all plays $q_{\mathrm{in}} \xrightarrow{o_0} q_1 \xrightarrow{o_1} \ldots$ of $\mathcal{S}$ are such that $o_0 o_1 \ldots$ is in the recognized language of $\mathcal{B}$.*

Proof. It is well-known that positional strategies are optimal [36]. In particular, if a positional Player strategy π_0 wins against all positional Opponent strategies, then it wins against all (general) Opponent strategies $\pi_1 \colon G^* G_1 \to G$ that map each play to a next state. Assuming that π_0 is a winning strategy, given a run $q_{\mathrm{in}} \xrightarrow{o_0} q_1 \xrightarrow{o_1} \ldots$ of $\mathcal{S}$, we define

$$\pi_1((q_{\mathrm{in}}, b_{\mathrm{in}}), (q_1, o_0, b_{\mathrm{in}}), \ldots, (q_n, b_n)) = (q_{n+1}, o_n, b_n).$$

Because π_0 wins against π_1, the induced play visits $F_g = \{(q, b) \mid b \in F\}$ infinitely often, so $b_{\mathrm{in}} \xrightarrow{o_0} b_1 \xrightarrow{o_1} \ldots$ is an accepting run of $\mathcal{B}$, and therefore $o_0 o_1 \ldots$ is in the recognized language of $\mathcal{B}$. $\qquad\square$

Putting Theorems 1, 2, and 3 together, we get the following corollary.

Corollary 3. *Given a dynamical system Σ, a symbolic model $\mathcal{S}$ that soundly represents Σ (constructed as in Sect. 3.2), and a continuous-time LTL formula φ, if $\mathcal{G}_{\mathcal{S} \times \mathcal{B}_\varphi}$ is winning, then for all trajectories σ of Σ from x_{in}, $\sigma, 0 \vDash \varphi$.*

This gives a sound algorithm for Problem 1. If the game is winning, then all trajectories σ of Σ from x_{in} are such that $\sigma, 0 \vDash \varphi$, but otherwise we cannot conclude that there exists a trajectory such that $\sigma, 0 \nvDash \varphi$. The completeness

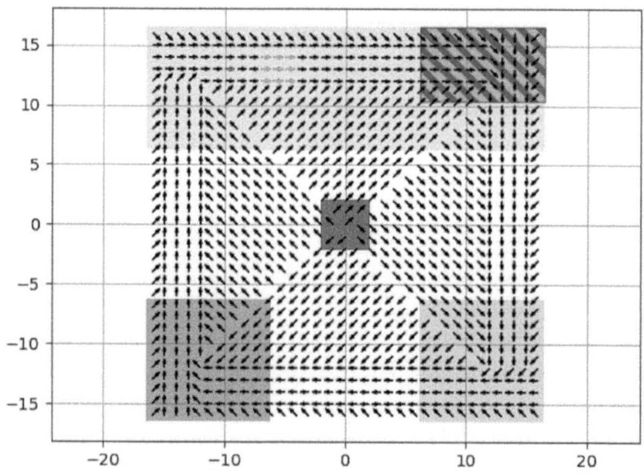

Fig. 4. A surveillance drone system flying from the position $(-10, 13)$ (base of the red arrow). The atomic propositions are assigned to xy-coordinates as follows: c (cyan) for $y \geqslant 6.21$, b (blue) for $(x, y) \geqslant (6.21, 10.32)$, p (pink) for $(x, y) \leqslant (6.21, 6.21)$, g (green) for $x \geqslant 6.21$ and $y \leqslant 6.21$, and r (not red) for $|x| > 2.1$ and $|y| > 2.1$. The states reached in a single transition from the initial state are at the bases of the green arrows. (Color figure online)

Specification	$\mathcal{B}_\varphi$		Game construction		Game solving	Total
	Size	Time(s)	Size	Time(s)	Time(s)	Time
$\Box\,r$	2	0.01	651 + 642	0.23	0.35	1.34
$\Diamond\,p$	5	0.01	757 + 680	0.52	0.46	1.75
$c\,\mathsf{U}\,b$	7	0.04	830 + 691	0.69	0.55	2.04
$b\,\mathsf{R}\,c$	7	0.04	814 + 685	0.69	0.53	2.03
$\Diamond\Box\,r$	6	0.02	1,933+1,924	0.60	2.05	3.44
$\Box\Diamond\,g$	7	0.02	4,640+2,631	1.93	2.48	5.20
$\Diamond(g \wedge \Diamond\,p)$	33	0.40	4,856+2,687	8.98	3.05	13.19
$\Box\,r \wedge (\Diamond\,p \wedge \Diamond\,c)$	46	51.39	7,723+4,144	29.66	7.54	89.36
$\Box\,r \wedge \Diamond(g \wedge \Diamond\,p)$	49	53.86	7,279+4,030	25.49	7.06	87.18

Fig. 5. Sizes (number of states) and construction times (averaged over 10 runs) for the deadlock-free reachable parts of $\mathcal{B}_\varphi$ and the corresponding parity games. For the games, sizes are reported as the total number of states controlled by Player (angelic nondeterminism in $\mathcal{B}_\varphi$) and Opponent (demonic nondeterminism in $\mathcal{S}$). The table also shows average game construction times for the deadlock-free reachable parts, game-solving times, and total times. Total times include the construction of the symbolic model $\mathcal{S}$, which has 1,089 states and takes an average of 0.77 s to build.

of this result cannot be guaranteed, as the exact values of atomic propositions along trajectories are lost during the discretization of the system's state space. To mitigate this theoretical limitation, we demonstrate the practical feasibility of our approach by verifying several specifications in Sect. 6.

6   Illustrative Example

To illustrate a potential application of the proposed structure, we present an illustrative application example of verifying a surveillance drone system. As shown in Fig. 4, the drone flies in an area of $33 \times 33\mathrm{m}^2$ and can move in eight directions: the four cardinal directions and the four diagonal directions, following linear dynamics at a speed of 4m/s. The system's nondeterminism comes from environmental disturbances impacting the drone's speed and direction. Its speed may vary by up to 0.1m/s and its angle by up to 0.08 radians.

We construct a symbolic model $\mathcal{S}$ using $\eta = 1\mathrm{m}$ and $\tau = 1\mathrm{s}$ (which satisfies Lemma 1), and fix the moving direction for each symbolic state as depicted by the arrows in Fig. 4. We implement Zielonka's algorithm [36] to solve the game described in Sect. 5. We implement the algorithm in Python 3.11.2 and run it on a MacBook Pro (Apple M2 Max, 64 GB). We verify the formulas in Fig. 5.

For complex specifications, the main bottleneck lies in the construction of the AP-observation automaton, whose size is exponential in the number of sub-formulas. For example, the formula $\Box\,r \wedge \Diamond(g \wedge \Diamond\,p)$ has ten subformulas. Here, we check the consistency of all 4^{10} valuations before pruning deadlocked states and minimizing the automaton. This implementation serves as a simple baseline to demonstrate the feasibility of the method, and we leave it as future work to optimize it, for example, by considering only valuations at reachable states.

7   Conclusions

We have introduced a novel translation of LTL formulas to AP-observation automata, which is specifically designed for verification of continuous-time systems by abstracting truth values on an interval to four possible patterns. We have presented a verification algorithm that uses this translation for the abstraction-based verification of nonlinear, nondeterministic, continuous-time, continuous-state systems without global stability assumptions.

In the future, we plan to adapt this framework to tackle the symbolic controller synthesis problem. We also want to weaken the constraints imposed on the system, specifically that when an atomic proposition holds, it should continue to hold for a certain amount of time. This can be done by introducing other observation patterns, which makes the construction more complex.

Acknowledgments. The authors would like to thank Jérémy Dubut for letting them reuse part of his implementation.

References

1. Pnueli, A.: The temporal logic of programs. In: 18th Annual Symposium on Foundations of Computer Science (SFCS 1977), pp. 46–57. IEEE (1977)
2. Kern, C., Greenstreet, M.R.: Formal verification in hardware design: a survey. ACM Trans. Des. Autom. Electron. Syst. (TODAES) 4(2), 123–193 (1999)
3. Pnueli, A.: Applications of temporal logic to the specification and verification of reactive systems: a survey of current trends. In: Current Trends in Concurrency: Overviews and Tutorials, pp. 510–584 (2005)
4. Rozier, K.Y.: Linear temporal logic symbolic model checking. Comput. Sci. Rev. 5(2), 163–203 (2011)
5. Belta, C., Bicchi, A., Egerstedt, M., Frazzoli, E., Klavins, E., Pappas, G.J.: Symbolic planning and control of robot motion [grand challenges of robotics]. IEEE Robot. Autom. Mag. 14(1), 61–70 (2007)
6. Belta, C., Sadraddini, S.: Formal methods for control synthesis: an optimization perspective. Ann. Rev. Control Robot. Auton. Syst. 2(1), 115–140 (2019)
7. Banerjee, A., Choppella, V.: Challenges and opportunities in the industrial usage controller synthesis tools: a review of LTL-based opensource tools for automated control design. Results Control Optim. 100511 (2025)
8. Vardi, M.Y., Wolper, P.: An automata-theoretic approach to automatic program verification. In: 1st Symposium in Logic in Computer Science (LICS). IEEE Computer Society (1986)
9. Gerth, R., Peled, D., Vardi, M.Y., Wolper, P.: Simple on-the-fly automatic verification of linear temporal logic. In: Dembiński, P., Średniawa, M. (eds.) PSTV 1995. IAICT, pp. 3–18. Springer, Boston, MA (1996). https://doi.org/10.1007/978-0-387-34892-6_1
10. Gastin, P., Oddoux, D.: Fast LTL to Büchi automata translation. In: Berry, G., Comon, H., Finkel, A. (eds.) CAV 2001. LNCS, vol. 2102, pp. 53–65. Springer, Heidelberg (2001). https://doi.org/10.1007/3-540-44585-4_6
11. Ogata, K., et al.: Modern Control Engineering. Prentice Hall India (2009)

12. Khalil, H.K., Grizzle, J.W.: Nonlinear Systems, vol. 3. Prentice Hall, Upper Saddle River (2002)
13. Gu, K., Niculescu, S.-I.: Survey on recent results in the stability and control of time-delay systems. J. Dyn. Syst. Meas. Contr. **125**(2), 158–165 (2003)
14. Sastry, S., Bodson, M.: Adaptive Control: Stability, Convergence and Robustness. Courier Corporation (2011)
15. Ames, A.D., Xu, X., Grizzle, J.W., Tabuada, P.: Control barrier function based quadratic programs for safety critical systems. IEEE Trans. Autom. Control **62**(8), 3861–3876 (2016)
16. Doherty, P., Kvarnström, J., Heintz, F.: A temporal logic-based planning and execution monitoring framework for unmanned aircraft systems. Auton. Agent. Multi-Agent Syst. **19**, 332–377 (2009)
17. Jha, S., Raman, V., Sadigh, D., Seshia, S.A.: Safe autonomy under perception uncertainty using chance-constrained temporal logic. J. Autom. Reason. **60**, 43–62 (2018)
18. Arechiga, N.: Specifying safety of autonomous vehicles in signal temporal logic. In: 2019 IEEE Intelligent Vehicles Symposium (IV), pp. 58–63. IEEE (2019)
19. Tabuada, P.: Approximate simulation relations and finite abstractions of quantized control systems. In: Bemporad, A., Bicchi, A., Buttazzo, G. (eds.) HSCC 2007. LNCS, vol. 4416, pp. 529–542. Springer, Heidelberg (2007). https://doi.org/10.1007/978-3-540-71493-4_41
20. Pola, G., Girard, A., Tabuada, P.: Approximately bisimilar symbolic models for nonlinear control systems. Automatica **44**(10), 2508–2516 (2008)
21. Tabuada, P.: An approximate simulation approach to symbolic control. IEEE Trans. Autom. Control **53**(6), 1406–1418 (2008)
22. Meyer, P.-J., Dimarogonas, D.V.: Hierarchical decomposition of LTL synthesis problem for nonlinear control systems. IEEE Trans. Autom. Control **64**(11), 4676–4683 (2019)
23. Pruekprasert, S., Eberhart, C., Dubut, J.: Fast synthesis for symbolic self-triggered control under right-recursive LTL specifications. In: 2021 60th IEEE Conference on Decision and Control (CDC), pp. 1321–1328. IEEE (2021)
24. Macoveiciuc, E., Reissig, G.: On-the-fly symbolic synthesis with memory reduction guarantees. IEEE Trans. Autom. Control **68**(4), 2576–2583 (2022)
25. Ren, W., Jungers, R.M., Dimarogonas, D.V.: Zonotope-based symbolic controller synthesis for linear temporal logic specifications. IEEE Trans. Autom. Control **69**(11), 7630–7645 (2024)
26. Pruekprasert, S., Eberhart, C., Dubut, J.: Symbolic self-triggered control of continuous-time non-deterministic systems without stability assumptions for 2-LTL specifications. In: 2020 16th International Conference on Control, Automation, Robotics and Vision (ICARCV), pp. 548–554. IEEE (2020)
27. Zamani, M., Pola, G., Mazo, M., Tabuada, P.: Symbolic models for nonlinear control systems without stability assumptions. IEEE Trans. Autom. Control **57**(7), 1804–1809 (2012)
28. Hashimoto, K., Dimarogonas, D.V.: Synthesizing communication plans for reachability and safety specifications. IEEE Trans. Autom. Control **65**(2), 561–576 (2019)
29. Alur, R., Courcoubetis, C., Henzinger, T.A., Ho, P.-H.: Hybrid automata: an algorithmic approach to the specification and verification of hybrid systems. In: Grossman, R.L., Nerode, A., Ravn, A.P., Rischel, H. (eds.) HS 1991-1992. LNCS, vol. 736, pp. 209–229. Springer, Heidelberg (1993). https://doi.org/10.1007/3-540-57318-6_30

30. Bak, S., Beg, O.A., Bogomolov, S., Johnson, T.T., Nguyen, L.V., Schilling, C.: Hybrid automata: from verification to implementation. Int. J. Softw. Tools Technol. Transfer **21**(1), 87–104 (2019)
31. Pruekprasert, S., Eberhart, C.: AP-observation automata for abstraction-based verification of continuous-time systems (extended version) (2025). https://arxiv.org/abs/2509.08343
32. Lygeros, J., Johansson, K.H., Simic, S.N., Zhang, J., Sastry, S.S.: Dynamical properties of hybrid automata. IEEE Trans. Autom. Control **48**(1), 2–17 (2003)
33. Panagou, D., Stipanović, D.M., Voulgaris, P.G.: Distributed coordination control for multi-robot networks using lyapunov-like barrier functions. IEEE Trans. Autom. Control **61**(3), 617–632 (2015)
34. Baier, C., Katoen, J.-P.: Principles of Model Checking. MIT Press, Cambridge (2008)
35. Chatterjee, K., Henzinger, M.: Efficient and dynamic algorithms for alternating büchi games and maximal end-component decomposition. J. ACM (JACM) **61**(3), 1–40 (2014)
36. Zielonka, W.: Infinite games on finitely coloured graphs with applications to automata on infinite trees. Theor. Comput. Sci. **200**(1–2), 135–183 (1998)

Cryptography and Choreography

Efficient AND Protocols Resistant to Maliciously Revealing a Single Card

Koichi Koizumi[1] ⓘ, Minato Abe[1] ⓘ, Eikoh Chida[2](✉) ⓘ, and Takaaki Mizuki[3] ⓘ

[1] National Institute of Technology, Fukushima College, Iwaki, Japan
[2] National Institute of Technology, Ichinoseki College, Ichinoseki, Japan
chida+lncs@g.ichinoseki.ac.jp
[3] Cyberscience Center, Tohoku University, Sendai, Japan

Abstract. In card-based cryptography for performing secure computation, after each player places an input commitment consisting of two face-down cards, all players cooperate to manipulate a sequence of cards according to a protocol. In the presence of a malicious player who does not follow the protocol, prior work has considered the active card-revealing attack and defined the t-secureness as the ability to prevent information about the input from being leaked even if at most t cards are turned over illegally. In this paper, we first propose an efficient 1-secure AND protocol: our proposed protocol uses only eight cards and one shuffle, whereas the existing protocol requires 16 cards and eight shuffles. Our 1-secure AND protocol is quite simple and easy to implement. We next design a committed-format 1-secure AND protocol by adding four more cards; a committed-format protocol produces its output in the same format as its inputs.

Keywords: Card-based cryptography · Secure computation · Card-revealing attack

1 Introduction

Secure computations, which involve performing computations while keeping the inputs secret, have been extensively studied and developed (e.g. [4,32,46]). Many secure computation protocols have been devised in the field of card-based cryptography [11,21,26,38]; such a card-based protocol uses a deck of cards to physically perform a secure computation. Most of the existing card-based protocols assume that all players are semi-honest. Therefore, if a malicious player cheats without following the protocol, the confidentiality of the input, i.e., the security of such protocols, is generally compromised. There have been several studies that address such issues [12,16,25,42]; among them, this paper focuses on the "active card-revealing attack" formulated by Takashima et al. [42].

1.1 Active Card-Revealing Attack

Takashima et al. [42] introduced an active attack assumption, considering a situation in which an attacker is willing to turn over cards illegally and does not hesitate even if detected, which they call the *active card-revealing attack*.

Z. Liu et al. (Eds.): ICTAC 2025, LNCS 16237, pp. 359–377, 2026.
https://doi.org/10.1007/978-3-032-11176-0_21

Card-based protocols that implement secure computations typically use black ♣ and red ♥ cards, and handle bit values according to the following encoding rule:

$$\boxed{♣}\boxed{♥} = 0, \quad \boxed{♥}\boxed{♣} = 1. \tag{1}$$

Two cards placed face down according to this encoding (1) for a given bit $x \in \{0, 1\}$ are called a *commitment* to x, and expressed as

$$\underbrace{\boxed{?}\boxed{?}}_{x} ,$$

where the pattern on the back of every card is assumed to be the same $\boxed{?}$ throughout this paper.

Typically, each player participating in a protocol secretly creates a commitment to their own private bit (unseen by other players). For example, suppose that Alice and Bob have private bits $a \in \{0, 1\}$ and $b \in \{0, 1\}$, respectively, and wish to securely compute their AND value $a \wedge b$. In this case, they first each make input commitments secretly:

$$\underbrace{\boxed{?}\boxed{?}}_{a} \quad \underbrace{\boxed{?}\boxed{?}}_{b} .$$

The first card-based protocol in history, namely the *five-card trick* [2] invented by Den Boer, adds one red card ♥ between the two commitments and outputs only the value of $a \wedge b$:

$$\underbrace{\boxed{?}\boxed{?}}_{a}\boxed{♥}\underbrace{\boxed{?}\boxed{?}}_{b} \rightarrow \cdots \rightarrow a \wedge b,$$

although the detailed steps are omitted here.

If an active card-revealing attack were to be launched against this protocol, turning over one of the cards comprising the input commitments would immediately reveal whether one of the private inputs of Alice and Bob is 0 or 1. Therefore, not only the five-card trick, but also any protocol that prepares and places input commitments according to the encoding rule (1) is not secure against illegally revealing a single card.

Thus, Takashima et al. [42] defined the "t-secureness" as the property that no information about the input is leaked even if at most t cards are turned over illegally, and they constructed protocols that satisfy this requirement. We assume here that once a malicious player illegally turns over some cards, the protocol is stopped (and the players do not execute the remaining steps).

1.2   The Existing Protocols

As seen in Sect. 1.1, if Alice places a commitment

$$\underbrace{\boxed{?}\boxed{?}}_{a}$$

to her own private input $a \in \{0, 1\}$ on the table, it is no longer 1-secure (because revealing one card would immediately leak the value of a). To solve this issue, Takashima et al. [42] utilized the idea of *secret sharing* [37]. Specifically, instead of creating a single commitment to a, Alice randomly generates two bits a^1 and a^2 such that $a = a^1 \oplus a^2$ to split a into two "shares," and places these two commitments as Alice's input:

$$\underbrace{\boxed{?}\boxed{?}}_{a^1}\ \underbrace{\boxed{?}\boxed{?}}_{a^2} .$$

In this case, the value of a is not leaked even if at most one card is turned over. In this paper, these four cards are referred to as a *split commitment* to a, and a^1 and a^2 are referred to as *shares* or *share commitments*. We sometimes denote a split commitment to $x \in \{0, 1\}$ by

$$\underbrace{\boxed{?}\boxed{?}\boxed{?}\boxed{?}}_{x} .$$

Based on the above idea, Takashima et al. [42] proposed a 1-secure AND protocol using 16 cards and 8 shuffles. Note that each of Alice's and Bob's split commitments uses four cards as described above, and hence we require eight additional cards:

$$\underbrace{\boxed{?}\boxed{?}\boxed{?}\boxed{?}}_{a}\underbrace{\boxed{?}\boxed{?}\boxed{?}\boxed{?}}_{b}\boxed{\clubsuit}\boxed{\heartsuit}\boxed{\clubsuit}\boxed{\heartsuit}\boxed{\clubsuit}\boxed{\heartsuit}\boxed{\clubsuit}\boxed{\heartsuit} .$$

We will introduce this protocol in Sect. 2.

In addition, for $t \geq 2$, Takashima et al. [42] proposed a t-secure AND protocol using $8t + 12$ cards and $2t^2 + 7t + 2$ shuffles.

These existing protocols require multiple runs of the other existing protocols, such as the copy protocol [27] and the AND protocol [25], making them more complex to execute compared to the other AND protocols that do not consider the t-secureness (e.g. [2, 20, 27, 40]). Therefore, it is desirable to develop protocols that can be executed more easily. Especially, a simpler 1-secure AND protocol using fewer cards and shuffles is solicited.

1.3   Our Contribution

In this paper, we first propose a new 1-secure AND protocol based on a different idea from the existing protocol. Like the existing protocol, our protocol uses eight cards for input split commitments to Alice's private bit a and Bob's private bit b, but does not require any additional cards; the number of shuffles is only one:

$$\underbrace{\boxed{?}\boxed{?}\boxed{?}\boxed{?}}_{a}\underbrace{\boxed{?}\boxed{?}\boxed{?}\boxed{?}}_{b} \rightarrow \text{ one shuffle } \rightarrow a \wedge b .$$

As will be seen in Sect. 3, this protocol, which we call Protocol A, is extremely simple, and thus, it is easy to implement.

We next present another protocol, called Protocol B, which produces as output a split commitment to $a \wedge b$, given two split commitments to a and b:

$$\underbrace{\boxed{?}\boxed{?}\boxed{?}\boxed{?}}_{a}\underbrace{\boxed{?}\boxed{?}\boxed{?}\boxed{?}}_{b}\boxed{\clubsuit}\boxed{\heartsuit}\boxed{\clubsuit}\boxed{\heartsuit} \rightarrow \cdots \rightarrow \underbrace{\boxed{?}\boxed{?}\boxed{?}\boxed{?}}_{a \wedge b} .$$

Thus, Protocol B requires four additional cards aside from the eight cards for input split commitments. As will be seen in Sect. 4, it uses two shuffles. Protocol B is classified as a *committed-format* protocol (because it produces a commitment). A committed-format protocol is useful; for example, executing Protocol B repeatedly $n - 1$ times provides us a secure computation of the n-variable AND function. Note that neither Protocol A nor the existing protocols given by Takashima et al. [42] are committed-format ones.

Table 1 shows the numbers of required cards and shuffles for the existing 1-secure AND protocol and ours. Both of our protocols, i.e., Protocols A and B, can be executed with fewer cards and fewer shuffles than the existing protocol.

Table 1. Comparison of 1-secure AND protocols

	# of cards	# of shuffles	committed
Takashima et al. [42]	16	8	no
Our Protocol A (Sect. 3)	8	1	no
Our Protocol B (Sect. 4)	12	2	yes

Although we omit the details due to the page limitation, our Protocol B can be extended to a t-secure AND protocol for any $t \geq 2$.

1.4 Situations of Use of t-Secure Protocols

Here, we mention three scenarios where t-secure protocols would be useful.

- Suppose that Bob has malicious intent when Alice and Bob execute a protocol; then, he illegally flips at most t cards. In this case, Alice's input is not leaked (thanks to the t-secureness). Since the trust between Alice and Bob is lost, the protocol will never be executed by these two again.
- Even if a malicious third party illegally flips at most t cards, neither Alice's nor Bob's input will be leaked. After the third party is dismissed, both the players restart the protocol with new input commitments.
- A simple mistake, in which a player unintentionally flips over a few cards during a card operation[i], is common, especially among players who are not familiar with card operations. In this case, neither Alice nor Bob's input is leaked (as long as the number of mistakenly opened cards is at most t). Each player then makes a new input commitment and restarts the protocol from the beginning.

1.5 Related Work

As mentioned above, several studies have explored active attacks or related concepts. Koch and Walzer [12] addressed active attacks on card-based protocols, focusing on

---

[i] Another operative error was discussed in [22].

the use of envelopes to prevent malicious actions. Manabe and Ono [16] also employed envelopes to construct protocols resistant to malicious players. Mizuki and Shizuya [25] considered information leakage due to scuff marks on cards and proposed countermeasures. Morooka et al. [28] presented three-player protocols designed to prevent malicious actions by observers.

Card-based cryptography is a dynamic field with a growing body of research. Recent areas of interest include: zero-knowledge proof protocols for Sudoku [44], other puzzles [5,6,19,31,34,36], games [15], and graph problems [43]; private set intersection protocols [3]; private-model protocols using standard decks [10,17,29]; applications of 3D printers [8]; shuffle-efficient protocols based on garbled circuit [30,45]; efficient protocols for symmetric functions [33,41]; and applications to card games [23,35,39].

1.6   Organization of This Paper

The remainder of this paper is organized as follows. In Sect. 2, we describe the existing 1-secure AND protocol [42]. Next, in Sect. 3, we present a new 1-secure AND protocol (i.e., Protocol A), which is much simpler than the existing protocols. Then, in Sect. 4, we develop a committed-format 1-secure AND protocol (i.e., Protocol B). Finally, in Sect. 5, we conclude with our results.

2   Existing 1-Secure Protocol

In this section, we introduce the 1-secure AND protocol proposed by Takashima et al. [42].

As noted above, this protocol uses the idea of secret sharing to conceal the value of each player's input bit. That is, instead of directly creating a commitment to a based on the encoding rule (1), Alice splits her private bit as in $a = a^1 \oplus a^2$, and creates a split commitment to a:

$$\underbrace{\boxed{?}\,\boxed{?}}_{a^1}\;\underbrace{\boxed{?}\,\boxed{?}}_{a^2}\;=\;\underbrace{\boxed{?}\,\boxed{?}\,\boxed{?}\,\boxed{?}}_{a}\;.$$

For example, if $a = 1$, there are two options: $(a^1, a^2) = (1, 0)$ and $(a^1, a^2) = (0, 1)$, from which Alice chooses one uniformly at random. Similarly, Bob creates a split commitment to b satisfying $b = b^1 \oplus b^2$:

$$\underbrace{\boxed{?}\,\boxed{?}}_{b^1}\;\underbrace{\boxed{?}\,\boxed{?}}_{b^2}\;=\;\underbrace{\boxed{?}\,\boxed{?}\,\boxed{?}\,\boxed{?}}_{b}\;.$$

With these split commitments, if one of their cards is illegally turned over, only one of the shares that make up a or b will be known, and hence, the values of a and b themselves cannot be identified from there[ii]. Given such two split commitments along with eight additional cards, the existing 1-secure AND protocol [42] proceeds as follows.

[ii] As assumed, once a card is turned over illegally, the protocol is stopped immediately.

The Existing 1-Secure AND Protocol [42]

1. Place the two input split commitments, i.e., four share commitments, as follows:

$$\underbrace{\boxed{?}\boxed{?}}_{a^1}\ \underbrace{\boxed{?}\boxed{?}}_{a^2}\ \underbrace{\boxed{?}\boxed{?}}_{b^1}\ \underbrace{\boxed{?}\boxed{?}}_{b^2}\ .$$

2. Duplicate each of the share commitments to b^1 and b^2 using the existing copy protocol [27] (which requires four free cards ♣♥♣♥):

$$\underbrace{\boxed{?}\boxed{?}}_{a^1}\ \underbrace{\boxed{?}\boxed{?}}_{a^2}\ \underbrace{\boxed{?}\boxed{?}}_{b^1}\ \underbrace{\boxed{?}\boxed{?}}_{b^2}\ \longrightarrow\ \underbrace{\boxed{?}\boxed{?}}_{a^1}\ \underbrace{\boxed{?}\boxed{?}}_{a^2}\ \underbrace{\boxed{?}\boxed{?}}_{b^1}\ \underbrace{\boxed{?}\boxed{?}}_{b^2}\ \underbrace{\boxed{?}\boxed{?}}_{b^1}\ \underbrace{\boxed{?}\boxed{?}}_{b^2}\ .$$

3. Obtain commitments to $a^1 \wedge b^1$ and $a^1 \wedge b^2$ from commitments to a^1, b^1, and b^2 using the existing AND protocol [25] (which requires four free cards ♣♥♣♥); similarly, obtain commitments to $a^2 \wedge b^1$ and $a^2 \wedge b^2$:

$$\underbrace{\boxed{?}\boxed{?}}_{a^1}\ \underbrace{\boxed{?}\boxed{?}}_{b^1}\ \underbrace{\boxed{?}\boxed{?}}_{b^2}\ \underbrace{\boxed{?}\boxed{?}}_{a^2}\ \underbrace{\boxed{?}\boxed{?}}_{b^1}\ \underbrace{\boxed{?}\boxed{?}}_{b^2}\ \longrightarrow\ \underbrace{\boxed{?}\boxed{?}}_{a^1\wedge b^1}\ \underbrace{\boxed{?}\boxed{?}}_{a^1\wedge b^2}\ \underbrace{\boxed{?}\boxed{?}}_{a^2\wedge b^1}\ \underbrace{\boxed{?}\boxed{?}}_{a^2\wedge b^2}\ .$$

4. Use the 4-bit XOR sub-protocol (see [42] for details) to compute $(a^1 \wedge b^1) \oplus (a^1 \wedge b^2) \oplus (a^2 \wedge b^1) \oplus (a^2 \wedge b^2)$, which is equal to $a \wedge b$.

This is the 1-secure AND protocol proposed by Takashima et al. [42]. This protocol requires eight additional cards in addition to eight cards for input split commitments. Therefore, the total number of required cards is 16. The number of required shuffles is eight although the details are omitted (see [42]).

In the next section, we present a very simple 1-secure AND protocol that can be executed with only eight cards and one shuffle.

3   Our Simple 1-Secure AND Protocol

In this section, we propose a simple 1-secure AND protocol that does not require any additional cards and uses only one shuffle (namely, Protocol A shown in Table 1).

In Sect. 3.1, we discuss the idea behind our protocol. We then describe the protocol in Sect. 3.2 and its pseudocode in Sect. 3.3. In Sect. 3.4, we show the correctness and security of our protocol.

3.1   Idea

In this subsection, we briefly explain the idea behind our protocol.

Assume that we have two split commitments:

$$\underbrace{\boxed{?}\boxed{?}\boxed{?}\boxed{?}}_{a}\underbrace{\boxed{?}\boxed{?}\boxed{?}\boxed{?}}_{b}\ .$$

Remember that the four cards of each split commitment satisfy the following patterns, depending on its value:

0	1
♣ ♥ ♣ ♥ or ♥ ♣ ♥ ♣	♣ ♥ ♥ ♣ or ♥ ♣ ♣ ♥

For example, if $a = 0$, the four cards are ♣♥♣♥ or ♥♣♥♣ (each occurs with a probability of $1/2$).

Let us exchange the positions of the second and third cards of the split commitment to a:

$$\underbrace{\boxed{?}\,\boxed{?}\,\boxed{?}\,\boxed{?}}_{a}\;\underbrace{\boxed{?}\,\boxed{?}\,\boxed{?}\,\boxed{?}}_{b} \;\rightarrow\; \boxed{?}\,\boxed{?}\,\boxed{?}\,\boxed{?}\;\underbrace{\boxed{?}\,\boxed{?}\,\boxed{?}\,\boxed{?}}_{b},$$

where we attach numbers (from 1 to 4) to the four cards for convenience sake. Then, the four cards (related to a) become as follows:

$a = 0$	$a = 1$
♣ ♥ ♣ ♥ → ♣ ♣ ♥ ♥	♣ ♥ ♥ ♣ → ♣ ♥ ♥ ♣
♥ ♣ ♥ ♣ → ♥ ♥ ♣ ♣	♥ ♣ ♣ ♥ → ♥ ♣ ♣ ♥

Now let us compare the four-card sequence related to a with the four-card sequence of the split commitment to b; especially, focus on the Hamming distance (which can be naturally defined, based on $\{♣, ♥\}$). For instance, the Hamming distance between ♣♣♥♥ ($a = 0$) and ♣♥♣♥ ($b = 0$) is 2. Somewhat surprisingly, when $a \wedge b = 0$, the Hamming distance is always 2. Furthermore, when $a \wedge b = 1$, the Hamming distance is either 0 or 4. The following table enumerates the Hamming distances for all cases:

b \ a	♣♣♥♥	♥♥♣♣	♣♥♥♣	♥♣♣♥
♣♥♣♥	2	2	2	2
♥♣♥♣	2	2	2	2
♣♥♥♣	2	2	0	4
♥♣♣♥	2	2	4	0

Thus, the Hamming distance between these two four-card sequences tells us the value of $a \wedge b$. Since we want to know only the Hamming distance, we will apply a shuffle while keeping their distance unchanged, as will be seen in the next subsection.

3.2 Description of Protocol

In this subsection, we give a complete description of our 1-secure AND protocol.

Given split commitments to a and b, our protocol proceeds as follows.

1. After placing the input split commitments as below, swap the second and third cards of the split commitment to a and make four two-card piles as follows:

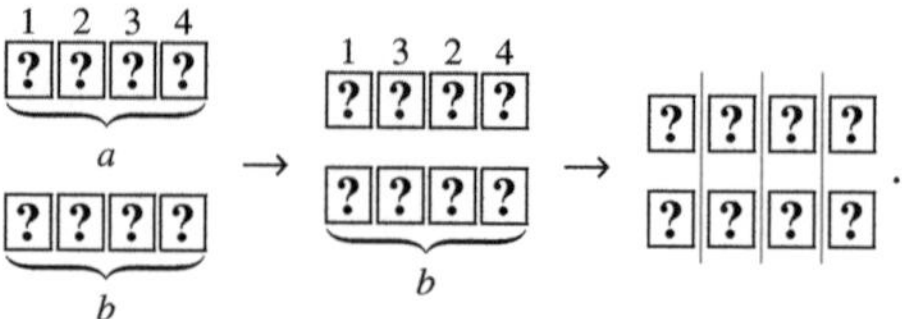

2. Apply a *pile-scramble shuffle* [7]:

$$\left[\begin{array}{cccc} \boxed{?} \boxed{?} \boxed{?} \boxed{?} \\ \boxed{?} \boxed{?} \boxed{?} \boxed{?} \end{array}\right] \rightarrow \begin{array}{cccc} \boxed{?} \boxed{?} \boxed{?} \boxed{?} \\ \boxed{?} \boxed{?} \boxed{?} \boxed{?} \end{array},$$

   which permutes the four two-card piles uniformly at random, resulting in one of the 4! possibilities with a probability of 1/4!. Note that the Hamming distance between the upper four-card sequence and the lower four-card sequence has been unchanged. (This shuffle can be implemented, for example, by placing each pile of cards in an envelope and stirring the four envelopes uniformly at random.)
3. Turn over all the cards, and let HD be the Hamming distance between the upper and lower four-card sequences. If HD = 0 or HD = 4, then $a \wedge b = 1$; if HD = 2, then $a \wedge b = 0$.

   This is our 1-secure AND protocol. It uses only eight cards and one pile-scramble shuffle.

   Our 1-secure AND protocol works correctly and securely because the Hamming distance surely reveals the value of $a \wedge b$ and the pile-scramble shuffle erases any information more than the value of $a \wedge b$. Moreover, the active card-revealing attack can be done at Step 1 or 2, but revealing a single card does not leak any information about a or b. A more formal treatment will be given in the following subsections.

3.3 Pseudocode

In this subsection, we describe our protocol more formally, based on the computational model of card-based protocols [24].

   In general, a protocol is supposed to achieve a desired functionality by permuting, shuffling, and/or turning over cards. We explain these three actions briefly: (perm, π) permutes the sequence of cards according to a given permutation π; given a set of permutations Π, (shuf, Π) chooses $\pi \in \Pi$ uniformly at random and applies π to the sequence of cards; and (turn, T) turns over every t-th card with $t \in T$, given a set T of indices.

   The following is a pseudocode of our 1-secure AND protocol, where $PSS_{(4,2)}$ represents the permutation set corresponding to the pile-scramble shuffle for four two-card piles.

Input:

1: (perm, (2 3))
2: (perm, (2 3 5) (4 7 6))
3: (shuf, $PSS_{(4,2)}$)

4: (turn, $\{1, 2, 3, 4, 5, 6, 7, 8\}$)
5: **if** $HD = 2$ **then**
6:     (result, "$a \wedge b = 0$")
7: **else**
8:     (result, "$a \wedge b = 1$")
9: **end if**

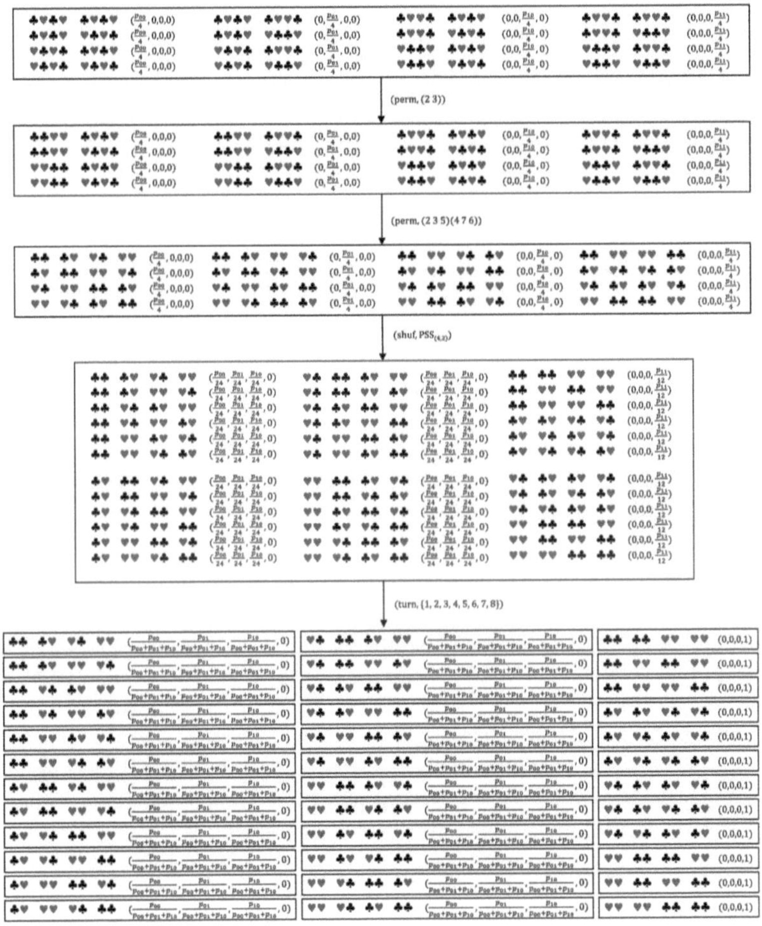

Fig. 1. KWH-tree of non-committed-format 1-secure AND protocol.

3.4   Correctness and Security

In this subsection, we use the modified version [22] of the *KWH-tree* [13] to show the correctness and security of our protocol more formally. Figure 1 is such a KWH-tree for our protocol, which we explain, as below.

Let p_{ij} for every $(i, j) \in \{0, 1\}^2$ denote a probability that input (a, b) (of Alice and Bob) is equal to (i, j). For example, if $(a, b) = (0, 0)$, the input sequence

$$\underbrace{\boxed{?}\,\boxed{?}\,\boxed{?}\,\boxed{?}}_{a}\ \underbrace{\boxed{?}\,\boxed{?}\,\boxed{?}\,\boxed{?}}_{b}$$

is one of the following four possibilities:

$$\clubsuit\heartsuit\clubsuit\heartsuit\ \clubsuit\heartsuit\clubsuit\heartsuit,\quad \clubsuit\heartsuit\clubsuit\heartsuit\ \heartsuit\clubsuit\heartsuit\clubsuit,\quad \heartsuit\clubsuit\heartsuit\clubsuit\ \clubsuit\heartsuit\clubsuit\heartsuit,\quad \heartsuit\clubsuit\heartsuit\clubsuit\ \heartsuit\clubsuit\heartsuit\clubsuit;$$

each of these occurs with a probability of $\frac{p_{00}}{4}$ (before the protocol). Thus, we write this (partial) 'status' as

$$\clubsuit\heartsuit\clubsuit\heartsuit\ \clubsuit\heartsuit\clubsuit\heartsuit\ (p_{00}/4, 0, 0, 0) \qquad \clubsuit\heartsuit\clubsuit\heartsuit\ \heartsuit\clubsuit\heartsuit\clubsuit\ (p_{00}/4, 0, 0, 0)$$

$$\heartsuit\clubsuit\heartsuit\clubsuit\ \clubsuit\heartsuit\clubsuit\heartsuit\ (p_{00}/4, 0, 0, 0) \qquad \heartsuit\clubsuit\heartsuit\clubsuit\ \heartsuit\clubsuit\heartsuit\clubsuit\ (p_{00}/4, 0, 0, 0),$$

where a four-tuple $(q_{00}, q_{01}, q_{10}, q_{11})$ along with a card sequence means that the probability that $(a, b) = (i, j)$ and the card sequence occurs is q_{ij} for every $(i, j) \in \{0, 1\}^2$. Considering also the remaining three cases $(a, b) = (0, 1), (1, 0), (1, 1)$, we obtain the topmost box in Fig. 1 as the initial (full) *status*.

The initial status (and succeeding statuses) are transformed into another status by an action, such as $(\mathsf{perm}, (2\,3))$, $(\mathsf{perm}, (2\,3\,5)(4\,7\,6))$, and $(\mathsf{shuf}, \mathrm{PSS}_{(4,2)})$, as shown in Fig. 1. In particular, the final action $(\mathsf{turn}, \{1, 2, 3, 4, 5, 6, 7, 8\})$ results in 36 "leaf" statuses.

Note that in each of the topmost four statuses depicted in Fig. 1, the (coordinate-wise) sum of all tuples is equal to $(p_{00}, p_{01}, p_{10}, p_{11})$; this guarantees that no information about the input (a, b) will be leaked. Regarding the 36 leaf statuses, each of them has only one element, which is either $\left(\frac{p_{00}}{p_{00}+p_{01}+p_{10}}, \frac{p_{01}}{p_{00}+p_{01}+p_{10}}, \frac{p_{10}}{p_{00}+p_{01}+p_{10}}, 0\right)$ or $(0, 0, 0, 1)$; this guarantees the correctness and also implies that any information other than the value of $a \wedge b$ will not be leaked.

Now, let us consider an active card-revealing attack. Assume for example that the leftmost card is illegally turned over after $(\mathsf{perm}, (2\,3))$, i.e., apply $(\mathsf{turn}, \{1\})$ instead of $(\mathsf{perm}, (2\,3\,5)(4\,7\,6))$. Then, we have the following status:

$$\clubsuit\clubsuit\heartsuit\heartsuit\ \clubsuit\heartsuit\clubsuit\heartsuit\ (p_{00}/2, 0, 0, 0) \qquad \clubsuit\heartsuit\heartsuit\clubsuit\ \clubsuit\heartsuit\clubsuit\heartsuit\ (0, 0, p_{10}/2, 0)$$

$$\clubsuit\clubsuit\heartsuit\heartsuit\ \heartsuit\clubsuit\heartsuit\clubsuit\ (p_{00}/2, 0, 0, 0) \qquad \clubsuit\heartsuit\heartsuit\clubsuit\ \heartsuit\clubsuit\heartsuit\clubsuit\ (0, 0, p_{10}/2, 0)$$

$$\clubsuit\clubsuit\heartsuit\heartsuit\ \clubsuit\heartsuit\heartsuit\clubsuit\ (0, p_{01}/2, 0, 0) \qquad \clubsuit\heartsuit\heartsuit\clubsuit\ \clubsuit\heartsuit\heartsuit\clubsuit\ (0, 0, 0, p_{11}/2)$$

$$\clubsuit\clubsuit\heartsuit\heartsuit\ \heartsuit\clubsuit\clubsuit\heartsuit\ (0, p_{01}/2, 0, 0) \qquad \clubsuit\heartsuit\heartsuit\clubsuit\ \heartsuit\clubsuit\clubsuit\heartsuit\ (0, 0, 0, p_{11}/2).$$

Since the (coordinate-wise) sum of all tuples is still equal to $(p_{00}, p_{01}, p_{10}, p_{11})$, no information about the input (a, b) is leaked (and the protocol aborts here). This is true for the other statuses (or the final statuses reveal all the cards), and hence, we can confirm that our protocol is 1-secure.

4   Our Committed-Format 1-Secure AND Protocol

In this section, we focus on committed-format protocols, which mean that their input and output formats are consistent. The existing protocol explained in Sect. 2 and our simple 1-secure AND protocol presented in Sect. 3 are not committed-format ones. Here, we propose a committed-format 1-secure AND protocol that can be executed with four additional cards (namely, Protocol B in Table 1).

In Sect. 4.1, we provide the idea behind the protocol. In Sect. 4.2, we describe the randomization sub-protocol used in the proposed protocol. The details of the protocol and its pseudocode are described in Sects. 4.3 and 4.4, respectively. We then confirm its correctness and security in Sect. 4.5.

4.1   Idea

First of all, we borrow the idea behind the Mizuki–Sone AND protocol [27], which is based on the following equation:

$$a \wedge b = \begin{cases} 0 & \text{if } a = 0, \\ b & \text{if } a = 1. \end{cases} \tag{2}$$

Thus, we prepare a split commitment to 0 in addition to input split commitments to a and b:

$$\underbrace{\boxed{?}\boxed{?}\boxed{?}\boxed{?}}_{a}\ \underbrace{\boxed{?}\boxed{?}\boxed{?}\boxed{?}}_{0}\ \underbrace{\boxed{?}\boxed{?}\boxed{?}\boxed{?}}_{b}\ .$$

As Eq. (2) implies, depending on the value of a, either 0 or b should be the output of an AND protocol. Since directly turning over the split commitment to a would leak its value, it is also necessary to perform randomization as in the Mizuki–Sone AND protocol. This will be detailed in Sect. 4.3.

Additionally, since either the split commitment to 0 or the split commitment to b will be the output, it is necessary to perform randomization to erase prior information about the orders of the cards in these split commitments. This will be introduced in the next subsection.

4.2   Randomization Sub-Protocol

As explained in the previous subsection, either a split commitment to 0 or b will be the output of our protocol. Consider a split commitment to b placed by Bob:

$$\underbrace{\boxed{?}\boxed{?}\boxed{?}\boxed{?}}_{b}\ =\ \underbrace{\boxed{?}\boxed{?}}_{b^1}\ \underbrace{\boxed{?}\boxed{?}}_{b^2}\ .$$

Since Bob knows both shares, b^1 and b^2, of the split commitment to b, he knows whether it is

$$\underbrace{\boxed{?}\boxed{?}}_{b}\ \underbrace{\boxed{?}\boxed{?}}_{0}\ \text{or}\ \underbrace{\boxed{?}\boxed{?}}_{\bar{b}}\ \underbrace{\boxed{?}\boxed{?}}_{1}\ .$$

To eliminate such Bob's prior knowledge, we want to add a random bit r_1 as follows:

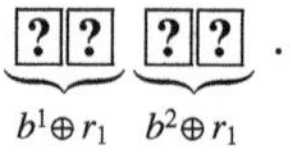

$$\underbrace{\boxed{?}\boxed{?}}_{b^1 \oplus r_1} \; \underbrace{\boxed{?}\boxed{?}}_{b^2 \oplus r_1} \;.$$

Similarly, for a split commitment to 0, we want to add a random bit r_2:

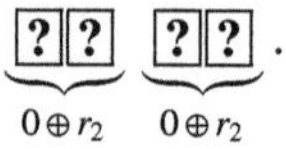

$$\underbrace{\boxed{?}\boxed{?}}_{0 \oplus r_2} \; \underbrace{\boxed{?}\boxed{?}}_{0 \oplus r_2} \;.$$

In our protocol, since only one of the split commitment to b and the split commitment to 0 is used as output, it is not necessary to use both random bits r_1 and r_2 simultaneously. Therefore, it suffices to add a common random bit r to both 0 and b.

The following randomization sub-protocol achieves this: given two split commitments to x and y, it adds a common random bit r.

Randomization Sub-protocol

1. Given two split commitments to $x = x^1 \oplus x^2$ and $y = y^1 \oplus y^2$:

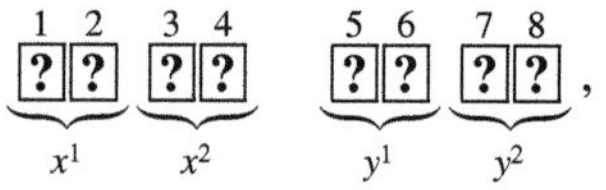

$$\underbrace{\overset{1 \;\; 2}{\boxed{?}\boxed{?}}}_{x^1} \; \underbrace{\overset{3 \;\; 4}{\boxed{?}\boxed{?}}}_{x^2} \quad \underbrace{\overset{5 \;\; 6}{\boxed{?}\boxed{?}}}_{y^1} \; \underbrace{\overset{7 \;\; 8}{\boxed{?}\boxed{?}}}_{y^2} \;,$$

place each share from top to bottom as follows, and apply a pile-scramble shuffle (i.e., randomize only the column positions while maintaining each of the two vertical columns on the left and right):

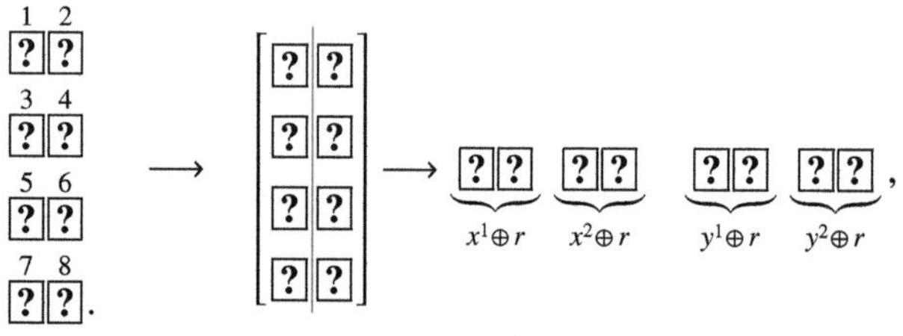

$$\begin{array}{l} \overset{1 \;\; 2}{\boxed{?}\boxed{?}} \\ \overset{3 \;\; 4}{\boxed{?}\boxed{?}} \\ \overset{5 \;\; 6}{\boxed{?}\boxed{?}} \\ \overset{7 \;\; 8}{\boxed{?}\boxed{?}} \end{array} \; \longrightarrow \; \begin{bmatrix} \boxed{?}\boxed{?} \\ \boxed{?}\boxed{?} \\ \boxed{?}\boxed{?} \\ \boxed{?}\boxed{?} \end{bmatrix} \; \longrightarrow \; \underbrace{\boxed{?}\boxed{?}}_{x^1 \oplus r} \; \underbrace{\boxed{?}\boxed{?}}_{x^2 \oplus r} \quad \underbrace{\boxed{?}\boxed{?}}_{y^1 \oplus r} \; \underbrace{\boxed{?}\boxed{?}}_{y^2 \oplus r} \;,$$

where r is a uniformly distributed random bit, generated by the shuffle.

4.3 Description of Protocol

In this subsection, we present our committed-format 1-secure AND protocol.

Given input split commitments to a and b along with four additional cards

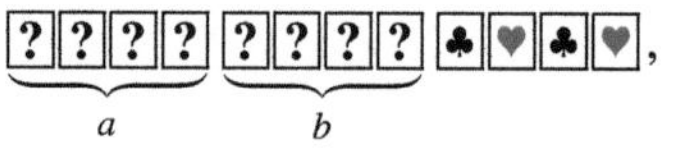

$$\underbrace{\boxed{?}\boxed{?}\boxed{?}\boxed{?}}_{a} \underbrace{\boxed{?}\boxed{?}\boxed{?}\boxed{?}}_{b} \boxed{\clubsuit}\boxed{\heartsuit}\boxed{\clubsuit}\boxed{\heartsuit} \;,$$

our protocol proceeds as follows.

Committed-Format 1-Secure AND Protocol

1. Place the input split commitments, and make a split commitment to 0, as follows:

$$\underbrace{\boxed{?}\boxed{?}\ \boxed{?}\boxed{?}}_{\substack{a^1 \quad\ a^2 \\ a}}\ \underbrace{\boxed{?}\boxed{?}\ \boxed{?}\boxed{?}}_{\substack{\clubsuit\heartsuit \quad \clubsuit\heartsuit \\ 0}}\ \underbrace{\boxed{?}\boxed{?}\ \boxed{?}\boxed{?}}_{\substack{b^1 \quad\ b^2 \\ b}}\ .$$

   Note that if $a^1 \oplus a^2 = a = 0$, then the four cards in the middle have the same value as $a \wedge b (= 0 \wedge b = 0)$. If $a^1 \oplus a^2 = a = 1$, then the rightmost four cards have the same value as $a \wedge b (= 1 \wedge b = b)$.

2. Apply the randomization sub-protocol explained in Sect. 4.2 to the split commitments to 0 and b; then we obtain

$$\underbrace{\boxed{?}\boxed{?}\ \boxed{?}\boxed{?}}_{\substack{a^1 \quad\ a^2 \\ a}}\ \underbrace{\boxed{?}\boxed{?}\ \boxed{?}\boxed{?}}_{\substack{r \quad\ r \\ 0}}\ \underbrace{\boxed{?}\boxed{?}\ \boxed{?}\boxed{?}}_{\substack{b^1\oplus r \quad b^2\oplus r \\ b}}\ .$$

   From now on, we apply the idea behind the Mizuki–Sone AND protocol [27] to the three split commitments to a, 0, and b.

3. Place the two cards of the share a^1 as shown below, i.e., the left card is placed above the split commitment to 0, and the right card is placed above the split commitment to b, as follows, and apply a pile-scramble shuffle:

$$\overbrace{\boxed{?}\qquad\quad\ \boxed{?}}^{a^1}\quad\longrightarrow\quad \left[\ \boxed{?}\ \Big|\ \boxed{?}\ \right]\quad\longrightarrow\quad \overbrace{\boxed{?}\boxed{?}}^{a^1\oplus r'}$$

$$\underbrace{\boxed{?}\boxed{?}\boxed{?}\boxed{?}}_{0}\ \underbrace{\boxed{?}\boxed{?}\boxed{?}\boxed{?}}_{b}\ . \qquad \left[\ \boxed{?}\boxed{?}\boxed{?}\boxed{?}\Big|\boxed{?}\boxed{?}\boxed{?}\boxed{?}\ \right] \qquad \underbrace{\boxed{?}\boxed{?}\boxed{?}\boxed{?}}_{x}\underbrace{\boxed{?}\boxed{?}\boxed{?}\boxed{?}}_{y}\ ,$$

   where

$$(x, y) = \begin{cases} (0, b) & \text{if } r' = 0, \\ (b, 0) & \text{if } r' = 1. \end{cases}$$

4. Turn over the commitments to a^2 and $a^1 \oplus r'$ to compute $a^2 \oplus (a^1 \oplus r') = a \oplus r'$.
   - If $a \oplus r' = 0$, then x is a split commitment to $a \wedge b$.
   - If $a \oplus r' = 1$, then y is a split commitment to $a \wedge b$.

   This is our committed-format 1-secure AND protocol. It uses 12 cards and two pile-scramble shuffles. Since this is a committed-format protocol, it is useful; for example, a secure AND computation with more than two inputs can also be realized.

4.4   Pseudocode

The following is a pseudocode of our committed-format 1-secure AND protocol, where the result action specifies the positions of the output split commitment.

Input:

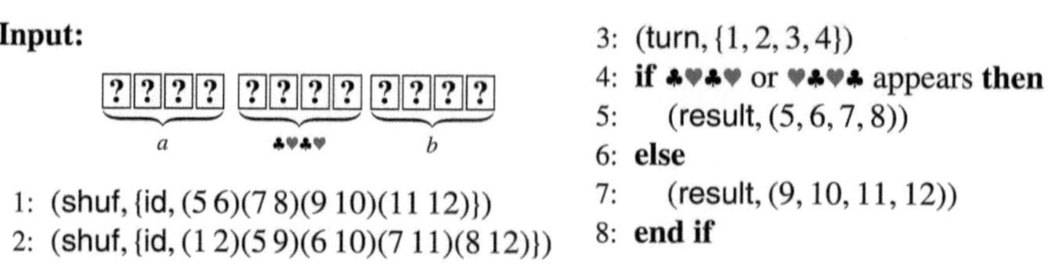

1: (shuf, {id, (5 6)(7 8)(9 10)(11 12)})
2: (shuf, {id, (1 2)(5 9)(6 10)(7 11)(8 12)})

3: (turn, $\{1, 2, 3, 4\}$)
4: **if** ♣♥♣♥ or ♥♣♥♣ appears **then**
5:     (result, $(5, 6, 7, 8)$)
6: **else**
7:     (result, $(9, 10, 11, 12)$)
8: **end if**

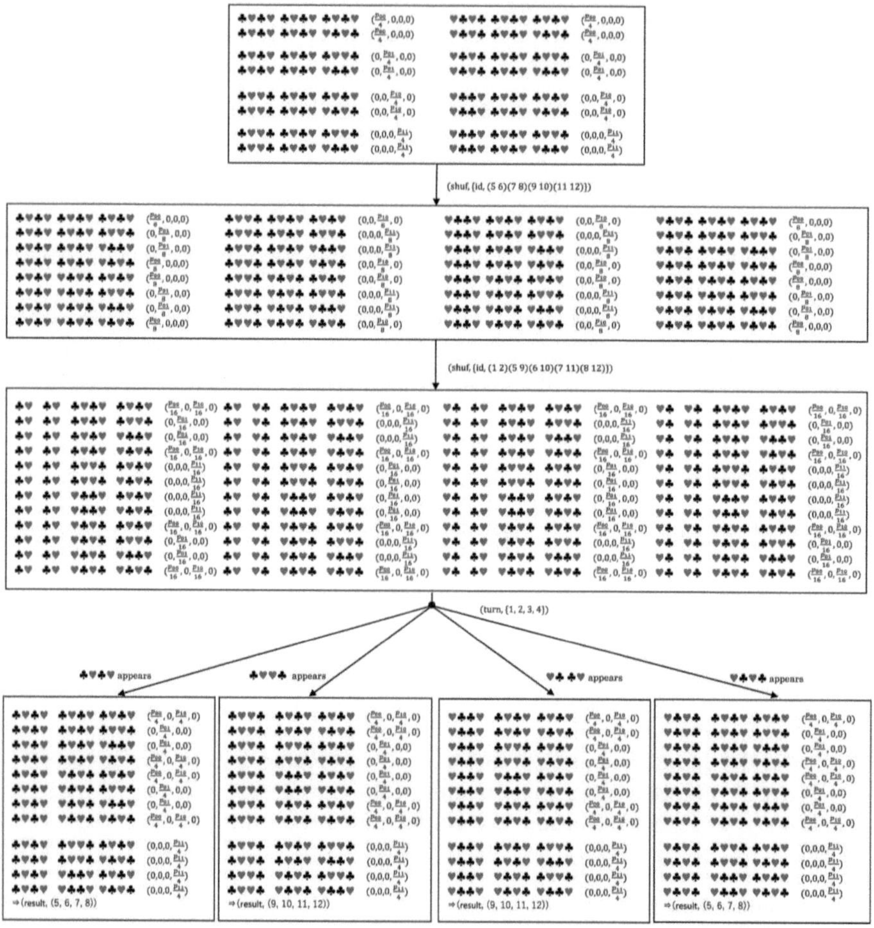

Fig. 2. KWH tree of committed-format 1-secure AND protocol.

4.5 Correctness and Security

Basically, the correctness and security of our protocol come from the Mizuki–Sone AND protocol [27]. More formally, we depict the KWH-tree in Fig. 2.

There are seven statuses in the KWH-tree. Similar to our non-committed-format protocol, i.e., Protocol A, the topmost status consists of 16 elements. The status is changed by the actions. In each status, the sum of all tuples is equal to $(p_{00}, p_{01}, p_{10}, p_{11})$, which ensures that no information about the inputs a and b is leaked. In the four final statuses, we can confirm the correctness (i.e., the value of $a \wedge b$ is surely computed). Furthermore, one can confirm that if any illegal $(\mathsf{turn}, \{i\})$ is applied anywhere, it results in a status whose sum is $(p_{00}, p_{01}, p_{10}, p_{11})$, implying the 1-secureness.

5 Conclusion

In this paper, we designed a simple 1-secure AND protocol using a novel approach compared to the existing protocols. Our proposed protocol uses only eight cards, i.e., it does not require any additional cards beyond the input split commitments. The number of shuffles is only one. We believe that our protocol is easy to implement, as illustrated in Fig. 3 with real physical cards. Furthermore, we also proposed a committed-format 1-secure AND protocol that can be executed with four additional cards, bringing the total number of cards to 12. The number of shuffles is two.

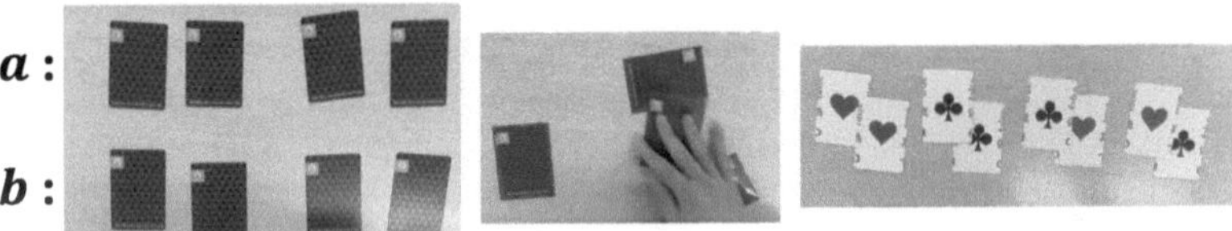

Fig. 3. Execution of our protocol.

As shown in Table 1, both of the proposed protocols can be executed with fewer cards and fewer shuffles than the existing protocols, making them more practical and easy to understand. Although this paper focuses on designing only 1-secure AND protocols, the assumption of $t = 1$ may suffice to protect against casual attacks or operational errors. In addition, our 1-secure committed-format AND protocol can be extended to a t-secure protocol for any $t \geq 2$.

Our contributions provide significant improvements in the efficiency and practicality of card-based protocols. Future work could explore further optimizations, expansions to other computations (beyond the AND function), and applications of these protocols in various secure computation scenarios, as well as investigate their robustness against other types of attacks. Since our protocols use pile-scramble shuffles, constructing protocols using the random cut [1,2], which is an easier shuffing operation, would be a desired direction for future work. Expanding our ideas to devise protocols using other familiar tools such as coins [14,18] and a balance scale [9] presents an interesting challenge for future work.

Acknowledgments. We thank the anonymous reviewers, whose comments have helped us improve the presentation of the paper. We thank Kazumasa Shinagawa for his helpful comments on the sub-protocol described in Sect. 4.2. This work was supported by JSPS KAKENHI Grant Numbers JP23H00479 and JP24K02938.

References

1. Abe, Y., Mizuki, T., Sone, H.: Committed-format AND protocol using only random cuts. Nat. Comput. **20**(4), 639–645 (2021). https://doi.org/10.1007/s11047-021-09862-2
2. Boer, B.: More efficient match-making and satisfiability *the five card trick*. In: Quisquater, J.-J., Vandewalle, J. (eds.) EUROCRYPT 1989. LNCS, vol. 434, pp. 208–217. Springer, Heidelberg (1990). https://doi.org/10.1007/3-540-46885-4_23
3. Doi, A., et al.: Card-based protocols for private set intersection and union. New Gener. Comput. **42**, 359–380 (2024). https://doi.org/10.1007/s00354-024-00268-z
4. Gentry, C.: Fully homomorphic encryption using ideal lattices. In: Proceedings of the Forty-First Annual ACM Symposium on Theory of Computing, STOC 2009, pp. 169–178. Association for Computing Machinery, New York (2009). https://doi.org/10.1145/1536414.1536440
5. Hand, S., Koch, A., Lafourcade, P., Miyahara, D., Robert, L.: Efficient card-based ZKP for single loop condition and its application to Moon-or-Sun. New Gener. Comput. **42**, 449–477 (2024). https://doi.org/10.1007/s00354-024-00274-1
6. Hatsugai, K., Ruangwises, S., Asano, K., Abe, Y.: NP-completeness and physical zero-knowledge proofs for Sumplete, a puzzle generated by ChatGPT. New Gener. Comput. **42**, 429–448 (2024). https://doi.org/10.1007/s00354-024-00267-0
7. Ishikawa, R., Chida, E., Mizuki, T.: Efficient card-based protocols for generating a hidden random permutation without fixed points. In: Calude, C.S., Dinneen, M.J. (eds.) UCNC 2015. LNCS, vol. 9252, pp. 215–226. Springer, Cham (2015). https://doi.org/10.1007/978-3-319-21819-9_16
8. Ito, Y., Shikata, H., Suganuma, T., Mizuki, T.: Card-based cryptography meets 3D printer. In: Da-Jung Cho, J.K. (ed.) Unconventional Computation and Natural Computation. LNCS, vol. 14776, pp. 74–88. Springer, Cham (2024). https://doi.org/10.1007/978-3-031-63742-1_6
9. Kaneko, S., Lafourcade, P., Mallordy, L.B., Miyahara, D., Puys, M., Sakiyama, K.: Balance-based ZKP protocols for pencil-and-paper puzzles. In: Mouha, N., Nikiforakis, N. (eds.) Information Security, pp. 211–231. LNCS, Springer, Cham (2025). https://doi.org/10.1007/978-3-031-75757-0_11

10. Kobayashi, N., Manabe, Y.: Card-based cryptographic protocols for three-input functions with a standard deck of cards using private operations. In: Garcia-Alfaro, J., et al. (eds.) Computer Security. ESORICS 2024 International Workshops. LNCS, pp. 94–111. Springer, Cham (2025)

11. Koch, A.: The landscape of security from physical assumptions. In: IEEE Information Theory Workshop, pp. 1–6. IEEE, NY (2021). https://doi.org/10.1109/ITW48936.2021.9611501

12. Koch, A., Walzer, S.: Foundations for actively secure card-based cryptography. In: Farach-Colton, M., Prencipe, G., Uehara, R. (eds.) Fun with Algorithms. LIPIcs, vol. 157, pp. 17:1–17:23. Schloss Dagstuhl, Dagstuhl, Germany (2020). https://doi.org/10.4230/LIPIcs.FUN.2021.17

13. Koch, A., Walzer, S., Härtel, K.: Card-based cryptographic protocols using a minimal number of cards. In: Iwata, T., Cheon, J.H. (eds.) ASIACRYPT 2015. LNCS, vol. 9452, pp. 783–807. Springer, Heidelberg (2015). https://doi.org/10.1007/978-3-662-48797-6_32

14. Komano, Y., Mizuki, T.: Coin-based secure computations. Int. J. Inf. Secur. **21**, 833–846 (2022). https://doi.org/10.1007/s10207-022-00585-8

15. Komano, Y., Mizuki, T.: Physical zero-knowledge proof protocols for Topswops and Botdrops. New Gener. Comput. **42**, 399–428 (2024). https://doi.org/10.1007/s00354-024-00272-3

16. Manabe, Y., Ono, H.: Card-based cryptographic protocols with malicious players using private operations. New Gener. Comput. **40**, 67–93 (2022). https://doi.org/10.1007/s00354-021-00148-w

17. Manabe, Y., Ono, H.: Card-based cryptographic protocols with a standard deck of cards using private operations. New Gener. Comput. **42**, 305–329 (2024). https://doi.org/10.1007/s00354-024-00257-2

18. Minamikawa, Y., Shinagawa, K.: Coin-based cryptographic protocols without hand operations. IEICE Trans. Fundamentals **E107.A**(8), 1178–1185 (2024). https://doi.org/10.1587/transfun.2023EAP1082

19. Miyahara, D., Robert, L., Lafourcade, P., Mizuki, T.: ZKP protocols for Usowan, Herugolf, and Five Cells. Tsinghua Sci. Technol. **29**(6), 1651–1666 (2024). https://doi.org/10.26599/TST.2023.9010153

20. Mizuki, T.: Card-based protocols for securely computing the conjunction of multiple variables. Theor. Comput. Sci. **622**(C), 34–44 (2016). https://doi.org/10.1016/j.tcs.2016.01.039

21. Mizuki, T.: Preface: special issue on card-based cryptography 3. New Gener. Comput. **42**, 303–304 (2024). https://doi.org/10.1007/s00354-024-00280-3

22. Mizuki, T., Komano, Y.: Information leakage due to operative errors in card-based protocols. Inf. Comput. **285**, 104910 (2022). https://doi.org/10.1016/j.ic.2022.104910

23. Mizuki, T., Kuzuma, T., Hirano, T., Oshima, R., Yasuda, M.: Gakmoro: an application of physical secure computation to card game. In: Unconventional Computation and Natural Computation. LNCS. Springer, Cham (2025, to appear)

24. Mizuki, T., Shizuya, H.: A formalization of card-based cryptographic protocols via abstract machine. Int. J. Inf. Secur. **13**(1), 15–23 (2014). https://doi.org/10.1007/s10207-013-0219-4

25. Mizuki, T., Shizuya, H.: Practical card-based cryptography. In: Ferro, A., Luccio, F., Widmayer, P. (eds.) Fun with Algorithms. LNCS, vol. 8496, pp. 313–324. Springer, Cham (2014). https://doi.org/10.1007/978-3-319-07890-8_27

26. Mizuki, T., Shizuya, H.: Computational model of card-based cryptographic protocols and its applications. IEICE Trans. Fundam. **E100.A**(1), 3–11 (2017). https://doi.org/10.1587/transfun.E100.A.3

27. Mizuki, T., Sone, H.: Six-card secure AND and four-card secure XOR. In: Deng, X., Hopcroft, J.E., Xue, J. (eds.) FAW 2009. LNCS, vol. 5598, pp. 358–369. Springer, Heidelberg (2009). https://doi.org/10.1007/978-3-642-02270-8_36

28. Morooka, T., Manabe, Y., Shinagawa, K.: Malicious player card-based cryptographic protocols with a standard deck of cards using private operations. In: Meng, W., Yan, Z., Piuri, V. (eds.) Information Security Practice and Experience. LNCS, vol. 14341, pp. 332–346. Springer, Cham (2023). https://doi.org/10.1007/978-981-99-7032-2_20

29. Nakai, T., Iwanari, K., Ono, T., Abe, Y., Watanabe, Y., Iwamoto, M.: Card-based cryptography with a standard deck of cards, revisited: Efficient protocols in the private model. New Gener. Comput. **42**, 345–358 (2024). https://doi.org/10.1007/s00354-024-00269-y

30. Ono, T., Shinagawa, K., Nakai, T., Watanabe, Y., Iwamoto, M.: Single-shuffle card-based protocols with six cards per gate. In: Seo, H., Kim, S. (eds.) Information Security and Cryptology. LNCS, vol. 14562, pp. 157–169. Springer, Singapore (2024). https://doi.org/10.1007/978-981-97-1238-0_9

31. Otsuji, T., Fulla, P., Fukunaga, T.: NP-completeness and physical zero-knowledge proof of Hotaru Beam. In: Chen, Y., Gao, X., Sun, X., Zhang, A. (eds.) Computing and Combinatorics, pp. 239–251. Springer, Singapore (2024). https://doi.org/10.1007/978-981-96-1090-7_20

32. Parter, M.: Secure computation meets distributed universal optimality . In: 2023 IEEE 64th Annual Symposium on Foundations of Computer Science (FOCS), pp. 2336–2368. IEEE Computer Society, Los Alamitos, CA, USA (2023). https://doi.org/10.1109/FOCS57990.2023.00144. https://doi.ieeecomputersociety.org/10.1109/FOCS57990.2023.00144

33. Ruangwises, S.: The landscape of computing symmetric n-variable functions with 2n cards. In: Ábrahám, E., Dubslaff, C., Tarifa, S.L.T. (eds.) Theoretical Aspects of Computing – ICTAC 2023. LNCS, vol. 14446, pp. 74–82. Springer, Cham (2023). https://doi.org/10.1007/978-3-031-47963-2_6

34. Ruangwises, S., Iwamoto, M.: Printing protocol: physical ZKPs for decomposition puzzles. New Gener. Comput. **42**, 331–343 (2024). https://doi.org/10.1007/s00354-024-00266-1

35. Ruangwises, S., Shinagawa, K.: Simulating virtual players for UNO without computers. In: Unconventional Computation and Natural Computation. LNCS. Springer, Cham (2025, to appear)

36. Sasaki, S., Shinagawa, K.: Physical zero-knowledge proof for Sukoro. New Gener. Comput. **42**, 381–398 (2024). https://doi.org/10.1007/s00354-024-00271-4

37. Shamir, A.: How to share a secret. Commun. ACM **22**(11), 612–613 (1979). https://doi.org/10.1145/359168.359176

38. Shinagawa, K.: On the construction of easy to perform card-based protocols. Ph.D. thesis, Tokyo Institute of Technology (2020). https://t2r2.star.titech.ac.jp/cgi-bin/publicationinfo.cgi?q_publication_content_number=CTT100817272

39. Shinagawa, K., Miyahara, D., Mizuki, T.: How to play Old Maid with virtual players. Theory Comput. Syst. **69**(1) (2025). https://doi.org/10.1007/s00224-024-10203-w

40. Stiglic, A.: Computations with a deck of cards. Theor. Comput. Sci. **259**(1–2), 671–678 (2001). https://doi.org/10.1016/S0304-3975(00)00409-6

41. Takahashi, Y., Shinagawa, K., Shikata, H., Mizuki, T.: Efficient card-based protocols for symmetric functions using four-colored decks. In: ACM ASIA Public-Key Cryptography Workshop, pp. 1–10. ACM, New York (2024). https://doi.org/10.1145/3659467.3659902

42. Takashima, K., Miyahara, D., Mizuki, T., Sone, H.: Actively revealing card attack on card-based protocols. Nat. Comput. **21**(4), 615–628 (2021). https://doi.org/10.1007/s11047-020-09838-8

43. Tamura, Y., Suzuki, A., Mizuki, T.: Card-based zero-knowledge proof protocols for the 15-puzzle and the token swapping problem. In: ACM ASIA Public-Key Cryptography Workshop, pp. 11–22. ACM, New York (2024). https://doi.org/10.1145/3659467.3659905

44. Tanaka, K., Sasaki, S., Shinagawa, K., Mizuki, T.: Only two shuffles perform card-based zero-knowledge proof for Sudoku of any size. In: 2025 Symposium on Simplicity in Algorithms (SOSA), pp. 94–107. SIAM (2025). https://doi.org/10.1137/1.9781611978315.7

45. Tozawa, K., Morita, H., Mizuki, T.: Single-shuffle card-based protocol with eight cards per gate and its extensions. Natural Comput. **24**(1), 131–147 (2025). https://doi.org/10.1007/s11047-024-10006-5
46. Yao, A.C.: Protocols for secure computations. In: 23rd Annual Symposium on Foundations of Computer Science (FOCS 1982), pp. 160–164 (1982). https://doi.org/10.1109/SFCS.1982.38

Pomsets for Process Management: A Healthcare Case Study

Sourabh Pal[1,2(✉)], Roberto Guanciale[3], Ivan Lanese[1,2], Emilio Tuosto[4], and Massimo Clo[5]

[1] University of Bologna, Bologna, Italy
sourabh.pal2@unibo.it
[2] Centre Inria d'Université Côte d'Azur, Valbonne, France
[3] EECS and Digital Futures, KTH Royal Institute of Technology, Stockholm, Sweden
[4] Gran Sasso Science Institute, L'Aquila, Italy
[5] Area ICT e Transizione digitale dei servizi al cittadino - Direzione Generale Cura della Persona, Salute e Welfare, Emilia Romagna, Bologna, Italy

Abstract. Complex coordination protocols are necessary to manage complex organisations. The healthcare management sector is no exception, since different authorities, users, and systems have to interact with each other in order to achieve their organisational goals. In this paper we consider a case study on the authorisation and accreditation of healthcare structures in the Emilia Romagna region in Italy. We specify the case study using *global choreographies* so to enable the analysis of the correctness of its communication patterns using the PomCho tool. This requires to refine PomCho and its underlying theoretical framework. First, we extend PomCho to support not only asynchronous communication, but also synchronous one. Moreover, in both the cases, we provide *a more efficient algorithm* to check closure properties ensuring realisability of choreographies. The new algorithm allows us to check realisability of larger pomsets than before, which makes our approach viable for complex systems such as our case study.

1 Introduction

Distributed systems present a main tension: while the decomposition of functionality across multiple components helps managing complexity and improves efficiency, it also scatters execution contexts and states across the computational environment. This makes it difficult to guarantee global properties. Centralised coordination avoids this problem but introduces performance bottlenecks and single points of failure. Choreographic specifications [18] offer a high-level way to describe desired interactions by presenting a global view of possible execution traces. This global perspective aims to simplify the modelling of interactions and their ordering constraints. In contrast, the

Work partially supported by PRIN project FREEDA (CUP: I53D23003550006), by French ANR project SmartCloud ANR-23-CE25-0012, by INdAM GNCS 2025 project MARQ, code CUP E53C24001950001, by European Union - NextGenerationEU PNRR Mission 4, Component 1, Investment 4.1 (DM 351/2022) - Public Administration, by the PRIN PNRR project DeLICE (F53D23009130001) and by the MUR dipartimento di eccellenza 2023–2027. We thank the reviewers for their comments and suggestions.

Z. Liu et al. (Eds.): ICTAC 2025, LNCS 16237, pp. 378–395, 2026.
https://doi.org/10.1007/978-3-032-11176-0_22

expected behaviour of each component can be captured by formal models such as Communicating Finite State Machines [5] or programming languages featuring message-passing (e.g., Erlang or GoLang).

Not every choreography admits a correct realisation, namely a realisation as a set of participants whose sequences of possible interactions match the ones specified in the choreography. We provide a language-independent solution based on some realisability conditions on global views. Concretely, we employ partially ordered multisets (pomsets) as an abstract representation of global specifications. A pomset exposes the causal relationships among communication events –namely sends and receives of messages– without prescribing a total order and it is suitable for reasoning about synchronous rendezvous and asynchronous semantics. Our realisability conditions can be checked directly on pomsets, eliminating the need to enumerate interleavings or translate into a particular choreography language.

Contributions and Structure of the Paper. We extend the framework in [14, 15] (summarised in Sect. 2) through the analysis of a comprehensive, realistic case study borrowed from the process management domain (cf. Sect. 3) whose size challenges both the theory [14] and the implementation in [15]. We refine the pomset framework to encompass synchronous communication, defining new realisability conditions for rendezvous-style send/receive primitives (cf. Sect. 5). This generalisation ensures that our method applies seamlessly whether components use blocking sends and receives or non-blocking, unordered message queues.

Verifying realisability over large pomsets can be unfeasible. To mitigate this, we introduce an algorithm (cf. Sect. 6) that identifies a "sufficient prefix", the largest subset of events that captures all relevant causal constraints, and can prune unnecessary pomsets. In many realistic specifications, these optimisations reduce the verification effort exponentially, making our approach viable for more complex systems (cf. Sect. 7).

Taken together, these contributions yield a unified, semantically grounded framework for verifying the realisability of scenario-based specifications in both the asynchronous and synchronous settings. By operating directly on pomsets, we enable designers to detect and eliminate coordination mismatches at design time, rather than discovering them as costly implementation bugs.

The tool, all the examples, and the full details on our case study are available in [25].

2   A Bird-Eye View of Choreographies

Choreographies allow one to describe distributed systems composed of multiple participants which interact via message-passing, like formalisms such as *Message Sequence Charts* (MSC) [12, 20], multiparty session types [17], and BPMN choreographies [21]. Following the choreographic approach to system design (see, e.g., [18]), distributed systems can be represented using two complementary views, namely a single *global view* or multiple *local views*, one per participant. The global view describes the order in which messages can be exchanged inside a system from a global point of view. It provides both a syntactic and a diagrammatic representation of a distributed communication system. A single global view corresponds to multiple local views, each of which defines the behaviour of a participant. Broadly speaking, the global view is more

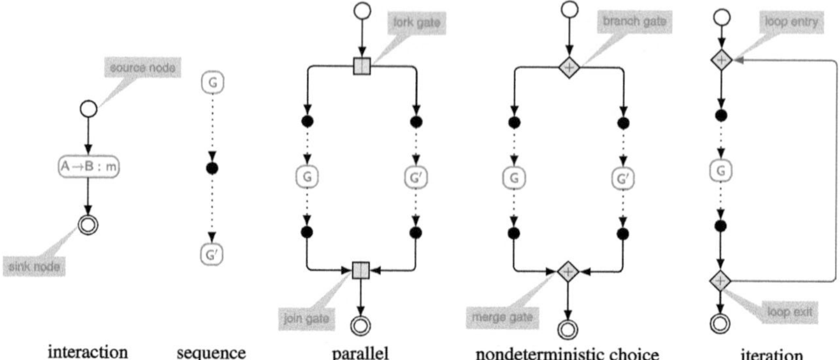

Fig. 1. Diagrammatic Representation of the Syntax of Global Choreographies

suitable for specification and understanding, while the local view is closer to the final implementation. Both views focus on communication, abstracting away computation.

Our choreographic framework consists of *global choreographies* (or g-choreographies for short) [30] for global views and *Communicating Finite State Machines* [5] for local views. A g-choreography is a term derivable from the following grammar:

$$G ::= A{\rightarrow}B : m \mid G;G' \mid G \mid G' \mid G + G' \mid \textit{repeat } G$$

The main building block of a g-choreography is an interaction between two participants, written $A{\rightarrow}B : m$, where participant A sends a message m to participant B, which in turn receives it. G-choreographies can be composed in sequence, in parallel, in nondeterministic choice, or iterated.

Each g-choreography in the syntax above has a graphical representation that can be formally derived by induction on the syntax of the g-choreography. Instead of a formal definition, we show how to achieve this using the sketches in Fig. 1. Intuitively, G can be depicted as a graph rooted in a *source* node ○ and having a single *sink* node ◎. Connecting nodes represent interaction, branch or fork points, or else looping points; this is immediate in the representation of interactions in Fig. 1. Besides interaction nodes, our graphical notation uses *gate* nodes ▢ and ◇ to identify fork and branch or iteration as well as their corresponding "closing" points. Gate nodes and dotted edges allow us to compose the diagrams; more precisely, a dotted edge from ● to a boxed G (the diagrammatic representation of G) means that the gate connected to the source node of G should be connected to the gate entering in ● and that the source node of G is removed; similarly, a dotted edge from a boxed G to ● means that the gate arriving in the sink node of G has to be connected to the gate after ● and that the sink node of G is removed. For instance, in the graph for the sequential composition, the top-most edge identifies the sink node of G and the other edge identifies the source node of G'.

We will describe the asynchronous and synchronous semantics of choreographies in terms of pomsets in Sects. 4 and 5, but the intuition above should be enough to understand the modelling of our case study, described in the next section.

3   Case Study: Process Management in Italian Healthcare

We study and analyse the realisability of a case study on healthcare management, focusing on authorisation and accreditation of the private and public healthcare structures in the Emilia Romagna region (Italy), which we dub A&A after *Accreditation and* Authorisation. The protocol describes the interactions among eleven participants, namely the actors and organisations involved in the process. The first task in the protocol is the nomination of the regional coordinator (RCOO) followed by the steps needed to allow RCOO to operate. Afterwards, the protocol describes five concurrent tasks, each of which concerns the iterative execution of a sub-protocol. We focus on the most complex sub-protocol where authorisation or accreditation to the private or public healthcare authorities (LHA) are granted or denied based on investigation reports of the technical teams i.e., evaluators (EV) and expert technicians (ET).

The analysis of A&A based on Choreographic Automata (CAs) [3] and the Corinne tool [22,24] in [23] cannot model concurrent flows of execution in a suitable way. Here, we therefore use *global-choreographies* (g-choreographies) to model A&A and the PomCho tool for the analysis since they natively support concurrency.

The g-choreography modelling A&A takes the form $G_I; (G_T \mid G_A)$ where[1]

$$G_I = \text{GDH} \rightarrow \text{RC}: \text{fndCor}; \text{GDH} \rightarrow \text{RCOO}: \text{assRes}; \text{GDH} \rightarrow \text{RCOO}: \text{perFunc};$$
$$\text{RCOO} \rightarrow \text{RC}: \text{mkPropRHS}; \text{RC} \rightarrow \text{RHS}: \text{gvCrite}$$

$$G_T = repeat\ \text{RCOO} \rightarrow \text{GDH}: \text{proAcc}$$
$$\mid repeat\ (\text{RCOO} \rightarrow \text{AC}: \text{chkOut}; \text{AC} \rightarrow \text{RCOO}: \text{rptinvs})$$
$$\mid repeat\ (\text{RCOO} \rightarrow \text{GHD}: \text{chkPol}; \text{GHD} \rightarrow \text{RCOO}: \text{confChkPol})$$
$$\mid repeat\ (\text{RC} \rightarrow \text{OTM}: \text{proCriteEv}; \text{RC} \rightarrow \text{OTAM}: \text{confCriteEv})$$

$$G_A = repeat\,(\text{LHA} \rightarrow \text{GDH}: \text{seekAcc}; \text{GDH} \rightarrow \text{RCOO}: \text{forAcc};$$
$$\text{RCOO} \rightarrow \text{HAS}: \text{perInvs}; \text{HAS} \rightarrow \text{RCOO}: \text{rtpinvs}; \,($$
$$\text{RCOO} \rightarrow \text{LHA}: \text{decAcc}$$
$$+$$
$$(\text{RCOO} \rightarrow \text{LHA}: \text{gnrtAcc} \mid \text{RCOO} \rightarrow \text{OTA}: \text{manVer});$$
$$G'_A;$$
$$(\text{RCOO} \rightarrow \text{GDH}: \text{sndPro}$$
$$+$$
$$\text{RCOO} \rightarrow \text{GDH}: \text{rptMon}; \text{GDH} \rightarrow \text{LHA}: \text{takAct})))$$

Figure 2 reports the g-choreography of A&A[2] using the visual representation[3] of g-choregraphies (cf. Sect. 2). Both the syntactic and visual representation of A&A show that the most complex part of the protocol is G_A, the g-choreography with highlighted background in Fig. 2. Below we comment on G_A, except for G'_A which is a sequence of interactions immaterial for the rest of the paper.

---

[1] Assume that $\_;\_$ takes precedence over $\_ + \_$.

[2] Acronyms are defined according to our English translation of the Italian descriptions in [16, 19]; the interested reader can find the correspondence in [23].

[3] See [26] for the g-choreography rendered by PomCho.

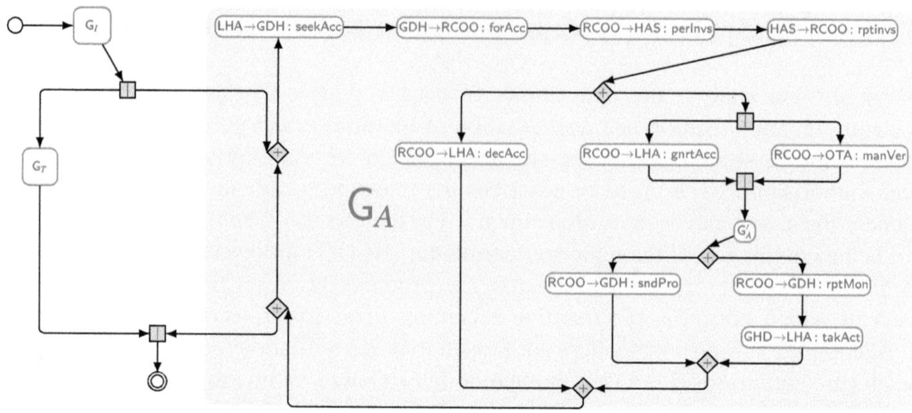

Fig. 2. G-choreography for Regional Coordination for Authorisation and Accreditation

The g-choreography is a refinement of the CA model in [23] amended from some inaccuracies with the help of domain experts. The CA model was also approximating the actual protocol due to the impossibility of handling the combinatorial explosion arising from the necessary explicit enumeration of all interleavings of concurrent activities. This problem was avoided in [23] by turning some concurrent computations into non-deterministic choices. Since such computations were loops, it means that the sub-protocols were executed one at the time instead of in interleaving. Besides imprecision, this model yields false positives in the analysis, since non-deterministic composition is subject to stricter conditions than parallel one.

Let us turn our attention to the remarkable structure of G_A. Indeed, G_A is an iterative process where, after the sequence of interactions on top, participants engage in a choice. The right branch is the sequential composition of two activities in parallel, followed by the interactions in G'_A, and finally a nested choice. As we will see in the rest of the paper this is both a source of complexity and the source of subtle glitches in the protocol.

4   Asynchronous Semantics

The asynchronous semantics of a g-choreography is modelled using *partially ordered multisets* (pomsets) [28]. Essentially, a pomset r corresponds to a partial order $\leq_r$, called *happens-before* relation, that specifies the causal dependencies among some events; if $e \leq_r e'$ then e' causally depends e in the pomset r. Instead of the formal definition of pomsets of g-choreographies (which can be found in [14,30]), we give an intuitive presentation of the main concepts.

Our pomsets order events labelled by communication actions. More precisely, actions of the form $A \cdot B\,!\,m$ label events where A sends message m to B, while actions of the form $A \cdot B\,?\,m$ label events where B receives message m from A. The semantics of a g-choreography G is then given by associating the set of pomsets $[\![G]\!]$ corresponding to the resolutions of each choice in G. This semantics can be defined by induction on the syntactic structure of G. The base case being $A{\rightarrow}B : m$ for which

$[\![A \rightarrow B : m]\!]$ is a singleton set containing a pomset where an event labelled with $A \cdot B\,!m$ (dubbed *output event*) precedes the one labelled $A \cdot B\,?m$ (dubbed *input event*). For the inductive cases, the semantics of a choice $G + G'$ is the union of the semantics of G and G' (that is $[\![G + G']\!] = [\![G]\!] \cup [\![G']\!]$); the semantics of $G; G'$ merges the pomsets obtained by the Cartesian product of the pomsets of $[\![G]\!]$ and $[\![G']\!]$, adding dependencies that force events of the same participant in G to precede those in G'; the semantics of $G \mid G'$ is obtained by merging the pomsets obtained by the Cartesian product of $[\![G]\!]$ and $[\![G']\!]$, without adding any dependencies. Finally, the semantics of iteration is given by taking the union of the semantics of the finite unfoldings of G, namely $[\![repeat\ G]\!] = \bigcup_{n>0} \underbrace{[\![G]\!]; \dots; [\![G]\!]}_{n-\text{times}}$.

Example 1. Consider the choreography (inspired by A&A) $G_1 = G + G'$, where $G = \mathsf{OTA} \rightarrow \mathsf{LHA} : \mathsf{decAcc}$ and $G' = (\mathsf{RCOO} \rightarrow \mathsf{LHA} : \mathsf{grntAcc} \mid \mathsf{OTA} \rightarrow \mathsf{RCOO} : \mathsf{manVer})$; $\mathsf{OTA} \rightarrow \mathsf{OTAM} : \mathsf{chkAutAcc}$. The graphical representation of the g-choreography and its asynchronous semantics are as follows:

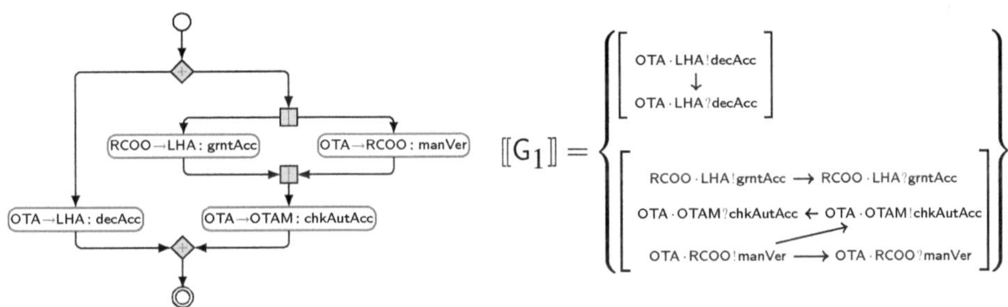

The g-choreography G_1 comprises two branches in a choice. The only interaction in the left branch is $\mathsf{OTA} \rightarrow \mathsf{LHA} : \mathsf{decAcc}$, while the right branch consists of the parallel interactions $\mathsf{RCOO} \rightarrow \mathsf{LHA} : \mathsf{grntAcc}$ and $\mathsf{OTA} \rightarrow \mathsf{RCOO} : \mathsf{manVer}$, followed by the interaction $\mathsf{OTA} \rightarrow \mathsf{OTAM} : \mathsf{chkAutAcc}$.

Hence, $[\![G_1]\!]$ consists of a pomset where LHA must consume the decAcc from OTA and another where participants LHA and RCOO may receive messages grntAcc and manVer in any order. Note that the sending of message chkAutAcc depends only on the sending of message manVer, since they are the only interactions in different components of the sequential composition done by the same participant.   ◇

A *linearisation* of a pomset r is a sequence $\{e_i\}_i$ of its events that respects the happens-before relation of r, namely if $i < j$ then $e_j \not\leq_r e_i$. The language of a g-choreography is the union over of the sequences of labels of all the *linearisations* of the pomsets of its semantics. A g-choreography among participants $a_1,\dots,a_n$ is implemented via a *communicating system* [5], that is an assignment to each participant a_i of a *communicating finite-state machine* (CFSM) [5] (i.e., a finite-state automaton whose transition labels are communication actions of a_i). In our asynchronous model of communicating systems, a configuration is a tuple $(q_1,\dots,q_n,M)$, where q_i is the current state of the CFSM of a_i and M is an unordered multiset of (pending) messages. The firing of a transition $q_i \xrightarrow{\mathsf{A_i \cdot B\,!\,m}} q_i'$ yields the new configuration $(q_1, \ldots, q_i', \ldots, q_n, M \uplus \{A_i \cdot B\,!\,m\})$, where $\uplus$ denotes multiset union. If $M = M' \uplus \{B \cdot A_i\,!\,m\}$ then the firing of a transition $q_i \xrightarrow{\mathsf{B \cdot A_i\,?\,m}} q_i'$ yields the new configuration $(q_1, \ldots, q_i', \ldots, q_n, M')$. The language of a system of CFSMs is the set of all sequences of labels on runs starting from its initial state.

Some g-choreographies are not properly implementable. For example, in G_1 (from Example 1), participants must agree on whether to take the left or the right branch. However, RCOO is not involved in the left branch, and can decide autonomously to move on the right branch sending message grntAcc, while participant OTA may send decAcc taking the left branch. This leads to an erroneous computation, not expected from the choreography G_1. Formally, a g-choreography G is *realisable* if there exists a communicating system S such that $\mathcal{L}(S) = \mathcal{L}(G)$, where $\mathcal{L}(G)$ is the set of all linearisations of the pomsets in $[[G]]$. This ensures that every run of S conforms to at least one linearisation of a pomset of the g-choreography and vice-versa.

Two sufficient closure conditions for the realisability of a set of pomsets under the asynchronous semantics have been described in [14]. We introduce some auxiliary notation to state them (see Example 2 for concrete uses of the notations below). A pomset r_1 is a prefix of a pomset r_2 if its events are a subset of the events of r_2 and it is downward closed w.r.t. the happens-before relation of r_2 (i.e., if $e \leq_{r_2} e'$ and $e' \in r_1$ then $e \in r_1$) and equipped with the projection of the happens-before relation of r_1. Under the asynchronous semantics, a pomset is *well-formed* if[4]:

- each output event $\mathsf{A \cdot B\,!\,m}$ (resp. input event $\mathsf{A \cdot B\,?\,m}$) has at most (resp. exactly) one immediate successor input event $\mathsf{A \cdot B\,?\,m}$ (resp. immediate predecessor output event $\mathsf{A \cdot B\,!\,m}$);
- whenever an event e is an immediate predecessor of another event e', then e and e' are labelled either by communication actions of the same participant or by matching output and input actions; and
- for any two distinct outputs e and e' with the same label and e' causally depending on e, no immediate-successor matching input of e' may precede any immediate-successor matching input of e.

The projection of a pomset r onto a participant A, denoted $r\!\restriction_\mathsf{A}$, is the sub-pomset consisting of all events in r that are labeled with communication actions involving A. Given a set of pomsets R over participants $\mathcal{P}$, we define the set of *branch assignments on R* as the set Π_R of functions such that $\pi(\mathsf{A}) \in \{r\!\restriction_\mathsf{A} \mid r \in R\}$ for $\mathsf{A} \in \mathcal{P}$. Intuitively, a branch assignment $\pi \in \Pi_R$ chooses, for each to participant $\mathsf{A} \in \mathcal{P}$, a pomset $r \in R$ (corresponding to a resolution of a g-choreography) and assigns $r\!\restriction_\mathsf{A}$ to A. Note that π can choose different resolutions for different participants. We use $\cup_\mathsf{A} \pi(\mathsf{A})$ for the pomset obtained by merging the pomsets in the codomain of π. Finally, the *inter-participant closure* of a pomset, denoted $\Box(r)$, is the set of all pomsets that can be constructed by adding dependencies to connect individual output events with their corresponding input events across participants. The resulting pomsets in $\Box(r)$ represent all valid ways of linking outputs to inputs. A pomset r is *more permissive than* another pomset r' if r has

---

[4] These conditions are adapted from the ones in [1].

the same events and labels of r' and its happens-before relation is a subset of the one of r' (namely, r imposes fewer causal dependencies than r'). The closure conditions CC2 and CC3 below jointly guarantee relisability. Intuitively, CC2 requires that if a set of executions (i.e., a pomset) cannot be taken apart by any participant from the executions (i.e., pomsets) of R, then those executions must be part of R. Intuitively, CC3 requires that if a set of executions (i.e., a pomset) can be consistently represented as a prefix R' of another pomset in R, indicating that some participants will terminate earlier while matching the executions of R, then those prefixes R' must be part of R.

Definition 1 (Closure conditions). *A set of pomsets R satisfies **CC2** if for all well-formed $r \in \{\Box(\cup_A \pi(A)) \mid \pi \in \Pi_R\}$ there is $r' \in R$ that is at least as permissive as r; R satisfies **CC3** if for all R' set of prefixes of R and all well-formed $r \in \{\Box(\cup_A \pi(A)) \mid \pi \in \Pi_{R'}\}$, there is a prefix r' of a pomset in R such that r' is at least as permissive as r.*

The closure conditions in Definition 1 are adapted from the realisability criteria for MSCs [1] and avoid the explicit computation of the languages of the choreography.

Example 2. We illustrate our closure conditions on the semantics of G_1 from Example 1. Since $[\![G_1]\!]$ consists of two pomsets involving participants RCOO, LHA, OTA, and OTAM, Π_R contains 2^4 functions, one for each possible combination of the projections of these pomsets on the four participants.

It is straightforward to see that only two functions of Π_R have a well-formed inter-participant closure: the ones where all participants have chosen the same pomset of R. For example, in one of the other cases, if the participant RCOO chooses the first pomset and OTA chooses the second one, the input $OTA \cdot RCOO?manVer$ has no corresponding output. Since the two well-formed pomsets coincide with the choreography semantics, the CC2 condition is met.

However, CC3 is not satisfied. In fact, let $\pi(RCOO) = [RCOO \cdot LHA!grntAcc]$ (i.e., prefix of the first branch), $\pi(LHA) = [RCOO \cdot LHA?grntAcc]$ (i.e., first branch), $\pi(OTA) = [OTA \cdot LHA!decAcc]$ and $\pi(OTAM) = []$ (i.e., both second branch). The inter-participant closure yields the well-formed pomset $r = [RCOO \cdot LHA!grntAcc \rightarrow RCOO \cdot LHA?grntAcc \quad OTA \cdot LHA!decAcc]$, however no prefix of pomsets in R is more permissive than r. Pomset r (as any other where RCOO chooses one branch and OTA chooses the other one) demonstrate the lack of direct or indirect (via other participants) communication between OTA and RCOO to select the proper branch.   ◇

Note that condition CC3 does not imply condition CC2, as proved by the counterexample in [27].

5   Synchronous Semantics

In order to cope with different communication models, we extend the framework to support synchronous message passing. The synchronous semantics of a g-choreography G, denoted as $[\![G]\!]^s$, is defined by induction on the syntactic structure of G. The only difference w.r.t. the asynchronous semantics is the case for $G; G'$, which adds the dependencies necessary to model the handshake between sender and receiver: (1) events of a participant in G must precede the events of the same participant in G'; (2) events in G'

that depend on an output in G must also depend on the corresponding input in G; (3) events in G preceding an input in G′ must also precede the corresponding output in G′. The synchronous semantics of a choreography can be computed by adding the missing dependencies to its asynchronous semantics: for every pomset and for every output e and its matching successor input e' every predecessor of e' must be a predecessor of e and every successor of e must be successor of e'. Example 3 below shows a pictorial representation of the translation from asynchronous to synchronous semantics.

Example 3. The synchronous semantics of the g-choreography of Example 1 is $[\![G_1]\!]^s$, which is as follows:

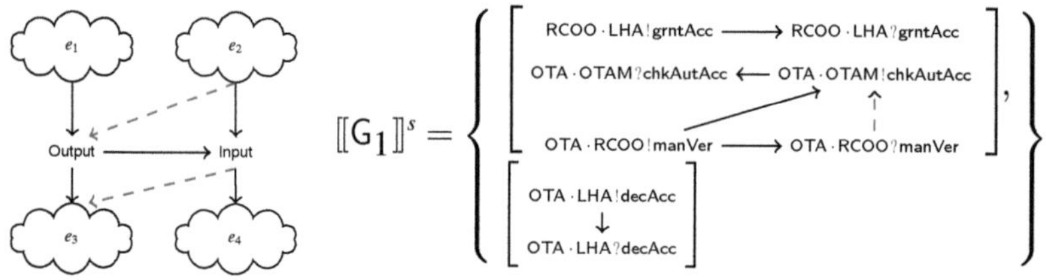

$$[\![G_1]\!]^s = \left\{ \begin{array}{l} \text{RCOO} \cdot \text{LHA!grntAcc} \longrightarrow \text{RCOO} \cdot \text{LHA?grntAcc} \\ \text{OTA} \cdot \text{OTAM?chkAutAcc} \longleftarrow \text{OTA} \cdot \text{OTAM!chkAutAcc} \\ \text{OTA} \cdot \text{RCOO!manVer} \longrightarrow \text{OTA} \cdot \text{RCOO?manVer} \\[4pt] \text{OTA} \cdot \text{LHA!decAcc} \\ \downarrow \\ \text{OTA} \cdot \text{LHA?decAcc} \end{array} \right\}$$

In the synchronous setting, every successor of the event OTA·RCOO!manVer (here just OTA·OTAM!chkAutAcc) must be a successor of OTA·RCOO?manVer as well, hence the additional dashed red arrow in picture. The events corresponding to the interaction OTA→OTAM: chkAutAcc remain however independent from those events for RCOO→LHA: grntAcc since no participant is involved in both the interactions. Moreover, the events for RCOO→LHA: grntAcc and the ones for OTA→RCOO: manVer are independent of each others since they belong to different threads.   ◇

The choice of modeling interactions also in the synchronous case with two distinct events (send and receive) while preserving independence of concurrent threads allows us to reuse the same theory and machinery of the asynchronous semantics, which is grounded on the work in [1] on Message Sequence Charts. However this results in each interaction (e.g., OTA→RCOO: manVer) being modeled by a two-way handshake (e.g., OTA·RCOO!manVer and OTA·RCOO?manVer) that cannot be interleaved by other messages of the same participants on the same thread (e.g., OTA·OTAM!chkAutAcc), but can be interleaved by other messages on other threads (e.g. RCOO·LHA!grntAcc). An alternative semantics could maintain distinct events per interaction, thus still benefiting from the asynchronous machinery, while also preventing interleaving of other threads between the send and receive events of a single interaction. This would require generating two pomsets per interaction, each enriched with specific dependencies to reflect thread-level ordering. E.g., we would have: one pomset with the additional edge OTA·RCOO?manVer → RCOO·LHA!grntAcc and one pomset with the additional edge RCOO·LHA?grntAcc → RCOO·LHA!manVer.

To avoid introducing new labels, the two-way handshake scheme described above is reflected in the LTS for the synchronous semantics of communicating systems by "overloading" the communication labels to let them represent handshaking. More precisely, the realisation of the synchronous semantics of a g-choreography involving participants

$A_1, \ldots, A_n$ can be attained through a *synchronous communicating system*, where a configuration is a tuple of length n whose i-th element is either the current state of (the CFSM of) A_i or the *handshake point* $[q_i l]$ with q_i a state of A_i and l a label on a transition from q_i; call *stable* configurations that do not have handshake points. Let $(q_1, \ldots, q_n)$ be a stable configuration such that $q_i \xrightarrow{A_i \cdot A_j !m} q_i'$ is a transition of A_i and $q_j \xrightarrow{A_i \cdot A_j ?m} q_j'$ is a transition of A_j then the synchronous LTS will have the transitions

$$(q_1, \ldots, q_i, \ldots, q_j, \ldots, q_n) \xrightarrow{A_i \cdot A_j !m} (q_1, \ldots, [q_i A_i \cdot A_j !m], \ldots, [q_j A_i \cdot A_j ?m], \ldots, q_n)$$

$$\xrightarrow{A_i \cdot A_j ?m} (q_1, \ldots, q_i', \ldots, q_j', \ldots, q_n)$$

(and similarly for the configuration $(q_1, \ldots, q_j, \ldots, q_i, \ldots, q_n)$). The language of a system of CFSMs is the set of all sequences of labels corresponding to the transitions of runs from the initial configuration.

In order to check realisability in the synchronous setting, we define synchronous well-formedness of pomsets: (i) the pomset is well-formed w.r.t. the asynchronous semantics; (ii) each output event $A \cdot B !m$ has exactly one matching immediate-successor input $A \cdot B ?m$. Since the verification conditions over pomsets are parametrised on well-formedness, to check realisability in the synchronous case it is enough to check the closure conditions (cf. Definition 1) using the synchronous well-formedness.

Notice that some choreographies are realisable in the synchronous model while they are not realisable in the asynchronous one. For instance the g-choreography of Example 1 does not satisfy **CC3** in the asynchronous case as seen in Example 2, but it does in the synchronous semantics. In fact, the counterexample used for the asynchronous case $r = [\text{RCOO} \cdot \text{LHA}!\text{grntAcc} \to \text{RCOO} \cdot \text{LHA}?\text{grntAcc} \text{OTA} \cdot \text{LHA}!\text{decAcc}]$ is not well-formed in the synchronous model, since the output $\text{OTA} \cdot \text{LHA}!\text{decAcc}$ has no corresponding input, and therefore it is not considered for the closure condition in the synchronous case. Intuitively, the g-choreography of Example 1 can be implemented in the synchronous model since OTA and RCOO must synchronise in the right thread of the right branch, making impossible for them to choose two different branches.

Some choreographies are also not realisable in the synchronous model. For instance, replacing the interaction $\text{OTA} \to \text{LHA} : \text{decAcc}$ with $\text{OTAM} \to \text{LHA} : \text{decAcc}$ in the g-choreography in Example 1 yields the g-choreography G_5' with semantics

$$[\![G_5']\!]^s = \left\{ \begin{bmatrix} \text{RCOO} \cdot \text{LHA}!\text{grntAcc} \longrightarrow \text{RCOO} \cdot \text{LHA}?\text{grntAcc} \\ \text{OTA} \cdot \text{OTAM}?\text{chkAutAcc} \longleftarrow \text{OTA} \cdot \text{OTAM}!\text{chkAutAcc} \\ \uparrow \\ \text{OTA} \cdot \text{RCOO}!\text{manVer} \longrightarrow \text{OTA} \cdot \text{RCOO}?\text{manVer} \end{bmatrix}, \begin{bmatrix} \text{OTAM} \cdot \text{LHA}!\text{decAcc} \\ \downarrow \\ \text{OTAM} \cdot \text{LHA}?\text{decAcc} \end{bmatrix} \right\}$$

where the left pomset is as in $[\![G_1]\!]^s$, whereas the other consists of $\text{OTAM} \cdot \text{LHA}!\text{decAcc}$ followed by $\text{OTAM} \cdot \text{LHA}?\text{decAcc}$. Since there is no coordination among the participants OTAM and LHA in the latter pomset with the participants OTA and RCOO of the first interaction of a thread of the former pomset, the execution can result in OTAM and LHA taking a branch different than the one taken by OTA— and RCOO. Consider the prefixes $\pi(\text{RCOO}) = [\text{OTA} \cdot \text{RCOO}?\text{manVer}]$ and

$\pi(\mathsf{OTA}) = [\mathsf{OTA} \cdot \mathsf{RCOO\,!manVer}]$ of the projections of the first branch and the projections of the second branch $\pi(\mathsf{LHA}) = [\mathsf{OTAM} \cdot \mathsf{LHA\,?decAcc}]$ and $\pi(\mathsf{OTAM}) = [\mathsf{OTAM} \cdot \mathsf{LHA\,!decAcc}]$: there is no prefix of R that is at least as permissive as the well-formed pomset in the inter-participant closure of $\bigcup_{\mathsf{A} \in \mathcal{P}} \pi(\mathsf{A})$, namely

$$[\mathsf{OTA} \cdot \mathsf{RCOO\,!manVer} \rightarrow \mathsf{OTA} \cdot \mathsf{RCOO\,?manVer}$$
$$\mathsf{OTAM} \cdot \mathsf{LHA\,!decAcc} \rightarrow \mathsf{OTAM} \cdot \mathsf{LHA\,?decAcc}]$$

6 Verifying Realisability

The closure conditions must be verified on finite pomsets. Therefore, we consider a bounded unrolling of loops in the implementation, limited to two iterations. This approach allows us to detect coordination issues such as: a message from one loop iteration being confused with a message from the next; participants disagreeing on the number of iterations executed; a message occurring after the loop being mistaken for one within the loop; and events from a loop iteration being reordered with respect to messages in the subsequent iteration. The main source of complexity in verifying closure conditions is that we have to check prefix-language inclusion and in the size of inter-participant closures. The next two sections tackle these problems.

6.1 Avoiding Pomset Compositions Explosion

Given a set of pomsets R over participants $\mathcal{P}$, the main challenge in checking CC2 arises from the exponential growth of the number of elements in the set of branch assignments Π_R with the size of $\mathcal{P}$. For example, consider the choreography $\mathsf{G_{xy}} = \mathsf{G_x} + \mathsf{G_y}$, where:

$$\mathsf{G_x} = \mathsf{A_1} {\rightarrow} \mathsf{A_2} : \mathsf{x};\, \mathsf{A_2} {\rightarrow} \mathsf{A_3} : \mathsf{x} \ldots;\, \mathsf{A_{n-1}} {\rightarrow} \mathsf{A_n} : \mathsf{x}$$
$$\mathsf{G_y} = \mathsf{A_1} {\rightarrow} \mathsf{A_2} : \mathsf{y};\, \mathsf{A_2} {\rightarrow} \mathsf{A_3} : \mathsf{y};\, \ldots;\, \mathsf{A_{n-1}} {\rightarrow} \mathsf{A_n} : \mathsf{y}$$

Here, n participants sequentially exchange either x or y. There are two possible projections per participant, one for each branch, so the set Π_R consists of 2^n combinations.

The key observation is that most of the pomsets in Π_R are either non-well-formed or share the same largest well-formed prefix relevant for CC3. Moreover, suppose we are given two pomsets r_A and r_B from the projections of participants $\mathsf{A}, \mathsf{B} \in \mathcal{P}$. If the dependencies in the union of r_A and r_B cannot be augmented to match an input of B from A, then the well-formedness condition will be violated in every $\pi \in \Pi_R$ containing r_A and r_B, regardless of the pomsets chosen for the other participants.

These observations lead to the new procedure for CC2 in Algorithm 1.1, which checks well-formedness incrementally, pruning invalid partial candidates instead of computing the full Π_R explicitly. Line 4 initialises two variables: variable $\mathcal{P}'$ keeps track of the set of already processed participants, while R' keeps track of the valid partial candidates: pomsets in $\{\Box(\cup_\mathsf{A} \pi(\mathsf{A})) \mid \pi \in \Pi_{R_{|\mathcal{P}'}}\}$ that are well-formed w.r.t. $\mathcal{P}'$.

Algorithm 1.1. A new algorithm for CC2

```
1   CC2(R, P):
2       let R_A = {r|_A | r ∈ R} for A ∈ P
3       choose A ∈ P
4       (R', P') = (R_A, {A})
5       while P \ P' ≠ ∅
6           choose A ∈ P \ P'
7           R'' = ∅
8           for r' ∈ R', r ∈ R_A:
9               for r'' ∈ □(r ∪ r'):
10                  if ∀A' · A''?m ∈ r'' such that (A',A'') ∈ (P' × {A}) ∪ ({A} × P')
11                      ∃ immediate predecessor A' · A''!m ∈ r'':
12                      # For synchronous case also check
13                      # ∀A' · A''!m ∈ r'' ∃ immediate successor A' · A''?m ∈ r''
14                          R'' = R'' ∪ {r''}
15          (R', P') = (R'', P' ∪ {A})
16      return ∀r ∈ R' ∃r' ∈ R as permissive as r
```

In practice, the algorithm starts with an initial participant (line 3) and selects the next participant (line 6) as the one that can resolve the largest number of pending input/output dependencies in R'. This heuristic is also applied in the CC3 check, where instead of pruning non-well formed pomsets we keep only the largest well-formed prefixes w.r.t. the processed participants.

When processing the next participant A, the algorithm merges every partial candidate with every projection of A (line 8), iterates over their interparticipant closure (line 9), and adds only the resulting new candidates that satisfy well-formedness w.r.t. all events that involve A (checked on lines 10–11 through a condition that implies well-formedness due the fact that pomsets are obtained by the inter-participant closure of the projection of the well-formed pomsets of R). Finally, the algorithm verifies the existence of a more permissive pomset in R for every final candidate in R'.

The heuristic above is relevant since the order in which participants are chosen (line 6) significantly affects the efficiency of pruning. For instance, if in G_{xy} above participants are chosen in order $A_1, A_2, \ldots, A_n$ then the size of R' remains 2 throughout the execution. In contrast, a processing order like $A_1, A_3, \ldots, A_{2m+1}, \ldots$ can cause the size of R' to grow up to 2^m pomsets after m iterations, due to the lack of direct interactions between the first m selected participants.

6.2 Avoiding Prefix Explosion

There is a combinatorial blowup to check CC3 due to the examination of all the prefixes of the pomsets in the choreography's semantics, whose number grows exponentially with the number of events across concurrent threads. For example, given the partial order $[e_1 \to e_2 \quad e_1' \to e_2']$, there are seven distinct non-empty proper prefixes: $[e_1]$, $[e_1']$, $[e_1 \quad e_1']$, $[e_1 \to e_2]$, $[e_1' \to e_2']$, $[e_1 \to e_2 \quad e_1']$, and $[e_1 \quad e_1' \to e_2']$. This becomes especially costly in asynchronous semantics, since the sequential composition of interactions targeting different receivers makes the corresponding receive events concurrent.

The main observation is that if r is a counterexample (i.e., r is well-formed and no prefix of R is more permissive than r), then every well-formed $r' \in \{□(\cup_A \pi(A)) \mid \pi \in$

Algorithm 1.2. A new algorithm for CC3

```
1    CC3(R, P):
2        let R_A = {r|_A | r ∈ R} for A ∈ P
3        choose A ∈ P
4        (R', P') = (R_A, {A})
5        while P \ P' ≠ ∅
6            choose A ∈ P \ P'
7            R'' = ∅
8            for r' ∈ R', r ∈ R_A:
9                for r'' ∈ □(r ∪ r'):
10                   while ∃e = A' · A''?m ∈ r'' s.t.  (A', A'') ∈ (P' × {A}) ∪ ({A} × P')
11                       and ∄ immediate predecessor A' · A''!m ∈ r'':
12                       # For synchronous case also check
13                       # e = A' · A''!m ∈ r'' and ∄ imm. succ. A' · A''?m ∈ r'':
14                       r'' = r'' \ subgraph from e
15                   R'' = R'' ∪ {r''}
16               (R', P') = (R'', P' ∪ {A})
17       return ∀r ∈ R' ∃r' ∈ R as permissive as r
```

$\Pi_{R'}\}$ such that r is a prefix of r' is also a counterexample. Moreover, every pomset admits a unique largest well-formed prefix, which can be obtained by removing all non-well-formed events together with their descendants.

Based on this insight, the new approach in Algorithm 1.2 avoids explicitly enumerating all prefixes of R. Instead, it performs the interparticipant closure $R'' = \{\Box(\cup_A \pi(A)) \mid \pi \in \Pi_R\}$, then it computes the largest well-formed prefixes R''' of R'', and finally checks that, for every $r''' \in R'''$, there exists a prefix of R that is more permissive than r'''.

In the actual algorithm, similarly to CC2, we do not explictely compute the interparticipant closure or the largest well-formed prefix. Instead, we build the largest prefixes incrementally. The variable R' keeps track of the largest prefixes of $\{\Box(\cup_A \pi(A)) \mid \pi \in \Pi_{R|_{P'}}\}$ that are well-formed w.r.t. P'. When processing a next participant A, we merge R' with the projections of A and we extend the candidates with the largest well-formed prefixes. Computing the largest well-formed prefix of a pomset (lines 10-14) is straightforward: we iteratively remove non-well-formed events that involve A along with all events causally dependent on them (i.e., input events without a corresponding immediate predecessor output, and in the synchronous case, output events without a corresponding immediate successor input), until only well-formed events remain.

7   Evaluation

We integrated Algorithms 1.1 and 1.2 in a new version of PomCho dubbed PomCho+. We now describe the application of PomCho+ to A&A and compare it to PomCho.

7.1   Verifying the closure conditions on A&A

The application of our analysis to A&A shows that it is realisable neither under the asynchronous nor the synchronous semantics. The main reason for this is the choice at the end of the loop in G_A (cf. Fig. 2, or the extract A&A below). One branch of the choice contains RCOO→GDH: sndPro, while the other one contains the interactions RCOO→GDH: rptMon; GDH→LHA: takAct. Note that participant LHA is only involved in the latter case, hence if the other branch is taken LHA does not know whether the loop has ended or not. This issue is made worst since LHA is the sender in the first transition of the loop, hence it does not know whether to trigger a new iteration by sending a seekAcc message to GDH or to wait for a message in the current iteration.

The above is the main issue flagged by our analysis, but the analysis in [23] hid it among many false positives given by the treatment of parallel composition and late join (cf. [23, Sections 5-6]). Domain experts confirmed that the CA model in [23] was not faithful to the specification which indeed requires a notification to LHA on both the branches. Adding such notification makes the protocol realisable under both the synchronous and the asynchronous semantics. The realisable protocol is available in [25].

The error was induced by the fact that in case of a report (right branch) the LHA needs to react. Hence this communication is more emphasised in the informal description [19] on which our model is based. Even if the analysis has not revealed a real bug in the protocol, it has highlighted an error in the model contributing to its refinement. The absence of false positives was also key to highlight real issues.

We give a snippet $\hat{G}$ of our model that constitutes a minimal example illustrating the problem described above. This allows us to identify a reasonably small pomset flagging the issue instead of analysing the large one corresponding to our full case study.

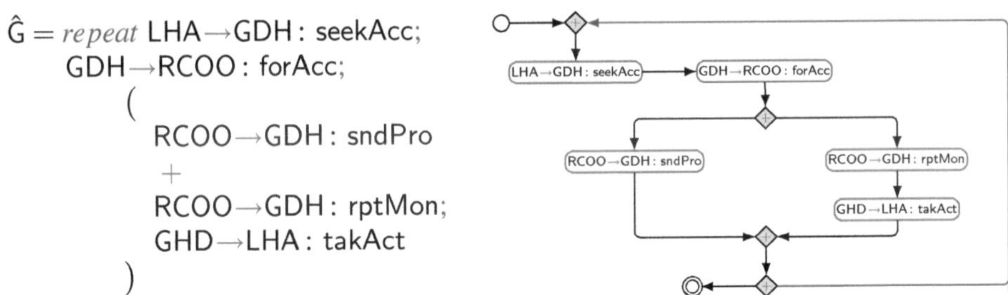

The counterexample of the semantics $[\![\hat{G}]\!]$ and $[\![\hat{G}]\!]^s$ (blue edge is only part of synchronous semantics) of the g-choreography $\hat{G}$ is

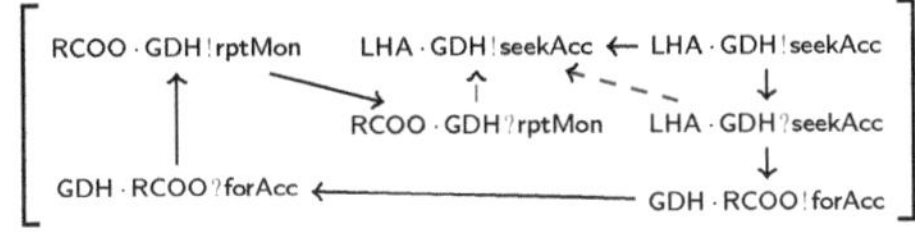

The pomset above is constructed from the projection of LHA that corresponds to the left branch for the first loop iteration, while all projections of the other participants correspond to the right branch. This counterexample shows that LHA can initiate the second iteration (i.e., second LHA · GDH!seekAcc) without waiting the message takAct from GDH. Therefore, the temporal dependency between RCOO · GDH?rptMon and the second LHA · GDH!seekAcc (i.e., the missing red edge) is violated. For this reason,

Table 1. Benchmarks ($\star$ indicates timeout without success after 1800 s)

	# WF			# Pomsets			# CEx			Time (ms)		
	Old	New	Sync	Old	New	Sync	Old	New	Sync	Old	New	Sync
G_1	16	2	2	2 26	2 3	2 2	0 3	0 1	0 0	8 43	6 10	7 9
$\hat{G}$	216	12	12	7 56	7 7	7 7	1 20	1 3	0 1	228 1091	91 133	130 145
G_{xy}	32K	2	2	2 $\star$	2 2	2 2	0 $\star$	0 0	0 0	35K $\star$	139 809	157 1165
G_5	1	1	1	1 441	1 1	1 1	0 0	0 0	0 0	26 22K	24 14	28 29
A&A	$\star$	480	480	$\star$ $\star$	224 112	224 112	$\star$ $\star$	32 80	16 8	$\star$ $\star$	863K 439K	968K 445K
A&A †	$\star$	416	416	$\star$ $\star$	192 80	192 64	$\star$ $\star$	0 0	0 0	$\star$ $\star$	1055K 402K	1048K 334K

there is no pomset in $[\![\hat{G}]\!]$ or $[\![\hat{G}]\!]^s$ that has a prefix more permissive than this counterexample.

7.2 Benchmarking Our Algorithms

We benchmark our algorithms against those in [13] on examples from previous sections, including A&A. Previous work only supported asynchronous semantics, so we have no synchronous reference. Table 1 reports the results of our benchmarks, conducted on a Macbook Air M2, operating system Ubuntu 22.04.5 LTS with 64 bit, Kernel: Linux 5.19.5-10-asahi, arm64 architecture, and 8GB RAM. Each row corresponds to the g-choreography in the first column. The remaining columns report the results on the algorithms considered (sub-columns Old and New for the asynchronous algorithm in [30] and ours, respectively, and Sync for our synchronous algorithm). More precisely, # WF yields the number of analysed combinations of well-formed pomsets; # Pomsets the number of pomsets in the inter-participant closure for CC2 and of prefixes analysed for CC3 (highlighted); # CEx the number of pomsets that do not satisfy the condition for CC2 and CC3 while Time yields the total running time to check CC2 and CC3.

For small examples, such as G_1 of Example 1 and $\hat{G}$ of Sect. 7.1, the new algorithms achieve speedups ranging from $1.4\times$ to $8.4\times$, due to the reduced number of prefixes analysed and the preventive pruning of non-well formed candidates. Notice that G_1 is realisable in the synchronous model only.

We assessed the contribution of the individual optimisations via dedicated examples. The g-choreography G_{xy} of Sect. 6.1 with $n = 15$ allows us to evaluate the impact of the number of participants: PomCho+ achieves a speedup of $272\times$ for CC2 since it maintains only two well-formed pomsets during the whole execution, while the size of Π_R computed with PomCho is $2^{15} = 32768$. It is not possible to compute the speedup for CC3, since the size of the set of branch assignments makes PomCho timeout on CC3. We have experimented with different values of n. The old algorithm can compute neither CC2 nor CC3 when $n > 10$. The proposed algorithm checks both CC2 and CC3 for all $n \leq 35$ and times-out for $n = 36$ with a timeout of 1800. The g-choreography G_5 is a variant of G_{xy} from Sect. 6.1, where in G_x (resp. G_y) participant A sequentially sends messages x_1, x_2, x_3, x_4, and x_5 (resp. y_1, y_2, y_3, y_4, and y_5) to B. As described in Sect. 6.2, the semantics of this choreography consists of one pomset with 20 distinct events with 10 events in each thread. This pomset has 441 prefixes, which have to be computed explicitly by the old approach. The new algorithm is able to maintain only one single largest prefix and achieve a speedup of $1603\times$.

The old implementation is incapable to analyse A&A. Since there are on average about 16 branches for each of the 11 participants, the size of the set of branch assignments would be $16^{11} \approx 1.7 \times 10^{13}$. Each pomset would also have a large number of prefixes, due to the four threads. In contrast, PomCho+ maintains up to 480 partial well-formed pomsets while analysing CC2, and 112 prefixes while analysing CC3. Similar considerations arise for A&A †, which is A&A updated so to make it realisable.

8   Conclusion, Related, and Future Work

This work builds on [23], where the analysis on the case study in Sect. 3 uses CAs [3] and the Corinne tool [22,24]. A main drawback of CAs (and, consequently, of Corinne) is that concurrency is modelled by explicitly representing all interleavings. This makes both the diagrammatic representation and the analysis quickly unfeasible for highly concurrent cases, such as A&A. The problem was avoided in [23] by turning some concurrent computations into non-deterministic choices. This approach has two drawbacks; firstly it does not faithfully model A&A, secondly, it produces false positives since non-deterministic choice is subject to stricter conditions than parallel composition.

Hence, to provide a satisfactory analysis of A&A, we turned to g-choreographies that compactly capture parallelism. This is convenient also because computations of g-choreographies can be compactly expressed as pomsets, which are the structures used in the tool PomCho [15] to check the closure conditions ensuring well-formedness of g-choreographies. However, A&A also challenges PomCho since the check of the closure conditions is implemented as a brute force algorithm. To overcome this issue we introduced optimisations of the algorithms and implemented them in PomCho. The verification of A&A initiates the usability analysis of PomCho advocated in [15].

The closure conditions proposed in [14] take inspiration from those in [1] and allow a more efficient analysis [15]. We extend the approach in [14] to synchronous interactions and adapt PomCho to support the new closure conditions. These results are instrumental to tackle the complexity of our case study.

The theories underlying PomCho and Corinne have common aims but different formalisations; we plan to investigate their relation in future work.

In [4] a mechanism to statically detect realisability in MSCs (a formal model of global specifications) has been proposed; the analysis is based on notions of non-local choices and of termination that are less permissive than our verification conditions since intra-participant concurrency is not allowed and termination awareness is not enforced.

Realisation of global views allowing interactions between multiple senders and multiple receivers is considered in [29]. Two notions of realisability are discussed, depending on whether local actions include the name of involved participants or not. Tool support is provided by the Ceta [7] tool.

Partial order models of choreographies akin to pomsets have been recently proposed in [6,9–11]. The pomset semantics of g-choreographies in [14,15] has inspired *branching pomsets* [9–11], which enable a more compact representation of choices. Whether this representation offers better algorithms for checking closure conditions is an open problem. Similar considerations apply to the results in [8], which proposes an optimisation of the pomset representation of concurrent computations.

The platform in [2] offers a framework for the top-down development of message-passing applications with low-level features (e.g., binding of components, or security aspects) but has limited functionalities for the analysis of global specifications.

As mentioned, our synchronous semantics and analysis build on the asynchronous ones. The reason was to reuse as much as possible previous PomCho implementation. One could instead represent synchronous communication as a single interaction event, labelled $A \rightarrow B : m$. This enables to halve the number of events (obtaining a corresponding speedup), but requires an extensive rework of both the tool and the theory.

The current integrated approach could also help to exploit both the synchronisation mechanisms in a same model. This would allow to study heterogeneous systems. We leave this research direction for future work.

References

1. Alur, R., Etessami, K., Yannakakis, M.: Inference of message sequence charts. IEEE Trans. Software Eng. **29**(7), 623–633 (2003)

2. Autili, M., Di Salle, A., Gallo, F., Pompilio, C., Tivoli, M.: CHOReVOLUTION: automating the realization of highly–collaborative distributed applications. In: Riis Nielson, H., Tuosto, E. (eds.) COORDINATION 2019. LNCS, vol. 11533, pp. 92–108. Springer, Cham (2019). https://doi.org/10.1007/978-3-030-22397-7_6

3. Barbanera, F., Lanese, I., Tuosto, E.: Choreography automata. In: Bliudze, S., Bocchi, L. (eds.) COORDINATION 2020. LNCS, vol. 12134, pp. 86–106. Springer, Cham (2020). https://doi.org/10.1007/978-3-030-50029-0_6

4. Ben-Abdallah, H., Leue, S.: Syntactic detection of process divergence and non-local choice in message sequence charts. In: Brinksma, E. (ed.) TACAS 1997. LNCS, vol. 1217, pp. 259–274. Springer, Heidelberg (1997). https://doi.org/10.1007/BFb0035393

5. Brand, D., Zafiropulo, P.: On communicating finite-state machines. J. ACM **30**(2), 323–342 (1983)

6. Castellani, I., Dezani-Ciancaglini, M., Giannini, P.: Event structure semantics for multiparty sessions. In: Boreale, M., Corradini, F., Loreti, M., Pugliese, R. (eds.) Models, Languages, and Tools for Concurrent and Distributed Programming. LNCS, vol. 11665, pp. 340–363. Springer, Cham (2019). https://doi.org/10.1007/978-3-030-21485-2_19

7. Ceta Tool. https://github.com/arcalab/choreo/tree/ceta

8. Edixhoven, L.: Shuffling posets on trajectories (technical report). CoRR, abs/2309.09189 (2023)

9. Edixhoven, L., Jongmans, S.-S.: Realisability of branching pomsets. In: Tapia Tarifa, S.L., Proença, J. (eds.) Formal Aspects of Component Software, FACS 2022. LNCS, vol. 13712, pp. 185–204. Springer, Cham (2022). https://doi.org/10.1007/978-3-031-20872-0_11

10. Edixhoven, L., Jongmans, S.-S., Proença, J., Castellani, I.: Branching pomsets: design, expressiveness and applications to choreographies. J. Log. Algebraic Methods Program. **136**, 100919 (2024)

11. Edixhoven, L., Jongmans, S.-S., Proença, J., Cledou, G.: Branching pomsets for choreographies. In: Aubert, C., Di Giusto, C., Safina, L., Scalas, A. (eds.) Proceedings 15th Interaction and Concurrency Experience, ICE 2022, Lucca, Italy, 17th June 2022. EPTCS, vol. 365, pp. 37–52 (2022)

12. Gaudin, E., Brunel, E.: Property verification with MSC. In: Khendek, F., Toeroe, M., Gherbi, A., Reed, R. (eds.) SDL 2013. LNCS, vol. 7916, pp. 19–35. Springer, Heidelberg (2013). https://doi.org/10.1007/978-3-642-38911-5_2
13. Guanciale, R., Tuosto, E.: Realisability of pomsets via communicating automata. In: Proceedings 11th Interaction and Concurrency Experience, ICE, pp. 37–51 (2018)
14. Guanciale, R., Tuosto, E.: Realisability of pomsets. J. Logic Algebraic Methods Program. **108**, 69–89 (2019)
15. Guanciale, R., Tuosto, E.: Pomcho: a tool chain for choreographic design. Sci. Comput. Program. **202**, 102535 (2021)
16. Healthcare Authorization and Accreditation protocol. https://salute.regione.emilia-romagna.it/ssr/strumenti-e-informazioni/autorizzazione-e-accreditamento/autorizzazione-e-accreditamento-sanitario
17. Honda, K., Yoshida, N., Carbone, M.: Multiparty asynchronous session types. J. ACM **63**(1), 9:1–9:67 (2016)
18. Hüttel, H., et al.: Foundations of session types and behavioural contracts. ACM Comput. Surv. **49**(1), 3:1–3:36 (2016)
19. Legge Regionale 06 Novembre 2019. https://demetra.regione.emilia-romagna.it/al/articolo?urn=er:assemblealegislativa:legge:2019;22
20. Formal description techniques (FDT) - Message Sequence Chart (MSC). Recommendation ITU-T Z.120 (2011). http://www.itu.int/rec/T-REC-Z.120-201102-I/en
21. Object Management Group. Business Process Model and Notation (2011). http://www.bpmn.org
22. Orlando, S., Di Pasquale, V., Barbanera, F., Lanese, I., Tuosto, E.: Corinne, a tool for choreography automata. In: Salaün, G., Wijs, A. (eds.) FACS 2021. LNCS, vol. 13077, pp. 82–92. Springer, Cham (2021). https://doi.org/10.1007/978-3-030-90636-8_5
23. Pal, S., Lanese, I., Clo, M.: Choreographic automata: a case study in healthcare management. In: Castellani, I., Tiezzi, F. (eds.) COORDINATION 2024. LNCS, vol. 14676, pp. 3–19. Springer, Cham (2024). https://doi.org/10.1007/978-3-031-62697-5_1
24. Pal, S., Lanese, I., Tuosto, E.: Corinne-3. https://github.com/lanese/corinne-3
25. pomcho+ Tool repository. https://bitbucket.org/sourabhphd/chorgram/src/ICTAC_2025/
26. pomcho+ Tool repository: A&A rendered by pomcho+. https://bitbucket.org/sourabhphd/chorgram/src/ICTAC_2025/ICTAC_Examples/Healthcare_Case_Study/choreography.png
27. pomcho+ Tool repository: An example that satisfies CC3 but not CC2. https://bitbucket.org/sourabhphd/chorgram/src/ICTAC_2025/ICTAC_Examples/CC2CC3/
28. Pratt, V.: Modeling concurrency with partial orders. Int. J. Parallel Prog. **15**, 33–71 (1986)
29. ter Beek, M.H., Hennicker, R., Proença, J.: Realisability of global models of interaction. In: Ábrahám, E., Dubslaff, C., Tarifa, S.L.T. (eds.) ICTAC 2023. LNCS, vol. 14446, pp. 236–255. Springer, Cham (2023). https://doi.org/10.1007/978-3-031-47963-2_15
30. Tuosto, E., Guanciale, R.: Semantics of global view of choreographies. J. Logic Algebraic Methods Program. **95**, 17–40 (2018)

Algorithms and Complexity

Ulam's Metric in Higher Dimensions

Sebastian Bala and Andrzej Kozik[(✉)]

Institute of Computer Science, University of Opole, pl. Kopernika 11a, Opole, Poland
`{sebastian.bala,andrzej.kozik}@uni.opole.pl`

Abstract. Ulam's metric defines the minimal number of moves (extraction followed by re-insertion of permutation elements) to go between a given pair of permutations, and determination of moved elements resolves the Longest Common Subsequence problem. The extensive research that followed Ulam's work provided many influential discoveries in computer science, mathematics, statistics and physics. In this paper, motivated by successful industrial applications of k-tuples of permutations, we extend Ulam's original definition to provide a framework of multidimensional metric and study its complexity and approximability.

Keywords: Ulam's metric · Longest Common Subsequence · computational and parametrized complexity · approximation · intractability

1   Introduction

A permutation $\sigma \in S_n$ is a sequence $(\sigma(1), \sigma(2), \ldots, \sigma(n))$ representing an arrangement of the elements of set $[n] \triangleq \{1, \ldots, n\}$. The possibility of expressing a linear ordering of set elements makes permutations foundational objects of combinatorics [6]. At the same time permutations are of great practical importance, as they model solutions to many real-life problems, e.g., in the fields of scheduling [22] or routing [25]. Taking into account the significance and the applications of permutations, a vast body of research tackled them from different angles, sides, and points of view.

In particular, Stanisław Ulam's research into the combinatorics of permutations addressed two principal questions [26]. Firstly, what is the minimum number of *insert* moves required to transform one permutation in S_n to another one, where an insert move consist in changing the position of exactly one element in the permutation? Secondly, what is the asymptotic distribution of this number as $n \to \infty$?

The answer to the first question is provided by *Ulam's metric* $U(\sigma_s, \sigma_t)$, where $\sigma_s, \sigma_t \in S_n$. Let $\sigma = (\sigma(1), \sigma(2), \ldots, \sigma(n))$ be a permutation in S_n, and let $s = (\sigma(i_1), \sigma(i_2), \ldots, \sigma(i_m))$ be a sub-sequence of σ, where $1 \le i_1 < \ldots < i_m \le n$. We say that a sequence $(b_1, \ldots, b_l)$ is the *B-induced* subsequence of $\sigma \in S_n$, $B \subseteq [n]$, if $(b_1, \ldots, b_l)$ is a subsequence of σ and $\{b_1, \ldots, b_l\} = B$;

Z. Liu et al. (Eds.): ICTAC 2025, LNCS 16237, pp. 399–416, 2026.
https://doi.org/10.1007/978-3-032-11176-0_23

we write $\sigma|B$ to denote the B-induced subsequence of σ. A common subsequence $CS(\sigma_s, \sigma_t)$ of two permutations $\sigma_s, \sigma_t \in S_n$ is a sequence $(\sigma_s(i_1) = \sigma_t(j_1), \sigma_s(i_2) = \sigma_t(j_2), \ldots, \sigma_s(i_m) = \sigma_t(j_m))$, where $1 \leq i_1 < \ldots < i_m \leq n$ and $1 \leq j_1 < \ldots < j_m \leq n$. For a given pair (σ_s, σ_t) of permutations $(\sigma_s, \sigma_t \in S_n)$, we say, that a subset $B \subseteq [n]$ *induces* a common subsequence if $\sigma_s|B = \sigma_t|B$. We write $LCS(\sigma_s, \sigma_t)$ to denote a *Longest Common Subsequence* (LCS) of σ_s and σ_t. Finally, we define

$$U(\sigma_s, \sigma_t) = n - |LCS(\sigma_s, \sigma_t)|. \tag{1}$$

As an example, consider $\sigma_s = (4, 3, 1, 6, 2, 5)$ and $\sigma_t = (5, 3, 1, 6, 4, 2)$. Then, $LCS(\sigma_s, \sigma_t) = (3, 1, 6, 2)$ and $U(\sigma_s, \sigma_t) = 2$, i.e., two insert moves are needed to transform σ_s into σ_t - moving 5 from the last position to the first, resulting in $(5, 4, 3, 1, 6, 2)$, and then moving 4 from the (now) second position to the 5-th, resulting in σ_t.

Fredman [10] showed that LCS can be computed using $n \log n - n \log \log n + O(n)$ comparisons in the worst case, and no algorithm has better worst-case performance. Later, Hunt and Szymanski [13] improved this bound to $O(n \log \log n)$.

Ulam's second question has attracted the attention of many researchers over the past 50 years, leading to numerous non-trivial results and establishing some surprising connections between different areas of mathematics, physics and statistics. See, for example [1,7,23] and especially the so called *final answer* in Baik, Deift and Johansson [2]. The latter showed, that the expected value of the length of $LCS(\sigma_s, \sigma_t)$ for σ_s and σ_t drawn uniformly at random from S_n equals $2\sqrt{n} - 1.77108n^{1/6} + o(n^{1/6})$.

According to Ulam's original motivation, $U(\sigma_s, \sigma_t)$ is often interpreted as the minimal number of moves needed to sort a hand of bridge cards σ_s as to obtain their σ_t ordering. Observe, cards in $LCS(\sigma_s, \sigma_t)$ form a longest run of correctly ordered cards, and the remaining cards needs to be sequentially taken (removed) from hand and inserted back into a desired position (as in σ_t).

But given the potential of expressing solutions of many combinatorial optimization problems as permutations, S_n spans a solution space in which Ulam's metric defines an optimal (shortest) path connecting any two solutions using insert moves. Existence and properties of such paths are especially important for metaheuristic algorithms [3,5], performing effective exploration of the solution space based on elimination and explorative properties. The efficiency of such methods is based on the connectivity property of a neighborhood - the assumption that every solution in the space can be reached from every other via finite sequence of moves. Therefore, algorithms computing Ulam's metric can be immediately applied as crossover operators in evolutionary and path-relinking metaheuristics [5], i.e., given a shortest path between two solutions, a result of their crossover could be either a midpoint, the best, or even all solutions on that path as an offspring.

In this paper, we generalize Ulam's first question to higher dimensions: what is the length of the shortest path between two tuples of permutations in S_n^k, $S_n^k = \underbrace{S_n \times \ldots \times S_n}_{k \text{ times}}$, the k-dimensional space of permutations?

This question is not merely of theoretical interest, as even 2-tuples of permutations have many successful industrial applications. For example, they are used to describe non-overlapping packings of rectangles on a plane as the *Sequence Pair* (SP) representation [20]. In the context of physical layout synthesis of VLSI circuits, pairs of permutations model a placement of transistors, leaf-cells and macro-blocks on a silicon die [15]. On the other hand, SP can be a solution space for multiprocessor scheduling problems with various definitions of cost functions and constraints [14,18,19]. As another example, 3 and 5-tuples of permutations has been used to model 3D packings [24].

An another interpretation of the generalized Ulams's metric arises in the utility-theory field: given the rankings of two persons for n items with respect to k metrics, compute the maximum size of a subset of items on which the two persons' orders agree on all metrics.

In this paper, we formulate a multi-dimensional analogue of Ulam's metric and study its hardness, approximability, and parameterized complexity. To the best of our knowledge, Ulam's metric in S_n^k has not been considered in the scientific literature so far. Instead, studies have been carried out in the field of the complexity and algorithms for longest common subsequences of two or more permutations (sequences), see e.g. [4].

The rest of the paper is organized as follows. The next section precisely defines U_k - Ulam's metric for k-tuples of permutations and LFS_k (the multidimensional analogue of LCS) and gives its application example. In Sect. 3, optimization problems kU and kLFS of computing U_k and LFS_k are defined, respectively. Then, we outline the landscape of foundational complexity results: membership in NP (Theorem 1) and NP-hardness (Theorem 2) of kU and kLFS; inapproximability of kU within approximation factors better than $1+1/40$ (Theorem 3); inapproximability of nLFS within an $n^{1-\epsilon}$ factor (Theorem 4); inapproximability of nU up to a $(2-\epsilon)$ factor (Theorem 5); inapproximability of $n^{1/c}$LFS up to an $n^{1-\epsilon}$ factor (Theorem 6), inapproximability of $n^{1/c}$U up to a $(2-\epsilon)$ factor (Theorem 7); kU belongs to FPT (Theorem 8); kLFS belongs to W[1] (Theorem 8); and finally, W[1] hardness for $n^{1/c}$LFS (Theorem 9). Section 4 concludes the paper.

2   Ulam's Metric in Higher Dimensions

Let $\Gamma \in S_n^k$ be a k-tuple of permutations of $[n]$, i.e., $\Gamma = (\sigma^1, \ldots, \sigma^k)$, $\sigma^i \in S_n$, $i = 1, \ldots, k$. Say an *insert move* of $v \in [n]$ in Γ consists of changing the position of v in each of Γ permutations, i.e., it consists of k independent sub-moves of v - one in each permutation of Γ. Note, some sub-moves can be *identity moves*, in which v is removed from a permutation and then inserted back into the same position. Define an insert neighborhood of Γ, $\mathcal{N}(\Gamma)$, as a set of permutation tuples obtained by performing all possible insert moves of $[n]$ elements in Γ.

Define a *path* between Γ_s and Γ_t in S_n^k as a sequence $\Gamma_0 = \Gamma_s, \Gamma_1, \ldots, \Gamma_{m-1}$, $\Gamma_m = \Gamma_t$ s.t. $\Gamma_{i+1} \in \mathcal{N}(\Gamma_i)$, $i = 0, \ldots, m-1$; let m be the length of that path. Then $U_k(\Gamma_s, \Gamma_t)$, Ulam's metric in S_n^k, is the length of the shortest path between

Γ_s and Γ_t, i.e., the minimal number of insert moves transforming Γ_s into Γ_t, where $\Gamma_s, \Gamma_t \in S_n^k$.

Let $\Gamma_s = (\sigma_s^1, \ldots, \sigma_s^k) \in S_n^k$ and $\Gamma_t = (\sigma_t^1, \ldots, \sigma_t^k) \in S_n^k$. A set $B \subseteq [n]$ is a *Fixed Subset* of Γ_s and Γ_t if it induces a common subsequence in all corresponding pairs (σ_s^i, σ_t^i) of permutations of Γ_s and Γ_t, i.e. $\sigma_s^i|B = \sigma_t^i|B$, $i = 1, \ldots, k$. Define $\Gamma|B \triangleq (\sigma^1|B, \ldots, \sigma^k|B)$ as a k-tuple of B-induced sequences of Γ. Let $FS_k(\Gamma_s, \Gamma_t)$ be a set of all Fixed Subsets of Γ_s and Γ_t, i.e., $FS_k(\Gamma_s, \Gamma_t) \triangleq \{B \subseteq [n] : \Gamma_s|B = \Gamma_t|B\}$. Then, following [1], it is not hard to show that

$$U_k(\Gamma_s, \Gamma_t) = n - |LFS_k(\Gamma_s, \Gamma_t)|, \tag{2}$$

where $LFS_k(\Gamma_s, \Gamma_t)$ is a *Largest Fixed Subset* of Γ_s and Γ_t.

As an example, consider $\Gamma_s = ((4, 3, 1, 6, 2, 5), (6, 5, 3, 4, 1, 2))$ and $\Gamma_t = ((5, 3, 1, 4, 6, 2), (6, 3, 5, 1, 2, 4))$. Then we have $LFS_2(\Gamma_s, \Gamma_t) = \{1, 2, 3, 6\}$, i.e., (i) $\Gamma_s|\{1, 2, 3, 6\} = ((3, 1, 6, 2), (6, 3, 1, 2))$, (ii) $\Gamma_t|\{1, 2, 3, 6\} = ((3, 1, 6, 2), (6, 3, 1, 2))$, (iii) $\Gamma_s|\{1, 2, 3, 6\} = \Gamma_t|\{1, 2, 3, 6\}$ (iv) $U_2(\Gamma_s, \Gamma_t) = 2$, i.e., two insert moves are needed to transform Γ_s into Γ_t - the move of 5 resulting in $((4, 5, 3, 1, 6, 2), (6, 3, 4, 5, 1, 2))$ followed by the move of 4.

Using Sequence Pair representation [20], U_2 can be interpreted similarly to Ulam's original U_1 (sorting cards) as a transformation of some rectangle packing into another, in which in each step a single rectangle (not in LFS_2) is taken (removed) from a packing and re-inserted in desired place. An example transformation is shown in Fig. 1.

Observe, for the case U_1 where $\Gamma_s, \Gamma_t \in S_n$, (2) is equivalent to (1) for permutations σ_s^1 and σ_t^1 and can be computed in polynomial time. Subsequently, we show that for any $k \geq 2$ determination of U_k is strongly NP-hard.

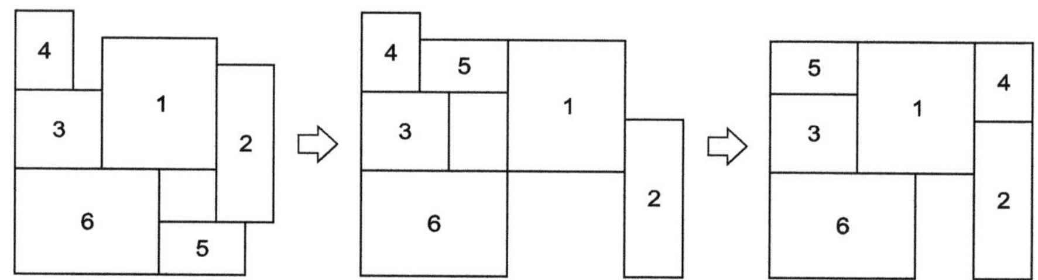

Fig. 1. A sample path in S_6^2 between $\Gamma_s = ((4, 3, 1, 6, 2, 5), (6, 5, 3, 4, 1, 2))$ and $\Gamma_t = ((5, 3, 1, 4, 6, 2), (6, 3, 5, 1, 2, 4))$; a midpoint $((4, 5, 3, 1, 6, 2), (6, 3, 4, 5, 1, 2))$ can be a result of their crossover. Each 2-tuple of permutations represents a non-overlapping packing of rectangles corresponding to elements of [6] (rectangles are of arbitrarily chosen dimensions; see [20] for Sequence Pair representation details).

3   The Complexity of Ulam's Metric in HD

A convenient form of defining an NP optimization problem A is its presentation as a fourtuple $(\mathcal{I}(A), fso_A, cost_A, type_A)$ [8], where: $\mathcal{I}(A)$ is a set of valid instances of A, fso_A is a function such that given an instance $x \in \mathcal{I}(A)$, $fso_A(x)$ is a set of feasible solutions for x. Moreover the question if $y \in fso_A(x)$? is verifiable in polynomial time with respect to the size $|x|$ of x. Given an $x \in \mathcal{I}(A)$ and a feasible solution y of x, $cost_A(x, y)$ is a positive integer measure of y, computable in polynomial time. Additionally $type_A \in \{\min, \max\}$.

Let A be a maximization problem. We use $Opt_A(x)$ to refer to the cost of optimal solution for $x \in \mathcal{I}(A)$. An algorithm $\mathcal{A}$, for A, computes a cost $\mathcal{A}(x)$ for feasible solution of an instance x. Define $F(\mathcal{A}, x) = \frac{Opt_A(x)}{\mathcal{A}(x)}$. Function $r : \mathbb{Z}^+ \mapsto \mathbb{R}^+$ is an *approximation factor* of $\mathcal{A}$ if for any $x \in \mathcal{I}(A)$, $F(\mathcal{A}, x) \le r(|x|)$. We say that algorithm $\mathcal{A}$ is $r(n)$-approximation algorithm. If A is an minimization problem then $F(\mathcal{A}, x) = \frac{\mathcal{A}(x)}{Opt_A(x)}$.

A *reduction* of an optimization problem A to an optimization problem B is a pair of polynomially computable functions (f, g) that satisfy two conditions: $(r1)$ $x' = f(x) \in \mathcal{I}(B)$ for any $x \in \mathcal{I}(A)$, $(r2)$ $y = g(x, y')$ is feasible solution of x, for any y' which is feasible solution of x'. A reduction (f, g) of an optimization problem A to an optimization problem B is an *S-reduction* if $(s1)$ $Opt_A(x) = Opt_B(x')$ for any $x \in \mathcal{I}(A)$, where $x' = f(x)$, and $(s2)$ $cost_A(x, g(x, y')) = cost_B(x', y')$, for any $x \in \mathcal{I}(A)$ and y' which is feasible solution of x' [8]. We write $A \le_S B$ to denote that there exists S-reduction from A to B.

A decision problem A is a *parametrized problem* if it is extended by function κ_A that assigns nonnegative integer to each instance x of A. An algorithm which decides if $x \in A$ in time $f(\kappa_A(x))p(|x|)$ is called *fpt-algorithm*, where f is a computable function and p is a polynomial. An R is an *fpt-reduction* of A to B if for any $x \in \mathcal{I}(A)$, $R(x)$ is an instance of B, moreover $(p1)$ $x \in A$ iff $R(x) \in B$; $(p2)$ R is computable by an fpt-algorithm with respect to κ_A; $(p3)$ There is computable function h such that $\kappa_B(R(x)) \le h(\kappa_A(x))$ for any $x \in \mathcal{I}(A)$.

The *k-dimensional Largest Fixed Subset Problem* ($kLFS(n)$) is formally defined as follows. The $\mathcal{I}(kLFS(n)) \triangleq S_n^k \times S_n^k$ is a set of all valid pairs of tuples of permutations. Let $\Gamma = \langle \Gamma_s, \Gamma_t \rangle \in \mathcal{I}(kLFS(n))$ be an instance of $kLFS(n)$. A set $B \subseteq [n]$ is a *feasible solution* of Γ ($B \in fso_{kLFS(n)}(\Gamma)$) if B is a Fixed Subset of Γ_s and Γ_t. The cost function $cost_{kLFS(n)}$ satisfies $cost_{kLFS(n)}(\Gamma, B) = |B|$. The $type_{kLFS}(n)$ is *max*, this means that the goal of $kLFS$ is to determine the largest $B \subseteq [n]$ such that B is a feasible solution of Γ.

The decision version of *k-dimensional Largest Fixed Subset Problem* ($kLFSD(n)$) is answering the question if for given nonnegative integer l and $\Gamma \in \mathcal{I}(kLFS(n))$ there exists $B \subseteq [n]$, such that $|B| = l$ and B is a feasible solution of Γ.

By $kU(n)$ we denote a dual problem to $kLFS(n)$ which satisfies: (i) $\mathcal{I}(kU(n)) = \mathcal{I}(kLFS(n))$, (ii) for any $x \in \mathcal{I}(kU(n))$, $B \in fso_{kLFS(n)}(x)$ if and only if $[n] \backslash B \in fso_{kU(n)}(x)$, (iii) $cost_{kU(n)}(\Gamma, Y) = |Y|$, (iv) $type_{kU(n)}$ is *min*. A $kUD(n)$ is the decision version of the $kU(n)$ problem.

Throughout the rest of the paper, we omit the parameter n in $kLFS(n)$, $kU(n)$, $kLFSD(n)$ and $kUD(n)$ when it is understood to be n. In such cases, we simply write $kLFS$, kU, $kLFSD$ and kUD.

Throughout the paper we will also refer to well known problems: In the MaxClique problem (for brevity MC) we are given undirected graph $G = (V, E)$ and the task is to find a fully connected subgraph (a clique) of maximum size. The decision version of MC - the Clique problem consists in checking for a given m if the graph contains a clique of size m. For the MinVertexCover problem (for brevity MVC) the task is to find a subset $B \subseteq V$ of the smallest size such that, for every $\{u, v\} \in E$, $u \in B$ or $v \in B$. The VertexCover problem denotes decision version of the MinVertexCover problem.

Solutions of the MaxClique and the MinVertexCover problem are related to each other in the following way: subset B of V is a minimum vertex cover if and only if $V \backslash B$ is a maximum clique in $\overline{G}$, where $\overline{G} = (V, V^2 \backslash E)$, for $V^2 = \{\{i, j\} \mid i \neq j$ and $i, j \in V\}$.

Fact 1. *A set $B \subseteq [n]$ is a vertex cover of $\overline{G}$ iff $[n] \backslash B$ is a clique for G.*

Fact 2. *A set $B \subseteq [n]$ is a feasible solution of kU problem for instance $\Gamma = \langle \Gamma_s, \Gamma_t \rangle$ if and only if $[n] \backslash B$ is a feasible solution of the kLFS problem for the same instance Γ.*

Lemma 1. *For any $k \in [n]$ there exist S-reductions from kLFS to MaxClique and from kU to MinVertexCover.*

Proof. For a given $\Gamma = \langle \Gamma_s, \Gamma_t \rangle = \langle (\sigma_s^1, \ldots, \sigma_s^k), (\sigma_t^1, \ldots, \sigma_t^k) \rangle$ we define a graph $G = (V = [n], E)$, where iEj if and only if for all $r \in [k]$ there are $\alpha_s, \beta_s, \alpha_t, \beta_t \in [k] : \alpha_s < \beta_s$, $\alpha_t < \beta_t$ and either $\sigma_s^r(\alpha_s) = i, \sigma_s^r(\beta_s) = j, \sigma_t^r(\alpha_t) = i, \sigma_t^r(\beta_t) = j$ or $\sigma_s^r(\alpha_s) = j, \sigma_s^r(\beta_s) = i, \sigma_t^r(\alpha_t) = j, \sigma_t^r(\beta_t) = i$. This condition establishes the function f transforming any given Γ, that is an instance of kLFS into G which is an instance of MaxClique. The function f satisfies (r1).

Remark 1. Any clique C of $f(\Gamma)$ induces a common subsequences for all pairs σ_s^i, σ_t^i. Hence $C \in fso_{kLFS}(\Gamma)$.

Proof. Suppose to the contrary, that C does not induce a common subsequence for some σ_s^i and σ_t^i. The clique C has at least two elements. Let τ_s, τ_t be the C-induced subsequences of σ_s^i and σ_t^i, respectively. If τ_s, τ_t are two different sequences, then there is the smallest index d such that $\tau_s(d) \neq \tau_t(d)$. Therefore $\sigma_s^{-1}(\tau_t(d)) > \sigma_s^{-1}(\tau_s(d))$ and $\sigma_t^{-1}(\tau_t(d)) < \sigma_t^{-1}(\tau_s(d))$, or vice versa. The reduction has been defined in such a way that there is no edge $(\tau_s(d), \tau_t(d)) \in E$. This is contradiction - C cannot form a clique in $f(\Gamma)$. $\square$

Thus, a function $g : S_n^k \times 2^V \mapsto 2^V$, for which equality $g(\Gamma, C) = C$ holds for any clique C of $f(\Gamma)$, satisfies condition (r2).

So far we have proved that there is reduction from kLFS to MaxClique. Note that $cost_{MC}(f(\Gamma) = G, C) = |C|$ for any clique C of G. Additionally, $cost_{kLFS}(\Gamma, g(\Gamma, C) = C)$ can be defined as $|C|$ for any C which is a clique. Hence, the (s2) condition of the S-reduction definition is satisfied.

Remark 2. A maximum clique $C \subseteq [n]$ of the graph $f(\Gamma)$ is a maximum solution of the kLFS instance.

Proof. To prove this assume to the contrary that there exists $D \subseteq V$ which induces common subsequences for all pairs (σ_s^i, σ_t^i) and $|C| < |D|$ for all cliques C of G. Therefore there are different $i, j \in D$ such that $\neg iEj$. By definition of the reduction there exists r, such that either $\sigma_s^r(\alpha_s) = i, \sigma_s^r(\beta_s) = j, \sigma_t^r(\alpha_t) = j, \sigma_t^r(\beta_t) = i$ or $\sigma_s^r(\alpha_s) = j, \sigma_s^r(\beta_s) = i, \sigma_t^r(\alpha_t) = i, \sigma_t^r(\beta_t) = j$, for some $\alpha_s < \beta_s$, $\alpha_t < \beta_t$. This contradicts the fact that i, j are elements of common sequence induced by D. $\qquad\square$

By the above Remark, also $Opt_{\mathrm{MC}}(f(\Gamma)) = Opt_{kLFS}(\Gamma)$ for any $\Gamma = \langle \Gamma_s, \Gamma_t \rangle$. Therefore, the property (s1) holds, and consequently the (f, g) is an S-reduction from kLFS to MAXCLIQUE.

Consider a pair (f', g') which for any $\Gamma \in \mathcal{I}(k\mathrm{LFS}) = \mathcal{I}(k\mathrm{U})$ satisfies equation $f'(\Gamma) = \overline{f(\Gamma)}$ and $g'(\Gamma, B) = [n] \backslash g(\Gamma, [n] \backslash B)$. The $f'(\Gamma)$ is a graph $\overline{G}$ with $V = [n]$, hence it is an instance of MINVERTEXCOVER ((r1) holds). By Fact 1, $B \in fso_{\mathrm{MVC}}(f'(\Gamma))$ if and only if $[n] \backslash B \in fso_{\mathrm{MC}}(f(\Gamma))$. By previously proven fact that (f, g) is reduction, $g(\Gamma, [n] \backslash B) \in fso_{kLFS}(\Gamma)$. By definition of kU, we have the Fact 2. Thus, $[n] \backslash g(\Gamma, [n] \backslash B) \in fso_{kU}(\Gamma)$. Hence (r2) holds.

By condition (s2) for an S-reduction (f, g) we have that $cost_{kLFS}(\Gamma, g(\Gamma, [n] \backslash B)) = cost_{\mathrm{MC}}(f(\Gamma), [n] \backslash B) = n - |B|$ if $[n] \backslash B$ is a clique of $f(\Gamma)$. $cost_{kLFS}(\Gamma, g(\Gamma, [n] \backslash B)) = cost_{kLFS}(\Gamma, [n] \backslash g'(\Gamma, B)) = n - cost_{kU}(\Gamma, g'(\Gamma, B))$. The second equation is due to Fact 2. By Fact 1 we have $cost_{\mathrm{MC}}(f(\Gamma), [n] \backslash B) = n - cost_{\mathrm{MVC}}(f'(\Gamma), B)$, and consequently $cost_{\mathrm{MVC}}(f'(\Gamma), B) = cost_{kU}(\Gamma, g'(\Gamma, B))$ for $B \in fso_{\mathrm{MVC}}(\overline{G})$. Thus, (s2) holds for (f', g').

The minimum vertex cover B for graph $\overline{G}$ corresponds to $V \backslash B$ which is a maximum clique of G. Hence $Opt_{\mathrm{MC}}(f(\Gamma)) = n - Opt_{\mathrm{MVC}}(f'(\Gamma))$. Similarly, one can conclude that, if $[n] \backslash B \in fso_{kLFS}(\Gamma)$ is a maximum feasible solution, then B is a minimum solution of the kU problem for instance Γ. Hence, $Opt_{kLFS}(\Gamma) = n - Opt_{kU}(\Gamma)$. Thus, we have (s1) for (f', g'). This ends the reasoning leading to conclusion that (f', g') is an S-reduction from kU to MINVERTEXCOVER. $\square$

An *S*-reduction is stronger than *L*-reduction, *AP*-reduction and *PTAS*-reduction [8], that are often used for proving the membership to the *APX* class. Furthermore, if $A \leq_S B$ and B is approximable with some factor, then A is approximable with the same factor. Therefore, by Lemma 1 and the fact that there exists 2-approximation algorithm for MINVERTEXCOVER [27], we obtain that there is 2-approximation algorithm for the kU problem.

For verification, if a set $Y \subseteq [n]$ is a feasible solution for $x \in \mathcal{I}(k\mathrm{LFS})$ one can iteratively check if consecutive elements of σ_s^i are in Y. These iterations put consecutive elements to the new sequence τ_s^i only if they are in Y. The same can be done for σ_t^i, obtaining τ_t^i for all $i \in [k]$. At the end we check if $\tau_t^i = \tau_s^i$ for each $i \in [k]$. This can be implemented within $O(kn \log(|Y|))$. Then feasible solutions are verifiable in polynomial time. Since $cost_{kLFS}(\Gamma, Y) = |Y|$, $cost_{kLFS}$ is obviously computable in polynomial time. As a conclusion we obtain:

Theorem 1. *The kLFS problem is an optimization problem in NP for any $k \in [n]$. For any $k \in [n]$ there exists 2-approximation algorithm for kU.*

Lemma 2. *There exists an S-reduction from the* MAXCLIQUE *problem to the* nLFS *problem and from the* MINVERTEXCOVER *problem to nU problem.*

Proof. Let $G = (V, E)$ be an undirected graph, $V = [n]$, $\Gamma = \langle \Gamma_s, \Gamma_t \rangle$, where $\Gamma_s = (\sigma_s^1, \ldots, \sigma_s^n)$ and $\Gamma_t = (\sigma_t^1, \ldots, \sigma_t^n)$. Let $V^{-i} = V \backslash \{i\}$ and let $P^i = \{j \in V^{-i} \mid jEi\}$ and $N^i = \{j \in V^{-i} \mid \neg jEi\}$ split V^{-i} into two disjoint sets.

Here and in the rest of the paper we will be using some additional notation. For two given finite sequences a and b, their concatenation is denoted by $a \cdot b$. By (i), we denote a sequence that consists of a single element i. A sequence a is *non repeating* if no element in a occurs twice (or more). Let, for each $i \in [n]$, a_i and b_i be increasing non repeating sequences of all elements from N^i and P^i, respectively. Then, we define σ_s^i as $(i) \cdot a_i \cdot b_i$ and σ_t^i as $a_i \cdot (i) \cdot b_i$, $i \in [n]$.

Remark 3. Set K is a clique in the graph G iff K is feasible solution of $\langle \Gamma_s, \Gamma_t \rangle$.

Proof. We consider two cases (1) if $i \in K$ and (2) if $i \notin K$. A *conditional split* of K is defined to be a pair of disjoint sets K_i^+ and K_i^- that satisfy the following conditions: (1) $K_i^+ = K \cap P^i$, (2) $K_i^- = K \cap N^i$.

We will denote by α_i the non repeating sequence of all elements from K_i^- in the increasing order, by β_i the non repeating sequence of all elements from K_i^+ in the increasing order. It is easily seen that depending on if $i \in K$ or $i \notin K$ the join sequence $\alpha_i \cdot \beta_i$ has either $|K| - 1$ or $|K|$ elements.

Let K be a clique. Notice that in case $i \in K$ the sequence α_i is empty and β_i consists of elements from $K \backslash \{i\}$. In this case σ_s^i contains subsequence $(i) \cdot \beta_i$. In permutation σ_s^i element i appears as the first element of the sequence. Since β_i contains elements from K_i^+ and K_i^+, by definition, is a subset of P^i and both b_i and β_i have the same order, then β_i is subsequence of b_i. Permutation σ_t^i contains subsequence $(i) \cdot b_i$ in this case. Thus σ_t^i also contains subsequence $(i) \cdot \beta_i$. Hence both permutations σ_s^i and σ_t^i contain subsequence $(i) \cdot \beta_i$. The common subsequence $(i) \cdot \beta_i$ is K-induced subsequence for both σ_s^i and σ_t^i.

Consider the case $i \notin K$. In this case α_i does not have to be empty sequence, unlike it was previously. Since $K_i^- \subseteq N^i$ and $K_i^+ \subseteq P^i$, the sequence α_i is subsequence of a_i and β_i is subsequence of b_i. In permutation σ_s^i, element i precedes $a_i \cdot b_i$, $\alpha_i \cdot \beta_i$ is subsequence of $a_i \cdot b_i$. Hence $\alpha_i \cdot \beta_i$ is subsequence of $(i) \cdot a_i \cdot b_i = \sigma_s^i$. By definition $\sigma_t^i = a_i \cdot (i) \cdot b_i$. Hence $\alpha_i \cdot \beta_i$ is subsequence of σ_t^i. Thus $\alpha_i \cdot \beta_i$ is K-induced subsequence for σ_s^i and σ_t^i. Now, by definition, K is a feasible solution of $\langle \Gamma_s, \Gamma_t \rangle$.

Now assume that a set $K \subseteq [n]$ induces common subsequences for all (σ_s^i, σ_t^i), where $i \in [n]$. Let γ_i be a subsequence of $\sigma_s^i = (i) \cdot a_i \cdot b_i$ and $\sigma_t^i = a_i \cdot (i) \cdot b_i$. Let $i \in K$. It is easy to see that i is the first element of γ_i, hence $\gamma_i = (i) \cdot \gamma_i'$, where γ_i' is the subsequence of b_i. By definition of b_i all its elements are in P_i. This means that iEx for all $x \in \mathcal{D}(\gamma_i')$. Since $\mathcal{D}(\gamma_i') = K \backslash \{i\}$, for all different $i, x \in K$ iEx. This means that K is a clique in G. $\qquad\square$

Remark 4. If the size of maximal clique in graph G equals m, then $\langle \Gamma_s, \Gamma_t \rangle$ has no feasible solution of length greater than m.

Formally, the reduction is defined by the following equations: $f(G) = \Gamma$, $g(G, K) = K$. The (r1) follows immediately from definition of f. By Remark 3, for given a feasible solution K of the nLFS problem for instance Γ, $g(G, K)$ is feasible solution of the MaxClique problem for instance G. Thus (r2) holds. By Remarks 3 and 4, $Opt_{\mathrm{MC}}(G) = Opt_{n\mathrm{LFS}}(\Gamma)$. For MaxClique as well as nLFS cost of feasible solution is the cardinality of a set which constitutes the feasible solution. Hence $cost_{n\mathrm{LFS}}(\Gamma, K) = |K| = |g(G, K)| = cost_{\mathrm{MC}}(G, g(G, K))$. Thus (r2) holds and consequently (f, g) is an S-reduction from MaxClique to nLFS.

Let us define (f', g') by the following equations: $f'(\overline{G}) = f(G)$ and $g'(\overline{G}, K) = [n] \backslash g(G, [n] \backslash K)$ for any $[n] \backslash K \in fso_{n\mathrm{LFS}}(\Gamma)$. By definition of g and by Facts 2, 1, we obtain $g'(\overline{G}, K) = K$ for any $K \in fso_{n\mathrm{U}}(\Gamma)$ and $K \in fso_{\mathrm{MVC}}(\overline{G})$. Hence (r2) holds. Since $f'(\overline{G}) \in S_n^n$, (r1) holds. Hence (f', g') is a reduction from MinVertexCover to nU.

By condition (s2) for an S-reduction (f, g) we have that $cost_{n\mathrm{LFS}}(f(G), [n] \backslash K) = cost_{\mathrm{MC}}(G, g(G, [n] \backslash K)) = n - |K|$ if $[n] \backslash K \in fso_{n\mathrm{LFS}}(f(G))$. By Fact 2 we have that $cost_{n\mathrm{LFS}}(f(G), [n] \backslash K) = cost_{n\mathrm{LFS}}(f'(\overline{G}), [n] \backslash K) = n - cost_{n\mathrm{U}}(f'(\overline{G}), K)$ for $K \in fso_{n\mathrm{U}}(f'(\overline{G}))$. By Fact 1, we have $cost_{\mathrm{MC}}(G, g(G, [n] \backslash K)) = n - cost_{\mathrm{MVC}}(\overline{G}, [n] \backslash g(G, [n] \backslash K)) = n - cost_{\mathrm{MVC}}(\overline{G}, g'(\overline{G}, K))$. Therefore, $cost_{n\mathrm{U}}(f'(\overline{G}), K) = cost_{\mathrm{MVC}}(\overline{G}, g'(\overline{G}, K))$. Thus, (s2) holds for (f', g').

The minimum vertex cover K for graph $\overline{G}$ corresponds to $V \backslash K$ which is a maximum clique of G. Hence $Opt_{\mathrm{MC}}(G) = n - Opt_{\mathrm{MVC}}(\overline{G})$. Similarly, one can conclude that, if $[n] \backslash B \in fso_{k\mathrm{LFS}}(\Gamma)$ is a maximum feasible solution, then K is a minimum feasible solution of the kU problem for instance Γ. Hence, $Opt_{k\mathrm{LFS}}(f(G)) = n - Opt_{k\mathrm{U}}(f'(\overline{G}))$. Thus, we have (s1) for (f', g'). $\square$

Theorem 2. *The* 2LFSD *and* 2UD *are NP-complete.*

Proof. By the existence of an *S*-reduction (Lemma 1) from kLFS to MaxClique and from kU to MinVertexCover, we get that for any $k \in [n]$, the kLFSD and the kUD are reducible to the Clique problem and the VertexCover problem, respectively, by polynomial time reductions. Hence kLFSD and kUD are in NP and in particular 2LFSD and 2UD are in NP.

It remains to show that 2LFSD is NP-hard. Let $\varphi = c_1 \wedge \ldots \wedge c_m$ be a boolean formula in $3CNF$ form, where $3CNF$ means that each clause c_i has three literals. Let $x_1, \ldots, x_n$ be all variables that occur in φ. Assume that variable x_i occurs α times in φ as a positive literal and β times as negative one. We construct polynomial time reduction by encoding a satisfiability of φ as 2LFSD. We introduce a new set of symbols $x_i^{(1)}, \ldots, x_i^{(\alpha)}, \neg x_i^{(1)}, \ldots, \neg x_i^{(\beta)}$, where $x_i^{(j)}$ stands for the j-th positive literal of x_i and symbol $\neg x_i^{(j)}$ stands for the j-th negative literal of x_i. Let $C_i = \{x_i^{(1)}, \ldots, x_i^{(\alpha)}, \neg x_i^{(1)}, \ldots, \neg x_i^{(\beta)}\}$ and $C = \bigcup_{i=1}^{n} C_i$. Let κ be a bijection from C onto $[3m]$. Create $\Gamma(\varphi) = \langle \Gamma_s, \Gamma_t \rangle = \langle (\sigma_s^1, \sigma_s^2), (\sigma_t^1, \sigma_t^2) \rangle$ which is an instance of 2LFSD having solution m if and only if φ is satisfiable.

The definition of $\Gamma(\varphi) = \langle \Gamma_s, \Gamma_t \rangle$ in the presented reduction should preclude the case that if Z induces common subsequences for (σ_s^1, σ_t^1) and (σ_s^2, σ_t^2) then both $\kappa(x_i^{(r)})$ and $\kappa(\neg x_i^{(p)})$ appear in Z for any $i \in [n]$ and r, p. It can be realized in the following way: Permutations σ_s^1 and σ_t^1 consist of blocks of substrings $A_i = \left(\kappa(x_i^{(1)}), \ldots, \kappa(x_i^{(\alpha)}) \right)$ and $B_i = \left(\kappa(\neg x_i^{(1)}), \ldots, \kappa(\neg x_i^{(\beta)}) \right)$. We define $\sigma_s^1 = A_1 B_1 A_2 B_2 \cdots A_n B_n$ and $\sigma_t^1 = B_1 A_1 B_2 A_2 \cdots B_n A_n$.

Remark 5. If a set Z induces a common subsequence of σ_s^1 and σ_t^1 then at most one of $\kappa(x_i^{(r)})$ and $\kappa(\neg x_i^{(p)})$ is in Z because (1) $\kappa(x_i^{(r)})$ appears before $\kappa(\neg x_i^{(p)})$ in σ_s^1, (2) $\kappa(x_i^{(r)})$ appears after $\kappa(\neg x_i^{(p)})$ in $,\sigma_t^1$ for any i, r, p.

Let $c_j = x_{j1}^{(a)} \vee x_{j2}^{(b)} \vee x_{j3}^{(c)}$ be the j-th clause in φ, where $x_{j1}^{(a)}, x_{j2}^{(b)}, x_{j3}^{(c)}$ are literals. Define a permutation σ_s^2 as concatenation of blocks $E_1 E_2 \cdots E_m$ where $E_j = (\kappa(x_{j1}^{(a)}), \kappa(x_{j2}^{(b)}), \kappa(x_{j3}^{(c)}))$ and $\sigma_t^2 = E_1^R E_2^R \cdots E_m^R$, where $E_j^R = (\kappa(x_{j3}^{(c)}), \kappa(x_{j2}^{(b)}), \kappa(x_{j1}^{(a)}))$.

Remark 6. If a set Z induces a common subsequence of σ_s^2 and σ_t^2 then $|Z| \leq m$. If $|Z| \geq m + 1$, there would exist literals x, y belonging to the same clause such that $\kappa(x), \kappa(y) \in Z$. Literals $\kappa(x), \kappa(y)$ that occur in σ_s^2, appears in reverted order in σ_t^2. Hence Z does not induce a common subsequence of σ_s^2 and σ_t^2.

Any choice of literals, one from every clause forms the sequence, which is *witness of satisfiability* of φ if the set of chosen literals is consistent.

Remark 7. Assume that φ is satisfiable and the set $\{y_1, \ldots, y_m\}$ is a witness of its satisfiability. Then the sequence $(\kappa(y_1), \kappa(y_2), \cdots, \kappa(y_m))$ is a common subsequence of σ_s^2 and σ_t^2.

Note that if $y_1, \ldots, y_m$ is a witness of satisfiability then $\{\kappa(y_1), \kappa(y_2), \ldots \kappa(y_m)\}$ induces a common subsequence of σ_s^1 and σ_t^1. Indeed, by consistency of $\{y_1, \ldots, y_m\}$ there is no i, j, k such that $\kappa(y_i)$ occurs in A_k and $\kappa(y_j)$ occurs in B_k. Hence, $\kappa(y_i)$ and $\kappa(y_j)$ occur in the same order in both σ_s^1 and σ_t^1. Therefore, by Remark 7, $\{\kappa(y_1), \kappa(y_2), \ldots \kappa(y_m)\}$ induces common subsequences for pairs (σ_s^1, σ_t^1) and (σ_s^2, σ_t^2) of length m. By Remarks 5 and 6 the lengths of induced subsequences are not greater than m. Thus, the induced subsequences are of the maximal length.

By the above reduction φ is satisfiable iff the solution of $\langle \Gamma_s, \Gamma_t \rangle$, as the instance of the the 2UD problem is of the size not greater than $2m$. Hence 2UD is NP-hard. $\qquad\square$

For a given boolean formula φ in $3CNF$, the MAX-3SAT problem consists of finding a maximal possible number of clauses that can be satisfied in φ. Note that the reduction, that were presented in the previous proof is an S-reduction from the MAX-3SAT problem to the 2LFS problem. In the reduction we use the $3CNF$ with exactly three literals in every clause. It has been proved in [12] that MAX-3SAT is inapproximable with factor better than $\frac{7}{8}$. Since our reduction is an S-reduction also 2LFS cannot have a better approximation. Inapproximability result can easily be generalized to the kLFS for $k \geq 2$, because it is enough to repeat construction with $\sigma_s^j = \sigma_s^2$ for $j > 2$.

Analyzing the same reduction and using the same inapproximability result [12], it can be proven that there is no approximation for the 2U problem with an approximation factor better than $\frac{41}{40}$ unless $P = NP$.

Theorem 3. *There is no polynomial time approximation algorithm for the* 2U *problem with approximation factor better than* $1 + \frac{1}{40}$ *unless* $P = NP$.

Proof. Assume that there is a polynomial time approximation algorithm $\mathcal{A}$ for the 2U problem with the factor $1 + \frac{1}{40} - \epsilon$ for some $\frac{1}{40} > \epsilon > 0$. For a $3CNF$ formula φ, let $\mathcal{A}(\Gamma(\varphi))$ be a solution for the instance $\Gamma(\varphi) = \langle \Gamma_s, \Gamma_t \rangle$ of the 2U problem. Denote by $|\mathcal{A}(\Gamma(\varphi))|$ the size of the set returned by $\mathcal{A}$ on the input $\Gamma(\varphi)$.

Let $2m + k$ be the cardinality of the optimal solution for instance $\Gamma(\varphi)$ of the 2U problem, where m is the number of clauses in φ which was encoded in $\Gamma(\varphi)$ in the proof of Theorem 2. $2m + k$ is the size of the smallest feasible solution for $\Gamma(\varphi)$ if and only if $m - k$ is the maximal number of clauses that can be satisfied in φ. Let $opt_\varphi = m - k$ We have that

$$|\mathcal{A}(\Gamma(\varphi))| \leq (2\,m + k)\left(1 + \frac{1}{40} - \epsilon\right) \tag{3}$$

Let $\mathcal{A}'(\Gamma(\varphi))$ be an algorithm that executes $\mathcal{A}$ on the input $\Gamma(\varphi)$ and returns $[3m]\backslash Z$, whereas $\mathcal{A}$ returns Z on the input $\Gamma(\varphi)$. $[3m]\backslash Z$ is a feasible solution for instance $\Gamma(\varphi)$ of the 2LFS problem as well as the $\kappa^{-1}(Z)$ is the satisfiablity witness for at least $|[3m]\backslash Z|$ clauses of φ. Since $\mathcal{A}(\Gamma(\varphi)) = Z$ and by inequality (3) we have:

$$|\mathcal{A}'(\Gamma(\varphi))| = |[3\,m]\backslash Z| \geq (m - k) - \left(\frac{1}{40} - \epsilon\right)(2\,m + k) \tag{4}$$

If φ is a formula in the $3CNF$ form, then there exists an assignment that satisfies at least half of the φ clauses.

$$\left(\frac{1}{8} - \frac{2}{40}\right)(m - k) \geq \left(\frac{1}{8} - \frac{2}{40}\right)\left(\frac{1}{2}m\right) = \frac{3}{40}\left(\frac{1}{2}m\right) \geq \frac{3}{40}k \tag{5}$$

We use this fact to obtain inequalities (5). Indeed, $m - k$ is the maximal number of clauses of φ which can be satisfied, then $m - k \geq 1/2m$ and and also $1/2m \geq k$. Therefore

$$(m - k) - \frac{1}{40}(2\,m + k) \geq \frac{7}{8}(m - k) \tag{6}$$

It is easy to note that

$$\epsilon(2\,m + k) \geq \epsilon(m - k) \tag{7}$$

Adding inequalities (6) and (7) by sides we obtain:

$$(m - k) - \left(\frac{1}{40} - \epsilon\right)(2\,m + k) \geq \left(\frac{7}{8} + \epsilon\right)(m - k) = \left(\frac{7}{8} + \epsilon\right)opt_\varphi \tag{8}$$

The left side of inequality (8) is equal to the right side of inequality (4). Thus $|\mathcal{A}'(\Gamma(\varphi))| = |[3m]\backslash Z| \geq \left(\frac{7}{8} + \epsilon\right) opt_\varphi$.

We have shown that $\mathcal{A}'$ is an approximation algorithm for MAX-3SAT with an approximation factor $\frac{7}{8} + \epsilon$ for some $\frac{1}{40} > \epsilon > 0$. By the result from [12] it is possible only under assumption that $P = NP$. Hence our assumption about the existence of an approximation algorithm with a factor $1 + \frac{1}{40}$ for the 2U problem can be true only under the assumption that $P = NP$. $\qquad\square$

Let $\mathcal{A}_{LFS}$ be an approximation algorithm solving nLFS. Since MAXCLIQUE $\leq_S n$LFS (Lemma 2), there exists an S-reduction (f, g) where both f and g are polynomially computable. We have shown previously, that the g can be defined by equation $g(G, C) = C$. This means, that if $\mathcal{A}_{LFS}(\Gamma)$ returns C, which is feasible solution of $\Gamma = f(G)$, then C is a clique in G. Since optimal solutions of G and $f(G)$ have the same costs, the algorithm which simply returns $g(G, C)$ solves the MAXCLIQUE problem and has the same approximation factor as $\mathcal{A}_{LFS}$. By [11] and [28] results, which establishes that approximation of MAXCLIQUE within factor $n^{1-\epsilon}$ is NP-hard, we obtain the following nonapproximability theorem:

Theorem 4. *For $\epsilon > 0$, the approximation of nLFS within $n^{1-\epsilon}$ is NP-hard.*

Since there is an S-reduction from MINVERTEXCOVER to nU (by Lemma 2), the lower bound for the approximation factor of MINVERTEXCOVER is also the lower bound for the approximation factor of nU. As a conclusion from [16] result we obtain:

Theorem 5. *There exists no polynomial time $(2 - \epsilon)$-approximation algorithm for the nU problem unless The Unique Game Conjecture is not true.*

In the proof of the next theorem, we develop approach for permutations in S_n^k, analogous to the approach presented in [21], Chap. 13, Lemma 13.1 for graphs. This approach uses directed product of graphs to prove inapproximability of the MAXCLIQUE problem with an approximation factor better than $\sqrt{n}$.

Theorem 6. *For any constant $c \in \mathbb{N}$, it is NP-hard to approximate the $n^{1/c}$LFS problem within $n^{1-\epsilon}$, for any $\epsilon > 0$.*

Proof. Let c and ν be integers. Assume that $n = \nu^c$ and $c > 1$. Let $\Gamma = \langle(\sigma_s^1, \ldots, \sigma_s^\nu), (\sigma_t^1, \ldots, \sigma_t^\nu)\rangle$, where $\sigma_s^i, \sigma_t^i \in S_\nu$. For $i \in [\nu]$, let $f_i^c : [\nu^{c-1}] \mapsto [i\nu^{c-1}]\backslash[(i-1)\nu^{c-1}]$ satisfy equation $f_i^c(k) = (i-1)\nu^{c-1} + k$. Let $\lambda = (a_1, \ldots, a_i) \in S_{\nu^{c-1}}$. If $[\nu^{c-1}]$ is the domain of f and the function is total over its domain, we write $f(\lambda)$ to denote a tuple $(f(a_1), f(a_2), \ldots, f(a_i))$.

We will denote by $\odot$ the generalized concatenation of sequences. If $a = (i_1, i_2, \ldots, i_\alpha) \in S_\alpha$ is a sequence of indexes, $\lambda_1, \lambda_2, \ldots, \lambda_\alpha$ are finite sequences, then $\underset{k \to a}{\odot} \lambda_k$ denotes a concatenation $\lambda_{i_1} \cdot \lambda_{i_2} \cdots \lambda_{i_\alpha}$.

We define $\Lambda = T^c = \langle(\lambda_s^1,\ldots,\lambda_s^\nu), (\lambda_t^1,\ldots,\lambda_t^\nu)\rangle$ recursively using Γ and $T^{c-1} = \langle(\tau_s^1,\ldots,\tau_s^\nu),(\tau_t^1,\ldots,\tau_t^\nu)\rangle$, where $\tau_s^i, \tau_t^i \in S_{\nu^{c-1}}$. For $c = 1$, $T^c = \Gamma$. The $\lambda_s^i, \lambda_t^i \in S_{\nu^c}$ are defined by the following equations

$$\lambda_s^i = \bigodot_{k\to\sigma_s^i} f_k^c(\tau_s^i) \qquad \lambda_t^i = \bigodot_{k\to\sigma_t^i} f_k^c(\tau_t^i).$$

Remark 8. Assume that Γ has a feasible solution of size m and T^{c-1} has a solution of size m^{c-1}. Then Λ has a solution of size m^c.

Proof. Let $B^{c-1} \subseteq [\nu^{c-1}]$ be a set, which induces common subsequence for all (τ_s^x, τ_t^x). Let $B \subseteq [\nu]$ be a set, which induces common subsequence for all (σ_s^x, σ_t^x). Any pair of different elements $i, j \in B$ appears in the same order in σ_s^x and σ_t^x for all $x \in [\nu]$. This means that i occurs in the earlier position than j in σ_t^x if and only if i occurs in the earlier position than j in σ_s^x. Similar remark holds for all pairs $(\tau_s^x, \tau_t^x) \in S_{\nu^{c-1}}^2$ and $k, l \in [\nu^{c-1}]$.

We claim that $B^c = \{(j-1)\nu^{c-1} + k \mid j \in B, k \in B^{c-1}\}$ is solution of Λ. On the contrary, suppose that B^c does not induce common subsequence of all pairs $(\lambda_s^x, \lambda_t^x)$. Thus we may find y such that B^c-induced sequences ρ and γ, for λ_s^y and λ_t^y, and $\rho \neq \gamma$, respectively. Then there are elements $(i-1)\nu^{c-1} + l$ and $(j-1)\nu^{c-1} + k$ that cause first difference in ρ and γ. Thus either $i \neq j$ or $i = j$. For the first case, by definition of λ_s^y and λ_t^y, without loss of generality, one can assume that in the sequence $\bigodot_{r\to\sigma_s^y} f_r^c(\tau_s^y)$, element $(i-1)\nu^{c-1}+l$ appears before element $(j-1)\nu^{c-1} + k$ and in the $\bigodot_{r\to\sigma_t^y} f_r^c(\tau_t^y)$ they are in the opposite order. This holds for any $l, k \in [\nu]$ because all elements from $f_i^c([\nu^{c-1}])$ appear before elements from $f_j^c([\nu^{c-1}])$ if i appears before j in σ_s^y. Elements i, j are in the opposite order in σ_t^y. By definition of B^c; $i, j \in B$ and we assumed at the beginning that B induces common subsequence in all (σ_s^x, σ_t^x), in particular in (σ_s^y, σ_t^y). This is contradiction.

In the case $i = j$, element $(i-1)\nu^{c-1} + l$ appears before $(i-1)\nu^{c-1} + k$ in $f_i^c(\tau_s^y)$ and in the $f_i^c(\tau_t^y)$ they are in the opposite order. This means that l, k are in different orders in τ_s^y and τ_t^y. By definition of B^c, $k, l \in B^{c-1}$, but it is assumed B^{c-1} induces common subsequence for all (τ_s^x, τ_t^x), in particular in (τ_s^y, τ_t^y). This is contradiction. $\qquad\square$

Define auxiliary functions $block^c$ and $inblock^c$ of type $[n = \nu^{c+1}] \mapsto [\nu]$ and $[\nu^{c+1}] \mapsto [\nu^c]$, respectively: $block^c(s) = ((s-1) \div \nu^c)+1$, $inblock^c(s) = ((s-1) \bmod \nu^c)+1$. For a given $J \subseteq [\nu^c]$ let $W^c(J) := \{block^{c-1}(r) \mid r \in J\}$, $H^c(l, J) := \{inblock^{c-1}(r) \mid r \in J$ and $l = block^{c-1}(r)\}$, $\alpha^c(J) = \max\{|H^c(l, J)| \mid l \in [\nu]\}$, $\beta^c(J) := \max\{l \mid |H^c(l, J)| = \alpha^c(J)\}$.

Remark 9. Assume that $c > 1$ and Λ has a feasible solution J. $W^c(J)$ is feasible solution of Γ and $H^c(\beta^c(J), J)$ is feasible solution of T^{c-1}. Moreover, T^{c-1} has a feasible solution of the size at least $|J|^{(c-1)/c}$ of the form $H^c(\beta^c(J), J)$, or Γ has solution of size $|J|^{1/c}$ of the form $W^c(J)$.

Proof. Assume that there is $J \subseteq [\nu^c]$ of the size m^c that is solution of Λ. $W^c(J)$ is a set which is feasible solution of Γ and $H^c(l, J)$ is feasible solution of T^{c-1}. In particular if l be chosen to make $H^c(l, J)$ of maximal size then l be equal $\beta^c(J)$.

By definition of W^c, for any different $p, r \in W^c(J)$ there are $\pi = (p-1)\nu^{c-1} + k, \rho = (r-1)\nu^{c-1} + l \in J$. By definition of λ_s^i, λ_t^i, if π and ρ appear in the same order in λ_s^i, λ_t^i then p and r are in the same order in σ_s^i and σ_t^i. Thus, indeed $W^c(J)$ is a solution of Γ.

For any $a, b \in H^c(l, J)$, there are $\pi, \rho \in J$ such that $a = inblock^{c-1}(\pi)$, $b = inblock^{c-1}(\rho)$, $l = block^{c-1}(\pi)$ and $l = block^{c-1}(\rho)$. By definition of $block^{c-1}$ and $inblock^{c-1}$, $\pi = (l-1)\nu^{c-1} + a$ and $\rho = (l-1)\nu^{c-1} + b$. For all $i \in [\nu]$, numbers π and ρ occur in the same order in λ_s^i and λ_t^i. Sequences $f_l^c(\tau_s^i)$ and $f_l^c(\tau_t^i)$ are substrings of λ_s^i and λ_t^i, respectively. Moreover π and ρ occur in $f_l^c(\tau_s^i)$ and $f_l^c(\tau_t^i)$ in the same order. It means that, for each $i \in [\nu]$, a and b appear in the same order in τ_s^i and τ_t^i (by definition of f_l^c). Thus, if $a, b \in H^c(l, J)$, then a and b appear in the same order in τ_s^i and τ_t^i. Therefore, for all $l \in [\nu]$, $H^c(l, J)$ is feasible solution of T^{c-1}.

Let $R(l) = \{s \in J \mid inblock^{c-1}(s) \in H^c(l, J)\}$. First, notice that $J = \bigcup_{l \in W^c(J)} R(l)$ and $R(l)$ are pairwise disjoint sets. It is easy to see if $|W^c(J)| < |J|^{1/c}$, then there exists l such that $|R(l)| \geq |J|^{(c-1)/c}$. In case $W^c(J) < |J|^{1/c}$, $R(\beta^c(J)) \geq |J|^{(c-1)/c}$, this implies that $H^c(\beta^c(J), J) \geq |J|^{(c-1)/c}$. $\square$

Now we will show, that if there exists a polynomial algorithm solving the $n^{1/c}$LFS problem, with an approximation factor within $O(n^{1-\epsilon})$ for some $0 < \epsilon < 1$, then there exists a polynomial time algorithm that approximates νLFS(ν) with factor $\nu^{1-\gamma}$ for some $0 < \gamma < 1$. Assume the existence of a polynomial time algorithm $\mathcal{C}$ that approximates $n^{1/c}$LFS with a factor $n^{1-\epsilon}$ and let the polynomial be denoted by p. Approximation algorithm $\mathcal{B}$ for νLFS(ν) works as follows: 1. Create $\Lambda = \langle (\lambda_s^1, \ldots, \lambda_s^\nu), (\lambda_t^1, \ldots, \lambda_t^\nu) \rangle$ as it was defined previously. 2. Run algorithm $\mathcal{C}$. Assume that it has returned the set $J \subseteq [n]$. 3. Execute recursive procedure ExtractLFS(Λ, c, J).

One can prove, by induction on c, that for input $\Lambda = T^c$ and its solution J the procedure ExtractLFS(Λ, c, J) returns a solution of Γ of size not less than $|J|^{1/c}$. In the inductive proof we use Remark 9 and the fact that $T^1 = \Gamma$ (for the first step of induction). For $c = 1$, ExtractLFS returns $J_1 = J^{1/1} = J$. Suppose that the following is true:

Assumption 1. *Let J be a solution of νLFS(ν^{c-1}) for instance T^{c-1}. Then* ExtractLFS$(T^{c-1}, c-1, J)$ *returns a feasible solution of Γ of size not less than $|J|^{1/(c-1)}$.*

By Remark 9, $W^c(J)$ is feasible solution of Γ. If its size is at least $|J|^{1/c}$ it is returned by ExtractLFS(T^c, c, J) in the fifth line. Otherwise T^{c-1} has feasible solution $H^c(\beta^c(J), J)$ of the size not less than $|J|^{(c-1)/c}$. By the inductive hypothesis ExtractLFS$(T^{c-1}, c-1, J^{(c-1)/c})$ returns a feasible solution for Γ of the size not less than $|J|^{(c-1)/c \cdot 1/c-1} = |J|^{1/c}$. This ends the inductive step.

Algorithm 1. Procedure $\textsc{ExtractLFS}(\Lambda_c, c, J_c)$

1: **if** c=1 **then**
2: **return** J_c
3: **if** $W^c(J_c) \geq |J_c|^{1/c}$ **then**
4: **return** $W^c(J_c)$;
5: **else**
6: $J_{c-1} = H^c(\beta^c(J_c), J_c)$;
7: $\Lambda_{c-1} = T^{c-1}$;
8: **return** $\textsc{ExtractLFS}(\Lambda_{c-1}, c-1, J_{c-1})$;

Corollary 1. *If Λ has a feasible solution of size $|J|$, then Γ has a feasible solution of size at least $|J|^{1/c}$.*

The time complexity of the presented reduction depends on the time complexity of the T^c construction, the complexity of $\textsc{ExtractLFS}(T^c, c, J)$ and $\mathcal{C}$. The complexity of the transformation T^{c-1} into T^c can be estimated by $O(\nu^2 \cdot \nu^{c-1})$. The cost of building $f_k^c(\tau)$ costs $O(\nu^{c-1})$ because it depends on the length of τ element. This cost is multiplied by $O(\nu)$ in the process of the concatenation of $f_k^c(\tau)$ components and the whole outcome is created ν times during λ components construction. Since the whole construction starts from $\Gamma = T^1$ the overall cost is $\Sigma_{i=2}^c O(\nu^{i+1})$. This is $O(\nu^{c+1})$ assuming that c is a constant. The complexity of $\textsc{ExtractLFS}(\Lambda, c, J)$ depends on how $\alpha^c(J)$, $W^c(J)$, and $H^c(\beta^c(J), J)$ are determined. The rough estimation of the upper bound for those costs is $O(\nu^{2c})$. The complexity of $\mathcal{C}$ is $O(p(\nu^{c+1}))$. The complexity of all three steps of the reduction is $O(p(\nu^{2c})) = O(p^2(n))$. We assume that degree of p is at least 1.

Now let estimate the approximation factor. By the assumption about the approximation factor of $\mathcal{C}$, we have $\frac{|Opt_{n^{1/c}\mathrm{LFS}}(\Lambda)|}{|\mathcal{C}(\Lambda)|} \leq n^{1-\epsilon} = \nu^{c(1-\epsilon)}$ for any instance Λ. The outcome of algorithm $\mathcal{B}$ satisfies $|\mathcal{B}(\Gamma)| \geq |\mathcal{C}(\Lambda)|^{1/c} = |J|^{1/c}$ But also by Remarks 8 and Corollary 1 the following equation holds $|Opt_{\nu\mathrm{LFS}}(\Gamma)| = |Opt_{n^{1/c}\mathrm{LFS}}(\Lambda)|^{1/c}$. Therefore $\frac{|Opt_{\nu\mathrm{LFS}}(\Gamma)|}{|\mathcal{B}(\Gamma)|} \leq \left(\frac{|Opt_{n^{1/c}\mathrm{LFS}}(\Lambda)|}{|\mathcal{C}(\Lambda)|}\right)^{1/c} \leq \left(\nu^{c(1-\epsilon)}\right)^{1/c} = \nu^{1-\epsilon}$. It means that the νLFS problem has a polynomial time approximation algorithm with factor $\nu^{1-\epsilon}$. This contradicts Theorem 4. $\square$

Theorem 7. *For any constant $c < n$, there exists no polynomial time $(2 - \epsilon)$-approximation algorithm for the $n^{1/c}\mathrm{U}$ problem unless The Unique Game Conjecture is not true.*

Proof. (Sketch). Let $n = \nu^c$. Instances of the $\nu\mathrm{U}$ problem are of the form $\Gamma = \langle \Gamma_1, \Gamma_2 \rangle$, where $\Gamma_1, \Gamma_2 \in S_\nu^\nu$. Consider the following reduction from $\nu\mathrm{U}$ to $n^{1/c}\mathrm{U}$. For a given instance $\Gamma = \langle (\sigma_s^1, \ldots, \sigma_s^\nu), (\sigma_t^1, \ldots, \sigma_t^\nu) \rangle$ of $\nu\mathrm{U}$, let

$$\lambda_s^i = \bigodot_{k \to (1, \ldots, \nu^{c-1})} g_k(\sigma_s^i) \qquad \lambda_t^i = \bigodot_{k \to (1, \ldots, \nu^{c-1})} g_k(\sigma_t^i).$$

In this proof, $g_k(p) = (k-1)\nu + p$. The $\Lambda = \langle(\lambda_s^1,\ldots,\lambda_s^\nu),(\lambda_t^1,\ldots,\lambda_t^\nu)\rangle \in S_n^\nu$ is an instance of $n^{1/c}\mathrm{U}$. It is easy to note, $\nu^{c-1}Opt_{\nu\mathrm{U}}(\Gamma) = Opt_{n^{1/c}\mathrm{U}}(\Lambda)$. If there exists algorithm $\mathcal{C}$, that returns a feasible solution J whose size is not greater than $(2-\epsilon)Opt_{n^{1/c}\mathrm{U}}(\Lambda)$. Then, for $M = \mathrm{argmin}_{k\in J}|H^2(k,J)|$ and $l \in M$, $H^2(l,J)$ is a feasible solution of Γ and $|H^2(l,J)| \leq (2-\epsilon)(Opt_{n^{1/c}\mathrm{U}}(\Gamma)/\nu^{c-1}) = (2-\epsilon)Opt_{\nu\mathrm{U}}(\Gamma)$. Consider algorithm $\mathcal{B}$ which constructs Λ from an input Γ, next executes $\mathcal{C}(\Lambda)$ receiving J as an output, and finally finds minimum set $H^2(l,J)$ for $l \in [\nu^{c-1}]$. That algorithm is an $(2-\epsilon)$-approximation algorithm which solves $\nu(U)$. By Theorem 5, this either contradicts of existence of such $\mathcal{C}$ or The Unique Game Conjecture [17] is not true. $\qquad\square$

Consider an S-reduction (f,g) from an optimization problem A to an optimization problem B. There is a canonical way to present standard parameterized version $p{-}A$ of an optimization problem A with parameter k: For given $x \in \mathcal{I}(A)$, decide whether $Opt_A(x) \geq k$ if $type = max$ or $Opt_A(x) \leq k$ if $type = min$. Formally, natural parametrization function κ_A is defined by $\kappa_A((x,k)) = k$, for $x \in \mathcal{I}(A)$ and $k \in \mathbb{N}$. Hence, set of instances for $p - A$ is $\mathcal{I}(A) \times \mathbb{N}$. Let R be defined by $R((x,k)) = (f(x),k)$ for $(x,k) \in \mathcal{I}(A) \times \mathbb{N}$.

Note that for any $(x,k) \in \mathcal{I}(p-A)$, $R((x,k)) \in \mathcal{I}(p-B)$. Moreover, for any (x,k), $(x,k) \in p - A$ iff $R((x,k)) \in p - B$, (p1) because $Opt_A(x) = Opt_B(x)$ by (s1). Computational complexity of the R is polynomial (p2) because depends on the polynomial complexity of the f on x and linear complexity on the parameter k. The function h defined as identity satisfies (p3) $\kappa_B(R((x,k))) \leq \kappa_A((x,k))$. Hence the R we have defined is an $fpt-$reduction from $p-A$ to $p-B$. Therefore, $p - k\mathrm{LFS} \leq_{fpt} p - \mathrm{MaxClique}$ and $p - k\mathrm{U} \leq_{fpt} p - \mathrm{VertexCover}$. Since $\mathrm{MaxClique}$ is in $W[1]$, $\mathrm{VertexCover}$ is in FPT and both parameterized classes $W[1]$ and FPT are closed under fpt-reductions [9] we obtain:

Theorem 8. *The $p-k\mathrm{LFS}$ problem is in $W[1]$ class for any $k \in [n]$. The $p-k\mathrm{U}$ problem belongs to the FPT class for any $k \in [n]$.*

Theorem 9. *For any constant c, the $p - n^{1/c}\mathrm{LFS}$ problem is $W[1]$-hard.*

Proof. (Sketch). By Lemma 2 $\mathrm{MaxClique} \leq_S n\mathrm{LFS}$ and consequently holds $\mathrm{p\text{-}MaxClique} \leq_{fpt} p-n\mathrm{LFS}$. Since the $p - \mathrm{Clique}$ is $W[1]$-hard then $p-n\mathrm{LFS}$ is $W[1]$-hard under fpt-reductions.

In the proof of Theorem 6 we defined polynomial time reduction r which for a given instance Γ of $\nu\mathrm{LFS}$ returns an instance Λ of $n^{1/c}\mathrm{LFS}$, where $n = \nu^c$. Let R be defined by $R((x,k)) = (r(x),k^c)$, for all $x \in \mathcal{I}(\nu\mathrm{LFS})$. By Remark 9 and Corollary 1, the Λ has solution of the size m^c iff the Γ has solution of the size m. Therefore, $Opt_{\nu\mathrm{LFS}}(x) \geq k$ iff $Opt_{n^{1/c}\mathrm{LFS}}(r(x)) \geq k^c$ (p1). The $r(x)$ and k^c are polynomially computable with respect to (x,k), then (p2) holds. In order to satisfy (p3), the h is defined as $h(k) = k^c$. Thus $p - \nu\mathrm{LFS} \leq_{fpt} p - n^{1/c}\mathrm{LFS}$. $\qquad\square$

4 Conclusions

In this paper, we formulated a multi-dimensional analogue of Ulam's metric and provided foundational results for its hardness, approximability, and parameterized complexity, as a basis for future research in this area.

Given hardness results for $k \geq 2$ and possible applications, e.g., in the rectangles packing problems, design of efficient algorithms computing U_k, the parameterized complexity of kLFS and the analogue of Ulam's second question will constitute our future research directions.

Acknowledgments. We would like to thank the anonymous referees of ICTAC and MFCS for their insightful comments and suggestions that improved the quality of the paper.

References

1. Aldous, D., Diaconis, P.: Longest increasing subsequences: from patience sorting to the Baik-Deift-Johansson theorem. Bull. Am. Math. Soc **36**, 413–432 (1999)
2. Baik, J., Deift, P., Johansson, K.: On the distribution of the length of the longest increasing subsequence of random permutations. J. Amer. Math. Soc. **4**, 1119–1178 (1999). https://doi.org/10.1090/S0894-0347-99-00307-0
3. Blum, C., Aguilera, M., Roli, A., Sampels, M.: Hybrid metaheuristics. an emerging approach to optimization. Stud. Comput. Intell. **114** (2008)
4. Blum, C.: Solving longest common subsequence problems via a transformation to the maximum clique problem. Comput. Oper. Res. **125**, 105089 (2021). https://doi.org/10.1016/j.cor.2020.105089
5. Blum, C., Roli, A.: Metaheuristics in combinatorial optimization: overview and conceptual comparison. ACM Comput. Surv. **35**(3), 268–308 (2003)
6. Bona, M.: Combinatorics of Permutations. CRC Press, Inc, Bocaraton (2004)
7. Corwin, I.: Commentary on "Longest increasing subsequences: from patience sorting to the Baik-Deift-Johansson theorem" by David Aldous and Persi Diaconis. Bull. Am. Math. Soc. **55**, 363–374 (2018). https://doi.org/10.1090/bull/1623
8. Crescenzi, P.: A short guide to approximation preserving reductions. In: Proceedings of the Twelfth Annual IEEE Conference on Computational Complexity, Ulm, Germany, June 24-27, 1997, pp. 262–273. IEEE Computer Society (1997). https://doi.org/10.1109/CCC.1997.612321
9. Flum, J., Grohe, M.: Parameterized Complexity Theory. Texts in Theoretical Computer Science. An EATCS Series, Springer (2006). https://doi.org/10.1007/3-540-29953-X
10. Fredman, M.: On computing the length of longest increasing subsequences. Discret. Math. **11**, 29–35 (1975)
11. Håstad, J.: Clique is hard to approximate within $n^{1-\epsilon}$. In: 37th Annual Symposium on Foundations of Computer Science, FOCS'96, Burlington, Vermont, USA, 14-16 October, 1996, pp. 627–636. IEEE Computer Society (1996). https://doi.org/10.1109/SFCS.1996.548522
12. Håstad, J.: Some optimal inapproximability results. J. ACM **48**(4), 798–859 (2001)
13. Hunt, J., Szymanski, T.: A fast algorithm for computing longest common subsequences. Commun. ACM **20**(5), 350–353 (1977)

14. Imahori, S., Yagiura, M., Ibaraki, T.: Improved local search algorithms for the rectangle packing problem with general spatial costs. Eur. J. Oper. Res. **167**, 48–67 (2005)
15. Kahng, A., Lienig, J., Markov, I., Hu, J.: VLSI Physical Design: From Graph Partitioning to Timing Closure. Springer, New York (2011)
16. Khot, S., Regev, O.: Vertex cover might be hard to approximate to within $2 - \epsilon$. J. Comput. Syst. Sci. **74**(3), 335–349 (2008). https://doi.org/10.1016/j.jcss.2007.06.019
17. Khot, S.: On the power of unique 2-prover 1-round games. In: Proceedings of the Thiry-Fourth Annual ACM Symposium on Theory of Computing, pp. 767–775. Association for Computing Machinery (2002). https://doi.org/10.1145/509907.510017
18. Kozik, A.: Handling precedence constraints in scheduling problems by the sequence pair representation. J. Comb. Optim. **33**(2), 445–472 (2015). https://doi.org/10.1007/s10878-015-9973-8
19. Kozik, A.: Scheduling under the network of temporo-spatial proximity relationships. Comput. Oper. Res. **84**, 106–115 (2017). https://doi.org/10.1016/j.cor.2017.03.011
20. Murata, H., Fujiyoshi, K., Nakatake, S., Kajitani, Y.: VLSI module placement based on rectangle-packing by the sequence pair. IEEE Trans. on CAD of ICs. **15**, 1518–1524 (1996)
21. Papadimitriou, C.: Computational complexity. Addison-Wesley, Reading, Massachusetts (1994)
22. Pinedo, M.: Scheduling. Theory, Algorithms, and Systems. Springer, New York (2012)
23. Romik, D.: The Surprising Mathematics of Longest Increasing Subsequences. Cambridge University Press, New York (2015)
24. Sheng, Y., Takahashi, A., Ueno, S.: 2-Stage Simulated Annealing with Crossover Operator for 3D-Packing Volume Minimization (2021)
25. Toth, P., Vigo, D.: The vehicle routing problem. Society for Industrial and Applied Mathematics, Philadelfia (2002)
26. Ulam, S.: Some ideas and prospects in biomathematics. Ann. Rev. Biophys. Bioeng. **1**, 277–292 (1972)
27. Vazirani, V.: Approximation Algorithms. Springer, Heidelberg (2001)
28. Zuckerman, D.: Linear degree extractors and the inapproximability of max clique and chromatic number. Theory Comput. **3**(1), 103–128 (2007). https://doi.org/10.4086/toc.2007.v003a006

The Spiral of Silence in Multi-agent Models for Opinion Formation

Jesús Aranda[1], Juan Francisco Díaz[1], David Gaona[1(✉)], and Frank Valencia[2,3]

[1] Universidad del Valle, Cali, Colombia
`david.gaona@correounivalle.edu.co`
[2] CNRS-LIX, École Polytechnique de Paris, Palaiseau, France
[3] Pontificia Universidad Javeriana Cali, Cali, Colombia

Abstract. We generalize the classic multi-agent DeGroot framework for opinion dynamics by incorporating the Spiral of Silence theory from political science, which posits that individuals may withhold their opinions when they perceive them to be in the minority. As in the original DeGroot model, the social network is represented as a weighted directed graph encoding how agents influence one another. However, agents holding minority opinions become *silent*, meaning they do not express their views.

We introduce two families of models. In *Silence Opinion Memoryless* (SOM$^-$) models, agents update their opinions by averaging those of their *non-silent* neighbors. In *Silence Opinion Memory-based* (SOM$^+$) models, agents average the opinions of *all* neighbors, but for silent ones, only the most recently expressed opinion is used. We show that SOM$^-$ models guarantee consensus on clique graphs but, unlike the classic DeGroot model, not on all strongly connected aperiodic graphs. For SOM$^+$ models, even cliques may fail to reach consensus, illustrating that even minimal memory can significantly affect opinion dynamics. Finally, we validate our models through large-scale simulations on small-world networks with over *two million* agents. The results support the Spiral of Silence theory and reveal inherent limitations to consensus in more realistic settings.

1   Introduction

Social networks play a significant role in *opinion formation* often having strong impact on polarization and the ability to reach *consensus*. Broadly, the dynamics of opinion formation in social networks involve users expressing their opinions, being exposed to the opinions of others, and potentially adapting their own views based on these interactions. Modeling these dynamics enables us to glean insights into how opinions form and spread within social networks.

The DeGroot framework [15] is one of the most prominent formalisms for opinion formation and consensus-building in social networks. In the models of this framework, a social network is represented as a weighted directed graph, where edges denote the

This work has been partially supported by the SGR project PROMUEVA (BPIN 2021000100160) under the supervision of Colombian Ministry of Science, Technology and Innovation (Minciencias) and by the CNRS project TOBIAS under the MITI interdisciplinary program.

degree to which individuals (i.e., *agents*) influence one another. Each agent holds an opinion, expressed as a value in $[0, 1]$, indicating their level of agreement with an underlying proposition (e.g., *"AI is a threat to humanity"*). Agents repeatedly update their opinions by taking the weighted average of their opinion differences with those who influence them (i.e., their *contacts*). There is empirical evidence validating the opinion formation through averaging of the model in controlled sociological experiments [10].

Consensus, i.e., convergence to a common opinion, is a central property in models of social learning and opinion formation [18]. In fact, difficulties in achieving consensus are a sign of a polarized society. A fundamental result for (classic) DeGroot models shows that agents converge to consensus if the influence graph is strongly connected and aperiodic. The DeGroot framework continues to be a focus of research for constructing frameworks for understanding opinion formation dynamics in social networks (e.g.,. [2–4,11,12,14,16,18,23,31,32]).

Nevertheless, the classic DeGroot formalism makes an assumption that could be overly constraining within social network contexts. It assumes that *all agents express their opinions at each time unit*. This assumption, which renders models tractable, may hold in some controlled scenarios as participants are often encouraged to express their views freely and consistently. However, in many real-world situations, some individuals may choose not to express their opinions due to personal choice or social pressure.

Indeed, the *Spiral of Silence* [24] is a well-established social theory that describes how individuals may be unwilling to express their opinions when they perceive themselves to be in the minority. This reluctance can lead to the *reinforcement of dominant views* within a social network. The theory asserts that individuals have a natural tendency to avoid social isolation and seek acceptance within their social groups. When people believe their opinions are unpopular or likely to be met with disapproval, they may opt to remain silent.

The relevance of the Spiral of Silence has been validated in social media environments. Large-scale empirical studies show that *social media platforms do not offer alternative spaces for minority opinion expression*, but instead reinforce silencing behaviors [19]. Meta-analyses confirm that the link between perceived opinion support and willingness to speak out remains strong in digital contexts [22]. Recent work finds that users are particularly sensitive to perceived disagreement among their online contacts, leading to self-censorship that can *spill over into offline behavior* [19,27]. During the COVID-19 pandemic, individuals frequently conformed publicly to dominant narratives while privately holding dissenting views, further illustrating the theory's enduring relevance [7]. These findings suggest that the dynamics of opinion suppression described by The Spiral of Silence not only persist but may be exacerbated in digital social networks.

In this paper, we generalize DeGroot models into a framework where agents may choose to remain silent at a given time following the Spiral of Silence. We consider two possibilities, leading to the two families of models described below.

Memoryless Framework SOM^-. In these models, silent agents are excluded from the opinion updates of the agents they would otherwise influence. Additionally, agents become silent at a given time if their views do not align with the majority of their non-silent contacts. This framework is called the *silence opinion memoryless* (SOM^-)

models, as the previous opinions of silent agents are not retained. This corresponds to a social scenario in which opinions (e.g., expressed in posts) are removed once they have been accessed.

Notice that ignoring silent agents at a given time unit amounts to removing certain edges from the influence graph at that time. Thus, a fundamental distinction from DeGroot models is that SOM^- models exhibit *dynamic influence* as edges may disappear and reappear during opinion evolution.

Memory-Based Framework SOM^-. In these models, agents choose to be silent if their opinion does not align with the most recent public opinions of *the majority of* their contacts. Unlike in SOM^+ models, silent agents *are not excluded* from the opinion updates of the agents they influence: when their current opinion is unknown, their most recent public opinion is taken into account in the update. This framework is called the *silence opinion memory-based* (SOM^+) models, as the most recent opinion of each agent is retained.

A property that distinguishes SOM^+ models from classic DeGroot models (and SOM^- models) is that the latter are *Markovian* processes: The next state depends on the current state but not the past states. Thus, SOM^+ models are *history-dependent* but with very limited memory; only most recent public opinions are remembered. We will show that this minimal notion of memory has an impact on consensus.

Contributions. We make the following theoretical and experimental contributions:

1. We generalize the DeGroot model to incorporate key aspects of the Spiral of Silence theory. To the best of our knowledge, this is the first extension of the DeGroot framework to do so.
2. We show that in SOM^-, convergence to consensus is guaranteed in clique graphs (i.e., fully connected graphs) with more than two agents. This result highlights that consensus remains possible under Spiral of Silence dynamics, even when silent agents are excluded from updates.
3. We prove that, unlike in the classical DeGroot model, SOM^- does not guarantee consensus in all strongly connected aperiodic graphs.
4. We demonstrate that SOM^+ fails to guarantee consensus even in clique graphs. This negative result underscores that the limited memory in SOM^+ can significantly alter the dynamics, making consensus harder to achieve under Spiral of Silence assumptions.
5. We validate our models through examples and large-scale simulations involving over *two million agents* on randomly generated networks with small-world properties typical of real social systems. These simulations support core claims of the Spiral of Silence theory, particularly the *reinforcement of dominant views in social networks*. The simulation code is available at: https://github.com/DavidGaona/belief_evolution_simulator.git

All in all, this paper highlights the impact of silence dynamics and memory on opinion formation and highlights the limitations of consensus in more nuanced models.

The paper is organized as follows: The new silence opinion models are introduced in Sect. 2. The study of consensus for these models is presented in Sect. 3. Our large-scale simulations and case studies emerging from our models and highlighting the spiral of silence effect are presented in Sect. 4. The concluding remarks are given in Sect. 5. For the sake of space, all proofs have been moved to the Appendix.

2 Opinion Models

In the DeGroot framework [15], each agent updates their opinion by taking the weighted average of the opinions of those who influence them. The models of this framework, however, do not account for the social phenomenon known as the Spiral of Silence [24], where some agents may choose to become or remain silent if their opinion does not align with the majority. As a result, their *current* opinion may not influence their contacts.

In this section, we generalize the DeGroot framework to take into account the Spiral of Silence. If an agent j decides to be silent, there are at least two natural options when updating the opinions of the agents having j as a contact: (1) agent j is simply ignored in the update since their current opinion is unknown (or not public), or (2) the most recent opinion when j was not silent is taken into account in the update. The former corresponds to a scenario where, for privacy purposes, opinions (messages) are removed once they have been accessed. The latter represents a typical scenario in social networks where previous opinions are kept and thus continue to influence others despite the agent's current silence.

The above options lead us to the two generalizations of DeGroot models studied in this paper: the *silence opinion memoryless* (SOM$^-$) models, where previous opinions are forgotten, and the *silence opinion memory-based (or history-dependent)* (SOM$^+$) models, where previous opinions are remembered. In both, agents become silent by a majority rule for each case. Below we introduce the elements of the models.

2.1 The Influence Graph

In social learning models, a *community/society* is typically represented as a directed weighted graph with edges between individuals (agents) representing the direction and strength of the influence that one carries over the other. This graph is referred to as the *Influence Graph*.

Definition 1 (Influence Graph). *An (n-agent) influence graph is a weighted directed graph $G = (A, E, I)$, where $A = \{1, \ldots, n\}$, $E \subseteq A \times A$, and $I : A \times A \to [0, 1]$ a weight function such that $I(i, j) = 0$ iff $(i, j) \notin E$ and for each $i \in A$, $\sum_{j \in N_i \cup \{i\}} I(j, i) = 1$ where $N_i = \{j \in A \backslash \{i\} : (j, i) \in E\}$.*

The vertices in A represent n agents of a given community or network. The set of edges $E \subseteq A \times A$ represents the (direct) influence relation between these agents; i.e., $(i, j) \in E$ means that agent i *(directly) influences* agent j. The value $I(i, j)$, for simplicity written I_{ij}, denotes the strength of the influence: 0 means no influence, and a higher value means stronger influence. The normalization condition ensures that the total influence on each agent sums to 1. The set N_i represents the *neighbors* of agent i.

We recall some notions from graph theory [17]. A sequence in E of the form $(i, i_1)(i_1, i_2) \ldots (i_{m-1}, j)$ is a path (of length m) from i to j. The graph G is said to be *strongly connected* if for every pair (i, j) of distinct nodes in A, there is a path from i to j. A graph G is a *clique* if for every pair (i, j) of distinct nodes in A, $(i, j) \in E$. A cycle is a path $(i, i_1)(i_1, i_2) \ldots (i_{m-1}, i)$ with all $i, i_1, \ldots i_{m-1}$ being distinct. Finally, G is *aperiodic* if the greatest common divisor of the lengths of its cycles is one.

2.2 Silence Opinion Models

To incorporate the Spiral of Silence into the DeGroot framework, we will model the evolution of agents' opinions alongside their decisions to remain silent about a given underlying *statement* or *proposition*. Such a proposition could include controversial statements like, for example, *"AI poses a threat to humanity"* or *"pineapple belongs on pizza"*. Thus, the state of the agents (system) with respect to the proposition involves both the *state of opinion* and the *state of silence*.

The *state of opinion* of all agents is represented as a vector in $[0, 1]^n$. If $\mathbf{B}$ is a state of opinion, then $\mathbf{B}_i$ denotes the opinion of agent i with respect to a given proposition. If $\mathbf{B}_i = 0$ ($\mathbf{B}_i = 1$) agent i completely disagrees (agrees) with the proposition. The higher the value, the stronger the agreement.

The *state of silence* is represented as a vector in $\{0, 1\}^n$. If $\mathbf{S}$ is a state of silence, $\mathbf{S}_i = 1$ ($\mathbf{S}_i = 0$) means that agent i is *speaking* (is *not* speaking; i.e., agent i is silent).

At each time $t \in \mathbb{N}$, every agent $i \in A$ updates their opinion and their silence state. We shall use $\mathbf{B}^t$ and $\mathbf{S}^t$ to denote the state of opinion and silence at time t. We can now define a general Silence DeGroot opinion model as follows.

Definition 2 (SO Models). *A* Silence Opinion (SO) model *is a tuple* $(G, \mathbf{B}^0, \mathbf{S}^0, \mu_G)$ *where* $G = (A, E, I)$ *is an n-agent influence graph,* $\mathbf{B}^0$ *the initial state of opinion,* $\mathbf{S}^0$ *the initial state of silence,* $\mu_G : [0, 1]^n \times \{0, 1\}^n \times \mathbb{N} \to [0, 1]^n \times \{0, 1\}^n$ *the state-transition function, called* (state) update function. *For every $t \in \mathbb{N}$, the state of the system at time $t + 1$ is* $(\mathbf{B}^{t+1}, \mathbf{S}^{t+1}) = \mu_G(\mathbf{B}^t, \mathbf{S}^t, t)$.

The update functions can be used to express any deterministic and discrete transition from one state to the next, possibly taking into account the influence graph, the current and even previous states. These functions are typically expressed by means of equations between states. In what follows, we will define particular update functions that take the spiral of silence into account.

2.3 Spiral of Silence Models

To build intuition we recall that the opinion update from the DeGroot model states that each agent adopts the weighted average of the opinions of the agents that directly influence them. This update can be equivalently expressed in terms of opinion differences with their neighbors, as shown in the rightmost formula of the following equation:

$$\mathbf{B}_i^{t+1} = \sum_{j \in N_i \cup \{i\}} I_{ji} \cdot \mathbf{B}_j^t = \mathbf{B}_i^t + \sum_{j \in N_i} I_{ji} \cdot (\mathbf{B}_j^t - \mathbf{B}_i^t) \tag{1}$$

for each $i \in A$, $t \in \mathbb{N}$. Thus, in the DeGroot model each agent updates their opinion with the weighted average of the opinion differences with their neighbors.

We now generalize the above DeGroot update (Eq. 1) as opinion update functions that depend not only on the current state of opinion but also on the state of silence and, possibly, on previous states.

Memoryless Update. Our first update corresponds to the first option mentioned at the beginning of Sect. 2: The opinions of silent neighbors are ignored in the update. This can be realized by modifying Eq. 1 as shown in the following opinion update equation:

$$\mathbf{B}_i^{t+1} = \mathbf{B}_i^t + \sum_{j \in N_i} I_{ji} \cdot \mathbf{S}_j^t \cdot (\mathbf{B}_j^t - \mathbf{B}_i^t) \tag{2}$$

We now define the corresponding silence update function following the Spiral of Silence Theory. First, we need some notation. Let $x, y, \tau \in [0,1]$. The τ-proximity relation $x \sim_\tau y$ holds true iff $|x - y| \leq \tau$, i.e., if x and y are within a tolerance radius τ. Also, let $N_i^t = \{j \in N_i : \mathbf{S}_j^t = 1\}$ be the sets of non-silent neighbors of i at time t. The silence update function is given as follows:

$$\mathbf{S}_i^{t+1} = \begin{cases} 1 & \text{if } \mathcal{M}_i \cdot |N_i^t| \leq |\{j \in N_i^t \mid \mathbf{B}_i^t \sim_{\tau_i} \mathbf{B}_j^t\}| \\ 0 & \text{otherwise} \end{cases} \tag{3}$$

For each agent i, the constants $\tau_i, \mathcal{M}_i \in [0,1]$ represent the agent's *tolerance radius* and *majority threshold* i.e., the minimum proportion of neighbors required for a group to be regarded as a majority by agent i.[1]

Intuitively, an agent i considers the opinion of j to be close enough to theirs if it is within their tolerance radius τ_i. Agent i decides to speak iff at least a fraction $\mathcal{M}_i$, their majority threshold, of their *non-silent* contacts have opinions close enough to theirs.

We can now define the memoryless models for the spiral of silence.

Definition 3 (SOM⁻). *Let* $M = (G, \mathbf{B}^0, \mathbf{S}^0, \mu_G)$ *be an SO model with* $G = (A, E, I)$. *Then* M *is said to be a* SO Memoryless *(SOM⁻) model if for each* $i \in A$ *and* $t \in \mathbb{N}$, $\mu_G(\mathbf{B}^t, \mathbf{S}^t, t) = (\mathbf{B}^{t+1}, \mathbf{S}^{t+1})$ *where* $\mathbf{B}_i^{t+1}$ *and* $\mathbf{S}_i^{t+1}$ *are determined by Eq. 2 and Eq. 3, respectively.*

Clearly, we can recover the DeGroot update (Eq. 1) by setting each tolerance radius constant τ_i in Eq. 3 to 1 (or by setting each majority threshold $\mathcal{M}_i$ to 0) and the initial state of silence $\mathbf{S}^0$ to the unit vector $\mathbf{1}_n = (1, 1, \ldots, 1)$ of size n.

Remark 1. The dynamic nature of the influence graph in SOM⁻ models sets them apart from the static influence in the DeGroot model. Silencing an agent j at a given time amounts to removing all edges $(j, i) \in E$ from the graph at that moment. This allows for more complex opinion formation behaviors.

Furthermore, we could have normalized the sum in Eq. 2 by dividing it by $\sum_{j \in N_i^t} I_{ji}$ when this divisor is not equal to zero.[2] While this would not impact our

---

[1] Although the constraint $\mathcal{M}_i \geq 0.5$ may seem natural, we neither require nor assume it in our technical results or simulations.

[2] Notice we are using N_i^t as index set in the summation rather than N_i.

technical results in Sect. 3, it would amplify the influence of the non-silent neighbors of i at time t, which may seem unnatural. Instead, notice that from Eq. 2 we get:

$$\mathbf{B}_i^{t+1} = \mathbf{B}_i^t + \sum_{j \in N_i} I_{ji} \cdot \mathbf{S}_j^t \cdot (\mathbf{B}_j^t - \mathbf{B}_i^t) = (1 - \sum_{j \in N_i} I_{ji} \cdot \mathbf{S}_j^t) \cdot \mathbf{B}_i^t + \sum_{j \in N_i} I_{ji} \cdot \mathbf{S}_j^t \cdot \mathbf{B}_j^t. \quad (4)$$

Thus, the influence I_{ji} of a silent agent j at time t may be seen as increasing the weight of agent i's opinion at that time. This can be interpreted as agent i increasing confidence in their own opinion in the absence of external influence from agent j.

Memory-Based Update. We now introduce the models corresponding to second option in the beginning of Sect. 2: If j is silent at time t, the opinion update takes into account the opinion they had the last time unit u (where $u \leq t$) when they were not silent. For this to be well-defined, we assume that initially all agents are not silent; i.e., $\mathbf{S}^0 = \mathbf{1}_n$.

Let $\bar{t}_j = \max\{u \leq t \mid \mathbf{S}_j^u = 1\}$. The *public state of opinion* at time t is a state of opinion $\mathrm{pub}\mathbf{B}^t$ such that $\mathrm{pub}\mathbf{B}_j^t = \mathbf{B}_j^{\bar{t}_j}$ for each $j \in A$. The following opinion update equation captures the above intuition:

$$\mathbf{B}_i^{t+1} = \mathbf{B}_i^t + \sum_{j \in N_i} I_{ji} \cdot (\mathrm{pub}\mathbf{B}_j^t - \mathbf{B}_i^t) \quad (5)$$

The corresponding silence update tells us that an agent i becomes or remains silent at time $t+1$ precisely when the public opinion of the majority of *all* their neighbors are not close enough to their own. More precisely:

$$\mathbf{S}_i^{t+1} = \begin{cases} 1 & \text{if } \mathcal{M}_i \cdot |N_i| \leq |\{\, j \in N_i \mid \mathbf{B}_i^t \sim_{\tau_i} \mathrm{pub}\mathbf{B}_j^t \,\}| \\ 0 & \text{otherwise} \end{cases} \quad (6)$$

where $\tau_i, \mathcal{M}_i \in [0, 1]$ are the *tolerance radius* and the *majority threshold* constants, respectively, for agent i. The memory-based models are defined thus:

Definition 4 (SOM$^+$). *Let* $M = (G, \mathbf{B}^0, \mathbf{S}^0, \mu_G)$ *be an SO model where* $G = (A, E, I)$ *is an n-agent influence graph. Then M is said to be an SO memory-based (SOM$^+$) model if* $\mathbf{S}^0 = \mathbf{1}_n$ *and for each* $i \in A$ *and* $t \in \mathbb{N}$, $\mu_G(\mathbf{B}^t, \mathbf{S}^t, t) = (\mathbf{B}^{t+1}, \mathbf{S}^{t+1})$ *where $\mathbf{B}_i^{t+1}$ and $\mathbf{S}_i^{t+1}$ are determined by Eq. 5 and Eq. 6, resp.*

The DeGroot update (Eq. 1) is a particular case of the SOM$^+$ opinion update (Eq. 5): We only need to set each tolerance radius constant τ_i in Eq. 6 to 1 since $\mathbf{S}^0$ is already required to be the unit vector of ones $\mathbf{1}_n$ in SOM$^+$ models.

Remark 2. The main difference between SOM$^+$ and the DeGroot and SOM$^-$ models is that the latter two are *Markovian* processes. The next state depends on the current state but not past states. In fact, much of the tractability of DeGroot models derives from its connection to Markov chains. Nevertheless, the next state in SOM$^+$ models does not depend on the entire state history but just on the most recent public opinions. In the next sections, we will see the impact of this limited amount of memory on opinion evolution.

3   Results on Consensus

Consensus is a central problem in social learning models. Often, an inability to reach a consensus is a sign of polarization. In the DeGroot framework, consensus represents convergence to the same opinion value over time.

Definition 5 (Consensus). *Let $(G, \mathbf{B}^0, \mathbf{S}^0, \mu_G)$ be an SO model with $G = (A, E, I)$. We say that the agents in A converge to consensus if there exists a value $v \in [0, 1]$ such that for all $i \in A$, $\lim_{t \to \infty} \mathbf{B}_i^t = v$.*

Conversely, we refer to the lack of (convergence to) consensus as *dissensus*, which occurs when agents fail to converge to a single opinion value.

In this section, we explore consensus for both types of models on two different graph topologies: *clique* and *strongly connected* graphs. We show that consensus can only be guaranteed in arbitrary SOM$^-$ models on clique graphs. In all other cases, consensus cannot be guaranteed due to the existence of *perpetual silence* in the case of SOM$^-$ models and public opinions in the case for SOM$^+$ models.

Due to space limitations, in this section we provide only sketches of the proofs for the lemmas and theorems; the complete proofs can be found in the full version of this paper available on arXiv [6].

3.1   SOM$^-$ Properties

A key property of SOM$^-$ models is that if all agents become silent at time t, they will all speak up at the very next round $t + 1$. The following lemma formalizes this property:

Lemma 1. *Let $(G, \mathbf{B}^0, \mathbf{S}^0, \mu_G)$ be an SOM$^-$ model with $G = (A, E, I)$. For any $t \in \mathbb{N}$, if $\mathbf{S}_i^t = 0$ for all $i \in A$ then for all $i \in A$, $\mathbf{S}_i^{t+1} = 1$.*

From Lemma 1, in SOM$^-$ models we cannot have all agents silent forever.

Corollary 1. *Let $(G, \mathbf{B}^0, \mathbf{S}^0, \mu_G)$ be an SOM$^-$ model with $G = (A, E, I)$. For every $t \in \mathbb{N}$, there exist $i \in A$ such that $\mathbf{S}_i^t = 1$ or $\mathbf{S}_i^{t+1} = 1$.*

We will now prove that the sequences of maximum and minimum opinion values, $\{\max(\mathbf{B}^t)\}_{t \in \mathbb{N}}$ and $\{\min(\mathbf{B}^t)\}_{t \in \mathbb{N}}$, are (bounded) monotonically non-increasing and non-decreasing, respectively, so they must converge to some opinion value, say U and L with $L \leq U$. In Sect. 3.2, we will prove that, under certain conditions, $U = L$, which implies that the model converges to consensus.

First, we show that the opinion values in a state are bounded by the extreme opinions in the previous state.

Lemma 2 (Opinion Bounds). *Let $(G, \mathbf{B}^0, \mathbf{S}^0, \mu_G)$ be an SOM$^-$ model with $G = (A, E, I)$. For any $t \in \mathbb{N}$, $min(\mathbf{B}^t) \leq \mathbf{B}_i^{t+1} \leq max(\mathbf{B}^t)$ for all $i \in A$.*

Notice that monotonicity does not necessarily hold for the opinion values of agents. Nevertheless, it follows from Lemma 2 that $max(\mathbf{B}^t)$ is monotonically non-increasing and $min(\mathbf{B}^t)$ is monotonically non-decreasing with respect to t.

Corollary 2 (Monotonicity of Extremes). *Let* $(G, \mathbf{B}^0, \mathbf{S}^0, \mu_G)$ *be an SOM$^-$ model with* $G = (A, E, I)$. *For all* $t \in \mathbb{N}$, $max(\mathbf{B}^{t+1}) \leq max(\mathbf{B}^t)$ *and* $min(\mathbf{B}^{t+1}) \geq min(\mathbf{B}^t)$.

The monotonicity (and boundedness) of extremes and the Monotonic Convergence Theorem [28], lead us to the existence of limits for the opinion values of extreme agents.

Theorem 1 (Limits of Extremes). *Let* $(G, \mathbf{B}^0, \mathbf{S}^0, \mu_G)$ *be an SOM$^-$ model with* $G = (A, E, I)$. *There must exist* $U, L \in [0, 1]$ *such that* $\lim_{t \to \infty}\{max(\mathbf{B}^t)\} = U$ *and* $\lim_{t \to \infty}\{min(\mathbf{B}^t)\} = L$.

Henceforth, U and L refer to the limit values from Theorem 1. Notice that if the limits for the opinion values of extreme agents are the same (i.e., $U = L$) and by the squeeze theorem [28], we can conclude that all the agents converge to consensus.

3.2   Consensus in SOM$^-$ Cliques

In this section, we show that consensus is guaranteed for SOM$^-$ models whose influence graphs are cliques with at least three agents.

We consider the *minimum influence* of the underlying (clique) graph $G = (A, E, I)$, defined as the constant $I_{min} = \min_{(i,j) \in E} I(i, j)^3$ and the difference between the maximum and minimum opinion values at time t, defined as $R_t = max(\mathbf{B}^t) - min(\mathbf{B}^t)$, notice that $R_t \in [0, 1]$ at any time t.

The proof strategy is based on the following key observations: (*a*) From any time t onwards, there will always be non-silent agents (Corollary 1). (*b*) The maximum and minimum opinion values, which are monotonically non-increasing and non-decreasing respectively, must converge to some value, say U and L respectively, with $L \leq U$ (Theorem 1). (*c*) As the graph is a clique, the non-silent agents will influence, through the update function, all other graph agents infinitely often (Corollary 1). In each such update, the span between the maximum and minimum opinions is multiplied by at most the constant $1 - I_{min} < 1$ (Lemma 3). Since this contraction recurs infinitely often, the span tends to zero, which forces all opinions to converge to a common value (Theorem 2).

To prove consensus (i.e., $U = L$), we now demonstrate how the difference between the maximum and minimum opinion values is reduced over different time units.

Lemma 3 (Convergent Extremes Differences). *Let* $(G, \mathbf{B}^0, \mathbf{S}^0, \mu_G)$ *be an SOM$^-$ model with an n-agent influence graph* $G = (A, E, I)$ *where* G *is a clique with* $n \geq 3$. *For all* $m \in \mathbb{N}$, *there exists* $t \in \mathbb{N}$ *such that* $R_t \leq R_0 \cdot (1 - I_{min})^m$.

As the difference between the maximum and minimum opinions reduces over time, approaching zero, we can now state our consensus result for cliques with at least three agents.

Theorem 2 (Consensus in SOM$^-$ Cliques). *Let* $(G, \mathbf{B}^0, \mathbf{S}^0, \mu_G)$ *be an SOM$^-$ model with an n-agent influence graph* $G = (A, E, I)$ *where* G *is a clique. If* $n \geq 3$, *then the agents in* A *converge to consensus.*

---

^{3} Notice that $I_{min} > 0$ since we are assuming that the underlying graph is a clique.

Remark 3. Notice that for 2-agent cliques ($n = 2$) consensus is not guaranteed; let us consider a clique with two agents: Agent 1 and Agent 2, where the opinions are $\mathbf{B}_1^0 = 1$ and $\mathbf{B}_2^0 = 0$, the influences are $I(1,2) = I(2,1) = 1$, the tolerance radii are $\tau_1 = \tau_2 = 1$ and the majority thresholds are $\mathcal{M}_1 = \mathcal{M}_2 = 0.5$. In this case, the opinion evolution of agent 1, starting with opinion 1, and agent 2, starting with opinion 0, always alternates between the values 1 and 0. Figure 1 illustrates the opinion evolution of this clique.

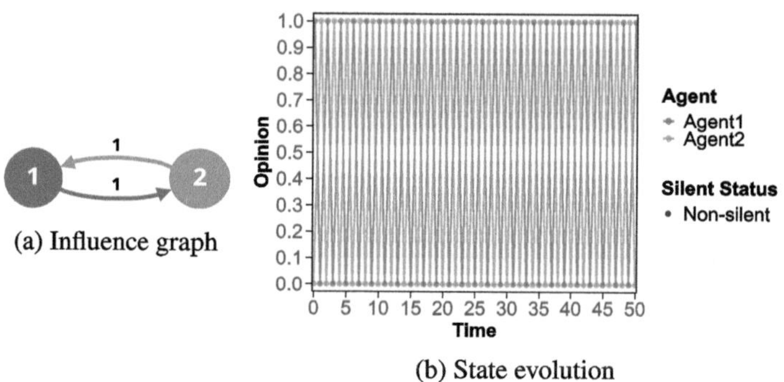

(a) Influence graph

(b) State evolution

Fig. 1. 2-agent clique opinion evolution; $\mathbf{B}^0 = (1,0)$, $\tau_i = 1$, $\mathcal{M}_i = 0.5$, $i \in \{1,2\}$.

3.3 Dissensus in SOM$^-$ Models

In strongly connected aperiodic graphs, the SOM$^-$ models differs from DeGroot models by no longer guaranteeing consensus. Agents can enter a state of perpetual silence, effectively disrupting opinion propagation as if severing connections from the graph. This phenomenon is particularly critical when silent agents form bridges between connected components. Their opinions, influenced by opposing connected components, may remain below their majo threshold indefinitely. As a result, they prevent opinion exchange between components, obstructing the possibility of achieving consensus. The following example illustrates this scenario by showing the agents state evolution and influence graph.

Remark 4. For visual clarity, self-influences are omitted. As a result, the visible incoming influences for each agent may not sum to one. Nevertheless, self-influences are implicitly present to ensure conformity with Definition 1. Readers can infer an agent's self-influence by subtracting the sum of its visible incoming influences from one.

In the example shown in Fig. 2, Agent 3 serves as the sole bridge connecting two distinct graph components: {Agents 1, 2} and {Agents 4, 5}. Due to the tolerance radius and majority threshold parameters, Agent 3 becomes effectively isolated due to its central position. Specifically, Agent 3's belief (0.5) lies outside the tolerance radius of agents in both components, causing it to have no neighbors with sufficiently similar opinions. Consequently, Agent 3 becomes perpetually silent after the first round.

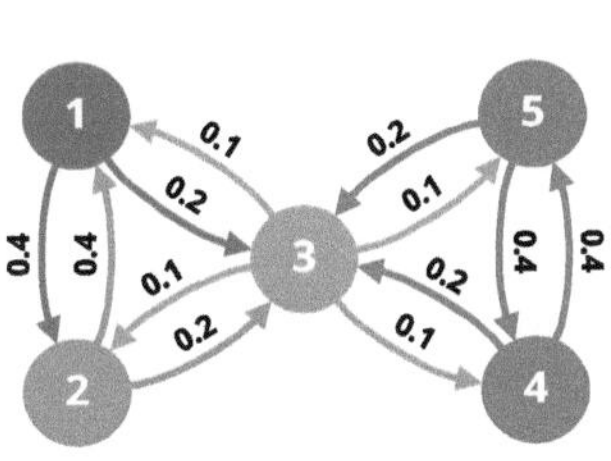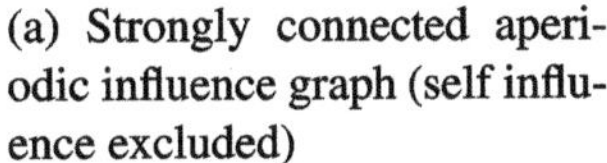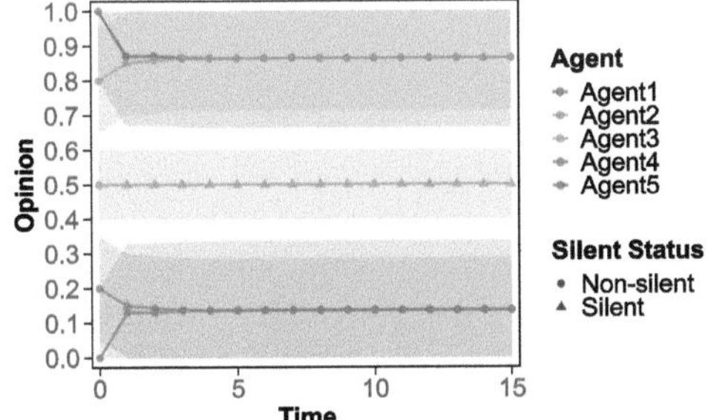

(a) Strongly connected aperiodic influence graph (self influence excluded)

(b) Each plot shows agents' state evolution over time.

Fig. 2. Examples of Dissensus in SOM$^-$ Models. Triangles represent silent agents, circles non-silent ones. Colored areas indicate opinion values within each agent's tolerance radius. Initial state vector: $\mathbf{B}^0 = (1.0, 0.8, 0.5, 0.2, 0.0)$; tolerance radii $\tau = (0.2, 0.15, 0.1, 0.15, 0.2)$; majority thresholds equal to 0.5 for each agent.

Meanwhile, the opposing influences from both components on Agent 3's belief update equation cancel each other out the "pull" from the left component (Agents 1, 2) is balanced by an equal and opposite "pull" from the right component (Agents 4, 5). This results in Agent 3's belief remaining fixed while it stays silent. In contrast, agents within each component maintain beliefs within each other's tolerance radii (after the first round), ensuring they continue to speak and influence one another. As a result, each component converges to its own local consensus, while the perpetually silent Agent 3 can no longer transmit influence between them. The graph thus becomes effectively disconnected, preventing global consensus despite the original strong connectivity.

3.4 Dissensus in SOM$^+$ Models

We now prove through an insightful counterexample that, unlike in the *memoryless* SOM$^-$ models, consensus is not guaranteed in SOM$^+$ models for clique graphs. This negative result shows that incorporating a minimal yet natural memory mechanism (where only the most recent public opinions are considered) can actually hinder consensus.

While SOM$^+$ models share similarities with SOM$^-$ ones regarding perpetual silence, it introduces a unique phenomenon where the entire graph can enter and indefinitely remain in a silent state. This distinction stems from how silent agents influence the opinion update in SOM$^+$.

Recall from Sect. 2.3 that $\mathrm{pub}\mathbf{B}^t$ is the public state of opinion at time t and represents the most recent public opinion of each agent. Henceforth, we will refer to $\mathrm{pub}\mathbf{B}_i^t$ as the *public opinion of agent* i. In SOM$^+$, speaking agents influence the opinions of their neighbors as in SOM$^-$. Nevertheless, unlike in SOM$^-$, silent agents influence their neighbors with their public opinion.

Hence, if agent i's opinion converges to a value where most recent public opinions of more than a fraction $\mathcal{M}_i$ of its neighbors fall outside its tolerance range, the agent will remain perpetually silent. This leads to scenarios where agents withdraw from discourse, while other agents continue to be influenced by these outdated public opinions.

Unlike SOM$^-$, where opinions of silent agents are disregarded, SOM$^+$ allows for the persistence of unchanged public opinions indefinitely. This can result in dissensus (i.e., lack of convergence to a consensus) due to the formation of public opinions that no longer reflect the current opinions of silent agents.

Counter-Example to Consensus. Consider the SOM$^+$ model $M = (G, \mathbf{B}^0, \mathbf{S}^0, \mu_G)$ with G as the Clique in Fig. 3a and $\mathbf{B}^0 = (1.0, 0.9, 0.1, 0.0)$, tolerance radius $\tau_i = 0.1$, majority threshold $\mathcal{M}_i = 0.5$ for each agent i in G. All agents initially have more than half of their neighbors' opinions outside their tolerance radius. Consequently, all agents become silent at $t = 1$. At this point, each agent's updated opinion places all other agents' opinions outside its tolerance radius. The agents' opinions then converge to distinct values, determined by the initial opinions $\mathbf{B}^0$, which perpetuates the condition for silence. This state persists indefinitely, as the convergence values maintain the silence condition for all agents. This results in dissensus as illustrated in Fig. 3b .

The above counter-example demonstrates how the SOM$^+$ models can lead to complete silence and opinion divergence in a clique, preventing the possibility of consensus.

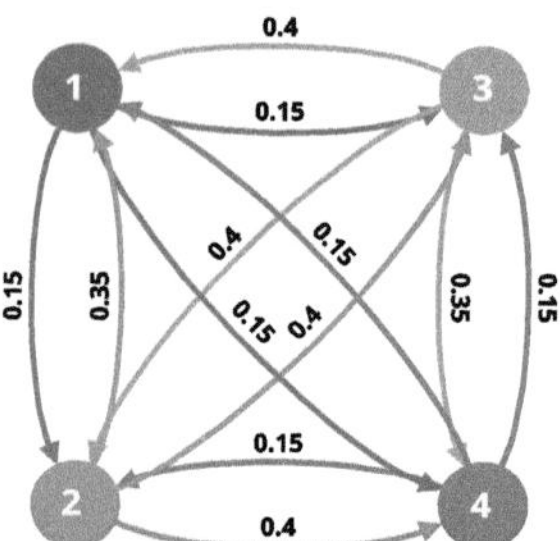

(a) Clique influence graph (self influence excluded)

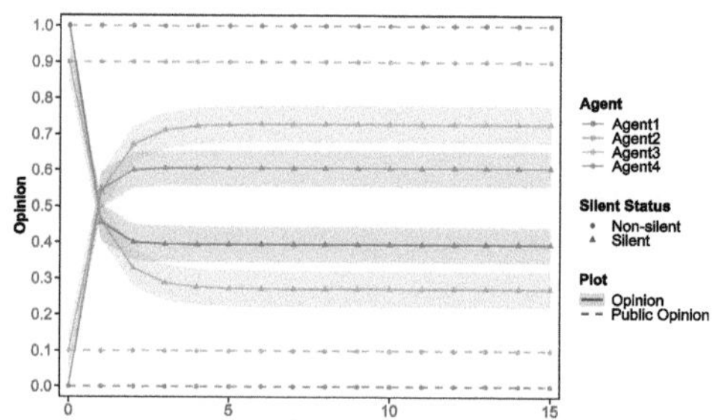

(b) Each plot shows agents' state evolution over time.

Fig. 3. Counter-Example to Consensus in an SOM$^+$ Model. Triangles represent silent agents, circles non-silent ones. Colored areas indicate opinion values within each agent's tolerance radius. Initial state vector: $\mathbf{B}^0 = (1.0, 0.9, 0.1, 0.0)$, tolerance radius and majority threshold equal to 0.1 and 0.5 for each agent.

4 Experimenting with the Spiral of Silence

This section demonstrates how SOM$^-$ and SOM$^+$ models can capture key dynamics of the spiral of silence through agent-based simulations. We first showcase an SOM$^-$

model that reinforces dominant opinions, enabling vocal minorities to disproportionately influence public discourse despite numerical inferiority. Next, we illustrate an SOM$^+$ model revealing an apparent dichotomy: agents privately converge to *consensus* while maintaining *divergent* public stances, mirroring social environments where outdated expressions mask underlying agreement [19].

To validate scalability, we simulate networks ranging from 4 to over 2.1 million agents (2^2 to 2^{21}) with varying connectivity, leveraging a modified version of Ross et al.'s algorithm [25] to generate networks with power-law ("rich-get-richer") degree distributions and small-world properties. Small-world properties are characterized by short average path lengths between nodes while maintaining high local clustering. This reflects *real social networks*' structure where information spreads efficiently despite limited local connections, making our simulations more realistic for studying opinion dynamics. Indeed, studies have shown social networks exhibit 6 degrees of separation [29], that is, any one person is on average 6 connections away from any other.

4.1   Reinforcement of Dominant Views

Figure 4 illustrates how SOM$^-$ models capture the essence of the Spiral of Silence theory. In this strongly connected graph, a vocal minority effectively dominates the discourse, causing the silent majority to converge toward the perceived majority opinion.

The network has two groups: Group 1 (Agents 1, 2, 3, 6, 7, and 8) with opinions in the lower half of the spectrum, and Group 2 (Agents 4 and 5) with opposing views near the higher end. Despite Group 1 being the actual majority, the network topology and differing tolerance radii τ lead to Group 2 dominating the opinion dynamics. Group 1 agents lack intra-group connections but are all linked to Group 2 agents. Also, Group 2's significantly larger tolerance radii allow them to remain non-silent more frequently.

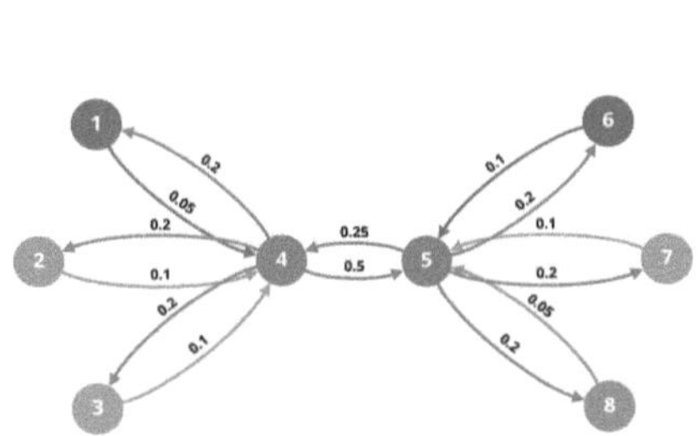
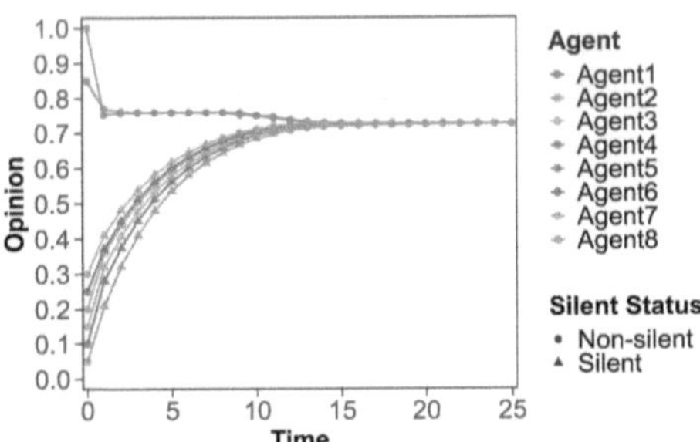

(a) Aperiodic strongly connected influence graph (self influence excluded)

(b) Each plot shows agents' state evolution over time.

Fig. 4. Silent Majority vs. Vocal Minority: Opinion Dynamics in SOM$^-$. Triangles represent silent agents, circles non-silent ones. Colored areas indicate opinion values within each agent's tolerance radius. Here $\mathbf{B}^0 = (0.1, 0.2, 0.15, 1.0, 0.85, 0.25, 0.3, 0.05)$ and $\tau = (0.1, 0.05, 0.1, 0.85, 0.6, 0.05, 0.1, 0.05)$ and majority thresholds are set to 0.5.

This configuration results in the vocal minority (Group 2) disproportionately influencing the network. The silent majority (Group 1) remains quiet for most of the update process, only becoming active when opinions have already shifted closer to the perceived majority view. This example demonstrates how the SOM$^-$ models can simulate scenarios where a minority opinion, through strategic positioning and persistent vocalization, can shape the overall opinion landscape, even when numerically outnumbered.

4.2   Hidden Consensus in SOM$^+$ Models

SOM$^+$ models reveal a noteworthy phenomenon: the possibility of reaching a consensus that remains undetected by the agents themselves. Figure 5 illustrates this scenario using a clique graph with four agents.

Initially, the agents hold diverse opinions ($\mathbf{B}^0 = (1.0, 0.9, 0.1, 0.0)$). However, due to the graph's influence structure, all agents become silent after $t = 0$. Despite this silence, their private opinions converge to a common value over time. Crucially, this convergence occurs without any further public expression of opinions, leaving each agent unaware of the emerging consensus. This hidden consensus phenomenon mirrors real-world scenarios in social media where individuals may unknowingly share common views while perceiving disagreement due to outdated public expressions [19].

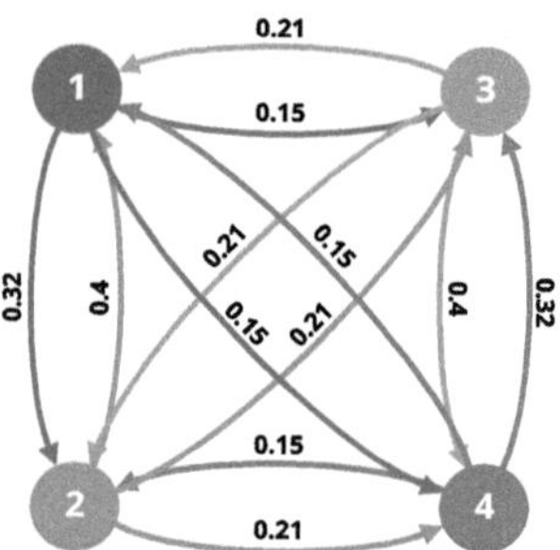
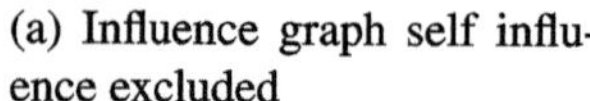
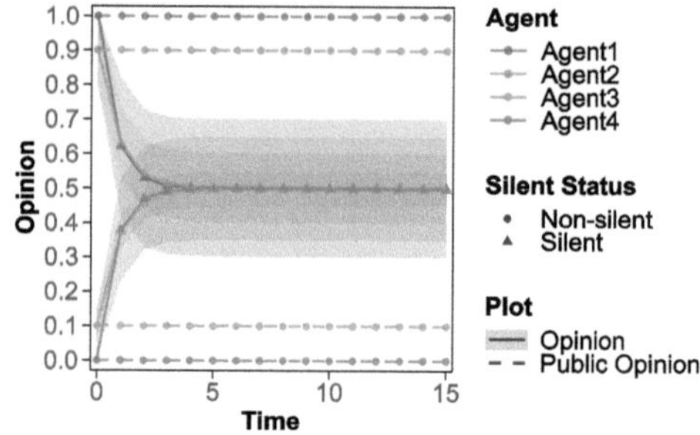

(a) Influence graph self influence excluded

(b) Each plot shows agents' state evolution over time.

Fig. 5. Silent Consensus Scenario. Triangles represent silent agents, circles non-silent ones. Colored areas indicate opinion values within each agent's tolerance radius. Initial state vector: $\mathbf{B}^0 = (1.0, 0.9, 0.1, 0.0)$; tolerance radii $\tau = (0.2, 0.1, 0.05, 0.15)$; majority thresholds equal to 0.5 for each agent.

4.3   Scaling to Large-Scale Network Simulations

While small-scale simulations illustrate core mathematical behaviors, they do not capture the complexity of real-world social networks. To bridge this gap, we developed a scalable simulation platform supporting networks of over 2.1 million agents (2^{21}), enabling analysis of emergent phenomena in realistic settings.

Our implementation combines a modified preferential attachment algorithm [1] to generate networks with small-world properties [30] and power-law (rich-get-richer) degree distributions. To address computational intensity, we employ parallel processing via Scala and Akka Actors [20,21], with results persisted in PostgreSQL for efficient querying. For each experiment, we generated networks with *density* (minimum neighbor count) ranging from 1 to 15, executing 1,024 simulations per parameter combination. Consensus rates were then calculated across all runs for statistical significance. All agents have their tolerance radius and majority threshold set to 0.1 and 0.5, respectively, and their initial beliefs as random uniformly distributed values from 0 to 1. The code is available here.

Contrasting Silence Opinion Models. The SOM^+ and SOM^- models exhibit dramatically opposing behaviors in consensus formation as seen in Fig. 6. For SOM^+ models, consensus becomes increasingly rare beyond 512 agents (2^9), occurring in only 0.097% of simulations (1/1024 runs) at this threshold, exclusively for density 4. Beyond this scale, no simulations reached consensus. This aligns with social media dynamics where persistent disagreement emerges, as agents' historical opinions create perception gaps between private consensus and public expression [19]. Even a minimal notion of memory (retaining only most recent public opinions) proves sufficient to sustain dissensus.

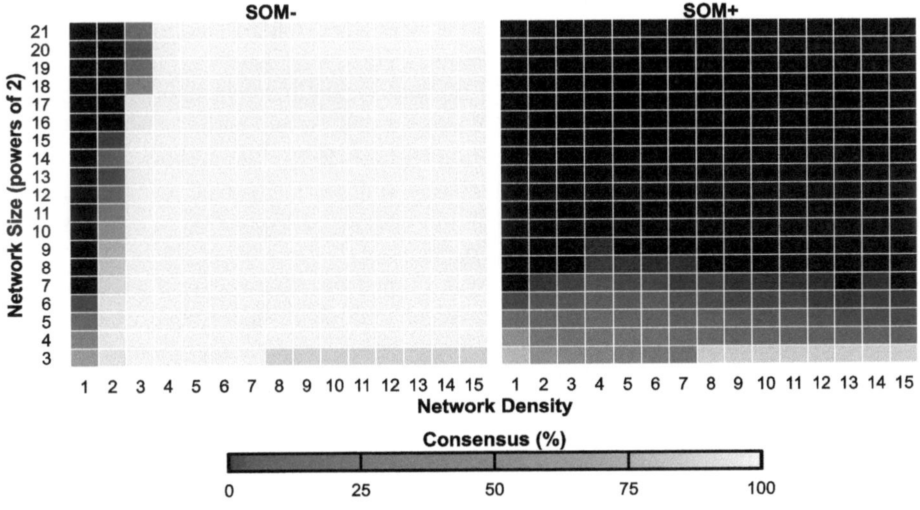

Fig. 6. Heatmap indicating consensus % across different network sizes (y-axis) and densities (x-axis) for both SOM^+ and SOM^- models. Lighter hues indicate a higher rate of consensus, while darker hues indicate a lower rate. All tolerance radii and majority thresholds are equal to 0.1 and 0.5 resp.

Conversely, SOM^- models exhibit the opposite scalability behavior. Once a certain density threshold is reached, consensus consistently emerges in all simulations. Larger networks require slightly higher connectivity: for 2,048 agents (2^{11}), a density of 3 suffices, while for 2.1 million agents (2^{21}), a density of 4 is needed. This highlights how the spiral of silence depends on network structure. In sparse networks, some agents may remain silent indefinitely due to critical bridge nodes (see Sect. 3.3). In contrast, denser networks make it increasingly unlikely for bridges to be disconnected, since disrupting consensus would require silencing more than d agents (for density d)—a rare occurrence in networks of this type.

5 Conclusions and Related Work

We extended the classical DeGroot framework to incorporate key social dynamics described by the Spiral of Silence. Our contributions highlight how the addition of memory, even in a limited form, as in SOM$^+$ models, introduces significant complexity to consensus-building processes. We demonstrated that consensus, while achievable for cliques in SOM$^-$ models, is no longer guaranteed, in contrast with DeGroot models, in arbitrary strongly-connected aperiodic graphs. This points to the impact that silence and memory can have on opinion formation in social networks. It also offers insights into the challenges of converging to consensus in real-world scenarios. We also discuss simulations reflecting predictions of the Spiral of Silence, such as the reinforcement of dominant views and hidden consensus. Finally, we discussed the simulation in our models of large-scale graphs reflecting the small-world topology of real social networks.

Related Work. To our knowledge, no prior work has extended DeGroot-based models to incorporate the Spiral of Silence. Some recent studies have examined the Spiral of Silence in agent-based networks. E.g., [25] models manipulative actors in social networks using agents with fixed binary opinions (agree/disagree) who choose whether to express them based on the prevailing opinion climate. In [9], the authors explore how the number of communities and their connectivity influence perceived opinion climates. However, these studies do not address opinion updates, convergence to consensus, or memory, which are central aspects of this paper.

In [13,34] the stabilization property was studied in majority-based opinion models, where individuals adopt the most prevalent opinion in their social circles (their neighbors). Although these works focus on majority-based opinion dynamics, similar to models inspired by Spiral of Silence, their models are exclusively memoryless with only two-value discrete opinions.

Recent studies [8,26,33] explored conflict, disagreement, and polarization using the Friedkin and Johnsen (FJ) model. This model extended DeGroot's by adding a fixed internal opinion and modeling stubbornness, where agents' expressed opinions reflected their internal beliefs. While silent agents in SOM$^+$ and stubborn agents in the FJ model shared some similarities, their behavior differed. In SOM$^+$, silent agents could later become active, allowing their public opinions to change. In contrast, stubborn agents in the FJ model did not shift in this way. Thus, although neither model guaranteed consensus, their opinion dynamics diverged.

The exclusion of silent agents in SOM$^-$ models amounts to having edges (influences) disappearing and reappearing during opinion evolution which reflects the dynamic influence nature of this model. There are several works studying dynamic influence in opinion formation. The work [16] introduces a version of the DeGroot model in which self-influence changes over time while the influence on others remains the same. The works [11,12] explore convergence and stability, respectively, in models where influences change over time. The work [5] demonstrates how asynchronous communication, when combined with dynamic influence, can prevent consensus. None of this work deals with the dynamics derived from the Spiral of Silence.

References

1. Albert, R., Barabási, A.L.: Statistical mechanics of complex networks. Rev. Mod. Phys. **74**(1), 47–97 (2002). https://doi.org/10.1103/RevModPhys.74.47

2. Alvim, M.S., Amorim, B., Knight, S., Quintero, S., Valencia, F.: A multi-agent model for polarization under confirmation bias in social networks. In: Peters, K., Willemse, T.A.C. (eds.) FORTE 2021. LNCS, vol. 12719, pp. 22–41. Springer, Cham (2021). https://doi.org/10.1007/978-3-030-78089-0_2

3. Alvim, M.S., Amorim, B., Knight, S., Quintero, S., Valencia, F.: A formal model for polarization under confirmation bias in social networks. Logical Methods Comput. Sci. (2023). https://doi.org/10.46298/lmcs-19(1:18)2023, https://hal.science/hal-03872692

4. Alvim, M.S., Gaspar da Silva, A., Knight, S., Valencia, F.: A multi-agent model for opinion evolution in social networks under cognitive biases. In: Castiglioni, V., Francalanza, A. (eds.) Formal Techniques for Distributed Objects, Components, and Systems, pp. 3–19. Springer, Cham (2024). https://doi.org/10.1007/978-3-031-62645-6_1

5. Aranda, J., Betancourt, S., Díaz, J.F., Valencia, F.: Fairness and consensus in an asynchronous opinion model for social networks. In: Majumdar, R., Silva, A. (eds.) 35th International Conference on Concurrency Theory, CONCUR 2024, September 9-13, 2024, Calgary, Canada. LIPIcs, vol. 311, pp. 7:1–7:17. Schloss Dagstuhl - Leibniz-Zentrum für Informatik (2024). https://doi.org/10.4230/LIPICS.CONCUR.2024.7

6. Aranda, J., Díaz, J.F., Gaona, D., Valencia, F.: The sound of silence in social networks (2025). https://arxiv.org/abs/2410.19685

7. Atanesyan, A., Hakobyan, A., Reynolds, B.: Communicating COVID-19 on social media: the effects of the spiral of silence. University of Helsinki Research Portal (2023). https://researchportal.helsinki.fi/en/publications/communicating-covid-19-on-social-media-the-effects-of-the-spiral-

8. Biondi, E., Boldrini, C., Passarella, A., Conti, M.: Dynamics of opinion polarization. IEEE Trans. Syst. Man, Cybern. Syst. **53**(9), 5381–5392 (2023)

9. Cabrera, B., Ross, B., Röchert, D., Brünker, F., Stieglitz, S.: The influence of community structure on opinion expression: an agent-based model. J. Bus. Econ. **91**(9), 1331–1355 (2021). https://doi.org/10.1007/s11573-021-01064-7

10. Chandrasekhar, A.G., Larreguy, H., Xandri, J.P.: Testing models of social learning on networks: Evidence from a lab experiment in the field. Working Paper 21468, National Bureau of Economic Research (2015). https://doi.org/10.3386/w21468

11. Chatterjee, S., Seneta, E.: Towards consensus: some convergence theorems on repeated averaging. J. Appl. Probab. **14**(1), 89–97 (1977). https://doi.org/10.2307/3213262

12. Chen, Z., Qin, J., Li, B., Qi, H., Buchhorn, P., Shi, G.: Dynamics of opinions with social biases. Automatica **106**, 374–383 (2019). https://doi.org/10.1016/j.automatica.2019.04.035

13. Chistikov, D., Lisowski, G., Paterson, M., Turrini, P.: Convergence of opinion diffusion is pspace-complete. In: Proceedings of the AAAI Conference on Artificial Intelligence, vol. 34, pp. 7103–7110 (2020)

14. Dandekar, P., Goel, A., Lee, D.: Biased assimilation, homophily and the dynamics of polarization. Proc. Nat. Acad. Sci. United States of America **110** (2013). https://doi.org/10.1073/pnas.1217220110

15. DeGroot, M.H.: Reaching a consensus. J. Am. Stat. Assoc. **69**(345), 118–121 (1974)

16. DeMarzo, P.M., et al.: Persuasion bias, social influence, and unidimensional opinions. Q. J. Econ. **118**(3), 909–968 (2003). http://www.jstor.org/stable/25053927

17. Diestel, R.: Graph Theory, 5th edn. Springer, Cham (2017)

18. Golub, B., Sadler, E.: Learning in social networks (2017). Available at SSRN 2919146

19. Hampton, K.N., Rainie, L., Lu, W., Dwyer, M., Shin, I., Purcell, K.: Social media and the 'spiral of silence'. Technical report, Pew Research Center, Washington, DC (2014). https://www.pewresearch.org/internet/2014/08/26/social-media-and-the-spiral-of-silence/

20. Hewitt, C.: Actor model for discretionary, adaptive concurrency. CoRR **abs/1008.1459** (2010). http://arxiv.org/abs/1008.1459

21. Hewitt, C., Bishop, P., Steiger, R.: A universal modular ACTOR formalism for artificial intelligence. In: Proceedings of the 3rd International Joint Conference on Artificial Intelligence, pp. 235–245. Morgan Kaufmann Publishers Inc., Stanford, CA (1973)

22. Matthes, J., Knoll, J., von Sikorski, C.: The "spiral of silence" revisited: a meta-analysis on the relationship between perceptions of opinion support and political opinion expression. Commun. Res. **45**(1), 3–33 (2018). https://doi.org/10.1177/0093650217745429

23. Mossel, E., Tamuz, O.: Opinion exchange dynamics. Probab. Surv. **14**(none), 155–204 (2017). https://doi.org/10.1214/14-PS230

24. Noelle-Neumann, E.: The spiral of silence: a theory of public opinion. J. Commun. **24**(2), 43–51 (1974). https://doi.org/10.1111/j.1460-2466.1974.tb00367.x

25. Ross, B., Pilz, L., Cabrera, B., Brachten, F., Neubaum, G., Stieglitz, S.: Are social bots a real threat? an agent-based model of the spiral of silence to analyse the impact of manipulative actors in social networks. Eur. J. Inf. Syst. **28**(4), 394–412 (2019). https://doi.org/10.1080/0960085X.2018.1560920

26. Shirzadi, M., Zehmakan, A.N.: Do stubborn users always cause more polarization and disagreement? a mathematical study. arXiv preprint arXiv:2410.22577 (2024)

27. Sohn, D.: Spiral of silence in the social media era: a simulation approach to the interplay between social networks and mass media. Commun. Res. **49**(1), 139–166 (2022). https://doi.org/10.1177/0093650219856510

28. Sohrab, H.H.: Basic Real Analysis. Birkhauser Basel, 2nd edn. (2014). https://doi.org/10.1007/0-8176-4441-5

29. Travers, J., Milgram, S.: An experimental study of the small world problem. Sociometry **32**(4), 425–443 (1969)

30. Watts, D.J., Strogatz, S.H.: Collective dynamics of 'small-world' networks. Nature **393**(6684), 440–442 (1998). https://doi.org/10.1038/30918

31. Chen, X., Tsaparas, P., Lijffijt, J., De Bie, T.: Opinion dynamics with backfire effect and biased assimilation. PLoS ONE **16**(9), e0256922 (2021). https://doi.org/10.1371/journal.pone.0256922

32. Xia, W., Ye, M., Liu, J., Cao, M., Sun, X.M.: Analysis of a nonlinear opinion dynamics model with biased assimilation. Automatica **120**, 109113 (2020). https://doi.org/10.1016/j.automatica.2020.109113

33. Xu, W., Zhu, L., Guan, J., Zhang, Z., Zhang, Z.: Effects of stubbornness on opinion dynamics (2022). https://arxiv.org/abs/2208.04160

34. Zehmakan, A.N.: Majority opinion diffusion in social networks: an adversarial approach. In: Proceedings of the AAAI Conference on Artificial Intelligence, vol. 35, pp. 5611–5619 (2021)

Tool and Short Papers

Explicit Model Checking Engine for Reachability Analysis of Colored Petri Nets

Emil Normann Brandt, Jens Emil Fink Højriis, Kira Stæhr Pedersen, and Jiří Srba[✉]

Aalborg University, Aalborg, Denmark
srba@cs.aau.dk

Abstract. Unfolding colored Petri nets into place/transition (P/T) nets is a standard approach for model-checking, leveraging established tools and techniques for basic Petri nets. However, the unfolding process often leads to a combinatorial explosion in the number of places and transitions, creating a significant bottleneck in analyzing complex colored Petri nets. We introduce a new verification engine for Petri nets with finite color domains that bypasses the costly unfolding process. Our engine employs an explicit, on-the-fly state-space exploration, utilizing an optimized binding generator and linear programming-based approximation techniques to enhance performance. Integrated into the open-source TAPAAL model checker, our engine is evaluated on an extensive benchmark from the Model Checking Contest (MCC) 2024. It demonstrates superior performance over the state-of-the-art unfolding approaches.

1 Introduction

Distributed systems are inherently complex, posing significant challenges to correct design and analysis. Petri nets (PNs) [24] have emerged as a powerful formalism for modeling complex distributed behaviors. To enhance their expressiveness and applicability, various extensions have been proposed. Among these, colored Petri nets (CPNs), suggested by Kurt Jensen [15], introduce token colors, enabling more compact and flexible modeling of complex systems.

Colored Petri Nets (CPNs) are susceptible to the state-space explosion problem, particularly when large color types are used. Any CPN with finite color types is expressively equivalent to an ordinary Petri Net (PN), meaning it can be unfolded [22] into its PN counterpart. Unfolding is advantageous because it enables the direct application of existing PN optimization techniques and a large selection of tools. However, unfolding introduces a significant overhead, and the resulting PN may become so large that it exceeds time and memory constraints. On-the-fly (or explicit) verification techniques enable gradual exploration of the state space, allowing the identification of reachable markings with specific properties without requiring to complete the unfolding process.

© The Author(s), under exclusive license to Springer Nature Switzerland AG 2026
Z. Liu et al. (Eds.): ICTAC 2025, LNCS 16237, pp. 437–447, 2026.
https://doi.org/10.1007/978-3-032-11176-0_25

We present a novel explicit verification engine for colored Petri nets that enables efficient reachability analysis on large nets without requiring their unfolding. We outline the design choices and implementation details that make our engine both efficient and competitive with state-of-the-art unfolding approaches. Specifically, we detail the critical code components for successor marking generation and describe over-approximation techniques based on linear programming, which often enable fast resolution of negative reachability queries. Additionally, we present a method for handling fireability queries (checking transition enabledness) which are typically more challenging than pure cardinality queries.

We experimentally evaluate the performance of our explicit verification engine on a benchmark of colored Petri nets and queries from the annual Model Checking Contest (MCC) [1]. We compare its performance with the unfolding approach implemented in TAPAAL [4,9,14], the winner in the reachability category at MCC'24 [19] and MCC'25 [20]. Our results demonstrate a 9% improvement in the number of queries answered by our explicit engine compared to unfolding.

Related Work. The state-of-the-art CPN model checkers that competed in the model checking contest during the past years, including ITS-Tools [25], Lola [27] and TAPAAL [14] are solely based on the unfolding approach [1]. Additionally, it has been shown that TAPAAL unfolding implementation for the reachability analysis is currently the most efficient unfolding approach [4], compared to the MCC unfolder [8] (used also by TINA [2] and LoLA [27]), ITSTools unfolder [25] and Spike unfolder [7] (also used by MARCIE [12] and Snoopy [11]).

CPN-Tools [16] is a popular tool for modelling, simulation and state-space exploration of CPNs with complex color data structures and guards defined in standard ML, however, it does not require finiteness of the color types and reachability analysis is in general undecidable. While the state-space analysis is via unfolding, the tool ASAP [26] aimed at providing an explict exploration engine, however, neither the binary nor the source code of ASAP is accessible/maintained anymore and hence we cannot compare with its performance.

2   Colored Petri Nets

In our verification engine as well as in the MCC competition [1], we consider colored Petri nets over a finite set *Colors* of all possible colors and finitely many color types, each associated with a subset of *Colors*. More precisely, we support color types with integer ranges as well as finite enumeration color types with an ordering relation on their colors and cyclic successor and predecessor operations $++$ and $--$, respectively. Products of color types are supported as well and each color type can have a number of associated variables. By arc expressions AE_τ we understand the set of all multisets over colors and variables in the color type $\tau \in CT$. If we e.g. have a color type with two colors a and b then $(2'a + 3'b) - 1'(a++)$ is a notation for an arc expression that represents the multiset $\{a, a, b, b\}$. Let $AE = \cup_{\tau \in CT} AE_\tau$. By $\mathcal{G}$ we denote the set of guard

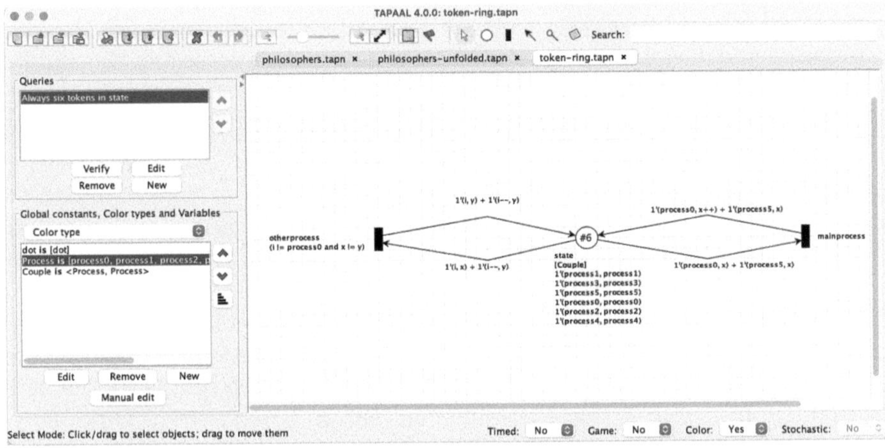

Fig. 1. Token ring [21] CPN example

expressions, i.e. Boolean combinations of atomic predicates comparing colors and variables using the standard comparison operators $<, \leq, =, \neq, \geq, >$.

Definition 1. *A CPN is a tuple $\mathcal{N} = (P, T, CT, \mathbb{V}, C, \mathcal{A}, \mathcal{I}, G, M_0)$ where*

- *P and T are finite sets of places and transitions s.t. $P \cap T = \emptyset$,*
- *CT is a finite set of color types and $\mathbb{V}$ is a finite set of variables,*
- *$C : P \to CT$ is a function assigning color types to places,*
- *$\mathcal{A} : (T \times P) \cup (P \times T) \hookrightarrow AE$ is a partial function assigning arc expressions to arcs connecting places and transitions and respecting the color type of the connected place, i.e. $\mathcal{A}(t, p) \in AE_{C(p)}$ and $\mathcal{A}(p, t) \in AE_{C(p)}$ for all $p \in P$ and $t \in T$ where the functions are defined,*
- *$\mathcal{I} : P \times T \to \mathbb{N}^{\infty}$ is an inhibitor arc weight function,*
- *$G : T \to \mathcal{G}$ is a function assigning guard expressions to transitions, and*
- *M_0 is the initial marking where a marking $M : P \to \mathcal{B}(Colors)$ is a function assigning multisets of colors to places while satisfying that $M(p)$ only contains colors from the color type $C(p)$ for every $p \in P$.*

Figure 1 depicts a CPN example in TAPAAL GUI [9], modelling a token ring [21]. The color type Process is an enumeration of six elements (process0 to process5) and Couple is a product color type containing pairs of processes. There are three variables x, y and i of the color type Process. The place 'state' contains six tokens in the initial marking and there are two transitions in the net. The transition 'otherprocess' is the only one that can fire in the initial marking M_0. In order for it to fire, we need to bind the variables to the concrete colors while satisfying the transition guard and at the same time the resulting multiset of colors on the connected arc expressions must be a subset of the colors present in the place 'state'[1]. For example, if we assume the binding $b(i) = \text{process1}$, $b(x) =$

---

[1] Our example has no inhibitor arcs; should an inhibitor arc (p, t) be connected to a transition t then in order to fire t we additionally require that $M_0(p) < \mathcal{I}(p, t)$.

process1 and $b(y) = $ process0, we obtain a valid binding that satisfies the guard $i \neq$ process0 and $x \neq y$. We can fire the transition 'otherprocess' in this binding, which removes two tokens (process1, process1) and (process0, process0) from the place 'state' and adds the tokens (process1, process0) and (process0, process0). We denote such a transition firing by $M_0 \xrightarrow{t,b} M$ where M is the marking after removing and adding the two tokens.

A P/T net is a colored Petri net with one color type called *dot* and a single color $\bullet$, no variables and all guards being *true*. The classical verification method for CPNs with finite color types is by unfolding [22] the colored net into an equivalent P/T net. Here for every place in the CPN we create a copy for every possible color from its color type. Similarly, for every transition and valid binding, we create a new transition and connect them by arcs accordingly. In our token ring example from Fig. 1, the unfolding contains 36 places, 156 transitions and 624 arcs. Hence unfolding nets with large number of colors, in particular product colors, can result in very large P/T nets and the unfolding process itself can exceed the time and memory limits. We instead avoid the unfolding step and implement a direct (explicit) model checking engine.

We are interested in reachability analysis, asking whether there exists a marking M reachable from the initial marking M_0, such that M satisfies a given *cardinality* γ^c or *fireability* γ^f formula defined by the following abstract syntax

$$\gamma^c ::= p \bowtie n \mid \textit{true} \mid \textit{false} \mid \gamma^c \wedge \gamma^c \mid \gamma^c \vee \gamma^c \mid \neg \gamma^c$$

$$\gamma^f ::= t \mid \textit{true} \mid \textit{false} \mid \gamma^f \wedge \gamma^f \mid \gamma^f \vee \gamma^f \mid \neg \gamma^f$$

where $p \in P$, $n \in \mathbb{N}$, $\bowtie \in \{<, \leq, \geq, >, =, \neq\}$ and $t \in T$. To evaluate a formula on a marking M, we replace p with $|M(p)|$ (number of tokens in p) and t with true/false, depending on whether t is enabled in M or not.

3   Optimizations Implemented in the Verification Engine

We shall now outline three most-impactful techniques implemented in our tool.

Successor Generator. The most critical part of the engine is the generation of marking successors as this operation is constantly repeated during the state-space search. We implement several improvements to the basic idea of iterating over all transitions and all possible bindings in order to identify the successor markings. The main components are summarized in Algorithm 1.

As the number of valid bindings for a transition can be large, we generate the successor markings one by one while storing the information about the last binding used on a given transition. We assume that both for transitions T and a set of bindings $\bar{\mathbb{B}}(M, t)$ in a marking M for a transition t, there is a function *first* that returns the first element of these sets (in some implicit order) and a function *next* that returns the next element or $\top$ if no further element exist.

Each call to `NextSuccessor`(M) at line 2 recovers from the global map the pair (t, b) of a transition and a binding to be explored next. As long as $t \neq \top$,

---

Algorithm 1: NextSuccessor(M) - successor generator

```
   /* store is a globally available map linking a marking M with
      transition-binding pair, initially (first(T), first(B̄(M,first(T)))) */
1
      Input   : A marking M
      Output : A successor marking M' of M or ⊤ if no further successor exists
2     (t,b) ← store[M] ;
3     while t ≠ ⊤ do
4         if |M(p)| > I(p,t) ∨ |M(p)| < min-cardinality(A(p,t)) for some p ∈ P
          then
5             | go to line 15;              /* t cannot become enabled in M    */
6         end
7         while b ≠ ⊤ do
8             if M ──t,b──→ M' for some M' then
9                 | b ← next(b, B̄(M,t));
10                | store[M] ← (t,b);
11                | return M';
12            end
13            b ← next(b, B̄(M,t));
14        end
15        (t,b) ← (next(t,T), first(B̄(M,t)));
16    end
17    store[M] ← (t,b);
18    return ⊤ ;
```

---

we perform at line 4 an inexpensive optimization by testing whether some of the inhibitor arcs disables t or whether the number of tokens (irrelevant of the color) in some place is strictly smaller than the lowest possible cardinality of the corresponding arc after substituting variables with colors (this is precomputed and cached). If the test succeeds, we know that t cannot be enabled under any binding and we jump to line 15 where we consider the next possible transition together with its first binding. Otherwise, we cycle through the possible bindings for the transition t in order to discover possible successors. A major performance gain is achieved by constructing $\bar{\mathbb{B}}(M,t)$ (used at line 9) using an interval analysis of possible colors that each variable can be bound to in order to enable the transition t in the marking M, instead of naively iterating through all possible colors of variables. Each time a new successor is discovered, we save the next possible candidate in the global map (to be used in the next call to the successor generator) and return the discovered successor marking M' at line 11.

Our optimized successor generator guarantees that the sequence of markings obtained by successive calls to **SuccessorGenerator**(M) eventually contains the value $\top$ and enumerates all successor markings of M .

Overapproximation by Color Removal. The idea of removing information about the concrete colors in markings and hence overapproximating the CPN behavior was presented in [18], however, without correctly dealing with arc expressions containing subtraction. We improve the technique to also work for expressions of the form $2'a - 1'x$ where $2'a$ stands for two tokens with color a from which the color that the variable x binds to is subtracted—depending on the binding of x, this arc expression evaluates to either one (if x binds to a) or two (if x binds to a different color) tokens of color a. In general, for any arc expression ae present in the CPN, we precompute the interval $[min\text{-}cardinality(ae), max\text{-}cardinality(ae)]$ such that the number of tokens required by ae is within this interval for any possible binding. Our tool then constructs the *color ignorant* P/T net where each transition is replaced by a number of new transitions for each possible permutation of cardinalities for incoming and outgoing arcs. Let $t \in T$ and let $perm_t : (\{t\} \times P) \cup (P \times \{t\}) \rightarrow \mathbb{N}^0$ be a function that takes a place-transition pair and returns the cardinality for the appropriate arc s.t. $min\text{-}cardinality(\mathcal{A}(t,p)) \leq perm_t(t,p) \leq max\text{-}cardinality(\mathcal{A}(t,p))$ and similarly $min\text{-}cardinality(\mathcal{A}(p,t)) \leq perm_t(p,t) \leq max\text{-}cardinality(\mathcal{A}(p,t))$. The set of all valid permutations for a transition $t \in T$ is denoted by $Permutations_t$.

For a given *colored Petri Net* (CPN) $\mathcal{N} = (P, T, CT, \mathbb{V}, C, \mathcal{A}, \mathcal{I}, G, M_0)$, our tool constructs the color ignorant P/T net $\mathcal{N}^i = (P^i, T^i, \mathcal{A}^i, \mathcal{I}^i, M_0^i)$ where

- $P^i = P$ and $T^i = \{t_{perm_t} \mid t \in T, perm_t \in Permutations_t\}$,
- $\mathcal{A}^i(t_{perm_t}, p) = perm_t(t,p)'\bullet$ and $\mathcal{A}^i(p, t_{perm_t}) = perm_t(p,t)'\bullet$,
- $\mathcal{I}^i(p, t_{perm_t}) = \mathcal{I}(p,t)$, and
- $M_0^i(p) = |M_0(p)|'\bullet$.

The construction forgets the concrete colors of tokens and accounts for all combinations of how the number of tokens can change. Hence the method preserves that for every marking M reachable in the CPN $\mathcal{N}$ there is a marking M' reachable in the color ignorant net $\mathcal{N}^i$ s.t. $|M(p)| = |M'(p)|$ for all $p \in P$.

This implies that if a cardinality formula is not reachable in the color ignorant net (we use here the fast state equation check using linear programming [10, 23]) then it is not reachable in the original colored net either. In many cases this allows us to conclude on negative reachability queries in a fraction of time that is otherwise required by the explicit state-space exploration.

Simplification of Fireability Propositions. When evaluating fireability formulae that contain the enabledness check of a transition t in $\mathcal{N}$, we can replace t with $\bigvee_{perm_t \in Permutations_t} t_{perm_t}$ when exploring the color ignorant net. For performance reasons, our tool replaces t with a single transition $t_{min} \in \{t_{perm_t} \mid perm_t \in Permutations_t\}$ that minimizes $perm_t(p,t)$ and $perm_t(t,p)$ for all $p \in P$ and $t \in T$. Clearly, t_{min} is enabled in a marking if and only if $\bigvee_{perm_t \in Permutations_t} t_{perm_t}$ evaluates to true.

A fireability predicate in a P/T net can be encoded as a cardinality one (as a conjunction of the minimum number of required tokens in places that enable a given transition) and we can therefore apply the overapproximation technique to quickly establish that a transition cannot be enabled. However, this technique cannot be used to determine that a transition is enabled in some reachable marking of a CPN as this requires information on the specific colors.

$$\Psi(t) = \begin{cases} \bot & \text{if } M \not\models t_{min} \text{ for all reachable markings } M \text{ in } \mathcal{N}^i \\ ? & \text{otherwise} \end{cases}$$

$$\Psi(\textit{true}) = \top \qquad \Psi(\textit{false}) = \bot$$

$$\Psi(\gamma_1^f \wedge \gamma_2^f) = \begin{cases} \top & \text{if } \Psi(\gamma_1^f) = \top \text{ and } \Psi(\gamma_2^f) = \top \\ \bot & \text{if } \Psi(\gamma_1^f) = \bot \text{ or } \Psi(\gamma_2^f) = \bot \\ ? & \text{otherwise} \end{cases} \qquad \Psi(\neg\gamma^f) = \begin{cases} \top & \text{if } \Psi(\gamma^f) = \bot \\ \bot & \text{if } \Psi(\gamma^f) = \top \\ ? & \text{if } \Psi(\gamma^f) = ? \end{cases}$$

Fig. 2. Definition of fireability query simplification function Ψ

In our tool, we evaluate subexpressions of the fireability formula and use the color ignorant net for efficient reachability checks by using the state equations and linear programming before we perform a state-space exploration of the color ignorant net (which is cheaper than exploring the original CPN).

Let Ψ be a function, defined in Fig. 2, that for a given fireability formula returns either the value $\top$ (reachable), $\bot$ (unreachable) or ? (inconclusive). We can see that if $\Psi(\gamma^f) = \top$ then γ^f is reachable in the original CPN and if $\Psi(\gamma^f) = \bot$ then γ^f is not reachable in the original CPN. In case of an inconclusive answer, the explicit state-space exploration is executed.

4   Implementation and Experiments

The explicit verification engine is implemented in C++ as part of the open source project verifypn [14]. The engine supports four search strategies BFS, DFS, random DFS and a heuristic search, using the successor generator described in Sect. 3 as well as its variant that evenly cycles through all transitions in the net. Our benchmarking showed that the latter one together with random DFS is the best performing variant and is therefore used in our experiments.

As input, our engine accepts CPN descriptions in the standard Petri Net Markup Language (PNML) [5] and formula queries in XML syntax as used in MCC [1]. The reachability search algorithm compresses the passed list of already visited markings using the PTrie data structure [17].

The tool can return traces that certify the reachability of a marking satisfying a given formula; in order to save memory the bindings in the trace are stored in a compressed format. TAPAAL GUI allows us to visualize the returned traces. The engine also implements a simulation mode with a communication protocol, allowing the user to simulate the behaviour of CPNs without unfolding the net. The source code of our explicit verification engine is available on GitHub [13].

Experiments. We benchmark the performance of our engine on all of the colored models from the Model Checking Contest (MCC) [19] 2024. There are 272 CPN models in the dataset, each with 16 cardinality and 16 fireability reachability queries, giving a total of 8 704 queries in each category. Each query is run on a single core of an AMD EPYC 9334 processor with clock speed 2.7 GHz, restricted to 16 GB of memory and a five minute timeout.

Engine	Total answers			Cardinality			Fireability		
	All	+	−	All	+	−	All	+	−
Unfolding	6697	3557	3140	3745	1192	2553	2952	2365	587
Explicit	7291	4055	3236	4040	1418	2622	3251	2637	614

(a) Number of answered queries (+ for positive and − for negative answers)

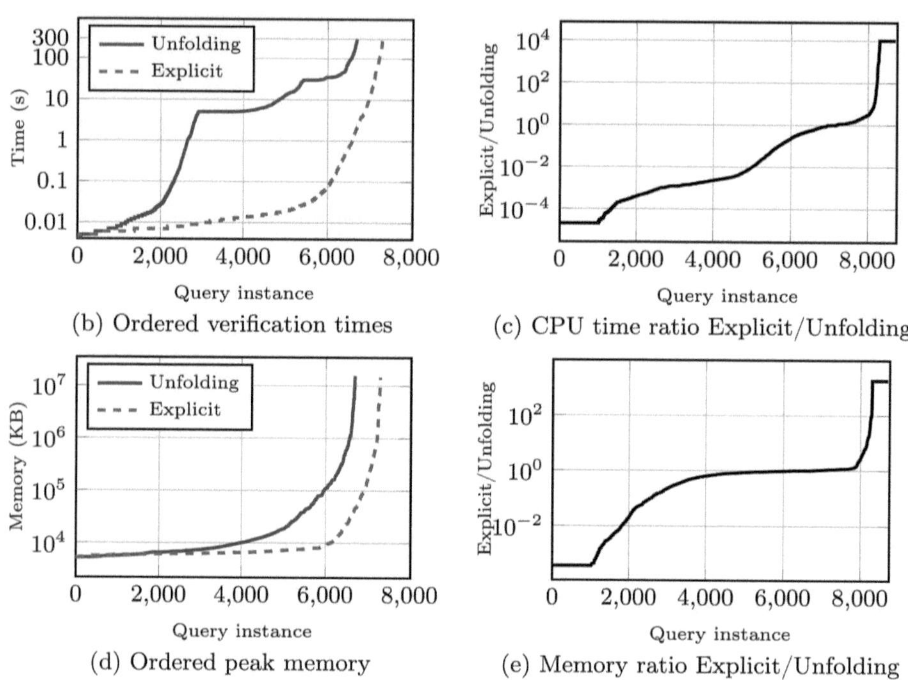

(b) Ordered verification times

(c) CPU time ratio Explicit/Unfolding

(d) Ordered peak memory

(e) Memory ratio Explicit/Unfolding

Fig. 3. Comparison of the explicit and unfolding approach

We compare the performance against the unfolding approach implemented in TAPAAL, the MCC 2024 winner in the reachability category and currently the leading unfolding tool [3], using the best (default) parameters of the unfolding engine. Reproducibility package is available at [6].

Figure 3a depicts the total number of answers that the unfolding and explicit engines solve within the time and memory constraints, including details about the cardinality and fireability subcategories and the distribution of positive queries (where a trace exists) and negative ones. Our explicit engine improves the number of answers in all columns. A more detailed insight is provided in the cactus plot in Fig. 3b where the query instances (on the x-axis) are independently sorted by their running times (on y-axis). This shows large improvements in the running time—almost three times as many queries are solved within one second using the explicit approach compared to the unfolding. The sudden slope change

Table 1. Answered queries and the total percentage in the MCC setup

MCC Script	Answers	Cardinality	Fireability
MCC'24 competition script (without explicit)	7088 (82%)	4051 (93%)	3037 (70%)
With explicit engine running for 120 s	7862 (91%)	4267 (98%)	3595 (83%)

in the unfolding curve is caused by a 5 s timeout of the color partitioning [4] technique in the unfolding approach. Similarly, Fig. 3c offers query by query comparison of the performance, showing that on a large majority of queries, the explicit approach achieves several order of magnitude improvements. Similar conclusions can be drawn from Figs. 3d and 3e regarding the peak memory consumption.

Finally, Table 1 depicts the comparison in the MCC setup (run locally on our cluster computer) with the 2024 competition script (running for 60 min) and its variant where we added 120 s of explicit state-space exploration using our engine before the unfolding approach (still finishing within 1 h). It shows that we increased the number of solved queries from 82% to 91% and the improvement is particularly pronounced in the fireability category (increment by 13% points). These additional answers were an important factor for TAPAAL defending its first place also in MCC'25 [20].

Acknowledgement. We thank to Peter Gjøl Jensen for his technical coding assistance.

References

1. Amat, N.: Behind the scene of the model checking contest, analysis of results from 2018 to 2023. In: Beyer, D., Hartmanns, A., Kordon, F. (eds.) TOOLympics Challenge 2023, pp. 52–89. Springer Nature Switzerland, Cham (2025)
2. Berthomieu, B., Ribet, P.O., Vernadat, F.: The tool TINA – construction of abstract state spaces for Petri nets and time Petri nets. Int. J. Prod. Res. **42**, 2741–2756 (2004)
3. Bilgram, A., Jensen, P., Pedersen, T., Srba, J., Taankvist, P.: Methods for efficient unfolding of colored Petri nets. Fund. Inform. **189**(3–4), 297–320 (2023)
4. Bilgram, A., Jensen, P.G., Pedersen, T., Srba, J., Taankvist, P.H.: Improvements in unfolding of colored Petri nets. In: Bell, P.C., Totzke, P., Potapov, I. (eds.) Reachability Problems, pp. 69–84. Springer International Publishing, Cham (2021)
5. Billington, J., et al.: The Petri net markup language: concepts, technology, and tools. In: 24th International Conference on Applications and Theory of Petri Nets, pp. 483–505. LNCS, Springer (2003)
6. Brandt, E.N., Højriis, J.E.F., Pedersen, K.S., Srba, J.: Reproducibility package for "Explicit Model Checking Engine for Reachability Analysis of Colored Petri Nets" (2025). https://doi.org/10.5281/zenodo.17077809
7. Chodak, J., Heiner, M.: Spike – Reproducible simulation experiments with configuration file branching. In: Bortolussi, L., Sanguinetti, G. (eds.) CMSB 2019. LNCS,

vol. 11773, pp. 315–321. Springer, Cham (2019). https://doi.org/10.1007/978-3-030-31304-3_19

8. Dal Zilio, S.: MCC: a tool for unfolding colored petri nets in PNML format. In: Janicki, R., Sidorova, N., Chatain, T. (eds.) PETRI NETS 2020. LNCS, vol. 12152, pp. 426–435. Springer, Cham (2020). https://doi.org/10.1007/978-3-030-51831-8_23

9. David, A.: TAPAAL 2.0: integrated development environment for timed-arc petri nets. In: Flanagan, C., König, B. (eds.) TACAS 2012. LNCS, vol. 7214, pp. 492–497. Springer, Heidelberg (2012). https://doi.org/10.1007/978-3-642-28756-5_36

10. Esparza, J., Melzer, S.: Verification of safety properties using integer programming: beyond the state equation. Form. Methods Syst. Des. **16**(2), 159–189 (2000). https://doi.org/10.1023/A:1008743212620

11. Heiner, M., Herajy, M., Liu, F., Rohr, C., Schwarick, M.: Snoopy – a unifying petri net tool. In: Haddad, S., Pomello, L. (eds.) PETRI NETS 2012. LNCS, vol. 7347, pp. 398–407. Springer, Heidelberg (2012). https://doi.org/10.1007/978-3-642-31131-4_22

12. Heiner, M., Rohr, C., Schwarick, M.: MARCIE – model checking and reachability analysis done efficiently. In: Colom, J.-M., Desel, J. (eds.) PETRI NETS 2013. LNCS, vol. 7927, pp. 389–399. Springer, Heidelberg (2013). https://doi.org/10.1007/978-3-642-38697-8_21

13. Højriis, J.E.F., Brandt, E.N., Stæhr Pedersen, K.: Github with source code of the explicit engine in verifypn (2025). https://github.com/TAPAAL/verifypn

14. Jensen, J.F., Nielsen, T., Oestergaard, L.K., Srba, J.: TAPAAL and reachability analysis of P/T nets. In: Koutny, M., Desel, J., Kleijn, J. (eds.) Transactions on Petri Nets and Other Models of Concurrency XI. LNCS, vol. 9930, pp. 307–318. Springer, Heidelberg (2016). https://doi.org/10.1007/978-3-662-53401-4_16

15. Jensen, K.: Coloured Petri nets and the invariant-method. Theoret. Comput. Sci. **14**(3), 317–336 (1981). https://doi.org/10.1016/0304-3975(81)90049-9

16. Jensen, K., Kristensen, L.M., Wells, L.: Coloured Petri nets and CPN tools for modelling and validation of concurrent systems. Int. J. Softw. Tools Technol. Transf. **9**(3–4), 213–254 (2007)

17. Jensen, P., Larsen, K., Srba, J.: PTrie: data structure for compressing and storing sets via prefix sharing. In: Proceedings of the 14th International Colloquium on Theoretical Aspects of Computing (ICTAC'17). LNCS, vol. 10580, pp. 248–265. Springer (2017). https://doi.org/10.1007/978-3-319-67729-3_15

18. Klostergaard, A.H.: Efficient Unfolding and Approximation of Colored Petri Nets with Inhibitor Arcs. Master's thesis, AAU (2018). https://projekter.aau.dk/projekter/files/281079031/main.pdf

19. Kordon, F., et al.: Complete Results for the 2024 Edition of the Model Checking Contest (2024). https://mcc.lip6.fr/2024/results.php

20. Kordon, F., et al.: Complete Results for the 2025 Edition of the Model Checking Contest (2025). https://mcc.lip6.fr/2025/results.php

21. Marechal, A.: Token ring CPN model, available at https://mcc.lip6.fr/2024/models.php

22. McMillan, K.L.: Using unfoldings to avoid the state explosion problem in the verification of asynchronous circuits. In: Computer Aided Verification, pp. 164–177. Springer (1993)

23. Murata, T.: Petri nets: properties, analysis and applications. Proc. IEEE **77**(4), 541–580 (1989)

24. Petri, C.A.: Kommunikation mit automaten (1962). https://api.semanticscholar.org/CorpusID:117254333

25. Thierry-Mieg, Y.: Symbolic model-checking using its-tools. In: Tools and Algorithms for the Construction and Analysis of Systems, pp. 231–237. Springer, Berlin, Heidelberg (2015)
26. Westergaard, M., Evangelista, S., Kristensen, L.M.: ASAP: An extensible platform for state space analysis. In: Franceschinis, G., Wolf, K. (eds.) PETRI NETS 2009. LNCS, vol. 5606, pp. 303–312. Springer, Heidelberg (2009). https://doi.org/10.1007/978-3-642-02424-5_18
27. Wolf, K.: Petri net model checking with LoLA 2. In: Application and Theory of Petri Nets and Concurrency, pp. 351–362. Springer, Cham (2018)

PRoTECT: <u>P</u>arallelized Const<u>R</u>uction <u>o</u>f Safe<u>T</u>y Barri<u>E</u>r <u>C</u>ertificates for Nonlinear Polynomial Sys<u>T</u>ems

Ben Wooding$^{(\boxtimes)}$, Viacheslav Horbanov, and Abolfazl Lavaei

School of Computing, Newcastle University, Newcastle upon Tyne, UK
{ben.wooding,v.horbanov2,abolfazl.lavaei}@newcastle.ac.uk

Abstract. We develop an open-source software tool, called PRoTECT, for the parallelized construction of safety barrier certificates (BCs) for nonlinear polynomial systems. This tool employs sum-of-squares (SOS) optimization programs to systematically search for polynomial-type BCs, while aiming to verify safety properties over four classes of dynamical systems: (i) discrete-time *stochastic* systems, (ii) discrete-time *deterministic* systems, (iii) *continuous-time* stochastic systems, and (iv) *continuous-time* deterministic systems. In particular, PRoTECT is the first software tool that designs stochastic barrier certificates. PRoTECT is implemented in Python as an application programming interface (API), offering users the flexibility to interact either through its user-friendly graphical user interface (GUI) or via function calls from other Python programs. PRoTECT leverages *parallelism* across different barrier degrees to efficiently search for a feasible BC.

1   Introduction

Motivation for PRoTECT. [1] Formal verification of dynamical systems has become a focal point over the past several years, primarily due to their widespread integration into safety-critical systems [13]. Barrier certificates (BCs) [19,20], also known as *barrier functions*, have emerged as a fundamental solution approach, offering assurances regarding the safety behavior of diverse classes of systems. Specifically, BCs can be employed to directly assess the behavior of systems across *continuous-state spaces* with an uncountable number of states, without resorting to discretization, which contrasts with abstraction-based approaches [15]. This aspect is particularly noteworthy when considering *safety*, (*a.k.a. invariance*) properties, wherein the state transitions of the system remain within a region labeled as "safe", ensuring no transitions occur to any region labeled "unsafe". In particular, barrier certificates, akin to Lyapunov functions, are functions established over the system's state space, fulfilling specific inequalities concerning both the function itself and the one-step transition (or the flow) of the system. A suitable level set of a BC can segregate an unsafe

---

[1] For Open Science, PRoTECT v1.3 (Python 3.10), the version available at the time of publication, is permanently preserved at: https://doi.org/10.5281/zenodo.11085376.

© The Author(s), under exclusive license to Springer Nature Switzerland AG 2026
Z. Liu et al. (Eds.): ICTAC 2025, LNCS 16237, pp. 448–458, 2026.
https://doi.org/10.1007/978-3-032-11176-0_26

region from all system trajectories originating from a specified set of initial conditions. Hence, the presence of such a function offers a formal (probabilistic) certification for system safety.

Related Work. A comprehensive overview of barrier certificates can be found in [3,27]. BCs can verify systems with polynomial dynamics, designing polynomial BCs using sum-of-squares techniques, *e.g.*, via SOSTOOLS [21]. Some alternative approaches explore verifying nonpolynomial systems, such as counterexample guided inductive synthesis (CEGIS), leveraging satisfiability modulo theories (SMT) solvers (e.g., Z3 [8] or dReal [10]). Other techniques encompass neural barrier functions [17,29] and genetic programs [25]. While we focus on using BCs for *safety* specifications, they also hold significant value for addressing other temporal logic specifications [4,16].

The most significant tool dedicated to the construction of barrier certificates is FOSSIL [1,9]. FOSSIL designs barrier certificates for discrete- and continuous-time *deterministic* systems using the CEGIS approach, while facilitating verification and control synthesis for specifications including safety, reachability, and reach-while-avoid. However, FOSSIL lacks support for *stochastic* systems, whereas PRoTECT provides support for both discrete- and continuous-time *stochastic* systems. Recently, two new tools for constructing barrier certificates have been introduced. TRUST [11] is a *data-driven* tool that generates barrier certificates for deterministic systems with *unknown* polynomial dynamics, using only a single trajectory of collected data. In addition, CBFKIT [7] is a toolbox designed for safe robotic planning. It supports both deterministic and stochastic *continuous-time dynamics* but requires the user to provide a barrier function *a priori*, which it then verifies for correctness—unlike PRoTECT, which automatically synthesizes a barrier certificate to meet the required conditions.

Original Contributions. The primary contributions and noteworthy aspects of our tool paper are as follows:

(i) We propose the first tool, employing SOS optimization techniques, that verifies the safe behavior of *four classes of dynamical systems*: (i) discrete-time *stochastic* systems (dt-SS), (ii) discrete-time *deterministic* systems (dt-DS), (iii) *continuous-time* stochastic systems (ct-SS), and (iv) *continuous-time* deterministic systems (ct-DS). In particular, PRoTECT is the first software tool that offers stochastic barrier certificates.

(ii) PRoTECT is implemented in Python using SumOfSquares [28], and leverages *parallelization* to efficiently search for BCs of different degrees, aiming to satisfy the desired safety specifications.

(iii) PRoTECT supports *normal, uniform,* and *exponential* noise distributions for dt-SS, as well as *Brownian motion* and *Poisson processes* for ct-SS.

(iv) PRoTECT offers advanced GUIs for all four classes of models, enhancing the tool's accessibility and user-friendliness.

The source code for PRoTECT, along with detailed guidelines on installation and usage, including tutorial videos, are available at:

https://github.com/Kiguli/PRoTECT

2   Problem Description

Safety Barrier Certificates. Consider a state set X in an n-dimensional space, denoted as $X \subseteq \mathbb{R}^n$. Within this set, we identify two specific subsets: $X_\mathcal{I}$ and $X_\mathcal{U}$, which represent the *initial and unsafe* sets, respectively. The primary objective is to construct a function $\mathcal{B}(x)$, termed the *barrier certificate*, along with constants γ and λ as the *initial* and *unsafe* level sets of $\mathcal{B}(x)$, as illustrated in Fig. 1. Specifically, the design of the BC incorporates two conditions concerning these level sets, in conjunction with a third criterion that captures the *state evolution* of the system. Collectively, satisfaction of the conditions provides a (probabilistic) guarantee that the system's trajectories, originating from any initial condition $x_0 \in X_\mathcal{I}$, will not transition into the unsafe region $X_\mathcal{U}$. We now formally introduce the safety specification that we aim to investigate in this work.

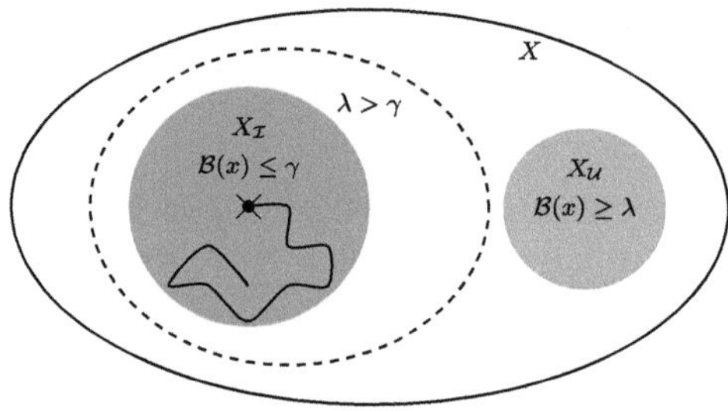

Fig. 1. A barrier certificate $\mathcal{B}(x)$ for a dynamical system. The dashed line denotes the initial level set $\mathcal{B}(x) = \gamma$.

Definition 1 (Safety). *A safety specification is defined as* $\varphi = (X_\mathcal{I}, X_\mathcal{U}, \mathcal{T})$, *where* $X_\mathcal{I}, X_\mathcal{U} \subseteq X$ *with* $X_\mathcal{I} \cap X_\mathcal{U} = \emptyset$, *and horizon* $\mathcal{T} \in \mathbb{N} \cup \{\infty\}$. *A dynamical system* Σ *is considered safe over an (in)finite time horizon* $\mathcal{T}$, *denoted as* $\Sigma \models_\mathcal{T} \varphi$ *if all trajectories of* Σ *starting from the initial set* $X_\mathcal{I}$ *never reach the unsafe set* $X_\mathcal{U}$. *If trajectories are probabilistic, the primary goal is to compute* $\mathbb{P}\{\Sigma \models_\mathcal{T} \varphi\} \geq \phi$, *with* $\phi \in [0, 1]$.

Overview of PRoTECT. PRoTECT offers functionalities that automatically generate BCs and verify the safety property across *four distinct classes of systems*. The description of the system serves as an input to the tool, triggering the appropriate function. These functions are named as `dt-SS`, `dt-DS`, `ct-SS` and `ct-DS`. Additionally, the geometric characteristics for sets of interest, which define the safety specification according to Definition 1, constitute another input

---

Algorithm 1: *Parallel* Construction of BCs

Data: system Σ, maximum polynomial degree P, *required* parameters K_{req}, *optional* parameters K_{opt}

```
1 temp = [];
2 choose function func for Σ to identify the class of system;
3 forall the p ∈ {2, 4, ..., P} in parallel do
4     barrier = func(p, K_req, K_opt);
5     if barrier is SOS then
6         temp.append(barrier);
7         if Σ is deterministic then
                // terminate all parallel processes
8         end
9     end
10 end
   // return element with highest confidence in temp
11 B(x) = max(temp);
```

Result: barrier certificate $\mathcal{B}(x)$, level sets γ, λ; confidence ϕ and constant c (for dt-SS and ct-SS)

---

to the tool. While a GUI is designed to enhance the user-friendliness of PRo-TECT, the BCs may also be verified via configuration files executed through the command line. As the output, PRoTECT returns BC $\mathcal{B}(x)$, level sets γ and λ, and, for stochastic systems, the value c and the confidence level ϕ (cf. Sect. 3).

Utilizing methodologies from the *sum-of-squares* (SOS) domain, facilitated by the SumOfSquares Python toolbox [28], PRoTECT adopts polynomial structures for BCs expressed as $\mathcal{B}(x) = \sum_{j=1}^{z} q_j p_j(x)$, with basis functions $p_j(x)$ that are monomials over x, and unknown coefficients $q = [q_0, \ldots, q_z] \in \mathbb{R}^z$ that need to be designed. PRoTECT leverages parallelization techniques to facilitate the *simultaneous* verification of multiple BCs, differentiating them based on their polynomial degrees, where degrees must be even [23]. In deterministic systems, upon finding a feasible BC, the parallel processing is terminated and the valid BC is returned to the user. Conversely, for stochastic systems, PRoTECT awaits until all potential solutions are fully processed, subsequently selecting and returning the BC that offers the highest probabilistic confidence. This process is detailed in the provided pseudo-code, illustrated in Algorithm 1.

Remark 1 Due to space limitations, this work focuses on the presentation of dt-SS, given its complexity when handled by our tool. However, the other classes, Python code snippets, and a comparison between FOSSIL and PRoTECT for the deterministic classes can be found in the extended version of this work [26].

3 Discrete-Time Stochastic Systems

In this section, we define the notion of barrier certificates for discrete-time stochastic systems (dt-SS). A dt-SS is a tuple $\Sigma_d^\varsigma = (X, \varsigma, f)$, where: $X \subseteq \mathbb{R}^n$

is a Borel space as the state set, ς is a sequence of independent and identically distributed (i.i.d.) random variables from a sample space Ω to a measurable set $\mathcal{V}_\varsigma$, *i.e.*, $\varsigma := \{\varsigma(k) \colon \Omega \to \mathcal{V}_\varsigma,\ k \in \mathbb{N}\}$, and $f \colon X \times \mathcal{V}_\varsigma \to X$ is a measurable function characterizing the *state evolution* of the system. For a given initial state $x(0) \in X$, the state evolution of Σ_d^ς is characterized by

$$\Sigma_d^\varsigma \colon x(k+1) = f(x(k), \varsigma(k)), \quad k \in \mathbb{N}. \tag{1}$$

The stochastic process $x_{x_0} \colon \Omega \times \mathbb{N} \to X$, which fulfills (1) for any initial state $x_0 \in X$ is referred to as the *solution process* of dt-SS at time $k \in \mathbb{N}$. PRoTECT accommodates *additive noise* types across a range of distributions, including *uniform*, *normal*, and *exponential* distributions. The notion of barrier certificates for dt-SS is provided by the subsequent definition [20].

Definition 2 (BC for dt-SS). *Consider the dt-SS $\Sigma_d^\varsigma = (X, \varsigma, f)$ and $X_\mathcal{I}, X_\mathcal{U} \subseteq X$. A function $\mathcal{B} \colon X \to \mathbb{R}_0^+$ is known as the barrier certificate (BC), if there exists constants $\lambda, \gamma, c \in \mathbb{R}_0^+$, with $\lambda > \gamma$, such that*

$$\mathcal{B}(x) \leq \gamma, \quad \forall x \in X_\mathcal{I}, \tag{2}$$

$$\mathcal{B}(x) \geq \lambda, \quad \forall x \in X_\mathcal{U}, \tag{3}$$

$$\mathbb{E}\Big[\mathcal{B}(f(x,\varsigma)) \mid x\Big] \leq \mathcal{B}(x) + c, \quad \forall x \in X, \tag{4}$$

where $\mathbb{E}$ denotes the expected value of the system's one-step transition, taken with respect to ς.

We now leverage the BC in Definition 2 and quantify a lower bound confidence over the safety of dt-SS [12,14,20]. This lemma, commonly found in the literature (e.g. [24]), provides the safety confidence for stochastic systems. The same confidence formula applies to *continuous-time* stochastic systems (see extended version [26, Section 6]).

Lemma 1 (Confidence ϕ). *For dt-SS Σ_d^ς, let there exist a BC as in Definition 2. Then the probability that trajectories of dt-SS starting from any initial condition $x_0 \in X_\mathcal{I}$ will not reach the unsafe region $X_\mathcal{U}$ within a finite time horizon $k \in [0, \mathcal{T}]$ is quantified as*

$$\phi = \mathbb{P}\Big\{x_{x_0}(k) \notin X_\mathcal{U} \text{ for all } k \in [0, \mathcal{T}] \mid x_0 = x(0)\Big\} \geq 1 - \frac{\gamma + c\mathcal{T}}{\lambda}. \tag{5}$$

Under the assumption that f is a polynomial function of state x and sets $X_\mathcal{I}, X_\mathcal{U}, X$ are semi-algebraic—*i.e.*, representable by polynomial inequalities—the extended version [26] provides a reformulation of (2)(4) as an SOS optimization program for designing a polynomial-type BC.

Remark 2 PRoTECT is equipped to accommodate any *arbitrary number* of unsafe regions $X_{\mathcal{U}_i}$, where $i \in \{1, \ldots, m\}$. In such scenarios, condition (3) should be reiterated and enforced for each distinct unsafe region.

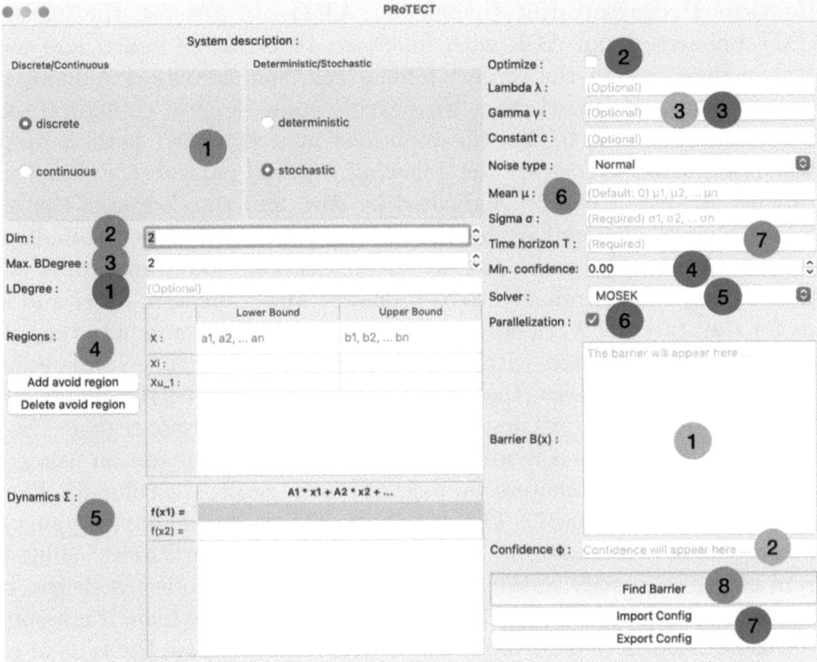

Fig. 2. PRoTECT GUI for dt-SS, where required parameters, optional parameters, and outputs are marked with blue, red, and yellow circles, respectively.

Graphical User Interface (GUI). To enhance accessibility and user-friendliness of the tool, PRoTECT offers the Model-View-Presenter architecture incorporating a GUI. Specifically, a GUI strengthens user-friendliness by abstracting away implementation details for the code, allowing for a push-button method to construct barrier certificates. In Fig. 2, colors and numbers are used to denote labels. While PRoTECT provides GUIs for all four classes of systems (see Fig. 2 (blue-1)), we only depict it for dt-SS due to space constraints. Our tool offers two implementations, either serial or parallel (red-6). The tool processes the information entered into the GUI before executing the desired function upon pressing the *Find Barrier* button (blue-8). Outputs of barrier certificate $\mathcal{B}(x)$, confidence ϕ, level sets γ and λ, and constant c are displayed at (yellow-1), (yellow-2), and (yellow-3), respectively. Optionally, the GUI allows for the import and export of configuration parameters in JSON format using the *Import Config* and *Export Config* buttons (red-7), with examples available in the folder `/ex/GUI_config_files`.

Application Programming Interface (API). In general, the backend of PRoTECT behaves as an API, with functions that can be called and used in any python program. In the project folders /ex/benchmarks-stochastic and /ex/benchmarks-deterministic, we provide some generic configuration files which demonstrate how to use the functions in a standard python program. The user is expected to provide the following *required* parameters: dimension of the state set $X \subseteq \mathbb{R}^n$ (blue-2), indicated by dim, and the degree of the barrier certificate (blue-3), denoted by b_degree. The lower and upper bounds of the initial region $X_\mathcal{I}$, labeled as L_initial and U_initial; lower and upper bounds of the unsafe region $X_\mathcal{U}$, referred to as L_unsafe and U_unsafe; lower and upper bounds for the state set X, denoted as L_space and U_space; where the value of each dimension is separated with a comma (blue-4). Due to possible scenarios with multiple unsafe regions, the unsafe region is passed to the functions as a numpy array of numpy arrays describing each individual unsafe region. The transition map f is written as a SymPy expression[2] for each dimension using states x1,x2,... and noise parameters varsigma1,varsigma2,... (blue-5). The time horizon $\mathcal{T}$, noted as t (blue-7). The distribution of the noise, NoiseType, can be specified as either ''normal'', ''exponential'', or ''uniform'' (blue-6).

Users may also specify *optional* parameters, these include the degree of the Lagrangian multipliers $l_i(x), l_u(x), l(x)$: l_degree (red-1), which, if not specified (i.e., set to None), will default to the same value as b_degree; the type of solver: solver (red-5), that can be either set to ''mosek'' [6] or ''cvxopt'' [5]. The confidence level ϕ in (5) can be optimized using optimize (red-2), if set to True. In this case, due to having a bilinearity between γ and λ in (5), the user is required to resolve this, *e.g.*, select $\lambda = 1$ (red-3). The tool will then optimize for the other decision variables including γ and c to provide the highest confidence level ϕ. Alternatively, the user can select a minimum confidence level ϕ (red-4) they require using confidence, so that PRoTECT attempts to search for a BC satisfying that confidence level. The parameters for the distributions should be specified as follows (blue-6): for normal distributions, the mean μ can be set using mean, and the diagonal covariance matrix σ can be provided using sigma. For exponential distributions, the rate parameter for each dimension can be set using rate. For uniform distributions, the boundaries for each dimension can be set using a and b. We provide two functions for dt-SS (red-6): the first dt_SS finds a barrier for a single degree, and the second parallel_dt_SS runs the first function in parallel for all barrier degrees up to the maximum barrier degree specified (also called b_degree).

---

[2] https://docs.sympy.org/latest/tutorials/intro-tutorial/basic_operations.html.

Table 1. Efficiency evaluation in BC construction for *stochastic systems* via PRoTECT. We present case studies for the barrier degrees 4, optimizing for the barrier with the highest confidence. Parameters γ and c are designed via SOS optimization and λ is fixed a priori. VDP denotes the stochastic Van der Pol oscillator. All experiments were conducted on a desktop computer (Intel i9-12900).

	n	system	T	b_degree	One Shot Stochastic Systems				
					γ	λ	c	ϕ	time (sec)
RoomTemp [18]	1	ct-SS	5	4	$4.8e^{-5}$	10	$9.6e^{-6}$	0.99	0.16
RoomTemp [18]	1	dt-SS	5	4	$4.4e^{-5}$	10	$8.9e^{-6}$	0.99	0.25
VDP [2]	2	dt-SS	5	4	N/A	1000	N/A	N/A	1.65
ex_lin_1 [19]	2	ct-SS	5	4	1.39	10	0.26	0.73	0.61
ex_nonlin_1 [19]	2	ct-SS	5	4	3.34	10	0.53	0.40	0.61
TwoTanks [22]	2	dt-SS	5	4	$1.0e^{-6}$	10	$3.4e^{-8}$	0.99	1.25
RoomTemp [24]	3	dt-SS	3	4	$1.1e^{-8}$	10	$7.5e^{-9}$	0.99	29.1
hi-ord_4 [1]	4	ct-SS	3	4	0.02	10	0.02	0.99	68.1

4 Benchmarking

Table 1 and Table 2 employ PRoTECT for stochastic benchmarks. In the 'One Shot' setting with a fixed barrier degree of 4, as shown in Table 1, PRoTECT optimizes all parameters, γ and c, during the SOS formulation, while λ is fixed a priori. Notably, the VDP example cannot find a barrier certificate with degree 4. Alternatively, the user can set a maximum degree and run computations in parallel up to this degree, returning the barrier certificate with the highest confidence. We call this the "Parallel" setting, as shown in Table 2, where λ is once again fixed a priori. Consequently, stochastic case studies typically require longer completion times compared to the "One Shot" setting or parallelism for deterministic systems (see extended version [26]), but at the gain of offering a higher confidence, *e.g.* example ex_nonlin$_1$ has a confidence improvement of 32%. This is a trade-off the user should navigate based on their particular setting. The parallelism introduces minimal overhead, and running the degrees in parallel is 19–27% faster than computing degrees (2, 4, 6) sequentially.

Remark 3 In Table 1, the VDP case does not yield an optimized solution for $\lambda = 1000$. However, by *setting the minimum confidence level* to $\phi = 0.8$ (as shown in red-4 in Fig. 2), feasible values for λ, γ, and c can be identified with confidence exceeding the specified threshold. These results are omitted from Table 1 to maintain consistency in the comparison.

Table 2. Efficiency evaluation in BC construction for *stochastic systems* via PRoTECT. We present case studies across three barrier degrees (2, 4, and 6), returning the barrier with the highest confidence. Parameter λ is fixed to a certain value and then γ and c are designed via SOS optimization. VDP denotes the stochastic Van der Pol oscillator. All experiments were conducted on a desktop computer (Intel i9-12900).

	n	system	$\mathcal{T}$	b_degree	Parallel Stochastic Systems				
					γ	λ	c	ϕ	time (sec)
RoomTemp [18]	1	ct-SS	5	6	$1.1e^{-6}$	10	$2.3e^{-7}$	0.99	0.33
RoomTemp [18]	1	dt-SS	5	6	$4.4e^{-7}$	10	$1.0e^{-7}$	0.99	0.53
VDP [2]	2	dt-SS	5	6	97.5	1000	3.53	0.88	14.3
ex_lin_1 [19]	2	ct-SS	5	6	0.34	10	0.04	0.95	1.73
ex_nonlin_1 [19]	2	ct-SS	5	6	1.84	10	0.2	0.72	1.81
TwoTanks [22]	2	dt-SS	5	4	$1.0e^{-6}$	10	$3.4e^{-8}$	0.99	5.14
RoomTemp [24]	3	dt-SS	3	4	$1.1e^{-8}$	10	$7.5e^{-9}$	0.99	1501
hi-ord_4 [1]	4	ct-SS	3	6	$1.8e^{-3}$	10	$1.2e^{-3}$	0.99	1308

5   Conclusion

This work introduced PRoTECT, a pioneer software tool utilizing *SOS optimization* to explore polynomial-type BCs for verifying safety properties across *four classes of dynamical systems*: dt-SS, dt-DS, ct-SS, and ct-DS. In particular, PRoTECT is the first software tool that designs stochastic barrier certificates. The tool is developed in Python and incorporates a user-friendly GUI to enhance its usability. Additionally, PRoTECT offers *parallelization* to concurrently search for BCs of different degrees, ensuring an efficient construction. In the future, PRoTECT will be expanded to incorporate reachability and reach-while-avoid specifications, along with designing controllers using SOS optimization techniques.

References

1. Abate, A., Ahmed, D., Edwards, A., Giacobbe, M., Peruffo, A.: FOSSIL: a software tool for the formal synthesis of lyapunov functions and barrier certificates using neural networks. In: Proceedings of the 24th International Conference on Hybrid Systems: Computation and Control, pp. 1–11 (2021)
2. Abate, A., et al.: ARCH-COMP20 Category Report: Stochastic Models (2020)
3. Ames, A.D., Coogan, S., Egerstedt, M., Notomista, G., Sreenath, K., Tabuada, P.: Control Barrier Functions: theory and Applications. In: 2019 18th European Control Conference (ECC), pp. 3420–3431. IEEE (2019)
4. Anand, M., Lavaei, A., Zamani, M.: Compositional synthesis of control barrier certificates for networks of stochastic systems against ω-regular specifications. Nonlinear Analysis: Hybrid Systems **51** (2024)
5. Andersen, M.S., Dahl, J., Vandenberghe, L., et al.: CVXOPT: A Python package for convex optimization. Available at cvxopt.org **54** (2013)
6. ApS, M.: MOSEK Optimizer API for Python (2022)

7. Black, M., Fainekos, G., Hoxha, B., Okamoto, H., Prokhorov, D.: CBFKIT: A Control Barrier Function Toolbox for Robotics Applications. arXiv preprint arXiv:2404.07158 (2024)
8. De Moura, L., Bjørner, N.: Z3: An efficient SMT solver. In: Proceedings of the International conference on Tools and Algorithms for the Construction and Analysis of Systems, pp. 337–340 (2008)
9. Edwards, A., Peruffo, A., Abate, A.: Fossil 2.0: Formal Certificate Synthesis for the Verification and Control of Dynamical Models. arXiv:2311.09793 (2023)
10. Gao, S., Avigad, J., Clarke, E.M.: δ-complete decision procedures for satisfiability over the reals. In: Automated Reasoning, pp. 286–300. Lecture Notes in Computer Science (2012)
11. Gardner, J., Wooding, B., Nejati, A., Lavaei, A.: TRUST: StabiliTy and Safety ContRoller Synthesis for Unknown Dynamical Models Using a Single Trajectory. In: Proceedings of the 28th ACM International Conference on Hybrid Systems: Computation and Control, pp. 1–16 (2025)
12. Jagtap, P., Soudjani, S., Zamani, M.: Formal synthesis of stochastic systems via control barrier certificates. IEEE Trans. Autom. Control $66(7)$, 3097–3110 (2020)
13. Knight, J.C.: Safety critical systems: challenges and directions. In: Proceedings of the 24th international conference on software engineering, pp. 547–550 (2002)
14. Kushner, H.J.: On the stability of stochastic dynamical systems. Proc. Natl. Acad. Sci. $53(1)$, 8–12 (1965)
15. Lavaei, A., Soudjani, S., Abate, A., Zamani, M.: Automated verification and synthesis of stochastic hybrid systems: A survey. Automatica 146 (2022)
16. Lindemann, L., Dimarogonas, D.V.: Barrier function based collaborative control of multiple robots under signal temporal logic tasks. IEEE Trans. Control Netw. Syst. $7(4)$, 1916–1928 (2020)
17. Mathiesen, F.B., Calvert, S.C., Laurenti, L.: Safety certification for stochastic systems via neural barrier functions. IEEE Control Syst. Lett. 7, 973–978 (2022)
18. Nejati, A., Soudjani, S., Zamani, M.: Compositional abstraction-based synthesis for continuous-time stochastic hybrid systems. Eur. J. Control. 57, 82–94 (2021)
19. Prajna, S., Jadbabaie, A., Pappas, G.J.: Stochastic safety verification using barrier certificates. In: 2004 43rd IEEE conference on decision and control (CDC). vol. 1, pp. 929–934. IEEE (2004)
20. Prajna, S., Jadbabaie, A., Pappas, G.J.: A framework for worst-case and stochastic safety verification using barrier certificates. IEEE Trans. Autom. Control $52(8)$, 1415–1428 (2007)
21. Prajna, S., Papachristodoulou, A., Parrilo, P.A.: Introducing sostools: A general purpose sum of squares programming solver. In: Proceedings of the 41st IEEE Conference on Decision and Control, 2002. vol. 1, pp. 741–746. IEEE (2002)
22. Ramos, J.A., Dos Santos, P.L.: Mathematical modeling, system identification, and controller design of a two tank system. In: 2007 46th IEEE Conference on Decision and Control, pp. 2838–2843. IEEE (2007)
23. Reznick, B.: Some concrete aspects of Hilbert's 17th problem. Contemp. Math. 253, 251–272 (2000)
24. Salamati, A., Lavaei, A., Soudjani, S., Zamani, M.: Data-driven verification and synthesis of stochastic systems via barrier certificates. Automatica 159, 111323 (2024)
25. Verdier, C.F., Mazo, M.: Formal synthesis of analytic controllers for sampled-data systems via genetic programming. In: 2018 IEEE Conference on Decision and Control (CDC), pp. 4896–4901. IEEE (2018)

26. Wooding, B., Horbanov, V., Lavaei, A.: PRoTECT: Parallelized Construction of Safety Barrier Certificates for Nonlinear Polynomial Systems. arXiv pp. 1–27 (2024). https://doi.org/10.48550/arXiv.2404.14804
27. Xiao, W., Cassandras, C.G., Belta, C.: Safe Autonomy with Control Barrier Functions: Theory and Applications. Springer (2023)
28. Yuan, C.: SumOfSquares.py. https://github.com/yuanchenyang/SumOfSquares.py
29. Zhao, H., Zeng, X., Chen, T., Liu, Z.: Synthesizing barrier certificates using neural networks. In: Proceedings of the 23rd international conference on hybrid systems: Computation and control, pp. 1–11 (2020)

On Computational Aspects of Ordered Matching Problems

Michal Čertík[1]([✉])[iD], Andreas Emil Feldmann[2][iD], Jaroslav Nešetřil[1][iD],
and Paweł Rzążewski[3][iD]

[1] Computer Science Institute, Faculty of Mathematics and Physics, Charles
University, Prague, Czech Republic
`michal.certik@matfyz.cuni.cz`, `nesetril@kam.mff.cuni.cz`
[2] Department of Computer Science, University of Sheffield, Sheffield, UK
`feldmann.a.e@gmail.com`
[3] Warsaw University of Technology and University of Warsaw, Warsaw, Poland
`pawel.rzazewski@pw.edu.pl`

Abstract. Ordered matchings, defined as graphs with linearly ordered
vertices, where each vertex is connected to exactly one edge, play a crucial
role in the area of ordered graphs and their homomorphisms. Therefore,
we consider related problems from the complexity point of view and
determine their corresponding computational and parameterized complexities. We show that the subgraph of ordered matchings problem is
NP-complete and we prove that the problem of finding ordered homomorphisms between ordered matchings is NP-complete as well, implying
NP-completeness of more generic problems. In parameterized complexity
setting, we consider a natural choice of parameter - a number of vertices
of the image ordered graph. We show that in contrast to the complexity
context, finding homomorphisms if the image ordered graph is an ordered
matching, this problem parameterized by the number of vertices of the
image ordered graph is FPT, which is known to be W[1]-hard for the
general problem. We also determine that the problem of core for ordered
matchings is solvable in polynomial time which is again in contrast to the
NP-completeness of the general problem. We provide several algorithms
and generalize some of these problems into ordered graphs with colored
edges.

Keywords: Computational Complexity · Parameterized Complexity ·
Ordered Graphs · Homomorphisms · Ordered Matchings · Ordered
Core

1 Introduction

An *ordered graph* is a graph whose vertex set is totally ordered. For two ordered
graphs G and H, an *ordered homomorphism* from G to H is a mapping f from
$V(G)$ to $V(H)$ that preserves edges and vertices ordering, that is,

---

P. Rzążewski—Supported by the National Science Centre grant 2024/54/E/ST6/00094.

Z. Liu et al. (Eds.): ICTAC 2025, LNCS 16237, pp. 459–467, 2026.
https://doi.org/10.1007/978-3-032-11176-0_27

1. for every $uv \in E(G)$ we have $f(u)f(v) \in E(H)$,
2. for $u, v \in V(G)$, if $u \leq v$, then $f(u) \leq f(v)$.

Note that the second condition implies that the preimage of every vertex of H forms a segment or an *independent interval* in the ordering of $V(G)$.

We define an *Ordered Matching* as an ordered graph in which every vertex is incident to precisely one edge.

Let us continue with the definition of an *Ordered Retraction* of G to H being an ordered homomorphism $f : G \rightarrow H$ such that $f(v) = v$ for all $v \in V(H)$. If this ordered retraction of G to H exists, we say that G *order-retracts* to H or that H is an *order-retract* of G. Notice that, as for digraphs (see [15]), if ordered retraction exists, we have ordered homomorphism of G to H and inclusion-ordered homomorphism of H to G, therefore G and H are (ordered) homomorphically equivalent.

Let us now define *an Ordered Core* as an ordered graph that does not retract to a proper ordered subgraph. We show in [10] that, as for unordered digraphs (see [15]), an ordered graph G is an ordered core if and only if there is no ordered homomorphism from G to a proper ordered subgraph of G, and that every ordered graph is homomorphically equivalent to a unique ordered core.

Further on we may call an independent interval simply an interval, and an ordered graph, ordered homomorphism, ordered core, and ordered matching simply graph, homomorphism, core and matching, respectively.

The forthcoming full version of the article [11] will contain the complete list of results along with their proofs.

2 Motivation

Ordered graphs naturally arise in several situations: Ramsey theory ([17], [14], [3]), extremal theory ([12,19]), category theory ([14], [18]) and others. Recently, the notion of twin width of graphs has been shown to be equivalent to NIP (or dependent) classes of ordered graphs ([4], [5]) thus meeting graph theory and model theory.

Homomorphisms of ordered graphs confirm and complement the above line of research: they are more restrictive (than standard homomorphisms, see, e.g. [15]) but display richness on its own (see, e.g. [1,13]). In [16] it has even recently been shown that ordering problems for graphs defined by finitely many forbidden ordered subgraphs capture the class NP.

The significance of ordered matchings is known in the domain of ordered graphs and their homomorphisms (see, e.g., [3], [2], [12], [7]). Even within homomorphisms of ordered relational structures, analogues or ordered matchings play a critical role (see [8]). Therefore, we examine associated problems with the aim of determining their computational and parameterized complexities.

3 Subgraphs of Ordered Matchings

We start with a definition of the problem of determining whether an input ordered matching G is a subgraph of an input ordered matching H.

Problem 1.

$$\mathrm{SUB}^M_{\le}$$

Input: Ordered matchings G and H.
Question: Is G a subgraph (resp. an induced subgraph) of H?

We show that the problem $\mathrm{SUB}^M_{\le}$ is NP-complete even for the following specific class of ordered matchings.

For an ordered graph G with vertices ordered as follows $V(G) = (v_1, \ldots, v_n)$, an *i-th cut* $C = (S, T)$ is a partition of $V(G)$ of a graph G into two subsets $S = (v_1, \ldots, v_i)$ and $T = (v_{i+1}, \ldots, v_n)$. Then we say that an edge e *goes across* the i-th cut $C = (S, T)$ if and only if one vertex of the edge e belongs to S and another endpoint of the edge e belongs to T.

An ordered graph G is *separated* if there exists $i \in [|V(G)| - 1]$ such that all edges go across the i-th cut.

Theorem 1. *Given two separated ordered matchings M and N, it is* NP-*complete to decide whether N is a subgraph (resp., an induced subgraph) of M.*

Proof. We reduce from the Permutation Pattern Matching Problem (see, [6]). There we are given two permutations $\pi : [n] \to [n]$ and $\Pi : [m] \to [m]$, where $m \ge n$, and we ask whether Π contains π as a sub-permutation (i.e., whether there are n elements whose relative positions in Π are as in π). As shown in [6], this problem is NP-complete.

Let M be the m-edge matching, consisting of the edges $(i, m + \Pi(i))$ for $i \in [m]$. Similarly, let N be the n-edge matching, consisting of the edges $(i, n + \pi(i))$ for $i \in [n]$. We claim that N is a subgraph of M if and only if Π contains π.

First, suppose that Π contains π, that is, there are $1 \le i_1 < \ldots < i_m \le n$ such that Π restricted to $(i_1, \ldots, i_n)$ is π. We claim that the subgraph of M induced by $X = \bigcup_{j \in [n]} \{i_j, \Pi(i_j)\}$ is isomorphic to N. For contradiction, suppose otherwise. Clearly, $N[X]$ is a separated n-edge matching. In addition, the right endpoints of the edges are ordered according to π. Thus, $M[X]$ is indeed a copy of N.

Now suppose that N is a subgraph of M. Note that since both M and N are matchings, this subgraph must be induced. Let $X \in [2n]$ be such that $M[X]$ is isomorphic to N. Then π, defined by the edges $(j, n + \pi(j)), j \in [n]$ of $M[X]$, is clearly a subpermutation of Π, defined by the edges $(i, m + \Pi(i)), i \in [m]$ of M, as Π restricted to $M[X]$ is π.

4   Finding Homomorphisms of Ordered Matchings

It is easy to see that for a fixed ordered graph H, the (ordered) H-coloring problem, defined as the problem of finding an ordered homomorphism from a given ordered graph G to a fixed ordered graph H, is in P (see, e.g. [7], [9]).

In this section, we will therefore focus on the $\mathrm{HOM}_<$ computational problem, where H is not fixed and is part of an input. Let us start with a definition of $\mathrm{HOM}_<$ for ordered matchings, whose input is a pair of ordered matchings G and H, and we ask if G admits an ordered homomorphism to H.

Problem 2. $\textsc{Hom}_{<}^{M}$

$\textsc{Hom}_{<}^{M}$

Input: Ordered matchings G and H.
Question: Does there exist an ordered homomorphism $f : G \to H$?

We now show that the $\textsc{Hom}_{<}^{M}$ problem is NP-complete.

Theorem 2. *Given two ordered matchings M and N, it is NP-complete to decide whether $N \to M$.*

Proof. We again reduce from the Permutation Pattern Matching Problem.

Let M consist of the m-edge matching, consisting of the edges $(i, m + \Pi(i))$ for $i \in [m]$ (as in 1) and the following edge set. Take the $2m$ vertices i, ordered naturally, created by the previous m-edge matching and add the vertices a_i and $b_i, a_i < b_i$ between the vertices i and $i + 1, i \in [2m - 1]$. Add vertices c_m and $d_m, c_m < d_m$ between vertices b_m and $m + 1$. The positions of the vertices a_i and $b_i, i \in [2m - 1]$ and c_m and d_m are uniquely defined. Create an edge between the vertices a_i and $b_i, i \in [2m - 1]$ and create an edge between the vertices c_m and d_m. The ordered graph M is an ordered matching with $3m$ edges.

Similarly, let N consist of the n-edge matching, consisting of the edges $(i, n + \pi(i))$ for $i \in [n]$ and the following edge set. Take the $2n$ vertices i, ordered naturally, created by the previous n-edge matching and add the vertices a_i and b_i between the vertices i and $i + 1, i \in [2n - 1]$. Add vertices c_n and d_n between vertices b_n and $n + 1$. Create an edge between the vertices a_i and $b_i, i \in [2n - 1]$ and create an edge between the vertices c_n and d_n.

We claim that there exists an ordered homomorphism $N \to M$ if and only if Π contains π. Denote the edges $(i, n + \pi(i))$ for $i \in [n]$ as *permutation edges* and edges in between a_i and $b_i, i \in [2n - 1]$ and c_n and d_n by *auxiliary edges*. We adopt the same notation for the edges in M.

First, suppose that Π contains π, that is, there are $1 \le i_1 < \ldots < i_m \le n$ such that Π restricted to $(i_1, \ldots, i_m)$ is π. From Theorem 1 we know that the subgraph of M induced by permutation edges of M must contain a graph $M[X]$ isomorphic to a subgraph of N induced by permutation edges of N. Auxiliary edges in N ensure that this mapping must be injective.

For contradiction, suppose otherwise. Suppose that two permutation edges of N map to one permutation edge of M. This cannot happen, as there is always an auxiliary edge in between the ends of the permutation edges. Now suppose that a permutation edge e in N maps to an auxiliary edge e' in M. This cannot happen either, as there are always at least two auxiliary edges between the ends of e in N and there are no edges between the ends of an auxiliary edge e' in M. Therefore, the permutation edges of N map injectively to an induced subgraph $M[X]$ of M.

It remains to show that the auxiliary edges of N can also always be mapped to the edges of M. But this is also obvious, as there are always auxiliary edges between the permutation edges $M[X]$ in M.

Now suppose that there exists an ordered homomorphism $N \to M$. We showed that the mapping of the permutation edges of N must be injective to the permutation edges of M. Therefore, this mapping defines an induced subgraph $M[X]$ of M, where $M[X]$ is isomorphic to N. But then we follow the same argument as in Theorem 1, showing that Π restricted to $M[X]$ is a subpermutation π, Π and π defined by permutation edges of M and N, respectively.

5 Parameterized Complexity of Homomorphisms of Ordered Matchings

Let us show that the $\mathrm{HOM}_<$ problem, when parameterized by $|V(M)|$ for an ordered matching M, is FPT.

Theorem 3. *Let G be an ordered graph and M be an ordered matching. Then deciding whether there exists an ordered homomorphism $G \to M$ is fixed-parameter tractable with respect to $|V(M)|$.*

Proof. We start by constructing the smallest possible ordered matching G' out of G, by mapping the subgraphs of G into disjoint edges.

Let G have g vertices and let M have m vertices. We denote these vertices in G by $1, 2, \ldots, g$.

Let us construct the smallest possible ordered graph G', in the number of edges g' in G'.

Take an interval of independent vertices $i, i+1, \ldots, j$ in G, which have their neighbors only among the vertices $j+1, j+2, \ldots, g$. We can determine whether edges incident with the vertices $i, i+1, \ldots, j$ can be mapped to only one edge in G as follows. Let us denote a set of vertices connected to vertices $i, i+1, \ldots, j$ as V_{ij}. Then we can map the edges incident with the vertices $i, i+1, \ldots, j$ to one edge in G if and only if the set of vertices V_{ij} form an interval in the ordering of G. The check whether the vertices in V_{ij} form an interval in the ordering of G can, of course, be performed in polynomial time.

Now we define the following greedy algorithm.

Algorithm 1.

Input: An ordered graph G.
Output: The smallest ordered matching G', such that $G \to G'$.
Method: Iterate on the vertices in the given order and map the ordered subgraphs of G to an edge whenever possible.

1. Set $A = \emptyset$ and $i = 1$.
2. Add i to A and set $a_{max} = i$
3. For $j = i+1$ to g
   3.1 Add j to A
   3.2 If any of the vertices in A are connected or if j is connected to any of the vertices $1, 2, \ldots, i-1$, exit the loop

    3.3 If the edges incident with vertices in A can be mapped to one edge in G, set $a_{max} = j$
4. Map all the edges incident with the vertices $i, i+1, \ldots, a_{max}$ to one of these edges and set $i = a_{max}$
5. For $j = i + 1$ to g
    5.1 if j is connected only to vertices among $j + 1, j + 2, \ldots, g$ then set $i = j, A = \emptyset$ and go to step 2.
    5.1 If $j = g$ stop

We note that if there exists an ordered homomorphism $G \to M$, then G can be partitioned into disjoint subgraphs that each map to an edge. We also notice that if the ordered subgraph G' of G resulting from the greedy Algorithm 1 above has the minimum number of edges (minimum with respect to a number of edges of other ordered matching subgraphs of G, where G could map) and is ordered matching, then it must be an order-retract of G as if every subgraph of G maps to an edge, then this edge must be a part of that subgraph. Here we note that this is the reason this approach works only for the matchings (since if e.g. two disjoint edges map into a path of length two, this might not be an ordered subgraph of the original ordered graph). We also note that if G' is an ordered matching and is minimum with respect to the number of edges (again minimum with respect to the number of edges of other ordered matching subgraphs of G, where G could map), then G' is the core of G.

Therefore, if G is not a core or G is not an ordered matching and there exists an ordered homomorphism $G \to M$, then in the ordered retraction $f : G \to G$, there exists at least one subgraph in G, containing at least three vertices, that maps to a single edge in G. In addition, if there are two or more subgraphs in G that map to an edge in G, these mappings can be performed consecutively and independently of each other.

Denote a subgraph of G by G_e. We note that the only way that the G_e in G can map to an independent edge in G' is if and only if G_e can be partitioned into two sets of independent vertices $i, i+1, \ldots, j$ and V_{ij}, where both of these sets are independent intervals and $i, i+1, \ldots, j$ is only connected to V_{ij}, and vice versa. The subgraphs G_e in G that can map to a single edge in G can therefore be uniquely determined by the set $i, i+1, \ldots, j$.

We see that if there exists a subgraph G_e with more than two vertices in G that can be mapped to a single edge, the algorithm finds it and performs the mapping (since these subgraphs can be mapped to edges independently). Therefore, if the core of G is an ordered matching G', the resulting ordered graph G' at the conclusion of the algorithm is equal to G' (of course, minimum with respect to g'). The algorithm again runs in $\mathcal{O}(g^{\mathcal{O}(1)})$ steps.

Now we can compare the number of disjoint edges g' in G' and the number h of disjoint edges in M.

If $g' > h$, then we know that there is no ordered homomorphism $G' \to M$, as G' is minimal with respect to g'. Then, of course, there is no ordered homomorphism $G \to M$.

If $g' \leq h$, then we know that we can find the ordered homomorphism $G' \to M$ by examining all 2^h possible choices of edges in M and seeing if any of them is isomorphic to G' (the isomorphism check in the case of ordered graphs is, of course, in P). If we find such a match, we know that there is an ordered homomorphism $G' \to M$ and therefore also $G \to M$ (by transitivity). If none of the combinations gives us a graph isomorphic to G', then we know that there does not exist an ordered homomorphism $G' \to M$ (here we also use the fact that G' is minimal with respect to g' and G' is a core).

We notice that we can also perform 2^m possible choices of vertices of M (to derive the complexity stated in the theorem), knowing that if we do not consider one vertex in an edge in M, we might not consider the whole edge, since G' is an ordered matching.

As the whole procedure takes at most $\mathcal{O}(2^m g^{\mathcal{O}(1)} g'^{\mathcal{O}(1)})$ steps, the result follows.

Let us now define a *colored ordered graph* as an ordered graph with colored edges and *colored ordered homomorphism* as an ordered homomorphism that preserves the colors of edges.

We define in the same way a colored ordered homomorphism generalization of the $\text{HOM}_<$ problem and determine the parameterized complexity of this problem parameterized by $|V(H)|$ for colored ordered matchings. We omit the proof of Corollary 1, which will be included in the forthcoming full version of the article.

Problem 3.

$\text{COLHOM}_<$

Input: Colored ordered graphs G and H.
Question: Does there exist a colored ordered homomorphism from G to H?

Corollary 1. $\text{COLHOM}_<$ *parameterized by* $|V(H)|$, *where* G *is a colored ordered graph and* H *is a colored ordered matching, is fixed-parameter tractable.*

We will now generalize the notion of ordered matching. Let H_0 be an ordered graph. We define an *ordered H_0-matching* as an ordered graph H that is a disjoint union of H_0. For example, taking $H_0 = K_2$, the resulting ordered H_0-matching is an ordered matching. In the following, we may denote ordered H_0-matching simply as H_0-matching.

The following then determines the parameterized complexity of $\text{HOM}_<$ problem parameterized by $|V(H)|$, where H is H_0-matching. The proof for Theorem 4 is not included here, but will be provided in the forthcoming full complete version of the article.

Theorem 4. *Let* H_0 *be a fixed connected ordered core and* G *be an ordered graph. Then deciding whether there exists ordered graph* H, *such that* H *is a disjoint unions of the graphs* H_0, *and* G *admits an ordered homomorphism to* H *is fixed-parameter tractable with respect to* $|V(H)|$.

6   Matchings Core Problems

Let us define the following problem, which we denote CORE$_<$.

Problem 4.

CORE$_<$

Input: Ordered graph G.
Question: Is there a non-surjective ordered homomorphism $G \to G$?

The following corollary then follows directly from the proof of Theorem 3 for the special case of CORE$_<$, where the core of an input ordered graph G is a matching.

Corollary 2. *Let G be an ordered graph. Then, if an ordered matching M is the core of G, finding M is in P.*

The following is then a related colored ordered homomorphism problem (generalization of CORE$_<$). Details of the proof of Corollary 3 are omitted but will be provided in the complete version of the upcoming article.

Problem 5.

ColCORE$_<$

Input: Colored ordered graph G.
Question: Is there a non-surjective colored ordered homomorphism $G \to G$?

Corollary 3. *Let G be an ordered colored graph. Then, if an ordered colored matching M is the core of G, finding M is in P.*

These results are in contrast with the NP-completeness of the general CORE$_<$ problem (and therefore also ColCORE$_<$), which we show in the article [10].

We also show in [9] that the parameterized Hom$_<$ problem, where input graphs are any ordered graphs, is W[1]-hard. We observe that while the ordered graphs G and H in [9] can be quite complex, the ordered graphs G and H in Theorem 4 are rather restricted and simple.

Therefore, it remains to fill the gap between these classes of ordered graphs and categorize which of the classes of ordered graphs makes Hom$_<$ parameterized by $|V(H)|$ in W[1]-hard and which of them in FPT. We shall not address it in this article.

References

1. Axenovich, M., Rollin, J., Ueckerdt, T.: Chromatic number of ordered graphs with forbidden ordered subgraphs. Combinatorica **38**, 1021–1043 (2016). https://api.semanticscholar.org/CorpusID:7776173
2. Balko, M., Cibulka, J., Král, K., Kynčl, J.: Ramsey numbers of ordered graphs. Electron. J. Comb. **27**(1) (2020). https://doi.org/10.37236/7816
3. Balko, M., Poljak, M.: On off-diagonal ordered Ramsey numbers of nested matchings (2022)
4. Bonnet, É., Giocanti, U., de Mendez, P.O., Simon, P., Thomassé, S., Toruńczyk, S.: Twin-width IV: ordered graphs and matrices (2021)
5. Bonnet, É., Nešetřil, J., de Mendez, P.O., Siebertz, S., Thomassé, S.: Twin-width and permutations (2024)
6. Bose, P., Buss, J.F., Lubiw, A.: Pattern matching for permutations. In: Dehne, F., Sack, J.-R., Santoro, N., Whitesides, S. (eds.) WADS 1993. LNCS, vol. 709, pp. 200–209. Springer, Heidelberg (1993). https://doi.org/10.1007/3-540-57155-8_248
7. Čertík, M., Nešetřil, J.: Duality, $\chi^<$-Boundedness and Order Density of Ordered Graphs (2024)
8. Čertík, M., Nešetřil, J.: Duality and $\chi^<$-Boundedness of Ordered Relational Systems (2025)
9. Čertík, M., Feldmann, A.E., Nešetřil, J., Rzążewski, P.: Complexity Aspects of Homomorphisms of Ordered Graphs (2025)
10. Čertík, M., Feldmann, A.E., Nešetřil, J., Rzążewski, P.: On Computational Aspects of Cores of Ordered Graphs and Hypergraphs (2025)
11. Čertík, M., Feldmann, A.E., Nešetřil, J., Rzążewski, P.: On Computational Aspects of Ordered Matchings (2025)
12. Conlon, D., Fox, J., Lee, C., Sudakov, B.: Ordered Ramsey numbers (2016)
13. Duffus, D., Ginn, M., Rödl, V.: On the computational complexity of ordered subgraph recognition. Random Structures & Algorithms **7**(3), 223–268 (1995). https://doi.org/10.1002/rsa.3240070304
14. Hedrlín, Z., Pultr, A., Trnková, V.: Concerning a categorial approach to topological and algebraic theories. In: General Topology and its Relations to Modern Analysis and Algebra, pp. 176–181. Academia Publishing House of the Czechoslovak Academy of Sciences (1967). http://eudml.org/doc/220068
15. Hell, P., Nešetřil, J.: Graphs and Homomorphisms. Oxford University Press (2004). https://global.oup.com/academic/product/graphs-and-homomorphisms-9780198528173?cc=cz
16. Kun, G., Nešetřil, J.: Dichotomy for orderings? arXiv (2025). https://doi.org/10.48550/arxiv.2504.13268
17. Nešetřil, J.: Ramsey theory, pp. 1331–1403. MIT Press, Cambridge (1996)
18. Nešetřil, J., de Mendez, P.O.: Towards a characterization of universal categories (2016)
19. Pach, J., Tardos, G.: Forbidden paths and cycles in ordered graphs and matrices. Israel J. Math. (2006). https://doi.org/10.1007/BF02773960

Safe Multi-agent Reinforcement Learning Using Formal Runtime Enforcement: A Case Study

Vedanta Mohapatra, Ayush Anand, and Srinivas Pinisetty(✉)

Indian Institute of Technology Bhubaneswar, Bhubaneswar, India
`{20cs02001,a23cs09003,spinisetty}@iitbbs.ac.in`

Abstract. Cyber-Physical Systems (CPSs) are increasingly used in safety-critical tasks like search and rescue missions. They are often combined with machine-learning algorithms like Reinforcement Learning (RL) for improved performance and accuracy. There is a pressing need to ensure the safety of such learning-enabled CPSs. In recent research, the Runtime Enforcement (RE) approach has been very successful in formally ensuring the safety of learning-enabled CPS. RE is a formal verification technique that dynamically guarantees the safety of a system.

We present a runtime enforcement mechanism for safeguarding a Multi-Agent Reinforcement Learning (MARL) enabled drone swarm CPS. We discuss the enforcement strategies that prevent drones from collision and boundary breach. We show how RE combined with MARL, in addition to guaranteeing safety, improves the overall performance of the swarm system.

Keywords: Runtime Enforcement · MARL · CPS · Automata

1 Introduction

Cyber-Physical Systems (CPSs) combine the digital computations and physical processes by enabling the digital controller to interact with its physical environment via sensors and actuators [14]. CPSs are used in intelligent transportation system, medical devices, smart grids, sensor networks *etc.* [5]. In a recent study, Herdel *et al.* [10] identified 'emergency' as the most prominent domain in drone (a potential CPS) application.

A drone swarm systems involves multiple drones working synchronously towards a common objective. Rule-based algorithm for control often lack the intrinsic ability to accomodate dynamic and unpredictable behaviour of environments. Thus, CPSs like drone swarm are often complimented/enabled with

V. Mohapatra acknowledges the support of IndiaAI Fellowship given by IndiaAI - a research division under Digital India Corporation, Govt. of India.

Z. Liu et al. (Eds.): ICTAC 2025, LNCS 16237, pp. 468–478, 2026.
https://doi.org/10.1007/978-3-032-11176-0_28

Machine Learning (ML) algorithms (often termed as swarm intelligence [27]) to enhance functional capabilities and adaptibility of the system [30].

Multi-Agent Reinforcement Learning (MARL) is a machine learning technique where a multi-agent system [29] uses reinforcement learning based algorithms to learn new behaviours by interacting with its dynamic environment [4,12,25,26]. The adaptive nature of reinforcement learning (RL)-based drone swarms introduces behavioral uncertainty and safety risks. These risks include potential inter-drone collisions, unsafe dispersal patterns, and failure to cover critical regions. Thus research on verification of RL-based systems has become prominent [13].

Scalibility of verification techniques (of RL methods) is still a challenge, although there exist works that show promising results [3]. Runtime Verification (RV) and Runtime Enforcement (RE) methods offer solutions for verifying an RL-enabled CPS. RV [6] is a light-wieght formal verification technique that verifies system properties during execution. RE [16] is an extension of RV method, where the verfication monitor, along with verifying the property, edits the execution of the system in order to guarantee the property satisfaction. RE methods for CPS is an active area of research [18,20,21]; however, the RE of ML-enabled cyber-physical systems remains an underexplored area of research.

In a recent work, Vuppala *et al.* [28] present an approach for ensuring the safety of RL-based controllers (in a CPS) using RE techniques. They use a simple q-learning RL algorithm and show how RE guarantees the algorithm's safe behaviour. Our work focuses on ensuring the safety of a more complex MARL-based control algorithm.

Problem Discussion: In this paper, we address the safety assurance problem of MARL-based drone swarm control by applying RE techniques. We specifically consider the case study of autonomous drone swarms conducting ocean search and rescue operations for drowning victims. MARL presents a promising solution for coordinating multiple drones to efficiently search expansive areas by learning optimal collaborative strategies through environmental interaction.

Through a reward mechanism, the MARL agents learn to coordinate search patterns based on evolving probability matrices that model ocean currents and victim drift patterns, rather than following fixed search protocols. However, their adaptive nature introduces critical safety concerns like drone-to-drone collisions, and boundary violations. We use RE techniques to address these concerns. We express safety requirements as a set of safety automata that prevent collisions, and boundary breaches. Enforcers based on these automata formal guarantee of safety during the entire learning process.

Contributions: (1) We propose a formal approach for safe MARL in dynamic environments, by integrating it with RE. This is the first application of RE to MARL-based swarm control. (2) We present a comprehensive case study of ocean search and rescue operations using drone swarms, showing how RE combined with MARL guarantees safety. (3) We implement and evaluate the proposed framework in the Drone Swarm Search Environment (DSSE) [8], demonstrating that runtime enforcement not only ensures safety but also improves learning outcomes, achieving 86.20% mission success rate compared to 74.90% without enforcement. (4) We show that the enforcer's intervention rate decreases over time (from initial high corrections to only 0.87% of actions requiring intervention), indicating that the MARL policy successfully internalizes safe behaviors through the enforcement-guided learning process.

2 Preliminaries

We briefly recall the RE problem for synchronous programs, and related notations and formalism from [21]. A finite word over an alphabet Σ is a sequence $\sigma = a_1 \cdots a_n$ of members of Σ, Σ^* denotes the set of all finite words over Σ, and $|\sigma|$ denotes its length. The empty word over Σ is denoted by ϵ_Σ, or ϵ. $\sigma \cdot \sigma'$ denotes *concatenation* of two words $\sigma, \sigma' \in \Sigma$. We write $\sigma' \preccurlyeq \sigma$ if $\exists \sigma'' \in \Sigma$ such that $\sigma = \sigma' \cdot \sigma''$, where σ' and σ are called *prefix* and *extension* of the other respectively.

A reactive system with a finite ordered sets of Boolean inputs $I = \{i_1, \cdots, i_n\}$ and Boolean outputs $O = \{o_1, \cdots o_m\}$ is considered. $\Sigma_I = 2^I$ denotes the input alphabet, $\Sigma_O = 2^O$ denotes the output alphabet, and the input-output alphabet is $\Sigma = \Sigma_I \times \Sigma_O$. Given an input-output word $\sigma = (x_1, y_1) \cdots (x_n, y_n) \in \Sigma^*$, $\sigma_I = x_1 \cdots x_n \in \Sigma_I^*$ is a projection on inputs obtained from σ, and $\sigma_O = y_1 \cdots y_n \in \Sigma_O^*$ is the projection on outputs. A property φ over Σ defines a set $\mathcal{L}(\varphi) \subseteq \Sigma^*$, $\sigma \models \varphi$ iff $\sigma \in \mathcal{L}(\varphi)$. φ is a *prefix-closed* policy iff $\forall w \in \mathcal{L}(\varphi), w' \preccurlyeq w \implies w' \in \mathcal{L}(\varphi)$. Policies are formalized as *safety automata* defined next.

2.1 The Safety-Automaton Model

Definition 1 (Safety Automaton). *A safety automaton (SA) $\mathcal{A} = (Q, q_0, q_v, \Sigma, \rightarrow)$ is a tuple, where Q is the set of locations or states, $q_0 \in Q$ is a distinct starting location, $q_v \in Q$ is a distinct non-accepting (violating) location, the alphabet is $\Sigma = \Sigma_I \times \Sigma_O$, and the transition relation is $\rightarrow \subseteq Q \times \Sigma \times Q$. All locations, except q_v, are accepting locations.*

A word σ is accepted by $\mathcal{A}$ if it ends in $q \in \{Q \setminus q_v\}$, when processed by $\mathcal{A}$ (starting from q_0). $\mathcal{L}(\mathcal{A})$ is the set of all words accepted by $\mathcal{A}$.

Definition 2 (Input SA $\mathcal{A}_{\varphi_I}$). *Given φ, specified as SA $\mathcal{A}_\varphi = (Q, q_0, q_v, \Sigma, \rightarrow)$, by discarding outputs on the transitions, input SA $\mathcal{A}_{\varphi_I} = (Q, q_0, q_v, \Sigma_I, \rightarrow_I)$ is derived from $\mathcal{A}_\varphi$. For every transition $q \xrightarrow{(x,y)} q' \in \rightarrow$, where $(x, y) \in \Sigma$, there is a transition $q \xrightarrow{x} q' \in \rightarrow_I$, where $x \in \Sigma_I$. $\mathcal{L}(\mathcal{A}_\varphi)$ is $\mathcal{L}(\varphi) \subseteq \Sigma^*$, and $\mathcal{L}(\mathcal{A}_{\varphi_I})$ is $\mathcal{L}(\varphi_I) \subseteq \Sigma_I^*$.*

When there are multiple policies to enforce, we enforce the product of their SA. Given two SAs $\mathcal{A}_{\varphi_1}$ and $\mathcal{A}_{\varphi_2}$ (which are deterministic and complete), $\mathcal{A}_{\varphi_1} \times \mathcal{A}_{\varphi_2}$ (which is also deterministic and complete) recognizes $\mathcal{L}(\mathcal{A}_{\varphi_1}) \cap \mathcal{L}(\mathcal{A}_{\varphi_2})$ [21].

Given φ, specified as $\mathcal{A}_\varphi = (Q, q_0, q_v, \Sigma, \rightarrow)$, and $\mathcal{A}_{\varphi_I} = (Q, q_0, q_v, \Sigma_I, \rightarrow_I)$ be derived from $\mathcal{A}_\varphi$ by discarding outputs, the *edit functions* [21], required by the enforcer to edit an erroneous input-output event are:

- **editl$_{\varphi_I}(\sigma_I)$:** Given $\sigma_I \in \Sigma_I^*$, editl$_{\varphi_I}(\sigma_I)$ is a set of input events $x \in \Sigma_I$ s.t. the word obtained by concatenating x after σ_I satisfies policy φ_I. Consider the SA $\mathcal{A}_{\varphi_I} = (Q, q_0, q_v, \Sigma_I, \to_I)$ defining φ_I, and let $q \in Q$ be the location reached in $\mathcal{A}_{\varphi_I}$ upon σ_I. Formally, editl$_{\varphi_I}(\sigma_I)$ considering $\mathcal{A}_{\varphi_I}$ is defined as follows: editl$_{\mathcal{A}_{\varphi_I}}(q) = \{x \in \Sigma_I : q \xrightarrow{x}_I q' \wedge q' \neq q_v\}$. If editl$_{\mathcal{A}_{\varphi_I}}(q)$ is non-empty, then nondet $-$ editl$_{\mathcal{A}_{\varphi_I}}(q)$ returns an element (chosen randomly) from editl$_{\mathcal{A}_{\varphi_I}}(q)$ and is undefined if editl$_{\mathcal{A}_{\varphi_I}}(q)$ is empty.
- **editO$_{\varphi}(\sigma, x)$:** Given $x \in \Sigma_I$ and $\sigma \in \Sigma^*$, editO$_{\varphi}(\sigma, x)$ is a set of output events y in Σ_O s.t. the input-output word obtained by concatenating σ followed by (x, y) (i.e., $\sigma \cdot (x, y)$) satisfies policy φ. Consider the automaton $\mathcal{A}_{\varphi} = (Q, q_0, q_v, \Sigma, \to)$ specifying policy φ, and let $q \in Q$ be the location reached in $\mathcal{A}_{\varphi}$ upon σ. Formally, editO$_{\varphi}(\sigma, x)$ considering $\mathcal{A}_{\varphi}$ is defined as follows: editO$_{\mathcal{A}_{\varphi}}(q, x) = \{y \in \Sigma_O : q \xrightarrow{(x,y)} q' \wedge q' \neq q_v\}$. If editO$_{\mathcal{A}_{\varphi}}(q, x)$ is not empty, then nondet $-$ editO$_{\mathcal{A}_{\varphi}}(q, x)$ returns a random element from editO$_{\mathcal{A}_{\varphi}}(q, x)$, and if editO$_{\mathcal{A}_{\varphi}}(q, x)$ is empty nondet $-$ editO$_{\mathcal{A}_{\varphi}}(q, x)$ is undefined.

In this work, we consider the RE framework for policies specified as SA from [21]. The formal definition of the constraints, functional definitions, and the algorithm to obtain enforcers from policies specified as SA is detailed in [21].

Following are the constraints that an enforcer must satisfy. *Soundness:* the output of the enforcer always ensures the property. *Monotonicity:* the result of an enforcer can not be reversed. *Instantaneity:* each enforcer reacts instantaneously (essential requirement for reactive systems). *Transparency:* an enforcer modifies an incoming event iff its emission would certainly violate the property. *Causality:* for every input-output event the enforcer first processes the input part x into x' (using editl$_{\mathcal{A}_{\varphi_I}}$), and then it reads and transforms output (y to y' using editO$_{\mathcal{A}_{\varphi}}$).

3   Combining MARL with Runtime Enforcement

Our case study focuses on autonomous drone swarms conducting ocean search and rescue operations. We employ MARL to coordinate a swarm of four drones operating in a 40×40 grid environment, where they must collaboratively locate a shipwrecked individual. The system utilizes a probabilistic model that incorporates ocean dynamics. While MARL enables adaptive and efficient search strategies, the inherent unpredictability of learning-based systems introduces safety risks including potential drone collisions, and boundary violations. We use RE to ensure safety.

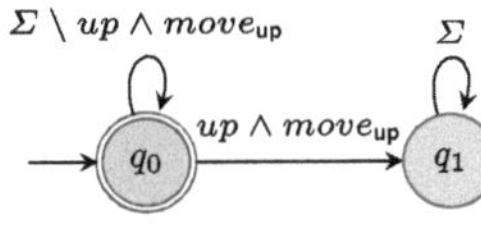

Fig. 1. $\mathcal{A}_{\varphi_1}$.

Each drone has four input variables - $\Sigma_I = \{up, down, left, right\}$, and four output variables - $\Sigma_O = \{move_{right}, move_{left}, move_{up}, move_{down}\}$. The input variables capture the occupancy status of four immediate neighbouring cells (1 for occupied by an obstacle or another drone and 0 for unoccupied). Any neighbouring cell outside the boundary is marked as occupied. The output variables tell the movement direction of the drone. If the value of an output variable is 1 or true, then the drone should move in that direction.

We have formulated four safety policies to counter collisions and boundary breaches: (1) policy φ_1 : *"up and move$_{up}$ cannot occur simultaneously"*; (2) policy φ_2 : *"down and move$_{down}$ cannot occur simultaneously"*; (3) policy φ_3 : *"left and move$_{left}$ cannot occur simultaneously"*; (4) policy φ_4 : *"right and move$_{right}$ cannot occur simultaneously"*. Figure 1 shows specification SA of φ_1.

Figure 2 represents a 2-drones swarm system embedded with bidirectional runtime enforcers. This can be extended to n-drones.

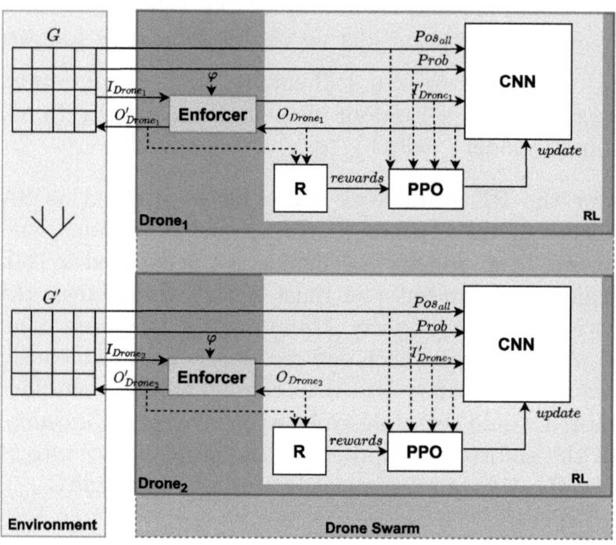

Fig. 2. MARL enabled 2-drones swarm system using RE.

Environment Layer: It consists the search gird G of size $g \times g$. This grid marks the boundary of the drone swarm. Each cell of the grid is identified by 2-D coordinate (x, y). Also, the occupancy status of each cell is given by a boolean value - 0 if the cell is unoccupied and 1 otherwise. The position of each drone in the grid is stored as an array of pairs $pos_{all} = \{(x_1, y_1), \cdots, (x_2, y_2)\}$. The grid also contains the probability of the target present (in each cell) as a $g \times g$ probability matrix *prob*.

Drone Swarm Layer: This layer consists of the drones. Each drone has an *Enforcer* and a RL based control system. The RL system incorporates a multi-input convolutional neural network (CNN) that inputs the occupancy status of its four neighbouring cells (i'_{dr}), the position of all agents (pos_{all}), and the probability matrix ($prob$). The CNN outputs the control signal o_{dr} to move the drone (to one of its neighbouring cells). The *Enforcer* sits in between the RL system and the environment, and ensures that the incoming input (from the environment) and the output (by the RL system) satisfies the given property φ. The safety policies (φ_1-φ_4) are formulated on the status of neighbouring cells and the movement (control) actions, and therefore the enforcer monitors and edits (when necessary): input i_{dr} to i'_{dr}, and output o_{dr} to o'_{dr}. The RL system also consists of a reward generator (R) and a proximal policy optimization module (PPO). R processes original action o_{dr} and enforced action o'_{dr} to generate multiple *rewards* including direct feedback, enforcement penalties, and bonuses for rapid target discovery. The *PPO* is responsible for updating the *CNN* parameters at regular intervals. It collects experience tuples[1] in a buffer, and upon reaching the buffer capacity, it performs gradient descent method via clipped surrogate objective optimization to update the *CNN* parameters through advantage estimation and value function learning [24]. An online algorithm for safe MARL-enabled system using RE is given below:

1: **Input** N instances of $\mathcal{A}_\varphi$, Interval I of training
2: $t \leftarrow 0$ ▷ t keeps track of the time-step (tick)
3: **for** $k = 1$ to $k = N$
4:     $q_k \leftarrow q_0$ ▷ $\forall \mathcal{A}_\varphi$, initialize current state with the initial state q_0
5: **while** true
6:     **for** $k = 1$ to $k = N$
7:        $i_{dr_k}, prob, pos_{all} \leftarrow$ observer()   ▷ observer() reads inp. from env.
8:        **if** $i_{dr_k} \notin$ editl$_{\mathcal{A}_{\varphi_I}}(q_k)$: $i'_{dr_k} \leftarrow$ nondet $-$ editl$_{\mathcal{A}_{\varphi_I}}(q_k)$
9:        **else:** $i'_{dr_k} \leftarrow i_{dr_k}$
10:       $o_{dr_k} \leftarrow$ CNN$(i'_{dr_k}, prob, pos_{all})$
11:       $rewards \leftarrow$ R(o_{dr_k}, o'_{dr_k})
12:       **if** t mod $I = 0$: PPO(expr_buffer)   ▷ PPO updates CNN parameters
13:       **if** $o_{dr_k} \notin$ editO$_{\mathcal{A}_\varphi}(q_k, i'_{dr_k})$: $o'_{dr_k} \leftarrow$ nondet $-$ editO$_{\mathcal{A}_\varphi}(q_k, i'_{dr_k})$
14:       **else:** $o'_{dr_k} \leftarrow o_{dr_k}$
15:       release(o'_{dr_k})   ▷ release() emits outp. to env.
16:       $q_k \leftarrow \delta(q_k, (i'_{dr_k}, o'_{dr})), t \leftarrow t + 1$

4 Implementation and Evaluation

This work focuses on ensuring safe behaviour of the MARL control, and therefore we implement enforcement of output actions only. However, the framework easily supports extending the scenario/set of policies enforced that also requires enforcement of input signals.

We utilize the DSSE simulator [8] to model and evaluate our approach. The simulation environment consists of a 40×40 grid world containing four autonomous drones tasked with locating a single target representing a ship-wrecked individual in oceanic conditions. It incorporates realistic search dynamics through a probability matrix that encodes the likelihood of target presence in each grid cell. Initially, the matrix assigns a probability of 1.0 to the target's last known position.

Each drone agent observes both the global probability matrix and its own spatial coordinates. The agents can execute movement actions or hover at their current location (*i.e.* when values of all four actions are 0).To assess the effectiveness of the proposed RL algorithm, we compared its performance with and without the runtime enforcer. We evaluated a baseline greedy algorithm equipped

---

[1] An experience tuple is $\{(pos_{all}, prob, i'_{dr}), o_{dr}, rewards, (pos_{all_{nxt}}, prob_{nxt}, i'_{dr_{nxt}}), done\}$, where $(pos_{all_{nxt}}, prob_{nxt}, i'_{dr_{nxt}})$, *done* is the status of search (1 for target found and 0 for not found).

with the same enforcement strategy to benchmark the RL approach. For each training iteration, the RL policy was updated and then evaluated by running 1000 independent agent simulations under consistent environmental conditions. All the results are computed as averages over 1000 simulations.

Average Steps to Find the Target: Figure 3a shows the average number of steps taken to find the target across training iterations.

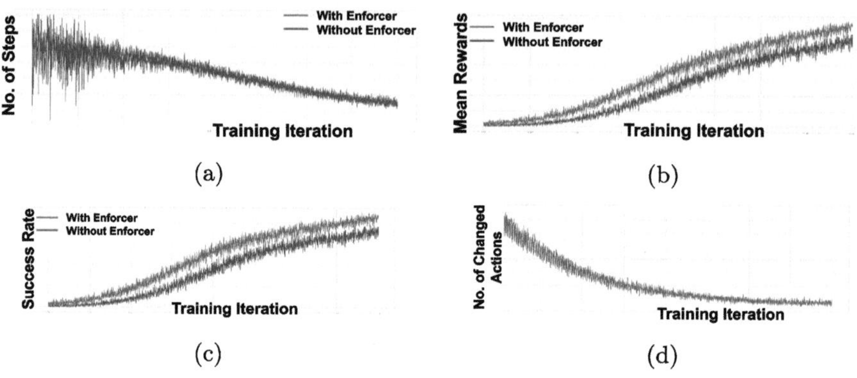

Fig. 3. Experimental results.

Table 1. Comparison of simulation results.

Parameters	RL (Enforcer)	RL (No Enforcer)	Greedy
Total simulations	1000	1000	1000
Success rate (%)	86.20	74.90	40.30
Average reward	1.32	1.15	0.66
Average steps (when found)	46.56	47.1	74.59
Average changed Actions by Enforcer(%)	0.87	N/A	N/A
Average safety policy φ violation (%)	0.00	0.20	NA

Reward Rate During Training: As shown in Fig. 3b, the reward rate steadily increases with training, indicating improved learning. The reward function rw is defined as $rw = 1 + [1 - (steps/100)]$, where *steps* is the no. of steps taken to find the victim; $rw = 0$ if $steps > 100$.

Success Rate Across Episodes: Figure 3c depicts the success rate of the agents in locating the target.

Changes in Agent Actions by Enforcer: Figure 3d illustrates how often the enforcer intervened to change actions.

The experimental results (in Fig. 3) show the tangible benefits of integrating RE into RL-driven drone swarm search operation. Firstly, the average number of steps required to locate the target decreases steadily throughout the training process across all configurations, with minimal difference between enforced and non-enforced cases. The setup with RE achieves significantly higher success rates in the latter half of training. This improvement reflects the influence of the enforcer, which helps avoid behaviors that could derail mission progress. The reward rate also improves steadily with training, and is consistently higher in the setup with RE. This supports that RE not only safeguards the system, but also guides the learning policy toward more reward-optimal behaviors.

Lastly, the number of changed actions (by the enforcer) decreases over time. This indicates that the policy internalizes safe behavior patterns. It also shows the enforcer's ability to provide corrective guidance to avoid critical failures like collisions and boundary violations. Overall, these results demonstrate that, along with guaranteed safety, combining the adaptability of MARL with the reliability of RE, the system's learning stability and mission success rate is improved. The simulation results, is summarized in Table 1. The RL agent with RE (success rate of 86.20%) outperforms both the counterparts. The average number of steps to locate the target is the lowest (46.56) in the enforced setting. The *average changed actions* by the *enforcer* remains low (0.87%), this implies selective intervention. It also suggests that the policy has internalized safe behaviour. The *average safety violation*, as expected, is *zero* in the case with *enforcer*, while the setup without *enforcer* experiences collisions and boundary breach.

5   Related Work

In order to correct/edit system's execution and avoid violation of properties being monitored, the enforcer uses actions like *halt, delay, suppress, store and reorder* [7,15,16,19,22,23]. However CPSs such as drone swarm are built on reactive system architecture [1,9] that demand instantaneous action on system's execution (for property satisfaction). Research on runtime enforcement mechanisms for reactive CPSs has been propitious in recent times [17,18,20,21,28], which allow instantaneous edit.

Combining RE with Reinforcement Learning: In [11] Jansen *et al.* propose construction of a probabilistic *shield* for property enforcement in RL-based systems. In another work [2], Alshiekh *et al.* introduce the concept of *shield learning* that assures (during learning and execution) a given set of system's specifications in an RL-based control system. They propose two alternative ways of shielding - preemptive and post-posed shielding. In [28], Vuppala *et al.* propose a bi-directional runtime enforcement framework for CPS that uses RL-based control. They use the case study of a pacemaker controlled and operated by an RL algorithm to showcase how combining RE with the RL enhances safety. The RL agent uses Q-learning algorithm to learn decision making. We extend the RE framework for multi-agent RL algorithms.

## 6	Conclusion

Cyber-physical systems with reinforcement learning-based control are increasingly used in real-world applications. However, their uncertain behaviour associated with their *"black-box"* nature makes them unreliable, posing a formidable challenge in ensuring safety, especially in safety-critical settings. In this work, we present a formal approach for ensuring the safety of such CPSs using an RE framework. We use a MARL-enabled drone swarm as our case study to illustrate how combining RE with a MARL-based control algorithm guarantees key safety properties like avoiding collisions and boundary breaches. Consequently, RE also enhances the success rate/efficacy of the MARL-enabled drone swarm system.

For future work, we would like to study runtime enforcement approach for enforcing regular properties in ML-enabled CPSs. We would also like to explore the possibility of combining RE with other RL algorithms like Monte Carlo methods, deep Q-networks, actor critic methods *etc.* .

References

1. Aceto, L., Ingólfsdóttir, A., Larsen, K.G., Srba, J.: Reactive Systems: Modelling. Specification and Verification. Cambridge University Press, Cambridge (2007)
2. Alshiekh, M., Bloem, R., Ehlers, R., Könighofer, B., Niekum, S., Topcu, U.: Safe reinforcement learning via shielding. In: Proceedings of the Thirty-Second AAAI 2018, New Orleans, Louisiana, USA, February 2–7, 2018, pp. 2669–2678 (2018). https://doi.org/10.1609/AAAI.V32I1.11797
3. Amir, G., Schapira, M., Katz, G.: Towards scalable verification of deep reinforcement learning. In: 2021 Formal Methods in Computer Aided Design (FMCAD) (2021)
4. Busoniu, L., Babuska, R., De Schutter, B.: A comprehensive survey of multiagent reinforcement learning. IEEE Trans. Syst. Man Cybern. Part C (Appl. Rev.) **38**(2), 156–172 (2008). https://doi.org/10.1109/TSMCC.2007.913919
5. Chen, H.: Applications of cyber-physical system: a literature review. J. Ind. Integr. Manage. **02**(03), 1750012 (2017). https://doi.org/10.1142/S2424862217500129
6. Falcone, Y., Havelund, K., Reger, G.: A tutorial on runtime verification. Eng. Dependable Softw. Syst. 141–175 (2013)
7. Falcone, Y., Mounier, L., Fernandez, J.C., Richier, J.L.: Runtime enforcement monitors: composition, synthesis, and enforcement abilities. Formal Methods Syst. Design **38**(3), 223–262 (2011)
8. Falcão, R.L., de Oliveira, J.C.C., Andrade, P.H.B.A., Rodrigues, R.R., Barth, F.J., Brancalion, J.F.B.: DSSE: an environment for simulation of reinforcement learning-empowered drone swarm maritime search and rescue missions. J. Open Source Softw. **9**(99), 6746 (2024). https://doi.org/10.21105/joss.06746
9. Harel, D., Pnueli, A.: On the development of reactive systems. In: Logics and Models of Concurrent Systems, pp. 477–498. Springer (1984)
10. Herdel, V., Yamin, L.J., Cauchard, J.R.: Above and beyond: a scoping review of domains and applications for human-drone interaction. In: Proceedings of the 2022 CHI Conference on Human Factors in Computing Systems, pp. 1–22 (2022)

11. Jansen, N., Könighofer, B., Junges, S., Serban, A., Bloem, R.: Safe reinforcement learning using probabilistic shields (invited paper). In: 31st International Conference on Concurrency Theory, CONCUR 2020, September 1–4, 2020, Vienna, Austria (Virtual Conference), pp. 3:1–3:16 (2020). https://doi.org/10.4230/LIPICS.CONCUR.2020.3

12. Kaelbling, L.P., Littman, M.L., Moore, A.W.: Reinforcement learning: a survey. J. Artif. Intell. Res. **4**, 237–285 (1996)

13. Landers, M., Doryab, A.: Deep reinforcement learning verification: a survey. ACM Comput. Surv. **55**(14s), 1–31 (2023)

14. Lee, E.A.: Cyber physical systems: design challenges. In: 2008 11th IEEE International Symposium on Object and Component-Oriented Real-Time Distributed Computing (ISORC), pp. 363–369 (2008).https://doi.org/10.1109/ISORC.2008.25

15. Ligatti, J., Bauer, L., Walker, D.: Run-time enforcement of nonsafety policies. ACM Trans. Inf. Syst. Secur. **12**(3) (2009)

16. Ligatti, J., Reddy, S.: A theory of runtime enforcement, with results. In: Gritzalis, D., Preneel, B., Theoharidou, M. (eds.) ESORICS 2010. LNCS, vol. 6345, pp. 87–100. Springer, Heidelberg (2010). https://doi.org/10.1007/978-3-642-15497-3_6

17. Panda, A., Baird, A., Pinisetty, S., Roop, P.S.: Incremental security enforcement for cyber-physical systems. IEEE Access **11**, 18475–18498 (2023). https://doi.org/10.1109/ACCESS.2023.3246121

18. Pearce, H.A., Pinisetty, S., Roop, P.S., Kuo, M.M.Y., Ukil, A.: Smart I/O modules for mitigating cyber-physical attacks on industrial control systems. IEEE Trans. Ind. Informatics **16**(7), 4659–4669 (2020). https://doi.org/10.1109/TII.2019.2945520

19. Pinisetty, S., Falcone, Y., Jéron, T., Marchand, H., Rollet, A., Nguena Timo, O.: Runtime enforcement of timed properties revisited. Formal Methods Syst. Design **45**(3), 381–422 (2014). https://doi.org/10.1007/s10703-014-0215-y

20. Pinisetty, S., Roop, P.S., Smyth, S., Allen, N., Tripakis, S., von Hanxleden, R.: Runtime enforcement of cyber-physical systems. ACM Trans. Embed. Comput. Syst. **16**(5s), 178:1–178:25 (2017). https://doi.org/10.1145/3126500

21. Pinisetty, S., Roop, P.S., Smyth, S., Tripakis, S., von Hanxleden, R.: Runtime enforcement of reactive systems using synchronous enforcers. Proceedings of the 24th ACM SIGSOFT International SPIN Symposium on Model Checking of Software, Santa Barbara, CA, USA, July 10–14, 2017, pp. 80–89 (2017). https://doi.org/10.1145/3092282.3092291

22. Pradhan, A., Akil, C.G.M., Pinisetty, S.: Runtime enforcement with event reordering. In: Anutariya, C., Bonsangue, M.M. (eds.) Theoretical Aspects of Computing - ICTAC 2024 - 21st International Colloquium, Bangkok, Thailand, November 25–29, 2024, Proceedings. Lecture Notes in Computer Science, vol. 15373, pp. 386–407. Springer (2024). https://doi.org/10.1007/978-3-031-77019-7_22

23. Schneider, F.B.: Enforceable security policies. ACM Trans. Inf. Syst. Secur. **3**(1), 30–50 (2000). https://doi.org/10.1145/353323.353382

24. Schulman, J., Wolski, F., Dhariwal, P., Radford, A., Klimov, O.: Proximal policy optimization algorithms. arXiv preprint arXiv:1707.06347 (2017)

25. Sen, S., Weiss, G.: Learning in multiagent systems. Multiagent Syst. Mod. Approach Distrib. Artif. Intell. **6**, 259–298 (1999)

26. Sutton, R.S., Barto, A.G., et al.: Reinforcement Learning: An Introduction, vol. 1. MIT Press, Cambridge (1998)

27. Tang, J., Liu, G., Pan, Q.: A review on representative swarm intelligence algorithms for solving optimization problems: applications and trends. IEEE/CAA J. Automatica Sinica **8**(10), 1627–1643 (2021)

28. Vuppala, S.R.H., Allen, N., Pinisetty, S., Roop, P.S.: A formal approach for safe reinforcement learning: a rate-adaptive pacemaker case study. In: Runtime Verification - 24th International Conference, RV 2024, Istanbul, Turkey, October 15–17, 2024, Proceedings, pp. 3–21 (2024). https://doi.org/10.1007/978-3-031-74234-7_1
29. Weiss, G.: Multiagent Systems: a Modern Approach to Distributed Artificial Intelligence. MIT Press, Cambridge (1999)
30. Zeng, Q., Nait-Abdesselam, F.: Multi-agent reinforcement learning-based extended boid modeling for drone swarms. In: ICC 2024-IEEE International Conference on Communications, pp. 1551–1556. IEEE (2024)

Correction to: Weighted Automata for Exact Inference in Discrete Probabilistic Programs

Dominik Geißler and Tobias Winkler

Correction to:
**Chapter 16 in: Z. Liu et al. (Eds.): *Theoretical Aspects of Computing – ICTAC 2025*, LNCS 16237,
https://doi.org/10.1007/978-3-032-11176-0_16**

The chapter 16 was originally published with a typographical error in Tables 1 and 2. These have been corrected in the updated version.

The updated version of this chapter can be found at
https://doi.org/10.1007/978-3-032-11176-0_16

Author Index